S0-BYR-246

sustainable communities, sustainable development

Writing Past Colonialism is the signature book series of the Institute of Postcolonial Studies, based in Melbourne, Australia. By postcolonialism we understand modes of writing and artistic production that critically engage with and contest the legacy and continuing mindset and practices of colonialism, and inform debate about the processes of globalization. This manifests itself in a concern with difference from the Euro-American, the global, and the norm. The series is also committed to publishing works that seek "to make a difference," both in the academy and outside it.

OUR HOPE IS THAT BOOKS IN THE SERIES WILL

- engage with contemporary issues and problems relating to colonialism and postcolonialism
- attempt to reach a broad constituency of readers
- address the relation between theory and practice
- be interdisciplinary in approach as well as subject matter
- experiment with new modes of writing and methodology

ipcs

INSTITUTE OF POSTCOLONIAL STUDIES | WRITING PAST COLONIALISM

sustainable communities, sustainable development

OTHER PATHS FOR PAPUA NEW GUINEA

Paul James, Yaso Nadarajah, Karen Haive, and Victoria Stead

with

Albert Age, Peter Annear, Sama Arua, Kelly Donati, Jean Eparo, Beno Erepan,
Julie Foster-Smith, Zarnaz Fouladi, Betty Gali-Malpo, Damian Grenfell, Elizabeth Kath,
Andrew Kedu, Paul Komesaroff, Leo Kulumbu, Ronnie Mamia, Lita Mugugia, Martin Mulligan,
Gibson Oeka, Jalal Paraha, Peter Phipps, Leonie Rakanangu, Isabel Salatiel, Chris Scanlon,
Helen Smith, Sabine Spohn, Pou Toivita, Kema Vegala, Naup Waup, Mollie Willie, and
Joe Yomba

 University of Hawai'i Press   Honolulu

The authors wish to thank the following sponsors for subsidizing this volume: Department for Community Development, PNG, and the Asian Development Bank, with smaller amounts from AusAID and the Australian Research Council.

© 2012 University of Hawai'i Press
All rights reserved
Printed in the United States of America

17 16 15 14 13 12   6 5 4 3 2 1

Library of Congress Cataloging-in-Publication Data

Sustainable communities, sustainable development : other paths for Papua New Guinea / Paul James ... [et al.].
    p. cm. — (Writing past colonialism)
  Includes bibliographical references and index.
  ISBN 978-0-8248-3588-0 (hardcover : alk. paper) — ISBN 978-0-8248-3640-5 (pbk. : alk. paper)
  1. Sustainable development—Papua New Guinea.   2. Community development—Papua New Guinea.   3. Papua New Guinea—Social conditions.   4. Papua New Guinea—Economic conditions.   I. James, Paul (Paul Warren). ----------- II. Series: Writing past colonialism series.
  HC683.5.Z9E587 2012
  338.9953'07—dc23

                                                                2012014465

University of Hawai'i Press books are printed
on acid-free paper and meet the guidelines
for permanence and durability of the Council
on Library Resources.

Series design by Leslie Fitch
Printed by Sheridan Books, Inc.

For strongim pipol and strong communities

CONTENTS

NOTE ON AUTHORS

PAUL JAMES is director of the Global Cities Institute, RMIT University, and author or editor of twenty-four books including *Globalism, Nationalism, Tribalism* (2006).

YASO NADARAJAH is a senior fellow in the Globalism Research Centre, RMIT University, and co-author of *Rebuilding Communities in the Wake of Disaster* (2012).

KAREN HAIVE is former assistant deputy secretary in the Department for Community Development, Papua New Guinea.

VICTORIA STEAD is a Ph.D. student in the Human Security Program, RMIT University.

THIS BOOK COMES OUT OF a much larger project of global ethnography conducted in Australia, Papua New Guinea, Malaysia, India, Sri Lanka, and elsewhere.[1] It emphasizes three major themes: community sustainability, community livelihoods, and community learning. Our overriding concern is to map the complex intersection—the tensions, both destructive and creative—of ontologically different formations as they work in and through each other in the contemporary globalizing world. The long-term objective of this ongoing project is to contribute broadly to social sustainability—culturally, politically, economically, and ecologically.

More particularly, here in Papua New Guinea, we focused on ways of supporting and building the base-level foundations for enhancing the resilience and vibrancy of communities under threat.[2] In effect, we wanted to rewrite the mainstream development literature by emphasizing the possibilities for revitalizing nonformal economies, restructuring health practices, and providing alternative pathways to community development through informal learning. One of the core strategies suggested by the research involves drawing on the existing strengths of communities and working in partnership with government and civil society organizations to create networks of community learning centers.

The book is one outcome of a long-term, collaborative research partnership between a team of academic researchers and the national Department for Community Development (DFCD) in Papua New Guinea, a partnership that from the outset aimed to contribute toward the development of a new, national policy for strengthening and enhancing local communities and local livelihoods in a country of extraordinary diversity and contradiction. The publication of this volume marks the end of the first stage of a research engagement that is far from complete.

Most pointedly, the project provided background research to support the development of an ongoing policy framework for community development in Papua New Guinea. The project was set within a community-engaged research framework to finalize the DFCD's community development policies. It involved a consultative process across local, provincial, and national levels. In local communities throughout Papua New Guinea a community-consultation process provided the basis for our research. Our research framework meant, for example, paying careful attention to the protocol of Organic Law while we waited for a letter to get off a provincial desk and into the hands of a district liaison officer. It meant waiting in a pressing crowd to get on an overnight boat to a distant island because our flight booking had not worked. It meant explicitly confronting embarrassing questions of monetary compensation, power broking, and gender inequities. The research rarely went in the way that we first intended, and it was never without initial setbacks, failures, and problems, but it was always conducted with committed care.

There have been many interconnected parts to the Papua New Guinea (PNG) project—from local research training to writing a series of government reports. Perhaps most significant, drawing upon field research in local communities and on policy work done in the Department for Community Sustain-

Karen Haive, Department for Community Development

ability by Karen Haive, Marian Jacka, Mollie Willie, and others, we worked to draft the Integrated Policy for Community Development for circulation to the provincial ministers, chairs, and advisors in preparation for the First National Ministerial Forum in October 2006. The eighth draft was completed in late 2006, with the final version of the policy document accepted by the Parliament as policy in early 2007. During the same period, community mapping was initiated in eleven locations comprising about forty villages across four provinces of Papua New Guinea—Central, Morobe, Madang, and Milne Bay. We subsequently documented the roll-out of the district focal points in a series of further places: Vanimo-Green District (Sandaun Province), Bialla District (West New Britain Province), Madang Town District (Madang Province), Wosera Gawi District (East Sepik Province), Rigo District and Moresby South (Central Province), Pomio District (East New Britain), and Sohe District (Oro Province), although this was done with much less depth than was the case with the community mapping sites.

The present community mapping project is unique in that a comprehensive national government policy and implementation process had been based on iterative, collaborative research and consultation with diverse communities across the nation.[3] This was the first time in Papua New Guinea that research with policy outcomes was planned in association with repeated visits to an extensive and intentionally diverse range of communities—urban, hinterland, and remote. And the project was unusual in bringing together a government department and an outside collaborating team to develop policy guidelines that were both taken back to communities and into the department for further discussion and debate. This second round of consultation occurred in 2007 and across 2008 into early 2009.

The logistics were complicated, and we did not always live up to our own expectations. For example, we had planned to include two other provinces in the community mapping process, but, because of political violence and a declared state of emergency in the Southern Highlands and administrative issues including funding delays in relation to Manus Island, those two provinces were reluctantly dropped from the ethnographic part of the study. The Southern Highlands subsequently became central to the Liquefied Natural Gas Project, with more violence ensuing. We remain acutely aware of the weakness that in the community-mapping chapters there is no Highland community and that working in eleven primary locations provides only a partial picture of such a complex country. We have been assiduous in drawing on the secondary-literature research including ethnographic studies that covered the whole of Papua New Guinea.

Our approach, drawing on what can be called "engaged theory," comes together around a number of core principles:

- That the global research is locally engaged and committed to making a difference;
- That the research always aims to move creatively between on-the-ground inquiry and generalizing theory;
- That the research is reflexive. Engaged reflexive research entails stepping back from the subjective immediacy of on-the-ground engagement. In other words, the passion of engagement needs to be carefully qualified by the reflexive dimension of objective distance;
- That the research involves a mutual and slowly negotiated relationship between researchers and other participants, including, where relevant, local communities. All participants are to be involved where possible as partners in a dialogue of exchange and mutual learning;
- That there is a duty of care to the people with whom we work to protect privacy and security where appropriate, to negotiate the boundaries of knowledge, to properly acknowledge sources where public, and to return the outcomes of our work to the community in a reciprocal relationship of mutual learning.

Alongside consultation in communities, background document-based and library research was conducted on the major themes of community development, health issues including HIV/AIDS, the informal sector, informal learning, and community learning centers. A project of this nature necessarily draws on a wide range of literatures, touching on diverse fields of both scholarly and applied research. One of the hallmarks of the kind of exploratory work undertaken here is the need for interdisciplinary engagement as well as the capacity to work across a diverse range of terrains and community groups. Our work has thus been informed by literatures in the social sciences and humanities, the human and biomedical sciences, and economics and development, and we owe an enormous amount to all those researchers who are listed in the endnotes.

This is a large range of fields to draw on, and the researchers involved in the project brought overlapping knowledge and methodological skills to the task at hand. Our second major weakness is that, though the book has been redrafted and redrafted, in working across many fields we have exposed many possible cracks in our own expertise. Moreover, because we are addressing multiple audiences across multiple fields—local people reading about their own communities, national and global policy makers, anthropologists and theorists of community development—some readers will find some sections difficult or not to have an immediate resonance, and other readers will want more depth. We have tried to keep significant sections of the book accessible to general readers. For example, the chapters concerning the community profiles are not exercises in deep anthropology. However, they have been critically read by community leaders in Papua New Guinea to make sure that they pass a basic test: "Does the writing properly represent *my* community in all its strengths and weaknesses?"

This publication, which builds on the draft reports that we presented in 2007 and 2009 to Dame Carol Kidu, then minister for the Department for Community Development, Papua New Guinea, is the outcome of a massive undertaking and collaboration among many people over a number of years. Julie Foster-Smith, herself both an Aboriginal Australian and a Papua New Guinean, played a crucial role in establishing the initial contact between Dame Carol and the Globalism Research Centre, through Paul James, Martin Mulligan, and Peter Phipps. Julie Foster-Smith mediated the Melbourne two-day exchange in 2004, and other experts on Papua New Guinea such as Martin Syder and Roger Southern contributed to setting up the project. Julie continued on with the project as a central advisor on community engagement and methodology questions. Despite poor health she contributed significantly on numerous difficult research sojourns until she could no longer travel.

Dame Carol was a constant inspiration—both personal and intellectual—and an ongoing source of guidance that was crucial to the changing nature of

Dame Carol Kidu, former minister for Community Development

our engagement across the complex boundaries of government, civil society, and communities. Secretary Klapat was wonderfully generous with his time and wisdom. We could not have done the work without his support, including his leadership in thinking through policy development and how the DFCD-Globalism research team might contribute to that process. Joseph and Dame Carol generously allowed us the independence and space to do much more than provide a basis to a pressing policy process. Whatever rigor this document has reflects the engagement they supported.

One intellectual home of the work is the Globalism Research Centre, and we warmly thank our colleagues there—in particular Todd Bennet, Damian Grenfell, Anne McNevin, Martin Mulligan, Tom Nairn, Heikki Patomaki, Peter Phipps, Andy Scerri, Helen Smith, Manfred Steger, Anna Trembath, Erin Wilson, and Chris Ziguras. Another intellectual setting for the project is the Community Sustainability Program within the Global Cities Institute at the Royal Melbourne Institute of Technology. Here we particularly thank Supriya Singh, research leader of the Community Sustainability Program within which this project falls, as well as Frank Yardley and Michelle Farley for their administrative support. The imaginative source of our thinking that Papua New Guinea could and can be otherwise came from writings years ago in *Arena Journal* by people such as Nonie Sharp and Utula Samana. A third important intellectual setting for our work is the international organization Global Reconciliation—a number of the coauthors of this book are involved in that organization—and we acknowledge the inspiring work of Ian Campbell, Robert Costa, Michael Drapac, Kushil Gunesekera, David Lurie, Elizabeth Reid, Paul Sheehan, and John Zelzer, among others. A further intellectual setting is the UN Global Compact Cities Programme, which developed the circles of sustainability method used in the present approach. Here we acknowledge the work of Andy Scerri, Liam Magee, and Martin Mulligan.

Many, many people have contributed to the researching and writing of this report. Peter Phipps managed the project across 2005–2006, Kate Cregan in late 2006–2007, and then Victoria Stead in 2008–2009. Apart from managing the project in late 2006, Kate provided research and writing for Chapters 7 and 12, for which we thank her warmly. She withdrew from the project in early 2007. Apart from the main authors, a number of persons contributed major sections of writing or chapters upon which the report was based: Peter Annear (health equity), Kelly Donati (development issues), Helen Smith (informal learning), Sabine Spohn (microfinance), and Zarnaz Fouladi (HIV/AIDS).

Many others contributed to the research on the ground, by providing advice or by doing background work on particular issues, and we also acknowledge them with gratitude: Albert Age, Sama Arua, Kelly Donati, Jean Eparo, Beno

Joseph Klapat, secretary of the Department for Community Development

Erepan, Julie Foster-Smith, Betty Gali-Malpo, Elizabeth Kath, Andrew Kedu, Max Kep, Paul Komesaroff, Leo Kulumbu, Stephanie Lusby, Karen Malone, Ronnie Mamia, Lita Mugugia, Martin Mulligan, Gibson Oeka, Jalal Paraha, Peter Phipps, Leonie Rakanangu, Elizabeth Reid, Isabel Salatiel, Chris Scanlon, Pou Toivita, Kema Vegala, Naup Waup, Mollie Willie, and Joe Yomba. Others have provided important administrative and logistic support, ideas, and friendship: Kila Aoneka, Jenny Kidu, Albert Obia, and Gibson Oera. Other research support came from Wasana Weeraratne, Alex Stott, and Mardi O'Connor in compiling the bibliography and checking references.

Colleagues have expertly and thoroughly commented on sections of the book, and we particularly thank Phillip Darby, Andy Scerri, Martha Macintyre, and Thomas Strong for their insightful contributions. Collaboration with the remarkable Phillip Darby has been fundamental to this book. This volume is a contribution to a lifelong project with Phillip and the Institute of Postcolonial Studies, which aims to get beyond the postmodern turn in postcolonial studies and to ground theory in the lives of people. Nonie Sharp read the manuscript with her usual generous care and was always an inspiration in our thinking about engaged ethnography and theory. We thank Jim Robins at the National

Research Institute, Papua New Guinea, for advice at crucial junctures. We also thank Steffen Wirth at the Asian Development Bank for offering both encouragement and material support. His gentle cynicism about the achievability of our project aims was matched by his generosity of spirit in making it possible. And we thank the University of Hawai'i Press, in particular director William Hamilton and editor Susan Stone for their careful and considerate attentions.

Our work in communities was conducted with a number of leaders and activists who facilitated discussions, organized community forums and conversations, and coordinated the feedback on community profiles and recommendations. We thank in particular Gerard Arua, Vanapa, Central Province; Monica Arua, Yule Island, Central Province; Viki Avei, Boera, Central Province; Sunema Bagita, Provisional Community Development Advisor, Milne Bay Province; Mago Doelegu, Alotau, Milne Bay Province; Clement Dogale, Vanagi, Central Province; Jerry Gomuma, Alepa, Central Province; Alfred Kaket, Simbukanam/ Tokain, Madang Province; Yat Paol from the Bismarck Ramu Group, Madang Province; Joseph Pulayasi, Omarakana, Milne Bay Province; Bing Sawanga, Yalu, Morobe Province; Alexia Tokau, Kananam, Madang Province; and Naup Waup, Wisini village, Morobe Province. They became our formal research leaders in their respective communities.

And last, but very important, we thank the communities and individuals of Alepa, Boera, Divinai, Inuma, Kananam, Omarakana, Tokain, Vanagi, Vanapa, Wisini, Yalu, and Yule Island for their generosity and openness in receiving us into their homes. Our hope is that in the years ahead we will remain intimate outsiders to your communities and *wantoks* in the mutual struggle for developing *other* pathways to sustainable living. All royalties from this book will go to communities in Papua New Guinea.

The title of the book, *Sustainable Communities, Sustainable Development: Other Paths for Papua New Guinea*, expresses the nature of the project. It points to the broad canvas of the work: exploring the manner in which other development strategies may contribute to community-building and, by implication, to the sustainability of communities through a connective process of learning across different knowledge systems—customary tribal, traditional cosmological, and modern analytical. In this emphasis, processes of development and community sustainability are not seen as separate concerns but as interdependent. What we mean by "*other* paths" has very different rationale and politics from what was proposed by writers in the lineage of Hernando de Soto, whose book *The Other Path* excited a generation of development economists.[4] Though there are points of overlap in our mutual interest in informal economies and informal institutions, instead of advocating the harnessing of the informal sector for market-based and profit-and-loss ends in the movement toward a modern integrated national economy, we are interested in the reproduction, intersection, and enhancement of different life-worlds in all their complexity. The concept of "other"—as in "other paths"—is thus used here in a pointed way. *Other* paths, we argue, need to take into account different ontological formations, including customary relations. Rather than either assuming or advocating the virtue of modernization as a one-dimensional process of development, or even arguing for "another modernity," we present a case for negotiation between different constituencies across the formations of social life. The book thus advocates something that those of us immersed in a culture of modern consumption or modern education will experience as *other* to what we take for granted as the way of the world.

PAUL JAMES, October 2011

Notes

1. The larger team includes Damian Grenfell, Paul James, Martin Mulligan, Yaso Nadarajah, Peter Phipps, Victoria Stead, Anna Trembath, and Mayra Walsh, all part of the Globalism Research Centre, as well as Supriya Singh and others.

2. We started with the Department for Community Development (DFCD) document *New Policy Direction: Revitalizing Local Communities and the Nation* (DFCD, Port Moresby, 2004). The first stage of the research used broad-ranging techniques including social profiling, a well-being questionnaire, photo-narratives, and strategic interviews to elucidate issues of economic and cultural development. The Department for Community Development was the executing agency, and the research and policy development stage was conducted under the auspices of the Employment-Oriented Skills Development Project backed by the Government of Papua New Guinea and the Asian Development Bank. The research team for the first stage was drawn from the Globalism Institute (now the Globalism Research Centre) and the Department for Community Development. In the current stage, as we move from taking findings back to local communities for further rounds of discussion and on to the implementation stage, the Globalism Research Centre continues to work closely with members of the Department for Community Development and to engage with the communities themselves.

3. There have in the past been a number of remarkable community consultation and social mapping projects. For example, the Social Feasibility Study of the Bismarck-Ramu Conservation and Development Project is a case in point (see Flip Van Helden, *Between Cash and Conviction: The Social Context of the Bismarck-Ramu Integrated Conservation and Development Project*, National Research Institute, Boroko, 1998). However, as extensive as it was, that report was based on one area and not directly tied into national policy development.

4. Hernando de Soto, *The Other Path: The Invisible Revolution in the Third World*, Harper and Row, New York, 1989.

I   COMMUNITIES IN CONTEXT

Chapter 1

Postcolonial Development and Sustainability

THE INDEPENDENCE OF Papua New Guinea was marked by both bold an-
ticipation and uncomfortable ambivalence. The Constitution of the Independent
State of Papua New Guinea (1975) brought the nation-state into being on the basis of a set of careful principles as far-reaching as its constitutional ancestors, including the Declaration of the Rights of Man (1789) and the Constitution of the
United States (1861). It has often been noted that the beginning of the Republic
of France, framed by its principles of *liberté, égalité,* and *fraternité,* represented
a faltering but long-term reorganization of sovereignty around the centrality of
a new political constituency—*the people*. The recognition of the category of "the
people" and the enunciation of the ideals of liberty, equality, and fraternity sig-
nified a turning point in political history. It was also an important milestone
in naming the conditions for the formation of nation-states across the globe.
The new hopes were carried forward in the Constitution of the United States,
as signaled by the brilliantly simple naming of the authors of the Constitution
as "We the People." For all their limitations, both documents as part of a global
shift toward written constitutions confirmed the "community of all citizens" as
the basis for modern political life. It might seem strange to begin a discussion of
Papua New Guinea by referring to eighteenth-century constitutional theory, but
it has a crucial point. The Constitution of Papua New Guinea was just as searching as those documents and in important respects went much further.

Alongside principles that, at least in theory, afforded the people dynamic
self-determination, social equity, and communality, the PNG Constitution emphasized the importance of ecological sustainability, grass-roots economic viability, and respect for customary ways of life. As a postcolonial nation it recognized a continuing "prehistory." This was a history that could not be expressed
as a singular narrative of becoming a nation-state. Whereas most constitutions

2

are one-dimensionally modern and center on the nation-state as the most im-portant level of community and polity, the PNG Constitution proclaimed a more complex aspiration. It gave expression to two possible basic reformations of the modern nation-state. First, it reconfigured modern ideals of the community-polity in relation to the continuing importance of tribal and traditional ways of life. Second, it placed the nation-state in a continuing relation to other social institutions—in particular, local community and family. Unlike, for example, France, the United States, and Australia, the country was not legally conceived as a nation of individuals. The importance of these reformulations cannot be underestimated.

The Constitution of Papua New Guinea was a doubly extraordinary docu-ment given that it was written in the context of a prevailing global orthodoxy of large-scale capitalist development and megaprojects. Most mainstream develop-ment writers, including the author of a book titled *How It All Began: Origins of the Modern Economy*, published in the same year as the Constitution, presented the normal path to development as systematic capitalism leading to "high-mass consumption."[1] To the contrary, according to the PNG Constitution, economic development in Papua New Guinea would be built on a different foundation:

1. A fundamental re-orientation of our attitudes and the institutions of gov-ernment, commerce, education and religion towards Papua New Guinean forms of participation, consultation, and consensus, and a continuous re-newal of the responsiveness of these institutions to the needs and attitudes of the People; and
2. Particular emphasis in our economic development to be placed on small-scale artisan, service and business activity; and
3. Recognition that the cultural, commercial and ethnic diversity of our people is a positive strength, and for the fostering of a respect for, and appreciation of, traditional ways of life and culture, including language, in all their rich-ness and variety, as well as for a willingness to apply these ways dynamically and creatively for the tasks of development; and
4. Traditional villages and communities to remain as viable units of Papua New Guinean society, and for active steps to be taken to improve their cul-tural, social, economic and ethical quality.[2]

The arguments of the present book conform to the terms of those articles but suggest that, given the slow crisis in contemporary Papua New Guinea, ac-tive processes are needed to make them possible.[3] The Constitution reflected the hopes of an emerging postcolonial state and was intended to enable Papua New Guinea to develop in a way that was self-determining and self-orienting.

It reflected what was loosely called the "Melanesian Way"—sometimes an empty cliché, sometimes a romantic allusion, and occasionally a glimmer of an alternative.

The country was to be developed with landownership rights for the people, focusing on small locally owned and run enterprises. The Constitution explicitly articulated an understanding of society in which "individual and community *interdependence* are basic principles" (emphasis added) and in which development would occur "primarily through the use of Papua New Guinean forms of social and political organization." The cultural, political, and ecological formations of individual communities were to drive economic development in ways that reflected "small-scale artisan, service and business activity." Development was to be built on the peoples' skills and resources. This was part of an explicit concern to mitigate the risk that the wrong kind of economic development could encourage "dependence on imported skills and resources," undermine Papua New Guinea's "self-reliance and self-respect," or promote dependency on donor countries.[4] The framers of the Constitution could not have been more prescient about the dangers. Many of the problems they identified have been realized—some tragically, some as farcical reruns of earlier tragedies, and some as manageable problems endemic to any development process.

Constituting a State of Nonconforming Communities

One problem that the constitutional framers overlooked was the variable forms of customary tribal and traditional political authority—from "big man" societies to paramount chiefdoms—and how these were to be accommodated within a unitary modern state with a stable party system. On the eve of Papua New Guinea's independence, many individuals—resident expatriates, overseas observers, and local Papua New Guineans—were deeply skeptical about the future of an independent Papua New Guinea. Some people in the New Guinea Highlands were apprehensive of being dominated by better-educated coastal and island people, while Papuans around the capital Port Moresby feared being swamped by immigration from the Highlands, a sentiment that continues today.

A series of microseparatist and local protest groups arose in the 1970s, ranging from the Kabisawali movement in the Trobriands led by John Kasaipwalova (who now lives an hour's walk from one of the communities featured in this book), to Papua Besena in Central Province led by Josephine Abaijah, to the Highlands Liberation Front, which was begun far from the Highlands in Port Moresby at the University of Papua New Guinea.[5] The Mataungan Association in Tolai East New Britain, which after independence joined the newly formed coalition government, projected Tolai autonomy unless Whites ultimately left the country.[6] Shortly before independence, a Bougainville secessionist group led by Leo Hannett and Father John Momis (de facto chairman of the Constitutional Planning Committee) unsuccessfully declared the independence of the "North Solomons Republic." This movement among others became one of the key pressures for forcing the emergent state to devolve power to the provinces.

In the cities such as Lae, Rabaul, and Moresby, this process was complicated in the period before independence as different groups used the climate of political acuity to voice their various grievances, including issues of general social inequity and the pay and conditions of workers in the public service and teaching professions. The month of June 1974 in Port Moresby and Lae was marked by postindependence street demonstrations. One demonstration, extending over two days, was organized by the United Church Women's Fellowship in Hohola. It was intended to voice concerns about racism, social conditions in the city, and emerging postcolonial class differences as locals took over from departing Australians in positions of power. Two thousand women were reported to have joined the march. The Konedobu office of the chief minister, Michael Somare, was stoned and windows smashed. Without really understanding the background to the demonstration and the nature of the Papua Besena movement, the *Sydney Morning Herald* attributed the event to "Papua's separatist firebrand, Miss Josephine Abaijah."[7] Commentators, looking to the general experience of postcolonial states elsewhere, spoke of the likelihood of political anarchy, an army coup, or authoritarian single-party dominance, and of economic collapse.

During the late twentieth century, Papua New Guinea did not follow any of those predicted paths to debilitating crisis or collapse. However, neither did the country follow the spirit of its own constitution. By any measure, the years from independence to the present have been hard. Instead of a complex but reflexively negotiated meld of customary and modern modes of governance, a modern compromise was entered into that accentuated and distorted one form of customary governance—the "big man" as a position of accumulated status— inside a liberal-democratic state that gave out money to politicians to embody that status. Instead of a complex meld of customary and modern development, the two forms of politics existed in ugly tension with each other, often to the detriment of local communities. As politicians reached out to mainstream ideas of development, the state became dependent on an unfortunate mixture of foreign aid and extraction industries.

Despite early assertions that postcolonial Papua New Guinea should not become dependent on foreign intervention for its development, aid remains fundamental to civil investment. Australia remains the most significant aid donor to Papua New Guinea, with approximately $330 million in aid for 2007–2008, $390 million for 2008–2009, and $457 million for 2010–2011.[8] Australia's large and complex development industry in Papua New Guinea comprises several interrelated government departments and agencies as well as private companies contracted out to deliver aid projects. The Department of Foreign Affairs and Trade (DFAT) funds both AusAID and the Australian Centre for International Agricultural Research (ACIAR), which, in turn, support development projects ranging from infrastructure construction and health campaigns to agricultural research and extension programs. In the latest round, the main AusAID delivery process in Papua New Guinea, Strongim Pipol, Strongim Nesen (Empower the People, Strengthen the Nation), with funding of up to $100 million over five years, is managed by URS, a massive engineering corporation headquartered in San Francisco and one of the top fifty contractors in the Iraq and Afghanistan "reconstruction" process.

Public policy think tanks, such as the Canberra-based Centre for Independent Studies (CIS), the Lowy Institute, and the Australian Strategic Policy Institute (ASPI) also play a role by contributing policy advice and commentary to government departments in Australia. Each of these development agencies, companies, think tanks, and consultants is responsible not only for informing the delivery of Australia's aid, but also for ensuring that the aid program addresses Australia's economic and strategic national interests. This is part of the problem. Many individuals working in this area may have different views from the dominant policy directions, but at an institutional level conventional notions of modern capitalist "development" and the Australian "national interest" prevail.

Now, more than three decades since the vision for a Melanesian form of development was first articulated—though never substantially enacted in practice—the nation-state of Papua New Guinea has entered a period of what might be called "slow crisis." We have to be careful in using such a condensed and potentially loaded term and to be precise about its meaning. First, the polity across all levels of government continues to be fragile with counterproductive and fragmented relations down into local communities and limited capacity at the local levels to deliver basic services or consistent rule of law. It is a *fragile state*. We do not mean to suggest, as many definitions of the term imply, that as a fragile polity Papua New Guinea faces the prospect of becoming a *failing* or *failed state*.[9] The PNG political process remains firmly democratic *in procedure*, with Organic Law reforms around local-level government, party stability, and preferential voting systems making some (minimal) difference to improving stability and accountability.[10] Corruption permeates the activities of some individual state administrators, politicians, and business operators, but active attempts are being taken to curtail both political and economic corruption, and it is far from accurate to say that a state of corruption defines the polity.

Second, while the nation remains fragmented, with little sense of common vision beyond general enunciations of the Melanesian Way or state-based consensus on some economic goals as spelled out in the Medium Term Development Strategy, it is not the case that the nation-state of a thousand tribes is in danger of breaking up. With care, Papua New Guinea could develop an integrating ideology of "unity in diversity" that has none of the authoritarian implications of the concept as it has been used in Indonesia and more depth than achieved under the rhetoric of multiculturalism in Australia or the melting pot in the United States. National sentiment might be a superficial layer over profound cultural differences, but this can be seen in some ways as an advantage rather than a problem.

Third, the nation's diverse local communities are being placed under increasing pressure. This process is facing communities across the Global South and North in different ways; older intersecting forms of solidaristic integration are being hollowed out, with community resilience and capacity to respond to change more and more dependent on outside resources. In Papua New Guinea, communities have never conformed to the modern romantic notion of islands of rural idyll (see Part II), but they are increasingly challenged by different expectations and ways of life. These conflicting expectations are compounded by the weakness of the state in paradoxical tension with a *modern* "cargo-cult" mentality that treats the state, or rather politicians, as intermittent providers of "good things"—albeit with no trust in them delivering.[11] However, while processes of global change such as financial crises and commodity-price fluctuations increasingly affect communities in Papua New Guinea, they were not subject to the same intensity of effect that ravaged communities in other parts of Southeast Asia after the Asian Financial Crisis in 1997–1998. At the level of local and informal economies, for example (Chapter 7), Papua New Guinea was relatively resilient in the face of the 2008–2010 "global financial meltdown." Even NASFUND, the key national superannuation fund for Papua New Guinea, remained relatively secure through the massive global fluctuations.[12] Increasing food insecurity in certain parts of the country, for example, appears to be more a function of increasing population numbers, reliance on store-bought commodities, and climate fluctuation than an intrinsic vulnerability.

The concept of "slow crisis" is used here drawing upon the classical and more ambiguous sense of a turning point (a *krisis*) that requires a response. It does not imply that a single decision will be sufficient to enhance the resilience of communities and political institutions in the face of massive change. Rather, it is to say that the cultural, political, and economic fabric of PNG communities around the country, still strong in many places, is being slowly weakened by uneven processes that are affecting local lifeways across the globe—the intensification of rapacious forms of globalizing capitalism, the overriding of production cultures by consumerism, the steady pull of unsustainable kinds of urbanization, the proselytizing reach of globalizing religions, together with effect of population increases and the continued degrading of the base environment.

In many cases these processes are invited in, and in some cases they are sustainably managed. However, in Papua New Guinea, local manifestations of the slow crisis continue to press into people's lives: sporadic but chronic violence, creeping civil decay, uncontrolled rural-urban migration, insidious political corruption, misplaced interventions from the outside, and a continuing overemphasis on large-scale corporate-led development such as through palm oil production, or logging and mining.[13]

The slow crisis always teeters on the edge of turning into a general disaster. The latest megaproject, the Liquefied Natural Gas project, has, in the tradition of Ok Tedi and Bougainville, created much hyperbole about potential social returns, but it may also be the basis for cultural disaster as communities fight over the spoils. An infrastructure and building boom has ensued in Port Moresby, but the construction will be concluded by 2014, and the project has uncertain long-term benefits. Such pressures present increasingly difficult challenges to the well-being of the nation-state even if a superficial sense of nationhood continues to be reproduced in the language and practice of "our country"—from the rhetoric of politics and sport to the advertising slogans of global soft drink manufactures.[14] Some of the more obvious expressions of problems coming home to affect the fundamental conditions of life include low life-expectancy rates, high infant and maternal mortality, chronic sexual violence,[15] debilitating urban crime, police violence, and an increasing incidence of HIV/AIDS.[16] In the face of this horror, some remarkable individuals, communities, and organizations in Papua New Guinea are working together to respond to such issues—these are our source of hope.

Defining Development and Sustainability

Development in this part of the world, as elsewhere in the Global South, continues to be a struggle. The lives of the people that corporate or state-led development is meant to enrich are often being made more difficult by the very developmental process that purports to help them. It remains true in Papua New Guinea as elsewhere that, despite well-intentioned attempts to the contrary, most development projects do not know how to engage with the complexity of community life. In many cases, while a paradigm shift from "things" to "people" has been discussed and encouraged, it has not been translated into practice. A consensus has emerged among commentators in the fields of education, anthropology, community development, and political ecology that sustainable development is something that comes from within communities rather than something that can be imposed from the outside. This nevertheless leaves many questions.

Within a landscape changed by the colonial experience and beset by the forces of globalization—most pressingly a global demand for natural resources—how are issues of self-determination, social equity and communality, ecological sustainability, grass-roots economic viability, and respect for customary ways of life to be negotiated in practice? From the most remote of the Highlands to the island communities to the densely compact settlements of Port Moresby, what paths to development are sustainable, practical, and appropriate? How can Papua New Guinea accommodate an indigenous and organic concept of "development" that takes account of the country's history, the rich diversity of its human experiences, and the changing nature of a society that is being unevenly shaped by processes of postcolonial change? Why do some community groups remain resilient—despite pressing and sometimes insurmountable odds—while others fall apart, becoming increasingly fragmented or at the worst resorting to sometimes the most heinous forms of violence? These are questions to which we intend to make a contribution.

The term "development" itself is complex and difficult. In the corporate sphere, it usually refers to the generating of physical infrastructure, political stability, and workforce training that will enhance company profit taking. In the state-led model of development, it commonly means building layers of civil administration and providing the legislative, infrastructural, and educational framework for economic-based development, all understood in terms of the nation-building program. In the area of community and civil-society studies, ideas of development range from getting more things to the people or building social capital, to alternative notions of the enhancement of community sustainability, resilience, security, and adaptability. Will there be space in Papua New Guinea for maintaining alternate patterns of development? How are the concepts of "development" and "development rights" to be understood, or even renegotiated, in communities where no such terms exist in their everyday languages?

Here we define development as *social change—with all its intended or unintended outcomes—that brings about a significant and patterned shift in the technologies, techniques, infrastructure, and/or associated life forms of a place or people.* There is no presumption in this definition that development entails modernization, but neither is there any suggestion of a "return to the past" except in the sense that certain *forms* of practice enacted in the past can be chosen in the present. There is no suggestion that all development is good. And given the possibility of unintended consequences, reversals, and counterproductive outcomes, there is no suggestion that all "good development" is sustainable.

Nor, it should be said, is all "sustainable development" good development. This last point is one rarely made in the mainstream Global North. In Papua New Guinea, activists, constantly confronting the rhetoric of development, tend to distinguish between "real development...about local people" and "*giaman* development"—that is, development characterized by false (*giaman* in Tok Pisin) short-term or meaningless promises about roads, jobs, and cash.[17] Papua New Guinea is unfortunately rife with the *giaman* development.

Related to this, Marshall Sahlins gives us the concept of "develop-man," drawing on the Tok Pisin term *defelopman,* to describe the indigenous tendency in the Pacific to actively use the material outcomes of capitalism to reassert a fetishized version of customary relations and rituals fueled by the modern. Big men become bigger, but the process of customary reproduction becomes more fragile. Speaking with sad irony, he suggests that in the passage from develop-man to modern economic development, customary people have had "to pass through a certain cultural desert to reach the promised land of 'modernization': they had to experience a certain humiliation."[18] Rather, in order to treat sustainable development in a holistic way, we draw on an orienting method called "circles of sustainability" that suggests that the social can be understood in terms of four domains: economy, ecology, politics, and culture.[19] These different domains are then considered in the context of layers of changing dominant formations of social life. In relation to the passage of develop-man toward modern economic development, Joel Robbins picks up on the paradoxical developmental outcome of this layering within a framework of dominance. Christianity in Papua New Guinea, in some forms, not only makes humiliation of tribal practices and belief "part of the coherent story of self-development, it goes so far as to give it a positive valence....Once it has done so in a particular locale, the era of develop-man in that place has in important respects come to an end." Moreover, "it encourages converts to become conscious of their 'culture,' a hypostatized image of their past way of life. Once people have reified their culture, it is but a short step for them to begin making conscious efforts to discard it and replace it with something new."[20]

The classic 1987 report *Our Common Future,* more commonly known as the Brundtland Report, defined sustainable development as "development that meets the needs of the present without compromising the ability of future generations to meet their own needs."[21] This definition still works, though its meaning turns on the undefined implications of the word "needs" and the assumed importance of cultural, political, and ecological needs rather than just economic material needs. The notion of "community sustainability" is a more recent one. Depending on how it is defined, it can be both a more specific and a more expansive concept than that of "sustainable development." It is more specific in that it looks at the practices and actions that are needed in relation to existing communities to achieve sustainable development, yet it is more expansive in that it has the potential to move beyond schematic or instrumental accounts of sustainable development to encompass the various domains of the social, including cultural aspects of how communities cohere through time. Beyond such general accounts, however, there is little agreement on what it means or entails, particularly in integrated social terms. While much research has been carried out on community sustainability from an economic or even ecological standpoint,[22] little work exists on the potential of cultural practices in strengthening communities.

Some writers point to the vagueness of the concept of "community sustainability." Voth and Moon, for example, identify four broad categories of contributors to the relevant research literature.[23] These are *designers,* including architects and planning professionals, who frame community sustainability in terms of planning processes; *practitioners,* including politicians, local government officials, and community groups and organizations, for which community is defined primarily in terms of municipalities or similar administrative units, and the focus of sustainability are ecological issues; *visionaries,* including agriculturalists, economists, architects, and planning professionals, who define communities in terms of association and interest and focus on issues of economic development, appropriate use of technology, and energy conservation; and, finally, *activists,* including environmentalists, people interested in bioregionalism, social ecologists, and others, whose focus is on community impacts on the natural environment. Despite the ever-burgeoning literature that touches on community sustainability, noting many of its positives, including the emphasis on community as agents of change and participatory decision-making processes, Voth and Moon conclude that "the idea of community sustainability *per se* hardly exists.... Vague abstractions like 'social capital' are discussed, but few details are provided about what really makes a community sustainable in terms of infrastructure, economics, culture, decision-making processes, and so on."[24]

Here we define community sustainability as *the long-term durability of a community as it negotiates changing practices and meanings across all the domains of culture, politics, economics, and ecology.* Again, it should be clear that communities can be sustainable without being good places to live.

Part of the significance of the present project, then, lies in its attempt to address the gaps in the current literature on community sustainability and to extend theoretical observations about a new qualitative conception of community sustainability informed by substantial and innovative empirical research. In this context, sustainability is conceived in terms that include not just practices tied to development, but also forms of well-being and social bonds, community-building, social support, and infrastructure renewal. In short, the concern with sustainability here entails undertaking an analysis of how communities are sustained through time, how they cohere and change, rather than being constrained within discourses and models of development. From another angle, this project presents an account of community sustainability detached from instrumental concerns with narrow economic development. While concerns about production and exchange continue to be imperative for community sustainability, this project will suggest that an approach driven by economistic concerns has a tendency to be reductive and will fail to account for the real complexity of interactions and effects produced by the matrix of cultural, political, economic, and ecological practices.

Defining Formations of Community

Ever since Ferdinand Tönnies introduced the terms "gemeinschaft" and "gesellschaft" to describe a shift from a society dominated by relatively stable, mainly nonurban, communities that emphasized mutual obligation and trust (gemeinschaften) to more mobile, highly urbanized societies in which individual self-interest comes to the fore (gesellschaften), commentators have been interested in the ever-changing nature of community.[25] Until recently, belonging to a community was usually seen as unqualifiedly positive. While community is now seen in more circumspect terms, the erosion of community is still predominantly interpreted as being the cause of social problems.[26] However, defining community is not straightforward, and this complexity has become an abiding concern of scholars of Melanesia.

In the West, the term "community" is often used interchangeably with "neighborhood" to refer to the bonds that come with living cheek by jowl with others in a shared space. Alternatively, it is used to refer to people bound by a particular identity defined by nation, language group, ethnicity, clan, race, religion, or sexual orientation. Or, again, it refers to groupings of mutual self-interest such as a profession or association. Cutting across all of these, community can also be defined by a particular mode of interaction, such as virtual or online communities. Community often seems to be whatever people say it is, potentially incorporating every conceivable form of human grouping, even those that might otherwise strike one as contradictory.

In the context of the supposed new "fluidity" of global interchange, community has come in for sustained critique in relation to its effects on social well-being. The feminist scholar Iris Marion Young has argued that the desire for community is oppressive in that it seeks to nullify difference and, as a consequence, validates gender discrimination, racism, and ethnic chauvinism.[27] Similarly, Zygmunt Bauman has argued that communitarianism creates an ideal of community that is like the "home writ large," in which there is no room for the homeless and which can also turn into an unexpected "prison" for many of the residents.[28] Bauman is more optimistic than Young in thinking that a new kind of unity is possible—"a unity put together through negotiation and reconciliation, not the denial, stifling or smothering out of difference."[29] However, under conditions of what he problematically calls globalizing "liquid modernity," he sees community as entirely a matter of individual choice—a desire to redress the growing imbalance between individual freedom and security. This is clearly not the case in Papua New Guinea. Arjun Appadurai has gone further in saying that he far prefers the "detachment of a postcolonial, diasporic, academic identity" to the "ugly realities of being racialized, minoritized, and tribalized in my everyday encounters" in local community.[30] And he looks forward to the time when externally and internally oppressive national states will give way to "transnational social forms."[31] In all these cases, community as such is seen to be source of the problems of exclusion and conflict. It is our contention, however, that the theorists of this "postmodern fluid world" fail to understand the enduring, if changing and variable, possibilities of existing communities—from the local to the global.

The metaphor of fluidity has even overcome some writers on Papua New Guinea. In a book provocatively called *Fluid Ontologies: Myth, Ritual and Philosophy in the Highlands of Papua New Guinea,* the editors argue that the metaphors of "fire" and "water" best represent the nuances of mobility, flows, flux, and change.[32] By comparison, in our argument it is not the ontologies or the social forms that are fluid, but rather the content—sometimes subtly, sometimes dramatically fluid, but always within a dialectic of change and continuity. That means that the trope of "ground" or "earth" continues to be as important as the tropes of fire and water. Ontologies are changing but not just as water carves the landscape or fire brings life through destruction: also as the tension between fire and physical exhaustion, water and ground.

In the contemporary world—whether it be Port Moresby or Paris—an emerging sense that one's sense of community is changing and no longer lived as a "given" is in tension with powerful subjective continuities. That is, community is no longer a relationship that a person might be drawn into, or even born into, without being forced at some time to think about its meaning, although for the most part we take such social relations for granted. Given all the variations, retraditionalizations, continuities, and transformations, the distinction made by Tönnies between "the social" cast in terms of the predominance of stable and traditional gemeinschaften or the more fluid and displaced gesellschaften is too dichotomous to be useful. However, the metaphor of flows just reverses the previous misplaced emphasis on tribal and traditional societies as fixed. It is becoming clear that it is necessary to look at the ways in which forms of community identity are be-ing created and re-created in relation to continuities under changing circumstances, both objectively and subjectively. The definition of community thus needs to be generalizing across quite different settings, but without simply being a matter of subjective and changing self-definition and without including all forms of as-sociation or sociality that happen to be important such as the family.

Here we define community very broadly as *a group or network of persons who are connected (objectively) to each other by relatively durable social relations that extend beyond immediate genealogical ties and who mutually define that relationship (subjectively) as important to their social identity and social practice.* This defini-tion allows us to recognize that communities in Papua New Guinea do not have natural or singular boundaries. "Singular" village-based communities, to the extent that they ever existed in Papua New Guinea, were in part an outcome of the colonial period.

Communities in Papua New Guinea are located in places—in the termi-nology that we are about to develop, they are "grounded"—but the nature of those places is crossed by different and overlapping relations. The following discussion offers three ways of characterizing community relations: (1) *ground-ed community relations,* in which the salient feature of community life is taken to be people coming together in particular tangible settings based on face-to-face engagement; (2) *lifestyle community relations,* in which the key feature bring-ing together a community is adherence to particular attitudes and practices; and (3) *projected community relations,* in which neither particularistic relations nor adherence to a particular way of life are preeminent but rather the active establishment of a social space in which individuals engage in open-ended pro-cesses of constructing, deconstructing, and reconstructing identities and ethics for living.

Before elaborating these categories further, a couple of notes of caution ought to be sounded about how these different accounts of community relate to each other. First, we are distinguishing between forms of community rela-tions, not forms of communities. When in this discussion communities are so distinguished, it is only as a shorthand designation for a community constituted in the dominance of one or another of these forms of community relations, not a complete description. The distinctions between community relations as em-bodied, as a lifestyle, or as projected are intended as analytical distinctions *and* shorthand designations. For example, the PNG concept of *wantok* relations has its foundation in grounded community relations, but, like the Australian con-cept of "mateship," it has, at the same time, been lifted out of that context and can be used as a lifestyle relationship between relative strangers.

Second, it is not being claimed that the bundle of relations in a given community exist in practice as one or another of those pure variations. Rather, the terms are intended as offering a way into an analytical framework across which the dominant, coexistent, and/or subordinate manifestations of different community relations (and therefore different communities) can be mapped. Though one dimension of community relations can predominate in a given community—and a community can thus be designated as such—the temptation to pigeonhole this or that community into a single way of constituting community should be resisted. Such an approach can lead to a reductive approach in which the complexity of a particular community is reduced to just one of its dimensions. For example, Wisini village in the mountains of Morobe Province is a strongly grounded community, but to the extent that its people have taken on the Pariet Project of self-consciously exploring its customary foundations and trying to write its history, it has also become over the past decade an increasingly politically projected community.

Third, living in the same place as others does not automatically make a group of people a grounded community (or even, to make the point more precisely, a community characterized by the dominance of grounded community relations). To take an example, it might be expected that communities in which people live together in villages are archetypal embodied communities—and often they are. However, of itself, the simple fact of coming into regular face-to-face contact with others indicates little about how those embodied relations are structured. The experience of being pressed together in an urban settlement in Lae or Port Moresby, in which people from different places find common shelter, and the experience of walking together across customary ground where place and genealogy define the relationship of those walking are both instances of embodied interaction. However, they can be worlds apart in terms of how the social relations are structured, integrated, and enacted. In short, surface descriptions about how people *interact* with one another do not always reveal much about how such interactions and relations are *integrated*.

In the framework proposed here, then, the terms "grounded community," "lifestyle community," and "projected community" are used not as normatively charged descriptions but as shorthand terms to refer to the dominant forms of social relations that constitute a given community.[33] They refer to the way in which social relations are framed and enacted without making any implicit judgment about whether they are good or bad. The purpose here is to offer a way of thinking about how communities are constituted across different ways of living and relating to others: to see how communities are constituted through the intersection of different forms of social integration from the face-to-face to the institutionally extended or disembodied, forms that overlay and overlap with one another.

Grounded Community

Attachment to *particular* places and to *particular* people are the salient features of what we are calling "grounded community relations." In other words, relations of mutual presence and placement are central to structuring the connections between people. Except for periods of stress or political intensification—usually in response to unwanted interventions from the outside—questions about active social projection are subordinate in accounts and practices of grounded community. Such projection is usually seen in terms of what is already given and in place. In such a setting, questions about the nature of one's lifestyle are assumed to take care of themselves so long as a given social and physical environment is in place with appropriate infrastructure such as dwellings and amenities. As will be seen in Part II, "Communities in Place," grounded community relations can sometimes be extended over spatial distances, stretched, for example, between the city and the country, to the extent that the diaspora continues to be connected by abiding embodied relations such as through regular powerful ceremonies of birth, marriage, and death.

Thus, adherence to particular ways of life tends to spring from a taken-for-granted sense of commonality and continuity. It arises from the face-to-face bonds with other persons in one's locale rather than from thinking about the lifestyle itself. People do not have to read from community-development tomes, self-help books, or religious tracts to confirm how to act with one another. Norms of behavior emerge from people in meaningful relations as the habitus of their being.[34] Even when the religious observances of such communities break out of the confines of mythical time—in the sense that they transcendentally look forward to a world to come and go back to the beginning of time—the sense of community is strongly conditioned by local settings and is carried on through rituals and ways of living that are rooted in categories of embodiment and presence. Customary *tribal* communities and rural *traditional* communities are examples of communities in which grounded relations tend to be dominant.

Grounded community relations tend to be bounded, both socially and environmentally, though communities so characterized are not necessarily more environmentally or socially sustainable. The strengths of grounded community relations are also its weaknesses. Just as natural ecosystems can be seriously disrupted by population changes or the introduction of outside organisms, accounts of communal integrity that arise in such settings tend to point to the disruptive effects of external forces. At one extreme this can lead to xenophobia and suspicion of outsiders. At the other extreme communities can be undermined by the influx of strangers or, if the tangible resources that sustain the community are taken away, allowed to fall into a state of disrepair or restructured through processes over which the local community has no say or control. Something of the notion of gemeinschaft survives in many mainstream and romantic ideas of community, in which local communities are threatened by centralization and loss of local control to government or corporate bureaucracy. This conception of community finds expression in some environmental philosophy, where community is seen as allowing "human-scale" development. Here community is a place where a more "authentic" life is said to be able to flourish away from the world of the mass market, the media, telecommunications, and the state—a condition of community that in a globalizing world is increasingly impossible to sustain, even in the remotest areas of Papua New Guinea.

Lifestyle Community

In contrast with grounded community relations, where the emphasis is on the particularities of people and place as the salient features of community, there are accounts and practices of community that give primacy to particular ways of living. In practice, this tends to take one of three forms.

Morally framed community relations tend to arise wherever there are relationships of trust and mutual obligation between people who agree to abide by certain morally charged ways of life. They are formed around a specified normative boundary: norms of right and wrong, appropriate and inappropriate behavior. This is the form taken by many *traditional* religious communities. Community here is essentially a regulative space, a means of binding people into particular ways of living. Nikolas Rose, though not an advocate of such conceptions of normatively based community relations, provides a neat characterization of such communities as "a moral field binding persons into durable relations. It is a space of emotional relationships, through which individual identities are constructed through their bonds to micro-cultures of values and meanings."[35] In Papua New Guinea, the churches have acted to layer morally framed community relations over the older grounded communities of clans, tribes, and villages. This has given those churches extraordinary purchase on community life, even if the prior forms of grounded relations continue on and the two layers of social life are in profound tension.

Interest-based community relations form around an interest or aesthetic inclination, where lifestyle or activity, however superficial, is evoked as the basis of the relationship. In Papua New Guinea this includes sporting and leisure-based communities, which come together for regular moments of engagement, and expatriate or diaspora communities who share commonalities of lifestyle or interest.

Proximate community relations come together where neighborhood or commonality of association forms a community of convenience. This is not the same as a grounded community, even though both are based in spatial proximity. As distinct from conceptions of grounded community, the cultural embeddedness of persons in this or that place does not define the coherence of community, nor does the continual embodied involvement of its members with each other.

Since the salience of lifestyle community relations lies in their morally framed, interest-based, or proximate coherence, such communities can be delinked from particular groups of people and particular locales. In other words, they can be deterritorialized. Face-to-face embodied relations may be subjectively important to such communities, but they might equally be constituted through virtual or technologically mediated relations where people agree to abide by certain conventions and bonds. In this regard, it is a *potentially* more open and mobile form of community. This is its strength but also its weakness. On the one hand, it tends to generate culturally thinner communities than grounded relations. On the other hand, lifestyle relations tend to allow for more adaptability to change.

This kind of community has gained the recent attention of the discipline of sociology. Sociologists have become increasingly interested in ways in which communities have become more spatially dispersed.[36] Over forty years ago, the US sociologist M. M. Webber suggested that improvements to communications and transport technologies had facilitated the emergence of "communities without propinquity," that is, spatially dispersed communities that people can choose to belong to as a result of shared interests or shared values.[37] Many did not share Webber's enthusiasm for this "new" form of community, noting that, for people such as the elderly or women with children, the weakening of place-based grounded communities had led to greater social isolation. The subsequent acceleration in technology-assisted compressions of time and space further shifted attention toward the prevalence of nonlocal communities. Increasingly, a distinction has been drawn between the terms "community" and "neighborhood" on the assumption that better planning of neighborhoods can facilitate social interaction and the emergence of community identity for those who need it. Again the emphasis is on the conscious choices that people might make about when and where to participate.

The idea of community constituted as a space for ways of life can be seen in liberal communitarian accounts. Advocating what he calls a "new communitarianism," Amitai Etzioni defines community as "webs of social relations that encompass shared meanings and above all shared values."[38] This conception of community also underpins recent debates around social capital, where community is regarded as a means of generating *abstracted* relations of trust, reciprocity, and mutual obligation. Communities constituted in this way are claimed to be consonant with contemporary forms of globalization. Since webs of trust and cooperation can be enacted via highly mediated forms of communication—although it is questionable how sustainable this is—it is accurate to say that community can be disembedded from the particularities of people and place. For new communitarians such as Etzioni, this is a virtue since it wards against settled communities becoming oppressive to individuals or subgroups. If a particular community begins to exert undue control over its members, individuals have the capacity to withdraw from it and realize different connections. In Etzioni's words: "People are at one and the same time members of several communities, such as professional, residential and others. They can and do use these multi-memberships...to protect themselves from excessive pressure by any one community."[39]

Projected Community

Unlike the two other conceptions of community relations, the notion of a "projected community" is not defined by attachment to a particular place or to a particular group of people. Neither is it primarily defined by adherence to a shared set of moral norms, traditions, or mutual interests. The salient feature of projected community relations is that a community is self-consciously treated as a created entity. It is because of this primacy accorded to the created, creative, active, and projected dimension of community that the word "projected" is used. This is perhaps the most difficult idea of community to grasp, partly because it is a much more nebulous idea of community. For the advocates of projected communities, such relations are less about the particularities of place and bonds with particular others, or adherence to a particular normative frame, and more an ongoing process of self-formation and transformation. It is a means by which people create and re-create their lives with others.

Communities characterized by the dominance of projected relations can be conservative or radical, modern or postmodern. And they can be hybrid and uneven in their forms of projection. At one end of the spectrum, this process can be deeply political and grass-roots based (the term "grass roots," or *grasruts*, usually has a very positive meaning in Tok Pisin, despite occasional ironical self-derision: *grasruts* as "ignorant"). Projected communities, at least in their more self-reflexive political form, can take the form of ongoing associations of people who seek politically expressed integration, communities of practice based on professional projects,[40] or associative communities that seek to enhance and support individual creativity, autonomy, and mutuality.

At the other end of the spectrum, projected communities can also be trivial or transitory, manipulative or misleading.[41] They can be overgeneralized and more akin to advertising collations. They can live off the modern search for meaning rather than respond adequately to it. Realized in this way, notions of "community" might be projected by a corporate advertiser or state spin doctor around a succession of engagements in the so-called third place of a Starbucks café or a self-named "creative city" or "creative community." Here older forms of community relations dissolve into postmodern fluidity where notions of settled, stable, and abiding bonds between people recede into the background.

Unless projected relations are tied back into grounded ties or lifestyle commonalities, such communities tend be superficial and unstable, constantly dissolving and regenerating, despite the best of intentions otherwise.[42] Empty reflexivity—that is, treating oneself or one's community either as an abstracted object of projected development or as the romanticized subject of self-actualization—achieves little. Moreover, as will become apparent in our profiles of different PNG communities, unless reflexive projection of alternative pathways of development is linked to resources and negotiated outside support, it can end up in bitter frustration and counterproductive cynicism.

Thus, in summary, we have mapped the following kinds of community formations:

1. grounded community relations
2. lifestyle community relations
   community life as morally bounded
   community life as interest-based
   community life as proximately related
3. projected community relations
   community life as thin projection
   community life as reflexively projected (as uncritical self-actualization)
   community life as reflexively projected (as self-critical engagement)

What does this mean for Papua New Guinea? In terms of local community formation, it means that older relations of grounded identity and integration continue but are brought into tension with newer upheavals, including badly managed attempts at nation-building, mining development, industrial fishing, and commodity-based agriculture. More than four-fifths of people live in rural areas, and approximately 95 percent of land is under customary title. The population is sparsely spread, and while lines of intercultural trade and translocal movement of persons have long been a feature of the country,[43] people have traditionally been organized into distinct and relatively integral villages interchanging with one another across the separations of distance, environment, and language (there are over seven-hundred languages indigenous to Papua New Guinea). Because of this, forms of community in Papua New Guinea have been, and continue to be, fundamentally shaped by forms of social relationship such as reciprocity associated with village life and relationships to place. As James

Weiner suggests, place and landscape have a profound role in anchoring forms of sociality in Papua New Guinea.[44] In other words, Papua New Guinea is predominantly made up of grounded communities. What we are suggesting is that, notwithstanding the deep history of such communities, their resilience cannot be taken for granted—quite the opposite.

Communities are under threat, both from within and from outside. This makes the formation of a national community an incredibly complex process, particularly in the context of intensifying globalization. Historically nations have been formed as contradictory communities of strangers, projected communities that subjectively *present* themselves either as grounded communities (for example, the older "continuous" nations of Europe) or as lifestyle communities (the urbanized "settler" nations of the West). However, for Papua New Guinea, where grounded communities still continue to predominate at the local level, the transfer of the subjectivities of grounded loyalty and identity over to the national level is fraught.

Our argument is that the localized grounded communities of Papua New Guinea need to take on a level of self-conscious, self-critical, and politically reflexive projection in order to take the strengths of their *ground*—people and place—into a difficult and changing world. This is a world that no longer allows grounded communities to change incrementally and organically through the vagaries of fate, memory, or contingency. It is a world that uses romantic conceptions of place and people and instrumentalizes them for other purposes. A number of writers describe the late 1960s and 1970s as a time in Papua New Guinea when concepts and practices of modernism and traditionalism—called "new ways" and "old ways" by locals—intensified their claim on the indigenous culture.[45] Across the transition from the colonial and postcolonial experience, as discussed in the next chapter—where we use a less dichotomous understanding of intersecting ontological formations, namely, tribalism, traditionalism, modern, and postmodernism, as relations in tension—modernizing pressures certainly came into contention with both customary tribal (indigenous) and religious traditional (colonial) relations. And as different indigenous cultural practices were treated to varying levels of outlawing, protection, or encouragement by both colonial authorities and external religious and governmental influences, an essentializing view of culture, and thereby of community practices—good and bad, progressive and backward-looking—was also being put in place. Against this essentializing view, we are suggesting that the positive projection of community life cannot be achieved as a simple "return to the past" or to "old ways." It entails walking *knowingly* in more than one world at the same time—tribal, traditional, and modern.

Other factors as diverse as the coming of radio and rock-and-roll or the construction of roads and airstrips to mining lands and missions provided what many view as the social watershed that inaugurated "new times, new ways of thinking and living, new forms of social organization and settlement."[46] (By the same process, we constantly found that our own research activities—accruing ambivalent status by being a global research team with members from the national government—also engendered reflection on the present just by our being there.) Whether the pressures are positive or negative, this is the context in which reflexive projection becomes necessary for communities that do not want to be swept away into the dominant currents of change and hope to make choices about the form that development will take.

Reconciliation across the Frictions of Change

To summarize the entire book in a few words, most people in Papua New Guinea live in grounded communities, and these kinds of communities are under serious threat here, as they are across the world. This suggests both vulnerabilities and distinct possibilities for alternative paths. Our vision for possible alternatives has a number of underlying considerations that cross the various domains of the circle of sustainability.

The first consideration is a cry that passively standing still or even actively resisting change is not sustainable. Unless grounded communities, the dominant form of community in Melanesia, reflexively project how they want to live—that is, unless, grounded communities come to reflect on and to politically project the kinds of social development that are appropriate through extended local and public dialogue—they will either slowly disintegrate, at least as grounded communities, or come to depend up parochial boundaries or isolation to maintain the putative integrity of their community. Reflexivity means more than reflection: it entails critical reflection on the nature of the reflection, discussion of what is to be done, and interrogation of the processes of dialogue that will be used to make decisions.

The second consideration starts with a recognition of the complexity of the process. Extended dialogue and critical self-reflection are extraordinarily difficult to maintain in isolation. They are best conducted through processes of learning that draw upon both local and external expertise, and both customary and modern knowledges, including comparative exploration of continuing current ways of doing things and introducing other ways of doing things from communities in Melanesia and beyond. This, of course, is paradoxical. In order to project other paths—including the possibility of reproducing and revivifying practices associated with tribal and traditional lifeways—communities need to take on levels of reflexivity associated with processes of modern knowing. The process of "both-ways learning" across the differences of the tribal, the tradi-

tional, and the modern is not simple. It is elaborated upon in Chapter 11. Pick-
ing up on an apparent resonance with other writers in the field, some readers
have suggested that we are advocating what Ulrich Beck would describe as "reflexive modernization."[47] At this stage we will say no more than that any such
reference is unintended, and the distinctive differences between our use of the
term "reflexive" and Beck's will unfold as the book proceeds (see particularly
Chapter 12). Both-ways politics, in our view, entails not just *another* modernity
but a lived reconciliation—with all the continuing discomfort and tension that
such a process always entails—between ontologically different ways of doing
things: tribal, traditional, and modern. Reconciliation does not mean collapsing
different lifeways into (even) a Melanesian version of the modern. Rather, we are
talking about living with what James Tully calls "strange multiplicities."[48]

The third consideration concerns political and cultural sustainability. Although active projection of other paths to development can occur organically
and serendipitously within communities, it tends not to be sustainable without
some form of political institutionalization and support.[49] In other words, sustainability requires consideration of not just economics and ecology, but also
politics and culture. Reading through the discussion of different communities
(see Part II), it becomes apparent that there is a high degree of self-conscious-
ness about development issues in Papua New Guinea. However, this tends to
be uneven, unsupported, and, at times, a source of conflict between different
members of the community. In the context of contemporary Papua New Guinea,
politically sensitive institutionalization needs to provide an adequate interface
for negotiating a number of competing issues—most pressingly between tribal,
traditional, and modern formations of sociality, including governance, economic production, resource allocation, and learning. Customary leadership as it is
currently configured cannot provide such an interface. Neither, however, can
the modern state. Indeed, the usual form of institutionalization tends to set up
counterproductive and unintended consequences to the extent that it demands
overly simplifying and directly replicable procedures. "Seeing like a state"—that
is, looking for simple singular solutions, to use James Scott's phrase—is bound
to fail.[50] In short, any moves toward institutionalization need to be done in relation to local complexities.

Currently, institutionalizing development at the community level in Papua
New Guinea—the setting up of relatively enduring public bodies of practice—
has tended to be either relatively ad hoc and rolled out project by project, or
formalized and, at least in intention, channeled through local-level government.
The former has been hit and miss; the latter has been mired in politics and lack
of capacity. Hence we are proposing other paths that complement both reforms
in the process of delivering foreign aid and reforms in governance. The cen-

tral focus here is on institutionalizing what can be called "community learning and development centers." Such centers, whether they are centered on a rough *patapata* under a mango tree or a dedicated community building with extensive resources, should be located within communities and run by communities. At the same time, they should be recognized and given both state and nongovernmental support from the outside. Such centers should be local in their decision-making processes and dialogical in their politics, but more than that they need to become sites for negotiation (and partnership where appropriate) with "outsiders."

In effect, these centers could provide settings for different versions of deliberative democracy that recognize the intersecting structures of authority in the locale. They could become sites through which people in communities negotiate with institutions such as the state, aid agencies, churches, and other national and international organizations over possibilities for supporting the resourcing of local development projects and programs in basic areas such as livelihoods (Chapters 7 and 8), health (Chapters 9 and 10), and education (Chapters 11 and 12). Such centers as part of an integrated community development approach would thus provide an alternative to the corporate or welfare state model. This approach requires self-determination at the level of local communities but within a multilayered framework supported by others, including the state as representative of the larger community of the nation.

In the last few paragraphs we have in effect presented the conclusions to our overall project—not just this chapter. This should not suggest that these conclusions were clear to us as we began the journey. And even at the end of this stage they are finalized contingently for the purposes of communicating our thoughts and research findings. Our conclusions will potentially be changed and refined in the process of practical implementation and policy development over the coming years, but they are built upon carefully considered premises.

Too often in the past, policy has been based on taken-for-granted assumptions and implemented through top-down directives rather than as a mutual process of dialogue, research, policy writing, and implementation between communities, researchers, and policy makers. Hence the present project began with and continues to be based on a number of premises. Long-term and continuing research, including assessment and monitoring, is important to all development policies, projects, and their implementation. Most development projects in the Global South either falter soon after the resources are withdrawn or generate a complex of unintended and counterproductive consequences. Moreover, understanding communities and implementing good policy requires working across all levels of social extension from the local and regional to the national and global, from communities, community-based organizations, customary forms of governance, local nongovernment organizations (NGOs), churches and other religious groups, and local-level and provincial governments to the national and international levels, including national PNG government departments and international organizations. As one of the basic premises, we work on the understanding that the carefully qualified involvement of government policy and program officers (from national, provincial, and local-level government) in the research process will, *if handled well,* enhance the capacity for effective community engagement. It has the potential to enhance alignment between the policy and program delivery of different levels of government and the communities they serve and to contribute to the skills training of government officers through learning by doing. Government participants in the present project were inducted from the beginning into engaged research as part of the policy-development process by being involved from the very first articulation of the project overview.

Important ethical issues are raised when academics are engaged as consultants by government and industry in Papua New Guinea, and the difficulties this presents in terms of maintaining a critical distance from the industry and/or government position are manifold. Stuart Kirsch argues that rather than adopting the distanced, scientific stance of an impartial observer, academics undertaking research in Papua New Guinea, particularly those spending extended periods of time with local communities, have an obligation to act as community activists. In David Hyndman's words, "Activism is a responsible extension of the anthropological commitment to maintain reciprocal relations with the people with whom we work."[51] This argument, for us, needs to be teased out into its various dimensions. While the present project does not follow the community-activist path (see the discussion of action research in the next chapter), it is conducted within the ethos of reciprocity and mutuality, recognizing, for example, the complementarity of local and outside knowledges, the need for long-term engagement, and the requirement of returning the research to the communities. Elise Huffer takes a comparable line, suggesting that close collaboration between communities and researchers is an important and valuable means through which it is possible not only for outside interests such as scholars and consultants to develop an ethical framework for their own work, but also for communities themselves to become engaged in questions and discussions about their own ethical standards.[52]

Overall, *Sustainable Communities, Sustainable Development* begins as an inquiry into pressing political and economic concerns, but also goes beyond them to address issues and questions across all the domains of social life that take us into the subjectivity of living locally in places stretched and remade by reclaimed customary practices, national interventions, and global pressures. What are the stories and histories through which different groups of people are responding to their nation's development? What is the everyday social environment of very different communities of people—those in migrant settlements and urban villages compared with those in more remote communities—all of whom daily negotiate the legacies of tribalism, the colonial past, and the contemporary challenges of living? While newspaper articles abound, portraying urban centers as sites of criminal violence or depicting rural communities as places of unthinking primordialism, in this book we seek to contribute to a creative and dynamic grass-roots response to the demands of everyday life and local-global pressures.

While the overdeveloped world faces an intersecting crisis that cuts to the foundation of the human condition—global climate change, global financial crisis, contingency of meaning, and the breakdown of institutions that used to provide a haven in a heartless world—Papua New Guinea, with all its difficulties—redoubled in urban centers—still has the basis for responding to that manifold crisis. Its secret lies in what has been seen by most people as its weakness—"underdeveloped" economies and communities. Most persons in Papua New Guinea, for all the pressures they face, still live in sustainable community relations to each other and to the natural world. However, this is not a strength that can be taken for granted or romanticized. There is a lot of work to done if the possibilities are to be realized and sustained.

Notes

1. W. W. Rostow, *How It All Began: Origins of the Modern Economy*, McGraw-Hill, New York, 1975.

2. *Constitution of the Independent State of Papua New Guinea*, Papua New Guinea Consolidated Legislation, Constitutional Laws Library, http://www.paclii.org/pg/legis/consol_act/ cotisopng534/, accessed 21 May 2007.

3. For a sense of the complexity, see, for example, Utula Samana, *Papua New Guinea: Which Way?* Arena Publications, Melbourne, 1988, and his discussion of the Tuam five-year development plans in Morobe Province in the 1970s and 1980s.

4. *Constitution of the Independent State of Papua New Guinea*.

5. Ron May, ed., *Micronationalist Movements in Papua New Guinea*, Research School of Pacific Studies, Canberra, 1982.

6. Ian Todd, *Papua New Guinea: Moment of Truth*, Angus and Robertson, Sydney, 1974, pp. 48–53.

7. Anne Dickson-Waiko, "The Missing Rib: Mobilizing Church Women for Change," *Oceania*, no. 74, 2003, pp. 98–119.

8. Australian Agency for International Development (AusAID), "Papua New Guinea: Country Programs," http://www.ausaid.gov.au/country/papua.cfm, last accessed 24 July 2010.

9. For a critique of the "failed state" paradigm, see Terence Wesley-Smith, "Self-Determination in Oceania," *Race and Class*, vol. 48, no. 3, 2007, pp. 29–46. For a careful discussion of the perceived crisis by Papua New Guinean authors, see David Kavanamur, Charles Yala, and Quinton Clements, *Building a Nation in Papua New Guinea: Views of the Post-Independence Generation*, Pandanus Books, Canberra, 2003.

10. Ben Scott, *Re-Imagining PNG: Culture, Democracy and Australia's Role*, Lowy Institute, Double Bay, 2005, ch. 4.

11. In a way we are getting ahead of ourselves by using concepts such as "modern" so pointedly before the theoretical work has been done to define precisely how they are being used (see Chapter 2 on ontological formations—tribal, traditional, and modern). Here the adjective "modern" is used to qualify the concept of cargo-cult to distinguish the point being made here from the usual clichéd disparagement of tribal communities for any elaborated desire for material goods. As Frederick Errington and Deborah Gewertz argue in criticism of the usual approach to tribal acquisition (and, in particular, of Jared Diamond, *Guns, Germs, and Steel*, Vintage, London, 1998), "Things have value because they can be used in transactions to establish relationships of recognition and respect" (*Yali's Question: Sugar, Culture, & History*, University of Chicago Press, Chicago, 2004, pp. 22–23). Modern cargo-cultism in this sense refers to the way modern capitalist consumption comes to overlay and further complicate older practices of reciprocal exchange.

12. Superannuates received 8 percent net of tax return on an after-tax profit for NASFUND of 74.116 million kina, compared to negative returns of around minus 20 percent in Australian balanced funds. *NASFUND Newsletter*, February 2009.

13. Palm oil is the largest agricultural export-income earner with exports in 2006 at K660 million compared to logs at K490 million and coffee at K337 million. Local communities are becoming more aware of the social costs of palm oil. In 2008, for example, the people of Woodlark Island rejected an offer by Vitroplant, despite a feasibility study said that it was economically viable. In the area of logging, "impact projects" as part of the national government's recovery plan are required to establish 25,000 to 30,000 hectares of forest plantations, and so-called nonimpact projects are required to go into downstream processing. (*Gavamani Sivarai*, vol. 5, no. 1, 2008). Whether this occurs in practice is a different matter.

14. Robert J. Foster, *Materializing the Nation: Commodities, Consumption, and Media in Papua New Guinea*, Indiana University Press, Bloomington, 2002. It should be also noted that invocation of "our country" is often negative. See Joel Robbins, *Becoming Sinners: Christianity and Moral Torment in a Papua New Guinea Society*, University of California Press, Berkeley, 2004, pp. 170–174.

15. Ruth Randell, *Gender Equality and Democratic Governance in the City of Port Moresby*, UNIFEM Pacific, 2008.

16. Care needs to be taken in interpreting all of these issues: Maxine Pitts, *Crime,*

Corruption and Capacity in Papua New Guinea, Asia Pacific Press, Canberra, 2002; Gina Koczberski, George N. Curry, and John Connell, "Full Circle or Spiralling Out of Control? State Violence and the Control of Urbanisation in Papua New Guinea," *Urban Studies,* vol. 38, no. 11, pp. 2017–2036; and Gina Koczberski and George N. Curry, "Divided Communities and Contested Landscapes: Mobility, Development and Shifting Identities in Migrant Destination Sites in Papua New Guinea," *Asia Pacific Viewpoint,* vol. 45, no. 3, 2005, pp. 57–71. For an example of a superficial developmentalist take on the slow crisis, see Diana Cammack, *Chronic Poverty in Papua New Guinea,* Chronic Poverty Research Centre, Manchester, 2008. For all of its authoritative stance and apparent detailed research in-country, the report is thin and often misleading, but this does not mean that concerns about the slow crisis should not be taken seriously.

17. For example, from the poster distributed by the Bismarck Ramu Group NGO in Madang Province, "Industrial Logging is *Giaman* Development," first produced in 2003 and still being distributed more than five years later.

18. Marshall Sahlins, "The Economics of Develop-man in the Pacific," in Joel Robbins and Holly Wardlow, eds., *The Making of Global and Local Modernities in Melanesia: Humiliation, Transformation and the Nature of Cultural Change,* Ashgate, Aldershot, 2005, p. 37.

19. United Nations Global Compact, Cities Programme, *Circles of Sustainability: An Integrated Approach to Developing Sustainability Indicators,* UNGCCP, Melbourne and New York, 2008. Available at http://www.citiesprogramme.org, last accessed 14 January 2011. See also Andy Scerri and Paul James, "Communities of Citizens and 'Indicators' of Sustainability," *Community Development Journal,* vol. 45, no. 2, 2010, pp. 219–236; and Andy Scerri and Paul James, "Accounting for Sustainability: Combining Qualitative and Quantitative Research in Developing 'Indicators' of Sustainability," *International Journal of Social Research Methodology,* vol. 13, no 1., 2010, pp. 41–53.

20. Joel Robbins, "The Humiliations of Sin: Christianity and the Modern Subject," in Robbins and Wardlow, eds., *The Making of Global and Local Modernities in Melanesia,* pp. 46–47.

21. World Commission on Environment and Development, *Our Common Future,* Oxford University Press, Oxford, 1997, p. 8.

22. See for example, Maureen Hart, *Guide to Sustainable Community Indicators, Sustainable Measures,* Hart Environmental Data, North Andover, 2nd edition, 1999.

23. Donald E. Voth and Zola K. Moon, "Defining Sustainable Communities," Rural Infrastructure as a Cause and Consequence of Rural Economic Development and Quality of Life conference, 1997, Birmingham, Alabama. http://www.uark.edu/depts/hesweb/hdfsrs/sustcom.pdf, accessed 31 July 2003.

24. Ibid., p. 26.

25. Ferdinand Tönnies, *Community and Society,* Harper and Row, New York, (1887) 1963.

26. Jim Walmsley, "The Nature of Community: Putting Community in Place," *Dialogue*, vol. 25, no.1, 2006, pp. 5–12.

27. Iris M. Young, *Justice and the Politics of Difference*, Princeton University Press, Princeton, 1990; Iris M. Young, *Inclusion and Democracy*, Oxford University Press, Oxford, 2000.

28. Zygmunt Bauman, *Liquid Modernity*, Polity Press, Cambridge, 2000, pp. 171–172.

29. Ibid., p. 178.

30. Arjun Appadurai, *Modernity at Large: Cultural Dimensions of Globalization*, Minnesota Press, Minneapolis, 1996, p. 170.

31. Ibid., p. 177.

32. L. R. Goldman, J. Duffield, and C. Ballard, "Fire and Water: Fluid Ontologies in Melanesian Myth," in L. R. Goldman and C. Ballard, eds., *Fluid Ontologies: Myth, Ritual and Philosophy in the Highlands of Papua New Guinea*, Bergin & Garvey, Westport, 1998.

33. The theoretical framework of "engaged theory" that underpins the present project comes from Paul James, *Globalism, Nationalism, Tribalism: Bringing Theory Back In*, Sage Publications, London, 2006. The discussion of different forms of community is adapted from work done by Chris Scanlon and developed in Martin Mulligan, Paul James, Kim Humphery, Chris Scanlon, Pia Smith, and Nicky Welch, *Creating Community: Celebrations, Arts and Wellbeing within and across Local Communities*, VicHealth and the Globalism Research Centre, Melbourne, 2007, ch. 2.

34. The term "habitus" here comes from Pierre Bourdieu, *The Logic of Practice*, Polity, Cambridge, 1990.

35. Nikolas Rose, *Powers of Freedom: Reframing Political Thought*, Cambridge University Press, Cambridge, 1999, p. 172.

36. Walmsley, "The Nature of Community."

37. M. M. Webber, "Order in Diversity: Community without Propinquity," in L. Wirigo, ed., *Cities and Space*, Johns Hopkins University Press, Baltimore, 1963.

38. Amitai Etzioni, "Introduction: A Matter of Balance, Right and Responsibilities," in *The Essential Communitarian Reader*, Rowman & Littlefield Lanham, 1998, p. xiii.

39. Ibid., p. iv. See also G. Mulgan, *Connexity: How to Live in a Connected World*, Chatto and Windus, London, 1997, p. 229.

40. Etienne Wenger, *Communities of Practice: Learning, Meaning and Identity*, Cambridge University Press, Cambridge, 1998.

41. Gerhard Delanty, *Community*, Routledge, London, 2003.

42. See Paul James and Andy Scerri, "Globalizing Life-Worlds: Consuming Capitalism," in Phillip Darby, ed., *Postcolonializing the International*, University of Hawai'i Press, Honolulu, 2006.

43. Andrew J. Strathern and Gabriel Stürzenhofecker, eds., *Migration and Trans-*

formations: Regional Perspectives on Papua New Guinea, University of Pittsburgh Press, Pittsburgh, 1994.

44. James F. Weiner, "Introduction: Depositings," in Alan Rumsey and James F. Weiner, eds., *Mining and Indigenous Lifeworlds in Australia and Papua New Guinea,* Sean Kingston, Oxon, 2004.

45. See among others, Edward LiPuma, *Encompassing Others: The Magic of Modernity in Melanesia,* University of Michigan Press, Ann Arbor, 2001, ch. 2; Bruce Knauft, *Exchanging the Past: A Rainforest World of Before and After,* University of Chicago Press, 2002; Errington and Gewertz, *Yali's Question.*

46. Nicole Polier, "Culture, Community and the Crisis of Modernity in Papua New Guinea," *Political and Legal Anthropology Review,* vol. 22, no. 1, 1999, p. 58.

47. Ulrich Beck, Anthony Giddens, and Scott Lash, *Reflexive Modernization: Politics, Tradition, Aesthetics in the Modern Social Order,* Polity Press, Cambridge, 1994. Of the three authors our position is closest to that of Anthony Giddens, but even in this case there are profound differences, including in how we use the concept of "reflexivity." See Chapter 11 below.

48. James Tully, *Strange Multiplicity: Constitutionalism in the Age of Diversity,* Cambridge University Press, Cambridge, 1995.

49. "Institutions" as we define them are publicly enacted, relatively enduring bodies of practice, procedures, and norms, ranging from formalized legal entities such as states, corporations, or registered NGOs, to more informal but legally buttressed and abiding sets of practices and regimes such as "the capitalist market" or "the family." The key phrases here are "publicly enacted" and "relatively enduring." The phrase "publicly enacted" in this sense implies active projection, legal sanction, and, as often as not, some kind of opposition. An institution is constituted in relation to a res publica, a public domain beyond the individual. It requires some form of authorization, whether it is myth and custom, in the case of tribally formed societies; God, Nature, or the Sovereign, in the case of societies formed in the dominance of traditionalism; or more abstract processes of sanctioning and legitimation such as those offered by the modern state, in the case of societies formed in the dominance of modernism. The phrase "relatively enduring" does not preclude changes, or even basic transformations, in the form of an institution, but it does point to a central defining dimension that is continuous despite the changes.

50. James A. Scott, *Seeing like a State: How Certain Schemes to Improve the Human Condition Have Failed,* Yale University Press, New Haven, 1998. Scott argues that centrally managed social plans derail when they impose schematic visions that do violence to complex interdependencies that are not, and cannot be, fully understood. The success of designs for social organization depends primarily on the recognition that local, practical knowledge is as important as formal, epistemic knowledge.

51. David Hyndman, "Academic Responsibilities and Representation of the Ok

Tedi Crisis in Postcolonial Papua New Guinea," *The Contemporary Pacific*, vol. 13, no. 1, 2001, pp. 33–54, quote from p. 15; Stuart Kirsch, "Anthropologists and Global Alliances: Comment," *Anthropology Today*, vol. 12, no. 4, 1996, pp. 14–16; Brian Brunton, "The Perspective on a Papua New Guinean NGO," in Glenn Banks and Chris Ballard, eds., *The Ok Tedi Settlement: Issues, Outcomes and Implications, National Centre for Development Studies and Resource Management in Asia-Pacific*, National University, Canberra, 1997, pp. 167–182. The debate over the Ok Tedi mine intensified discussions about the responsibility of the researcher to act politically in response to exploitation and degradation. In our view, individual researchers may have a responsibility to act politically and if conducted ethically to use their research to do so; however, this does not make the research process itself a form of activism, participatory or otherwise.

52. Elise Huffer, "Governance, Corruption, and Ethics in the Pacific," *The Contemporary Pacific*, vol. 17, no. 1, 2005, p. 131.

Chapter 2

Engaged Theory and Social Mapping

RESEARCHING COMMUNITIES HAS long been beset with difficulties that are still being debated. How is it possible to delimit the spatial boundaries of a research locale? What determines the temporal frames of a study? How are the different standpoints of the researcher and the researched to be understood and related? What are the different kinds of power engendered by a research relationship? In relation to the spatial frame of a study, for example, the classical presumptions of studies of community, with their focus on bounded and stable social settings, were profoundly disrupted by intensifying social change. Direct pressures for new ways of researching came from social movements such as the liberation struggles of colonized peoples, the civil rights movements of discriminated groupings, and the assertions of the subaltern. Pressures for change also came in the context of broader social processes as researchers grappled to understand how local people responded to, contested, and actively appropriated modernizing and globalizing practices including capitalism. Anthropology and sociology were at the forefront of the social sciences' engagement in this social ferment. Anthropology, in particular, was challenged for its complicity with the administrative apparatus of colonialism. More broadly, from the middle of the twentieth century, the authority of the modern social sciences as objective truth-bearing practices was called into question, as were the power relations that had underwritten exchanges between researchers, the researched, and the uses of that research. At the same time, some of these social scientists were also presented—perhaps paradoxically, and with a further reinforcement of their authority—in roles as allies and sometime spokespersons for the socially dispossessed and marginalized. This chapter is written for those who want to understand the background to our attempt to surmount the various problems researchers of communities face. It is crucial to the larger scheme of things, but some readers interested only in Papua New Guinean development itself might want go directly to the next chapter.

The Complexity of Local-Global Research

Out of this web of interconnected issues have come some very different responses. One set of responses in sociology is to advocate "action" or "participatory research," where researchers are to be embedded as coparticipants in the social life of a place or community. However, for all its potential strengths, action research tends problematically to blur the continuing and necessary distinction between the skills and perspectives of outside researchers and the skills and hard-won insights of community members as "insiders." Insiders are putatively allowed to generate the direction of "action research." But given the continuing discrepancies in power, the reality is that research still tends to be directed (but now implicitly and illicitly) from the "inside" outsider. Long discussion of research methods might take place inside the community, but, given the different skills of academic researchers and community members, this is often done with insufficient epistemological consideration of the formulation and implementation of relevant research methods. Outsider researchers too quickly assume that they have become insiders, while the insiders often resent that the research does not necessarily have the consequences for their communities that they hoped for and that the outsiders end up with most of the credit for the completed research.

A second set of responses comes out of the discipline of anthropology.[1] In significant ways the multisite ethnography of George Marcus, the multilocal fieldwork anthropology of Ulf Hannerz, the "traveling theory" of James Clifford, and the global cultural studies of Arjun Appadurai and Carol A. Breckenridge's *Public Culture* journal project attempted to handle the issue of destabilized community settings.[2] For these cultural and social anthropologists, multisite ethnographies reflect the mobility and transnational interdependence of a highly globalized world. At times more akin to cultural studies than classic fieldwork anthropology, this global ethnography has the advantages of reflecting the mobility and interconnectedness of many of the societies now being studied. With this in mind, we follow something of the same path, though with a very different methodology. First, movement, hybridity, and diasporic connection are not treated as new phenomena. Second, though we are not interested in strictly defining the boundaries of a given community as such, we still seek to have people in specific locales describe to us what they understand their communities to be and what constitutes their mutual livelihoods.

This means that research *on* a single locale occurs *in* many places, including with people who are connected to a locale but no longer live there. For example, the village(s) of Inuma-Alepa continues to be localized but also includes persons living in urban Port Moresby who remain connected through remittances and social activism. The Inuma-Alepa villages themselves remain characterized for the most part by grounded community relations and subsistence livelihoods, but at the same time processes of modern exchange cut into and sustain the village economy. Even the word "subsistence" needs to be understood as occurring within a relatively local area rather than as just subsisting within the microlocale of the household or immediate village. Third, while this means that we are also interested in the global and local processes of production, exchange, communication, organization, and inquiry that cut through a particular locale, these processes are not treated so much as "disjunctive flows" as patterns of interchange in tension—structured layers of practice and subjectivity. This method of examining modes of practice gives some systematicity to what in Anna Tsing's beautiful metaphor can be called "frictions."[3] And fourth, despite considerable change in the patterns of power, we continue to take the institution of the nation-state seriously. Even in a country such as Papua New Guinea, where the nation-state came comparatively late to the understanding of identity and practice, it still has an important, even if secondary, bearing on social life.

For all its sophistication, global ethnography has with exceptions failed to live up to its own aspirations. It has in practice often failed to carry forward the depth and rigor sometimes achieved by classical anthropological ethnography—a depth to which we still aspire in the long term.[4] More than that, the dominant cultural studies framework tends to project a picture of fluidity and change taken as a snapshot of variable instances of places here and there. In other words, against earlier approaches that overemphasized the conditions of integration, contemporary dominant approaches overemphasize fluidity as an ideological presumption. By comparison, we are interested in the dialectic of continuity and discontinuity, with no presumption as to the strength of either. Further, even if our work suffers from the possibility of fragmentation and superficiality—given that it is conducted episodically and by a large number of researchers—by sustaining the work over a long period of engagement, by focusing on relatively continuous communities in chosen locales, by extending our work over time and space, and by using a consistent theoretically informed approach, we aim in time to make up for the weaknesses of our multisite research.[5]

It is understandable that most global ethnography, including our own, is often more of an aspiration than a rigorously sustained practice. Cross-community social mapping studies are difficult to sustain without large teams of researchers. Given that scholarly research in the social sciences tends to be an individualized affair, it is usually simply not practicable to do more than proclaim the need for such studies. The only way around this challenge is, first, by the development of committed research teams—dependence upon committed individuals is no longer enough. Second, those researchers must impose the discipline of a common methodological framework to allow for comparison across locales. And, they must go back to the same places time and again to allow for comparison across time. This is the aspirational form of our global ethnography, with members of our larger research team also working in Australia, India, Malaysia, Sri Lanka, and Timor Leste, among other countries.

While it is relatively common but by no means obligatory for individual researchers to maintain an ad hoc relationship with a community or individual informants over the duration of a career, such an overt commitment to "be there" for the long-term is unusual in social science research. This is in part because the classical model of information gathering from the field is a one-off, concentrated in-community exercise, sometimes ignoring the long-term reciprocal relationships and commitments this begins to entail. It also tends to be ad hoc because of the social and logistic difficulties associated with developing long-term relationships over periods of presence and absence. Lines of fracture include losing research project funding or changing employment, shifts in individual or disciplinary research priorities, loss of individual or disciplinary interest, interpersonal difficulties, and so on. Another of the fracture lines is the personal cost to the researcher. Substantially engaging over a long period with *anybody* else can be really hard, tiring work. Add to this the burden of linguistic and cultural differences as well as the physical and emotional challenges of living with marginal and underresourced people for any length of time, and it is understandable that "commitment" can wear thin. Solidarity across all manner of borders is a great aspiration, but it constitutes an emotionally and physically consuming practice that is difficult to sustain. Whether or not we are able to overcome these issues will depend on the test of time.

Defining Locales: From the Urban to the Remote

The challenge of development in a contemporary, postcolonial context is complicated by what is often a rapid and radical reconfiguration of social space. In attempting to understand that social space, we are confronted, first of all, with problems of definition. Debates and practices in the fields of anthropology, sociology, and ethnography confront us with one set of issues, and debates in the fields of human geography and demography present others. One concern is that mainstream demographic analyses of human settlements—whether they are by governments, intergovernmental organizations, economists, or NGOs—overwhelmingly use the urban-rural dichotomy as the dominant modality of categorizing locales and land use. The urban-rural distinction was first proposed in the early 1950s, and it was critiqued at the time for being overly simplistic. Nevertheless, it quickly entered into popular usage. It has persisted as the dominant classification system and is used by virtually all countries. Beyond that there are a number of significant problems with the widespread usage of the various settlement categories. First, there is no uniform approach to defining rural and urban settlements. The United Nations has taken the position that "because of national differences in the characteristics which distinguish urban from rural areas, the distinction between urban and rural population is not yet amenable to a single definition that would be applicable in all countries."[6] Thus, it is said to be best for countries to decide for themselves whether particular settlements are urban or rural. The OECD has adopted the same approach. However, while recognizing that it is a difficult task to create categories that are applicable to a diverse range of landscapes, contexts, and regional settings, the failure to define the terms being used simply means that there is an overabundance of opportunities for confusion and inconsistent use.

The usual urban-rural distinction also fails to account for the changing nature of human settlement across the globe. Graeme Hugo and his colleagues point to a number of significant changes, including changing forms of urbanization such as urban sprawl and the decentralization of nonresidential functions: for example, retail parks close to intercity highway junctions, massively increased levels of commuting between urban and rural areas, the development of communication and transport technologies, and the emergence of polycentric urban configurations.[7] While the urban-rural dichotomy was always oversimplistic, it is arguably more misleading today than it was half a century ago. In Papua New Guinea, as we will argue, it needs to be treated very carefully given the networks of exchange relations that intensively connect different locales, including through marriage and retirement relations.[8] In addition, the generality of the terms overwhelms the significant variation in settlement forms that exist between the extremes of the most urban and the most rural. "Rural" is in general use a catchall category for "not urban." The inadequacy of this has led to a number of intermediate categories being proposed, including suburban, periurban, exurban, and perimetropolitan. These new forms of categorization are intended to respond to the increasing complexity of settlement patterns, and they partly do so. The difficulty is that marking the differences is sometimes reduced to a set of arbitrary metrics. Lucatelli and his colleagues use two criteria— population density and accessibility—to distinguish between three categories of rural areas: periurban rural, intermediate rural, and remote rural. Rural areas are considered to be those with a population density lower than 150 inhabitants per square kilometer, while the three subcategories are defined according to the level of access to major services.[9] This methodology certainly marks differences, but the technical precision is pseudoscientific rather than in keeping with the present social mapping approach that takes objective and subjective dimensions of social life equally seriously. Coombes and Raybould identify three dimensions through which human settlements can be addressed, as opposed to the one-dimensional nature of the urban-rural distinction: settlement size, from hamlet to metropolitan center; concentration, from dense to sparse; and accessibility, from central to remote.[10]

Piecing together material from different sources, however, it is possible to get a basic framework for a general set of definitions that we will use throughout the book.[11]

A *city* or *urban area* can be defined as a human settlement characterized by a significant infrastructural base—economically, politically, and culturally—a high density of population, whether it be as denizens, working people, or transitory visitors; and what is perceived to be a large proportion of constructed surface area relative to the rest of the region. Within that area—Lae and Port Moresby provide obvious examples—may also be smaller zones of non-built-up, green or brown sites used for agriculture, recreational, storage, waste disposal, or other purposes.

A *suburban area* can be defined as a relatively densely inhabited urban district characterized by predominance of housing land use—as a residential zone in an urban area contiguous with a city center, as a zone outside the politically defined limits of a city center, or as a zone on the outer rim of an urban region (sometimes called a periurban area). For example, suburban Lae and Alotou are made up of village communities, sometimes edged by bushland; in suburban Moresby this also includes "settlements" or "squatter areas." In other words, we thus do not make the usual distinction made in PNG planning parlance between formal suburbs and informal settlements—they are in our terms different forms of suburbanization.

A *periurban area* is a zone of transition from the rural to urban. These areas often form the immediate urban-rural interface and may eventually evolve into being fully urban. Periurban areas are lived-in environments. The majority of periurban areas are on the fringe of established urban areas, but they may also be clusters of residential development within rural landscapes and along transport routes. Periurban areas in the Global North are most frequently an outcome of the continuing process of suburbanization or urban sprawl, though this is different in places where customary land relations continue to prevail. In the case of Papua New Guinea, where most people live in villages, a periurban area might have the appearance of being rural, but because of its immediate proximity to an urban area, its orientation to that center is more intense than even hinterland communities—hence the designation.

A *rural area* is an area that is either sparsely settled or has a relatively dispersed population with no cities or major towns. While agriculture still plays an important part in numerous rural areas, other sources of income have developed, such as rural tourism, small-scale manufacturing activities, residential economy (location of retirees), and energy production. A rural area can be characterized by either its constructed (though nonindustrial) ecology or its relatively indigenous ecology.

A *hinterland area* is a *rural area* that is located close enough to a major urban center for its inhabitants to relate a significant proportion of their activities to the dominant urban area that draws upon that area, as in the circum-Goroka area or villages such as Boera or Inuma-Alepa in relation to Port Moresby.

A *remote area*, like a *hinterland area*, can only be defined relatively and subjectively. That is, the term "remote" presumes a centering of power somewhere else. In this case it tends to be defined in terms of accessibility to major urban areas. A remote area is a rural area that is hard to get to from major cities and where access to major services and major urban centers is not viable for the majority of the area's population on more than an occasional basis, whether owing to geography, language barriers, political reasons, or socioeconomic resources. The Wisini group of villages in the south Highlands of Morobe are such an example, often with the roads cut in the wet season.

A *wilderness area* is an area (usually but not always remote) characterized by a lack of human inhabitation and a relative continuity of ecological complexity.

These terms will be used throughout the book to refer to different types of social formation within contemporary Papua New Guinea. The terms "city" or "urban center" here are perhaps the most important to qualify. As the definition implicitly intends, there is no sense in which the city necessarily becomes dominated by modern relations, while tribal relations are relegated to the rural and remote areas. The concept of the "Melanesian city" used by Utula Samana is relevant here, and the modern-tribal relation remains a question of choice for PNG communities and planners:

> There are three important aspects of what we are calling Melanesian cities: one is that they do not destroy or cut across the existing social organization of the villages themselves; secondly, that people can service their own welfare needs; and thirdly that they are integral in the sense that they spring out of the sort of organization that is growing out of the village level into the community government both at the political and the economic level.[12]

In the social profiles included in Part II, the focus communities are grouped according to the categories of urban, hinterland, and remote, but significantly what we find across these forms of settlement is a globalization of modern practices and sensibilities overlaying and creating tensions—both productive and destructive—that people are actively attempting to work though.

Defining Ontological Formations

In the previous chapter we spent some time defining different dominant formations of community. And we have just defined different forms of settlement in terms of spatial distance and geographical configuration—urban to remote. However, these ways of thinking about communities and locales need to be complemented by deeper layers of analysis. The spatial understanding of urban to remote communities that we have just described, for example, remains a flat understanding of spatiality unless it is accompanied by recognition of the possibility of the changing and layered nature of spatiality across all kinds of locales. In other words, beyond the question of the extension of social relations across space, there is also the question of how that space is lived. Thus, we also want to define some terms that are used loosely in the literature to distinguish different modes of living. As a shorthand designation different dominant patterns of such categories are distinguished here as different ontological formations: tribalism, traditionalism, modernism (and also postmodernism, though this is less crucial to our analysis in relation to community sustainability in Papua New Guinea). Such formations have already been used without definition through our earlier discussion. Apparently simple concepts such as "the modern" or seemingly innocuous adjectives such as "traditional" pass easily into narratives of development. With the exception of "the tribal," which is usually retranslated and hidden away under the heading of "the indigenous" or the "traditional," or put in quotes,[13] they sneak into many commentaries completely without definition.

However, there is a profound danger in leaving this complicated area ill-defined or subject to just passing discussion. Often narratives carry a taken-for-granted conception of "the modern" counterposed against other ways of life defined in the negative as "the premodern." In other words, those living as "premodern" communities do not have their dominant formations named except in the negative or in relation to the "higher order." Sometimes, by inference, "premoderns" become those who are on an inevitable or anticipated civilizational climb; they are defined as peoples who are yet come to a modern realization of their "past" identities and "future" potentialities. The politics here are so important that we need to take an uncomfortable dive into the depths of social theory for a few paragraphs.

The usual first step in overcoming this problem is to set up a divide between "the traditional" and "the modern." However, this quickly sets up the need to grapple with an earlier tendency across many fields of inquiry from political science to history and anthropology to set up a Great Divide between these ways of living. Most attempts to overcome bifurcation between the premodern and the modern are associated with a second form of blurring. The term "modernity" is problematically used as both an epochal period and a dominant ontological formation. For example, even as sophisticated a commentator in this area of "Melanesian modernity" as Edward LiPuma is prone to this problem:

> The dialectic of encompassment generates a far more intricate tapestry, history conspiring with chance to produce a modernity stamped by its multidimensionality, internal contradictions, and unpredictability. There is no easy historical and ethnographic navigation. The oppositional logics of modernity and tradition, domination and resistance, the local versus the world system, though they come all too easily to mind, do not begin to capture the signs and substance of what is going on here.[14]

He is right about the problem of the oppositional logics, but here Edward LiPuma at once uses the all-encompassing and epochal term "modernity" (albeit to summarize a complex outcome) and at the same time disavows the term, or at least points to the oversimplification entailed in making such a claim to a transition from tradition to modernity. He at once talks of the "globalization of modernity" as the most powerful force *encompassing* contemporary Melanesia and as producing a world that is now lived "*wholly* in the modern" (emphasis added),[15] and at the same time asserts the complex lines of this encompassment. We need to understand what he is trying to do by using this term "encompassing." He is rightly criticizing those who seek to find *authentic* original practices—in effect, pristine exotica—as distinct from modern-framed authentic practices in places such a Papua New Guinea. However, from our perspective, because of the limits of his methodological tools, his totalizing concept of "encompassing" entails rejecting what we hold theoretically dear—namely, the notion that it is possible *analytically* to separate out what is tribal *and/or* traditional from what is modern about any particular practice, even if *in practice* they are bound up with each other in a way that is more akin to a twisted jungle than a sedimented rock formation.

LiPuma's position assumes, moreover, a one-to-one correspondence between an ontological formation (the modern) and particular modes and institutions of practice (capitalism, nation-state, and so on). In his words: "All encompassed peoples will become capitalists.... And what holds for capitalism is also true for the nation-state, commercial culture, civic education, the mass media and much else."[16] It does not matter how much one clothes such a claim in qualifications about the unevenness of the process, as he does so subtly in his ethnographic analysis. The explicit writing does nothing to assuage the assumption that modernism equals capitalism, and therefore a single path of development prevails. To the contrary, as we have argued throughout this book, processes of modernization, even as they consolidate as a dominant ontological formation, do not negate the possibility of *other* paths of development. The concept of *other* here is intended, in part, to underline the notion of "other than one-dimensionally modern." It is the *other* that those constituted as modern/postmodern subjects tend to either find uncomfortable or wrap up in romantic clothing.

A method that treats the modern as all-encompassing makes it impossible to conceive of an alternative *projection* of a politics other than as subsumed by the modern. The concept of "projection" is key in our analysis. Projecting customary ways of life does not have to be yet another instance of simply embracing the modern, particularly if the community is trying to revivify *kastam* within a complex matrix of relations that it understands reflexively. It is true that any reflexive politics that "recognizes" itself as it enacts its political project is by definition drawing on a standpoint made possible by a process of lifting knowledge out of custom, but that is only at one level and in relation to one mode of practice—namely, inquiry. The epistemologies of modernism (and postmodernism) are formed in the analytical abstraction of knowledge, forcing a process of constant reflection on the meaning of things rather than providing a relatively stable set of analogical or cosmological answers. But the fundamental point here is that "encompassing," or what we describe as a constitutive overlaying of levels in dominance, is never totalizing. It is one level of the social. It is part a process of overlaying levels that may reconstitute prior practices and understandings and substantially dominate them, but it tends to generate ontological contradictions across the various intersecting levels of social being rather than simply to encompass or destroy all that has gone before.

In this alternative view, it is thus possible to use modalities of modern (and, to a lesser extent, postmodern) reflexivity to project ways of life that draw upon the strengths of other formations of being that are not modern. This is what the Pariet project in Wisini village and the Gildipasi project in the Tokain group of villages are doing (see Chapters 5 and 6) with all their tensions and faltering limitations. One of our readers has suggested that while we recommend greater reflexivity regarding community development, we "in fact document copious reflexivity and creativity already inhabiting the communities" we study. This is an astute comment and has prompted us to make very clear that the communities that we have been working with invited us "in" and therefore were already open to reflecting upon and rethinking the nature of development in their communities. As will also become clear, reflexivity without resources or negotiated support can lead to frustration rather than practical action.

This *other* pathway also works in a cross-cutting direction that makes it possible to project a different kind of "modernity." That is, it is also possible to draw upon tribal ways of understanding to negotiate and resubordinate the meaning and, to some extent, the consequences of the modern. As Bruce Knauft brilliantly shows in relation to a remote tribal grouping called the Gebusi, sensibilities of tribal exchange are being used to understand how the people can take up the trappings of the new and modern inside the familiarity of the old and the customary:

> Gebusi say they are exchanging their past for their future. In saying this, they use the same concept that they use for direct and reciprocal exchange in marriage, feasting or killing (*sesum degra*).... When Gebusi say that they are directly exchanging the customs of their past for those of their future, however, we are presented with a different order of exchange. This is not just reciprocity of people or valuables across time, but an exchange of different styles of life. It is not just an exchange *in* time, but an exchange *of* time itself—an exchange between different ways of relating to time, different modes of temporality.[17]

The present *engaged theory* approach—in which the concepts "tribal," "traditional," "modern," and "postmodern" are employed as provisionally useful designations of ontological difference—helps to make sense of this complexity.[18] That is, modes of social being from the tribal to the postmodern are defined in terms of how basic categories of the human condition are practiced, understood, and lived. Those basic categories are taken to be time, space, embodiment, and knowing. This is not to suggest that *tribalism* is the same in the Trobriand Islands and the New Guinea Highlands, let alone in Rwanda and Nunavut. Nevertheless, the social form called here "customary *tribalism*," distinguished as a mode of social being rather than as a distinct social practice, is thus defined by the dominance of particular socially specific modalities of space, time, embodiment, and knowing.

This customary tribal *mode of being* can be characterized by analogical, genealogical, and mythological practices and subjectivities. This includes notions of genealogical placement, the importance of mythological time connecting past and present, and the centrality of relations of embodied reciprocity. Expressed less abstractly in terms of *modes of practice,* in settings where tribalism is prevalent we tend to find the dominance of manual-embodied modes of production, reciprocal modes of exchange, oral-symbolic forms of communication, kinship or genealogically defined relations of organization, and perceptual-analogical-mythological modes of addressing nature and culture. For example, in relation to the dominant mode of inquiry, Nonie Sharp describes knowledge in the customary fishing cultures of the Torres Strait and Papua New Guinea as taking the form of genealogies of fish traps and *wauri* shells. For the Binandere people of Papua New Guinea, knowledge is "woven into a spiral within the limits of six generations from the 'head' (*opipi*), the terminal ancestor, to the 'tail' (*mai*), who is the youngest living descendent of the clan, to the Binandere cone-shaped fish trap (*sirawa*)."[19] Here the form of the knowledge, the form of generational relations, and the form of the shell are analogous.

While much more could be said, the key intention of this brief discussion is simply to begin to evoke different lifeways (modes of being) and different patterns of practice (modes of practice). In using the concept of "tribalism" or the adjective "tribal" we are not turning back to a search for "tribes" as discrete, spatially bound entities. But neither are we put off by the way in which the term "tribe" has become taboo in the field of anthropology. While the only time we will use the noun "tribe" in this study is when a community names itself or others as such, it is not so much an avoidance as based on a need for clarity. The term "tribe" tends to carry too much baggage about a singular bounded grouping. By contrast, in actively using the term "tribalism" or the adjective "tribal," we are talking about an ontological formation that may or may not exist in dominance in a particular locale or a particular practice or idea, and it is not defined by a spatial boundary. In postcontact societies—and this now pertains globally—tribalism exists intertwined with other formations. Tribal formations, practices, or meanings may be substantially reconstituted by more abstract formations such modernism. Or they may exist in an uneasy, uneven, and changing matrix of relations with traditionalism, modernism, and/or postmodernism across all or any one of its modes of practice. This is the case in many places in contemporary Papua New Guinea. Chapter 3 will elaborate on this process with an extended discussion of different modes of practice in different parts of the country.

As tribal communities (that is, communities formed in the dominance of tribalism) have fundamentally changed across modern history, having been confronted most pointedly by imperially extended colonization as well as by later forms of globalization, we have to treat tribalism as an ontological formation that is now framed in intersection with other formations. Hence we use adjectival terms distinguishing "*customary* tribalism" from "*traditional* tribalism" or "*modern* tribalism." At the same time, analytical distinctions can be made, as between tribalism and traditionalism, that are too often collapsed into each other. *Traditionalism* (as distinct from customary tribalism) abstracts from embodied nature and reframes the analogical and perceptual practices of tribalism in cosmological terms through entities such as God, Yahweh, or Nature. That is, some kind of Being (with a capital "B") comes to connect and make sense of prior forms of more fragmentary mythological thinking and practice. Such cosmologies are extended through metaphorical and political reworkings of kinship or culture-nature such as the Line of David or the Great Chain of Being that are constantly re-embedded within the "social whole." In terms of modes of practice, traditionalism tends to be associated with different dominant modes of production (overlaying manual production with techniques that abstract from direct muscle power), of exchange (extended barter and trade relations), of communication (scriptural and written forms of address), of organization (patrimonial role-divided relations), and of inquiry (cosmological framing of nature and culture).

Thus traditionalism can be characterized as carrying forward the prior ontological forms of tribalism—analogy, genealogy, and mythology—but reconstituted in terms of universalizing cosmologies and political-metaphorical relations. The keen relevance here to Papua New Guinea is the coming of the institution of the Christian Church. It may have modernized its practices of organization and become enmeshed in a modern monetary economy, but the various denominations of the Church, most manifestly its Pentecostal variations, remain deeply bound up with a *traditional* cosmology of meaning and ritual. The truth of Jesus is not seen as analytically relative. The irony of this is that contemporary Pentecostalism is a profoundly modern recursion. Indeed it can be argued that the Church gained its extraordinary power in Papua New Guinea by mediating tribal, traditional, and modern forms of practice and subjectivity while *officially* frowning on tribal "excess."

The various denominations thus may have varying and ambivalent relations to tribal and neotribal practices, but they are nevertheless the context for syncretic syntheses. For example, relevant to the discussions of HIV/AIDS later in the book (Chapter 10), Gogodola Christian women have for a several decades now formed fellowships known as prayer warrior groups. While intensely Christian, they continue to draw on their tribal sense of sickness as a visible form of counterembodiment—that is, to be sick is literally to not be yourself but a different person. In this context, HIV, in its pre-AIDS manifestation as a disease that does not always make you sick, cannot make sense to locals except—in a layering of tribal and traditional understandings—as a secret disease that can best be seen, and best be avoided, by those of sexual purity whose eyes are touched by the Holy Spirit. With all these ontological tensions it is understandable that "inexperienced" warrior women are themselves prone to having their eyes turned in another direction by "lying spirits." It is understandable how they become licentious and "go mad" or *daeladaele*.[20]

Modernism can in the same way be defined as carrying forward prior forms of being but fundamentally reconstituting (and sometimes turning upside

down) those forms in terms of technical-abstracted modes of time, space, embodiment, and knowing. Time, for example, becomes understood and practiced
not in terms of cosmological connection but through empty calendrical time-
lines that can be filled with the details and wonders of history—events made by
us. Space is territorialized and marked by abstract lines on maps—places drawn
by our own histories. Embodiment becomes an individualized project separated
out from the mind and used to project a choosing self. And knowing becomes
an act of analytically dismembering and resynthesizing information. In practice, modernism is associated with the dominance of capitalist production relations, commodity and finance exchange, print and electronic communication,
bureaucratic-rational organization, and analytic inquiry, but there is no necessary connection here. It is a historical connection that lurches from periods of
thriving to periods of crisis but in all cases naturalizes itself as the taken-for-
granted pathway to development. For example, when Angela Imbang, a sixth
grader at Chambri Community School in the Sepik region, subject to a modern
national curriculum, copies some notes about development into her social studies notebook, she believes that change will, through her choices, bring about a
better world in Papua New Guinea: "When there is development there is always
changes. We must choose the best way to cause the development."[21] Indeed we
must choose. We now have no choice. The question to which we will continually
return, however, is "What *other* paths can be chosen?"

Engaged Theory and Community-Engaged Research

The community-engaged approach of the present project thus attempts
to find a way past various problems, both theoretical and practical. While the
project cannot yet even pretend to have the depth of dedicated field ethnography, it has begun to develop some shreds of understanding through intense,
short episodes of careful engagement with communities set within a framework
of assurance that we will continue to be engaged. The long-term nature is a
further challenge, particularly given that increasingly academic research is set
within a neoliberal global culture with an emphasis on immediate outcomes
and KPIs (key performance indicators), governed by short-term funding cycles,
national-interest concerns, and the dominance of applied scientific and technical research over social science research, quantitative research over qualitative
research.

Community-engaged research intends to restore the distinctive roles of
insiders and outsiders, providing perhaps a more open and fruitful dialogue
between the research partners.[22] Such dialogue needs time, and it requires considerable negotiation, skill, and goodwill from both sides to move across cultural
and epistemological boundaries. This whole process of building relationships is

a process of face-to-face dealing with "the cultural other," whether from another ontological setting or even just another region. It is about acquiring deeper understanding and new perspectives through listening and talking—not just listening and gathering data. To come into conversation with a diverse group of people with different cultural and epistemological backgrounds and locations can be a disturbing thing, exposing and altering—but also imaginatively charging and positively transforming. In *Decolonizing Methodologies*, Linda Tuhiwai Smith, talks of the importance of the "seen face," turning up at cultural events, returning again and again to the community, and being aware of the indigenous and local protocols for being present.[23] Smith's notion of the "seen face" has inspired us with one important layer of our engaged social theory and relates strongly to our distinction between modes of social integration ranging from face-to-face relations to the disembodied relations at a distance. While *as researchers* we do not aspire to be *integrated* into communities at the level of the face to face—for example, as fictive kin or through ritual rites of passage—we do seek meaningful face-to-face interaction whereby we always return as *significant* outsiders.

The engaged methodology used for the present study involves a careful integration of both quantitative and qualitative methods, including both ran-

Engaged research deals with people's lives. Chris Clement Wagi Dogale died in the Port Moresby General Hospital, and we were drawn into his funeral.

dom and targeted questionnaires as well as lengthy strategic conversations with community members, government officials, and other nonprofit organizations such as churches and NGOs. The research also involves the collation of existing data relevant to each community that was part of this study—for example, government documents, local publications, community and NGO newsletters, and other published surveys and research materials. Condensed profiles relating to the history and character of eleven communities were compiled over three years. In each area, local people, including the leaders of community-based organizations with relevant skills, knowledge, and experience, were asked to comment and give feedback on the materials gathered, review the application of our research methods, and also provide advice about individuals and organizations we may have needed to consult further. Local consultants and members of the Department for Community Development played a significant role in providing appropriate focus and introductions to key community members in each site. They are among the coauthors of this book.

Social researchers often make a choice between using quantitative and qualitative research methods, and they often settle on one method only. The research methodology developed by the Globalism Research Centre involves a selective integration of quantitative and qualitative methods, set within an applied framework of community mapping. It aims to link data collection directly into a series of levels of analysis—empirical, conjunctural, integrational, and categorical—taking in both the objective and subjective dimensions of those levels. At the first level of empirical analysis, there is a strong need for well-founded data about how people feel and act—such as that collected through surveys—but we are also interested in the hermeneutics of the subjective dimension of those feelings and actions. At another level, moving beyond the experiential, a form of conjunctural analysis is employed aimed at relating local experiences to conjunctures of broader social processes and prevailing modes of practice. The analysis focuses on modes of production, exchange, communication, organization, and inquiry. Moving across different forms of analysis enables researchers to identify and understand the specificities of what is happening within the practice of everyday lived experiences to relate them to broader social themes such as the changing nature of community life in the contemporary world. Other, more abstracted modes of analysis—integrational and categorical levels of analysis—can also be applied, depending on the particular aims of the research. Integrational analysis takes us into the relations of interconnection and differentiation, emphasizing the way in which people relate to each other. Categorical analysis takes us into basic categories of being—time, space, embodiment, and knowing—to help understand different formations of being: tribalism, traditionalism, modernism, and postmodernism. In the present project the emphasis is on the first two levels of analysis, but the more abstract levels of analysis that sit beneath the surface occasionally come to the fore in important ways. [24]

Engaged Theory and Community Mapping

It would be false to give the impression that there are clear time-bound stages to community-engaged research because the processes are iterative.[25] However, the process of engagement in this project began with extensive discussion with officers in the Department for Community Development in order to decide which locales to focus on and to select a range of different places across different provinces of the country. After research locales and research themes were selected, the gathering of material started with publicly available documents and other relevant research. We then held community conversations in the research locations and began working with local collaborators before any of the field data was gathered from those places. This work became the basis of Part II of this book, which includes material from the fieldwork.

Community Conversations

Forums in the communities occurred at the beginning of the project (and then again after drafts of the reports and then the book were completed during the next few years). In the first instance, participation in the community sites involved a process of discussion and liaison through the Department of Community Development as well as with relevant community leaders and organizations in these places. Community forums were organized in each locale to discuss what form the research might take, to introduce the basic questions around sustainable livelihoods, community learning, including training needs, and to outline the research methods. Depending on the situation and the person speaking, discussions were conducted in a hybrid mix of Tok Pisin, local languages, and English with translation back and forth. The issues raised in these forums became important background for properly engaging in "strategic conversations" (see below) around themes of particular importance to each community. One of the important aspects of this research process was to be clear about the relationship with the community and what the project would and would not offer them. Negotiation was mainly facilitated through dialogue that explained what the project was about and how the information would be managed and used. Given the involvement of the state and its assumed authority, it was explicitly stated that there was no pressure for communities or community members to participate. Later community conversations also became an opportunity to gather and record background information as the basis of a brief community profile or general story of that community as an introduction to it.

(See the description of a "community profile" below and as written out for each of the research locations in Part II.)

Community conversations also occurred at the end of the writing process. Information from the survey was shared and reviewed by the communities themselves. Later forums continued the process of engagement and involvement, including discussion of the implementation of recommendations from the research process and project. What was an appropriate local way of doing this? Would it vary in different regions? The field trips in 2007 and 2008, which involved conducting return visits to the communities with a draft copy of the present monograph and the policy, were a key part of the process. As much as we could, we tried to elicit community feedback on draft material before the publication of this final expression of our writing. Sometimes the community conversations worked extraordinarily well; at other times they were restricted to a handful of community leaders or were delayed for weeks or months by events in the communities such as funerals.

Questionnaires

Surveys were conducted around key themes of contemporary community life as identified by the research teams in Australia and Papua New Guinea using a "Community Sustainability" questionnaire. The core module of that questionnaire is being used across a number of sites around the world, including Australia, Cambodia, Cameroon, East Timor, India, Israel, Malaysia, and Sri Lanka, as part of the Globalism Research Centre's larger Local-Global Project. The questionnaire uses five-point Likert scales, multiple-choice questions, and open-ended questions to elicit detailed information about key lifeworld themes. We began with a ten-point scale, but this was changed after pilot studies in Papua New Guinea and Australia showed the extended scale to be unwieldy. The finer discriminations required within the ten points sometimes led to vague arbitrations between the researchers and respondents on which number to choose. In the early stage the questionnaire was translated into local languages and used as a structured interview schedule with researchers reading out the questions to each interviewee. However, the translations were also shown by the pilot studies to be of limited use—for example, in Tok Pisin different words are used across the different locales in the country; in Motu the translation from an oral language into a written form had the effect of losing the nuance of terms or changing their meaning. In the end, conducting the survey depended on the skill of the interviewers either working in local languages themselves or training bilingual locals to help with each of the interviewees, working through the meaning of the question, discussing the interviewee's response, and recording the answers. It became a very slow process.

In total, approximately 1,600 questionnaires were completed over a period of direct visits to the identified eleven villages by the research team. With the pilot study questionnaires taken out as well as half-completed, ambiguously completed, and suspect or inconsistent questionnaires, just over 1,000 questionnaires were used for the analysis. This method gave us a reasonably solid statistical basis for understanding and comparing some of the needs and issues of importance to communities, although with all the usual caveats about the limitations of quantitative analysis of subjective responses to set questions. The questionnaire was designed to gather data from a statistically significant number of respondents in each of the chosen research locations. Completed questionnaires were analyzed using the statistical package SPSS, and key findings emerging from the qualitative research were discussed within the research team as well as with locals.

Strategic Conversations

At least five and up to twenty individuals were interviewed in each community. In selecting people who might be interviewed, a broad cross-section of the community was identified taking into account gender and age, language group and clan, and leadership roles. Each interview took between thirty minutes and three hours. The term "strategic conversation" indicates that an active dialogue is intended for each of the interviews and that ideally the interviewer and interviewee have extended each other's thinking based on some prior understanding of each other's views on the subject. This process requires that the researchers have some knowledge of the issues in the particular places. Each theme listed below, from Provision and Livelihood to Learning and Education, included broad questions covering the central issues of concern to the project (sustainable livelihoods and sustainable communities), and each was explored according to two aspects: how things are now and what supports or strengthens the things you value or want to change. Questions were broadly based on and around the following themes and questions:

1. Provision and Livelihood
    a. How do you contribute to the livelihood of your family/household?
    b. Would you like to change anything about how you provide this livelihood? Why?
    c. Could you better sustain your livelihood? How? Are there obstacles to this?
2. Work and Money
    a. Do you earn money? How do you earn money?
    b. How do you and your family use money? Where does most of it go?

    c. Would you like to change anything about the effects on you or your community of earning or spending money?

3. Organization and Community
    a. How is your community organized?
    b. What do you like about being part of your family and your community?
    c. Would you like to change anything about your family and community?
    d. If so, what?

4. Learning and Education
    a. How are local knowledges and special skills passed on in your community?
    b. What would strengthen skills and knowledge in your community?
    c. What skills and knowledge are needed that aren't there now?

Stories

In a process similar to that adopted for identifying the case-study projects for each of the communities, consultations with relevant people resulted in the construction of a list of local stories that seemed to be relevant to our research interests. Further rounds of consultation focused on the determination of the criteria that would enable the final selection of the stories to be compiled and analyzed. The aim was to collect two or three diverse stories from within each of the communities. These stories have been woven into this book rather than collected in a particular section. In particular, they have been used as an entry point in the social profiles written about each of the research locales. This approach to storytelling was surprisingly successful in eliciting material that was passed over by other methods. As Linda Smith writes: "Story telling, oral histories, the perspectives of elders and women have become an integral part of all indigenous research.... Such approaches fit well with the oral traditions which are still a reality in day-to-day indigenous lives."[26]

Photo Narrative

The photo-narrative method used in this research was adapted from a variety of research techniques that use cameras as a research tool. Other named approaches include "reflexive photography," "photo novella," and "photo voice."[27] At the basic level, photo narrative entailed distributing cameras to participants in the project and asking them to take images that expressed their sense of community or at least some aspect of their community. While some advocates of this kind of research method argue that it can empower participants, our aim was more modest in trying to find nonthreatening ways to explore the daily experiences of people living in the communities. Booth and Booth, for example, assert that photo narrative "challenges the established politics of representation

A Christian service at Omarakana village, Trobriands. This service is connected to one of the stories that we later relate.

by shifting control over the means for documenting lives from the powerful to the powerless, the expert to the lay-person, the professional to the client, the bureaucrat to the citizen, the observer to the observed."[28] To a limited extent this can be true, and such shifts in power are to be desired. However, such outcomes should not be seen as flowing effortlessly from photo-narrative research; simply handing cameras to community researchers does not necessarily or automatically challenge these binary structures. Nor does it necessarily challenge these structures in an effective manner.

We found that such a method can help people to give voice to experiences and perceptions that they may not have contemplated consciously before, and it can blur the boundary between research and self-expression. However, in the end we did not use the method systematically enough to really test its usefulness. One advantage for this project is that photography has an aesthetic dimension to it and the capturing of relevant images of lived experience is relevant to communities where visual literacy is much stronger than textual literacy. After the participants in the photo-narrative research took their photos, a research team member conducted semistructured interviews about their images lasting between ten and ninety minutes. This was found to be a nonthreatening process, with the recorded conversations more like a process of sharing and discussing photos than a formal interview.

Social Profiles

Profiles of the research locales and the community or communities who lived in the particular locations were developed at a number of stages. The preliminary stage involved working with the people in the chosen locales and knowledgeable outsiders to find out what and who actually constituted the community or communities in those places. There was no presumption about the status of communities—whether communities existed in the locales and, if they did exist, how they overlapped, faded into others, or were culturally and geographically bounded. The intention was to map the locales in relation to our chosen themes to document what people understand to be their social connections and potentially their community or communities. This information allowed us to refine our understanding of the different kinds of community and to develop social histories with a broader sense of a local community, looking at how they came to be and how they have been sustained through time. This stage was complemented by a second stage of research into the public record on these locales: official discourses of development; official documents and reports such as those produced by civic and professional organizations and representative bodies, particularly those that have a bearing on the sustainability of communities; and quantitative data on a series of objective indicators of population and demographic data. Framing all of these concerns was the question of how communities are sustained through time. There was surprisingly little public material available for the chosen locales, so fieldwork in particular communities became a substantial basis for the profiles that were finally written. The profiles are intended to draw a condensed but evocative picture of community life.

Publicly Available Material

While hardly any material was available on the research locales themselves, a vast amount of research has been done in Papua New Guinea across various fields. An ongoing dimension of the project entails collecting existing material, including policy documents, census and other statistics, research reports, social histories, geographical maps, and so on—anything relevant to the general themes of the project. It was essential to know what work had already been done in the chosen locales and on the chosen themes before going into the communities in order to avoid reinventing the wheel. Community leaders were often aware of previous government visits and research in their community, and they expected any subsequent researchers or officials to have done background work and to know about them. The National Research Institute and the University of Papua New Guinea were rich sources of information about the general themes of the project. Research officers in the Department for Community Development took on the task of gathering background material on the relevant themes, but their work was constrained by lack of time and perhaps also by lack of trust that the research was worthwhile or would have direct implications for their own portfolios. In the end, the thematic research came to rely on outside researchers in the Globalism Research Centre rather than local researchers. This did not make the thematic research any less strong but was an indication that the research partnership took a number of years to build and is still being developed.

Conclusion

Overall, then, how does one understand an individual's or group's everyday practices, their ways of operating or doing things? As Michel de Certeau has indicated, analysis shows that "a relation (always social) determines its terms, and not the reverse, and that each individual is a locus in which an incoherent (and often contradictory) plurality of such relational determinations interact."[29] The only problem with Certeau's description of the complexity is his use of the concept of "incoherent plurality." We would rather ask: what are the systems of patterned (and often contradictory) relations—what Certeau terms *les combinatoires d'opérations*—that also compose the culture-politics-economy-ecology of a place and people. In Papua New Guinea those patterns are complex. Relations of class, ethnicity, kinship, *wantok,* ceremonial partnership, religious denomination, gender, generation, and rural-urban living complicate a place already differentiated along tribal lines.[30]

There are always enormous complexities and difficulties involved in the comprehension across cultural boundaries. Fieldwork of this kind involves a dialectical process between slow reflection and immediacy.[31] Both are cultural constructs, and neither the subject nor the object remains static. It is an ongoing construction of experience and understanding, a realm of tenuous common sense and inquiry that is also constantly breaking down, being patched up, and being reexamined, over and over again. The various tools in our methodology—addressing both subjective and objective dimensions—were intended to sensitize us to that complexity while allowing us to draw out patterns (structures) of practice and meaning. Each of the tools used alone was inadequate to that task, but used in relation to each other we found them all helpful.

Notes

1. Material here is drawn from an article by one of the authors of this volume: Peter Phipps, "Community Sustainability Research: The Challenge of Reciprocity," *Local-Global Journal,* vol. 1, 2005, pp. 79–89.

2. Arjun Appadurai, *Modernity at Large: Cultural Dimensions of Globalization,* University of Minnesota Press, Minneapolis, 1996; Ulf Hannerz, "Many Sites in One," in Thomas Hylland Eriksen, ed., *Globalisation: Studies in Anthropology,* Pluto, London, 2003; George Marcus, "Ethnography in/of the World System: The Emergence of Multi-sited Ethnography," *Annual Review of Anthropology,* vol. 24, 1995, 95–117.

3. Anna Lowenhaupt Tsing, *Friction: An Ethnography of Global Connection,* Princeton University Press, Princeton, 2005

4. For an evocative book that begins to elaborate the possibilities of such an approach see Tsing, *Friction.*

5. This is not dissimilar to the extended case method elaborated in Michael Burawoy, et al., *Global Ethnography: Forces, Connections, and Imaginations in a Postmodern World,* University of California Press, Berkeley, 2000, except that our approach does not treat global forces as "constituted from a distance" and thus inevitably eliciting resistance, avoidance, or negotiation.

6. United Nations Statistics Division (UNSD), *Principles and Recommendations for Population and Housing Censuses,* series M, no. 67, rev. 1, UNSD, New York, 1998.

7. Graeme Hugo, Anthony Champion, and Alfredo Lattes, "Toward a New Conceptualization of Settlements for Demography," *Population and Development Review,* vol. 29, no. 2, 2003, pp. 277–297.

8. Michael Goddard, ed., *Villagers and the City: Melanesian Experiences of Port Moresby, Papua New Guinea,* Sean Kingston Publishing, Wantage, 2010.

9. S. Lucatelli, S. Savastano, and M. Coccia, "Health and Social Services in Rural Umbria," *Materiali UVAL,* issue 12, 2006, http://www.dps.mef.gov.it/documentazione/uval/materiali_uval/Muval12_Sviluppo_rurale_inglese.pdf, accessed 13 August 2007.

10. M. Coombes and S. Raybould, "Public Policy and Population Distribution: Developing Appropriate Indicators of Settlement Patterns," *Environment and Planning C: Government and Policy,* vol. 19, no. 2, 2001, pp. 223–248.

11. Here we have drawn heavily on the European Conference of Ministers Responsible for Spatial/Regional Planning (CEMAT), *Glossary of Key Expressions Used in Spatial Development Policies in Europe,* CEMAT, Lisborne, 2006, http://www.mzopu.hr/doc/14CEMAT_6_EN.pdf, accessed 15 August 2007.

12. Utula Samana, *Papua New Guinea: Which Way?* Arena Publications, Melbourne, 1988, p. 49.

13. See, for example, Bruce Knauft, *From Primitive to Postcolonial in Melanesia and Anthropology,* University of Michigan Press, Ann Arbor, 1999.

14. Edward LiPuma, *Encompassing Others: The Magic of Modernity in Melanesia,* University of Michigan Press, Ann Arbor, 2001, p. 19.

15. Ibid., quotes from pp. 19, 16.

16. Ibid., p. 6.

17. Bruce M. Knauft, *Exchanging the Past: A Rainforest World of Before and After,* University of Chicago Press, Chicago, 2002, p. 38. Emphasis in original.

18. The levels approach touched on here is the subject of Paul James' book *Globalism, Nationalism, Tribalism,* Sage Publications, London, 2006.

19. Nonie Sharp, *Stars of Tagai: The Torres Strait Islanders,* Aboriginal Studies Press, Canberra, 1993, p. 75.

20. Alison Dundon, "Warrior Women, the Holy Spirit and HIV/AIDS in Rural Papua New Guinea," *Oceania,* vol. 77, 2007, pp. 29–42.

21. Deborah B. Gewertz and Frederick K. Errington, *Twisted Histories, Altered Contexts: Representing the Chambri in a World System,* Cambridge University Press, Cambridge, 1991, p. 1

22. Material in this paragraph and the next draws upon the work of two of our authors: Martin Mulligan and Yaso Nadarajah, "Local-Global Relations and Community-Engaged Research," *Globalism Institute Annual Report,* 2007, pp. 11–22.

23. Linda Tuhiwai Smith, *Decolonizing Methodologies: Research and Indigenous Peoples,* Zed Books, London, 1999.

24. James, *Globalism, Nationalism, Tribalism.* Rather than attempting to explain the analytical intricacies, strengths, and weaknesses of this approach here, we will allow them to become apparent through the book.

25. The process of developing consistency in our work in relation to methods of social mapping has been led by Martin Mulligan, lead author of *Creating Community: Celebrations, Arts and Wellbeing within and across Local Communities* (Martin Mulligan,

Paul James, Kim Humphery, Chris Scanlon, Pia Smith, and Nicky Welch), VicHealth and the Globalism Research Centre, Melbourne, 2007.

26. Linda Tuhiwai Smith, *Decolonizing Methodologies*, pp. 144–145.

27. D. Harper, "Meaning and Work: A Study in Photo Elicitation," *International Journal of Visual Sociology*, vol. 2, no. 1, 1984, pp. 20–43; C. Wang and M. A. Burris, "Photovoice: Concept, Methodology and Use for Participatory Needs Assessment," *Health and Behaviour*, vol. 24, no. 3, 1997, pp. 369–387; C. Wang and Y. A. Redwood-Jones, "Photovoice Ethics: Perspectives from Flint Photovoice," *Health Education and Behavior*, vol. 28, no. 5, 2001, pp. 560–572; C. Wang and C. A. Pies, "Family, Maternal, and Child Health through Photovoice," *Maternal and Child Health Journal*, vol. 8, no. 2, 2004, pp. 95–102.

28. Tim Booth and Wendy Booth, "In the Frame: Photovoice and Mothers with Learning Difficulties," Disability and *Society*, vol. 18, no. 4, 2003, p. 432.

29. Michel de Certeau, *The Practice of Everyday Life*, translated by Steven Rendall, University of California Press, Berkeley, 1988, p. xi.

30. Henry Okole, "Political Participation in a Fragmented Democracy: Ethnic and Religious Appeal in Papua New Guinea," *Development Bulletin*, University of Papua New Guinea, Port Moresby, 2002.

31. Paul Rabinow, *Reflections on Fieldwork in Morocco*, University of California Press, Berkeley, 1977.

Chapter 3

Situating Communities

THE DECADES SINCE INDEPENDENCE HAVE SEEN substantial changes in Papua New Guinea's cultures, economies, politics, and ecologies. Many of these changes have been influenced or even dictated by external circumstances beyond the country's control, while much also reflects the efforts of its governments' attempts to build a capitalist economy and a sense of national identity and purpose. Where does all this leave the communities of Papua New Guinea? What is the nature of its multitude of different communities, many still partly customary in their way of life, as they live with the effects of a series of national development goals and plans, and move with and against pressures of modernization and globalization?

Cross-cutting moments of customary and modern culture are everywhere. Waiting in an airport departure lounge for five hours, we finally hear the announcement for the departure of our flight to Lae from Port Moresby. One of the locals, who had put a betel nut (*buai*) into his mouth almost an hour ago, proceeds to moisten a mustard stick with his tongue and to dip it into a bag of lime powder. "If you are cold, betel nut will make you warm; if you are down, it will bring you up," he quips as he adds the limed mustard to the chewed *buai*. Plastic signs carrying the international symbol for prohibition are displayed prominently around the room—a red circle with a diagonal line through it over the silhouette of a betel nut—but the traveler has a wide grin on his face as he begins chewing vigorously again.

> Betel nut...
> When I chew you
> You calm the waves of my mind

You raffle the waves of my stomach
They batter against the reef of my belly...[1]

Chewing betel nut is one seemingly trivial signifier of the complex layers of social practice. Betel nut is a common element across Papua New Guinea's numerous cultures, languages, and topography, and there is archaeological evidence from the Bosum Plateau that betel nut use goes back 5,500 years. A mildly euphoric stimulant, it is consumed in many countries throughout the Asia Pacific region.[2] In Papua New Guinea, it tends to be chewed with mustard sticks and lime powder, and the resultant red substance is spit out—hence the signs in almost every public building. Betel nut selling is a staple of the informal economy, and sharing betel nut can be an important cultural and social gesture. Its prevalence now in cities like Port Moresby, Mt. Hagen, and Lae is evident through the dark red stains splattered across the ground.

Another signifier of the "altered contexts" of the social is the concept of wantok.[3] It provides perhaps the most important way into understanding individual and community relations across the country. Wantok, a Melanesian term, refers to a person connected to others by a relationship of reciprocity, genealogy, or cultural affinity. Such relations have customarily been founded in kinship relations and in ethnicity or language groupings—wantok literally means "one talk" in Pidgin. Increasingly, however, wantok relations in contemporary urban settings can also be generated through modern friendship. The term wantok flows easily in moments of discussion in Papua New Guinea— almost too casually, like the term "community" here and in other parts of the world. Even with the interaction of strangers who have momentarily come together in a situation of adversity—an airport discussion about rescheduling caused by bad weather, a marketplace argument about special pricing—the sense of relating to a wantok seems comfortably positive and overwhelmingly connected over time and place. Through allowing for very flexible social interactions, the reciprocity of contemporary "wantokism" appears to undercut the need for permanent organizations, since individuals can elicit benefits through a range of relations from grounded community relations to ad hoc relationships of convenience.[4]

The wantok system represents a bond between people with a basic sense of community—perhaps a kinship-based grounded community speaking the same language or perhaps persons living in or coming from the one place or sharing common values. At its extreme, it excludes other groups who may not share common interests or values. The social strength of the tribal-modern wantok concept is first that it ambiguously crosses the various modalities of face-to-face relations—including consanguinal relations or ties of embodied genealogy, ritual relations or ties of ceremonial recognition, perceptual relations or ties of known affinity, and convivial relations or ties of spatial contiguity.[5] Second, the concept also allows for a loosening or abstracting of those ties to the extent that it becomes just a subjective naming. In short, calling a person a *wantok* can name a relationship on the basis of the condensed intersection of all of those face-to-face modalities, on the basis of just one of those modalities, or—as the meaning of social relations in Papua New Guinea is changing—on the basis of a subjective calling up of such a connection, however thin. It is the last of these possibilities in the modern context that has allowed for overt instrumental self-interest, and even corruption, to come to the fore.

The *wantok* system is thus founded on a tribal ethic of reciprocity, but it is no longer primarily constituted by it. With the layering of tribal, traditional, and modern relations in Papua New Guinea, particularly in urban settings, reciprocity can be undertaken as either a deep social obligation, a rationally calculated endeavor, or both at the same time. As an outsider to a transaction, it is hard to tell the difference. Primary *wantok* relationships are those defined by grounded dimensions such as shared language and common place of origin. But there are a range of relationships that may fall within the category of *wantok*, with distinctions being made between "true" and "honorary" *wantok*, or between close and more distant *wantok*. Levine and Levine note that Papua New Guinean understandings of ethnicity overwhelmingly emphasize the importance of place, as opposed to many anthropological and sociological understandings of ethnicity, which stress the importance of cultural similarity as the basic frame of reference. "In urban Papua New Guinea people often interact with reference to subjective beliefs in common origin … [they] do not emphasize considerations of custom. When discussing participants in relationships and events who are defined with reference to subjective beliefs in common origin, townsmen use an expandable spatial referent."[6] The extension of *wantok* to include friendship-based relationships also appears to be an urban development, significantly extending the meaning of a customary sociality.

The exchange of money between *wantoks* complicates this further. Michael Goddard has suggested that, when we situate small-scale usury in articulation between a Melanesian gift economy and a capitalist commodity economy *and* the transactions are written down, the whole ritual and cultural practice of moneylending primarily becomes one of profit making.[7] That is, when loans are written into books (*bukim mani*), the codification overrides reciprocity and customary wantokism. Profit locates even kinsfolk as "unrelated individuals." This indicates first how significant money has become to social relations and, second, how in many cases contemporary *wantok* relations have become abstracted from older forms of embodied integration. *Wantok* relations of this more abstracted and instrumental kind may be thus an alternative response to the demands of living in a densely populated place where the competition for jobs and living conditions is fierce and not getting any easier. It raises important questions about what will happen to Papua New Guinea's urban grass-roots support system given that it can no longer be based entirely on the rationale of a tribal-traditional *wantok* system of kin-ordered society. It also raises issues about the relationship between the city and rural settings.

Although not much detailed work has been done on the relation between the city and the country, it has become more or less axiomatic in anthropological discussions of urban living in Papua New Guinea that migrants bring to town with them the practices and ideologies of a kin-ordered society with its sense of socially related obligation and reciprocity. In urban situations, over time, this practice is seen to extend to embrace networks beyond the immediate clan or consanguinal relations of an individual in a rural setting. The *wantok* framework enables an individual in the city to draw on those individuals or groups that he or she considers a *wantok* for socioeconomic support. This becomes particularly important when urban living often involves at least a geographic extension of the social and cultural support structures of village life. However, while the term *wantok* is still the most common word used to describe this form of urban support network, we are also seeing the emergence of new forms of social relations, which are best understood as lifestyle communities.

Two major qualifications on this presentation of the stretching of relations from the village to the city can be made. First, the relationship also stretches the other way from the village to the city, with *wantok*s in the city drawn upon by those in the villages, particularly for monetary support. When the community at Inuma-Alepa wants to build a Seventh-Day Adventist church in their village, they use the organizational and financial capacity of their brethren in Port Moresby to raise thousands of kina. When a funeral service occurs in Vanapa, the community draws upon its *wantok*s in Port Moresby and Brisbane to provide money to buy the pigs for the feast. (See the social profiles on Alepa and Vanapa in Chapter 5.) Those individuals with resources who live at a distance but want to maintain a "place" in a community thus become obliged to share. Second, the unqualified assumption that all migrant and settlement communities are dominated by *wantok* sensibilities can no longer be made. Whereas researchers in the late colonial period found relatively homologous associations between regional groups and particular settlements including sections of low-covenant estates, or even company compounds, more recent research into conditions of continuing migration and population growth indicates a complex variety in the population of the settlements. Much of this variation depends on whether these settlements are populated with first-generation or multiple-generation settlers from rural areas. It also depends on how much knowledge is carried through to the next generation of customary life back in the village.

Deborah Gewertz and Frederick Errington argue that a middle class has also been emerging in developing Papua New Guinea with its significant and growing role inadequately understood because most research and study has focused on village-level issues.[8] These authors stress that, even though village-based communities typically shared an "egalitarian ethos," understanding contemporary Papua New Guinea now critically requires a focus on the new issue of class formation. The growing urban drift has created groupings of landless squatters living in settlements around urban areas, particularly Port Moresby and Lae. This other emerging class is living without customary land tenure and under the constant threat of eviction.[9] As the volume of urban drift increases and the bonds that once held spatial settlements—particularly rural settlements—are changing and sometimes dissolving, how, we should ask, are Papua New Guineans responding in the practice of their everyday living?

Although the notion of "sustainability" had not yet entered the taken-for-granted lexicon of government or industry, F. J. West predicted some fifty years ago many of the issues that would have an impact on the social and cultural fabric and compromise community sustainability in Papua New Guinea today:

> The rate of change…must not be so violent that the…native [is] left to face the impact of European penetration without the support of his traditional community. If too much land were to be alienated, the natives would not have sufficient for their own needs; some would be landless, and lacking land would lack the basis of their social organization.… If too many men leave a group…and return arrogant, contemptuous of those who know nothing of the great world beyond the group, and laden with white man's wealth, then the…result would be a large number of "de-tribalised" natives who would have lost their own culture without being absorbed into the European one.[10]

Within Papua New Guinea, capitalist ventures of various sorts have been uneven in their impact. Confronting a multiethnic, polyglot citizenry of predominantly rural ethnic groups, many of them engaged in subsistence and smallholder agriculture on the penumbra of a cash economy. Even for tribal groups living in the remote villages of Wisini in Morobe Province or Omarakana in the Trobriand Islands (see Chapter 6), such a heightened and uneven pace of development has become a multistranded process, perplexing and dismaying as much as it creates opportunistic possibilities. It is in this unsettling embrace of different ontological formations—customary tribalism, religious traditionalism, and developmentalist modernism—experienced as a crisscrossing of connections and misconnections, breakdowns and compromises, that the people of Papua New Guinea have to negotiate ways of living on a day-to-day basis.[11] People talk of the strain of walking in "two worlds," the tribal and the modern. Political posters depict bifurcated figures, carrying a briefcase in one hand and a spear in the other.[12] These depictions reduce the intersecting layers to a Great Divide between the tribal and the modern, but people nevertheless understand that these cartoon-quality caricatures are just that—attempts to illustrate a more complex reality. To provide a way into the patterns of practice in Papua New Guinea, in the following section we examine some of these layered processes in terms of three modes of practice: production, exchange, and inquiry.

Practices of Production: From Gardening to Mining

More than four-fifths of the Papua New Guinean population live in rural areas, and, apart from some cash cropping, most people rely on subsistence farming to meet their day-to-day needs. Here subsistence farming should be understood in terms of Marshall Sahlins' concept of "domestic mode of production" rather than as scratching out a meager living. It is production for livelihood rather than production for profit.[13] Overlaying this kind of production, the drive to integrate Papua New Guinea into the global capitalist economy has had significant consequences, sometimes profoundly negative. It has reinforced existing inequities between regions, challenged the nature of local identities, and put pressure on processes of national integration.

The immediate history of this process goes back to the period of colonial administration under Australian jurisdiction. Australia played a significant role in shaping not only the political system but also PNG's formal economy, emphasizing the extraction of natural resources and export commodities as the basis of financing economic development.[14] Such economic development was a significant objective partly due to a belief that it would "guarantee continued Australian influence in the Territories."[15] Colonial commentators such as O. H. K. Spate, advisor to the Australian minister for territories in the 1950s, wrote that the "extension of Australian control over a region so manifestly un-Australian in character (even though also un-Asian) as New Guinea can only be justified by the effective exploitation of its physical resources and by the advancement of its peoples."[16] For F. J. West, the "dual mandate" of colonial rule presented a dilemma for the Australian administrators of fulfilling its "obligation to rule as a sacred trust for native peoples" and still maintaining its "duty" to encourage modern capitalist development.[17]

Although Papua New Guinea's constitution clearly articulated an economic future based on local skills and knowledge, in the postcolonial period economic development based on cash cropping and the exploitation of natural resources such as minerals and timber has dominated formal sector development. Several writers remain skeptical of the long-term sustainability of formal sector development with less than a tenth of people employed in the formal sector in the early 1990s.[18] However, supporting the argument for further expansion of the formal sector has been the focus of many mainstream writers, academics, and policy commentators, particularly in Australia. They advocate a stronger shift away from the Melanesian tradition of subsistence production to rapid economic modernization. Anne Booth argues that the PNG government must focus on extracting economic value from the country's natural resources and "facilitate rather than impede the process of monetization."[19] The narrow emphasis here is on accelerating the rate of economic growth in ways that will contribute to Papua New Guinea's Gross Domestic Product. Ron Duncan and Ila Temu put forward similar arguments, suggesting that Papua New Guinea's future rests on its potential to mobilize the "huge, largely stagnant agricultural sector" while attracting foreign investment that would boost industry and generate jobs.[20]

In Australia, academics and researchers from right-wing public policy think tanks share the view that it is Papua New Guinea's customary land tenure system that is holding the nation back from economic growth and from becoming integrated into the global economy. Susan Windybank and Mike Manning, writing for the neoliberal Centre for Independent Studies, maintain that

> the system of communal land ownership that covers more than 90 percent of the country also remains an obstacle to sustained and widespread rural investment.... Individuals cannot buy or sell land as a commodity, so land cannot be turned into an asset to generate private wealth by using it as collateral for bank loans. Historical experience has shown that no country has developed with a communal land system.... This is at odds with the Melanesian tradition of communalism, but it must be addressed by Melanesians themselves if long-term development is to take place.[21]

This view that a customary land tenure system is detrimental to Papua New Guinea's development is shared by the neoliberal economist Helen Hughes, also of the Centre for Independent Studies, and by Tim Curtin, who has claimed that individual landownership is required to accelerate economic development.[22] The basis for Curtin's argument, aside from examples of how land privatization has worked well in other countries, is that agricultural production has failed to keep up with population growth under the customary tenure system. Very little of the literature putting forward the economic growth solution for Papua New Guinea refers to the country's own constitutional ideals or gives consideration to the sociocultural factors that make rapid economic development unrealistic and poorly suited to a Melanesian context. The pressure by outside ideologues is quite intense. Articles appear in the local newspapers from outside luminaries such as Mike Moore, former director general of the World Trade Organization, arguing that "secure property rights boosts investments...[and] safeguards them from predatory bureaucrats and local mafia....It is not rocket science," he says. "The pattern is clear."[23]

In this context, while outsiders push for the privatization of land, it is locally based philosophers and planners who have a more complex sense of the issues. They challenge the view that customary land in Papua New Guinea is unproductive. An anthology like *Culture and Progress: The Melanesian Philosophy of Land and Development in Papua New Guinea* gives some sense of this complexity, with most contributors arguing the need for new layers of governance of customary land rather than simply the replacement of tribal "ownership" by modern property rights.[24] As one variation on the developmentalist push, Hartmut Holzknecht advocates the establishment of incorporated land groups in which customary owners come together, if necessary, as recognized legal entities to secure access to loans in order to finance development programs within their communities. This ensures that development initiatives requiring new landholding arrangements "come from communities, from the grassroots, and then co-ordination with local government, provincial government and national government" to support the goals of rural communities.[25] This position, however, does not address the risk of communities losing their land if they are unable to make repayments.

Going deeper, much of the anthropological literature on the effects of economic development in Papua New Guinea suggests that the processes of capitalism are producing radically new conceptions of work, livelihood, and even identity.[26] This has been occurring over decades as communities struggle to situate themselves within changing global and national landscapes and strive to negotiate complex relations with powerful corporate and government interests. In particular, mining has been a favored form of economic development for its capacity to deliver results to the bottom line of the national economy. With the national government as a major stakeholder in the mining industry, mineral extraction has been seen as a source of economic promise, supposedly reducing the nation's dependency on Australian aid by stimulating the formal sector and providing opportunities for government revenue.[27] However, the effects of mining development have been far reaching, in many cases disrupting the social fabric and cultural networks that have customarily governed community life. Nonetheless, the promise of social services and increased prosperity means that large-scale mining projects are initially welcomed by those communities that have been included in the consultation process.[28] The rapid changes introduced by mining development and their long-term cultural, ecological, and economic implications are often poorly understood by local communities, and the infrastructural and economic benefits promised by mining companies are not always fulfilled.

The politics of representing this development has led in radically different directions. Nicole Polier, for example, has examined the radical social transformations of the Faiwolmin people of the North Fly River in Western Province. She suggests that as Faiwolmin men increasingly work as miners in a wage economy, labor that was previously expended on customary land for subsistence production has been supplanted by the need to earn money to buy imported food and commodities in the local supermarket introduced to the village by the mining company. The presence of the mine has created new migrations of men to the central mining township, while the work of tending gardens and building shelters is left to the women and older men. For Polier, the mining enclave has produced great uncertainties and raises challenging questions for the Faiwolmin as they seek to reconcile tribal identities with modern modes of production: "To what space does the Faiwolmin male, suspended between a subsistence sector and a shanty town, belong? Does he belong to the mountainside and cycles of male initiation? To a village? Does he belong to a nation that has displaced him, or a corporate, postcolonial parent that regards him as a squatter—a guest at best—in the land of his ancestors?"[29]

In Polier's analysis, the Faiwolmin are presented as disempowered recipients of development for whom self-determination is only a fantasy. In a contrasting perspective on how communities respond to mining development, Martha Macintyre and Simon Foale write that

> In the current economic climate of PNG one might add that it is almost impossible to convince people who long for the material benefits of logging or mining, that the direct and indirect damage to their environment might outweigh all the short-term benefits of compensation and employment. In addition to that, the fact that environmental damage can become a source of regular income (in the form of payments for dust pollution, water discoloration, etc.) means that it can even be seen as beneficial to those most affected.[30]

Based on work done in two locales, Misima and Lahir Islands, Macintyre and Foale describe local communities driven by a cynical and self-interested politics of acquisition. The views of locals are summarized as being based on either misconceptions about effects or lack of concern for environmental consequences. Not having conducted research in those locales, we cannot challenge those conclusions except to say that people in the locales in which we worked were

very different. It is certainly the case that different forms of adaptation are occurring across Papua New Guinea. Benjamin Imbun analyzes how a tribal workforce at the Porgera mine in a Highlands province are adapting to the shift from
"tribal to industrial" modes of production.[31] The mine was the Porgera people's
entry into a cash economy, producing a "strong sense of identity and common
interest in the mine which distinguished them from 'other' nationals."[32]

According to Imbun, the Porgerans more or less successfully integrated
their lives into the mine's various operations. However, Imbun makes no mention of the environmental problems resulting from the mine. This may be because his analysis deals with the Ipili people in Porgera and not the Duna, who
were largely excluded from any benefits received by the mine.[33] Imbun's interviews with local mine employees suggests that, though there was some anxiety
about what might happen to the village if the mine closed down, locals employed by the mine generally felt positively about the kind of development that
industry had brought to their village. Such an immediate subjective response
tells us little in the long term. What will become more important over time
is the sustainability of these communities as they move from production for
livelihood, through which they maintain a strong connection with the land and
landscapes of the ancestors, to capitalist production whereby the community is
drawn into the broader national project to become part of the global economy.

While Polier and others examine the imposed renegotiation of identity as a
product of colonialism and the capitalist expansion of a postcolonial Papua New
Guinea, Peter Kean's critique of postdevelopment theory attempts to resist both
the tendency to romanticize indigenous cultures and the assumption that there
are no benefits to be realized for tribal and traditional communities within the
cash economy. Kean examines local responses to development in the Siki Settlement Scheme of West New Britain, a center for oil palm production, arguing
against the notion that local communities are the passive recipients of economic
development. Kean instead reads Siki residents as active agents within the economic transformations of modernization occurring around them, in which the
shift to wage labor has not only provided the benefits of a source of cash income
but also released residents from village obligations that they found personally
burdensome. He asks, "In an economic environment irrevocably altered by participation in the global economy is it realistic to suggest that people can or would
want to embark on an inward-looking cultural alternative to development?"[34]

This is a legitimate question for settler communities with no access to customary land for domestic production or for communities where the dream of
employment opportunities and a cash income for the purchase of commodities
is an almost irresistible draw card for young people. However, there remain
basic problems with Kean's analysis. He does not address the issue that many

forms of economic development undermine the cultural and political fabric of communities, a fabric that both preserves the vitality and resilience of communities and provides a basis for enhancing their capacity to respond to change. While he acknowledges some problems in settlement communities, in particular, conflict between customary landowners and migrant communities over control of land resources, he does not question the assumption that conventional economic development is the best or only kind of development available to these communities. In Kean's analysis, development is something that communities respond to rather than something that emerges from within the communities themselves.

What is evident from Kean, Imbun, Macintyre, Errington, Gewertz, and others is that the relationship to resources including land is an important factor in how communities respond to economic development projects and to change in general. In his analysis of local responses to a mining project in the Strickland River area, Glenn Banks argues: "To understand community responses to mining in Melanesia requires dropping these Eurocentric divisions between the environment and the rest of one's life."[35] Banks examines the different community responses to the mine, concluding that the greatest resistance to the mining operation was not in those areas suffering the most significant environmental damage but in areas where consultation with the local communities was poorest and where communities felt most marginalized from decision making in the development process. Banks makes the case that, as communities along the Strickland River seek to negotiate the global forces that affect them at a local level (and from which they are largely marginalized), they will find new political strategies. From Banks' position, to suggest that Papua New Guinea is in the process of being recolonized by multinational interests (many of them Australian and Chinese) is to state the obvious; what is less evident, as writers such as Paige West also show, is how the environmental NGOs represent another colonizing force that sometimes privileges Western concerns for the environment over indigenous concerns for a relationship to resources (namely, land) and livelihood.[36]

While attempts by communities to control their own resources and to resist being marginalized within the processes of development must be understood as integral to local responses to globalization and to the sustainability of communities in general, Glenn Banks potentially overlooks how many PNG communities, in seeking to bring themselves closer to the "centres of state and company,"[37] are also active agents in appropriating the language of Western environmental discourses. Rather than merely recolonizing PNG communities, the environmental concerns of the West are used as a tool for bringing local interests into the center of more global debates about environmental responsibility as locals work toward more sustainable communities. Banks is critical of anthropologists such as David Hyndman and Stuart Kirsch who have argued that community protests against large-scale mining projects are not about economic concerns but about the ecological destruction of productive land.[38]

The localized impacts of mining and the experiences of mining communities are neither a question simply of economics or of environment but rather of livelihood, resources, and identity across all the social domains of culture, politics, economy, and ecology. Alison Dundon, an anthropologist who spent time with the Gogodala people along the Fly River, examined the way in which changes in the relationship between food and the environment presented a fundamental challenge to the Gogodala concept of *ela gi,* or "way of life."[39] In the mid-1990s, as mining tailings moved down the river, the Gogodala noted changes to their sago palms, which were of increasingly poor quality and often failed to mature. Food gardens irrigated with river water appeared sickly, and fish from the river and lagoons near the village had sores, growths, or little flesh on them.[40] As a result of these changes to their food and to the landscape, the Gogodala became increasingly reliant on store-bought foods such as tinned fish, white rice, flour, tea, sugar, and white bread. The consumption of these foods produced not only a change to their subsistence traditions, but also a radical reformulation of what it meant to be a Gogodala person: "those who 'live on store things' are characterised by their fat or soft bodies... they do not work as hard as others.... One man from a northern village... pointed out that some of them didn't even have gardens, instead spending their time begging for money or stealing or 'following songs from the radio. What sort of life is that? Well, it won't be a Gogodala life.'"[41] These changes clearly go beyond the level of environment. They are reshaping the social landscapes in general and the intertwined relationships between food, ancestors, land, and self.

In responding to changes around them and mobilizing in the face of their perceived exclusion or exploitation, community movements in contemporary Papua New Guinea have taken and will likely continue to take a diverse range of forms. It remains a strong possibility that movements will turn increasingly to more conventional methods of political and economic activity and thus be gradually incorporated within the system, at the provincial if not at the national level. Equally plausible, however, is that movements invoking a neotribal or traditional form of communal identity (and also perhaps cult-based millenarian movements) will continue to emerge, sporadically, as a form of protest among groups who consider themselves relatively deprived, slighted, or threatened.

This leaves three related questions: Are communities pursuing practices that are sustainable in economic, political, cultural, and environmental terms? How will they position themselves in the space between and across tribal and modern modes of production? And what resources and discourses will they

Children walking home with fresh fish bought at the market in Losuia, Trobriand Islands. Children enter into the exchange process at an early age.

draw upon in doing so? Thus we return to the basic issue. For all the discussion of mining and despite the predominance of modern extractive capitalism in terms of its framing of the national economy of Papua New Guinea, most people in the country depend for their livelihood on localized domestic production. Subsistence agriculture with all its customary and modern intersections continues to be a way of life. Any adequate approach to sustainable livelihoods in Papua New Guinea needs to directly address questions of how customary agricultural production can continue while adapting to pressures such as population increases, urbanization, and cultural fragmentation.

Practices of Exchange: From Kula to Money

Reciprocal exchange continues to be an important form of exchange in customary communities in Papua New Guinea, even if other forms of exchange coexist with it and are increasingly reframing it.[42] *Reciprocity,* in the sense used here, can be defined as exchange of goods—material and immaterial—*within a network of exchange relations* that carries the "spirit" of face-to-face integration between the persons involved in exchange and thus require some form of ritual recognition or *social* return. In contemporary Papua New Guinea, classic reciprocal exchange has tended to retreat into the more restricted circles of clan, family, and face-to-face *wantok* lineages. It can no longer be said to exist as an overarching system of exchange or even as long-term and stable circles of exchange. The classic example of a reciprocal exchange system is the Kula Ring in the Milne Bay region. When in the 1920s Bronislaw Malinowski famously documented a dual movement of gifts and countergifts passed in opposite exchange circles around a ring of Massim communities in Milne Bay, he was describing the system in more functional and formal ways than we intend by the concept.[43] As used here "reciprocity" is a more abstract way of talking about a mode of exchange than the way in which Malinowski described gift giving and it has a more profound subjective side than he was prepared to acknowledge. Gifts are *goods* that have, for a time, become the symbolic media within the broader complex of reciprocal exchange.[44]

There are also *currency objects* in customary communities—that is, objects acting as a kind of money. Within older tribal settings, currency goods such as salt money or kina shells were not available for impersonal exchange as capital until a further process of abstraction occurred. However, in the contemporary context this has become much more fluid. John Kasaipwalova, chief of the Kwenama clan on Kiriwina Island in the Trobriands, tells, for example, of leaving a *beku* stone—an object of wealth used in tribal gift exchange—with his lawyer, Beresford Love in Port Moresby, as collateral in the mid-1970s after the Kabisawalai self-help development movement collapsed, leaving a K120,000 debt. Now, such currency objects are as much valued by modern notions of "rarity" as by tribal conceptions of "social standing."

At another level, there are also bartering relations where goods are exchanged for other goods of approximate equivalence, and here the reciprocity tends to be more abstract and is conducted between people who can be relative strangers, acquaintances, or extended *wantoks*. In this process the relationship requires an immediate return. For example, when women meet early in the morning at the weekly Kara market, near Yule Island (Chapter 6), the island people bring fish, and the land people bring vegetables and fruit for exchange. Women carry the goods that they wants to exchange, and, with eye contact and body posture rather than words, they negotiate what they both believe is a fair trade. This process continues until all the goods are either exchanged or rejected. It is an exchange market that has been going on for as long as local people can remember.[45]

New understandings of currency and exchange have introduced other levels of social and cultural transformation in local communities. Notwithstanding

Women bartering fish for bananas in a cashless reciprocal exchange at the Kara market

continuities of some practices, the introduction of money has systematically cut across the diverse forms of currency, bartering, and reciprocal exchange in Papua New Guinea's tribal-traditional societies and has been remaking those communities for decades.[46] The church with its traditional/modern ambivalence about money provides one set of complications. In the plateau region of central New Ireland, which has a long history of Western contact and involvement in a cash economy as a result of a strong missionary presence, the Lelet have developed a worldview that is strongly informed by apocalyptic narratives of the Pentecostal Church, possessing an uneasy relationship with money that is at once socially desirable and tainted by the Antichrist. The apocalyptic world events are foretold by "evil" attempts on a global scale to establish a "new world" through the undoing of existing social and economic systems at the national and local levels.

A second set of complications came with the administrative use of money. For the colonial administrators, the use of money as the dominant *modern* medium of exchange played an important role in drawing local communities into the discourses of nationhood that supported the colonial project of economic development and the exploitation of the colony's natural resources. Drawing on Foster's analysis of the relationship between money and the nation, Richard Eves has argued that the promotion of money by the colonial authorities as the dominant currency produced a new form of community identity constituted through the "singular individual with his or her own money" as well as "a collective one which instantiates a distinctive nation as a unit of collective identity, with its own money."[47] Money came to signify the power of both Australian and Papua New Guinean governments to provide for the PNG people—or not. In the postcolonial period this extended to individual politicians. The distribution of money and goods during one's campaign became a significant basis for being elected to Parliament. Sam Kaima calls the phenomenon *Mipela istap long maket* (We are on sale).[48] The icons of money also became signifiers of national independence and state integration:

> Currency, the means of consumption, not only objectifies "the nation," wheth-er in the iconographic forms of pigs and pearl shells or of Michael Somare and the Parliament House—the 50-kina note depicted in the PNG Banking Corpo-ration (PNGBC) ad. Currency also symbolizes the nation-state as one entity in a system of such entities.... The use of currency, then, practically affirms the existence of a bounded community of consumers, the borders of which are defined by the extent to which the territorial state authorizes the currency as legal tender.[49]

Claims in the popular press that Papua New Guinea's economy is on the brink of collapse, along with theories in which international economic institu-tions such as the International Monetary Fund and the World Bank are part of a broader agenda for global dominance, have problematized the relationship to money and led to new articulations of national identity that imply "a passive acceptance of the state rather than active allegiance."[50] Richard Eves argues that this is consistent with a broader dissatisfaction among many Papua New Guin-eans with the national government, which has failed to live up to expectations that a strong and prosperous government, and therefore PNG society, would spring forth from independence. While many communities have responded positively to the sense that their participation in the formal economy is con-tributing to national well-being, some communities' experience of Papua New Guinea's economic and political uncertainties has shifted the symbolic signifi-cance of money and weakened its connection to nation-state identity.

In a parallel and equally complex overlaying of social forms in tension, some Christian communities around Papua New Guinea have also experienced the apocalyptic discourses of Pentecostal Christianity in ways that produce "a new collective identity that also transcends the boundaries of the nation."[51] Many Pentecostal communities have begun to understand their world as part of a broader traditional-modern cosmology. For instance, events such as drought are now, at one level, experienced locally as part of a modern sense of global climate change, but at another level they are also formulated in terms of a neo-traditionalist religious understanding of a "new geography of the world as an interconnected entity, in which local experiences and dilemmas are seen to be constituents of larger narratives."[52] Whether this means that some grounded communities are able to make sense of their own local histories and experiences within the context of globalization and therefore better understand the local and global interrelationships that shape their lives is dubious. As many other writers have suggested, such Pentecostalism involves both a process of world making and one of world breaking.[53]

Overall, the consequences of all these changes and pressures are profound. In the political domain, money has been drawn into a new kind of cargo cultism and an increasingly instrumental relationship to the state. In the cultural domain, the distribution and availability of money now sets the terms and timing for customary festivals as deep within local practices as the Mila Mala Festival on Kiriwina Island (Chapter 6). In the ecological domain, communities or sections of communities such as in Vanapa (Chapter 5) often feel the need to sacrifice their forests to loggers for short-term financial gain. And in the economic domain, money increasingly determines social life outside of customary agricultural production. As cash income has become increasingly important at the village level, young men in particular are pursuing opportunities for wage employment in urban areas. John Connell argues that "the outcome is that poverty is largely transferred from the country to the city and has thus become more visible."[54] Settlement communities arriving from rural areas have expanded, and customary landholders such as the Motu-Koita in the Central District are increasingly squeezed out of their own lands, making it increasingly "difficult to collect the rent-in-kinds or continue the personal exchange relationships that had been integral to the negotiations with the first small groups of settlers."[55]

Practices of Inquiry: From Training to Learning

The critique of development raises questions about community development and its relationship to the development of the nation. Formal and informal education often plays a critical role in community development and the forms that it takes. Papua New Guinea's colonial legacy is strongly reflected in its education system, with much of its curriculum derived from a Western education framework. As Pa'O H. Luteru and G. Robert Teasdale have written, the educational systems of most Pacific Island countries, including Papua New Guinea, "were not geared towards the needs of indigenous populations, but to satisfying the demands of expatriates and of local elites who were required to support

the administration and preserve the status quo."⁵⁶ The formal education system in Papua New Guinea, which was seen as critical to the process of national
development, was not engineered to support the needs of the rural sector and
the customary economic base but rather an administrative sector in the formal
economy. Education was designed to provide a flow of qualified graduates who
could participate in the project of nation-building. Papua New Guinea's education system would therefore only ever meet the needs of a minority of the population. Luteru and Teasdale highlight the influence that Australia had in many
aid-dependent countries in the South Pacific. Australian aid to countries such as
Papua New Guinea was also driven by Australia's own broader strategic interests
to develop education as an "export industry" by "maximizing the dependency of
developing countries on the Australian education system," and to facilitate the
kind of development in Papua New Guinea that would promote trade in ways
that were beneficial to Australia's economic interests.⁵⁷

Sheldon Weeks has pointed out that, although measures are taken to avoid
the problem of the "overproduction of school leavers," such as the establishment
of quota systems restricting the number of high schools students, Papua New
Guinea nonetheless faces the problem that many school leavers are unlikely to
find the employment opportunities in the formal sector that they had hoped
for.⁵⁸ Consequently, students who do make it through to the secondary level
often have to leave their communities for another village where they can attend
high school, placing a strain on both student and parents. Despite the sacrifices
made by parents to educate their children, completion of high school is not
guaranteed to result in gainful employment. Drawing on the concept developed
by Ronald Dore, Weeks describes the production of more school leavers than
can be absorbed by the formal economy as "diploma disease."⁵⁹

In his study of the values attached to education in Pere village in Manus,
Peter Demerath has argued that this situation has led many village residents
to become disillusioned about the benefits of education for their children and
therefore to disengage from the formal education system. For the Manus people, "Western knowledge, particularly literacy education, was the key to improving their standard of living, especially when they saw that schooling could lead
to white-collar employment in the formal sector."⁶⁰ Formal employment in the
cash economy conferred status upon extended family, even though village life
required only minimal cash to purchase items such as batteries and fish hooks
that could not be grown or produced by the villagers themselves. Because formal
education was proving to provide a poor "return on investment," as Demerath
puts it, parents invested less and less in their children's education, aside from
paying for school fees. Pere villagers viewed education, on the one hand, as part
of the process of becoming more "modernized" or "developed." On the other

hand, the disillusionment with the lack of opportunities for wage employment resulted in the residents of Pere village "adjusting themselves to lifestyles that required a minimum of money, valorizing a partially 'invented' village-based identity," which Demerath interprets as "creative and culturally mediated responses to the collective uncertainty and threatened marginalization posed by the process of 'modernization' in Papua New Guinea."[61]

While Peter Demerath observes a productive response in Pere village to the disappointments of formal education, one that reinforces village life and traditions, Francyne Huckaby's fieldwork in a village of Eastern Highlands Province points to more detrimental effects of Western education on community well-being. Huckaby argues that the education system imposed on Papua New Guinea during the colonial period reproduces "Western-based values of linearity, abstraction, and individuation" at the expense of local knowledge, learning systems, and values.[62] Students are organized and disciplined by teachers in ways that undermine customary forms of learning such as storytelling and devalue cultural systems of reciprocity and care of others. While Huckaby acknowledges that an education system in Papua New Guinea cannot be composed of an entirely village-based knowledge base, she argues that it must incorporate learning that is relevant to village life so that local knowledge is not subordinate to Western knowledge. In her analysis of the relationship between the founding principles of Papua New Guinea's constitution and the history of educational development and reform in Papua New Guinea, Beatrice Avalos puts forward a similar view, acknowledging that "building a nation means preparing high-level professionals and administrators to lead the country's development," while also "recognising that most of the country still lives in rural areas" and that "education has to assist self-reliance for village rather than for urban life."[63] This position was advocated by a Research and Curriculum Officer for the Department of Education who wrote in a policy statement in 1950:

> If we take out to the adults a sense of the importance of such skills and reading and writing, we should bring into the school an appreciation of the value of such skills as canoe-making and gardening. It is on such an appreciation, both inside the school and in the village outside the school, of the value of both the old and the new skills, that not only the material progress of the village, but also its present social harmony are dependent.[64]

This approach to educational policy in Papua New Guinea was referred to as the "blending of cultures," a concept that was advocated by colonial administrators as far back as 1935, even as schools were established around Papua New Guinea that reflected Australian curriculum priorities. Although several others advocated for the blending of modern and tribal-customary approaches to learning and education, it proved difficult to put into practice, as we argue in Chapter 11. Instead, Papua New Guinea has been left with an education system that poorly reflects the values, knowledge, or learning styles of Melanesian culture. At the same time, it also leaves young Papua New Guineans poorly prepared for a productive working life in the Western sense.

The subjugation of the local by Western education systems is not the exclusive practice of Western teachers working in a PNG context but often comes from Papua New Guinean teachers themselves. Wayne Fife conceptualizes this phenomenon as the "bureaucratization of consciousness," in Papua New Guinea, "that makes sense of dividing the world into hierarchically arranged sets of organizations in which individual placement seems to depend on abstract criteria rather than social relationships."[65] Fife draws on Michel Foucault's notion of knowledge systems as "technologies of power" in order to analyze the way in which Papua New Guinean school teachers become active participants in persuading "others that bureaucratic social forms are and should be the language of modernity."[66] In this sense, the culture of colonialism is reinforced through the abstraction and rationalization of social relationships and the natural world in the classroom.

This background suggests that the work of decolonizing Papua New Guinea's educational system is ongoing. It highlights the importance of incorporating indigenous epistemology into Papua New Guinean schools, particularly in village areas, and to Papua New Guinea's development trajectory in general. David Welchman Gegeo and Karen Ann Watson-Gegeo argue for models of community development that encourage young people to learn about their own culture rather than viewing education as a mechanism for inducting young Papua New Guineans into the modern world of the wage economy and formal sector. For Gegeo and Watson-Gegeo, education must play a more critical role in community development and village life: "In contrast to 'rural development' guided by outdated modernization models and ideas, development that is meaningful to rural people must be built on knowledge resources that the villagers already have, and the strategies they know for expanding that knowledge."[67]

Education is for life. It is a "means of developing skills, values and attitudes that allow students to understand and reflect on the community within which they live and be productive in it"; a positive pedagogy in their terms "is likely to promote a bottom-up approach to addressing education issues, where communities are closely involved in decision making processes."[68] From this perspective, a "productive life" encompasses more than participation in the wage economy, but also participation in the informal sector and in community life in general. This includes subsistence and small-scale cash-crop farming, child care, and the other activities that contribute to the well-being of family and community.

As a former colonial power and Papua New Guinea's most significant aid donor, Australia has significant influence over the country's development direction. It has a responsibility to consider the ethical implications of its aid program and the modes of development it encourages and facilitates. The solution to Papua New Guinea's problems must come from within Papua New Guinea itself—not through costly, large-scale, top-down projects that are developed and imposed from outside. Other pathways must emerge from within communities themselves in such a way that Papua New Guineans do not lose their longer-term political and cultural orientations. Practical strategies are needed that enable a return to the objectives of the nation's constitution and redress the fundamental inadequacies of Western-style economic development in a Melanesian context. This kind of alternative will require a volte-face for many policy experts, both in Papua New Guinea and in Australia, particularly those who maintain that countries such as Papua New Guinea must renounce their cultural traditions in the name of progress and development. Such an approach is doomed to fail in the long term as it undermines the cultural vitality of Papua New Guinean communities and their resilience and adaptability in the face of global change. If it were true, as is said colloquially, that "when an old man dies in a village, a whole library dies with him," then customary culture would have collapsed generations ago. Fortunately, many communities in Papua New Guinea still have a continuing basis for living with and through different formations of inquiry and learning.

The Place of Development

Urban Development

The popular discourse about settlement communities in the media and in some government publications is that they are the origin points of problems of lawlessness, disorder, and poverty in cities such as Port Moresby. Challenging the veracity of this assumption, Michael Goddard draws on a number of studies to argue that the *raskol* gangs responsible for much of the crime in the city are not always from settlement communities, nor are they necessarily unemployed (in the sense that they are seeking formal employment). Instead, many *raskols* are disillusioned individuals who can better support themselves through crime than through a low-paying job in the formal sector. This is an economic reality that is not confined to the settlement areas but is in fact a broader problem of low wages within the formal economy.[69] The cost of living in Port Moresby is high, and many jobs in the formal sector do not provide enough income to support a household, forcing many residents into the informal sector to supplement their income.[70]

The problems of urbanization in Port Moresby and Lae can partly be attributed to poor urban housing policy during the colonial period, when the city was developed according to the European notion of the city as the place for "urbanizing, modern and civilized societies" while villages were "rural, traditional and primitive."[71] Today government crackdowns on settlement communities and on participation in sections of the informal sector have been associated with a rise in police brutality. Residents of settlement communities are "portrayed as temporarily out of place and in an environment lacking the traditions, moral and positive community values of rural communities."[72]

While it is important not to romanticize urban village life as a bucolic and unproblematic existence, it is equally important to recognize that, in many cases, the kinship connections that continue to constitute urban community life do in fact impose some sense of governance and social structure, mitigating the worst problems of law and order that emerge outside of the context of community law and expectation. Urban people thus still tend to live as "villagers in town"—to use C. D. Rowley's classic phrase—except that, contrary to Rowley's descriptions in the 1960s, the longer-term rural migrants no longer see themselves as temporary.[73] What others might call "slums" are settled villages: some with major social problems but settled nevertheless. Moreover, on the one hand, there are fewer opportunities for a wage income in rural areas (with the exception of "development enclaves"), and urban connections to rural livelihood—that is based on subsistence and semisubsistence agriculture—remain possible through trading with *wantoks*. On the other hand, with increased pressure on land resources due to population increases and the expansion of cash cropping, the question of interconnected urban-rural livelihoods is becoming more difficult. In parallel, the changing expectations of younger generations begin to break the taken-for-granted rural-to-urban transmission lines of customary knowledge and authority. This situation presents a significant challenge for the PNG government in terms of its policy emphasis. If urban settlers are to be encouraged to remain connected in an ongoing way to their communities of origin or to return, they must have lines of connection and something to which they can return.

Rural and Remote Development

This conundrum also raises the perpetual question of how best to create opportunities for sustainable development in rural and remote communities or, more pertinently, what it is that communities mean when they call for development. In their study of conflicts between migrant communities and customary landowners in major oil-palm-producing regions of Papua New Guinea (West New Britain Province and Oro Province), Gina Koczberski and George Curry have highlighted a new set of social problems in regions where state land, alienated from customary landowners during the colonial period, is increasingly being settled by migrant communities from other parts of Papua New Guinea seeking opportunities for cash income and employment.[74] Oil palm, along with other export crops, has been touted as a marvel of sustainable development by the PNG government, the Asian Development Bank (ADB), and the Australian government alike. Rural development, in the form of large-scale cash cropping, is now being strongly encouraged as Papua New Guinea's economic future. In these settlement communities of West New Britain Province (WNBP) and Oro Province, tribal identity based on "land, place and belonging" is coming in conflict with the emerging identities of migrant communities in the new cultural borderlands created by development. The identities of landless migrant communities that have settled on or around state-alienated land are increasingly tied with national objectives to modernize Papua New Guinea's economy and integrate it with the processes of global capitalism: "a shared identity is gathering strength based, not on common descent, but on shared experiences, insecurities and a constructed history of their role in national development. In this collective settler identity, nation building and development are emphasised."[75]

Despite some of the economic successes for the industry, many seemingly intractable social problems are emerging around oil palm plantations. According to Koczberski and Curry, these include "rapid population growth, the illegal sale of customary land to migrants in WNBP, and rising demands by customary landowners for compensation" for oil palm land settlement schemes as well as alienation of children from their own indigenous languages.[76] Other problems not addressed adequately by Koczberski and Curry are the fact that employment of men in oil palm production is creating new tensions within families about the best way to spend and distribute income. This expenditure of labor on wage incomes further decreases the capacity of families to produce their own food. Women are often expected to tend food gardens on their own while the men are absent and, at the same time, to continue to fulfill the multitude of other social and familial obligations that play an important part in holding the community, clan, and family unit together. Food gardens are particularly important for practicing and demonstrating one's connection to the land. When laborers are too old or no longer fit enough to work for a cash wage, a tended garden is one way of maintaining a claim to the land.[77]

Although Koczberski and Curry acknowledge some of these social problems, Koczberski has become involved as a consultant in a community development initiative in an oil palm settlement. The Mama Lus Frut Scheme was established by an oil palm company and the Oil Palm Industry Corporation (OPIC), an extension service for oil palm growers, to find ways of involving women in oil palm production. The scheme has been presented by Koczberski as a community development initiative that is helping women to "reinforce, support and reassert their traditional power and identity within their households and communities" by enabling them to collect a small wage collecting the loose fruit on the ground after harvesting by the men.[78] However, as Koczberski herself suggests, the real problem for the oil palm industry was not the social problems on oil palm plantations but the fact that women were not participating in a way that maximized profits for the industry: "With women refusing to contribute labour to household oil palm production, the industry faced the problem of a high rate of loose fruit wastage among smallholders.... Because loose fruit collection is a gendered female task, estimates suggest that between 60 and 70 percent of loose fruit was left to rot on the ground, representing a substantial loss of revenue for the industry and income for smallholders."[79] That is, from the producer's perspective, the social problems emerging from settlement communities are highlighted as problems when they interfere with the productivity of the oil palm industry. This perspective fails to address the core of the combined problem of disputes over land resources between migrant and customary communities and a disruption in customary work patterns.

Whether the objective of the Mama Lus Frut Scheme is to empower women economically or to minimize inefficiencies within the industry, it is bringing about new gendered relations in the settlement community. According to several of our PNG informants in the NGO sector, the term *mama lus frut* has become a derogatory slang expression in Melanesian Pidgin for a woman who is unattached and therefore "loose fruit." While Koczberski has reported on the Mama Lus Frut Scheme as an example of economic empowerment that has allowed women to renegotiate their identities within the development process, it has been reported that men leave behind extra fruit on the ground for women laborers in exchange for sex. These reports have yet to be officially confirmed, and a study is projected. However, the problems facing oil palm settlements and many other parts of Papua New Guinea where large-scale development projects become the dominant livelihood highlight the complexities of anticipating how a reorientation of livelihoods away from domestic production and toward a wage economy will produce new gendered and ethnoregional relations between and within communities. (See the discussion in Chapter 10 on sex work and the ambiguities surrounding such practices.) Such examples highlight how the changes introduced by Western-style economic development are producing new contested spaces and identity formations within tribal communities operating within a global context.

Conclusion

The development trajectory embarked upon during the colonial period and then reinforced after independence has raised serious questions about the nature of development itself in Papua New Guinea. Are Papua New Guinea's problems a function of local bad management, the result of a misguided faith in the possibilities of modern capitalist development—both locally and internationally—or because of an unsustainable hybrid development? Attempting to answer that question all too often comes down to theatrical politics easily evoked with Manichean clarity but rarely expressed with a satisfactory sense of the cross-cutting currents. In 1986, the Seventeenth Waigani Seminar attempted to tackle the ethics of development, producing a number of diverging positions on the question of how ethics and development fit together. On the one hand, John Waiko understood ethical development as development that recognized and valued Papua New Guinea's unique cultural context and that could tackle difficult ethical questions about "the rights and wrongs of change."[80] On the other hand, Bill Hayden, Australian minister for foreign affairs at the time, focused on the Australia–Papua New Guinea aid relationship and the need for mutual obligation within the aid program—arguing that the "responsibility for effective aid lies also with those nations which receive it."[81] Paias Wingti adopted a critical position with regard to the nature of development, both during the colonial period and after independence:

> It saddens me when I look back at some aspects of our recent history since Western civilisation began creeping in and, sometimes without due care, gradually changed our people's lifestyles and systems—all in the name of development. Many of the first foreign settlers came with one major aim and that was to create wealth for themselves.... Plantations were established and villagers recruited to work on them. As traders the foreigners introduced new consumables which meant they took back the little money the workers earned. The small village farmers were restricted to servicing the interests of the traders.[82]

Even if we allow that, as a partial representation of the consequences of outside intervention in colonial Papua New Guinea, Paias Wingti's account is closer to the truth than Bill Hayden's effective deferral of responsibility, it cannot explain the course of the postcolonial nation-state. Wingti calls for the kind of development that the nation's founders envisaged at independence—development from within, not from without. Similarly, Gabriel Ramoi, the then PNG minister for communication, used the Waigani Seminar as an opportunity to launch a thinly veiled attack on Papua New Guinean leaders who failed to stick to the constitutional vision for development after independence and instead left the development of Papua New Guinea in the hands of outsiders: "The fool wants Papua New Guineans to be the masters of their own destiny but he gets foreigners to plan and direct the nation's development."[83] The problem remains, however, that the same kind of development in the hands of insiders rather than outsiders is still unsustainable.

While Wingti and Ramoi attempt to tackle the question of what kind of development is ethical and how it might be encouraged in Papua New Guinea, Serge Latouche challenges the very notion that development is good or desirable at all, posing an alternative question: "Is development ethical?" Latouche reads development as something "generated by the ideology of progress"—a concept grounded in Western political systems and reinforced by the Protestant work ethic, which serves to uphold the social and economic structures of capitalism.[84] Environmental degradation caused by unethical industrial practices, the rapid change from a subsistence to a cash economy, a breakdown in the organizing principles of community life, corruption in the political process, and migration from rural to urban areas—for Latouche, all these are not the product of bad development but of development itself:

> The search for well-being is really the obsessional question for addition to being. All human societies have to face the problem of being, of existence. They resolve it through their culture. The solutions are very diverse.... When non-Western cultures more or less spontaneously adopt the new standards of well-being and the gadgets of civilisation, this does not lead them to development's paradise, but more surely to underdevelopment's hell. What the anthropologists call deculturation—the destruction of the mental and social world that constitutes a culture—generates an explosion in the community the effects of which are almost entirely negative.... Sources of creativity and vitality are destroyed beyond recall.[85]

It is too easy to dismiss Latouche's critique of development theory and practice as being based on an overly critical idealism that fails to recognize the heterogeneity of development or the way that the principles of Northern-style development are undermined, or at least reinterpreted, at the level of the local. Latouche's critique appears most problematic when considered in light of various analyses of the willingness of local communities in Papua New Guinea to embrace the kinds of top-down, foreign-driven economic development projects that radically transform their modes of production, exchange, and organization. Nonetheless, it is impossible simply to discount Latouche's critique of development or, more important, to turn a blind eye to the environmental, political, educational, and health problems that he describes as "underdevelopment's hell."[86]

The problems that have emerged from the kind of development that communities in Papua New Guinea have experienced over the last thirty or forty years go to the heart of what undermines community sustainability.[87] Over the last twenty years there has been a fluctuation between a rhetoric of culturally sensitive, internally managed development and blind faith in mega–mining projects. The core problem—to address our question above—is that postcolonial Papua New Guinea has embarked on a pathway of unsustainable hybrid development that manages neither capitalist investment nor cultural re-creation well. While it is unrealistic and idealistic to suggest that communities should not change, it is essential that communities, in considering the nature of change, maintain reflexive control over the cultural, economic, political, and ecological resources that enable them to negotiate the transformations from the local to the global. This negotiation ranges from local agreements about the organization of everyday livelihoods to a national compact in relation to the more abstract political and economic structures that shape the movement of information and capital across the globe. While the mainstream notions of "development," "growth," and "progress" have proven problematic in both theory and practice, other developmental paths are worth exploring. There is a need for support systems that enable communities to respond to the changes around them in ways that are self-determining and sustainable in the long term. Whether this developmental path is referred to as "sustainable development," "community development," "people-centered development," or something else altogether, there is clearly a need for the destabilizing factors in Papua New Guinea's communities to be better understood and addressed. We do not have much time.

Notes

1. Kumalu Tawaii, *Signs in the Sky: Poems by Kumalu Tawaii*, Papua Pocket Poems, Port Moresby, 1970 (republished by University of Papua New Guinea, Port Moresby, 2006).

2. The betel nut, or areca nut in English, has many different names from East Africa to the Pacific, including *angiro* (Solomon Islands), *pugua* (Guam), *bu* (Yap), *bua* (Palau), *boa* (Bali), *buai* (New Ireland: Kuanua), *buei* (New Ireland: Pala), and *vua* (New Ireland: Lamekot).

3. The phrase comes from Deborah B. Gewertz and Frederick K. Errington, *Twisted Histories, Altered Contexts: Representing the Chambri in a World System*, Cambridge University Press, Cambridge, 2001.

4. Henry Okole, "Political Participation in a Fragmented Democracy: Ethnic and Religious Appeal in Papua New Guinea," *Development Bulletin*, University of Papua New Guinea, Port Moresby, 2002.

5. See Paul James, *Globalism, Nationalism, Tribalism,* Sage Publications, London, 2006, pp. 83–96.

6. Hal B. Levine and Marlene Levine, *Urbanization in Papua New Guinea,* Cambridge University Press, Cambridge, 1979, p. 60.

7. Michael Goddard, *The Unseen City: Anthropological Perspectives on Port Moresby, Papua New Guinea,* Pandanus Books, Research School of Pacific and Asian Studies, Australian National University, Canberra, 2005, ch. 5.

8. Gewertz and Errington's work has focused on issues involving the growing middle class of Wewak, the provincial headquarters of East Sepik Province. These authors over the past twenty-five years have focused on social issues such as personhood, regional relationships, and global processes, among others, consistently using local ethnographic data to attempt to place topics on the academic agenda. Deborah B. Gewertz and Frederick L. Errington, *Emerging Class in Papua New Guinea: The Telling of Difference,* Cambridge University Press, Cambridge, 1999.

9. United Nations Development Program (UNDP), *Millennium Development Goals: Progress Report for Papua New Guinea 2004,* UNDP, 2004, available at http://www.undp.org.pg/documents/mdgs/National_MDG_Progress_Report_2004.pdf, accessed 6 May 2008.

10. F. J. West, "Colonial Development in Central New Guinea," *Pacific Affairs,* vol. 29, no. 2, 1956, pp. 170–171.

11. On the concept of ontological formations—tribalism, traditionalism, modernism and postmodernism—see James, *Globalism, Nationalism, Tribalism.* It should be underlined again that we are careful here not to use terms like "modernity," which connote one-dimensional epochs, or to treat the modern/traditional divide as a dichotomous description of separate realms. See also Yaso Nadarajah, "A Community in Transition: Propagating a Yield of Conflict and Violence," in Alejandro Cervantes-Caron and Ilse Lazaroms, eds., *Meaning and Violence: Readings across Disciplines,* Inter-Disciplinary Press, Oxford, 2007.

12. See, for example, the poster with a large question mark over a divided figure distributed by Bismarck Ramu and signed Jada, produced in 2002 and still available in 2008.

13. Marshall Sahlins, *Stone Age Economics,* Tavistock, London, 1974.

14. David Hyndman, "Academic Responsibilities and Representation of the Ok Tedi Crisis in Postcolonial Papua New Guinea," *The Contemporary Pacific,* vol. 13, no. 1, 2001, pp. 33–54.

15. Peter Kean, "Economic Development in the Siki Settlement Scheme, West New Britain," *Critique of Anthropology,* vol. 20, no. 2, 2000, p. 158.

16. O. H. K. Spate, "Problems of Development in New Guinea," *Geographical Journal,* vol. 122, no. 4, 1956, p. 430.

17. F. J. West, "Colonial Development in Central New Guinea."

18. Nick Purdie, "Pacific Islands Livelihoods," in John Overton and Regina Scheyvens, eds., *Strategies for Sustainable Development: Experiences from the Pacific,* UNSW Press, Sydney, 1999, pp. 64–79; B. J. Allen, "Land Management: Papua New Guinea's Dilemma," *The Asia-Pacific Magazine,* no. 1, 1996, pp. 36–42. Here the figures are very approximate.

19. Anne Booth, "Development Challenges in a Poor Pacific Economy: The Case of Papua New Guinea," *Pacific Affairs,* vol. 68, no. 2, 1995, p. 230.

20. Ron Duncan and Ila Temu, "Papua New Guinea: Longer Term Developments and Recent Economic Problems," *Asian-Pacific Economic Literature,* vol. 9, no. 2, 1995, p. 50.

21. Susan Windybank and Mike Manning, "Papua New Guinea on the Brink," *Issue Analysis,* Centre for Independent Studies, no. 30, 2003, p. 8.

22. Tim Curtin, "Scarcity Amidst Plenty: The Economics of Land Tenure in Papua New Guinea," in T. Curtin, H. Holzknecht, and P. Larmour, eds., *Land Registration in Papua New Guinea: Competing Perspectives,* Research School of Pacific and Asian Studies, State Society and Governance in Melanesia Project, Discussion Paper 2003/1, Canberra, 2003, pp. 6–17; Helen Hughes, "Can Papua New Guinea Come Back from the Brink?" *Issue Analysis,* Centre for Independent Studies, no. 49, 2004, pp. 1–12.

23. Mike Moore, "Poverty Is Not Inevitable," *The National,* 29 February 2008.

24. Nancy Sullivan, ed., *Culture and Progress: The Melanesian Philosophy of Land and Development in Papua New Guinea,* DWU Press, Madang, 2002.

25. Hartmut Holzknecht, "Customary Land Tenure Systems: Resilient, Appropriate and Productive," in Curtin, Holzknecht, and Larmour, eds., *Land Registration in Papua New Guinea,* p. 21.

26. The most illuminating of these writings is Frederick Errington and Deborah Gewertz, *Yali's Question: Sugar, Culture, & History,* University of Chicago Press, Chicago, 2004.

27. Glenn Banks, "Landowner Equity in Papua New Guinea's Mineral Sector: Review and Policy Issues," *Natural Resources Forum,* no. 27, 2003, p. 224.

28. Leonard Lagisa and Regina Scheyvens, "Mining in Papua New Guinea," in John Overton and Regina Scheyvens, eds., *Strategies for Sustainable Development: Experiences From the Pacific,* UNSW Press, Sydney, 1999, p. 129.

29. Nicole Polier, "Of Mines and Min: Modernity and Its Malcontents in Papua New Guinea," *Ethnology,* vol. 35, no. 1, 1996, pp. 1–16.

30. Martha Macintyre and Simon Foale, "Politicized Ecology: Local Responses to Mining in Papua New Guinea," *Oceania,* vol. 74, no. 3, 2004, pp. 231–251, quote on p. 239.

31. Benjamin Y. Imbun, "Mining Workers or 'Opportunistic' Tribesmen? A Tribal Workforce in a Papua New Guinean Mine," *Oceania,* vol. 71, no. 2, 2000, p. 145.

32. Ibid., p. 147.

33. Glenn Banks, "Mining and the Environment in Melanesia," p. 50.

34. Kean, "Economic Development in the Siki Settlement Scheme."

35. Glenn Banks, "Mining and the Environment in Melanesia," p. 41.

36. Paige West, *Conservation Is Our Government Now: The Politics of Ecology in Papua New Guinea*, Duke University Press, Durham, 2006; Glenn Banks, "Marginality and Environment in Papua New Guinea: The Strickland River Area," *Asia Pacific Viewpoint*, vol. 41, no. 3, 2000, p. 228.

37. Glenn Banks, "Marginality and Environment," p. 227.

38. Hyndman, "Academic Responsibilities and Representation"; Stuart Kirsch, "Return to Ok Tedi," *Meanjin*, vol. 55, no. 4, 1996, pp. 14–16.

39. Alison Dundon, "Mines and Monsters: A Dialogue on Development in Western Province, Papua New Guinea," *Australian Journal of Anthropology*, vol. 13, no. 2, 2002, p. 139.

40. Ibid., pp. 146–147.

41. Ibid., p. 147.

42. David Akin and Joel Robbins, eds., *Money and Modernity: State and Local Currencies in Melanesia*, University of Pittsburgh Press, Pittsburgh, 1999.

43. Bronislaw Malinowski, *Argonauts of the Western Pacific: An Account of Native Enterprise and Adventure in the Archipelagoes of Melanesian New Guinea*, London, Routledge and Kegan Paul, (1922) 1972.

44. Here "goods" becomes the generic concept (as opposed to "bads") allowing us to talk of different categories of goods, ranging from the inalienable to the alienable. Expressed schematically the different kinds of goods can be taken to include the following: goods that are sacred, gift exchanged, precious, useful, and commodity exchanged. In this argument a particular good can pass from one category to another or belong to more than one category at the same time. Maurice Godelier, *The Enigma of the Gift*, Polity Press, Cambridge, 1999; Annette B. Weiner, *Inalienable Possessions: The Paradox of Keeping-While-Giving*, University of California Press, Berkeley, 1992; and C. A. Gregory, *Savage Money: The Anthropology and Politics of Commodity Exchange*, Harwood Academic Publishers, Amsterdam, 1997. See also Gregory's much more technical book, *Gifts and Commodities*, Academic Press, London, 1982.

45. Deborah B. Gewertz describes a similar barter market of fish for sago in the Sepik region, except in her description there is an apparent status difference in the transaction partners that we did not see at Kara market (*Sepik River Societies: A Historical Ethnography of the Chambri and Their Neighbors*, Yale University Press, New Haven, 1983, ch. 2).

46. See, for example, Michael French Smith's study of Kragur village during the period from independence to the late 1990s: *Village on the Edge: Changing Times in Papua New Guinea*, University of Hawai'i Press, Honolulu, 2002.

47. Richard Eves, "Money, Mayhem and the Beast: Narratives of the World's End

from New Ireland (Papua New Guinea)," *Journal of the Royal Anthropological Institute,* no. 9, 2003, p. 528.

48. Sam Kaima, "The Politics of 'Payback': Villager Perceptions of Elections in the Markam Open," a paper presented at the "Political Culture, Representation and Electoral Systems in the Pacific" conference, University of the South Pacific, Vanuatu, July 2004.

49. Robert J. Foster, "Print Advertisements and Nation Making in Metropolitan Papua New Guinea," in Robert J. Foster, ed., *Nation Making: Emergent Identities in Postcolonial Melanesia,* University of Michigan Press, Ann Arbor, 1995, p. 160.

50. Eves, "Money, Mayhem and the Beast," p. 543. For earlier material on violent millenarian rejections of the state, see Alexander Wanek, *The State and Its Enemies in Papua New Guinea,* Curzon Press, Richmond, 1996.

51. Eves, "Money, Mayhem and the Beast," p. 543.

52. Richard Eves, "Waiting for the Day: Globalisation and Apocalypticism in Central New Ireland, Papua New Guinea," *Oceania,* vol. 71, no. 2, 2000, p. 87.

53. Joel Robbins, "The Globalization of Pentecostal and Charismatic Christianity," *Annual Review of Anthropology,* vol. 33, pp. 117–143; Dan Jorgensen, "Third Wave Evangelism and the Politics of the Global in Papua New Guinea: Spiritual Warfare and the Recreation of Place in Telefolmin," *Oceania,* vol. 75, 2005, pp. 44–61.

54. John Connell, "Regulation of Space in the Contemporary Postcolonial Pacific City: Port Moresby and Suva," *Asia Pacific Viewpoint,* vol. 44, no. 3, 2003, p. 247.

55. Michael Goddard, "From Rolling Thunder to Reggae: Imagining Squatter Settlements in Papua New Guinea," *The Contemporary Pacific,* vol. 13, no. 1, 2001, p. 7.

56. Pa'O H. Luteru and G. Robert Teasdale, "Aid and Education in the South Pacific," *Comparative Education,* vol. 29, no. 3, 1993, p. 297.

57. Ibid., p. 294.

58. Sheldon G. Weeks, "Education in Papua New Guinea 1973–1993: The Late-Development Effect?" *Comparative Education,* vol. 29, no. 3, 1993, p. 266.

59. Ibid., p. 263.

60. Peter Demerath, "The Cultural Production of Educational Utility in Pere Village, Papua New Guinea," *Comparative Educational Review,* vol. 43, no. 2, 1999, pp. 165–166.

61. Ibid., p. 162.

62. Francyne M. Huckaby, "When Worlds Collide: A Critical Decolonizing View of Western-Based Schooling in Papua New Guinean Village Education," *Journal of Curriculum Theorizing,* vol. 20, no. 4, 2004, p. 88.

63. Beatrice Avalos, "Ideology, Policy and Educational Change in Papua New Guinea," *Comparative Education,* vol. 29, no. 3, 1993, p. 276.

64. Quoted in ibid., p. 277.

65. Wayne Fife, "The Look of Rationality and the Bureaucratization of Consciousness in Papua New Guinea," *Ethnology*, vol. 34, no. 2, 1995, p. 130.

66. Ibid., p. 131.

67. David Welchman Gegeo and Karen Ann Watson-Gegeo, "Whose Knowledge? Epistemological Collisions in Solomon Islands Community Development," *The Contemporary Pacific*, vol. 14, no. 2, 2002, p. 403.

68. Sarah Hopkins, Graham Ogle, Lisette Kaleveld, John Maurise, Betty Keria, William Louden, and Mary Rohl, "'Education for Equality' and 'Education for Life': Examining Reading Literacy and Reading Interest in Papua New Guinea Primary Schools," *Asia-Pacific Journal of Teacher Education*, vol. 33, no. 1, 2005, p. 79.

69. Goddard, "From Rolling Thunder to Reggae."

70. E. Kopel, "Street Vending in Port Moresby: A Positive Step towards Self-Help or an Eyesore for the City?" in D. Gladman, D. Mowbray, and J. Duguman, eds., *From Rio to Rai: Environment and Development in Papua New Guinea up to 2000 and Beyond*, Papers from the 20th Waigani Seminar, Port Moresby, vol. 6, UPNG Press, Port Moresby, 1996, pp. 153–165.

71. Goddard, "From Rolling Thunder to Reggae," p. 14.

72. Connell, "Regulation of Space," p. 252.

73. C. D. Rowley, *The New Guinea Villager: A Retrospect from 1964*, Cheshire, Melbourne, 1965.

74. Gina Koczberski and George N. Curry, "Divided Communities and Contested Landscapes: Mobility, Development and Shifting Identities in Migrant Destination Sites in Papua New Guinea," *Asia Pacific Viewpoint*, vol. 45, no. 3, pp. 357–371.

75. Ibid., p. 362.

76. Ibid., p. 360.

77. Polier, "Of Mines and Min," p. 8.

78. Gina Koczberski, "Pots, Plates and *Tinpis*: New Income Flows and the Strengthening of Women's Gendered Identities in Papua New Guinea," *Development: Local/Global Encounters*, vol. 45, no. 1, 2002, p. 91.

79. Ibid., p. 89.

80. John D. Waiko, "Introduction: A Plea for an Ethical Stocktake," in Susan Stratigos and Philip J. Hughes, eds., *The Ethics of Development: The Pacific in the 21st Century*, University of Papua New Guinea Press, Port Moresby, 1987, p. 2.

81. Bill Hayden, "The Ethics of Development: Aid—a Two Way Process?" in Stratigos and Hughes, *The Ethics of Development*, p. 54.

82. Paias Wingti, "The Power of the People," in Stratigos and Hughes, *The Ethics of Development*, pp. 84–85.

83. Gabriel Ramoi, "Ethics and Leadership," in Stratigos and Hughes, *The Ethics of Development*, University of Papua New Guinea Press, Port Moresby, 1987, p. 94.

84. Serge Latouche, "The Ethical Implications of Development: A Philosophic Reflection on an Economic Process," in Stratigos and Hughes, *The Ethics of Development*, University of Papua New Guinea Press, Port Moresby, 1987, p. 139.

85. Ibid., pp. 141–142.

86. Ibid.

87. The Twentieth Waigani Seminar held in August 1993 was remarkable for drawing attention to the rich complexity of these issues. The proceedings were published in six volumes. See Darren Gladman, David Mobray, and John Duguman, eds., From *Rio to Rai: Environment and Development in Papua New Guinea*, vols. 1–6, University of Papua New Guinea Press, Port Moresby, 1996.

II   COMMUNITIES IN PLACE

Chapter 4

Urban and Periurban Communities

Vanagi Settlement, Central Province

HOW CAN IT BE THAT SOURCES OF INSECURITY AND HOPE ARE BOUND UP WITH EACH OTHER?

Chris Clement Wagi Dogale died in the Port Moresby General Hospital in the early hours of Saturday, 20 October 2007. He was also known as Wadi, named after his uncle. He died in the same hospital where he had been born on a Saturday in June 1979. Twenty-eight years on, his father Clement Dogale was woken at 3:00 a.m. to come to Chris' bedside. Chris had been shot a few hours earlier, allegedly by police officers. The story of what happened has been told and retold by various people in the subsequent period, and our understanding of the events of that night is based on a patchwork of narratives. Chris had been in a stolen car with four other young men when they were stopped by police. What unfolded after that is murky. We know that the driver and one of the other passengers escaped. The remaining youths were apprehended and all three of them shot. One was shot and died immediately; a second was shot through the leg and fell; Chris was shot through the side of his chest. He fell onto the second youth, covering him with blood. They were left on the rugby field. Both Chris and the second youth were later taken to the hospital. After hours of waiting for treatment, the second youth left the hospital and later went into hiding. He later told others that it was because he was covered in Chris' blood that he had been presumed dead. His story forms part of the background to this account.

When Clement arrived at the hospital, his son tried to sit up in bed. Chris showed no sign of his pain, although his father could feel it. The young man didn't complain. Instead, he asked, "Are you cross with me?" Clement replied, "No, but I love you." It was one of the last things he said to his son, and he said later that he could see that Chris knew he was dying.

Two weeks later, after waiting for an autopsy to be finalized, the people of Vanagi Settlement and other relatives and friends gathered to mourn Chris' death. On the day of Chris' funeral, the settlement was quiet; people waited for his body to be brought back home. The coffin arrived on the back of an open truck. Clement and other men from the community who had accompanied the coffin carried it along the narrow lane to the family home. Frangipani and bougainvillea flowers were woven into the chain-link wire and corrugated iron fencing along the dusty path. Inside the house, family and friends gathered around the coffin, crying and moaning, while others sat and stood in silence outside. Women loudly called his cultural name—"Wadi, Wadi." Clement Dogale was wearing a T-shirt with the words "Learn today for better tomorrow" silk-screened on the back. A crying child came out of the house where Chris' body lay, and Clement held the child, saying, "You're a strong girl, strong girl."

After an hour or so, the men once again lifted the coffin, this time to take it to the community church—also the community learning center and the place where Clement, a retired teacher, runs the volunteer preschool for the young children in Vanagi. Chris' mother let out a piercing cry as her son's body left her home. People took her arms to help her stand and to comfort her. Then they and the other people at the mourning house walked behind the coffin as it was carried back past the bougainvillea and frangipani flowers tucked in the fence. The church was full of people sitting on the ground, and others stood looking in through the metal bars around the perimeter of the building. The coffin was placed in the middle of the room, and female relatives and children sat around it. Many of the women and men wore white tops, and the children's white T-shirts were printed with the words

> Kakzo madi,
> Born freely,
> Lived simply,
> Passed silently,
> Rest in peace.

Chris' mother wasn't crying now but sitting silently next to his coffin and leaning forward slightly with her shoulders hunched. Her eyes stared forward, and the full force of her grief was written in them. After an introduction by the deputy chairman of the community, Clement stood up to speak. He talked to the people assembled about his son's birth and how he saw Chris' head showing from his mother's body. He talked of his wife's pain in the birth and the strength of women. He talked

Clement's mother (*center*) beside the coffin of her son, Vanagi Settlement

about the short life of his eldest child and how in 1985, leaving the Salvation Army accommodation at Koki, the family had come to Vanagi Settlement, not knowing how long they would stay. It was here that his son grew up.

Chris won a place at Don Bosco Technical School, and his parents were proud. However, as Clement described it, Chris walked around with the wrong boys and often missed classes. His father gave him three chances but in the end took him out of school to be educated in the settlement. When he was in his mid-twenties Chris' life began to shift. He began spending time with the pastor, and he and his father grew closer. As Clement found out after his son's death, Chris had begun taking food to prisoners inside the Port Moresby Detention Centre. He had been writing poetry about his experiences. One poem talked about death and the pain it causes but also its ability to bring a community together. Reading it now, the poem had prescient meaning for his father.

In finishing his address, Clement spoke of his son's strength and of the things he had learned from him. He told the mourners, "I have been reborn today." Our hearts are breaking, he said, but we are strong too. We go on because there are things we have to do.

Through its Law and Order Committee, its school programs and community security arrangements, and its Village Court, Vanagi is doing a lot to address violence and safety in a settlement that was once one of the most dangerous in Port

Houses raised on stilts in Vanagi Settlement. Port Moresby with modern high-rise developments is visible on the hills behind.

Moresby. Some of Vanagi's sons and their friends have been called *raskol*s, but the term covers a multitude of sins, from organized crime to silly misdemeanors. The sadness is that there are too many communities in Papua New Guinea grieving the loss of their sons. Adversity has ironically strengthened this community, but it is not always the case.

PLACE—PAST AND PRESENT

Vanagi Settlement is a small, densely populated squatter community located in Port Moresby South in the National Capital District, nestled between the coast and the area of Koki. It was the first settlement ever established in Port Moresby and in 2002 became the first squatter community to be recognized by the National Capital District Commission (NCDC). It has a small but rapidly growing population, which was estimated at 376 in the 2000 national census (probably an underestimate) but has grown substantially since then owing to the birth rate within the community and the arrival of new settlers. It is now home to over a thousand persons. There are also cross-cutting communities in Vanagi, and we did not presume a general sense of belonging to the locale when we first began to spend time in the place, but nevertheless it can be said that Vanagi is a community in the sense of our definition—a group or network of persons who are connected (objectively) to each other by relatively durable social relations that extend beyond immediate genealogical ties and who mutually define that relationship (subjectively) as important to their social identity and social practice.

There are people in Vanagi who trace their relatives back to the original founders of the settlement. They tell stories of how the community was founded, about how the place where Vanagi is now built was originally a resting spot for fishermen from Hood Lagoon, Hula, and Aroma villages in Central Province. The men and their families would stop to rest after selling their catch at Koki market or while waiting for the tide to take them back out to sea or home to their villages. In the late 1950s two brothers from Keapara village in Hood Lagoon, Kamu Ma'a and Wala Ma'a, built homes and became the first settlers in this community. They were later joined by their sister Dau Ma'a, followed by other settlers from Hula, Hood Lagoon, and Aroma coastal villages. Since then, settlers have come from provinces across Papua New Guinea. Because the original inhabitants were people who lived, sailed, and fished on canoes, the settlement was named "canoe." Recently, the community changed its name to Vanagi, which is a Motu word meaning the same thing.

There are now around eighty to one hundred houses (some people say two hundred) within Vanagi, sharing a small area of land. They are mainly built with secondhand and reclaimed modern materials—wood, cement sheeting, unpainted weatherboards, louver windows, rusting corrugated iron, and sheet metal. Logs that come through extended village-to-village relations outside of Port Moresby are often used for stilts. Many homes are makeshift huts; a few are more substantial dwellings with satellite dishes. Many are raised high above the water extending out from the coast, with thin wooden walkways connecting them to each other and the shore. There are open stoves on some of the walkways, and clotheslines stretch between houses for hanging out laundry. Small canoes are pulled up onto the shore

A drain runs through the settlement carrying effluent from the semi-industrial zone above.

or stored on wooden platforms beneath the houses. Across the water, beyond the accumulating rubbish, Lade Kone Island is visible in the distance, and clusters of houses in other settlements can be seen dotted up and down the coast. In the other direction Vanagi extends inland toward Koki market and the business area of Port Moresby South. There are more houses, not as closely packed but still with little room between them. Many are built on reclaimed land created by filling in shallow waters with gravel, rocks, soil, and household rubbish.

A multipurpose building, built with concrete blocks and metal, stands at the center of the settlement. It serves as a learning center, preschool, church, meeting hall, and place for funerals. A number of trade stores are dotted around, along with small stalls, selling betel nut, candy, drinks, and food. There are no substantial vegetable gardens in the settlement, densely populated as it is, but banana palms and other plants and trees grow in places. Bougainvillea grows along fences and around some houses. Its bright pink and purple flowers stand out against the dusty ground and the piles of rubbish washed up on the shore and carried into Vanagi through open canals that run down to the sea from the business area and hills behind the settlement. Large buildings up on the hills—offices, apartment blocks, and residential compounds filled with expatriates and members of Papua New Guinea's emerging elite—stand visible in the distance.

ORGANIZATION AND GOVERNANCE

The nature of Vanagi as an urban settlement means that its organizational structure needs to accommodate the considerable ethnic and linguistic heterogeneity within the community. The four main founding groups within the settlement are the Aroma, Hula, Keapara, and Mailu ethnic groups, and belonging to one of these recognized founding groups carries with it a certain status within the community. In addition to these four groups, there are families and individuals who have entered into the community through migration or intermarriage. These include Kerema people from the Gulf, Mekeo people from Kairuku, Gorokas from the Eastern Highlands, Samarais from Milne Bay Province, people from the Sepik area, other Motuans from Central Province, and New Guinea Islanders. Overwhelmingly and unusually, they live together with a shared sense of community and belonging.

Continuing but subordinate tribal forms of organization are evident in the choices of persons to head the various community committees and the extended family and kinship networks that provide a crucial social security system in the face of high levels of unemployment and a minimal capacity for domestic agriculture within Port Moresby. Complex relationships of reciprocity—and connections through intermarriage—retain a central importance in the settlement despite the diversity of places of origin and the strong influence of modern economic and cultural forms and systems. Conversations with individuals and families in Vanagi over the period of four years from 2006 to 2009 indicated an abiding sense of attachment to the place and the community. This is notable given that Vanagi is an urban squatter settlement with a relatively short history of establishment; it is quite different from some of the settlements nearby that continue to be rife with disaffection. Residents described a localized community that in itself was *relatively* trouble-free—with a high level of respect for the property and well-being of others, reinforced by curfews and strict understandings of how to handle such issues as noise limits and alcohol use—but located in an extended neighborhood that is highly dangerous. The positive discussions often harked back to the dark days when violence was prevalent, as if now it had largely gone away. This is not quite true. Nevertheless, when residents do speak of the still regular incidents of disturbance and conflict, it is overwhelmingly in relation to perceived outsiders coming into the settlement from nearby suburbs.

The formal organizational structure in Vanagi is extensive. It was established in 1997 and includes an Executive Committee, a Community Improvement Committee, and a number of subcommittees that enjoy broad-based support and participation. The Executive Committee—consisting of a chairman, deputy chairman, treasurer, and secretary—meets monthly and also holds special meetings whenever urgent matters and commitments arise. The nine subcommittees are responsible for organizing around education, housing, law and order, church, women, youth, health and sanitation, electricity and water, and sports. Subcommittee meetings follow the monthly executive meetings, with the implementation of programs and activities involving the participation of committee members, community groups, elders, and other residents. It is remarkable. The subcommittees work cooperatively to organize community celebrations, particularly around Christmas and New Year's. Church-run activities and spiritual development programs also contribute to the organization of the settlement and processes of community-building. There are six main denominations in the community, namely, the United Church, the Catholic Church, the Seventh-Day Adventists, the Evangelical Alliance of Papua, the Assemblies of God, and the Pentecostal Church. All of them have strong standing, with none of them singularly dominant. This is perhaps reflective of the diverse ethnic, cultural, and geographic origins of the population.

Vanagi thus works well, despite being what outsiders would call a slum. A strong sense of community has emerged out of extreme adversity, but that cannot be the only reason that its politically conscious sense that life can be different is not shared by all the urban villages in the immediate vicinity. Part of the answer lies in its location in the Moresby South electorate of Dame Carol Kidu and the strong engagement of the community with the Department for Community Development and vice versa. A second reason is a strong cohort of leaders with no single person standing out. A single church denomination and its given authority structure, for example, has not come to stand in for plural local governance. A third reason is access to resources on a consistent basis, with this access dependent on the active community governance process. Since Vanagi Settlement is located within the boundaries of the National Capital District, people living there have better access to some services than those living in hinterland or more remote communities. The community is able to use basic educational, health, and postal services provided in Port Moresby. Approximately thirty-two households have electricity supplied to their residence, which they pay for. Similarly, thirty-four households pay for their use of a direct water supply. Community members express frustration at the lack of response by the National Capital District Commission to their requests for increased and improved services, but they have learned to make submissions as a community through its local governance processes.

Vanagi is now recognized by government and nongovernmental agencies as one of the better-organized communities in the National Capital District and is often held up as a model of successful community development in the city. Nevertheless, it faces a number of serious problems and challenges. On a practical level, there is the problem of rubbish and waste accumulation. A lack of adequate waste and sewage collection services is common throughout Port Moresby, and Vanagi faces the additional problem of waste washing up on its shores from elsewhere and being carried into the settlement from canals and sewers originating farther inland.

The water in the canals often turns a bright red color, suggesting that sewage or chemical waste is being released into the drains from the residential or commercial areas behind the settlement. Residents indicated that this is a cause for real concern given that fishing is a main source of livelihood and sustenance for many local people. Another practical problem facing the community is that of overcrowding. Already Vanagi is densely populated, and there is little room for the settlement to expand. The population is increasing steadily, and the rate of growth can only be expected to intensify in keeping with current trends and given the massive rate of rural-urban migration that is predicted across Papua New Guinea in the coming decades.

Primary among the social problems identified are drunkenness, fighting, and noise disturbances. As mentioned above, these are often perceived to be the result of infiltration of the community by outsiders, particularly male youth, although this may in part represent an unwillingness to admit to the misdemeanors of Vanagi's own youths. As one fifty-two-year-old man described it, adding the words "from outside" as an automatic explanation: "There are drinkers here, from outside, that come in. They start up trouble." The comments of other people throughout the community were much the same. Some of the older generation spoke fondly of the early years after the foundation of Vanagi and expressed the sense that the emergence of social unease in the community was linked to recent changes across Port Moresby. Lily Ma'a, a volunteer teacher at the preschool, said:

> Sometimes I go back and think about those ways, our olden times when our parents were living here. We used to play around, there was no trouble. We used to walk free and go to each other's houses and play around, and at midnight we used to come back. But nowadays I don't think guests would go to each other's houses and stay any more. Our area is all right, but the outsiders, they get drunk and come in and torment us. Now, young boys, they're going out and drinking home brews and [smoking] marijuana.

Like Lily, a number of people pointed to a decreased feeling of safety in the community, linked to incidents of brawling, problems caused by outsiders, and the increased use of alcohol and marijuana. Overall, however, responses to the Community Sustainability Questionnaire indicate that the sense of personal safety in the community is higher than in many of the other research sites. Seventy-nine percent of respondents said that they were satisfied or very satisfied with how safe they felt, compared to an overall average of 71 percent across all the sites including remote villages. And while participants in strategic conversations did identify particular social problems within the community, they also pointed to the presence of a number of coordinated community responses to these problems, including the

Law and Order Subcommittee, the presence of a magistrate, a village court at Koki, a peace officer, church-based programs and activities, cooperation between elders and community leaders, and youth-focused initiatives such as the organization of regular volleyball and rugby competitions.

LIVELIHOOD AND PROVISION

Fishing is the main form of livelihood in the community and has been since the settlement was first established, but it is not a strong industry, and attempts at microcredit or taught entrepreneurialism have failed (see Chapters 7 and 8). There are good fishermen within most families in the community, with fish providing a source of both sustenance and income but not with the same consistency as in the past. In addition to fish, the main staple foods are rice, bananas, and vegetables such as *kaukau* and yams. Some families have land on which to make small gardens, but most people rely on purchased food for their regular meals. There are a number of trade stores located in the settlement, and the busy Koki fresh-food market is close. The supermarkets in Port Moresby are also easily accessible, although their prices tend to be expensive. Thirty-two percent of respondents to the questionnaire listed local shops as the main place they got their food, with another 26 percent listing food markets. Twenty-three percent said that the supermarket was the main place they got their food. By contrast, the overall averages from all research sites were: 7 percent, local shops; 4 percent, food markets; and 5 percent, supermarkets. In Vanagi, only 11 percent of people said that their main source of food was work done on their own lands or fishing, compared to a figure of 78 percent overall.

There is a high rate of unemployment among residents, reflective of the general employment shortage within Port Moresby. Of those people surveyed, 30 percent said that they were receiving a wage from the state, receiving a wage from private business, were a casual laborer or service worker, or were running a business. These figures roughly correspond to those from the 2000 national census, which found approximately 35 percent of people in Vanagi aged ten years and older to be in paid employment. The wages of those with paid employment tend to be used to support their extended families and are supplemented by the informal sector work activities of other family members, including many children and youths. Conversations with residents revealed that among those community members in formal employment, occupations included primary school teaching, literacy teaching, medicine, plumbing, carpentry, welding, sign writing, screen printing, mechanics, cooking, building, and manual labor. This amounts to a considerable range of skills present within the community. However, with relatively few opportunities for formal employment and no real capacity to practice subsistence agriculture, small, informal income-generating activities are the main ways in which people in Vanagi sustain their livelihoods. Indeed, 37 percent of respondents to the survey indicated that their main way of making a living was selling goods at market, and another 16 percent said that they worked within the household. Another 12 percent said that they worked in another way outside of the formal economy.

Informal income-generating activities practiced by individuals and families include selling fish, betel nut, cigarettes; collecting and selling empty cans, copper wire, and scrap metal; collecting and selling firewood; growing and selling seasonal fruits such as mangoes; making coffins; sewing; operating trade stores; selling seashells; and selling live chickens and eggs. Many people selling small goods do so at Koki market, and a number also set up small stalls within the settlement or in its immediate surrounds. The main demands for cash are for the purchase of food, payment of school fees, and contributions to community funds and activities. Most families "own" their houses (though without formal legal title) and so do not have to make rental payments, unlike many people in the city.

LEARNING AND EDUCATION

There are a number of educational and learning initiatives within Vanagi. In addition to formal school education, there is a volunteer-run community preschool, a range of adult literacy and training programs, and the informal passing on of skills and knowledge through families. A key resource for many of these initiatives is the community hall, out of which the preschool is run along with a range of workshops and skills-training sessions. The larger space also serves as a space for meetings, community gatherings, and church services. The building includes a small room stocked with a few educational books, magazines, and reports.

When asked about the highest level of formal education they had completed, responses to the Community Sustainability Questionnaire in Vanagi were comparable to the overall results across all research sites, with people in Vanagi having just slightly higher levels of formal education than respondents in other sites. For instance, 3 percent of respondents in Vanagi had completed either a university undergraduate or postgraduate qualification, compared to an average of 2 percent for all the sites. Fifteen percent had completed some sort of trade training, compared to a 13 percent average for all the sites. Thirty-eight percent of respondents in Vanagi had completed either some or all of their secondary education, a little higher than the overall average of 32 percent. And 6 percent had not completed any level of formal education, an apparently high figure but less than the overall average of 9 percent.

Because of its central location in Moresby South, there are a number of elementary and secondary schools located close to the settlement. However, community leaders and residents expressed concern at the dropout rate for school-aged children. Many leave during their time at secondary school, often because of difficulties in paying school fees. In addition, children and youths are often required to work in order to contribute to their family's income, and many school-aged children can be seen around the settlement selling small goods at stalls.

One of the most successful initiatives in Vanagi has been the establishment of a community preschool. This development is the outcome of a program implemented in the late 1990s by the member of Parliament for the Moresby South electorate, Dame Carol Kidu. Under the program, short training courses in early-childhood teaching were offered throughout the Moresby South area for interested volunteers. After the three-week course, these volunteers returned to their homes to establish community preschools. The Vanagi community preschool opened in 1998 and is currently one of twenty-four located in the Moresby South area. They are coordinated through the Port Moresby South Community Preschool Association. Clement Dogale, a community leader in Vanagi and father of the late Chris Clement, is the president of the association and one of the teachers at the Vanagi preschool. A retired teacher, he described his sense of disillusionment at the continuing problems affecting youth in Papua New Guinea, despite the large amounts of money being spent by the government on youth-focused initiatives. When the training courses were offered, he went along, motivated in part by curiosity and by his feeling that things needed to happen in a different way:

> I was one of those who trained to become preschool teachers in our community. When I went in, it was an eye-opener for me. I found that it was the thing I was looking for. I saw that it was the way to change Papua New Guinea....We went in and did the training for three weeks only, came back, and started teaching children, with no pay, we just got interested and started teaching. Many of the children now are in the community schools, and they are ahead of other children. They are making a difference, which I am happy about.

Sixty-eight children enrolled in the Vanagi community preschool in 2006, with around thirty attending each day. The program's dependence on volunteers, however, makes it difficult to keep the preschool going. Some of the individuals who initially trained as teachers have left, leaving only Clement and one other core teacher. Some of the children bring twenty toea a day, which goes to support the teachers, and villagers support them with food. The preschool also receives some funding from the local Latter-Day Saints church, but it is not sufficient to pay an ongoing wage for the staff. Without this, it will be hard to ensure the continuity of the program.

Another important dimension of the learning and education processes in the community is the informal exchange of skills and knowledge—both customary and modern. Older men pass down their skills in fishing, making nets, and making customary canoes. Women pass down skills in sewing, cooking, and baking to their younger female relatives. Outside of extended families, skills are shared through fo-

Children at the Vanagi Settlement preschool run by Clement Dogali

rums such as the women's group and through workshops coordinated through the Education Subcommittee. Still, there is a sense that skills are slowly being lost, and both men and women express their frustration at not having access to adequate equipment with which to practice their skills, such as stoves, sewing machines, and tools for making canoes or mending fishing nets.

Within Vanagi, there is a strong desire for further training and education. Eighty-eight percent of people surveyed agreed or strongly agreed with the statement "More training is necessary for doing the work that I would ideally like to do." The types of training identified by these people as being most important were income generation and management. Respondents also expressed a desire for more training in family life as well as in technology and literacy. To a large extent, though, Vanagi is already a very skills-rich community. The variety of occupations in which residents are working and the experience and knowledge present within families amount to a significant resource for this small settlement to tap into. Despite the demand for more training and educational opportunities, and although many households struggle to meet their basic needs and desperately need a means of increasing their income, there is also a strong foundation on which to build. Within a place like Vanagi, one of the key tasks in enhancing and promoting community learning will be to identify and most effectively utilize the diverse skills and knowledge that already exist and then plan for educational and training programs to complement this existing base and provide new skills where they are needed.

Divinai Village, Milne Bay Province

WHY ARE LOCAL PROJECTS SO DIFFICULT TO SUSTAIN?

Several years ago Joseph Alex, a community leader in Divinai village, planted vanilla crops on his land on the advice of government officials from the Department of Primary Industries. A number of other villagers did the same, and, now that their crops are finally producing fruit, all have found themselves unable to sell the vanilla beans that they thought would be "green gold." Why did this initiative, like other cash-cropping projects in Divinai, fail to live up to expectations?

Markedly different from customary practices of *production for livelihood,* where surplus produce is sold within relatively localized systems of labor and exchange, the primary purpose of cash cropping is agricultural *production for profit* by selling into an extended national or global market. Most commonly cash crops are produced for the export market, drawing local communities like Divinai into global systems of trade and exchange. Cash cropping is expanding as an economic emphasis across all of Papua New Guinea, promoted by the national government and in turn by international financial institutions and donor countries such as Australia. The vanilla plots in Divinai are not the village's first attempt at cash cropping. For many years copra—the dried kernels of coconuts—was its principal cash crop, but declining world prices mean that it no longer provides a reliable source of income for people. Some people who used to produce copra moved to coffee or cocoa. Many returned to growing garden produce for their own consumption and small-scale selling in informal markets.

Then, in 2000, a cyclone wiped out much of the vanilla crop in the world's biggest producer, Madagascar. It sent world prices sky-rocketing and suddenly made vanilla production an enticing option for other "developing" countries. As Joseph puts it, "When they started looking at other markets, they thought that was an opportunity to get the idea of planting vanilla to the village people." Joseph planted vanilla after learning that it was returning profits to farmers in the Sepik region—"they were saying it was green gold." However, vanilla is possibly the most labor-intensive crop in the world, often requiring hand pollination and taking as long as five years after planting to produce aged extract. By the time Joseph's crops were ready for harvest, although he did not know it, production in Madagascar was starting to increase again, supplemented by production in countries such as Uganda, India, Costa Rica, and Colombia. Those countries, like Papua New Guinea, had entered the market in the wake of the Malagasy crisis. The arrival of these new players together with a concomitant increase in the use of synthetic agents by food manufacturers—synthetic vanillin now costs one-hundredth of the price of the natural product—meant that global prices for vanilla beans have slumped by over 90 percent from their peak in 2003 at US$200 per kilo. Currently, the price hovers around $20 a kilo, with farmers getting only around 10 percent of the traded commodity price, and destructive cyclones again in Madagascar in 2009 have not made much difference in that price. To put it bluntly, without the benefit of globally attuned commodity forecasting and analytically sensitive economic advice, seeking green gold is bound to fail.

The disappointment of the Divinai farmers, then, is the result of a complex set of factors including, among other things, global weather patterns, export-oriented development policies in Papua New Guinea and its donor countries, poor timing, agricultural production in other countries such as India, the increased use of synthetic vanilla extract in food manufacturing, and, perhaps most important, the fundamental volatility of global markets. In other words, local, national, and global issues all make a difference to village life—although most of the information relevant to these issues swirls around local Papua New Guinea as rumor rather than as expertly interpreted knowledge. Joseph's inability to find a market for his vanilla is not an uncommon story in Divinai or across Papua New Guinea for export cropping in general. In Joseph's words: "My uncle planted a hectare of cocoa, someone else has planted maybe a reasonable amount of coffee, but they're not even selling it because there's not a market.... I know these are good ideas that the government has told us to follow, to get into, but the big question is are they going to provide us the market?" The Department of Primary Industry station at nearby Bubuleta has now started distributing nutmeg seedlings, but there is anxiety among many of the villagers, who worry that they will again fail to find a market for their crops. Joseph, while recognizing in an amorphous way that the economy he is engaged in is complex and transnational, sees the lack of markets for his cash crops as a failure of the government to provide for its farmers. In truth, the vagaries of the international trade in agriculture are something the Papua New Guinean government is in no place to control, but it is encouraging local communities to grow cash crops with the assurance that they will provide a consistent and considerable source of income. Sometimes there are markets, and the crops become profitable as they were for the Sepik farmers who were able to harvest their vanilla crops and sell them before world prices plummeted. Other times, as has been the case in Divinai, local people are left at "the losing end of the whole thing," with crops they cannot sell and that their families cannot eat. The problem is not cash cropping in itself but the way in which it is held out as the way forward without consideration of how it integrates into a complex economy for livelihoods rather than a one-dimensional economy for profit.

PLACE—PAST AND PRESENT

Divinai village is a small community of around seven hundred people, located in Milne Bay Province on the coastline overlooking the Bismarck Sea, toward the far eastern tip of the Papua New Guinean mainland. Narrow black-sand beaches run along the Milne Bay coast, with mountains behind them and the Stirling Range to the north, rising to summits of five thousand feet. Thick jungle, scrub, mangrove, and sago swamps are key features of the province's environment. The land immediately around Divinai, however, is largely flat and dry, with poor soil and occasional drought. Coconut, sago, and betel-nut palms occupy much of the land, along with gardens and cash-crop plantations. The Divinai population is organized into just over one hundred households, with families living together in homes built mainly out of bush materials, located according to clan arrangements and matrilineal systems of landownership.

Central to the story of the place is the history of the missionaries and churches in the area. Samoan missionaries from the London Missionary Society first arrived in the region in the late nineteenth century. In 1891 the Reverend Charles Abel arrived to establish a base for the Missionary Society on Kwato Island, approximately three kilometers west of Samarai Island in the China Strait of Milne Bay. The island was envisaged as a "total society" for the Christian converts who lived there: isolated from the heathenism around them, they were trained to be evangelists, teachers, and players of cricket and football. The island community was dispersed with the outbreak of World War II, but the Kwato church continued on as the Kwato Extension Association. Villagers in Divinai—which is a short boat ride away from Kwato Island—still refer to "Mr. Abel" as if he were a present figure, active in their lives, and the Kwato church is still the central religious body in community life. In recounting its own history, the Divinai community draws attention to these early interactions with strangers, with Charles Abel and the Samoan missionaries before him. Mrs. William, an older villager woman whose grandmother was taught at the Kwato Island school, describes "something about this village that is very unique...a mixture of what we get from the outsider, from the foreigners who have been through the villages and the communities."

The provincial capital of Milne Bay, Alotau, is located just twenty minutes' drive northwest of Divinai. The proximity of the township—hence our designation of the community as periurban—and the quality of the road network in the area means that travel to and from the center is relatively easy, and the community is able to access the services located there, including the market, bank, medical services, post office, shops, and government and private sector offices. Gurney airport has daily flights connecting Alotau to Port Moresby, weekly flights to Popondetta in Northern Province, and flights three times a week to both Misima Island and Kiriwina Island in the province. Alotau itself was constructed in the late 1960s, shortly before independence, its location selected because of the existence of the Gurney airstrip. The airstrip is a legacy of the Second World War, built when Milne Bay became a site of strategic importance in the struggle for control over the Pacific. Beginning in July

1942, large numbers of Australian troops were stationed in the area, and a major battle between Allied and Japanese forces was fought in September and October of that year. The Papuan communities in Milne Bay suddenly found themselves in the midst of a cruel conflict being fought on their lands, one that took a heavy toll on them. Today, the wrecks of planes and ships that remain dotted around the area—both in the jungles and underwater in the bays off the coast—have become key attractions for a local tourist industry offering eco-lodge accommodation and scuba diving. Alotau itself is also a commercial center, a result of its accessibility via the Gurney airstrip and gold-mining operations on Misima Island.

ORGANIZATION AND GOVERNANCE

The Divinai community includes a significant number of migrants who have moved to the area as a result of intermarriage, and among respondents to the questionnaire, 27 percent indicated that they had lived in the area for five years or less. Many of those who have moved to Divinai are from nearby villages; shared language and extensive networks of kinship and intermarriage connect communities in the surrounding area. Mrs. William, a senior woman in the Divinai community, described it like this:

> Here, in this area—we call it the Tawala area—the same language that we speak here extends as far as East Cape and around there to Huhuna and right down here around the bay. We speak Tawala language, and we follow our mothers' side, matrilineal society. So we all fall back to our mother. And my daughter will be taking after me, if I go. She will continue to live on my land. I am sitting on my grandmother's land—I got it from my mother, and my daughter is going to get it from me.

The matrilineal system of community organization means that, upon marriage, it is the husband who moves to his wife's family lands. At death, however, his body returns to his mother's land for burial. Mourning rituals around death and burial play an important role in affirming customary ties to land, and it is through the burial ceremony that elders pass on and confirm the land rights of clans and families. Relationships of responsibility and reciprocity are reinforced through the ritual practices at times of death, as they are through the practices around marriage, bride price, birth, and initiation. As a result, there are strong relationships of kinship that include those members of the community who have migrated from other places. Extended families and clans provide support networks and collective identity, and community members credit the strong kinship relationships for the social cohesion within Divinai.

Organization and leadership within the community is provided through the coexisting structures of the chiefdom system, the churches, and the local-level government. As with land rights in the community, clan leadership is passed down along matrilineal lines, from uncles to their eldest nephews. The leaders of individual clans are united under a paramount chief, who is the highest authority within the customary-tribal system. In addition to guarding and passing on customary knowledge of rituals, stories, land boundaries, and history, the paramount chief and the clan chiefs are called upon to intervene in disputes within the community and matters relating to cultural, land, and marine resources. In cases where disputes cannot be resolved through the chiefdom system, however, they are now referred to the modern legal system to be adjudicated through the village courts. This practice accords with our argument for the intersection and reflexive articulation of different modes of being, including tribal, traditional, and modern relations, but mostly here occurs as just a fact of concurrence rather than through careful or consistent negotiation, and depends very much on the sensitivity of individuals.

Since the first arrival of missionaries in the area in the late nineteenth century, the tribal-customary governance and decision-making structures of the chiefdom system have existed concurrently with the traditional-modern authority structures of the Christian churches. Churches in Divinai and the Alotau area, particularly the Kwato church, play a fundamental role as a basis for communal life. When asked what they identified as their main source of community, 28 percent of respondents to the questionnaire in Divinai identified the place that they lived, which is consistent with the overall results across all the research sites and attests to the widespread importance of land and place. Significantly though, another 24 percent—much greater than the overall figure for all locations of 7 percent—identified their main source of community as being a "club, community, or religious center." This was confirmed and reiterated in more in-depth strategic conversations and interviews, in which individuals consistently referred back to the centrality of the church in the community.

There are four denominations in the area, although the Kwato church appears to be the dominant religious body and holds an important place in the history of the community. Under the church structure, the pastor is the leader of the congregation, with deacons acting under him. While the paramount chief and the clan chiefs continue to be respected as the guardians of customary knowledge and practices, leadership within the community also comes from the pastor and deacons who guide the community in their spiritual life and congregation. This relationship is rarely addressed directly. Clans continue to serve as crucial mediums for the organization of families and individuals, providing a source of identification through which people exist in relation to one another and through which land and forms of knowledge and practice are passed from one generation to another. However, the community is also organized and mobilized through the structures of the churches—through the women's fellowships, youth groups, community activities, and collective worship.

The continuing importance of customary rituals, practices, and forms of organization and identity exists concurrently with the importance accorded to the churches and Christian ideologies. In most ways, however, church ways frame prior customary relations. In other words, Christianity frames the way in which the contemporary relevance of customary practices is negotiated. So, when asked about the place of customary values in community life, people mentioned the centrality of systems of matrilineal landownership and the practices associated with marriage and death as "some of the customary things that we still retain." At the same time, they pointed to a move away from customary initiation rituals, of which sorcery and charming are key elements. The distinction is in their compatibility, or otherwise, with Christianity. "[Initiation] goes on with witchcraft, so we try to do away with that, according to the biblical principal. Whatever is against God we don't participate in very much." Clearly, though, there is some ambiguity in the shift between interpretation and practice. Initiation rituals and sorcery are still practiced but in a way that is less publicly and collectively sanctioned than, say, clan-based funeral feasts, which occur alongside Christian burial services.

Whereas Christianity and the customary dimensions of collective life seem to sit in a relatively harmonious, fluid relationship to each other, there are much sharper points of tension in the relationship between the churches and the local-level government. Under the 1995 Organic Law reforms, political power in Papua New Guinea was further decentralized from the provinces to local-level governments (LLGs), and Divinai is now one of twenty-nine wards in the Alotau LLG. The ward councilor in Divinai is, under this system, the overall head of the community and considered to be the representative of the government at the local level. He is supported by a committee of five people appointed by the community, and under his leadership they constitute the core group that does most of the planning in the ward. A Ward Development Committee brings together representatives from families and clans, key programs such as health and education, and groups such as the Women's Fellowship, youth, sporting clubs, and church groups. These representatives are responsible for taking back information and decisions from the committee and disseminating them throughout the community. The Ward Development Committee also has a number of subcommittees tasked with coordinating sports, law and order, youth activities, and women's activities in the community. In addition, it coordinates community workdays, held every Tuesday, at which community members are intended to contribute labor and time to the general upkeep and maintenance of the village. Collective tasks include the beautification and cleaning of the village cemetery and individual homes as well as of the church, local school, and other shared spaces. The cleaning and devegetation of roads is done under contract from the Department of Works and Implementation and earns the community some income. Attendance at community workdays is poor, however, and the community leaders appointed under the LLG system frequently encounter difficulties in mobilizing the community through the Ward Development Committee.

The stated goal of the 1995 Organic Law reforms was to create stronger links between the national government and community life, while making law and government responsive to local needs and realities, but the sentiment expressed by a number of people within Divinai is that the new structure has failed to meet the needs and demands of the local people. Referring to the 1995 reform, Joseph Alex, who is a leader within the Kwato church, described it as "something on paper alone—the practical part of it has never happened." He spoke of his frustration at the difficulties in accessing government services and the lack of responsiveness of government to the proposals put forward by community leaders. For him, the fact that he had put forward development proposals that had not been taken up by the councilor and the LLG was evidence of the failure of the government system. Doubtless there are a whole set of factors at play here—including political will, funding, available resources, and conflicting demands—but Joseph's comments illustrate the perception of government by many community members both here in Divinai and across Papua New Guinea. There is an abiding sense of disconnect between the experience of daily life at the local level and formal structures of government. Significantly, the argument that Joseph and other community members made was that the church is much more central in organizing and bringing people together than are the agencies of government. As he put it,

> The government does not bring people together.... How the people interact with each other is more or less through the churches. The churches play an active role in people's lives. When my councilor comes and tells me, "OK, village people get together; we are going to talk about this and this and this," I am going to guarantee you this; you will find five or ten people will attend... but when you talk about my pastor, he'll say, "People come, we gather round and do this," you'll find that the whole community's going to come around.

The structures of religious authority and organization thus carry a much greater importance within the Divinai community than do the formal structures of modern political authority. Where the churches and chiefdom system appear to coexist in a relatively harmonious way, the churches and local government sit in uneasy tension with one another. A commonly voiced sentiment was that there needed to be greater cooperation between the two and more respect for the churches in the development process.

Notwithstanding these tensions, however, the results of the Community Sustainability Questionnaire suggested that structures of leadership and decision making in Divinai have comparatively high levels of support from the community. When asked how much they agreed with the statement "I feel that decisions made about life in my neighborhood are made in the interests of the whole community," 77 percent of respondents to the questionnaire in Divinai either agreed or strongly agreed, and 15 percent disagreed or strongly disagreed. This is considerably more positive than the overall results across all the research sites, where only 62 percent agreed or strongly disagreed, and 20 percent disagreed or strongly disagreed. When researchers posed the statement "I feel that governments make decisions and laws that are good for the way I live locally," 52 percent of Divinai respondents agreed or strongly agreed. This is hardly a resounding expression of faith in government but still considerably higher than the overall result across all the research sites of 43 percent. It suggests that while the perception of government is poor within Divinai, as it arguably is across the country, the relationship between state and citizenry here is less strained than it is within many of the other places.

Overall, the results from the questionnaire and material gathered from community conversations, interviews, and ethnographic observation point to high levels of community well-being in Divinai. Eighty percent of survey respondents said that they were satisfied or very satisfied with their community neighborhood, and 84 percent said that they were satisfied or very satisfied with feeling part of their community. Seventy-nine percent were satisfied or very satisfied with their life as a whole, with 10 percent indicating they were dissatisfied or very dissatisfied. This compares favorably to the overall figures across the research sites of 72 percent and 14 percent respectively. Respondents in Divinai also reported a much higher feeling of safety within their community, with 81 percent saying they were satisfied or very satisfied with their feeling of safety, compared to an overall figure of 72 percent. Only 4 percent of Divinai respondents were dissatisfied or very dissatisfied with their feeling of safety, much lower than the overall result of 12 percent. A feeling of social cohesion, connectedness to the provincial capital in Alotau, and the strength of church and kinships relationships ranked highly among those things that community members and leaders identified as positive features of community life.

LIVELIHOOD AND PROVISION

Daily livelihood in Divinai is sustained through a variety of activities, the predominant ones being agriculture for subsistence and for sale at markets. The ocean too is an important source of food, and, as in coastal villages across the country, a wealth of knowledge about fishing has been passed down family lines for many generations. Within families, livelihood activities are frequently divided on the basis of age and gender. Women are the main income earners, and it is they who sit at market stalls in the local village market or at Alotau selling their families' produce and catch for a small income. In practice, it is the best fish and vegetables that are sold at market, with the rest retained for the family's own consumption. Many of the village women also engage in periodic small-scale income-generating activities such as selling handicrafts or baked goods like scones. As Mrs. William described it, "Any grass-roots woman can pick up something like a bundle of pumpkin tips or a coconut and sell it at the market—she gets one kina or two kina, something to buy kerosene—basic needs." In total, 52 percent of Divinai respondents to the questionnaire said that their main way of making a living was through work within the household. Another 21 percent identified selling goods at market or on the street. Eighty-nine percent of people surveyed said that their main source of food was work done on their own land or fishing, a figure significantly higher than the overall result of 78 percent across all the research sites. Five percent identified a supermarket, and 4 percent identified local shops as their main source of food.

The income that the women earn is distributed to cover the costs of immediate family needs such as school fees, health expenses, clothing and household goods, and community obligations like church contributions, funerals, feasts, and bride prices. A small microfinance initiative has been set up to enable women in the community to accrue some savings from the money they earn. However, unlike in the Tokain group of villages in Madang Province, being the primary income earner does not always ensure that women are able to control how the family's money is spent. Women in the village expressed concern about men spending family money on alcohol. The councilor and the Law and Order Committee have been asked to take up the issue, but it remains a matter of concern for community women.

In addition to gardening, fishing, and small-scale income-generating work such as marketing, a significant number of people in Divinai are engaged in livelihood activities within the formal sector. In the responses to the questionnaire, a much higher than average percentage of respondents from Divinai—26 percent as opposed to 14 percent across all the research sites—indicated that they were receiving a wage (either from the state or private business), ran their own business, or were paid a cash income as a casual service worker or laborer. A key reason for the high number is the proximity and accessibility to Alotau and accordingly with the commercial, political, and tourist activities based there. Additionally, the development of cash-cropping agriculture means that increasing numbers of villagers within Divinai are being drawn into formal sector employment—and the much broader systems of production and exchange within which such work is situated—through the growth of cash cropping as a livelihood activity. Often, though, this work is precarious and inconsistent, and families may revert to subsistence agriculture and the selling of small surpluses in the local informal markets when they are unable to find a market for the vanilla, cocoa, coffee, or copra they produce.

Formal sector employment, then, encompasses a broad range of activities, and accordingly there are significant variations in the lifestyles, status, and subjective self-understandings that these activities afford. Many of the people in formal employment work for relatively small incomes, with little to distinguish their lives from those of the majority of villagers who make their living from gardening, fishing, and selling goods in the informal markets. There are some, though, whose levels of income position them in sharp contrast to those they live around, providing them with conspicuously different lifestyles and according them particular status. The relationship between these people and the other Divinai villagers seems ambiguous. On the one hand, their incomes and housing are a marker of difference; on the other hand, they are connected through kinship and *wantok* relationships, and in some senses their presence is claimed as a way of elevating the status of the community at large. The provincial administrator for Milne Bay lives in the area, married to a village woman. So too do the assistant secretary for the Department for Primary Industries and other officials and business people: "all the tall people," as Mrs. William describes them. "They are in the bush here; they have big high-covenant houses. They're hiding in the bush, you won't see them! But in the morning if you are [outside] washing dishes, you'll see all these flashy cars driving out. So you will note that this village too has some tall people here."

LEARNING AND EDUCATION

Levels of education in Divinai are comparatively high in relation to Papua New Guinea as a whole. The presence of the community primary school in the village means that all people have completed at least a basic primary education. In fact, only 2 percent of respondents to the questionnaire in Divinai said that they had received no formal education, significantly lower than the overall figure of 9 percent across all the research sites. Fifty-four percent said they had completed primary school, compared to 42 percent across all eleven sites; however, the percentage of those who said they had completed some or all of their secondary education was lower than the overall figure, at 28 percent as opposed to 33 percent. Beyond the primary school level, access to formal education becomes much more difficult, and the expense is often too great for families to continue. However, the immediate proximity of the village to Alotau means that many people with skills training or higher-level education still reside in the community while employed in the urban center.

Outside of the formal education system, learning takes place within families—as skills and customary knowledge are passed down from one generation to the next—and through forums provided by faith-based and governmental agencies. Familial forms of learning are being emphasized by both tribal and modern-political community leaders as a remedy to the challenges facing youth in the community, including those posed by alcohol consumption, the lure of urban centers, and the struggle to retain customary ways in the face of the modern. The obligation falls on older family members to pass on local knowledge to the young men and women, in preparation for them to take on adult family and community responsibilities. Training for both young and older women comes as well from the churches, particularly through the Women's Fellowship. An agriculture station in the village has run some training sessions, especially on cash cropping. It could be used to assist the community in agricultural methods such as soil improvement and improved gardening skills. In 2006 a community resource center was constructed, and the hope was that it would also be a place for training and learning activities, but this has not been very successful.

There is a strong desire for greater access to learning and education within the community. When surveyed about what sort of training they desired, 52 percent of respondents agreed that agricultural training would be useful. Twenty-five percent selected training in income generation as desirable, and 23 percent wanted training in management skills. As was common in all of the communities where the questionnaire was conducted, training in family life and customary ways of doing things was also important to people, with 34 percent and 30 percent of respondents respectively expressing a desire for such education in these areas. The forms of education and training that are desired by people in the village correspond strongly to the nature of the community itself. The strong cultural basis of Divinai, rooted in its kinship and clan networks, means that customary forms of learning are highly valued. At the same time, though, people and families are negotiating the effects of social, cultural, and economic change. The desire for training workshops on customary family-life activities sits alongside the desire for skills training that will enable them to tap into the growing tourism industry in the region. People want more information on cash cropping and the functioning of the export market, but they also want to learn how to improve their subsistence gardening as population growth creates pressures on available land. They want to be able to access the knowledge held by outside experts while holding strongly to the knowledge of their tribal elders.

Kananam Community, Madang Province

WHAT DOES IT MEAN THAT OUTSIDERS WITH GRAND PLANS HAVE DONE
SO MUCH DAMAGE?

The path from the church building set within the grounds of the Alexishafen
mission is uneven and well trodden, but the land no longer belongs to the people.
The Gamarmatu clan, the main clan in these areas, has settled here for years. Families moved inland from the outlying islands after the heavy bombing during World
War II. In the mid-1990s, the Church handed the land back to the government rather
than to the Kananam people. The people feel a great betrayal, as they understood
that they had passed the land over to the missionaries in reciprocal exchange for
learning and ministry. The Kananam people were not made aware—until it was too
late—that the land was not to be handed back to them but instead was to be sold
privately. In the late 1990s the old Vidar plantation area around the harbor was
bought by a private company for three million kina and is now the site of the RD
Tuna Cannery, owned by a Philippines company. According to the villagers, the first
payment was handed over to the Catholic Church.

Directly across from Alexishafen is Sek, the largest island in the lagoon, composed of one large family of approximately one thousand people across twelve
hamlets. Other islands, such as Dumuseg and Ambusin, dot the lagoon; however
several have been abandoned because of rising water levels over the last ten years,
possibly owing to global climate change. Two islands have disappeared completely,
and others are in the process of being subsumed by the warm, blue waters of the
lagoon. Many of the islands have also become inhabitable, and lack of access to
fresh water supplies or fresh food, particularly the loss of fish from their once-
abundant waters, has exacerbated the process. A small community hall is set a little
way from the edge of the lagoon, and Papa Paul Buy's house is on the shoreline. He
is a village elder and a Gamarmatu elder in his seventies and lives with his wife. His
children are spread around him—an extended family dotted across different lanes
and corners in the areas edging the lagoon.

It was early afternoon, and Papa Paul Buy asked us how we possibly thought
we could help his people to come out of the apathy and depression into which they
have fallen. His voice rose in consternation as he talked of the dragging of the seas
by foreign fishing trawlers and the arrogance of people who simply took so much
from his people's lands and put nothing back. Suddenly he stopped and smiled,
and asked us if we were friends. Not quite sure how to respond to such a sudden
question, we looked at him. We had earlier asked him to tell us his story, and Papa
Paul Buy was keen to understand why we wanted it. He said to us, "My story is also
the story of my people. If I tell you, will you say it like I say it—should I trust you
like a friend?"

In the heavy denseness of the afternoon sun, squatting under a straggly tree for shade, we were unsure how to proceed. Then Papa Paul Buy started to speak. His sentences were short and in the local dialect. It seemed a long story, as many times Papa Paul Buy stopped and pointed out into the sea or stopped to reflect, sometimes with great sadness it seemed and sometimes with pride. A small group of local community members gathered and sat around us, including children.

> We are Mortonoau people, of the Gamarmatu clan. We came by canoe built by us, from the knowledge of our ancestors, the word of the ancestors. We came in canoes and boats that could move through the waves of the sea and the rumbles of the rains. We set upon Sec Island, grew our gardens and fished in the waters, and traded with our many people of this noble land, nation. The sea was our garden; it gave us much, it gave us our people, and we gave the sea our respect. Our law, the word of the elders ruled to keep peace, law, justness.
>
> When the bombs fell and the embankments we had built from corals from the sea broke around us, we took to our canoes and rowed to the mainlands. The church became a place, a home of sorts, and we served in many ways. Independence dawned, with it a new hope that our story of the Mortonoau, the word, the elders, be told—the spiritual fabric, the heart of our people here in this place near the sea. We had hoped that this, our story, would have been heard, lived again through this independence. But we are overcome—we are swallowed by that which is large, foreign to our sea, to our fish, our lives, and our word. We are faced with destruction, and our old ways cannot hold together in these times, as some of our elders themselves sell their soul and people. But we cannot lose hope. We live with hope, that one day our story will arise—and we will know ourselves, rule ourselves as we proclaimed in 1975 by the PNG colors.

The intensity of hope has gone up and down over the last decade, which has been a difficult period. RD Tuna opened its operations after a twenty-year agreement was signed in 1996 with the Papua New Guinean government. Some people in the village explained how, in the early years of the cannery, the village women exchanged fruit and coconut for "by-catch fish" with the Filipino men on the fishing boats. However, after some years, the fishermen began to reject the fruit and coconut, demanding sex. There is now a "fish for sex" trade in Kananam, and the women sell themselves for food. Seven Filipino–Papua New Guinean babies have been born into the area recently of such liaisons, and the mothers of these babies struggle alternately for survival and acceptance within the community, which is itself struggling to stay on its feet. In the last two years, there seems to be a growing number of HIV cases in the place, prompting concerned community leaders like Alexia and Alphonse to initiate and invite awareness and training programs such as the national-level Tingim Laip HIV Awareness Program. This program, funded primarily by AusAID, works in partnership with local groups and sites across the area. The Tingim Laip Madang Province document circulating in Kananam showed the RD Tuna Cannery workers—80 percent female—to be in the highest risk category for contracting the virus.

PLACE—PAST AND PRESENT

The Kananam community is situated on a lagoon, approximately fifteen minutes by road from the provincial capital of Madang town, with approximately three thousand people inhabiting the many villages scattered across the short stretch of coast and handful of islands. There are three main clans—the Sec clan, Gamarmatu clan, and Matanan clan—and two subclans—the Geonen clan and the Danu Fon clan. Like Divinai near Alotau, Kananam is so close to Madang that it can be described as a periurban in a rural setting. From a survey conducted in this region, we found that 64 percent of Kananam respondents had lived in the area their whole lives, significantly higher than the overall figure of 38 percent for the eleven other sites across different provinces of Papua New Guinea. In recent years, new settlers representing the Susubanis, Begis, and Dapu clans have also moved in and settled around the water edges, many also seeking jobs with the fishing companies in the area. Masses of mangroves and clusters of coconut trees are perched over the edge of the lagoon, framed by the misty Bismarck Ranges. Customary wooden canoes—made from a long, slender log with a smaller log that juts from the side as a counterbalance—move across the turquoise blue waters during the day. Mornings are a slightly busier time as children slowly make their way to school or villagers head out to catch some fish. The canoes that sit along the edge of coastal villages are an important mode of transport but also mark the uniqueness of every village. The shape and design of a canoe can only be borrowed from another village with the appropriate permissions, and compensation must be paid, often in the way of pigs, by those who fail to ask before copying a canoe design.

The manicured lawn and landscaped gardens of the Catholic mission at Alexishafen stand out conspicuously against the dense vegetation along the coastline. Still a significant physical presence over a century after missionaries' arrival, the Catholic mission remains a source of ire because it represents for most of the community the critical point in their recent history when they were first alienated from their customary land. This land called Vidar was heavily forested and was cut for swidden gardens. However, the church took over Vidar and used the forests for building houses and boats. Villagers described relations with the church as poor. The sisters at the Alexishafen mission later told us that, despite their attempts at building relations, they did not understand why they were despised by the villagers who sometimes stole food from their gardens. For the Kananam people, however, the problem was obvious. Augusta Nalun, the now unemployed local primary school teacher says angrily, "While my people here starve, the foreign companies scrape our seas bare and the government pockets get filled." A large protest against the trawling companies, organized by the local community in late 2006, drew more than three thousand community members, particularly irate over indiscriminate acts of exploitation and human rights abuses. One community member described the protest: "I got into the tiny boat, and we came right up to one of RD Tuna's large trawling boats. I used a large microphone and asked them to leave our young women alone. I screamed at them and asked them who was there to take care of the many illegitimate children who, because of our ways, were also now our children. We ourselves were struggling to put one decent meal on the mat." Nothing seems to have changed much for these people since that protest, though conversations with locally based NGO Bismarck Ramu revealed that this community protest brought the activities of RD Tuna to the attention of the European Union, one of the company's main markets. Following a visit a few months later by inspectors from Germany, their market sales in Europe have been dramatically reduced.

ORGANIZATION AND GOVERNANCE

The Kananam communities maintain customary systems of leadership and ways of doing things that have sustained their livelihoods throughout generations. However, family relationships are weakening, due to the scarcity of resources such as land and fish, and the declining daily practice of reciprocity through the exchange of fish and garden food. There is a weak sense of participation in community activities, especially by the young people. The older generation and parents expressed unhappiness because their children are showing less interest in family activities like gardening and fishing, and spend too much time lazing around the house or in the communities.

The hope of employment opportunities at RD Tuna is also attracting new settlers to the Kananam region from farther inland. This migration seems to be stretching the fragile fabric of the already-struggling community. Clan divisions are growing, especially as new settlers, equipped with money, buy land and set up new groups of settlements. The pressures on the customary models of organization and leadership are great. As the community feels increasingly marginalized from the benefits of development activities around what was once their land and way of life, there is increasing frustration and growing anger.

For many, the anger is the result of the lack of royalty payments and benefits by the church and the RD Fishing Company for the use of their land and the sea. The people also blame the government for not informing or involving them when they implemented development projects in the communities. The result has been the inability of the community to negotiate a better outcome for their people and place.

The simmering anger at the Catholic mission at Alexishafen compounds a rising tension, and community leaders speak of a growing disregard for new but short-term and underresourced government projects. Alphonse, a community leader in Kananam, argues that the biggest handicap for people is their lack of general information about their basic rights, the national Constitution, and the bureaucratic system, meaning that they are often unable to respond or act adequately. But even for the community leaders, it is difficult to find good or valid information, unless they are able to connect regularly with the Bismarck Ramu NGO, which has been campaigning against the tuna cannery for many years.

Many people also expressed a sense of disconnect from the systems of national and provincial government. Before 1975 and in the early years after independence, government extension officers regularly visited communities and worked with the people. However, Kananam community members say that these visits have now stopped. People express a desire for the government extension programs to be revived again on the basis that they made the government presence felt in the communities.

Results from the Community Sustainability Questionnaire indicated low levels of community well-being within the Kananam area. Whereas 78 percent of respondents across all the research sites said that they were satisfied or very satisfied with their community neighborhoods, only 50 percent of respondents in Kananam said so. Similarly, only 56 percent of Kananam people surveyed said that they were satisfied or very satisfied with their lives as a whole, much lower than the overall figure of 72 percent across all the sites. And again, when asked to what extent they agreed with the statement "I feel most people can be trusted," only 19 percent of Kananam respondents agreed or strongly agreed, compared to 34 percent across all eleven sites in Papua New Guinea. Forty-seven percent disagreed or strongly disagreed with the statement, much higher than the overall figure of 34 percent. Data such as these correlate strongly with the sentiments conveyed by community leaders and other villages, namely, that this is a community struggling to hold together its social and cultural fabric in the face of massive challenges.

LIVELIHOOD AND PROVISION

People's livelihoods depend heavily on resources from both the sea and the land. Both are fast becoming scarce owing to population increases and the acquisition of a good portion of these resources by the state and the Church. People in Kananam speak of dwindling fish stocks and marine resources contaminated by the heavy oil spills from the fishing vessels operated by the RD Tuna Cannery. They speak of the difficulties in making a living and sustaining the livelihoods and well-being of their families. The community members also tell of health problems, such as stomachaches after swimming in the water, chronic skin infections, coughing.

and diarrhea, which emerged with the arrival of the cannery. At Mataman, one of the leaders of the Bismarck Ramu Group—against which RD Tuna has already unsuccessfully tried to bring defamation charges—explained how the fishery was affecting his village. Less than half of people in Kananam were employed by the fishery, he said, and the numbers of fish in the lagoon dropped in the late 1990s with the arrival of the fishery.

The declining marine resources and the generally deteriorating quality of the marine environment affects not just the capacity of families to find sufficient food to feed themselves, but also the possibilities for small-scale income generation. Fishing and the collection of other marine resources like shellfish, shrimps, lobsters, and crabs is the main income-generating activity for the people in Kananam. Various reef fish are caught using fishing lines and hooks or spears, especially at night, and the fishermen know well the breeding sessions and grounds for the different species. Fishing skills and knowledge are passed through family lines, especially from fathers to sons, but the waters are yielding much less for the younger generations than they did for their parents.

Another source of income for families is the farming of cash crops. Because of current low market prices, copra processing is not occurring in Kananam at the moment, and most villagers expressed disappointment at this. There is, however, some cocoa farming, and growing betel nut and mustard also provides good sources of income. Families from the islands make their gardens on Ambusin Island, while those from mainland villages like Kananam and Tawei make their gardens on the mainland. Garden crops are mainly grown for the families' own consumption, but surplus produce will be sold at the food markets. Villagers note, however, that the garden surplus is diminishing with the loss of land. Reduced fish and garden yields are affecting social relations within and between communities, particularly in regard to exchange systems. Fish was once abundant and easily shared with others, and was often exchanged for garden food. Exchanging surplus produce for fish provided villagers who lived from their gardens with an important protein supplement for their diet and also, because garden produce is seasonal while fish stocks are available year round, provided important food sources when their own food supplies were low. With fish and garden food becoming scarcer, however, increasing numbers of people are turning to "development" to support their livelihoods, either working in paid employment at RD Tuna or in "spin-off" businesses. The community as a whole is becoming more and more dependent on income from the cannery, and the cash economy is supplanting former reciprocity-based systems of exchange and barter. Simultaneously, the decline in fish and garden resources means that supermarket food has become increasingly important. This in turn reinforces the need for a cash income.

Food is expensive, however, and when food costs are combined with the costs of school fees, medicines, and other staples, the result is that the community expe-riences intensely the squeeze of modern life. Wages at the fishery are very low and conditions poor. The company is increasingly taking over or creating its own "spin-off" businesses in breach of the commitment it made to the community when it first began its operations. The combined effect of an increased vulnerability in their food supply, indeed their livelihood, and the betrayal of the company's prior com-mitments explain why the community is so focused on the activities of the company for their survival. In 2003 a report by Nancy Sullivan concluded the following:

> Despite the social impact components inserted into the Environmental Plans of RD Tuna Canners Pty Ltd, and RD Fishing PNG, Pty Ltd, which generally dis-miss the possibility of substantive social effects, these companies have had a significant impact on the quality of life for their host communities. A number of environmental impacts have also had cultural effects, and despite complaints, the company has not made adjustments. Wastes disposal at both the Wharf and Cannery is making people sick, as are the noise and odor of these premises. Over-fishing has left little if any fish for these people to live on and conduct trade. Promises of material and developmental assistance from the company to the landowners have not been fulfilled. None of the schools, Aid Posts or churches has seen any real assistance since their arrival. The social breakdown of customary authority and family values is most alarming, and while some of this might be inevitable for any large development project, they have certainly been exacerbated by negligent company policies and the behavior of foreign company personnel. We find problems of workplace hygiene, social and sexual abuse of women, improper waste dumping, illicit sales of alcohol and ciga-rettes, disregard for landowner hiring preference practices, and the payment of sub-minimum wages.[1]

While we found nothing to suggest that company policies or behavior had substan-tially changed, the community is beginning to work out how it might respond and adapt in sustainable ways.

LEARNING AND EDUCATION

Within the Kananam communities, customary forms of learning and the pass-ing on of knowledge are weakening. Older members of the communities say that the younger generations lack interest in learning customary knowledge about things such as dancing, feasting, and festivals. While some skills continue to be passed down within families, there is a danger that many important forms of knowledge will be lost in part or in whole. At the same time, levels of formal education are not high. In comparison to the average results across all the research sites, there are few people in Kananam and its surrounds who have had no schooling. Only 3 percent of respondents to the questionnaire indicated that they had not completed any level of formal education. However, of those who have been educated within the formal system, the large majority—62 percent—have not progressed beyond the primary school level.

Some learning and training opportunities are available through government agencies, church programs, and nongovernmental organizations. Such opportunities, however, occur sporadically in response to particular issues arising in the region. Respondents to the questionnaire indicated a strong desire for more learning opportunities within their community. When asked which sorts of training would be useful for them, 65 percent of respondents said they would like training in family life, and 41 percent agreed that training in customary ways of doing things would be useful. In both instances, these figures were higher than the overall figures across all the research sites. Comparatively, respondents in Kananam were less likely to want training in agriculture and income generation, with 14 percent and 27 percent selecting these options. Smaller numbers again indicated a desire for training in technology, management, or literacy.

Partly in response to these community needs and as part of the ongoing response to social tensions and the presence of the cannery, community leaders have already initiated a Community Learning and Development Centre within Kananam. In a letter handed to the RMIT research team by Alexis Tokau in October 2007, it was apparent that the weight of responsibility was heavy and many community leaders were feeling something had to be done. Alexis wrote:

> I have taken this bold step to begin a CLDC (Community Learning and Development Centre) in the community....Our current leaders and the Councillor and SSD Cooperation have not come up with an alternative solution or action to address the issue. Further problem experience in the community is the divisions among clans (5 clans) and in families there is a strong influence on handful of elders who own spin-off business at RD Fishing and ignorant of the rest of the population. Confirm statement from our elders that the sex trade at RD Fishing Vidar is still continuing. Note that the company's operation is still continuing...females and school age children are being indirectly force to engage themselves in illegal activities. Lack of cooperation is a result of poor leadership....At the moment we are using the parish hall for our monthly meetings— *katholic mama group*. We can conduct training here...women are the backbone of families, communities and even the nation.

The sentiments expressed in the letter and the move to establish a Community Learning and Development Centre in Kananam correlate with the findings of the questionnaire, particularly the articulated need to build training around core issues affecting this community—the erosion of family and community life (see Chapter 12 on community learning centers). The letter also conveys the importance of women in organizing their community and responding to the forces threatening to pull it apart. Despite the many and varied challenges facing the villages in Kananam and its surrounds, the fact that the community is taking active responsibility to address them is exciting and points once again to the strengths existing in so many of Papua New Guinea's customary communities. If the determination and commitment of the community can be reinforced and supported through the findings of this research report, the Community Learning and Development Centre may well flourish. However, as subsequent developments indicate, this is not a straightforward process.

In 2007 Madang Township, fifteen minutes away, was chosen to be the site of a focal point for supporting community learning centers in the district. The first visit to Madang to meet with the provincial administration there took place in October 2007. Department for Community Development officers presented a draft version of the memorandum of agreement at that time, which was finalized during a second visit in January 2008. The provincial administrator directed the deputy administrator to take charge of the entire program and brought in a number of advisors from agriculture, health, education, community development, fisheries, and commerce, who were involved in the second round of negotiations. The provincial administration selected Madang town as the district for the focal point on the basis of its accessibility, and the district community development officer there became the focal point coordinator. The launch of the focal point took place in March 2008.

Significant problems emerged, however, with the model community learning and development center. Somehow, the site chosen to be the model community was not in fact a community but a physical space located within the Madang urban boundary, on which a building was constructed with funding from the Community Justice Liaison Unit, a PNG-based AusAID project. The site was on a road leading up to the prison camp, and the Community Justice Liaison Unit was hopeful that their staff would be able to use the space to run programs with young people in an effort to reduce law and order problems in the area. The involvement of the Community Justice Liaison Unit is in keeping with the vision for the Integrated Community Development Policy, but the selection of this site as a model community seems to indicate a misunderstanding of the community learning and development center concept. Community learning and development centers should be located within communities and established and operated by those communities. There is no problem with external funding being used to construct a building, but this essential feature of a community learning and development center is crucial to its sustainability. The role of the community itself is much more important than the building or facilities.

A customary dancer in Lae at one of the community development expos at which the Community Learning and Development Centre concept was developed

As it played out, there was insufficient consultation with the community on whose land the building was constructed. Far from them having a sense of ownership of it, conflicts emerged over the use of the land on which the focal point office was established. During a subsequent visit to the site, it was noticed that a line of young coconut trees had been planted, cutting off some of the land that the center was built on. Some community members mentioned that other elders were unhappy with the spot on which the center had been built. Shortly after that, the building was burned down. The effect was that no model community is operating in the district, and tensions have been generated among the local people. The progress since the building was burned down has been uneven.

Yalu Village and Surrounds, Morobe Province

IS IT POSSIBLE TO NEGOTIATE THE FUTURE BY GOING BACK TO THE PAST?

It is early afternoon at Yalu. The village is thick with discussion about reclaiming from the government what the people of Yalu see as nearly 359 acres of their customary land. One of the community leaders, Bing Sawanga, was at the helm of these negotiations as a representative of both the Aliwang Land Trust Committee and the Land Mobilization Committee. Buno Storm, an elder, comes out of one of the larger bush houses to greet us. Women busy themselves readying a meal. A hen scuttles past with one of the women in pursuit. "Your dinner," Buno Storm says, laughing loudly. As questions deepen around community responses to sustainability issues, Kolam Storm and Nawasi Bonnie, brother and youngest son of Buno Storm respectively, pick up the draft *Sustainable Communities* report and turn to the draft write-up of Yalu. They both pore over it—and every so often they talk between themselves.

Almost an hour passes—and, meanwhile, more people have started turning up at this end of the village. Many are women, and they sit around, talking to each other and sometimes with us. As we exchange stories of where we are from and of the different worlds we inhabit, Deckie Maino, leader of the local women's group and the village expert in making bread in local-made ovens, becomes reflective and asks us how we possibly thought we could understand what is happening in Yalu through such a short stay. It is hard to see how sharing food and talking might contribute to government policy supporting village sustainability. We explain why we have come back, this time with the draft report, and, in so doing, we are also learning more about the village. The other women nodded, and Deckie Maino laughed: "At least you come back and ask us whether you've got it right. We have to give you that. We must give you our famous chicken stew." There are loud responses that the stew is already on the fire.

As the food was eaten and then dishes cleared, the people gathered around. There were now about thirty people, and many settled back, chewing betel nut and looking toward Kolam Storm to begin. Earlier, we had asked if there was a particular story of their village and area that they wanted us to write into the profile of the place. There had been much discussion, and it seemed as if they had reached a consensus.

Long, long time ago in the time of our ancestors, one tribe-line lived in the mountains on top of the Yalu River. They called themselves the Ngalunuf. One day they went to see another family. The village was called Ngalugosol. They had a *sing-sing*—a *sing-sing* without drums, a *sing-sing* with *chuwen*.

Buno Storm explained that, when his ancestors heard the singing, they were surprised, as the people from Ngalugosol did not use a *kundu* (customary drum). Instead they were using something very different—a *chuwen*—a kind of a split drum made from black palm.

One day, the young men of Ngalunuf decided that they wanted to try the singing that they had heard the time when they went to Ngalugosol. Yet this time the people of Ngalunuf wanted to try these songs using the *kundu* drums. The young men waited until all the adults left the village to go and attend to their gardens. Once everyone had gone, the young men started singing and dancing what they had heard and seen from the Ngalugosol. A beautiful sound was created, which echoed throughout the surrounding area. Suddenly, realizing their singing and drumming could be heard, the young men stopped singing. The older men and women, returning from the gardens, asked these young men who was singing the beautiful songs in the village. The young men replied that they did not know who was singing.

These episodes continued many times, until one day the older men of Ngalunuf got tired and, wanting to find out who was singing, told an old lady to stay behind and hide in the house when all the men and women went to the garden. All the young men, thinking that everyone had gone to the garden as many times before, gathered together and began to sing. Little did they know that the old lady was watching them. In the late afternoon when all the men and women returned from their gardens, the old lady told the villagers what she had seen. She said that she saw all the young men singing and that they had all this time been hiding the truth. Once the men and women of Ngalunuf discovered that the young men of Ngalunuf were responsible for the singing, they became very angry.

Nawasi Bonnie, the young man, then continued the story.

The young men of Ngalunuf discussed what to do about the situation. They decided that, the next time that all the men went to the garden, the young men would get the married women and have their way with them. When the men came back from the garden that afternoon, the women told them of what had happened that day while they were at the garden and how the young men had assaulted them. The male elders of the village all met that night to discuss what punishment the young men deserved for the crime they had committed against the married women of the village. They decided that the young men should be banished from the village to go and live some place far away. The elders of the village called out for the young men to come and see them, telling them that because of the trouble they had caused, the young men were to leave the village forever and be banished far away from the village and find their own settling place. They heard their fate and left as requested and made a new home away from the village.

The young men stayed at their new home, yet the problem was that they had no women and could not create a new population for their new village. Then one day one of the young men went looking in the surrounding bush lands when he came across a bushman [magic man] called Mumulafa who held the ability to create black magic. Mumulafa was sitting up a tree with his powerful poison bag [a special *bilum,* or string bag, containing certain powers] hanging on a branch below. The young man quickly took the poison bag and ran as fast as he could all the way back to his village. When he arrived at the village, he informed the other young men of what had happened and told them to be ready to fight in case Mumulafa came back to retrieve his poison bag.

The young men waited on guard till it was nighttime, and the bushman arrived to be captured on arrival by the young men. Mumulafa pleaded not to be killed, and, in return for his poison bag, he would grant the young men what they needed for their survival. The bushman gave the young men many powers that they needed including the ability to create a productive garden, the ability to find animals easily while hunting, and also, most important, the ability to find women so as the tribe could grow and prosper. Mumulafa took back his poison bag as agreed and was about to leave when one of the young men shot Mumulafa with a bow and arrow and killed him. The other young men got up in anger and killed the young man who had killed Mumulafa. After the remaining young men used the magic that Mumulafa gave to them to get women, the young men were able to marry the girls and thus create the population for the new tribe. This village/clan to this day is called Ngaluwasuw [Mulamula].

Buno continued:

Our story tells of old ways and new beginnings—and also of old rules and new rules. But we are all linked, and we have to decide what rules to use and what stories to keep. This story was chosen by us to tell of our ways and of the ways we have to live with ourselves and with our new beginnings and endings. Even young people need rules. They have to make good rules themselves too.

The next day Nablu Sngat and Ezikiel Wallys, also of the Yalu village surrounds, gave us two written pieces of paper. "We have written out the story for you again in Pidgin, and this will help you to remember." The story recounted above is a combination of what we heard at the gathering at Yalu and what was retold in those two

pieces of paper. The story is an indirect telling of an ongoing process of social negotiation—including negotiation as basic as that involved in the setting up of clans in
the past. As in many of the stories we heard, there is an acute recognition of change
and the need to do something in the face of old and new complexities.

PLACE—PAST AND PRESENT

Yalu is located about seventeen kilometers out of the center of Lae along the
Lae-Madang and Highlands highway between the airport and the town. It is in the
Wampar local-level government, Huon District, in Morobe Province. Yalu is made
up of eight small community settlements ranging in population from nineteen to a
thousand people. These settlements, as in the story that Buno Storm and the others
unfolded to us, arose out of different circumstances and for different reasons. Yalu
village remains the central point, primarily because of its size and also because it
comprises members of the two most prominent clans—the Timkim clan and the
Konzorong clan. The settlements, according to the 2000 national population census report, include Yalu with 957 people in 160 households, Ambuasutz with 218
people in 33 households, Langalanga with 311 people in 62 households, Anund with
19 people in 3 households, Yalu Bridge with 184 people in 29 households, Parapi
with 326 people in 54 households, Yalu Plantation with 191 people in 42 households, and Junglik Plantation with 403 people in 76 households. In total, Yalu and
its surrounds consist of approximately 2,609 people and 460 households. These
settlements encompass the area where the Aliwang language has become the main
mode of communication. (According to one community member, "Aliwang" is a
word from the past. "Ali" refers to a shield made of wood, which was sometimes
used as a base to sleep on. "Wang" means to be on top, that is, to be ready to de-
fend your people.) The customary boundaries, now being negotiated, extend from
the ninth mile to the Nawaii Mountain boundary, from the back of West Taraka
down to the Markham River.

Yalu now has an estimated total population of 1,500. It is occupied by both the
local Aliwang people and settlers from other parts of Morobe, such as the Waingg
and Kabwum people, as well as people from other parts of the country. Yalu has
a large land area beginning at Nine Mile to Markham Bridge; extending over the
mountains to West Taraka, Bumayong, and Igam Army Barracks; and ending at
Muya Primary School along the Highlands highway. Because of this large unused
land area, most of it is occupied by settlers, especially from Nine Mile all the way
to Yalu along both sides of the highway. Landowners have until the recent past
"sold" their land to new settlers. The Aliwang people belong to thirteen main clan
groups. To list them is to give an impression of deep history, but they are also, as
we saw in the opening story, continuously in the process of change—the Ngalugosol (Timkim), Konzorong, Ngalukumbun, Chupeng, Alivis, Ngalumbas, Ngalunuf,

Ngalutumb, Ngaluwasuw, Mimin, Siwon, Zam, and Waril. Apart from the Aliwang language, Yalu people also speak the Yabem language, which is one of the two common languages spoken throughout the province along with Kote.

ORGANIZATION AND GOVERNANCE

People live in family groups and what they, using the language of contemporary anthropology, call "clans." A typical household comprises the elderly parents, their children, in-laws, and grandchildren. Some adult children have their own houses built next to their parents' homes. Young boys and unmarried men live in *haus bois*, which are usually in a central location close to the families. Girls and young women live with their parents in the family homes. Results from the Community Sustainability Questionnaire indicated that 59 percent of Yalu respondents identified their "neighborhood or place that you live" as their main source of community, as opposed to 28 percent overall across Papua New Guinea. Overall, respondents were much more likely to select "more than one of these" when given a list of possible sources of community (42 percent), suggesting that, in Yalu and its surrounds, there is perhaps a stronger identification with place as the locus of community than a particular group of persons. Almost all Yalu respondents (96 percent) were either satisfied or very satisfied with feeling part of the community, much higher than the overall PNG figure of 80 percent.

It was apparent that there was a great deal of community development activity in Yalu. On one of our visits, Ezkiel Wallys, coordinator of the women's group affiliated with Soroptimist Lae, an international NGO, provided a sheet of paper listing the number of activities and groups that are currently active in Yalu and the surrounds. These include six youth groups, Giamsao Women's Group, Aring Women's Group (affiliated with Soroptimist Lae), Aliwang Land Trust (affiliated with Ahi Land Mobilisation), law and order committees (twenty young men helping law and order committees as task officers),[2] small enterprises (Aliwang Holdings and Mopong Binis Group), Aliwang Cocoa Growers Association, twenty-one cocoa fermentaries,[3] with more in the pipeline, and a locally managed water control group that collects one kina per month for basic maintenance costs. The national Department of Health has also introduced and launched the "Healthy Island" concept to improve healthy living by building "VIP" ventilated pit toilets in the community. Like Vanagi Settlement in Port Moresby, this was a locale that had been the focus of a lot of government and NGO activity.

The community members were always ready to talk about local issues and to discuss how they were responding to these issues. As was common with other communities, the rise in local crime and youth-related violence was their main concern. Some of the women felt that there were now many more efforts to build new training programs and activities—currently the community was building a big training center on land that had been donated by the Timkim clan leader. The strong relationship with the local authorities was also evident in the number of programs and training activities that members of the community were able to attend or participate in as trainers.

LIVELIHOOD AND PROVISION

The majority of the people in Yalu are subsistence gardeners. They grow their own food, some look after chicken and pigs, and some grow cocoa and betel nut as cash crops. Some of the produce they consume themselves, and the surplus they sell at the main market in Lae. Some of the people rear chickens and pigs for local consumption, and a few have trade stores in the village. Many of the Yalu people earn their income through the sale of garden food at the market in Lae. When asked about their livelihood activities in the Community Sustainability Questionnaire, 74 percent of Yalu people said that they worked within the household, compared to 57 percent across all the research sites; 12 percent sold goods at market or on the street, compared to 23 percent overall; 9 percent received a wage from the state, compared to 7 percent overall; and 3 percent receive a wage from private business, which was on par with the overall average.

A number of local people earn income through a relationship with Niugini Table Birds, which has a huge factory a few kilometers down the highway. A contract with the company means building a chicken house and rearing the chickens that are provided by the company. It is an attractive contract, as the feed and everything else that is required in the rearing of the chickens is supplied. The income helps the family to buy other food and also to pay for expenses such as school fees and medicine. Twenty-one percent of people surveyed in Yalu said that the main place they got food was from local shops, and another 3 percent answered "food markets." At 70 percent, the proportion of people who got most of their food from their own lands or by fishing was lower than the overall result of 78 percent.

Overall, however, respondents in Yalu were largely positive about their households' economic well-being. Only 25 percent of respondents considered their household to be struggling financially, compared with 57 percent average across all locales. Seventy percent of respondents said they were comfortable, much higher than the overall 35 percent, and 5 percent said they were well off, compared to 8 percent across other locales. The proximity of Yalu to Lae and also its location immediately off the highway meant that there were better than average opportunities for travel to other places for jobs or to seek other sources of income. But the community as a whole is becoming more and more dependent on a cash income, and the cash economy was supplanting former reciprocity-based systems of exchange and barter. Young people were keen to experience life in the city, and there has been a slow increase in the number of young men and women seeking employment in Lae and also other places farther away.

LEARNING AND EDUCATION

Among respondents to the Community Sustainability Questionnaire, 46 percent of people in Yalu had completed primary school as their highest level of education, which was slightly higher than the overall figure of 42 percent. Levels of secondary education were lower, at 28 percent compared to 33 percent overall; however, a higher proportion of people in Yalu—17 percent compared to the overall average of 13 percent—had received some sort of trade training.

When asked what kinds of training or learning would be considered particularly helpful, agricultural training was most sought after by people in Yalu. Seventy-three percent of people thought this would be useful, compared to the figure of 53 percent across all the research sites. The next most popular area for training was in management, which 22 percent of people thought would be useful (just under the overall figure of 27 percent). Training in income generation was desired by 18 percent of people, which was considerably less than the 35 percent overall figure. Sixteen percent of people wanted training in technology, with the same percentage again expressing a desire for training in each of family life, customary ways of doing things, and literacy.

A few existing small-scale training activities are being run by nongovernmental organizations in the area, and the women in Yalu seem particularly active in building networks and partnerships with local government and organizations. In 2007, for instance, a learning center was being built, focusing primarily on training skills for women. This activity is coordinated by the Timkim clan, and the site for the center is on Timkim land. In October 2007, during one site visit by the research team, it was apparent that the basic structural foundations were in place. A couple of capable and strong community leaders were playing a critical part in organizing funding opportunities and addressing community needs, and two trained teachers were ready to teach adult literacy classes as soon as the building was ready. It was also evident in Yalu that, in addition to specific skills training and learning activities, a lot of activities take place related to educating and organizing people in dealing with the issues of landownership and the reclaiming of customary land.

Much education and learning takes place outside of formal schooling and modern training activity, and some of the most vital local knowledge and skills are passed down from fathers to sons and from mothers to daughters. Skills in making gardens and planting certain local vegetables, for instance, are passed down within families. Likewise, special skills like black magic and sorcery are also passed down through specific and selected individuals within the family group. Some of the people in Yalu, however, suggested that respect for elders and customary knowledge seem to be waning, and many of the elderly people said that the young people in the community are not interested in learning or knowing about customary things. They say young people have lost the respect and value of customs. Western values have influenced the way they behave, and customary values are slowly diminishing. They said customary values should be preserved within the community. Nevertheless, it is obvious that rituals and stories have not lost their place in community life. The retelling of the story of the young men of Ngalunuf—the ancient legend, as the storytellers called it—and the way it was considered relevant to contemporary times, gives a good indication of the continuing use of stories to negotiate change. Even more significant was the cross-generational collectivism that accompanied the recounting of the story to the people gathered around: while it was an old man who began the tale, it was a younger man who picked up the narration and continued with it.

Notes

1. Nancy Sullivan, N. T. Warr, Joseph Rainbubu, J. Kunoko, F. Akauna, M. Angasa, and Yunus Wenda, "A Social Impact Study of Proposed RD Tuna Cannery at Vidar Wharf, Madang," unpublished report for Bismarck Ramu Group and Gadens Ridgeway Attorneys at Law, 2003, p. 12. See also Nancy Sullivan, Joseph Rainbubu, Kritoe Keleba, Yunus Wenda, and Chris Dominic, *European Union's Rural Coastal Fisheries Development Project Baseline Study: Follow-up RRA for Madang*, Nancy Sullivan Ltd., Madang, 2004.

2. Interestingly, though, 39 percent of respondents from Yalu were dissatisfied or very dissatisfied with their feeling of safety, compared to 12 percent overall. It is possible that these task forces are new activities introduced to respond to the feelings of insecurity in the area and among the communities. The first visit and survey was conducted in early 2006, and the second visit was in mid-2007.

3. In 1950 approximately 150 "fermentaries" that had existed for fermenting cocoa were closed down by colonial authorities. In 1978 the village decided to rebuild, and currently there are 21 small ones functioning.

Chapter 5

Hinterland Communities

Tokain Group of Villages, Madang Province

CAN A STRONG SHARED IDENTITY PROVIDE A BASIS FOR PROJECTING A FUTURE?

The villagers are gathering slowly in the new community learning center, which they built themselves in early 2006. The people here are from the Tokain group of villages. There are three main villages in the Tokain group—Tokain 1, Tokain 2, and Simbukanam—and another cluster of villages in the surrounds—Malas, Dibor, Imbab, and Yambrik. These villages fall into wards 4 and 5 of the Sumgilbar local-level government within the Sumkar District on the northwest coast of Madang Province. The people who live in these villages are creating a shared identity together and increasingly call themselves the Gildipasi people. The name says it all. The word "Gildipasi" is drawn from the first letters of the Gilagil River, the Dibor River, Palesal Creek, the Sinkum Ranges, and the Iariniari Ranges—natural landmarks bordering the area where the Gildipasi clans live. In keeping with the complexity of the place, the name is a self-conscious and modern designation but one that builds on negotiated customary relations.

Gildipasi began in 1984 as an informal local community group in response to the impact of outside forces on community livelihood and customary ways of life. It is now a central community organization. Of particular concern to the group are the impacts of long-term logging in the area and proposed new deep-sea mining ventures. In responding to these threats, the Gildipasi people are drawing strongly on their customary values and ways of being in order to protect their right as a community to determine their own future. The new center that the Tokain 1 community have built is a place to gather, learn, and organize. It is also, the villagers say, for visitors: "So that they have a place of their own—and then are able to join us for our gatherings. It is not a long walk to the sea from here. The visitor can cross the road that divides Tokain 1 and Tokain 2, and go down to the river. Or else one can walk down from Simbukanam to the river from the other side."

It is a Sunday, and the community is walking toward the community center after their usual Sunday church service. The church is located at the end of Tokain 2—a large shed that has rows of benches and a slightly elevated platform at the top end. A photo of Christ and a crucifix on a small table seem to be the only signs of an altar. The hamlets of Tokain 1, Tokain 2, and Simbukanam are close to each other, though Simbukanam is located on the hill-ward side. Villagers gather at the church service from all of these places, representing the many clans that coexist in this place—Baine, Inong Gomang, Yadigam, Dimon, Dalem, Kalasika, Ameng, and Munuguwin. The service is attended by more than a hundred villagers, and the sermon is conducted by a local villager, an initiated preacher who speaks fierily about sin and redemption. On the way back to the learning center together with some members of the church, we visit a grieving household. A young couple has just lost their firstborn to a bout of malaria—a young child, five years old. Someone says that at least seven to eight children die every year from malaria in this small cluster of villages. The child, wrapped in a blanket, lies in her mother's arms, and the grief is intense. After a while with the family, we continue on to the community center in Tokain 1, and the walk is somber.

There are about forty villagers gathered at the community center when we arrive. They sit on the sand floor—some chewing betel nut and some eating fruits and nuts. They are mostly men, but slowly a group of older women come in and sit down, followed in about ten minutes by some younger women and children. After the austere service and the visit to the stricken family, the mood of the gathering is measured. But after a while the room fills up and the meeting begins. When they are more than eighty people in the center, one of the community leaders jumps up and introduces himself as Alfred Kaket, one of the leaders of the Gildipasi community movement. After introductions, Alfred plunges into the purpose for the gathering, which is to respond to the interim draft sustainable communities research report that we have brought back to the community groups for their feedback and input. Alfred tells us, "We like the way the communities you are working with have been written about, and we have suggestions on some changes. But so much has changed too. We are in the middle of new struggles to keep our lives together. Our lands, our rivers, our sea continue to be exploited, and we continue to be left outside any discussions by both the government and the development corporations."

One by one, community members get up to give their stories of changes and developments, of ways that they are trying to work together so that their lives in this small cluster of villages do not degenerate even further into "chaos" and "decay." Soon the discussion moves to questions of community and the diversity of communities that live in Papua New Guinea. "How do different groups and regions identify themselves?" "In what ways can people work collectively and effectively yet hold on to their own history, cultural identity, and rituals?" These questions spark many responses, and the women join in, saying that it is important for their children to know where they come from. Nobody seems keen to venture into the cities of Port Moresby and Lae, and they speak strongly of many young people who have been lost in the unrelenting, uncompassionate cities, plagued by crime and clan fights.

Suddenly one of the elders stands up and begins to speak about the old traditions and how the Gildipasi are trying to bring these back in a way that will help the people. We ask more questions and share our own stories of the cultural rituals in the places we come from, and there is laughter and cheering as these exchanges lead to theatrical expressions and impromptu performances. Pigs tusks, dogs teeth, shells from the back of native snails—the people try to describe these items of significant cultural importance. Soon Alfred Kaket stands up and says, "We will show you how we now will use these deep and important cultural items together as a way we wish to be seen in the modern world. Gildipasi will wear this as our emblem—the carrying of our old ways into the new world." He then turns to Papa Paul Kodang, an elder in the gathering, and requests him to show us what this emblem would look like. Papa Paul Kodang gets up and disappears from the community center. No one speaks during the time he is away, as if unsure whether he will return. He does return, holding some items in his hand. He removes his shirt and puts them around his neck, reciting a verse in Pidgin. The crowd cheers and stands up. There is a fever of excitement, a sense of camaraderie. We ask Alfred Kaket's nephew to help us write down what is said. He writes, "We are happy for you to take this as our symbol, our expression into the world as the Gildipasi people of Papua New Guinea." He speaks in a mixture of Tok Pisin and English:

> Dispela pig teeth na dok teeth na bilas blong em i stap wantaim. Insait long Gildipasi dispela pig teeth na dokteet em soim custom pasin bilong olgeta clans i kamap wanbel na wokbung wantaim long olgeta kainkain wok. Dispela pik teet na dok teet mipela I still usim nau, long dispela taim yet. Na dispela (symbol) sign em I powerful insaoit long Gildipasi.

These pig tusks, these dog teeth, and the decorations—they all belongs to us. Inside Gildipasi these pig tusks and dog teeth show everything about our culture and custom. It belongs to us, all the clans. It shows how we all work together as one in all sorts of ways and types of work. These pig tusks and dog teeth are still used before and still used for us today—and for a long time yet.

These dog teeth and pig tusks are a powerful symbol for Gildipasi now and for a long time to come.

PLACE—PAST AND PRESENT

To get to the Tokain group of villages from Madang, one has to drive along the coastal road for close to two hours. Tokain 1 consists of a circle of about twelve huts resting on stilts enclosed by a scanty belt of shrubs and straggly trees. A larger atypical hut rests on the ground; this is the new Community Gathering and Learning Center. Currently, five out of the eight Gildipasi-linked villages have built their own centers—the latest being the one at Tokain 2, which opened in November 2008. The old learning center at Simbukanam, the neighboring village, is now used more as a storage place. As the central meeting place for the activities of the cluster of villages, Tokain 1 is seen as the more strategic place to build a learning center. Just a short walk away is the beach and the small freshwater estuary that doubles as a washing place for the villagers, particularly the women.

There are two main clans in Tokain 1—the Baine and the Inong Gomang. In Tokain 2, the four main clans are the Yadigam, Dimon, Dalem, and Kalasika. And then in Simbukanam are the Ameng and Muniguwin. While the Gildipasi organization offers a modern structural response to developments and issues in the area, it is also evident that customary structures underpin the community fabric. Although Gildipasi rests on customary (clan) leadership, there is no singular paramountcy claim within the area; currently the Ameng and Baine clans have taken leadership roles in building the next stage of Gildipasi.

Customary land boundaries, rising from the Sinkum and Iarinyari Ranges and descending into the surrounding Gilagil and Dibor Rivers and Palesal Creek, are being recovered as the markers of a shared space within which the Gildipasi clans meet together to debate and discuss their livelihood and their responses to developments both from within and from outside of the province. At Tokain 1, a group of villagers gather around a small fire, which, apart from the moon, is the main source of light. As introductions abound, it is obvious that there are others here from the surrounding villages—Tokain 2, Simbukanam, Malas, Dibor, Imbab, and Yambarik. Conversation centers on developments in the area, particularly the selling of *buai* to the people from the Highlands. The elders here are worried about the discrepancies in the prices that locals are being paid for their *buai*, which are beginning to cause rifts among the clans.

A twenty-minute walk from Tokain 1 is Sumer, one of the hamlets of Simbukanam, named after the first breadfruit tree. Sumer mainly houses members of the Kaket family. Activity is centered on a main cooking and meeting place. Here many of the Kaket family members are involved late into the evening in the discussion around issues and opportunities in the area, as all of the brothers—Alfred, Lawrence, and Ortwin—are also leaders in the Gildipasi movement. Simbukanam is located on a small hill and has a population of about eighty people. This peaceful village experienced its share of negative impact from development projects, especially environmental destruction and associated social disorder as the result of logging in the early 1980s. According to the village leaders, their limited water system was polluted and almost destroyed, and social problems such as alcohol and drug abuse linked to the logging operations would have destroyed the peaceful livelihoods of the people if not for the actions of the community leaders.

ORGANIZATION AND GOVERNANCE

The community in the Tokain group of villages is a complex one, with multiple layers of organization and identification. The broad community brings together the residents of eight villages, with each village a distinct unit of identification, itself consisting of several clans. Within each village, family ties form the foundation of households, with groups of households bringing together entire extended families, including parents, grandparents, siblings, children, and brothers and sisters of spouses. The Kaket family is an example—making up the hamlet of Simbukanam. Multilayered connections and identities are maintained through complex relationships, from the everyday lived reciprocity of cooking, gardening, fishing, and child care within families through to the broader relationships of exchange and communication between villages and clans. There is an apparent ease in the way communities move across the eight villages and retain a sense of a collective place. In conversations, people are almost always introduced according to which village they come from and who they are related to, and it is easy to see the extensive connections between and across the different villages, created through intermarriages and involvement in the many community activities.

The community leaders believe in having recognized and respected structures blending customary and modern leadership roles. While they respect the customary leadership structure, they have also established community improvement committees to address concerns and issues brought about by the development processes. Leaders assist and complement one another in organizing and coordinating community activities. The committee consists of the two chiefs who advise on customary laws and two clan leaders who represent the people of their respective clan including children. Community-group representatives include the following:

- youth representative
- women's representative
- school board representative
- community health representative

- environment representative
- agriculture representative
- church representative
- law and order representative

Results of the Community Sustainability Questionnaire indicated high levels of well-being among villagers in the Tokain group of villages. Ninety percent of respondents were either satisfied or very satisfied with their community neighborhood, much higher than the figure of 72 percent recorded for all the research sites. Eighty-eight percent were satisfied or very satisfied with their feeling of safety. These results, together with the information gathered through qualitative conversations and interviews, point to a strong sense of community cohesion and shared identity.

Community activities are important in bringing people together from the different clans and villages in the area, and young people appear to be involved in these activities alongside adults. More than half of the people who attended the five-hour discussion held by researchers at the Tokain 1 community center were youth and young adults. They participated in the conversations and were keen to provide their input and ask questions. The story of the pig tusks and dog teeth emblem of the Gildipasi movement was narrated by a boy—who then spent an hour or so writing down the meaning for the researchers. The participation of community members in issues relating to their locality reflects a high level of engagement in local issues as well as an increasing disengagement with directives and promises that come from either logging companies or government representatives.

Bringing together all of the villages and clans, Gildipasi is now the dominant site of organization and community identity. It has also located itself at the center of community governance structures, underpinned by the existing forms of customary tribal leadership and organization. For instance, elders from the two more active clans in the area are at the center of the Gildipasi leadership. At the same time, Gildipasi is consciously responding to the forms of power and organization within the postindependence PNG state and nation. In a working document prepared by the Gildipasi people, they write:

> Gildipasi finds its roots in the original visions of Papua New Guinea's constitutional fathers, as stipulated in the preamble to PNG's national constitution and of PNG as a sovereign national state. Gildipasi does not stand alone, but as a people's initiative to actualize what the constitutional fathers wanted to see happen. And more specifically, Gildipasi is based on the fifth national goal of PNG—to achieve development primarily through the use of Papua New Guinean forms of social, political and economic organization. "We see true social security and happiness being diminished in the name of economic progress.

We caution therefore that large scale industries should be pursued only after very careful and thorough consideration of the likely consequences upon the economic, social and spiritual fabric of our people...." Gildipasi will not be registered. [The reference here is to the current agenda to register customary land.] As much as we want to move forward and keep up with rapidly changing times, we exist as a community collective, open to working with outsiders, as long as these outsiders do not push their agendas and motives.[1]

The community groups are highly conscious of the need to take responsibility for their own well-being and the sustainability of their environment, as many development projects continue to proliferate around them with an apparent disregard for genuine collaboration with the local communities who have lived here for generations. The community member Yat Paol from Tokain 1 village, who is one of the advisors for Gildipasi's executive group, works as an advocacy and campaigns officer with a local NGO called the Bismarck Ramu Group, located in Madang. Speaking to the research team in 2006, Yat said:

The most significant challenge in working with communities is the rate of change triggered by large-scale development. Community facilitation can be very time-consuming. It takes time to build strong relationships with communities. If another group comes in offering "projects," it can easily undermine their work. Globalization is part of this challenge. There is now a constant movement of information and people in and out of communities, which can influence the way that communities think about the present and their future. There is also a growing concern with new forms of exchange and trade—even at the very local everyday level of community life.

Yat gave as an example the new forms of global "environmentalism" such as carbon-credit schemes, whereby countries such as Papua New Guinea are made to believe that they will receive cash for preserving their forests. He emphasized that this is not appropriate development but a modern form of cargo culture. "Like an aid program, it means that some communities can receive cash for doing nothing at all."

In the Bismarck Ramu Group, as in Gildipasi, villagers and community members are operating with a critical and reflexive understanding of development, based on a sophisticated sense of the global and regional context shaping local well-being and livelihoods, even in such a remote and isolated part of Papua New Guinea. They also have a critical understanding of government and the state. As Yat Paol put it in an e-mail to one of the researchers involved in this project, "It is a thing these days that an NGO finds a reason to applaud government." This sentiment was echoed in the questionnaire results. When asked how much they agreed with the statement "Governments make decisions and laws that are good for the way I live locally," only 24 percent of respondents from the Tokain group of villages agreed or strongly agreed, compared to the overall figure of 43 percent across all the research sites. As many as 46 percent of respondents disagreed or strongly disagreed, as opposed to 35 percent across all the research sites.

Gildipasi asserts its right to determine its own future rather than have the PNG government and international and multinational organizations make decisions on their behalf. This right of self-determination includes not just economic independence, but also social security mechanisms and political autonomy (at the local level). The organization has structured its responses to incursions from the outside around the vital components that the Gildipasi people believe are the foundations of their community life. These include youth, women, culture, health, education, religion, law and justice, land and environment, agriculture and business, and governance.

When new leadership took over during the early 2000s, the Gildipasi Planning Committee became known for several years as the Gildipasi Welfare Foundation. Some community members joined to form a local cooperative, now named Gildipasi Resources Limited, which was then registered as a company with the Investment Promotion Authority. This company focuses on buying dried and processed copra from local farmers and growers within the Gildipasi area and selling this in bulk to the copra mill in Madang. As Peter Bunam, the chairman of Gildipasi, said:

> We no longer want to rely on outside forces to decide our lives. The Gildipasi Planning Committee, which began as a pressure group back in 1984, was an initiative of the people, by the people, and for the people. We believe in people power and in working together. We have had ups and downs—and the movement had its difficulties especially when our prominent leader passed away. But we revived ourselves in 2002, and, at a meeting on 13 January 2006, the executives of Gildipasi were elected by the people. Gildipasi was recognized and accepted by the people as Gildipasi business arm—and that the executive would act for the interest and well-being of the whole Gildipasi area.

Throughout our conversations, however, people stated that they still had a long way to go.

LIVELIHOOD AND PROVISION

The people of Gildipasi are primarily subsistence farmers using slash-and-burn swidden methods. Men and boys help to clear the bush on the new garden plots and burn the dried leaves and stacks, and the women and girls do the planting and weeding of the gardens. Men make banana gardens, while women and girls plant other vegetable gardens such as beans, greens, *kaukau*, taro, and tapioca. Among respondents to the Community Sustainability Questionnaire, 96 percent said that the main place they got their food was from work done on their own land or by fishing. Sixty-nine percent listed work within the household (including gardens) as their main way of making a living. Another 19 percent said they sold goods at market or on the street, while another 10 percent worked for a wage from a private business or the state, were a casual laborer or service worker, or ran a business. Many people also undertake informal income-generating activities such as selling betel nut, local fruits, clothes, or cooked food by the roadside, although these may happen sporadically and are not necessarily a main form of livelihood activity.

The main source of income for families in the community comes from marketing copra, cocoa, and garden produce. Crafts such as string bags are also a source of income. String bags (*bilums*) are made from the bark of special trees, softened and rolled by the women and then woven into the bags. *Bilum* making is one specific skill that the womenfolk are required to learn. Women have been involved in processing *noni* products (medicinal *Morinda citrifolia* also used in other villages such as Boera, discussed below) for use in bath soap and oil, which has a ready market. They are the main sellers at the local food markets. Decisions regarding the spending of family income are made by both parents, but many times women, being the main sellers, make independent decisions on spending money on the most needed items for their families, and the men respect those decisions.

A decade of logging in the area—which followed from a series of what are now seen as naive negotiations on the part of the community—has had a significant influence on the livelihoods of people in the Tokain area villages and the ways that they are reconstructing these now. Two Simbukanam clans (Ameng and Munuguwin) and one Imbap clan (Saingham) set up and signed the first conservation deed among themselves. The Gildipasi people set up the second conservation deed in Papua New Guinea and began earnestly to deal with the multitude of social and environmental problems that such intense logging has caused in their once pristine and dense rain forests. Working now with the new environmental "slow crises" of declining water quality, loss of access to fresh water, new types of weeds encroaching onto gardens, and chemical run-off, among other issues, they are only too aware of the hard work ahead. While they are not opposed to development itself, the central question is what form such development takes and how it can be negotiated by much more informed local communities, not just at the level of galvanized community leaders.

The growth of a cash economy and increased movement of people and goods across the region are other factors affecting the livelihood activities of the Tokain area people, sometimes with disturbing results. An interesting yet troubling new development is the growing corridors of resentment and contempt emerging around the selling of betel nut to the people from the Papua New Guinean Highlands, where betel nut is not available. People spoke of Highlanders buying betel nut for a low price from the local people only to sell it for a massive profit when they return home. What was once a relatively easy trade of a sack or two of betel nut from a collective household to a buyer from the Highlands is now much more complex, and social tensions are arising. This was illustrated when one of the research team members—a PNG resident from Morobe—went down to the river for a swim only to notice a number of local youths leave the river as soon as they saw him enter the water. Later, when they saw him at the discussions in the village, they came up and apologized, saying, "We thought that you were one of the people from the Highlands, and we don't want to bathe in the same river with the Highlanders. They are cheating us." These divisions are growing and echo the rumbling hostilities between Highlanders and Papuans in the Central Province region. Community members in Gildipasi described a climate of growing intimidation by the Highlanders but also noted that, while many betel-nut growers have felt unable to renegotiate their prices, some are now slowly responding to the price discrepancies by refusing to sell their betel nut to these buyers.

LEARNING AND EDUCATION

Within the Tokain group of villages, as across Papua New Guinea, the Church—here the Catholic Church—plays a major role in learning and education activities. Sundays are organized around the church service, and there is a flurry of activity as children are bathed and clothed in their formal church outfits for the service. Along the road to the church, greetings are exchanged and information is shared regarding the next meeting for *bilum*-making classes as well as other community activities. On one occasion, Alice Kodang, one of the graduates who had recently participated in literacy training, reminded some of the young children about the literacy class that they had missed recently. An adult literacy, teacher-training class had been conducted at Madang Open University campus in November 2006, and, with the support of Gildipasi, the eight young women who attended this class established literacy schools at Tokain 1, Dibor, Simbukanam, and Imbap. Alice is about twenty-two years of age. After finishing high school, she was trained locally through the Tokain learning center to run literacy classes for young children up to the age of twelve. But she is frustrated, wanting to move further in her studies and training skills. She is keen to become a primary school teacher, but rising expenses and a lack of security for young women in cities like Port Moresby and Lae where such training is available make this difficult. Alice awaits anyone who comes in from the outside, eager to absorb and learn anything new, anything useful that she can pass on to her young learners.

Several community development courses and skills training programs are regularly run in the area, stimulated by discussions at Gildipasi meetings and assisted through the community's partnership with the Bismarck Ramu Group NGO. Before the first research project visit in 2006, the community had just completed a weeklong awareness workshop on the World Bank and the International Monetary Fund run by the Bismarck Ramu Group. There are also workshops on health issues, food values, and cooking. Training sessions and workshops have shown participants how to use existing knowledge to enable small income-generating activities. Customary arts are highly valued in the community, and there is a keen interest to pass on customary knowledge to the younger generation. Such knowledge includes crafts such as *bilum* making, painting, and basket weaving but also the use of building materials such as rafters, "totem poles" (pillars), and boats.

Some of the women in the community discussed the need for more classes and skills training in a wide range of topics and areas. They mentioned cooking and sewing but also leadership, bookkeeping, report writing, awareness on the rights of women and children, combating violence against women, environmental issues, and basic literacy. Women also expressed a desire to build more confidence to participate actively in community development activities, including decision-making processes. The fact that one of the Gildipasi women was elected treasurer of the organization demonstrated that space was available for women to be involved, and women are slowly building the courage and capacity to take on leadership positions in the community.

Learning and education—formal, nonformal, customary, and modern—will continue to be a vital part of the Gildipasi struggle, providing the community with tools to better negotiate their place in a changing world. In the words of the chairperson of Gildipasi:

> What will we do? How will we move forward? These are our constant questions. We have good land, good working knowledge—and we are coordinated. We have managed to stop the main logging company and are alert to the subsidiary companies that they form to trick us. Many of our people have been led astray by the presence of money when the logging started. We have lost many, especially our older men, to drugs and alcohol. No more! We are alert!

Boera Village, Central Province

IS IT POSSIBLE TO NAVIGATE BETWEEN CUSTOMARY COSMOLOGIES,
TRADITIONAL BIBLICAL UNDERSTANDINGS, AND MODERN LEARNING?
On the *patapata* in front of Lady Moi's house in Boera village sat two books.
The first was *Buka Helaĝa, Taravatu Gunana bona Taravatu Matamatana* (Book of
God, Old and New). The second book, *Ane* (Song), was the hymn book of the Unit-
ed Church of Papua New Guinea and the Solomon Islands. Both are translated into
the local Motu language, and they reflect the strength and place of Christianity in
the local community. The first song in the hymn book is a simple four-line song:

Namo badina, Dirava,	It is good being beside God,
Iboudai aita hanmoa;	All of us should rejoice;
Toi tamona, Tamana,	Three in one, the Father,
Natuna, Lauma Helaĝa.	The Son, and the Holy Spirit.

Within the Boera community, the members of the three-hundred-strong Wom-
en's Fellowship do rejoice in the sense of common purpose they share. The fellowship is one of three ministries within the Boera church, forged from both a tribal-
traditional and a modern sense of the sacred. Like their mothers and grandmothers
before them, the women of the fellowship are strong. They rejoice in their faith, and
they rejoice in their ancestral connection to the land and the sea. Yet there is also
a deep sadness within the fellowship as it struggles to hold on to its customary
practices and keep its families safe.

For centuries, the women in Boera held their community tight as their menfolk
went off to fish and trade, sometimes for months on end. Now, there are new forces
pulling people away from the village—boarding schools, the lure of paid employment, the night lights of Port Moresby. But the pulling away is always matched by a
coming home of sorts. And today, a handful of women sit on the *patapata*, next to
the Bible and the hymn book waiting for the return of the body of a young woman,
a victim of Papua New Guinea's growing AIDS epidemic. She was one of a group of
women who moved to the city together, working as barmaids and sending money
home to their families in the village. In the last year alone, three of them have died
in the same terrible way. A fourth woman—still alive, but very sick—has also come
back to Boera.

In the past, when the men from the village went fishing, they took with them in
their *lakatoi*s (canoes) clay pots made by women in the village. The pots were used
for carrying water and food, and storing the fish that were caught. They were also
the central item in the famous Hiri trade between the Motuan people and those
of the Papuan Gulf villages. Along with the Trobriand Kula Ring (see Chapter 6)

Road repairs, seen on the way to Boera village, are being funded by the Chinese government's aid program. Papua New Guinea remains massively dependent on international aid. More recently, royalties from the Liquefied Natural Gas Project are being used to upgrade roads, but that revenue brings its own problems.

the Hiri trade is the most documented trade cycle in Papua New Guinea. William Robinson, writing in 1888, records that "with a fine wind Yule was soon passed, and at Delena they met four large canoes with Boera natives who had purposed going on to Maiva, but were told to return by the great Yule sorcerer, because he did not receive an arm shell large enough to satisfy him."[2] Once a year, groups of men set out in *lakatois* filled with clay pots to follow the southeast wind down to the Papuan Gulf, where they traded the pots for sago. This kept the men away for months. It was dangerous, too, and the stormy voyage home often brought with it the loss of life. Back then, clay-pot making was a sacred act. For those who partook in that business, there were certain moral values and obligations to follow. When the men set out in the *lakatoi*, their wives would remain inside the house, abstain from bathing in the sea, and not cut or comb their hair. They ate only vegetables and had their bodies tattooed with tribal designs. It was through their commitment to the sacred traditions and practices that their husbands were protected. If a woman acted outside the moral code, the men would not be successful and the *lakatoi* would not be safe. The women's strength and respect for the sacred was what ensured the safe return of the menfolk to the village.

Today, there is only one woman left in Boera who knows how to make clay pots in the old way. A whole generation of women missed out on the passing of the skills, drawn away from the village to study at boarding schools. Vicki Avei, a female leader in Boera and an active member of the Women's Fellowship, tells the story:

> It's a sad thing that most of us missed out on this. The education system came in, and all of a sudden the girls were beginning to understand and wanted to be educated. In those days our schools were always boarding schools, we never had a school in the village. The older women who were trying to teach the younger women could not, because they were not there. There's a big gap, and the gap is where I start from.

Cultural and ritualistic laws govern the passing of this customary skill. Only women from families whose *lakatoi*s were successful in the old voyages are able to be teachers, and there are limitations on who can learn and when. But Vicki and other women like her are coming back to Boera to try and fill the gap. The Women's Fellowship runs workshops to teach clay-pot making, along with other skills and practices that used to be shared among the women in the old times. And now there is a school in the village, so girls can be educated and still learn the customary skills.

Each week, the women in the Fellowship pool a percentage of the money they earn from selling the fish that their husbands catch. They use these funds to pay for training for women in the village, for a local health center, and for repairs to buildings in the community. Under the auspices of the church, they follow a service program—visiting hospitals, taking care of the sick and vulnerable, cleaning the school. And now, faced with a new threat to their community, they are organizing AIDS awareness programs, training women from all seven clans in Boera so they can disseminate that knowledge within their own families. Like their mothers and grandmothers before them, the women in Boera are holding their village tight. People will keep being pulled away—in search of fish, or work, or adventure—but it is the women who keep struggling for their safe return.

Later in the afternoon, the body of the young woman is brought back to the village. A number of the older women and the younger women are there to support her family. They cook, and bring the food to the mourning house where her body lays. They sit together outside the house, waiting, holding their community tight once more. Later she will be buried in the village cemetery, underneath the frangipani trees, just meters from the house where the old woman still makes her clay pots.

PLACE—PAST AND PRESENT

Boera is an indigenous Motu village nestled on the Papuan coast, about an hour's drive northwest from Port Moresby. It is a well-organized community, with a population of over nine hundred people from seven different clans. The roads leading into Boera from the main road are in poor condition (although that will change as the Liquefied Natural Gas project is developed), but the village does have electricity, running water, and a number of significant community assets. Its multipurpose community hall is one of the largest buildings on the Papuan coast and is used by people from throughout the area. Located next to it is a medical aid post, where government health workers provide treatment and medication. The aid post is adequately stocked with basic medical supplies, including equipment for pregnancy testing. In the center of the village are the church and the pastor's house.

To one side of the church, white sand leads down to the coast and the ocean; to the other side, the village stretches inland, with houses and gardens visible in the foreground and hills behind them. Motu people customarily built their houses on stilts extending over the sea—which offered protection from witchcraft and magic—and many of the houses in Boera are still built in this way, constructed from a combination of bush and modern materials. Increasingly, however, houses are being built inland, the result of a growing population and also a strategy for securing land and restricting the capacity of migrants to occupy customary lands.

Most of the inland area around Boera is covered by savannah grassland. Topographic work in a 1978 survey by the Royal Australian Survey Corps (RASC) indicated the presence of medium-level forest coverage across the hills at that time. The survey also showed a stream running from a catchment at the foot of the Udabada hill, through the village and down to the sea. Historically, the creek was an important resource for the Boera people, who used it to float timbers from the forest to build houses and *lakatoi* canoes as well as for drinking, cooking, and washing. Since the time of the RASC survey, however, the creek has all but dried up. Anecdotal evidence pointing to prolonged droughts and extended dry seasons might provide some explanation for this, but it is also likely the result of deforestation around the catchment area. The forests have been significantly depleted by the demand for timber for building and firewood, the clearing of forests for gardens, and the use of land for houses.

Boera is a customary Melanesian coastal village with many of its houses still built on stilts. This once peaceful village was recently the site of violence clashes over the proceeds of the Liquefied Natural Gas Project.

Despite the expansion of the village inland, however, this remains a community very much oriented toward the sea. Fishing remains the basis of most people's livelihoods, and the relationship to the ocean is at the heart of the Boera people's identity and history, even if the connection between current practices and that history is now attenuated. The Hiri trade between the Motuan and Kerema people of the Papuan Gulf was stopped by the colonial administration in the late 1950s. (See also the profile on Yule Island in relation to the origins of Boera.) Each year, men had traveled in *lakatois*, carried by the southeast wind, the *lahara*, down to the Gulf of Papua, where they traded clay pots. The men would spend two or three months in the Gulf doing repairs on their canoes and building relationships with the traders, waiting for the change in seasons that brought with it the west winds needed for the voyage home but also storms and heavy seas. The return trips were dangerous, and, laden down with extra cargo, *lakatois* often sunk on their way back up the coast.

According to the oral history of the Hiri trade, the first *lakatoi* was built by a man from Boera, Edai Siabo. When returning from a fishing trip one day, a huge eel appeared, dragging him under the surface of the sea. When the eel brought Edai back up, it instructed him to build a huge double-hulled canoe, fill it with clay pots, and follow the *lahara* southeast toward the Gulf. The first *lakatoi* was called *Bogebada* (which means sea eagle in Motu), and it was filled with pots made by Edai's wife. He instructed her to stay in the house for the whole period he was away, not to bathe in the sea, to keep track of the days he was away, to keep a fire burning, and to have her skin tattooed by an old woman. The crew was away for months, and the villagers assumed them dead. They mocked Edai's wife and told her to remarry, but she stayed true to his instructions. Then one day the *lakatoi* appeared out on the horizon. Edai's wife ran out of the house, washing herself in the ocean for the first time and dressing in her best costume. She began dancing, shouting, "*Hedihoroha Bogebada!*"

And so began the annual voyages, with both men and women adhering to the rituals set by Edai Siabo and his wife. The trade continued until the late 1950s, when a *lakatoi* sunk on its return trip to Boera, and the colonial authorities forbade the practice from continuing. After independence, an attempt was made to reclaim and celebrate the history of the Hiri trade. The Hiri Moale Festival is now held annually in Port Moresby. Timed to coincide with the PNG Independence Day celebrations in September, *lakatoi*s travel down from the coast to the city, and each year a Hiri Hanenamo (queen) is appointed—a young woman whose behavior and conduct show respect for the traditions first established by Edai's wife. She is chosen for her discipline, character, beauty, dancing, tattoos, and knowledge of customs; and the contest is regarded as a way of encouraging young women to take an active interest in Motuan history and culture.

However, this too has become increasingly vexatious. While the Boera people claim to be the original instigators of and principal actors in the Hiri trade, the history of the voyages has been absorbed into a broader Papuan narrative created in the postindependence era. This has given rise to contention over the past few decades, especially around the decision to hold the Hiri Moale Festival in Port Moresby, as opposed to in Boera, the birthplace of Edai Siabo. As a result, the Boera community has not fully participated in the Hiri Moale Festival. There has been talk recently of reasserting their ownership of the history of the Hiri trade by hosting a festival in the village at the original site of Davage Beach. But over the last few years the already considerable tension has been redoubled by the Liquefied National Gas project. The project has an anticipated value of Aus$15 billion and includes gas production and processing facilities in the Southern Highlands and Western Provinces, with liquefaction and storage facilities northwest of Port Moresby and more than seven hundred kilometers of pipeline. In 2009 the Motu-Koita Assembly withdrew funding for Boera "because of infighting between the Boera Gadona led by Sir Moi Avei and the Boera, Rearea, Porebada, Papa villagers regarding the LNG project."[3]

ORGANIZATION AND GOVERNANCE

Customary ownership of the land and sea is patrilineally passed down within families. The village is organized around a structure that weds the tribal clan system with the framework created by the arrival of Christianity in the late nineteenth century and the establishment of the United Church in Boera. The leadership structure consists of seven deacons, representing each of the seven major clans. From these deacons a village chairman is chosen through elections held every two years. The role of the chairman is to provide leadership and coordinate the deacons, who meet to make decisions on local questions and issues. The chairman also works closely with the pastor of the village church, who in turn coordinates three committees—the Women's Fellowship, the Youth Ministry, and the Children's Ministry—all of which have strong standing in the community.

A stone monument in the village commemorates the landing of London Missionaries at Boera in the 1880s, and in many ways the church and the pastor's house are the heart of the Boera community. The church organizes social, religious, and sporting activities, bringing together people from the different clans in Boera, while also strengthening relationships with the nearby villages of Porebada and Lealea. Most people in the village are involved in the church, particularly through participation in the three committees. The Women's Fellowship is particularly strong, acting as a social network while providing a space for the sharing of customary knowledge and cultural traditions. It also plays a key role in the economic organization and upkeep of the village. Women—who are generally responsible for selling produce in markets—contribute 30 percent of their income to the fellowship, and this provides a fund that is then used for building repairs and construction, running workshops and training sessions, and the upkeep of the medical center and community school. The committees in some sense reflect modern forms of social organizing introduced with the arrival of Christianity, but they also draw on the history of tribal and customary networks of Motuan men and women.

The Community Sustainability Questionnaire was conducted in Boera in August 2006. In total, there were 178 respondents, a sample that was broadly representative of the constituency of the village in terms of gender and age. Of those surveyed, 58 percent had lived in the village for twenty-one years or more. Another quarter had been in Boera between eleven and twenty years. That is, a large proportion of people within the community have long established connections to the place in which they live, which seems congruent with the fact that Boera is an indigenous village. However, only 36 percent of those surveyed indicated that they had lived in the village their whole lives. This would seem to indicate a relatively high level of mobility, which might be explained by the village's close proximity to Port Moresby.

In terms of its social makeup, Boera is largely ethnically homogenous, with a predominantly Motuan population. There are a significant number of migrants within Boera who are connected to locals through intermarriage or *wantok* relationships. However, many of these people are from nearby Motuan villages. As in many places throughout Papua New Guinea, how to respond to intermigration is an ongoing issue. Some people express the feeling that intermigration is a source of social problems and tension, and they point to what they see as major cultural differences between Motuan people and those from other provinces. In general, though, until recently relationships between locals and migrants have functioned well. Migrants who have established strong connections through intermarriage or *wantok* relationships are often granted rights to customary lands by locals in order to build houses and make gardens. However, efforts are being made to prevent the occupation of land by migrants who have not been explicitly granted rights of access, and the natural gas project has fueled contestation.

Another source of social tension relates to the use of alcohol and other drugs, particularly marijuana. There are extensive trading networks through which locals invite traders into the village to sell marijuana. Its relatively abundant supply makes it cheap, and villagers report high levels of regular consumption. Efforts to curb the supply have been unsuccessful. Likewise, attempts to curb the consumption of alcohol have had little effect. When one trade store owner attempted to obtain a license to sell alcohol, his application was blocked by the village councilor on the basis of health and social problems attributed to alcohol consumption. Nevertheless, both young and older men have regular access to home brew. It costs about five kina for a five hundred milliliter coke bottle filled with home brew, which is enough to get a person drunk, and brewing is both easy and inexpensive.

In 2006, overall, the strategic conversations, community meetings, and questionnaire results indicated a relatively high level of well-being within the village. Seventy-six percent of respondents said that they were satisfied or very satisfied with their community neighborhood, and a similar number were satisfied or very satisfied with feeling part of that community. The results also indicated a comparatively good level of physical health. When asked to describe their own health, 57 percent said it was "generally good." Another 38 percent said it was "sometimes good and sometimes poor," and less than 1 percent described their health as "generally poor." This compares well to the overall results from all research sites. However, in the years after 2006, this sense of well-being was sorely challenged.

LIVELIHOOD AND PROVISION

Fishing provides the dominant source of income-generating work and the basis for the staple diet. Men fish using *lakatois*—which carry three or four people at a time—or outboard motors, using nets and fishing line. Women primarily work collecting shellfish in shallows along the coast and are responsible for selling the catch that is not used for their family's own consumption. The fish is mainly sold at Gerehu market, which is twenty-three miles away from Boera on the way into Port Moresby. Women who sell at the market travel there and back each day by truck, paying a fee of three kina each way, which is a not insignificant cost. Locally owned

PMVs (public motor vehicles) run from Boera into town, although the poor state of the roads means that many of them have broken down.

Most of the money that is earned—through markets, raising animals, making craft items, or working in the formal sector—is spent within the village. For most people in the community, food is the biggest expense. There are three trade stores in the village operated by families as household businesses. Their prices tend to be comparable to those in the city, and, because of the costs of traveling to and from Port Moresby, most villagers depend on these stores for basic items such as soap, rice, tinned food, and biscuits. School fees are another big expense and can take a large chunk of a family's income. Other regular expenses include transport costs and contributions to the church.

In addition to fishing, families in Boera also make gardens, with the crops grown mostly for their own consumption and not for selling. While the long dry season makes continuous growing difficult, the inland soil is generally quite fertile. During the rainy season crops like corn, pumpkin, yams, peanuts, and green vegetables grow well. Fruits such as guava and pawpaw are also grown. Some drought-resistance crops, such as varieties of yam, banana, and cassava have been introduced and offer an important food source, particularly during the dry season. There are also experiments with agro-farming techniques, with a demonstration project initiated by Sir Moi Avei in his own garden, using modern farming techniques for growing crops such as cabbages, lettuces, tomatoes, eggplants, and melons. Villagers also grow customary herbs and plants such as noni (Morinda citrifolia), which has a long history of use throughout Southeast Asia and Polynesia and is believed to have significant and wide-ranging medicinal qualities, including antibacterial, antioxidant, antitumor, and anti-inflammatory properties.

Within the village, a number of families keep animals—chickens and pigs—for food, trade, and customary purposes. The chickens kept are mostly customary kinds, as opposed to modern breeds of meat chickens, which are more expensive to look after. Customary types of chickens can be kept freely in the backyards of houses and fed on food scraps instead of bought grain. Eggs provide an alternate source of protein to fish and can also be sold at market, fetching around seventy toea apiece. Pigs are kept mainly as a source of income for families. In addition to native pigs, which are kept freely in the village, there are a number of piggeries containing modern crossbreed pigs. These are fed on store-bought feed, and there is a high demand for them, particularly from Highlanders living in the city. Mature pigs can fetch over a thousand kina. They are also used for feasting and contributing to bride price.

In addition to fishing, agriculture, and keeping animals, there are a few other ways in which people in Boera make their living. A number of people in Boera are engaged in formal employment in the private and government sectors in Port

Moresby. A handful of these live in the village, and they commute daily using private or public vehicles. Some younger people move to the city in order to work and send money back to their families in the village. But, as is common throughout the country, formal sector employment amounts to only a small proportion of all the livelihood activities undertaken by families in the community.

Some people in the village make a living through their skills in arts and crafts. Carving and shaping shells to make ornaments and jewelry is the main livelihood activity for one family in the village, which makes necklaces, armbands, and earrings and sells them at market. Their skills are in high demand, with both locals and outsiders visiting them to place orders. As has been noted, Boera was historically a center of clay-pot making in Papua New Guinea, with pots used for trade as well as for cooking, storing water, and preserving food. Efforts are now being made to pass that skill on to a new generation of women. If the villagers are successful in ensuring that it is passed on, this could be a potential source of income-generating activity, particularly if Boera does initiate a festival at Davage Beach to commemorate the Hiri trade. Other people make string bags and sell these at markets as well. Roadside stalls are another source of income for some people, selling cigarettes, betel nut, store items, and fried food. They tend to occur infrequently, however, as the women who run them are usually busy with gardening, fishing, and daily household activities.

Two sets of resources in Boera have become contentious—water and land— and these are the reason that the community, once so strong, is now in crisis. The creek running through Boera has all but dried up, though there is, on the whole, a good level of access to fresh water in the village. Two modified customary wells are currently in use—reinforced with cement and wire mesh to prevent contamination—as well as a number of bore water pumps. One of these was established with donor support through the Health Department, while others are installed privately by families with the money to do so. In addition, an extensive Southern Cross solar pump system means that water is available from public taps located throughout the village. Water is drilled from the underground aquifer at a point between the two customary wells and pumped by a small generator to a reservoir located up the hill near the village community school. From there, water is piped through the village. The supply is controlled by the village Water Committee, and the reservoirs are opened at morning and night each day. Water is collected daily in containers and stored in homes for domestic use.

Conflicts have arisen over rights of usage and access. From 2006 to the present, disputes were observed relating to who had access to one of the wells providing drinking water. Because the well is located within the customary land of a group of families, those families were claiming exclusive access rights. Other villagers responded by trying to assert customary usage rights. Similarly, conflicts have arisen over the location of water pumps in the village, with customary landowners often claiming control over their usage. One, belonging to a former teacher, has been established as a user-pays pump, with villagers charged twenty toea per use—nominally for maintenance costs but believed by many to be a personal profit-making exercise. Such disputes are evidence of the conflicting imperatives of customary landownership and the establishment of public utilities, with questions of resource-usage rights being compounded by contemporary factors of growing population and land pressures. On the whole, however, water supplies in the community are relatively secure, and in this regard Boera is fortunate in comparison to many other Central Province villages, which often struggle to obtain sufficient water, particularly during the prolonged dry seasons that some associate with climate change.

Conflict has also become more intense over landownership in relation to the massive compensation payments expected from a liquefied natural gas project. The main operator is ExxonMobil, which holds 33.2 percent of the project, together with Oil Search (29 percent), the PNG Government (16.6 percent), Santos (13.5 percent), Nippon Oil Exploration (4.7 percent), and Petromin PNG Holdings Limited (0.2 percent). The remaining partnership is held by PNG customary landowners, with 2.8 percent. The liquefied natural gas plant site affects the villages of Boera, Papa, Lea Lea, Porebada, and Buruni. In February 2010, men from Porebada village launched a raid on Boera village following an earlier altercation with drunken youths from Boera, and four people died from gunshot wounds.[4] Three houses were set on fire, including Sir Moi's sister's house.

LEARNING AND EDUCATION

The community hall in Boera is regularly used as a community learning center for people in the village as well as from neighboring villages. Both government and NGO agencies use the space to conduct educational workshops, including training by the National Fisheries Authority on simple methods of fish harvesting and processing; and HIV/AIDS workshops conducted by the National AIDS Council and the United Nations Development Program. These training sessions and other short courses have had high participation rates. The construction and upkeep of the community building was funded by the Women's Fellowship, which also conducts a number of training and educational programs for women in the community. These range from basket making, to health and nutrition, to agricultural skills and financial management. In addition to workshops conducted in the village, the fellowship uses the funds pooled by its members to pay for individuals to participate in other training and educational courses outside of Boera.

Formal education levels in Boera are comparatively high compared to other sites where research was conducted. The highest level of education achieved for 28 percent of respondents to the questionnaire was primary school. Another 43 percent had had some secondary education or had completed it. Eight percent of respondents had completed a university undergraduate education, which is the highest figure from any of the research sites and significantly higher than the overall figure of 3 percent. The establishment of primary and secondary schools within the village means that children no longer have to leave their families and customary lands in order to receive an education. Having to leave the village to attend school was identified as one of the reasons for the loss of customary skills, so there is hope now that children and youth will be able to learn both modern and customary forms of knowledge without one coming at the expense of the other. Some community members commented, however, that the schools were not running well, with students often being sent home early in the day.

There is demand for more training and better educational opportunities within the community, both formally and informally. When asked about learning and skills training, 86 percent of respondents to the Community Sustainability Questionnaire in Boera either agreed or strongly agreed with the statement "More training is necessary for doing the work that I would ideally like to do." When asked what sorts of training they wanted, 48 percent thought that agricultural training would be useful, and 42 percent identified income generation as something they would like to receive training in. People also indicated a desire to have access to training about family life and customary ways of doing things.

People in Boera, particularly those of the older generations, talk with regret about the loss of customary skills and knowledge. One man, Paul, described the difficulty experienced in trying to run programs to teach the youth about their history and culture: "We used to have the old people go to the schools. The school had a program for customary knowledge, art and craft, and the old people would go to the school and teach. But these things have all dropped off. Mostly it is passed through the family, the immediate family. The young generation now are not so interested, they just wander off." Still, renewed efforts are being made through peer education and the Youth Ministry. Paul says, "We are trying to put the local knowledge together with whatever new knowledge is coming from the outside; trying to blend our local knowledge together...to keep the fire alive."

Inuma and Alepa Villages, Central Province

WHEN DOES CONSTRUCTING A MONUMENT CONTRIBUTE TO BUILDING
A COMMUNITY?

The villages of Inuma and Alepa are small, subsistence-based villages located four hours' drive out of Port Moresby, southeast on the Magi Highway. Inuma was originally part of the larger village, Alepa, an hour's walk away along a rough bush track. Inuma was established in the early 1980s when one of the Alepa clans—the Kwaruve—relocated to be closer to the newly constructed highway. There are now around twenty households in Inuma village, surrounded by savannah grassland hills and patches of forest. The village has a small shop, owned by a man who runs a PMV to and from the city, carrying passengers and bringing back foodstuffs and goods to sell. It has a tiny elementary school with one teacher; sixteen children learn mathematics, arts and crafts, religious education, community living, health, and language skills there. And then, just off to the side of the road, it has a massive, stunningly designed church, big enough to hold its entire population many times over. With its high ceiling and metallic-blue sloped roof, the church towers above all the other buildings in the village and dwarfs the tiny school that sits beside it. Understanding the process that lay behind the building of that church provides an entry point into the complexity of community relations that cross the usual renditions of the rural-city divide, qualifies conventional descriptions of clan relations

A church under construction in Inuma, supported by donations from Port Moresby

and bounded community life, and illustrates the social impact of something as apparently simple as a major road going through an area.

The construction of the church was organized and initiated by the Inuma community itself. In particular, they used local professional support as well as the *wantok* and denominational connections of community members now living in Port Moresby to raise significant amounts of funding. In doing so, they have been able to elevate the religious-institutional status of their own village within the Rigo area, and they have given it a relatively independent status in relation to the older tribal connections to Alepa. Planning for the church began many years ago. After the first of the Kwaruve clan left Alepa to establish Inuma, the local Seventh-Day Adventist mission requested that the district headquarters of the mission also relocate to the Inuma site in view of the increased accessibility offered by its location. The headquarters moved over in 1983, and a temporary church building was erected shortly after. In December 2000, when family members living in Port Moresby returned to the village to celebrate Christmas as they do every year, discussions began about the need to build a permanent church. A Building Committee was established, with Dickson Guina appointed as its chairman.

A number of the committee members, including Dickson, live and work in Port Moresby. In fact, around thirty members of the Inuma community are now based in the city, working in public service, private industry, and business. Charged with raising the money required to build the new church, the committee drew upon the connections of these community members and *wantok*. Over a period of several years, they held fund-raising events and corporate dinners, and invited their friends in the city to come to Inuma and see the work being prepared. Their friends included the then–National Capital District governor Wari Vele and his brother Anderson Vele, who was at that time the local member of Parliament for the Rigo area. Alphonse Moroi, the governor of Central Province, sent four representatives to a groundbreaking ceremony held in Inuma in 2005 to mark the beginning of construction. A customary welcome was organized for the invited guests, followed by the modern groundbreaking ceremony and the formal presentation of checks, which the national media outlets were invited to cover. Fund-raising efforts and contributions from strategically important individuals meant that, by the beginning of 2008, the Building Committee had raised in excess of 77,000 kina.

In the design and construction of the building, this tiny rural community also used the national and international training of its *wantok*s, both inside and outside of its own village. An architecture lecturer from the University of Technology in Lae—originally from a neighboring village in Rigo, and one of Dickson Guina's in-laws—was commissioned to draw up the plans for the church. Another of his in-laws—a chief estimator educated in Melbourne—drew up the list of materials based on the plans. A carpenter and builder from Abau village east of Inuma, educated at Madang Technical College, had previously built Dickson's house in Inuma, and based on that work the community decided that he should be engaged as the foreman and builder for the church. The bulk of the construction work, however, was taken on voluntarily by the community members themselves.

During the week, groups of villagers would take turns alternating between working in their own gardens and going to the bush land near the village to cut the timber required for the frame of the building. On Fridays the community rested, and on Saturdays they gathered for worship. Every Sunday they would go back to the bush and move the timbers back to the building site. Local kwila and *thon* woods were used for the main structure of the building. These are hardwoods, making them impervious to termites but also very heavy, and so most of the tall logs were transported down the Ormond River. Those that the villagers could manage to carry were moved that way. This work continued, week in and week out, for a year. Every household in Inuma contributed to the church's construction.

When the RMIT and DFCD research team visited Inuma for a second time in 2007, building on the church had already been going on for close to a year. The frame had been erected, and the huge timbers cut from the neighboring forests were supporting the high, metallic blue color-bond roof, bought in the city. At that stage the sides of the building were open, letting air flow through and allowing a clear view of the hills and trees leading out to the horizon. The Building Committee had plans to erect louvers along the sides, with glass panels at either end so the spaciousness and light remained a feature. The villagers were preparing then to lay the cement floor, but the building was already being used for twice daily services, with a main worship service held each Saturday.

The church is predominantly used for the Inuma community to gather and worship. However, the elevation of the local mission's status to that of district headquarters means that the building is also intended to be used by the broader Seventh-Day Adventist community in Rigo for big meetings, seminars, and workshops. For a tiny community of twenty households, which only established itself twenty-odd years ago, Inuma has successfully built upon its proximity to the Magi Highway and its connections to governmental and business circles in Port Moresby to create itself as a strategic center in the Rigo District.

Not every community in Papua New Guinea has thirty of its members employed in well-connected positions in the nation's capital. In building its church, Inuma was able to capitalize on strategic connections and advantages that it was fortunate to enjoy. The story of the Inuma church illuminates key factors that have shaped the nature of this particular community: the construction of the highway and the resultant increase in the strategic importance of the village within the wider Rigo area, the presence of a number of highly educated community members employed within the city and with access to key political and economic resources as a result, and cohesive structures of governance and organization within a community knit together through membership in a single clan. However, the story of the church also points to characteristics and dynamics that are affecting communities across Papua New Guinea in a period of change: the intersection of tribally based systems of social relations with those clearly informed by the modern; the profound centrality of religion and its capacity to mobilize communities; the spreading out of networks of social connection beyond local sites; and complex relationships between the urban and rural as familial, clan-based, and *wantok* relationships retain a deep importance in the face of growing urbanization.

PLACE—PAST AND PRESENT

Inuma village is located within the Rigo District in Central Province, southeast of Port Moresby. Historically, the villagers at Inuma were part of a larger community based in Alepa village, which is southeast of the town of Kwikila and about one hour's walk from the Hood Lagoon near the coast of the Coral Sea. The people who now form the Inuma community are members of the Kwaruve clan, which was originally one of a number of clans within Alepa village. Inuma was built on what their elders considered to be their proper tribal land passed down by their ancestors.

The land on which Inuma was built is green and lush, as it is throughout the Rigo area as a result of regular rainfall and the proximity of the Ormond River, which runs down into the sea. A network of smaller rivers runs across the area, flowing down in the valleys between the mountains and providing a source of irrigation for crops. The geography of the area is predominantly lowland mountains, with large areas of savannah grassland and smaller patches of forest. There are rain-forest areas toward the northwest, and the mountains there are more densely forested. The land is fertile, and gardens are filled with bananas, yams, cassavas, coconuts, and sweet potatoes. Inuma village itself is situated right on the side of the Magi Highway, which connects the Rigo District with Port Moresby.

The "big village"—Alepa—is much more geographically isolated than Inuma. Konako village sits between the two and is closely connected to Alepa. Another village, Varokogena, is a half to a full day's walk upstream from Inuma, heading northeast along the Ormond River. The fifth village is Abau, also within walking distance. These villages all speak a common language—the Rigo dialect—and Inuma is connected to each of them through family relationships and intermarriage. Inuma's proximity to the highway means it is by far the most accessible of the villages in the area. The secondary roads that lead to Alepa, Konako, Varokogena, and Abau are all in poor condition, and the primary mode of access is by foot. In contrast, Inuma has direct access to Port Moresby, with PMVs running the four-hour route daily as well as to Kwikila, which is an administrative center in the region with a large outdoor market, a supermarket, and other shops. The accessibility that Inuma enjoys shapes the nature of the place: its geographical proximity to Kwikila and Port Moresby gives it easier access to the cash economy within these places and makes the village a point of transit for others heading to and from the urban centers. Most people have family members who live in Port Moresby, meaning that there are ongoing connections between village and city and regular flows of people and resources back and forth

Within each of the villages, people live with their extended families in clusters of houses, with shared huts used for cooking and preparing food. Most households tend to have five or more people within them. The houses are built using wood from the forest as well as modern materials such as fibro-cement. Some people still make customary thatched walls, weaving bamboo slivers together according to colorful patterns passed down within families. There is no electricity, although many households do have access to running water. There are two aid posts within the cluster of villages and three elementary schools. For some people, access to these services means walking for hours along bush tracks. Communication networks have, for a long time, been dependent on the passing of oral messages through people traveling between the villages. The extension of mobile phone networks in Central Province, however, means that an increasing number of people are able to communicate with people outside their village via phone.

ORGANIZATION AND GOVERNANCE

The sense of community in Inuma is strongly defined by the fact that the village consists of just one clan. As community leader Dickson Guina described it, "We are from the same clan [so] we think the same, we do things—there is cooperation, there is understanding about the land use." The community is small and tightly coheres around shared family connections. The Inuma people's self-understanding of their community is reflected in the responses to the Community Sustainability Questionnaire, where 46 percent of respondents identified "a particular group of people" as their main source of community, a much higher figure than the overall average of 14 percent. Identification with land is important, as the Kwaruve clan had long-standing ancestral connections to the place to which they relocated. However, given the relatively short length of occupancy on the site and the centrality of clan connections in establishing the community, it is understandable that "a particular group of people" would rank highly as a source of community identification in the village.

What is interesting about the community in Inuma, however, is the nature of its relationship to the big village, Alepa. Inuma has its own systems of governance and organization, and there is little day-to-day contact between the two places. However, Inuma villagers still consider themselves part of Alepa, and their own village is known as the "small village" in relation to the "big village" from which they originally came. The two locations have a sense of common identity constituted through shared history, language, ancestors, and relationships of trade and intermarriage, even if those points of commonality are infrequently enacted in daily life. To some extent, the sense of common identity extends as well to the other villages in the surrounds of Inuma. Layered on top of the familial, village, and clan modes of identification is another layer of identity founded on common location within Rigo District. Located within relatively close proximity to each other, the five villages around and including Inuma have semiregular contact with each other, and the flows of people between them has been demonstrated in the process of the construction of the Inuma church.

Within the cluster of villages around Inuma, strategic conversations and the results of the Community Sustainability Questionnaire point to high levels of community well-being. For instance, 89 percent of respondents indicated that they were either satisfied or very satisfied with their community neighborhood, a figure higher than the average of 78 percent across all the research sites. Similarly, 86 percent of respondents said they were either satisfied or very satisfied with their feeling of safety in Alepa, again higher than the overall average of 72 percent. People talked about the strength of cooperative activities, such as the building of the new church and community celebrations and organized sports activities. Many community activities are organized through the churches. In particular, the United Church and Seventh-Day Adventist Church are prominent institutions and organize many of the cultural and social events that bring people together within their villages. It is through the churches, as well, that villagers contribute resources and income to buy communal assets such as chain saws and other tools and equipment.

As in many communities, the church has considerable influence and plays a major role in the organization and governance structures within Inuma. Elders are appointed by the church minister, and while other people have influence, it is these elders who carry the most power. The church elders from the wider Rigo area (now effectively standing in for the customary leaders) meet regularly to talk to each other about issues and problems within their communities and plan how to act and respond. When they reach consensus, decisions are passed down to all the people within the four villages. One of the recent focuses of the elders has been the efforts to curb the production and consumption of home brew—*steam*—which is considered by many villagers to be a source of social tension and disharmony within the community.

Some of the elders have also been working to change some of the blurred customary-modern practices in the community. Many wish to see changes in the practices associated with bride price. Increasingly, bride price is being measured and paid with cash as well as or instead of the crops, pigs, and other goods that were customarily used. The function of bride price as expressed by locals is to compensate the family of the bride—particularly the father—for the loss of their daughter through marriage. Women, it is said, further intoning modern notions of worth, are valuable assets within families—looking after gardens, cooking, keeping the house, and caring for other family members. However, as the people of Papua New Guinea negotiate the intersection of customary tribal, traditional Christian religious, and modern customs and practices—and particularly as bride price practices are increasingly influenced by the emerging cash economy—there is extensive discussion regarding its ongoing place and relevance in some communities. One woman described how her father, who is one of the founding members of Inuma village, has refused to set a bride price for her. Instead, he has said that he wants an assurance that his children will be able to come back to the village and look after him when he is old. In this sense, the discussions happening within the Alepa community and among the leaders of that community point to the negotiations around relationships, changing forms of family, and reciprocity that are taking place in communities in contemporary Papua New Guinea.

Forms of community organization and leadership appear to enjoy a broad level of support among people in Inuma. Eighty-one percent of respondents to the questionnaire either agreed or strongly agreed with the statement "Decisions made about life in my neighborhood are made in the interests of the whole community," with only 7 percent disagreeing. When compared to the overall average of 62 percent across all the surveyed sites, this suggests well-functioning structures of community governance.

Broadly, structures of organization and governance within Inuma are shaped by the influence of modern representative forms of leadership and the impact of the church. The systems of relationship embedded within the clan structure remain important, but they are changing and adapting within a complex social and political landscape. In other words, elders are central, as they always have been, but they are now, in effect, appointed through the church on the basis of traditional-modern considerations of faith and upstanding practice. Meanwhile the hereditary chief lives in Port Moresby and is largely absent from the village. As in many communities in Papua New Guinea, committees are increasingly adopted as the dominant modality of organization and leadership. Dickson Guina is chairman of the Building Committee, but he is also chairman of the Clan Committee, a role that draws subjectively on conceptions of customary leadership as well as being shaped by the modern. He describes some of the changes that have taken place:

> In our customary leadership, because of patrilineal society, our leadership is always the one who is the firstborn child—he becomes the leader. In this case, my dad is the firstborn child of our grandfather. So he is recognized to be a leader of our community, our clan. Now, time has changed. Because of our education,

and people separating, time has changed. And now they see who within the clan has the potential to be recognized as a leader. So in this case I was chosen to be the leader, because of the qualities in me, which my other brothers and cousins and uncles recognize that I can make a difference. So they decided, my elder brothers too, they agreed that I should get the leadership.

LIVELIHOOD AND PROVISION

Subsistence agriculture is the predominant form of livelihood activity for the large majority of households in Inuma and Alepa. Regular rainfall means that there is no shortage of water, and conditions are excellent for growing crops. Gardens are filled with banana palms, yam plants, and cassava, as well as other crops such as tapioca, corn, pumpkin, coconut, and papaya. These gardens are overwhelmingly the main source of food for households in the community. Across all the villages around Inuma, 92 percent of respondents to the questionnaire stated that the main way they got their food was through work done on their own land or by fishing. The other 8 percent identified food markets as their main source of food.

After crops are put aside for households' own consumption, surpluses are sold at markets in Kwikila or in the National Capital District. Predominantly, the crops sold are bananas, yams, and cassavas. There have previously been strong relationships of exchange between the people in Inuma and those in the surrounding villages. Once-a-month bartering systems took place, for instance, between the people in Alepa and Konako, and those in Inuma, where fish was exchanged for cooking bananas from the more inland areas. These forms of regular exchange ensured a diversity of foodstuffs for people within the community, while also serving to maintain the relationships between the different villages. Increasingly, though, the emerging cash economy is replacing form of barter exchange, and people's own garden produce is supplemented with rice, tinned fish, and other foodstuffs bought at trade stores.

Of those people surveyed by the research teams, 71 percent sold goods at market as their main form of work. Another 21 percent worked within the household, and only 4 percent listed their main way of making a living as being a casual laborer or service worker for cash. None of the respondents indicated that they worked for a wage from the state or from a business. We know, however, that there is a sizable contingent of the community living and working in Port Moresby, with regular and ongoing connections to family members in the village, and, because of the location-based use of the questionnaire in the initial round, these persons are not part of the respondent group. The community is multisited, and some people living in the village receive money from *wantoks* working in the city. Within the village, there are also some small-scale instances of informal-sector enterprise. For instance, Ben Giula operates a PMV that runs between Inuma and Port Moresby each day, transporting people and goods. Other households sell diesel, and some raise chickens or ducks for sale, advertising their goods with signs erected in view of the highway. On the whole, however, while there is an abundance of food, there is a scarcity of opportunities through which to generate income while living in the village. Most households consider themselves to be struggling financially.

LEARNING AND EDUCATION

Access to formal educational opportunities in Inuma is limited. There is a small elementary school, but students must travel to attend higher levels. Two other elementary schools are located within the cluster of five villages. Within the group of villages around and including Inuma, 15 percent of respondents to the Community Sustainability Questionnaire had not completed any level of formal education, compared to 9 percent across all the eleven research sites in Papua New Guinea. Forty-two percent had completed primary school, 23 percent had completed some secondary school, and only 12 percent had finished secondary school. Eight percent had completed some form of trade training, less than the overall average of 13 percent across all the sites, and none of the people surveyed had undertaken undergraduate or postgraduate study. The responses show significantly divergent levels of education, with a small highly educated and trained portion of the community—many of whom have now left the area for jobs in Port Moresby—and a majority with low levels of income and little formal education.

Beyond the formal education system, the communities have had relatively little in the way of skills training or other community development workshops. Villagers in Inuma have said that requests to the local administrative center for training, specifically in vanilla-growing techniques, have gone unmet. Local people expressed a sense of frustration at their lack of contact with administration officers from the Central Province Office despite their proximity to the Kwikila station. When asked about training and education in the community, 89 percent of questionnaire respondents either agreed or strongly agreed with the statement "I would like to learn how to do my current work better." Most of the respondents—76 percent—identified agriculture as a particular area where training was wanted. After this, the second most sought after type of training was in family life, with 15 percent of people expressing a desire for this. Relatively few people expressed a desire for training in literacy, management, or technology. In conversations with researchers, villagers in Inuma and Alepa identified a number of particular areas that strongly affect their livelihood activities. For instance, pests and diseases decrease the quality and quantity of the harvest. People have been told to buy chemicals to eradicate the pests, but the financial burden of regularly buying the chemicals themselves is creating new problems. Problems like these are particularly relevant to the people in these communities, and training in agriculture is undoubtedly a key priority.

Sibbie Dovabbie, the local teacher in Inuma, sits in the one-room elementary school. Students wanting to go on to higher levels of education have to travel outside the village.

Training and education initiatives need to be appropriate and responsive to the needs and conditions of local communities. In a predominantly subsistence community where livelihoods are dependent on the capacity of households to grow sufficient crops to feed themselves, training in agricultural skills and techniques is a natural priority for the people of Inuma and Alepa. Moreover, community learning strategies should ideally build on the strengths and skills already present in communities. Within Inuma, instances of collective activity, such as the building of the church, point to a diversity of existing skills and experiences that can be harnessed and used by the community.

Vanapa Area, Central Province

WHY ARE SETBACKS AND PROBLEMS IN DEVELOPMENT PROJECTS
INTERPRETED AS FAILURES?

In April 2001 the Disobai Naori project was established by clan elders and other individuals living in Vanapa West, a resource-rich area north of Port Moresby, in an attempt to find alternatives to the commercial logging of their customary forests. Elders from the Disobai Naori clan—which includes around ninety-five households from the Koiari tribal group—were being pressured to sign a logging agreement, but the community had witnessed the negative social, cultural, environmental, and economic impacts of large-scale logging in nearby Vanapa North and were reluctant to proceed. So they contacted a relative, Julie Smith, who lived in Australia and worked there as a consultant. She brought a team of Australian consultants over to Papua New Guinea, who worked with the community to establish an incorporated landowner group, the Disobai Naori Land Group Inc., and produced a comprehensive business plan detailing an alternative strategy for the sustainable management of the Vanapa West forest resources. Ultimately, however, the project fell apart before the plan could be implemented, the victim of interpersonal disputes and family politics. In seeking to paint a picture of the Vanapa community, the story of how the Disobai Naori project developed, and ultimately how it failed, is illuminating.

> The vision of the Disobai Naori people...is to care for the forest as our ancestors did and pass on this knowledge to our children. In the traditions of our ancestors, we will wisely use our forest and all our resources to sustainably provide for a stable social, cultural, and economic future for our whole people. We will learn from the past and work for improvements to our lives step by step, so that we can achieve a relaxed and happy life.

The purpose of setting up an incorporated landowner group and preparing a business plan was to create a framework for effective management of forest resources and to create an organizational structure that would ensure that the benefits of resource use were spread throughout the whole community. An initial two-day planning workshop for the project brought together forty-five community members. The workshop served to illuminate key priorities and areas of concern for the Vanapa West community, which then informed the development of the business plan. Community members articulated a wish for economic development and increased income generation through use of their forest resources, while simultaneously stressing the importance of environmental and cultural sustainability. They also identified social issues they felt needed to be addressed, including women's workloads and poor health, children's well-being and education, problems around alcohol and drug use, and the management of household incomes. People also expressed a desire to protect the many sacred and magical places within Vanapa West, particularly in the mountains, and to create opportunities for sharing knowledge with the younger generations, who are increasingly oriented toward Port Moresby and the promises of city life. In short, then, the community was looking to the Disobai Naori project for a plan that would address the social, cultural, and environmental as well as the economic dimensions of community well-being and development.

In response to these concerns, the Disobai Naori business plan was created by the team of consultants from Focus and Associates. The plan identifies and maps the location of different resources in the Vanapa West area, including heritage sites as well as sites of cultural and spiritual importance. For instance, the plan details the important story-places that connect people to their land, such as the cave where a man turned into a snake and a stone statue of a pig that is believed to be the origin point for all pigs. These story-places number among the resources of the forest. Economically, the plan establishes a framework for community-controlled ventures including commercial harvesting of rattan for sale to the Small Industry Development Center in Port Moresby and a block-making business, using the stone, gravel, and sand resources in the area, which would provide work and training for community members. A walk-about sawmill is proposed as an alternative to commercial logging, and opportunities are identified for limited commercial cropping alongside managed food gardens. Ecotourism is proposed as a means of generating income, employment, and training opportunities for community members. Plans for a community banking system are developed as a means for effective income management and community-wide investments, which also address women's concerns about the misuse of income within families and the community's desire to fund the education of their children. In all these instances, sustainability is a central concern, and the plan takes as its basis a multifaceted understanding of development and well-being that moves beyond the strictly economic.

The Disobai Naori project was potentially truly significant. It secured funding from the British High Commission to prepare the business plan, and AusAID, the European Commission, the Canada Fund, and PNG government agencies all expressed interest in supporting its implementation. Before the formation of the Disobai Naori project, people within the area had only known to go to churches for funding and support. This undertaking represented one of the first times that a customary landowning group was to be given money to initiate projects that would let them self-manage their own resources, and in this sense it was a radical departure from the entrenched norms and practices of the dominant development paradigm.

In the end, though, the project collapsed before it could be implemented. Interpersonal conflicts emerged between key figures in the Disobai Naori Land Group and a member of the Disobai Naori clan who held a position of customary leadership but resided in Australia. Some of the people involved in the project in Papua New Guinea have accused this individual of sabotaging the project to assert her own authority within the clan, while she in turn made allegations of self-interested behavior on the part of the consultancy group. Accounts of the conflict are murky and contradictory, but ultimately the project was shelved. Funding agencies were simply unwilling to release any funds unless the dispute was resolved. The dispute lingered; the money never came, and the plan was never implemented.

More interesting than the minutiae of the interpersonal conflict are the broader themes that the dispute tapped into. The development and collapse of the Disobai Naori project took place in the context of intersecting forms of organization, ideas, and assumptions relating to social mobilization and agency. The language and structures that the project used—business plans, incorporated landowner groups, boards, constitutions, and funding partnerships—often diverged markedly from the structures of chiefly authority, clan organization, and decision making that still operate within the Vanapa community. While the Disobai Naori Land Group took measures to engage respectfully and meaningfully with the chiefdom system, the conflict that was the catalyst for the collapse of the project can be seen, in part at least, as a result of a clash of two different authoritative structures. And, ultimately, the funding agencies and governmental bodies involved in moving toward the business plan's implementation were unable to accommodate the complexity of the relationships involved in customary tribal leadership and decision-making processes.

The collapse of the relationships with the funding agencies meant that none of the plans and dreams laid out in the Disobai Naori document have been realized. A small group of people from the original Disobai Naori group have now signed agreements with a logging company, and commercial logging has begun in parts of the mountainous area. The collective vision articulated by the community is no closer to reality than it was in 2001, despite all the promise of the project and the work and energy of those involved.

When the Disobai Naori group produced their business plan for their community, they wrote, "We believe our experience has much relevance to other communities throughout the country." And it still does. Indeed, the key challenges that the Disobai Naori project identified in the Vanapa West community are challenges that face communities around the country, and there is much to learn. The deferral of the project serves to illuminate some of the many potential challenges and pitfalls that are experienced in trying to realize sustainable, community-led development throughout Papua New Guinea. But the project also highlighted the wealth of resources within Papua New Guinean communities and possibilities that emerge from an alternative approach to development that embraces the importance of the cultural, social, and ecological dimensions and not just the economic. The vision of the Disobai Naori people still stands as a powerful image of strong, resilient, sustainable community life. The next question becomes, can a community treat such a "failure" to implement as a learning experience and return to basic principles in order to find another more sustainable path?

PLACE—PAST AND PRESENT

The Vanapa area is a large region north of Port Moresby and the National Capital District, adjacent to the coast of the Coral Sea. It is in Hiri District and falls under the jurisdiction of the Hiri local-level government. The community is bordered by the Veimauri River to the northwest, the Laloki River to the west, and the Brown River to the south. The main Vanapa River runs through the middle of the area, and the Hiritano Highway connects it to Port Moresby. The Vanapa community is in turn made up of numerous smaller communities that range in size and composition and are scattered throughout the area, including the villages of Kuriva, Kerea, Vekavu, Kanobaba, and Badiroho. Most of the communities are found near the banks of the Vanapa River and on either side of the highway. In addition to the local landowners, there are smaller groups of settlers from Goilala, Mekeio, Berena, the Sepiks, Morobe, and the Gulf. Many settlers occupy small areas of land within the area, while others have married into the villages and communities of landowning clans.

Driving into the Vanapa area from Port Moresby, the vegetation along both sides of the Hiritano Highway is primarily savannah grassland. As you move away from the highway—up and down the Vanapa River and farther inland—it changes to dense tropical rain forest. Mountains dominate the northern part of Vanapa and continue down through the eastern part of the area. Particularly in the north, there are large areas of deforestation due to significant commercial logging that has left the natural environment noticeably damaged. Rain-forest vegetation predominates in the south, along with areas of swampland. The area of Vanapa West, which belongs to the Disobai Naori people of the Koiari tribal group, includes 70,000 hectares of largely virgin rain forest bounded by the mountains and the Vanapa River. Action by the Disobai Naori group has largely stemmed the onslaught of commercial logging activities here, but there are reports of incursions, and some landowning groups have recently allowed logging to commence.

Materials from the forest are used in constructing houses and other buildings, but the community's relative proximity to the city means that it is also quite easy to source modern materials and transport them back. Many of the villages are clustered around the point where the Hiritano Highway crosses the Vanapa River. A steel bridge here is a key piece of infrastructure for the community and a central point of transit for those traveling to and from Port Moresby. There is a school building in Kerea and both a school and a health center in Kuriva. A network of roads and paths runs through the area, but the roads are in very poor condition. This is a major point of grievance within the community and makes travel and accessibility difficult, especially for the more remote and isolated villages.

ORGANIZATION AND GOVERNANCE

There are two major landowning groups in the Vanapa area, the Toura and the Koiari. Both speak their own language and are distinct ethnic groupings. Land is passed down within the two landowning clans on a patrilineal basis. These tribal groups have extensive relationships with other tribes in and around the Vanapa area. The Toura (sometimes also known as the Doura) are scattered up and down the Hiritano Highway, while the Koiari are the tribal landowning group of Vanapa West. The Koiari are also customary landowners in areas outside of Vanapa, including in Kokoda and other areas within the Owen Stanley Ranges. A number of settler communities are also part of the broader Vanapa community. These include families from Goilala, Berena, Mekeiou, and the Gulf. Some of these settlers have been in the community for up to three generations. They have houses and gardens in the community but no land rights.

Villages are organized around family groups and clans. Kanobaba, for instance, which is located on the Hiritano Highway near the main bridge over the Vanapa River, consists of the families of five brothers. The community in Vekavu village, which is farther down the highway south of Kanobabo, is made up of the people of the Naumaniaha clan, who live there with their clan chief. Households include parents and children and often grandparents or other extended family members. Eighty-six percent of respondents to the Community Sustainability Questionnaire lived in households with five or more people, and 23 percent lived in households with ten or more people. Living in family groups provides important social and economic support structures and is also a way for family groups to claim and look after their land. Within villages, children are raised with the support of immediate and extended family and that of the broader community.

Across the Vanapa area, there is a multilayered governance structure that brings together customary chiefs, elected community leaders, and traditional-modern religious authorities. Some people in the community have suggested that the chiefdom system is effectively broken down. While chiefs do exist and are recognized as such, they claim that the system of authority and decision making is not working. This is a point of contention, however, and others stress the ongoing importance of chiefly authority. Such debates can be understood within the broader context of rapid change in Papua New Guinea. The colonial powers were the first to disrupt tribal structures of leadership and authority, followed by the project of state- and nation-building that was launched with the country's independence in 1975. The PNG state is, in many ways, still struggling to consolidate its power across the country, and its bureaucratic structures of local-level, provincial, and national authority often sit in an uneasy relationship with the chiefdom system. In addition, the major Christian churches that are now entrenched in Papua New Guinean society have introduced their own models of leadership including elders, deacons, ministers, and church fellowships. And finally, village- and clan-based models of organization are being acted on by the forces of urbanization, increased movement between villages and urban centers, and a recent boom in mobile communications technologies that allow increasing connectivity between communities that were previously much more self-contained.

Within Vanapa, all of these factors are at play. The Catholic Church entered the region in the 1950s and occupies a strong place in the community. It runs adult literacy classes, women's fellowship programs, and other community activities. The United Church and the Assemblies of God are also present within Vanapa and coordinate other community organizations. Church leaders are respected as leadership figures. Vanapa's proximity to the National Capital District also means that it has semiregular contact with government services and officials and is connected to the political and social structures of the urban center through a back-and-forth flow of people and communications. At the same time, the Disobai Naori experience shows the continuing importance of the major families and customary landowners, who carry particular status and authority and are central to the social and cultural fabric of the community. The elected community leaders often come from these families, and one of Vanapa's strengths is the enthusiasm of these leaders, who have actively sought out engagement with experts from the National Agricultural Research Institute (NARI) and the Department of Primary Industries (DPI) in an effort to implement projects to improve livelihoods in the community.

Still, many attempts at initiating community-wide projects have ended unsuccessfully. Particularly, efforts to establish agricultural improvement projects and water-supply systems have struggled to get off the ground. An example is found in the rice harvester project that was begun several years ago and abandoned after one season. The project was an attempt to set up a small-scale commercial rice-growing enterprise that would generate some income for participants from the community. The rice was planted successfully, but before it was due to be harvested the slasher, used to cut the rice, broke down and could not be repaired. By the time that people were organized to harvest the rice manually, most of it had fallen from the plants into the water and was lost. Ultimately the return for those involved was far less than what had been hoped for and expected. The difficulties in finding an adequate response to the crisis suggest the dangers in a reliance on machinery and technology-driven projects but also point to problems in coordinating a community-wide strategy within Vanapa.

Strategic conversations with community members suggest possible reasons

why community-wide efforts are so difficult. It has often been hard to secure cooperation between the many different villages that together make up the Vanapa community. Villages can be relatively self-contained, and there can also be practical difficulties in organizing community-wide efforts when a community is spread out over
a large territory as Vanapa is. Differences in ethnicity, culture, and background may
also be factors. It has been suggested that the absence of a shared main language
is a factor in the lack of cross-village cooperation. The main ethnic groupings—the
Toura and the Koiari—both speak different languages, as do the Goilala settlers and
those from other areas. Communication is possible in Tok Pisin but not in people's
primary language. Whereas shared local dialect is a uniting factor in many communities in Papua New Guinea, the sense of communal identity in Vanapa needs to
accommodate the reality of considerable linguistic diversity.

The results form the Community Sustainability Questionnaire offer some in-
sight into the way that community operates in Vanapa. Eighty percent of respondents to the questionnaire indicated that they were either satisfied or very satisfied
with feeling part of their community, which is on par with the average across all research sites. Similarly, 79 percent said that they were satisfied or very satisfied with
their lives as a whole. One instance where the Vanapa results did deviate considerably from the overall results was in response to the statement "I feel comfortable
meeting and talking with people who are different to me." Seventy percent either
agreed or strongly agreed with the statement, compared to an overall average of 79
percent, and 10 percent neither agreed nor disagreed. Significantly, 20 percent of
respondents from Vanapa disagreed with the statement, nearly double the overall
result of 11 percent across all the research sites. These results seem to corroborate
the view that, while people living in the Vanapa area do consider themselves part of
a broad community, there are also underlying points of tension around perceived
differences between villages.

LIVELIHOOD AND PROVISION

People in Vanapa are mainly subsistence farmers, hunters, and gatherers.
Some used to be employed in the city and have since retired back to their villages,
while others have lived and worked in the community their whole lives. A small
number of people in the community are employed in the city and have a regular
wage, but by far the main source of income for households is from family members
selling garden produce at markets, particularly Gordon's Market in Port Moresby.
Forty-four percent of respondents to the questionnaire said that they sold goods
at market as their main way of making a living, with another 40 percent indicating
that they work within the household, including making gardens and looking after
animals. Gardening is also the main source of provision for families in the community, with 75 percent of respondents to the questionnaire indicating that they get

most of their food from work done on their land or by fishing. Any income earned is used to supplement this diet with products like rice, tinned fish, tea, and sugar and is also used to pay for children's school fees, clothes, transport, medical costs, and other basic living costs.

Gardens are passed down patrilineally within clans, and newly married couples establish new gardens with the approval of clan group members and the village chief. They are planted with *kaukau*, corn, cassava, bananas, tomatoes, pumpkin, watermelon, taro, *aibika* (tree spinach), peanuts, cucumbers, and greens. Companion planting is used to maximize the productivity of gardens, which are made according to a five-to-seven-year rotation and allowed to fallow after this period. Crops are generally planted at different times in a garden's life cycle. So, for instance, corn and *kaukau* are popular first crops for a new garden, while bananas are frequently planted in the last cycles of the garden. There is also some commercial planting of cashew nuts, coffee, cocoa, citrus, and rubber. Regular crop irrigation is difficult, however, due to the long dry season that affects Port Moresby and the area around it. Ensuring a reliable water supply for gardens and for household use is a big challenge for the community.

Much of the labor that goes into subsistence gardening is organized around a gendered division of labor. Yam farming, for instance, is exclusively done by men, who establish large gardens in which only yams are planted and that have yam houses built in the middle. During the period that they are preparing the gardens, the men are required to abstain from sexual activity and may also fast and perform rituals. Aside from yam farming, however, women overwhelmingly provide most of the labor in gardens, and they perform this difficult work in addition to running their households, preparing meals, and looking after children. As a result, many women experience periods of physical exhaustion and sickness caused by fatigue and malaria. The burden of women's work is one of the issues being taken up by women's groups in the community, which are now voicing a desire for tools, equipment, and new processes that can assist women in their work—and in doing so improve their health.

There are ongoing debates within Vanapa about agricultural methods and practices used in the community. In 2007 and 2008 there were extensive discussions regarding the use of agricultural machinery such as tractors. Tractors would make a huge increase in the productivity of farming and would reduce the labor time currently needed to plant and harvest gardens. At the same time, however, previous experiences such as the failed rice harvester project have made others wary of a reliance on machinery. Tractors and other pieces of agricultural equipment are expensive to buy and can be expensive to repair and maintain. Expected returns from the use of farming machinery are often thwarted when equipment breaks down, is stolen, or is not maintained properly.

In a similar vein, there are divergent views on the use of agricultural techniques such as grafting or the use of chemicals to control pests. Taro beetles are causing problems for taro crops, while fruit flies are damaging capsicum plants, beans and eggplants, and other vegetables. Outside experts from the National Agricultural Research Institute and the Department of Primary Industry have been brought by community leaders to run workshops on pest control and have recommended particular chemical solutions. Through demonstrations, they have shown how the chemicals work and how the plants grow bigger and stronger. But as the locals expressed after the visit of the agricultural scientists, the chemicals, fertilizers, and pesticides cost money, and they create situations of dependency where crops will fail without them. Similarly, techniques such as grafting can require the purchase of particular species of crops, often at significant expense. Because of this, other people in the community have been advocating alternative strategies for increasing agricultural productivity. Problems with pests, they say, can be solved with local methods such as pesticide solutions made from neem trees and companion planting with marigolds and garlic (globalized cropping plants originating in Central America and Central Asia respectively). Behind these debates about pesticides, chemical fertilizers, machinery, and farming equipment is the much broader question of the relationship between modern and customary forms of knowledge and production. The community is keen to receive the benefits that these new technologies and products promise, but they also return to what they describe as local knowledge. In this case, there is the irony that locals have forgotten that their knowledge is mediated by the Department of Primary Industry who introduced the neem tree (indigenous to India) to the area in the early 1980s.[5] Nevertheless, notwithstanding the hybridity of knowledge forms, the way in which knowledge is received, accommodated, and practiced in a locality continues to be fundamental.

Outside of the areas where houses and gardens are established, the natural environment in the Vanapa area is another important source of food and resources. People within the community, particularly those in the customary landowning clans, have an intimate knowledge of the forests, mountains, and river systems that surround their villages. The forests provide food sources including ferns and edible leaves, three varieties of *pit pit*, or bush asparagus, as well as gingers, edible bamboo, wild yams, figs, bananas, breadfruit, and other fruits. Timbers are used for construction and crafts, and the forests also contain perfumed trees that have medicinal and ceremonial uses. The forests are also home to wild pigs, *magani* (wallabies), deer, cassowaries, and game birds. The rivers and creeks contain eels, prawns, crayfish, crabs, barramundi, mullet, black bass, and catfish. These resources also provide opportunities for income-generating projects. For instance, the perfumed trees that grow in the forests also carry significant commercial value, while hunting and selling wild pigs is an important livelihood activity for many people,

A commercial logging company at Vanapa operating against community wishes

and others earn income through harvesting and selling rattan. However, while rattan is bought for K0.50 per meter by places such as the Small Industry Development Center in Port Moresby, local people are generally paid much less than this because of the role of middlemen. And while timber is a valuable resource, the villagers in Vanapa North can attest to the devastation that can be caused through large-scale commercial logging. The walk-about sawmill proposed by the Disobai Naori group was one attempt to ensure that use of the area's resources remained sustainable and in the control of the community itself. Projects like this have the potential to improve livelihoods within Vanapa without compromising the health of the natural environment and the rights of customary landowners.

LEARNING AND EDUCATION
Education within the Vanapa community includes both formal and informal aspects. In terms of formal education, there are two primary schools within the Vanapa area and secondary schools outside the area that are attended by some students. Informal training programs and workshops are run by the local churches and by agencies such as the National Agricultural Research Institute. In addition, there is a rich pool of customary skills and practices that are held by individuals and families and passed down to the younger generations according to tribal custom.

Customary practices, sacred beliefs, and relationships with their customary lands have an ongoing centrality in the day-to-day lives of the Vanapa people. In conversations with the research teams, individuals spoke of people in the community who possess knowledge in such things as healing snakebites, building canoes, making and stopping rain, hunting, and making gardens. People in the community learn these customary skills from their fathers and grandfathers, while other skills are passed from mothers to daughters. Sacred forms of knowledge are carefully guarded and can only be shared with particular people, but they are used for the benefit of the community at large—so too with knowledge related to ceremonies and sacred rituals.

Levels of formal education in the community are not high. Forty-one percent of people surveyed had completed primary school as their highest level of formal education, which is about on par with the overall average across all the research sites. However, 22 percent had not completed any level of schooling, which is much higher than the overall average of 9 percent. The percentage of those who had completed some or all of a secondary school education—27 percent—was also lower than the overall average, as was the figure for those who had some form of trade training. There are two primary schools in the area, in Kerea and Kuriva. However, these are at a distance from some of the villages. Students in years nine and above need to travel out of the area in order to attend school. These factors together with the difficulties many parents have in paying school fees mean that levels of education are often low. For instance, almost all the Koirari people at Badiroho village have no formal education, save for a few young people and children, as fees are simply too expensive for the people there. The desire to be able to fund their children's education was consistently voiced by people within the community and was often given as a motivating force for people seeking to improve their livelihoods.

Opportunities for skills training are available from a number of sources. Church-run educational programs offer opportunities for learning for those who are not accommodated within the formal school system. The Catholic Church runs adult literacy classes, and women's fellowship programs are a source of training for women. The National Agricultural Research Institute and the Department for Primary Industries also run workshops, as discussed above. Still, people within the community have expressed a strong desire for more training opportunities. Forty-three percent of questionnaire respondents felt that they did not have sufficient training to get the kinds of jobs that they wanted, and 92 percent said that they would like to learn to do their current work better. When asked what sort of training they would like, 67 percent nominated agricultural training as desirable. Twenty-eight percent wanted training in income generation, and the next most sought after training was in family life, which 15 percent of people identified as something they would like.

A strong desire for educational and learning opportunities is found throughout Vanapa. While the rice harvester project and the Disobai Naori project were unsuccessful a few years ago, people still discuss the prospects of establishing similar projects, taking into account the lessons they have learned from past experience. They talk too of fish-farming projects and other initiatives that could generate some income for families to use for their children's schooling and to raise their standards of living. As the Disobai Naori project made clear, there are many options for community-controlled, sustainable initiatives within Vanapa. Still, the difficulties in realizing some of these plans have dampened the hopes of some people within the community, and the lack of cooperation between villages remains something to be overcome. The challenge will be take the willingness of people to seek out and attempt new initiatives, the enthusiasm of community leaders, and the customary skills and knowledge present within the area and bring these strengths together in a community-wide effort.

Notes

1. "Gildipasi Community Organisation Working Document," October 2007.

2. William Robinson, *James Chalmers, Missionary and Explorer of Rarotonga and New Guinea*, F. H. Revell, New York, 1888.

3. "Boera Out of the Hiri Moale Festival This Month," *The National*, 7 September 2009.

4. Rowan Callick, "Clan Killings at PNG Gas Fields," *Australian*, 4 February 2010. The 110-page *PNG LNG Quarterly Environmental and Social Report* (First Quarter 2010) did not mention anything about social tension.

5. With thanks to Martha Macintyre for bringing this to our attention.

Chapter 6

Remote Communities

Wisini Group of Villages, Morobe Province

HOW CAN AN OLD DANCE BE PART OF THE CONCEPTION OF A NEW WORLD?

Children are hanging off of trees and rocks as the vehicle approaches Wisini village. It has come through Kassangare village and moves up to Wisini after crossing the Kassangare River, a tributary of the Biaru River, currently in flood. The villagers begin gathering around the vehicle—the exchanges of greetings are warm and friendly. Many of the children hang on to our hands and laugh. Their oversized T-shirts are printed with advertisements for electricity companies or instant noodles, or else with slogans promoting conservation efforts or empowering messages by international companies and groups. The elders and the tribal chiefs come out to welcome us back with dances and *kundu* drums. We are led to the space next to the vacant health building. Constructed by the villagers, the building remains empty with the community waiting for the local government to deliver on a long-standing promise of health officials for the region. In 2002 through 2003 the villagers initiated the idea of a medical center. The center was conceptualized as an aid post, and a *singsing* festival raised more than four thousand kina. The local-level government contributed three thousand kina. Villagers, encouraged by the prospect of medical service in their area, erected a dedicated building with living quarters for the visiting health officials. The person who arrived left after a couple of months, and, years later, the building remains vacant. The villagers have not occupied it, hoping that some day soon it will become an active health service center.

The elders begin to dance. It is a dance of conception, a difficult labor, and then the birth of the child. "This is the Pariet movement," Wata Kai says. He is an elder and an oral historian: "I am the holder of my people's stories. Pariet will be our way forward because it is a rebirth for us. This dance is our nurturing, the conception, the struggle, the birth, and now the responsibility to find our place in the world where we now live and must protect from harm."

Begun in the 1990s, the Pariet movement is a growing response to the rapidly advancing and destructive elements of development and isolation from mainstream Papua New Guinea. For the Pariet movement, the important questions they ask themselves seem to inform their way forward. Who are we? Where are we from? How do we work together? What are our weaknesses, our strengths? What has been taken away from us, our places? What do we need to get back our rights and entitlements in the current world? Why has the independence of Papua New Guinea not brought us a better life—or a collective sense of a people? What has gone wrong?

The Pariet movement has initiated a process of recording the oral histories of the Pariet tribe with a view to reclaiming customary land boundaries in order to be able to manage their own livelihood and way of life. Villagers talk of the increasing number of tribal communities who are seeking to join the movement, not just alongside the Biaru and Waria River boundaries, but now also extending into the Ramu, Wahgi, and Purari River areas into the Watut and Markham River regions. When asked what the Pariet movement means to her, one of the young women seated next to the group says, "I am Pariet. I know where my people come from, and you are here because of the Pariet people's work. Pariet is my mouth and eyes and future."

As the night progresses, there is an exchange of recent happenings and developments. Then. all of a sudden, Zureki Maigao, then chairperson of the Pariet movement, gets up. He has been listening to the conversations around him. Encouraged by some of the others around him, he initially hesitates, seemingly from shyness, and then speaks:

This is now our story. I have been chairperson for fifteen years. We are Pariet. We have been part of the Pariet story for more than fifteen years. It is slow, it is hard, and it is a struggle to find our roots, our ancestors after so much destruction. But we are stronger than ever before. Now under the tribal lineage of the Ammam people, we stretch far across the mountains and down through to the other side of the mountains. Pariet has helped us to see who we are. We want our independence and our own way to decide what is for our self-betterment. In my role, I speak with authority. Pariet will see us through. I have the Amman blood, and in my blood I know this is the way.

This rendition of an evening in historical time from our arrival to the voice of the Pariet chairperson is how, among many stories, the elders of the Pariet movement wanted their story to be told. It is a few paragraphs written down carrying the intersection of orality and print. It is both a contingent and a choreographed story of contemporary intersections as people look in two directions at once: back to a carefully reconstructed past and forward in modern time to the future that brings together different ways of being. Their story includes a symbolic journey by outsiders to their place, a modern chronicle of a political movement called Pariet, a tribal dance, and hidden stories that remain unrevealed here; and it ends with the words of their chairperson, "I speak with authority," old and new.

PLACE—PAST AND PRESENT

Wisini is a village located near the Biaru and the Wisini Rivers, within the Wau rural local-level government mandated region of Bulolo District in Morobe Province. According to Naup Waup, a local tribal elder (uniquely with tertiary qualifications from both Papua New Guinea and Australia), the first inhabitants of Wisini arrived from Porr about twelve generations ago. Two other clans—Kai and Kemkolkol—arrived first in other places and then later moved to Wisini:

> The elders speak of an unknown disease that affected the Wisini population four generations ago. People were dying in unexplainable circumstances, and only the people who left the area survived. The current village is built on a massive graveyard, and evidence of this is still very visible with fragments of human bones found on the ground. Upon the arrival of the missionaries, the Wisini people were asked to build their village again on the very same land, and the village as we know it today is still here in the unchanged location.

The village is a twelve-to-eighteen-hour journey south by four-wheel drive from Lae, the key provincial town of Morobe Province. The bitumen road, built through Australian aid, travels across the Markham River Bridge through Timini village and on to Bulolo. Timini is just a cluster of houses and a small market with people sitting by the roadside selling local fare and produce. From Timini one passes across relatively flat land up into low, striated mountains. The largest industry here is the Zenag Highland Products chicken farm and factory established in 1946. Zenag is close to the Kumalu River, which brought a mudslide down the mountainside in 2005, burying the small town of Mummery in silt and rocks. The only remaining signs of the town are the remnants of a church spire and an old store billboard sticking out of the rubble. The town of Bulolo on the Kumalu River has a small population serving the needs of large mining and timber companies in Morobe Province. From Bulolo the road moves upward to Wau—primarily a main street with two general stores owned by an Australian and one main gas pump—and finally to Werewere and Wisini. Mining along the Wau-Werewere route has lessened, but sporadic blasts are reminders that it still continues, if on a smaller scale.

The last part of the journey out of Wau is a hazardous one, and many places are virtually inaccessible except by walking or a powerful four-wheel-drive vehicle. A backhoe operator working on the Wau road was killed under an overturned vehicle two weeks after we used a road that he had cleared in July 2006. Massive potholes, half-collapsed bridges, landslides, road collapses, and river crossings slow travel and have been made worse by sections of deforestation and soil erosion. When the rains come, they slow or make impossible what is already an incredibly exhausting drive, with regular stops to dig the car out of yet another mud bath.

The Wisini group of villages includes the four main villages of Wisini Ward 17—Kassangare, Tauroro, Wisini, and Ilabu—and a loose network of other villages that are scattered along the Ono, Waria, and Biaru Rivers. These include the villages of Sim, Gerepo, Kauru, Koperaka, and Sumu. Since early 1992 these villages have begun to work together as a collective, driven in many parts by the Pariet mobilization project,and also by the increasing need to depend on a larger network of people and places as food sources diminish and access to primary services like health and education have either declined or ceased to exist. Once the aggressive phase of mining on this side of the mountain tapered off in the early 1990s, the primary community services and road maintenance that once existed to service these gold-mining companies disappeared with them.

Remote and isolated as they are, the villages in the Wisini area have had little in the way of government services and support, particularly from the provincial and national levels. The Kasangere Elementary School started in 2002 closed down in 2005. The Crisitan Elementary School started in 2004 and closed down in 2005. The only remaining school in this area is the Biaru Primary School, and many young children are unable to walk the minimum of three kilometers each way to get to the school. Pariet project efforts set up a small community school in the Koruma area called the Koruma Primary School, and this school struggles on with the help of volunteers and part-time teachers.

While the Papua New Guinean state has had little presence in Wisini, business-led "development" activities have taken place. The mountain overlooking the villages consists of steep, undulating slopes, interspaced with the slopes of old or recent landslides and crisscrossed with trails. Much of the once densely vegetated mountainsides have been significantly affected by the heavy explosives and open-cast mining methods used in large-scale resource extraction. Sporadic mining still occurs, and villagers spoke of new negotiations currently under way with the national government for licenses and services for the recommencement of mining around the region. This has sparked deep and grave concern among these villagers, particularly those located along the Watut and Langimar River areas. Speculations abound of gold being discovered in these areas, and the community knows well what to expect if this turns out to be the case.

The mountain is encircled by a rough dirt road that changes to mud after a night of rain. This road was the only land route for mining companies in the late 1970s to the late 1990s. Heavy bulldozers and tractors are now the main users. They come up to collect the tobacco and coffee produce from the villagers—the journey is slow and hazardous, but these are the only types of vehicles capable of traveling on the road. The vehicles have taken their toll on the road. In many places, potholes, some as deep as three feet, have become filled with rainwater. On one journey we came across two tractors that the Pariet members said had been there for more than a week. The driver was awaiting parts for the vehicle. There was a makeshift fence of saplings and branches around the tractor, and a man was asleep inside the main cabin. The tractor was being watched to prevent it from being vandalized. Gerry Krong told us, "Villagers are angry and confused— while they have to sell their coffee and tobacco, they are also angry that, instead of repairing the roads, the companies send such terrible vehicles. The road has become the only way to connect to the outside. Old paths and tracks have been

The road to Wisini from Wau is a four-wheel-drive track that is impassable with heavy rains.

destroyed or altered due to mining and logging activities and consequent soil ero-
sions and landslides."

ORGANIZATION AND GOVERNANCE

There were approximately 300 people officially recorded within the Wisini Ward
in the 2000 census. But the most current updated record by the Pariet project in
2006 records approximately 763 people.

There are six main subtribes or clans within the Pariet project or Ammam
tribe—the Naap, Kuiyap, Portutep, Kourtat, Huup, and Kemkolkol. In 2006 we
counted a total of five men's houses and forty-eight women's houses in Wisini village, complicating the notion of sixty-four households. The community around Wisini has a long history of religious influence, and evidence of this is easily seen in
the presence of two or more concrete buildings that function as churches with daily
religious practices and activities. Many of the villagers have taken Christian names
but, when they are introduced, also state their indigenous names and tribe. Different Christian denominations in the area include Lutheran (20 percent), Lutheran
Reform (2 percent), Baptist (25 percent), Four Square (25 percent), Seventh-Day Adventist (5 percent), ARC or Reformed Seventh-Day Adventist (2 percent), and finally
Sabbath (30 percent) and Kaumpis (1 percent), two local religions based on local
interpretations of the Bible—the second newly formed. The local inhabitants move
between different denominations, sometimes being simultaneously in two, and as
such the percentages from 2006 have subsequently fluctuated considerably. There
appears to be occasional consternation as each denomination strives to maintain
its dominance or assert its revival.

As within other PNG communities, familial relationships within the Wisini
group of villages form the basic foundations of the place, including strong extended family ties among the people. The huts in which the villagers live vary in size
across the surrounds, dictated by the size of the families rather than the wealth

Table 6.1 Figures from Pariet Project Village Records

	HOUSE-HOLDS	PERSONS	MALES	FEMALES	MEN'S HOUSES	WOMEN'S HOUSES
Tauroro village	19	95	72	23	2	4
Ilabu village	40	195	103	92	7	38
Kasangare village	33	172	96	76	9	52
Wisini village	64	301	156	145	5	48
Total: Wisini Ward (17 clans)	156	763	427	336	23	142

or income of the household. Community life is maintained through the everyday lived reciprocity of cooking, gardening, foraging or working in the forest, tending to small plots of coffee or tobacco, fishing in the rivers, and child care. In such a remote area, where there are no electricity, gas, or telecommunication services, villagers rely on one another to stay alive and safe. When the Community Sustainability Questionnaire was conducted in the Wisini group of villages in 2006, 47 percent of respondents indicated that they have lived in the same immediate area their whole life. Where people do move from their village of birth, it is often the result of marriages between the villages or a matter of relocation from one side of the river to the other.

It is apparent that the Pariet mobilization process is drawing together a wide network of tribal villages and elders, with the Wisini group of villages providing a form of headquarters or pulse for the movement. The process of mobilization is largely driven by the identification of key cultural stories and artifacts, the sharing of overlapping customary knowledge of land management and governance across tribes, and the mapping of these around the revival of an ancient text and sacred journey by a tribe called the Ammam People. This mapping has now slowly extended out from the Wisini village cluster, across river and settlements to the Garaina (Waria Bulolo District) and Watuk (Menyamya District), down to Hote Yamap and Yalu (Huon Gulf District). The mapping process is encouraging tribal elders across different tribal boundaries to draw lines of lineage, ancestry, and old intertribal connections and rivalries that had been dramatically disrupted by colonial occupation and subsequent large resource extraction activities. Old dances and songs—telling stories of resistance and determination, knowledge of food sources, and tales of greed and deceit—appear not just to be re-created but also recalled. A new theater group—called the Seventh Division Theatre dance group—is now further developing these dances and songs. Working closely with the Pariet movement, this dance group, drawing on traditional songs, poems, legends, and instruments, now focuses on educating and training young people.

LIVELIHOOD AND PROVISION

The tribal villagers in Wisini and surrounds are primarily subsistence farmers, tending their gardens though slash-and-burn methods. Cooking is done on a fire almost always in the front area outside the hut, mainly to boil taro (*Colocasia esculenta* and *Xanthosoma sagittifolium*) or yams (*Dioscorea* spp.). Among respondents to the Community Sustainability Questionnaire, 88 percent identified work done on their own land or fishing as their main source of food. Within their gardens, households grow a diverse range of crops that form the bulk of their diet. Tapioca, taro, and yams are important staples, but people also grow cabbage (the European version—family Brassicaceae), cucumber, onions, eggplant, pineapple, and papaya.

The rivers that run through the area—the Biaru River and its tributaries—are the only source of water within the villages. The rivers are also a source of food, but fish stocks have been severely depleted by the chemical run-off from the mines.

As well as providing food for their own consumption, gardening also provides a limited source of income for some families. The main activity of the local cash economy is coffee growing, followed by tobacco growing, peanut cultivation, and pig rearing. Other important cash crops are vanilla pods and avocado, but many of the avocado trees and vanilla plots have been sold off to outsiders in what are now seen as naive negotiations on the part of the community. Steady buyers of coffee include Wayamu, Danniel, Coffee Farmers Association, and Big Bean Coffee Limited. Coffee trees are scattered through the forest area, and data from 2005 given to us by the Pariet movement showed that there were only seventeen coffee tree owners across the area. Many of the other villagers earn a small income during the harvesting periods or through tending the trees. In 2005 coffee comprised 40 percent of earnings, tobacco 20 percent, peanuts 5 percent, and pigs 25 percent. Most of the cash earned was spent on school fees (70 percent), clothing (10 percent), trade store goods (15 percent), and savings (5 percent).

The day-to-day lives of the villagers today bear the mark of influence of more than thirty years of intensive logging and large-scale mineral extraction in the area. Working now to sustain their livelihoods, they do so facing a multitude of social and environmental problems. As they struggle through their everyday existence in a remote area, the villagers are now much more aware of the debris left behind from these massive activities—reduced water quality in the rivers, new types of weeds, chemical run-off.

LEARNING AND EDUCATION

There is a strong desire for learning and training within the Wisini group of villages. Among those surveyed, 91 percent said that they would like to learn how to do their current work better. Given the dominant agricultural base, it is perhaps not surprising that 72 percent wanted training in agriculture. Management was also an area in which many people—45 percent—expressed a desire for training. Literacy training, too, was in high demand, with 54 percent identifying this as something that would be useful for them, much higher than the overall figure of 19 percent across all the PNG sites in this project. In addition, there was a strong interest in forms of training that reflect the Pariet movement's concern with the strengthening of their customs and culture. Of the survey respondents, 46 percent wanted training in family life, while 52 percent wanted training in traditional ways.

As has already been mentioned, the Biaru Primary School is the only primary school left in the area, and one of the projects initiated by the Pariet mobilization has been the establishment of a small community school in the Koruma area, run

by volunteers and part-time teachers. However, the Pariet movement has also identified informal and customary-based learning and education as vitally important for
their community. The importance of engagement with the younger generations—
around matters of custom and culture as well as through formal education—is
felt keenly by people throughout the Wisini area. One woman in the community, a
recent widow with seven children, was asked in an interview to identify what she
thought made her community strong. She answered: "Coming together, sit around
together and talk about what is good for us, and looking after people like me and
others who need help. From custom to education—people are saying that education is more important than custom, to give children a better future. But custom
and education must go together—they must go together."

Education and development are seen as closely linked. A young man, said,
"Yes, people tell us we are rich in customs and land, but we are poor. We want
things to make our life better." Aru Kuskom is a high school student at Lae. He
boards with his aunt and travels back to Wisini for the holidays. Sometimes when
there is no truck or transport, he walks down to Wau and then tries to hitch a ride
up to Lae. Such transport is not always certain and changes with the weather and
the rains. He relies on his parents for his living and travel, and says that he relies
on his aunt in Lae for his boarding and food: "I like coming back to Wisini. This is
my village. I only live in Lae. Wisini is my home. I was born here and brought up
here—and I like my people. I want my people to have a better life. Make my community life better." When asked in what way better, he replied, "Better school, better
living here. There is only one primary school. I want a better school, higher school
for more study. More training for the other people. We have nobody to teach us new
things. When I am a pilot, I will take the plane for the people here in Wisini."

Similarly, education cannot be understood outside of the broader questions
of community livelihood and well-being. Many of the young men in Wisini and its
surrounds are frustrated and angry about the lack of educational facilities for them
and the lack of access to training centers or schools within their area. The nearest
places are in Lae—and getting there involves a good two-to-four-day walk down the
mountain. Many do not have the income to stay on in Lae, and those who leave the
village to look for work and education usually return, unable to sustain a decent way
of life in the city. The young women too expressed a great deal of helplessness. Sitting huddled together with a large group of women around the women's hut, Nancy
Paro, one of the older women, says, "Let the girls talk. They want to talk." And then
Nancy Karong, one the girls who had helped us earlier with the cooking, says,

> Yes, we never speak. We always listen. We are studying in the mission school. We
> like it there. But I don't know what to do after I finish. The books at the mission
> school talk to us about keeping good houses and clean clothes and sewing. But

we don't have even a sewing machine. So how can we sew?...I am nineteen years old. We are seventeen years, here this one is nineteen, and she is sixteen. I don't know this one. How old are you? We all go to school together. It is called the Biaru Primary School. It is not far from here. I am in grade 7. We learn how to sing and manners and English and some maths. I don't have money to go to Lae. If I go, it is not safe.

It is obvious as we converse with people involved in Wisini that, while community mobilization is strong, many of the questions and responses are framed by an increasing skepticism toward both local and Western interventions and their promises of improvements in everyday lived struggles. As one woman said:

We get so tired too; *yumi planti bagarap,* yes, yes. You and me, we women do get pretty exhausted. We are always working from the time our eyes open to when they cannot be open. There is so much to do, and we do the same thing every day. Sometimes the men listen, and sometimes they don't care what we say. But we also work in the garden. We also sell the coffee. We also walk to Lae and to

Naup Waup, an activist and social researcher from Wisini and a leader of the Pariet mobilization

Wau and everywhere to sell our coffee. Maybe one day the road will be better. No, I want a big school. I want to meet many people and live different.

The Pariet project of the Ammam tribal people represents a determined attempt by the local community to organize itself in the face of massive complex forces. It knows that it has a long way to go.

Omarakana and Kiriwina Island, Milne Bay Province

HOW COULD IT BE THAT A CELEBRATION, LONG PART OF THE CUSTOMARY CALENDAR, IS DISPLACED BY A GLOBALIZED EVENT ABOUT WHICH THE WORLD KNOWS NOTHING?

Omarakana is the village of the paramount chief of the Trobriand Islands. Each year on Kiriwina Island, the largest of the Trobriands, their annual harvest of yams is followed by a period of festivities known as Mila Mala. Yams are the staple crop on Kiriwina, but they are also items of great cultural and spiritual importance. Mila Mala celebrations occur when the harvest in a village is particularly good, and they are a means through which that community exhibits its wealth and standing to the other communities around it. The yams are collected, presented, and stored inside tall wooden yam houses painted with distinctive patterns in red, black, and white; and dancing and feasting occupy the community for several days. The elaborate sexuality of the celebrations was famously documented by the Polish anthropologist Bronislaw Malinowski in the early twentieth century and is partially responsible for the Trobriands' reputation as the "Islands of Love." More stories have been written about the Trobriands than perhaps any other region in Papua New Guinea, and the people of Kiriwina are practiced in rehearsing foundational stories about themselves to outsiders. The story we tell here, however, is not one of theirs but rather narrates the unfolding of two celebrations—one that did happen and one that did not. That is, it did not happen in a way that was continuous with the customary sense of the festival or in the modern sense of what had been planned. The juxtaposition of these two celebrations, the Mila Mala festival and World Youth Day, carries the full weight of social change in the Trobriands and the layers of the tribal, traditional, and modern.

In 2006 an Organizing Committee under the auspice of the Council of Chiefs and chaired by Kevin Kaidoga received funding to run the Mila Mala festival. The managed event was intended to attract tourism, showcase the Trobriands, and project community. As part of this process, the introduction of money fundamentally altered the celebrations and delayed the festival until a day in late September, long after harvesting. Where the organization of the celebrations previously had everything to do with social obligation, pride, and the customary understandings of status, it now also had to do with the receipt of a wage, access to resources like cars and travel allowances, and modern conceptions of status. Fixing a date and location for the festival meant overriding the prior cosmological situating of Mila Mala, in which place and time depend on the changing interrelationships between villages, the particularity of the seasons, and the outcomes of the harvest. There were allegations of corruption and abuse of power, and murmurings about the presence of "money talk" in the Organizing Committee. The 2006 festival nearly did not happen—that is, until John Kasaipwalova, chief of the Kwenama clan, drew upon his own money and called in reciprocal relations to hold a central festival at Bweka, about an hour's walk from Omarakana. The dancing was strong, but no tourists came, and the only nonlocal there, apart from six members of our research team, was Toby Neville, a bus driver whom some people said was there to take photos of the girls to make into postcards.

The following year Mila Mala—which has followed the annual yam harvest for as long as can be recalled through the oral history of the island—did not happen at all. Or, to be more precise, only one small festival was held at Oluweta village, and it neither had the sanction of the Council of Chiefs nor the imprimatur of the Mila Mala Organizing Committee. Kenneth Kalubaku (John Kasaipwalova's brother) said that his village refused to be part of the formal ceremonies because of the broken promises in 2006, and ironically Oluweta thus held the only feast that year that might be said to carry part of the customary spirit of Mila Mala.

In a second irony, in 2007, months after the harvest season, Oluweta became the scene of another celebration on Kiriwina, one rooted in a much more recent history. The revelry was in honor of Catholic World Youth Day celebrations occurring across the globe and instigated by Pope John Paul II in 1986. It involved a locally carved wooden cross journeying across the Milne Bay islands. As part of the global celebrations leading up to a Holy Mass celebrated by His Holiness Pope Benedict XVI in Sydney, Australia, in July 2008, a World Youth Cross had been traveling the world. It had visited some provinces in Papua New Guinea, but not Milne Bay. In response the Catholic Church in the province arranged for a special local cross to be built and carried across the region. It was not part of the official Catholic schedule, and Pope Benedict did not send an envoy, but it was a crucial event nevertheless.

Catholicism has entered deeply into social life and practice in this part of Papua New Guinea. The Catholic Church is not the only church on Kiriwina Island, but it has strong roots, particularly in the northern part of the island around Omarakana and Bweka, near where the mission station still operates. The cross that the provincial leadership of the Church commissioned was built out of local kwila—a honey-colored hardwood—and carved with intricate patterns by master carvers. Beginning in Alotau, on the eastern tip of the Papua New Guinea mainland, its journey had taken it to many of the Milne Bay islands clustered in the Solomon Sea. Now, it was on Kiriwina, the largest of the Trobriand Islands group, and had already spent time in the custodianship of several villages. It was being carried from Guseweta village to Oluweta, with a procession of two hundred or so people accompanying it. The weeks of preparation had included filling potholes in the road and laying down palm leaves.

When the wooden cross finally arrived at Oluweta village, the procession moved slowly, soberly, up the road. The cross itself was carried by five young men,

The wooden cross of Alotou being carried across Kiriwina Island as part of a major Catholic ceremony

who rested the weight of it on their shoulders and bowed their heads as they walked. Others—young women and men wearing white shirts and red scarves around their necks—carried religious icons, conch shells, and banners with biblical verses. The two women walking in front of the crossbearers held a banner that read, "CROSS OF JESUS: WAY * TRUTH * LIFE." Above the entrance to the village, which the crossbearers now approached, another banner hung between two trees. Written with white paint on black plastic were the words "St FRANCIS ASISI of Oluweta Solemnly Welcomes THE HOLY CROSS."

The people at Oluweta had been expecting to receive the cross early in the morning, but changes to the program for the day meant that its arrival was delayed. They waited for it patiently. Underneath the welcoming banner, a group of young singers had spent the morning seated on the ground at the side of the road, dressed in white shirts and blue pants and skirts. Opposite them, four young women stood where they had been for the past four and a half hours. They wore the tribal costume of young Trobriand dancers—short grass skirts with many layers, dyed mostly red but with patterns of yellow, blue, and white. Feathers and shell valuables were affixed carefully to their headdresses, earrings, and the bands around their waists and arms; and their backs and chests were sprinkled with yellow pollen. Dancing has long been part of customary celebrations and rituals in the Trobriands, and the elaborate costumes and adornments that dancers wear are important signifiers of status and social relationships. Normally, they would be worn at Mila Mala, but the celebrations had not happened last harvest. Now, the dancers had been arranged to greet the Catholic cross, and their presence gave some suggestion of the respect with which the event was endowed.

Finally, the kwila-wood cross was making its way along the dirt road leading in to Oluweta. The singers stood up. Past them, within the village, young children holding ferns and flowers were thrust into position along the side of the road. The procession was accompanied by a man playing a guitar, and as they walked toward the black banner welcoming the cross, their singing joined with the singing of the choir that had been awaiting their arrival.

Past the entrance, the procession continued to the village church. The young dancers walked in front, leading the way with focused seriousness. The people who had been waiting at the entrance now followed behind, while others were gathered in the open area in front of the church. Among them, old women wearing black funeral clothes with black fabric on their heads knelt on the ground, singing mourn-

A young woman dressed as for the Mila Mala Festival but this time to welcome the cross

ing songs in local language. As the procession reached them and the cross was lowered from the shoulders of the young men, they raised their hands above their heads to receive it. The people gathered around them knelt, many of them crying. Sounds of singing were mingled with sobs and soft moaning.

Later, there would be a service for those gathered, after which the cross would be interned inside the church. Dancing would follow, and feasting: the rituals of the introduced church manifested with and through the customary rituals that long predate its presence on the island.

The occurrence of the Catholic World Youth Day celebrations on Kiriwina thus matched in significance the Mila Mala celebrations of the year before. If the World Youth Cross celebrations were extraordinary in their local-global novelty, the yearly yam harvest was extraordinary for the relative absence of celebration. Both happenings have their roots in the various influences that have made their way into Trobriands society since the colonizing project began. Together, they paint a complicated picture of change and continuity on Kiriwina Island, of the dynamism of culture and the messy back and forth between the old and the new.

PLACE—PAST AND PRESENT

Located in the Solomon Sea beyond the eastern tip of the Papua New Guinea mainland, the Trobriand Islands are a collection of populated coral atolls and over a hundred unpopulated small islets that form part of Milne Bay Province. They were named for Denis de Trobriand, the first lieutenant in one of d'Entrecasteaux's frigates when this group of populated atolls and hundreds of islets was sighted in 1793. Other groups of islands surround them—including the D'Entrecasteaux Islands, the Amphlett Islands, and the Louissiade Archipelago—and although many of these island groups are geographically quite close to the mainland, the ocean around them and the high cost of travel have meant they remain remote places. There is great variety in cultural traditions and practices across the region, but interconnections between the islands and fundamental similarities mean that they are often considered together under the heading of "Massim" society. The largest of the populated islands in the Trobriands group is Kiriwina, which has around sixty villages in which over 25,000 people live. Although many young people leave the islands to find paid employment or to pursue education on the mainland, a large percentage of them eventually return to resume village life, and the population has grown considerably over recent decades. Set at the northern end of Kiriwina and about thirty minutes drive from the district administrative center of Losuia is Omarakana village.

Omarakana village is home to Paramount Chief Pulavasi Daniel, the highest customary authority in the Milne Bay area. The position of paramount chief is passed down matrilineally through the leading Tabalu clan. Today, the paramount chief's house is a large structure built out of modern blue-painted timber board and fibro. It is surrounded by smaller, customary-style huts with thatched pandanus roofs. In a clearing behind the house stands the chief's yam house. Trobriand yam houses, tall narrow wooden structures painted with distinctive red and white patterns, are one of the more immediately recognizable instances of Trobriand art and culture, with replicas found in hotel gardens in Port Moresby and miniature models sold in the city's tourist shops. Used to store the staple food that is harvested annually around midyear, the yam houses are also important cultural signifiers of wealth and status, and, while each village chief has his own, the paramount chief's should be the tallest and best kept. From 2005 to 2008 the chief's yam house degraded and was in need of major work; its thatch roof was broken. Nearby yam houses looked worse. The physical sense of the village changed as a whole during those few years, but the community also seemed much less resilient than on earlier visits going back to the late 1970s.

Physically, the Trobriand Islands are elevated coral atolls, and most, including Kiriwina, are flat. Tropical vegetation and rich soil allow for productive gardening, predominantly of yams. Roads connect most of the villages to each other, with their rough surface made of exposed coral. Off to the sides of these run thin dirt tracks leading to the yam gardens where women labor to produce the important crop. They are aided in this by regular, heavy rainfall, but periods of drought are not unknown, and, when they occur, they can result in severe food shortages.

Losuia, the district headquarters, has a post office, several administrative offices, and a number of trade stores. Kiriwina High School nearby provides education for day students (expensive, at a cost of 600 kina annually in 2008) and boarders (900 kina) from villages farther away. Also present on the island is a Catholic mission station in which three nuns—two from Italy and one from Myanmar—are currently based. An airstrip built by American soldiers during the Second World War is still functional, and planes fly from Port Moresby to Kiriwina twice a week. Also left over from the war are the wrecks of submarines and ships around the coast and an assortment of broken weaponry and other pieces of equipment that villagers regularly dig up when making new yam gardens or working in existing ones. In one of the two lodges on the island offering accommodation to tourists—some of whom come to dive in the shipwrecks or snorkel off the coast—shell casings are used as tiny vases to hold the frangipani flowers that decorate the dining room tables.

ORGANIZATION AND GOVERNANCE

A complex system of interlinked clans and tribes provides the basis for social organization in Kiriwina, as it does throughout the Milne Bay region. Connecting the tribes is a strong set of shared cultural practices, a common history with distinct but overlapping myths and stories of origin, established patterns of trade and festivities, and a shared language. The Kilivila language belongs to the Milne Bay family of Austronesian languages, and, although it is spoken on a few other Massim islands, Trobrianders are the major speakers. Kilivila takes the form of a number of local dialects, which are mutually understandable and have also absorbed a number of English words and terms in the period since first contact. Tok Pisin is rarely used, although many locals who travel beyond the island for work and education learn both it and Motu.

Matrilineal lines underpin systems of landownership and inheritance, and also determine social identity and relationships of responsibility and obligation. As one set of stories relates the structure, there are four main tribal groupings on the island, represented by different totems: the white pigeon, green parrot, eagle, and red and yellow parakeet. Cutting across these tribes are a number of clans, membership of which is passed matrilineally through family groups. The four primary clan groups are the Tabalu, from which the paramount chief is drawn; the Toruwaga, who are the rival clan to the Tabalus; the Kwenama; and the Mulabwema. A tribe will include members of different clans, but within each tribe there is a leading clan from which the chiefly line will be drawn. So, the Tabalu are the leading clan within the Malasi, or white pigeon tribe, and the Kwenama and Toruwaga clans are the two leading clans from which the chiefs of the green parrot tribe are drawn, while the Mulabwema are the chiefly clan of the eagle tribe (the chiefly clan of the red and yellow parakeet tribe is not represented within the whole-island chiefdom structure). Customarily, intermarriage within tribes was taboo, but now instances of marriage between people from the same tribal groupings are not uncommon.

Relationships of authority and responsibility exist within the parameters of the tribe. Tribal chiefs are drawn from the dominant clans within each tribe, and beneath them the other clans of the tribe are arranged in a hierarchy. Different clans are allocated different responsibilities in relation to the tribal chief, whether it be resourcing materials or producing the lime with which he chews his *buai*. Those in chiefly matrilineages, ranked among themselves, own rights to special prerogatives surrounding food prohibitions and taboos that mark spatial and physical separation as well as rights to wear particular feather and shell decorations and to decorate houses with ancestral designs and cowrie shells. The most important prerogative for chiefs is the entitlement to many wives. At least four of each wife's relatives make huge yam gardens for her, and this is the way a chief achieves great power. But, if a chief is weak, he will have difficulty finding women to marry. Chiefly entitlement also comes with reciprocal responsibilities to those in their tribes, including social obligations to host feasts and redistribute wealth.

While chiefs exert authority over their tribes, it is the paramount chief in Omarakana village who is the unquestioned ultimate authority on the island. In the central clearing in Omarakana, the place of the yam houses, Bwenaya, a sacred stone that is the respected goddess of the weather, is buried. Her precise location is known only to the paramount chief, and it is from the goddess that he draws his strength. Most, if not all, decisions affecting the island as a whole are made by him, such as those affecting feasts, festivities, and harvesting. He presides over the Kiriwina Council of Chiefs, which includes chiefs from the major clans across the island. He presides as well over the Kiriwina Local Government Council, which consists of local councilors elected under the modern local-level government political structure. The paramount chief's role in presiding over this forum is demonstrative of the continuing strength and influence of customary-tribal systems of political organization and authority, but it is also indicative of the ways in which modern structures of power are shaped and acted on through their incorporation into predominantly tribal social contexts.

The Catholic Church has been influential in Kiriwina society since the early days of colonial contact. As witnessed through events such as the recent World Youth Cross celebration, there are deeply felt affective ties connecting the church and local communities, but the presence of Catholicism and other Christian churches has not shaken the customary belief systems of Trobriand Islanders. The belief in and practice of magic is embedded in the day-to-day lifeworlds of Kiriwina. While sorcery is feared above all else, magic more broadly is an accepted part of most aspects of social life—love, beauty, gardening, weather, sailing, and skills such as carving or boat building. Knowledge and practice of magic, spells, charms, and incantations is determined by matrilineage, status, and relationships of *tambu* (from taboo but emphasizing prescriptions and restrictions in communication and marriage). On a festive occasion, for example, the ceremonial washing and decoration of dancers is undertaken by women of a special class, namely, those who stand to them in the relation of *tambu*. In other words, these women may be approved and suitable partners for passing intrigues or for more stable liaisons or for marriage. It is their duty to prepare the men for the dance; to deck them out with ornaments, flowers, and paint; and to perform the magic incidental to each stage of the proceeding. In this way, magic as practice becomes part of the way that social life in the community is ordered and understood.

The ritualistic dimensions of the practice of magic are indicative of the complex patterns of exchange and interaction that permeate all of Trobriand social life. Relationships of obligation and reciprocity bind people together, often over considerable distance and time. This is evident, for instance, in cultural practices surrounding death and burial. When a person dies, Trobriand Islanders believe the spirit goes to live on the distant island of Tuma, where the ancestors continue their existence. The mourning and exchanges following a death are the most lengthy and costly of all ritual events. When a person dies, an all-night vigil takes place in which men sing traditional songs, and the spouse and children of the deceased cry over the body. A series of food and women's wealth distributions take place after the burial, after which the close relatives of the spouse and the father of the dead person shave their hair and/or blacken their bodies while the spouse remains secluded. About six months later, those who have been in mourning are repaid by women of the deceased's matrilineage, who host a huge distribution of skirts and banana-leaf bundles among the many hundreds of mourners. Grass skirts and banana-leaf bundles are both important items of women's wealth, and skills in making them are highly valued, passed down within families from mothers and aunts to daughters and nieces. The status of big-woman is secured for those who distribute the most wealth, meaning that power and obligation remain tightly intertwined. When the deceased is an important person, an annual distribution of yams, pork, taro pudding, sugarcane, or betel nut take place each year following the death. At the end of the annual harvest period, it is believed that the ancestors of a matrilineage return to the Trobriands from the island of Tuma to examine the well-being of their kin, and, when a harvest is especially large, a villagewide distribution will be held to honor all the recently deceased from one clan.

The anthropologist Malinowski recognized the primacy of exchange rituals in Trobriand social life. Writing in 1922, he described the basis of what he called the "tribal economics" of the islands as being "that *the whole tribal life is permeated by a constant give and take;* that every ceremony, every legal and customary act is done to the accompaniment of material gift and counter gift; that wealth, given and taken, is one of the main instruments of social organisation, of the power of the chief, of the bonds of kinship, and of relationship in law."[1] The intricate webs of connection created through ritual practices of exchange are perhaps most vividly illustrated in the operation of the Kula Ring. Where funeral distributions and other social practices involve the exchange of women's wealth—banana-leaf bundles and grass skirts—Kula is the means of exchange of men's wealth, shell valuables. Networks of men extend across geographic space—extending beyond Kiriwina and the Trobriand Islands and encompassing most of the Milne Bay area—creating a "ring," or route, through which the shell valuables move in a complex pattern of gift and countergift. Shell necklace valuables, *soulava,* move clockwise through the ring, while arm shell valuables, *mwari,* move in a counterclockwise direction. Exchanges take place between individuals and their partners, and the numbers of partners a Kula participant has will vary according to his or her power and status. Partner relationships may be lifelong in their duration and entail obligations to provide hospitality, protection, and assistance. They can at times be fraught with conflict, but the time delay between the exchange of gift and countergift means that they also rely on trust and the strength of social obligation. In this sense, a crucial dimension of the Kula gift economy is its distinction from the bartering and trade of items of use value.

Within the Kula Ring, giving is always weighted more highly than receiving: as with women's wealth, objects hold significance in themselves, but it is the redistribution of those objects that secures the social status of the giver. The value of the objects themselves is ceremonial and lies in their being signifiers of status and connection. While a particular valuable is in the possession of a Kula participant, he will display it—often on the body of his wife, daughters, or nieces—and the necklace or armband brings status to his family through signifying the Kula relationships that have enabled him to acquire it. Slowness in passing on an object that one has received, however, is likely to tarnish the reputation of a participant, and so valuables are assured an ongoing movement through the ring.

While Malinowski praised the ceremonial gift exchange of the Kula Ring, he also predicted that it would eventually fall into demise. This has not happened, but, as with all dimensions of cultural and social life, the practices of Kula have changed over the years since the first colonial contact with the Milne Bay islands, and the ring is under pressure. In some instances, the contemporary Kula Ring has expanded across geographic space, with some items now held by individuals in Port Moresby and possibly even as far as Australia, cut off from the partner relationships that were maintained through seagoing travel between the islands. The introduction of a cash economy has affected the Kula tradition as well, with some participants suggesting that valuables are now being purchased for cash by individuals who keep them as their property, failing to pass them on and honor the customary obligations. When this happens or when the time lapse between gift and countergift is collapsed into a momentary cash transaction, the relationships created by the Kula exchange are lost. Politics have always been part of the ritual practices around Kula, but politics in the Trobriands are changing now; and gift economies such as the Kula Ring are being transformed through contact with new economies, ideologies, and forms of social being.

LIVELIHOOD AND PROVISION

Subsistence agriculture is the mainstay of the Kiriwina community. The staple crop, yams, carries a social and cultural significance far beyond their dietary function. The growing of yams—which includes planting, staking up the vines of the plants, and tending to them as they grow—is generally men's work, although it is not unheard of for a woman to make her own yam garden. Men also work building garden fences and are generally responsible for the yearly yam harvest that precedes the Mila Mala period of festivities. When a woman is married, her father and eventually her brothers must make yam gardens and produce a yearly yam harvest for her husband. This work is done in her name, as recognition of the matrilineal ownership of the land on which the yams are grown.

While yam growing is predominantly men's work, both men and women work together to clear new garden land, and women take responsibility for producing other garden foods. Taro, sweet potatoes, bananas, sugarcane, leafy greens, beans, tapioca, squashes, coconuts, and areca palms are all grown, and unlike yams their function is purely as a source of daily sustenance. The daily diet that these foodstuffs provide is supplemented with fish for those in coastal communities and those who trade with them. Pork is eaten occasionally, at times of special feasting. Like yams, pigs carry a social and cultural importance in Kiriwina society, and, as with yam farming, the butchering of pigs and preparation of pork for feasts is done by men. Daily cooking, though, is women's work.

The importance of subsistence agriculture for Kiriwina livelihoods is reflected in the results of the Community Sustainability Questionnaire. Of those surveyed, 95 percent indicated that fishing and work done on their own land was their primary source of food. Their responses also spoke to the demanding and time-consuming labor that is required for this work: 60 percent of respondents said that they worked for 60 or more hours a week, in contrast to an overall figure of just 24 percent across all the research sites. Another 13 percent of Kiriwinans surveyed said they worked for between forty and sixty hours a week. It is difficult to corroborate these figures without extensive surveys of individuals over periods of time, but it is significant that the estimations of their own labor time that people provided were much greater than those provided by respondents in many other communities, particularly less remote ones.

In more recent times, fishing has provided coastal men with limited access to a cash income, and a fishing cooperative has been successful on nearby Vakuta Island. In the last few years, a local market run by women has been established on Kiriwina, but there are few other sources of income generation. Isolated as the community is, relatively few outsiders come to the island, although the grounds around the tiny airstrip are filled with young men selling crabs and fish when the flight from Port Moresby comes in twice a week. There has been little success with cash-cropping enterprises, and, since colonization, government attempts at establishing such schemes have failed, save for a period of copra production.

The only other source of income comes from the few tourists who visit the island. In the 1970s weekend tourist charters resulted in increasing sales of the distinctive Trobriands wooden carvings, but over the past decade tourism has declined dramatically. The numbers of men trying to sell their intricate carved walking sticks and other pieces far outnumber the tourists on hand to purchase them. The ebony wood that is used to create them is now also greatly depleted and must be imported from other islands. A few Kiriwinans own successful trade stores, and there is one guest lodge run by a local man and his family. An additional guest lodge and two other trade stores are owned and run by expatriates. Today remittances from children working elsewhere in the country provide villagers with their main source of cash.

What little cash income is produced on the island or gotten through remittances from places like Alotau and Port Moresby on the mainland, goes toward purchasing rice, tobacco, kerosene, and cloth, and toward the payment of school fees. Women's bundles of dried banana leaves act as a limited currency. Villagers with access to cash will sometimes buy trade-store goods, which they sell to other villagers for payment in bundles, allowing those without cash to purchase Western merchandise.

Trade is another important means of acquiring goods that are not produced by Kiriwina villagers themselves, and it has a long history in the Milne Bay region. Massim men are skilled sailors, and canoes are still used to connect the Trobriand Islands to each other and to the island groups that surround them. Stone axe blades, another important item of men's wealth, were traded in from Muyua Island and polished in the Trobriands in the last century, and many still circulate today. Large cooking pots, also used in local exchanges, come from the Amphlett Islands, while canoes from Normanby and Goodenough Islands arrive periodically with sacks of betel nuts that are sold at the Kiriwina wharf. Regular Kula voyaging also facilitates regular trade and bartering in addition to the ceremonial exchange of shell valuables.

LEARNING AND EDUCATION

Levels of both literacy and formal education in Kiriwina are generally low compared to other remote islands in the province and other communities across the country. Of those surveyed through the Community Sustainability Questionnaire, 21 percent indicated that they had no formal schooling, much higher than the overall figure of 9 percent across all eleven communities where the questionnaire was conducted. Thirty-four percent had completed primary education, and 36 percent had completed some or all of their secondary education. Nine percent of respondents had some form of trade training, down again from the overall figure of 13 percent, and none of those surveyed had been to university. The low levels of formal education partly reflect the limited access to schools for children on the island. There is inadequate basic education provision and just one high school on the island, at the administrative center of Losuia. Some students from more distant parts of the island board at this school, while other children travel to the mainland, returning for holidays. Boarding, however, is expensive, and the limited access to cash makes affording school fees a challenge.

The lack of formal education also reflects the low priority given to primary and secondary education in comparison to the importance placed on agriculture and customary practices. This does not mean that learning and education are not valued but that learning activities are more strongly weighted toward the passing on of customary knowledge. Included among these are the skills associated with agriculture, farming, and fishing as well as dancing, canoe making, carving, weaving, and the use of magic. The gendered division of labor and customary practice is reflected in the processes through which knowledge is passed from generation to generation, with parents, aunts and uncles, and grandparents all participating in handing down the skills and information that enable both boys and girls to partake in social life.

The importance accorded to traditional aspects of Kiriwinan life is reflected in the results gathered through the surveying of villagers. Training in both family life and traditional ways of doing things were strongly desired, with 56 and 51 percent of respondents respectively indicating that these things would be useful. However there is also a strong desire for forms of training and education more specifically geared toward participation in modern social and economic realms. Fifty-eight percent of respondents said that they would benefit from agricultural skills training, 24 percent wanted training in management skills, and 31 percent considered training in income generation desirable.

The tenacity of customary skills and cultural practice together with the knowledge underpinning livelihood activities is one of the community's greatest strengths. There is, however, an evident gap in the provision of basic education and formal skills training opportunities. It is clear in Kiriwina that people are being called on to negotiate both tribal and modern forms of social, economic, and cultural life. The sustainable development of the community demands the capacity to move in and between these ways of being, and education and learning should be oriented toward this end. In practice, this means that more avenues for accessing formal schooling, training, and modern forms of knowledge need to be created. Such forms of learning cannot, in and of themselves, engender the resilience and adaptability that sustainable community development demands, but they form an essential dimension of a community education strategy that begins with celebrating and strengthening the strong traditions through which customary knowledge and skills are maintained.

Yule Island, Central Province

WHERE HAVE ALL THE LOBSTERS GONE, AND WHY ARE THE NATURAL
CYCLES CHANGING?

Local stories abound of toxic run-off from the gold mines, climate-change effects, and illegal foreign trawling across the migration path to Yule Island. We know that each year, beginning in August, sexually mature tropical rock lobsters from the Torres Strait begin a four-month migration northeast, through the Gulf of Papua, toward Yule Island, just off the Papua New Guinea mainland. Studies suggest that Yule Island is the farthest extent of the migratory path of *Panulirus ornatus,* the point of no return for the migratory adults. They die at the end of the season from the stress of migration and reproduction.[2] The eggs hatch after a month or so, again beginning the cycle, and planktonic phyllosoma larvae are thought to float back to the Coral Sea and into the Torres Strait on the Hiri boundary current. This is the same current that in conjunction with the *Laurabada* monsoon winds once brought the Hiri traders back to Boera village and the Roro *harima* traders back to Yule Island—that is until such trade was disrupted by World War II and faltered thereafter (see Chapter 5).

In the Papuan Gulf and around the island, the lobsters are caught alive by hand or with handheld nets or killed by divers with spears. For the communities on Yule Island, given the limited capacity for agriculture on the land, the lobsters have become an important commodity—as food but more so as an item for trade. With a growing need for cash to pay for school fees, trade-store goods, and petrol for the outboard motors that connect them to the mainland—and with few other viable economic activities on the island—selling the lobsters to a growing global market has also become a crucial means of earning income.

Lobster fishing as a cash industry goes back to the late 1960s. Residents on Yule Island today recall that, at about the same time that a commercial tropical rock-lobster fishery was established in the Torres Strait, an Australian man living on the island established the Yule Lobster Company. Monica Haia'o Arua from Paramakupuna village on the island recalls that in 1975 he returned to Australia, handing over the company to people from Roro village on the island and Paitana village on the mainland. Lobsters were sold to buyers from Japan, and, in the years before independence, livelihoods for the villagers were good. The island boasted an administrative headquarters in Siria village, with a trade store, a post office, and a bank. There were guesthouses for visitors and a small airstrip. The establishment of a fisheries industry and wharfs seemed to bode well for the island's future, but in the years after independence it began to slip into a chronic economic decline. The administrative headquarters moved to Bereina on the mainland, the bank closed, and the airstrip was steadily taken over by encroaching bush. The guesthouses are now derelict buildings, and there are very few visitors to the island these days. The Yule Lobster Company established by the Australian, which held so much promise at the time, did not last much past his departure. Shortly after in 1975 it changed its name to Yule Aperana Limited, and some time not long after that it went into liquidation. No one is entirely sure what happened or why, but, while the crayfish industry grows bigger and bigger—fueled by demand from China, Hong Kong, Japan, and the Philippines—the Yule Island community is struggling to benefit from it.

There was another attempt to set up a community lobster project in late 2006 and early 2007. Coordinated by Andrew Aisia, a Yule Islander who was previously an agricultural officer for the Department of Primary Industries, a pontoon was built off the coast, with the support of a Hong Kong–Chinese company operating with Filipino workers. Under the scheme, men and women would catch crayfish and crabs and take them to the pontoon, where they would be paid straight away. According to many accounts, the prices were fair—10 kina per kilogram for lobster and 4.50 kina per kilogram for crabs. The crayfish were kept in mesh cages in the water beneath the pontoon and fed daily. About once a month, the Filipino workers from the company would come and buy them all. The scheme lasted one season and was reportedly successful. But then, again for reasons not entirely clear, the project was stopped. And in October 2007 men could be seen on board the unused

The pontoon from a failed lobster project being dismantled, the materials to be taken back to Yule Island for use in housing construction

pontoon dismantling it and taking the materials to shore to use for constructing houses.

Several reasons were offered regarding why the project failed to continue. First, the materials with which the pontoon was built were of a poor quality: the floatation devices were weak, causing the structure to partially sink, and the wire used for the underwater cages was rusting away. As an explanation for the project shutting down, however, this does not seem sufficient. Infrastructure and equipment can be repaired, and the repairs seem a worthwhile venture given the community's lack of access to any other regular market where they could sell their catch. The second reason given was that the villagers experienced a notably bad crayfish season. It was suggested, in turn, that this could have been the result of commercial fishing ventures depleting stocks in the Torres Strait before the crayfish had time to complete their migration or of climate change affecting the water temperature, with indirect effects for breeding and migration. Recent data from the Australian Government Bureau of Rural Sciences indicates that the Torres Strait Lobster Fishery is, overall, not overfished. However, some localized depletion is occurring in the Papua New Guinea area of the fishery, and there are also anecdotal reports of illegal trawling occurring in some parts of the Papuan Gulf. With regard to the impacts of climate change, there simply is not enough information available to say definitively what

Fishing in the strait between Yule Island and the southern coast of the mainland

is happening. But the people of Yule Island have fished in the waters around their community for generations, and they have no doubt that the seasons and natural cycles are changing.

PLACE—PAST AND PRESENT

The small island originally called Rabao sits just off the Papua New Guinea mainland at the eastern end of the Papuan Gulf about 110 kilometers northwest of Port Moresby. White-sand beaches encircle its perimeter, with coral outcrops and coconut palms. Traditional canoes dot the ocean alongside small outboard motors that are used for fishing and transportation to and from the mainland. Houses are clustered together, mostly built with bush materials and elevated on big logs. Decks built underneath them—with logs and bamboo slats to allow the air to flow through—provide some escape from the intense heat. The dependence of Yule Islanders on the sea means that their villages are dotted along the coast, concentrated at the southern and northern tips of the long island. At the southern end, Opa village sits close to the Catholic mission station established in the 1880s. Above it on the western coast are Koko villages numbers one and two, then Koaekupuna or Abo village, then Oviapokina and Erierina villages, and past them the Yule Island airstrip and Siria village in the Kairuku area. At the northern tip of the island are the villages of Akere, Pinupaka, and Aivara. To encircle the entire island in an outboard motor takes about two hours, provided that enough fuel can be found and the tiny engines last the distance.

Monica Haiaʻo Arua tells this story of the island's history:

> I am a direct descendent of the paramount chief of Paramakupuna village, Elias Waraupi Aisi, on my father's side. On my mother's side I am the granddaughter of the chief of the warriors, Patrick Meauri Koae, from Koaekupuna, Yule Island. The history of Yule Island as told to me by my father and my grandfather and the elders of the village community is as follows: The three major clans were Koaekupuna, Oviapokina, and Paramakupuna. They are originally from Araho, which is on the mainland. The original inhabitants of Yule Island were the Motuan people of Apau, now known as Boera, in Central Province outside of Port Moresby. How the Boera people were displaced was through tribal fighting. The warriors of Koaekupuna and Oviapokina villages combined together and had a tribal fight against Apua people. They took possession of the island known at that time as Rabao, now known as Yule Island.

The three clans that Monica Arua names are still the major clans on the island, although many different people have come and gone since her ancestors ousted the Apua people. Prominent among these are the European Catholic missionaries, who arrived at Yule Island in the 1880s and established a mission there that would become the base for their evangelizing efforts throughout the country. The priests and brothers brought with them Filipino catechists, newly recruited and trained by the Catholic mission in the Philippines. With Anglican missionaries already established on the mainland, these lay missionaries were sent out to bring the Catholic Church up to speed in the battle for Papua New Guinean souls. Years later they returned to Yule Island, where many of them married local women and lived out the rest of their lives. Today, many Yule Islanders carry the Filipino family names and distinct features of their ancestors. The Catholic mission maintains a presence on the island, albeit on a smaller scale than it did through the late nineteenth and early twentieth centuries.

The extension of the colonial administration after World War I brought more newcomers—magistrates, teachers, and officials. An administration headquarters was established at Siria village in the Kairuku area, where the overgrown airstrip remains today. A government hospital was serviced by doctors who, according to the older Yule Islanders who remember them today, would fly in on the island's Cessna plane on Mondays, Wednesdays, and Fridays of each week. When the Kairuku station was moved to Bereina, on the mainland, in the early 1970s, the hospital, post office, and both of the island's Catholic high schools moved with it. In many ways the island has been in a state of steady decline since this point. There are few reasons now for people to travel to the island, and so there are no sources of goods and money beyond what can be secured through the trade of fish and seafood with the Yule Islanders' mainland neighbors. Attempts at establishing a small tourism industry have struggled. The sole remaining guesthouse following the closure of the Kairuku station—the Carmelite Convent—has now fallen into disrepair, and fledgling attempts at establishing homestays for visitors have floundered.

ORGANIZATION AND GOVERNANCE

The community of Yule Island is organized into three main clans, with eleven or so small villages clustered at the northern and southern tips of the island and at Kairuku on the southern west coast, where the administrative headquarters used to stand. There is a relatively low level of migration in and out of the community, isolated as it is. Of those people surveyed through the Community Sustainability Questionnaire, 79 percent said they had lived in the community for eleven or more years, and 38 percent said that they had lived in the area their whole lives. Land and place are important makers of identification, and people here know their land and their environment intimately.

However, the Yule Island community is also struggling to create a viable future for itself, with few income-generating activities and little access to health and community services. There are visible reminders of the points that used to connect the island to the mainland but have long been in decline. Overall, indicators of community well-being were lower in Yule Island than in many of the other research sites in this project. When asked to indicate their satisfaction with feeling part of their community, 76 percent of respondents to the questionnaire said they were satisfied or very satisfied, in comparison to a figure of 80 percent across all the research sites. Correspondingly, the number who replied that they were dissatisfied or very dissatisfied was higher, at 17 percent compared to an overall result of 11 percent. Similar sentiments were reflected when respondents were asked how satisfied they were with their community neighborhood, with 62 percent satisfied or very satisfied, compared to 78 percent across all the research sites. The figure for those dissatisfied or very dissatisfied was 16 percent, against a national figure of 11 percent. At the same time, however, high levels of well-being were recorded when respondents were asked to indicate their level of satisfaction with their life as a whole, with 76 percent saying that they were satisfied or very satisfied. This was slightly higher than the 72 percent recorded across all the research sites. Similarly, levels of satisfaction with the balance between work and social life were comparatively high, with 87 percent of Yule Island respondents satisfied or very satisfied, compared to 71 percent of all respondents.

Results from the Community Sustainability Questionnaire suggest comparatively low levels of confidence in authority structures and decision makers, in terms of both local-level governance and formal government bodies. When asked to indicate the level to which they agreed that "decisions made about life in my neighborhood are made in the interests of the whole community," only 56 percent agreed or strongly agreed, compared to 62 percent across all the research sites. Almost a third of Yule Island respondents disagreed or strongly disagreed. When asked whether they felt that formally educated experts could be trusted when dealing with local issues, only 13 percent indicated a positive response, the lowest result among all of the research sites. Likewise, the percentage of those who agreed or strongly agreed with the statement "Governments make decisions and laws that are good for the way I live locally"—18 percent—was the lowest across the research sites. Among respondents to the Community Sustainability Questionnaire, 38 percent indicated that they participated in community activities on a daily or weekly basis, less than the overall figure of 51 percent across all the research sites. Another 27 percent said they participated in such activities on a monthly basis.

This may provide an explanation for the high levels of satisfaction felt about "life as a whole" and work-life balance, and the lower levels of satisfaction with community and one's place in it. That is, there is a relatively high degree of well-being at the individual and household level, but forms of organization and identification at the community-wide level are under strain. Furthermore, there is a sense expressed by Yule Islanders, in response to the questionnaire and through interviews and community consultations, that the government is largely absent. The low level of confidence in state decision making and legislation reflects a perception of isolation from the government services that exist elsewhere in Central Province.

LIVELIHOOD AND PROVISION

Not surprisingly for a remote community, livelihood activities associated with subsistence agriculture and fishing constitute the dominant means of work in Yule Island. Fifty-one percent of questionnaire respondents noted that the main way that they made their living was through work in the household. Another 28 percent selected selling goods in the informal economy as their main livelihood activity. Subsistence agriculture also provides the main source of food for 84 percent of Yule Island respondents. This result was predictably higher than the overall figure of 78 percent across all the communities surveyed but lower than the figures in the other remote communities of Wisini village in Morobe (88 percent) and Omarakana village in the Trobriand Islands (95 percent). In Yule Island 4 percent of respondents said that supermarkets were the main place they got their food, another 4 percent selected local shops, and 3 percent identified food markets. This may reflect the limitations of the island's ecology, which provides fish and other seafood but is unsuitable for growing some staple crops such as bananas. Accordingly, trade and barter exchange with other Mekeo communities on the mainland provides important supplements to household diets.

Since well before the arrival of the first missionaries on the island in 1885, the annual crayfish season has provided villagers on Yule Island with access to a valuable resource, drawing them into relationships of exchange and trade with communities beyond their own. Before the emergence of a cash economy, women from the island would take lobsters—along with fish, crabs, and sometimes pottery—to barter markets on the mainland. The people of Yule Island learned to make pots from the Motu (another historical link to Boera, though we found no evidence of sacred pot making).[3] Women from other villages across the Mekeo region, and as far east as the Motuan villages around Port Moresby, would bring sago, bananas, yams, and taro. These forms of barter exchange still take place, and at Kara, on the point of the mainland coast closest to the southern tip of the island, the women still meet in the early hours of the morning once a week to swap their produce. Individually or in small groups, the women set out their produce on mats on the ground: bunches of bananas, a few smoked fish, crabs and lobster still alive with their claws and legs bound. There is other produce too: small piles of baby tomatoes, *buai*, and, nowadays, cans of soft drinks in cooler boxes and small individually wrapped sweets that sell for ten toea each. But the bulk of the trade is of seafood and bananas, which are exchanged without any money passing hands. Little is said between the women as they walk up and down looking carefully at the other goods laid out on display, some of them carrying their produce as they walk up and down the line of mats and foodstuffs. When one woman sees something she considers an appropriate item for exchange, she will carry over her own goods, and, if equally acceptable, the terms of the barter are quietly negotiated. The barter exchange begins early in the morning, and by 7:00 a.m. the traders are starting to pack up. Women from the mainland set off carrying their fish, either walking or piling into the trays of pickups or PMVs. Behind them, Yule Islander women load bunches of bananas into canoes and outboard motors and set off slowly for the hour or so trip back to their villages.

Increasingly, though, what is needed within the community is not just food, but cash, and traditional barter practices are now just one part of a complex system of commerce and trade, within which the Yule Island villagers are struggling to secure their livelihoods and future in the face of change. As with most communities in contemporary Papua New Guinea, the primary expenses include foodstuffs such as rice, cooking oil, and flour, which have become staples of village diets. The use of outboard motors also requires regular purchase of gasoline, and fishing is now frequently done with nets, which must be purchased and maintained. The remoteness of the island limits the community's access to income-generating activities and the informal cash economy. Surprisingly, 9 percent of respondents to the questionnaire indicated that they were in receipt of a wage from the state, which is higher than the overall figure of 7 percent across urban, hinterland, and remote communities. At the same time, however, subjective senses of financial well-being were very low. Seventy percent of questionnaire respondents said that they considered their households to be struggling financially, a figure significantly higher than the 57 percent recorded across all the research sites. The remaining 30 percent identified their household's financial status as comfortable, and none considered themselves to be well-off.

There are other big challenges facing the community, too, and principal among them is major environmental change. On the island, people speak about the massive problems being posed by the erosion of the coastline. Some of the older people in the community say that they have seen meters of the coast eroded in their lifetimes, and they describe rising sea levels leading to the salination of their underground water sources. Rising water tables mean that wells are now bringing up saltwater, and water tanks and pumps are rusting. Many people now travel on outboard motors or canoes to bring back containers of fresh water from the mainland, a practice that costs both time and resources. Villagers undertake it out of necessity, recognizing that it is an inadequate solution to their problem of resource insecurity.

The language of climate change is frequently invoked to account for the ecological challenges facing the community, and, while substantial scientific research is needed to ascertain what role global environmental shifts are playing in the Yule Island region, it is significant that this discourse is being used by people in an attempt

Water tanks like these on Yule Island rust out quickly because of increasing salination of the groundwater, attributed by locals to sea-level rise and climate change. People sometimes have to travel for hours to the mainland to bring back fresh water.

to understand the shifts that they are seeing in their lands and waters. It points to a sense in which people in this remote community understand themselves as situated within a broader regional and global context. However, the environmental insecurity felt on the island also has its roots in more localized, material conditions. The tanks that are rusted through are built with poor quality metal, not adequately lined and subject to rust as the water becomes more saline; water pumps stay broken because there are not the resources to repair and maintain them; the pontoon used in the latest lobster project was constructed with weak flotation devices that meant it partially sank. There are other factors, too, including patterns of land use, impacts of commercial fishing ventures, population growth, and possible environmental ramifications from nearby gold mining on the mainland, which are yet to be adequately understood. It this combination of material problems associated, first, with poor infrastructure resulting from ill-planned development projects and, second, with broader economic, social, and environmental dynamics outside the control of local communities that generates the precariousness attached to livelihoods in the Yule Island community. Creating sustainable livelihoods here requires an understanding of the interplay between these factors and the strengthening of local capacity to generate reflexive strategies to negotiate them.

LEARNING AND EDUCATION

As with other services in the community, formal education provision on Yule Island has been in decline since the administrative headquarters was moved to the mainland site of Bereina. When both the colonial and mission presences were at their strongest, there were three schools in operation on the island. St. Patrick's School provided elementary schooling for both boys and girls, with Our Lady of the Sacred Heart Girls High School and De La Salle Boys High School catering to those able to continue their education to secondary level. The missionaries also operated a teacher training center. A printing office run by the church mission enabled the production of school materials for all the Catholic schools in the region, which were distributed by their Cessna plane. When the Kairuku administration on the island closed, the two high schools were among the services transferred to Bereina by the Australian Administration. St. Patrick's remains operational on the island, but students wishing to proceed beyond grade eight must travel to Bereina to attend De La Salle High School, known as Mainohama, which is now coeducational. The time involved in traveling to the mainland makes this difficult for many, and the cost involved in purchasing fuel for the outboard motors is similarly prohibitive.

While access to secondary education has become difficult, the long-term missionary presence on the island has meant that levels of basic education in the community are quite high. The Catholic Church has been a key provider of education, and only 2 percent of questionnaire respondents said that they had received no formal education, compared to 9 percent of respondents across all the research sites. Over one-third of respondents had completed primary school as their highest level of formal education. Notably, another third had completed either some or all of their secondary education. Many of these people are adults who received their secondary education when the two high schools were still operating on the island, but the figures also suggest that some children are continuing to receive an education beyond the elementary level, notwithstanding the difficulties households encounter in facilitating this. Another quarter of respondents had completed some form of trade training, higher than the overall figure of 13 percent, and another 4 percent had completed a university qualification.

Adults expressed a strong desire for further educational opportunities, including informal skills and livelihoods training. Eighty-nine percent of respondents agreed that they would like to learn how to do their current work better, and 84 percent said that more training was necessary for them to do the work they would ideally like to do. Opportunities for learning and skills development are both highly in demand and much needed within the community. Faced with a natural environment under pressure and struggling to secure means of maintaining livelihoods in an isolated community, such opportunities may provide the key to developing the adaptive strategies that the Yule Island villagers will need to ensure the sustainability of their lives and their home.

Notes

1. Malinowski, *Argonauts of the Western Pacific,* p. 128; emphasis in original.

2. *Fishery Status Reviews: Torres Strait Lobster Fishery,* http://www.affashop.gov.au/ PdfFiles/03_FSR07_tslf.pdf (accessed 9 January 2009); Yimin Ye, Jim Prescott, and Dennis Darren, "Sharing the Catch of Migratory Rock Lobster (*Panulirus ornatus*) between Sequential Fisheries of Australia and Papua New Guinea," http://www.fish.wa .gov.au/docs/events/ShareFish/papers/pdf/papers/YiminYe.pdf (accessed 9 January 2009).

3. Patricia May and Margaret Tuckson, *The Traditional Pottery of Papua New Guinea,* University of Hawai'i Press, Honolulu, 2000, pp. 41–42.

III   COMMUNITY DEVELOPMENT

Chapter 7

Informal Economies and Community Livelihoods

JUST AS THE INFORMAL ECONOMY IS conventionally taken to exist outside the "real economy," studies of informal economic activities tend to be located outside the central currents of mainstream economic theory. In mainstream economic and development theory, informal economies have classically been treated as part of an irregular sector that either should be temporarily tolerated or harnessed and integrated into the economic center. In short, across the world such practices have been treated as "shadow economies." More recently, however, sociologists, anthropologists, and political economists have been giving increasing levels of attention to the informal economy as a phenomenon in itself.

Although the significance of the informal sector has varied in different periods and different countries, the study of this phenomenon has intensified and become generalized since the 1980s. In relation to Papua New Guinea, scholars began paying attention to the informal economic sector in the 1970s, though under a different name and never in a systematic way. After the economic crises of the early 1980s and with the fallout of demanding structural adjustment programs, attention was magnified as massive numbers of people in the world turned to informal survivalism. In many cities of the Global South, a fundamental shift occurred that saw informal livelihoods become the primary mode of economic reproduction.[1] Table 7.1 is representative of the broad sweeping nature of the study of this phenomenon. It reflects the challenges of distinguishing such a concept within its cultural context as well as considering this sector as a central aspect of its social and economic dynamics within a particular country. Even the dramatic figures in the table below completely underestimate the size of the informal economy in countries such as Papua New Guinea—estimated to

Table 7.1 The Informal Economy as a Percentage of GDP

REGION	1989/1990	1999/2000	2002/2003
OECD	13.2	16.8	16.3
Central European and Former Soviet		38.1	40.1
Africa		41.3	43.2
South America		41.1	43.4
Asia		28.5	30.4

Source: Johannes Jütting, Jante Parlevliet, and Theodora Xenogiani, *Informal Employment Re-Loaded*, OECD
    Development Centre, Paris, 2008, p. 15.
Note: Regional values are unweighted averages.

include around 70 percent of economic activity and engage much more than 90 percent of the population.

Many terms have been used to designate this phenomenon since it was first called the "informal sector" in the 1970s. The naming tends to turn on the geo-economic focus of the studies—that is, whether the focus is "developed" countries or "developing" countries.[2] For example, one writer has revealingly suggested that the informal sector should be called the "black economy" for developed countries, the "informal sector" for developing countries, and the "second economy" for transition countries.[3] In other words, the informal economic sector is commonly treated as a relatively enduring phenomenon in the poorest countries of the Global South, to be tolerated for the time being in transition countries, and simply bad in the capitalist North.

In a variation on that theme, another response is to assume that positive development is associated with a natural progression from different kinds of informal economies to a singular formal-if-lightly-regulated economy of capitalism. The worst writings in this genre emphasize labor deregulation as a heroic virtue allowing "flexible employment" with low wages or monetary return only on commission or based on profit (a euphemism in many cases for extreme poverty and exploitation). More sensitive writings acknowledge barriers to this progression—including the lack of access to funding, infrastructure, and training. However, despite acknowledgment of the creativity of the different informal economies, such writings still tend to assume that all aspects of the informal economy need to move toward increased formality through targeted policy reforms such as increased microfinancing, installation or improvement of infrastructure, and skills training.[4] Our concern in this chapter is not that such reforms are problematic—to the contrary, they are often very useful in urban informal economies when integrated with a well-considered community development and learning process (see Chapter 12). Rather, it is that such reforms tend to be accompanied by an assumption that, in order to "capture" the possibilities of "informal economies" for conventional developmental ends, capitalism as a single market system needs to override all other forms of market relations.

Our argument, to the contrary, is first that the informal sector includes both

Building a house with bush materials at Ilabu village, near Wisini in the remote mountains of Morobe Province

"unregulated" *capitalist* exchange and services (including modern petty entre-preneurialism) and *customary* production-exchange relations (including tribal subsistence and extended subsistence living). The latter does not tend to figure in the worldview of mainstream policy makers and economists. Second, there has emerged a new optimism about the informal sector that suggests that it will provide an unregulated dynamism and soak up all those that fall out of formal employment. Our argument, in qualification, is that the value of the informal sector depends on its nature and the kinds of support that it gets—both from state agencies and from local communities. This is the key. Unless local communities are central in negotiating the best way of addressing the development of informal economies, then state regulation and infrastructural support will fail or people will ignore that regulation.

Defining the Informal Sector

Identifying sections of the population involved in an informal labor force is not a new phenomenon. A number of authors have described a casual labor market in eighteenth- and nineteenth-century imperial and colonial cities from London and Shanghai to Osaka to Bombay.[5] The emergence of the concept of the "informal sector" is attributed to a study by Keith Hart in the context of contemporary Ghana.[6] Hart considered the informal sector to be almost synonymous with the sphere of self-employed individuals and small businesses or enterprises. The term then came to refer to ways of making a living outside the formal wage economy, either as an alternative to it or as a means of supplementing income earned within it.

While Hart's definition limits the informal sector to the economic activities of the self-employed, his introduction of the concept formally within academia made it possible to incorporate activities that were previously ignored in theoretical models of development and in national economic accounts.[7] It was a watershed in the formal study of this sector. The main contribution of the informal sector was seen as the provision of subsistence to families. In such a way, the informal sector was considered to have some positive effects on labor and thus, by extension, on national economies. However, in spite of this groundbreaking work, Hart's case study was confined to examining the state of employment in one country with all its specificities. Informality was mainly characterized by the avoidance of government regulations or taxes.

As the concept developed, it also took on new confusions. The informal economy, for example, began to be problematically referred to as "the traditional sector." This designation had its origins in dualistic theories of development that suggested that developing economies contained both a traditional sector—described as including subsistence and nonwage areas—and a modern sector based on market capitalism.[8] In this usage "traditionalism" as a form of production-exchange relations is wrongly defined in a way that draws into itself anything that is "not modern" *and* exists outside of the state-regulated parameters of capitalist market exchange, including many practices that are neither traditional nor tribal. Thus trading in cigarettes on the street without having paid import duties is considered part of the "traditional" sector even though it is a form of illicit petty-capitalist exchange and has nothing to do with the dominant form of trading in traditional societies.

More accurately, the trade of societies framed by *traditional* cosmologies and practices can be characterized as being based on long-distance trade in precious goods and local market exchange of basic goods (dominant, for example, in late-medieval Europe). Dominant tribal forms of exchange are different again. The trade of societies framed by *tribal* relations is based on reciprocal and barter exchange (both still important in remote Papua New Guinea). In terms of the approach that we have taken throughout this book, these layers of exchange can be clarified as follows:

- *Reciprocal exchange* constitutes the dominant form of exchange in customary tribal formations. Even when extended over large regions as, for example, is the case of the Kula Ring of Melanesia, this form of exchange is particularistic and drawn back into embodied relations and reciprocal ties to others (see the discussion of Kiriwina in Chapter 6). Here "reciprocal" is used very broadly as a concept to embrace relations of obligation and direct mutuality.
- *Barter exchange* is associated with both tribal and traditional social formations and is contained within relatively localized settings. Such relations often continue to operate alongside the emergence of money-based markets, as in the example of Yule Island (Chapter 6). However, interestingly, as money-based markets become dominant and are spatially extended, barter exchange tends to become more and more localized.
- *Money-based exchange* is associated with commodity exchange where money contributes to allowing increasing geographic extension of the relations of both production and exchange. This type of exchange allows long-distance trade, in the first instance in high-value goods associated with traditional empires, but also comes to be basic to modern capitalist exchange from the local to the global. Money-based markets can either be reembedded into customary settings (as some of the local food markets in Papua New Guinea are) or lifted out to a point where monetary exchange excludes other forms (as in the "supermarket" or "megamart" phenomenon across the globe). Even in Port Moresby, with all its cross-cutting forms of exchange, it is hard

to imagine a local gardener walking into Tabari Haus supermarket, Baroko, and bartering for rice with *kaukau*. In that place it is only money that speaks.

• *Capital-based exchange* is that form of exchange which includes but is abstracted beyond markets that simply use money in the transaction of goods. It is a form of market relations that takes for granted the entity of accumulated abstract value (capital) and at a certain point begins trading in capital itself. This can be relatively informal, as in the case of derivatives such as Over-the-Counter Transactions, or formal, as in the case of currency trading. This the level of the market at which, for example, the Papua New Guinea NASFUND operates, although in their case it is on the formal side of the capital-exchange market.

Informality thus has nothing to do with the defining differences between these various forms of exchange. A barter exchange system can be highly formalized (Yule Island), while some kinds of capital exchange can be relatively informal—that is, they may exist on the margins of taxation regimes and other forms of state regulation. In other words, questions of formality and informal-

The market spaces in the major towns, like this one at Koki in Port Moresby, tend to be state regulated, but, despite posted formal rules about conduct, they tend to remain central to the informal economy. Regulators are particularly concerned about contraband such as cigarettes that are smuggled into the country to avoid taxes.

ity are figured differently *within* different forms of exchange and production relations—all have different modalities of organization—and the nature of the regulation of those market forms from the outside by the modern state is variable. The key point here is that other forms of exchange-production relations need to be addressed seriously, not just those associated with capitalist exchange-production.

With the use of the term "informal economy" by an International Labour Organization report in the early 1970s, the area came to be clarified as a distinct sector of economic activity enacted by a distinct socioeconomic group. Over the next three decades, the definitions became more and more technical.[9] In most accounts the *formal* economic sphere came to include activities that are recognized and regulated in some way by the state.[10] By contrast, *informal* economies came to be defined as those that operate outside the regulations of governments, including labor legislation and taxation. As such, even though the informal sector can generate a significant proportion of labor and income, until recently it tended to be treated by policy makers as beyond access to subsidies, credit, or other forms of state assistance.[11] Furthermore, this way of approaching the sector, like most official statistics, tended to leave out subsistence agricultural production, forestry, and fishery, mostly because it is hard to account for such activities, as for labor in the home, in a conventional Gross Domestic Product analysis.[12] In most definitions, informal sector activities were said to include a wide range of economic activities such as street food selling or market vending; small-scale manufacturing as of garments, shoes, or handicrafts carried out by single operators; and also small automotive or machinery repair shops—in all of which the status of labor is not formally contracted with employment and social protection. However, the defining aspect of their informality should not be the small size of the operation or their hand-to-mouth quality. Such activities are part of the informal (modern capitalist) economy to the extent that they sit outside state-based systems of tax, duties, subsidies, health-and-safety regulations, and so on—and the informal economy should therefore include noncapitalist modes of production and exchange such as subsistence growing of yams and taro.

The extent to which the "informal" covers different economic realms continues to be debated, particularly in relation to its legality, extralegality and illegality. Writers such as Maghendra Reddy and Michael Todara claim that, while this sector includes a large number of small-scale production and service activities that are individually or family owned and that use labor-intensive and simple technology, it does not exclude illegal activities by individuals operating outside the formal sphere for the explicit purpose of evading taxation or regulatory burdens.[13] The informal sector is said, for example, to consist of "all small-scale activities that are normally semi-organized and un-regulated, and use simple labor-intensive technology undertaken by artisans, traders and operators in work-sites such as open yards, market stalls, undeveloped plots, residential houses and street pavements...not registered with the Register of Companies, they may or may not have licenses from local authorities for carrying out a variety of businesses."[14] Daniels defines the informal economy as "all income-earning activities that are not regulated by the state in social environments where similar activities are regulated."[15]

The relationship between the formal and informal sectors also remains a contested area. Urjit Patel and Pradeep Srivastava give a highly technical account of the macroeconometrics of the informal and formal sectors in a case study from India, which has had a long and continuous history of a strong informal sector.[16] Their conclusion, based on reviewing nearly three decades of statistics, is that the informal and formal sectors—at least in the case of much of India—while intimately linked, have an opposite response to government policy in their output.

Other studies have emphasized different issues. Portes, Blitzer, and Curtis conducted surveys in Uruguay to attempt to define the nature and extent of the informal sector in the mid-1980s. Uruguay has a very strong history of labor regulation, so there is a high degree of formalization, though there is also a sizable informal sector. They conclude that there is little difference in the contribution made to households from formal and informal activities—they are on a par in time and effort—but there is a big difference in the amount of income the activities bring in. Some commentators still cling to a notion that the formal and informal sectors are homogeneous, both inter- and intranationally, but the trend is now to suggest that, both within and across nations, the informal sector is heterogeneous and that the participants are as varied as any group of social beings in any social formation. In a practical sense, that means that policy and approaches to implementing change need to be formulated and applied with an appreciation of that variation, sometimes even responding on a case-by-case basis. It is interesting that, while the term "informal sector" was first coined in the 1970s, there continues to be considerable dispute over what the formal sector and the informal sector comprise. The disputes reflect the complicated, complex, and intricately interwoven nature of lifeworlds juxtaposed against the dominant development ideology of the simplifying state.

A further issue surrounding the concept is associated with the relationship between informality and poverty. Much of the literature implicitly assumes that the informal sector is closely connected with having common roots in abject poverty, insecure or customary land tenure, inadequate or absent education, and the marginalization of people from state development and economic activities.[17] However, such assumptions are not necessary to the definition nor are these things necessary consequences of informality. Some claim that the sector is closely associated with squatter settlement issues because of the inability of the modern economy to absorb the rising labor force in productive employment. It is equally possible to see such poverty and housing conditions as arising in response to an intensely competitive *formal* capitalist sector as massive social change brings rural people to the cities in increasing numbers. As such, informal economies have become more important in "megacities" of the Global South as a means of survival. The informal sector then includes various kinds of work—outworkers, sole traders, unincorporated businesses. These are basically all self-employed forms of legitimate or semilegitimate income generation, although they can also include illegal activities such as drug trading, prostitution, drug trafficking, and goods-and-people smuggling.

In most countries of the Global South, divisions of poverty and wealth have also increased owing to the related processes of globalization, urbanization, and capitalization. Lack of formal employment; straining and decaying infrastructures, including water supply, sewage, garbage disposal, and transport; an acute shortage of housing, education, and health services; and the growth of new and decrepit squatter settlements all pose major challenges to these countries.[18] Urbanization—the movement of people to cities began in the 1960s and has intensified over the last two decades—with all its challenges, faces each Pacific Island country.[19] Urban problems increase as the growth rate of an urban population supersedes the simultaneous growth of the urban sector. Poverty, crime, and environmental issues dominate, driven in part by growing issues of inadequate sanitation, housing, water, and provisions for waste disposal. The growth of the urban sector has been accompanied by the growth of the *recognized* informal sector—often the entry point to the city for migrants from villages and other rural and remote areas with the hope of finding some form of income in the city. Furthermore, as Yoshiaki Azuma and Herschel Grossman write, ill-directed regulation by the state can drive people to seek a way around that regulation and thus enter the informal economy:

> In many countries, especially poor countries, a heavy burden of taxes, fees, bureaucratic hassles, and bribes drives many producers into an informal sector. . . . We can attribute the existence of a large informal sector to the fact that, because productive endowments contain important unobservable components, the state cannot adjust the amounts that it extracts from producers in the formal sector finely according to each producer's endowment. Given this fact we find that, if either the distribution of endowments is sufficiently inegalitarian or the cost of producing private substitutes for public services is

sufficiently low, then the state extracts a large enough amount from producers in the formal sector that poorly endowed producers choose to work in an
informal sector.[20]

The growth of the urban informal sector is not independent of the formal
sector.[21] The informal sector has varying but considerable linkages with the formal sector, state institutions, and the wider economy and can also provide goods
and services at relatively low prices that often undercut prices offered by registered companies, reflecting the overhead and rentals that such companies have
to bear. The role that the informal sector plays in providing creative means for
employment and poverty alleviation is significant.[22]

Hernando de Soto extended the study of the informal sector, raising questions about the hidden impact of this sector and whether regulatory frameworks
such as the deregulation of the market, greater private property rights, and the
intervention of the state needed to be reframed to enable this sector to grow.[23]
As a neoliberal exponent of microenterprise with concern for alleviating poverty,
de Soto became very influential. Over the last couple of decades, his approach
has come to define the way in which the informal sector is understood and
related policy is enacted. Nevertheless, criticism has been strong, and we agree
with many of the points of contention of his critics. As Anaya Roy and Nezar
Alsayyad argue, in de Soto's work the very idea of the informal sector has been
framed within a neoliberal ideology, and at base he is pushing for privatization
of informal or customary landownership as a means of "liberating" private capital.[24] Roger Bromley and Chris Gerry argue that de Soto is naive in his push for
privatization. The categories of what is and is not legal fall apart when one looks
more closely at the interrelation of legal, illegal, and extralegal activity.[25] More
critical still, Mike Davis has written that de Soto's entire approach is based on a
series of fallacies:

> De Soto's bootstrap model of development...is especially popular because of
> the simplicity of his recipe: get the state (and formal sector unions) out of the
> way, add micro-credit for micro-entrepreneurs and land titling for squatters,
> then let markets take their course to produce the transubstantiation of poverty
> into capital. (De Soto's inspired optimism, in its most absurd version, has led
> some development aid bureaucrats to redefine slums as "Strategic Low-In-
> come Urban Management Systems"). This semi-utopian view of the informal
> sector, however, grows out of a nested set of epistemological fallacies.[26]

These fallacies are worth putting on the table. Although we do not conclude
as Davis does that the informal economy in all its guises is necessarily and always

a "living museum of human exploitation," Davis' "fallacies" are useful points to consider when discussing the informal sector in Papua New Guinea below: [27]

1. There is a "need to distinguish micro-accumulation from subsistence." This we have done very self-consciously in this chapter, distinguishing between informal capitalist exchange and services (that is, *modern* petty entrepreneurialism) and semisubsistence *customary* production-exchange. The point of this distinction is that microaccumulation is open to massive exploitation or abuse if not well regulated by the state, while customary economies are community based and therefore based on a different kind of regulation (and different kinds of possible exploitation). As we go through the next points, this distinction partly qualifies Davis' concerns, at least in relation to customary economies, because he is predominantly talking about petty entrepreneurialism. (See also the next chapter, Chapter 8, on microfinance.)

2. Notwithstanding "the stereotype of the heroic self-employed, however, most participants in the informal economy work for someone else (via the consignment of goods or the rental of a pushcart or rickshaw, for example." This statement is more relevant to economies in urban and hinterland India and China, and does not necessarily pertain in Papua New Guinea, where a customary informal economy is more prevalent than a petty entrepreneurial economy.

3. Informal employment "by its very definition…is the absence of formal contracts, rights, regulations and bargaining power. Petty exploitation (endlessly franchised) is its essence, and there is growing inequality *within* the informal sector as well as between it and the formal sector." Petty exploitation is not endemic to customary relations of exchange. It is true that urban Papua New Guinea is experiencing increasing inequalities within the informal sector and across the urban landscape as whole, but this is less relevant in the hinterland and remote communities.

4. "Informality ensures extreme abuse of women and children." This is not necessarily the case in Papua New Guinea even though it is an intensely patriarchal society.[28] The abuse or otherwise of women and children depends on many issues beyond the nature of employment.

5. The informal sector "generates jobs not by elaborating new divisions of labor, but by fragmenting existing work, and thus by subdividing incomes." Again this is more relevant to the phenomenon of microaccumulation within capitalist informal economies rather than customary food production and exchange, although it can be seen in the streets of Port Moresby and Lae with the proliferation of betel nut sellers competing with each other.

6. "Because they contend with such desperate conditions, it is perhaps not surprising that the poor turn with fanatic hope to a 'third economy' of urban subsistence, including gambling, pyramid schemes, lotteries and other quasi-magical forms of wealth appropriation." The turn to gambling, crime, and magic has relevance in Papua New Guinea, but research suggests that the turn is not necessarily due to desperate poverty.

7. "Under such conditions, it is not surprising that initiatives such as microcredit and cooperative lending, while helpful to those informal enterprises managing to tread water, have had little macro impact on the reduction of poverty." True, but this does not mean that all microcredit schemes are a waste of time.

8. "Increasing competition within the informal sector depletes social capital and dissolves self-help networks essential to the survival of the very poor." This has not been the case even in Port Moresby and Lae, where *wantok* ties are most stretched.

9. "And finally under such extreme conditions of competition, the neoliberal prescription...of making labor even more flexible is simply catastrophic...transmuted into ethnoreligious or racial violence." While this is true in some of the slums of South Asia and Latin America, it is not so extreme in Papua New Guinea, with interclan violence more usually associated with personal and political grievances rather than chronic market competition.

Qualified by the specificities of Papua New Guinea, these nine points remain important to keep in mind as we turn to a more detailed discussion of the country.

The Informal Sector in Papua New Guinea

Substantial work has been done on mapping and developing policies in relation to the informal sector in Papua New Guinea. In recognizing the importance of the informal economy, the Consultative Implementation and Monitoring Council of Papua New Guinea established the Informal Sector Committee in 1999.[29] The committee's primary responsibility was to promote and advocate for policy, legislation, programs, and projects that encourage and support the development of a vibrant informal economy that will contribute to the growth of Papua New Guinea. The Honorable Dame Carol Kidu, member for Moresby South and then minister for Community Development, was the first chairperson. Currently Max Kep is the chairperson—he is also the chair of the Urbanization and National Consultative Committee on Informal Economy. One of the significant contributions of the Informal Sector Committee has been the enactment by Parliament of the Informal Sector Development and Control Act,

2004. This act was an outcome of a study conducted in 2001 on "Reviewing Constraints to the Development of Informal Sector in Papua New Guinea" with funds from the Asian Development Bank, the United Nations Development Program, and the Government of Papua New Guinea. The act was embraced as a significant landmark for the PNG government, receiving recognition from the International Labour Organization. The act is meant to provide both rights and responsibilities for participants in the informal economy, clearly indicating the importance the government places on the informal economy.

Whether the Informal Sector Act is being successfully implemented in terms of considerations raised about different modalities of informality is unclear. The act was released in the absence of a national policy on the informal economy, and this has meant that the act lacked a clear national-level structure that could influence funding and implementation. In the absence of such an integrated policy on informal strategy that could provide a strategic direction and a clear structure to influence funding, the Department for Community Development is now working on a policy submission to the National Executive Council to develop a national-level policy on the informal economy. There appear to be a range of committees such as a Ministerial Committee on informal economy at the political level, a National Consultative Committee on the Informal Economy at the bureaucratic level, and a Technical Working Group to oversee this process. The PNG Government website indicates that the Technical Working Group and the National Consultative Committee met six times in 2007—and produced a concept paper on informal economy policy that integrated a 2007 International Finance Corporation–funded comprehensive study on the informal economy. The concept paper was endorsed by the National Consultative Committee in May 2008, and a range of government department consultations continued through 2009. One was held at the Lamana Hotel on 12 August 2008 and another at the Holiday Inn on 26 August 2008. This consultation work is being funded by AusAID.

Unclear in this development of policies and strategies is the extent of involvement of or consultation with local people from the informal sector and local organizations, including NGOs and community groups. Nevertheless, the Technical Working Group has assimilated the positive view of the informal sector seen in the global literature. A concept paper on Papua New Guinea's national economy policy prepared by the Working Group states the following:

> The informal economy provides a source of income for a large part of the population of PNG. Most estimates suggest that over eighty percent of workers are employed in the informal economy. The PNG National Human Development Report 1998 states that the informal sector accounts for seventy percent of

all economic activity. It is believed from studies that unfortunately, about five percent of approximately 80,000 annual school leavers obtain employment in the formal economy.

It is clear that the informal economy plays a crucial role in providing livelihoods for the people of PNG and a central role in income and employment generation. Its size means that the government ensures that it is an inevitable reality in respect of which the Government must put in place suitable policy responses for its development. Informal economic activity in many circumstances provides the only opportunity for individuals to earn an income. For this reason it will in all likelihood remain the most significant component of the PNG economy for the foreseeable future. [30]

The Working Group has made a significant leap in effectively recognizing rural and agricultural production as part of the informal sector. The formal sector in Papua New Guinea has conventionally been taken to encompass economic activity taking place within legal, governmental regulation—which includes acquiring land and working for a taxed wage or running an incorporated business. And, equally conventionally, the informal sector has been defined as consisting of "extralegal" housing and income generation outside formal regulation by government agencies. Those definitions continue, but it is indicative of a sea change in approach that the concept paper rewrites conventional understandings of the scope of the sector to include economies that are not easily measurable. By comparison, for example, John Connell's major book on the Papua New Guinean economy, written a little over a decade ago, only spends a couple of pages on what he calls the informal economy, emphasizing crime and security provision, betel nut selling, transport, market vending, and prostitution.[31] The Working Group, in recognizing that the bulk of economic activity in Papua New Guinea is based on family or group agricultural activity and the trading of food produce, has already moved toward recognizing a different kind of development from that which conventionally espouses two parallel paths to the future: the privatization of land, the deregulation of the labor market, and the creation of new entrepreneurs in the informal economy, along one line, and large substantially leveraged extraction and export-oriented industries in the formal economy, along the other.

In the remainder of this chapter, the informal sector will be discussed within the two broad areas of agriculture and trading, place, and housing. These are the areas that the government is also addressing, and they provide the most important evidence of the positive side of the informal sector in Papua New Guinea (the negative side includes illegal activities such as avoiding duties on cigarettes or chronic larceny). Agriculture and trade are already intimately linked in the informal economies of the country, as the majority of goods traded both within

A woman selling chickens that she has raised in her village at Wau roadside market

and outside urban centers—traded in village-based markets, but also more and more at roadside market centers—are agricultural products grown in people's gardens. In any sense, gardening or informal agriculture is central to life in Papua New Guinea. Allied to the desire to garden is the need for land, and, when that is put in an urban context, the issue of urban housing and the rise of squatter settlements is raised. Urban housing, as it quickly spreads beyond land that was covenanted in colonial times, tends in almost all cases to be built on land that is covered by customary right. Thus there arises a pressing and contentious dilemma: the need to house people and provide them with land for gardens, and the importance of doing so without disenfranchising customary custodians. The negative side of the informal sector—precarious employment on the edges of the formal sector such as prostitution, illicit trading, and crime from street violence to white-collar corruption—is given less prominence in the discussion that follows, but this is not because we define the informal sector as not including such activities. It is because we want to highlight in the next two chapters possibilities that leave communities at the center of the process of development. Here we are referring to community learning and development centers to support informal livelihoods (see Chapters 11 and 12).

Agriculture and Food Production

Capitalism and customary production have intersected in Papua New Guinea for over a century. The colonial presence from 1884 introduced practices of commodified labor with the recruitment of young men to work on plantations in the central Pacific and Queensland—sometimes by enticement, sometimes by blackbirding or kidnaping and indenture. Coastal areas such as Goodenough Island, Milne Bay, and the Sepik coastal region "exported" labor on a considerable scale. In the later part of the nineteenth century and the early part of the twentieth century, copra, cocoa, and teak plantations were established on the mainland coastal belt and on the Milne Bay islands. European influence and practices—primarily German, British, and then Australian—introduced an emphasis on the production of cash crops such as coffee and copra for metropolitan economies. In the early 1950s, for example, there was substantial commercial planting of coffee trees. This cash cropping placed increased burdens on subsistence farming, particularly as labor was drawn away from production for local needs. Subsistence farming carried the cost of reproducing labor, supporting families, and caring for the returnees from the plantations, all of which added and continues to add a considerable subsidy to plantations and mines. In parallel, much of the state expenditure on infrastructure, roads, airports, and harbors has been directed in response to plantation production and mining, adding a further subsidy to the formal economy.

The colonial presence brought with it many changes—not just regarding land use, but also shifts in farming techniques and the adoption of new values of time, labor, and consumption. New crops were introduced, primarily in the shift from subsistence crops to cash crops. There was much resistance to some of these new ways—yet there was also an amazing agility in the way the new practices and new kinds of trade were absorbed.[32] In 1966, after a tour across Papua New Guinea, Fisk commented,

> The overall picture that emerges is that of a low income country in which virtually all of the population have as much food as they want, are housed adequately by their own traditional standards, and have ample leisure for feasting, ceremonial and other pastimes. It is an economy that is potentially viable and self-sufficient at a level of primitive affluence, but which is almost entirely dependent on external aid, and on the importation of foreign skills and capital, for any advance beyond that very primitive level.[33]

This separation of questions of food security and formal capitalist development is important. Fisk goes on to add that the analytical distinction between what is a subsistence economy and a monetary sector must be maintained. While the monetary economy has spread across the entire country, he says—even into the most remote areas—"the use of money remains an irregular and peripheral factor, rather than an essential part of the business of living."[34] The monetary economy (informal and formal) has intensified since the period in which Fisk was writing, but his suggestion that the monetary economy is "peripheral" to the lives of many people does not give a complex enough sense of the layering of different kinds of exchange even then.[35] The informal economy predominated as it still does within rural and hinterland villages, but already money-based exchange was affecting something as fundamental as growing food in local gardens.

One of the mainstream arguments in discussions of agriculture—urban or rural—is the importance of maintaining food security and food sustainability. Our general conclusion is first that rural gardens remain basic to informal livelihoods. Food security is under threat in places such as the Trobriands, where a swidden system of gardening is becoming less able to cope as the population increases and the culture subtly shifts away from the taken-for-granted sense that yam gardening is the only way of life (see Chapter 6). Nevertheless, many gardeners are attempting to adapt to changing pressures. Second, urban gardens continue also to be a valuable source of background food security, although here the pressures are far more intense and the adaptation less successful. Urban people work in gardens for their cultural significance but also to make extra income. As the research of writers such as Karl Benediktsson, Malcolm Levett, and Marakan Uvano suggests—and also as evidenced in our follow-up work—there is a sustainable market in urban centers for informally grown fresh local fruit and vegetables.[36] Local markets are working. However, food is increasingly coming from outside the urban zones: urban home-garden production is decreasing in urban centers. One key issue that makes it difficult for urban poor to take advantage of the skills they already have in this regard is accessibility of land. For people living in densely populated squatter settlements such as Vanagi settlement in Port Moresby, there is little or no land available. We often heard from first- and second-generation migrants to Port Moresby from different climatic zones that the soil and rainfall patterns are not suitable in the Moresby area for gardening, and this is also an issue but simply requires different approaches to gardening more attuned to the local environment. Third, when people grow gardens on government or fallow clan land, this can lead to disputes and thefts. In our interviews a number of urban gardeners in villages such as Kira Kira, Pari, and Yalu talked of petty theft as becoming increasingly a way of life. A fourth issue is that locally produced food may have lower status than store-bought commodities, or it may be more perishable.

Based on a survey of 460 households in Morata and Waigani (Port Moresby), Malcolm Levett and Marakan Uvano conclude that garden produce was used mostly for home consumption. Selling produce in the market was at about the same level as exchanging between households. In the suburb of Gerehu (Port Moresby), the main reasons that people gave for gardening was their own subsistence, at 42 percent of respondents, and to reduce their cash outlay on fresh food, at 19 percent. Levett surveyed an additional 174 households across Port Moresby in 1993 to find out who buys what food and where. Staple foods, fruit, and vegetables when purchased came predominantly from the informal sector. Locally produced foodstuffs in the markets were cheaper than what was available in the supermarkets. People also responded that they preferred to buy locally grown produce, as long as it is sweet and juicy and that, if there were more available, they would buy locally grown.[37] Nearly two decades after that survey, local markets are still strong, but supermarkets have been bourgeoning in urban centers, and this suggests significant changes. As we wrote in the social profile on the settlement of Vanagi (Chapter 4), 32 percent of respondents listed local shops as the main place they got their food, with another 26 percent listing food markets. Twenty-three percent said that the supermarket was the main place they got their food. By contrast, the overall averages from all research sites including urban, periurban, hinterland, and remote communities were 7 percent, local shops; 4 percent, food markets; and 5 percent, supermarkets. By contrast, in Vanagi, only 11 percent of people said that their main source of food was work done on their own lands or fishing, compared to a figure of 78 percent overall for Papua New Guinea.

Across all of Papua New Guinea, apart from the most remote communities, consumption has increasingly turned to highly desired food goods that tend not to be locally produced—such as rice and canned beef. The introduction of rice during colonial occupation popularized it as a staple, much as flour and sugar were used as payment among Australia's Indigenous populations.[38] Papua New Guinea does not have an adequate means of producing rice, however, and in places such as Vanapa (Chapter 5) informal attempts to develop rice production have failed.[39] Apart from petroleum/oil, rice is by far Papua New Guinea's largest import (over 213,000 metric tonnes in 2004 according to the Food and Agricultural Organization of the United Nations,[40] theoretically enough for thirty-five kilos of rice per person in Papua New Guinea per year). As Tim Spencer and Peter Heywood remarked as early as the 1980s, "On the one hand there is rhetoric of self-reliance very clearly stated in the National Food and Nutrition Policy. On the other hand, there is the reality of a growing dependency on rice imported from Australia, a very efficient producer whose rice industry is highly motivated to maintain and expand the market in Papua New Guinea."[41]

Over time rice has become normalized as a staple and together with high-fat bully beef, meat flaps, canned tuna, and Chinese instant noodles is available in all but the most remote stores. However, it remains a high-cost import with a lower nutritional value than local root crops. In stores with freezers, the ubiquitous presence of imported lamb and beef flaps, brisket, and offal for human consumption is borne out by the import statistics that put secondary meat products as the second highest import behind rice. In Deborah Gewertz and Frederick Errington's phrase, for the flap-food nations such meat is a sought-after food of modern consumption.[42] Low-status commodities in the Global North thus developed a formal market in countries such as Papua New Guinea, and this market was extended from the 1980s on as freezers became more readily available.

Attempts at connecting the formal and informal economies in food have had mixed results. This is not because it is intrinsically a problem, but rather because the issues are rarely considered thoroughly. Robert Macadam opened up the issue of unexpected outcomes in his discussion of a CSIRO project that crossed the formal and informal sectors—in this case, locals became unemployed because they did not assimilate the training that was offered. He is optimistic that formal economic enterprises can readjust their mode of operation to take into account local needs.[43] Gina Koczberski and George Curry in their more recent study of the palm industry are a little more circumspect and emphasize the need for income diversification and the continuing importance of the informal economy in supporting basic living.[44]

The most damning account, however, is a major report on the Philippine RD Tuna Cannery in Madang that has had a disastrous effect on local informal trade and community health.[45] The privileging of big business in overwhelming a local resource has led to lowering of economic stability for local people and destructive interventions into local life: prostitution, substance abuse, fouled water, depleted local fishing, and now a protracted legal dispute. Most everyone in the nine villages we visited had described changes in their marine resources over the last decade. They felt there were fewer fish as a result of pollution in the lagoon (RD Tuna had, until recently, been dumping oil into the lagoon), noise pollution from the movement of large fishing liners in the lagoon, and dredging. Many villagers also described changes in health as a result of the pollution in the water: dysentery, skin problems, blood in their stool, and so on. (See the profile on Kananam in Chapter 4.) Nancy Sullivan writes:

> The economic repercussions of RD have been widespread. People have no money to pay their children's school fees, to pay clinic costs, or start up independent business ventures like trade stores or cash crop gardening. They have so little money, in fact, that they must remain in full-time employment just to subsist, whereas many would no doubt do better with part-time employment and the freedom to work their gardens. The company has not assisted these communities in basic social or infrastructural investments, either, so that market houses, feeder roads, aid posts, schools and churches have all been neglected and, far from upgraded, in many cases deteriorated. It is conceivable that small business enterprises that might otherwise have emerged (with vanilla, cocoa, trucking, canteens, for examples) would have benefited these community fundamentals. And, as many informants suggested, had wages been such that cash did flow back into these communities, and new ventures were begun, we might also assume the provincial government would have made related investments in schools, aid posts and infrastructure. This is only conjecture. But what is irrefutable is the current state of destitution that all these communities face seven years since RD's entry into the area. People cannot feed their families, cannot serve their traditional feasting, marriage and mortuary obligations, and cannot pay the minimum costs for educational and health services. There are workers who, literally, have taken home fortnight pay packets of K3 and K5, after deductions for NPF, transport, meals and uniforms. Their prospects are also dim: very little training has occurred, and so very few Papua New Guineans see themselves as having better skills or more managerial control down the line.[46]

The tale of the damage that commercial fishing has done to traditional life and the customary informal economy in Madang is a common one across the Global South. Monopoly markets in primary produce tend to harm informal efforts; the supposed trickle-down effect of international and/or commercial enterprises rarely materializes. That is, there is little improvement in employment and often adverse effects on the physical health and sociocultural well-being of the original custodians of the resources being exploited. Importation of food and price cutting by supermarkets disadvantages small traders and vendors, and consequently their customers—the larger population. Commercial fishing has had a detrimental effect on the customary informal economy without moving the wider population into the formal economy: they are caught both ways. People have turned to the negative side of the informal economy as by exchanging sex for food.

In response to this issue, William Vorley has brought together an excellent report on a long-term project on sustainable agriculture in developing countries funded through the International Institute for Environment and Development, London. Broadly, Vorley argues for increasing education programs and disaggregating and decentralizing policy (empowering local government). He warns against the lack of good governance in the implementation of decentralization, pressing for *appropriate* policies that are carefully implemented and followed through, guided by the question "Where are the public policy processes that work, and how can they be strengthened and spread further?"[47] Vorley argues for a much more attentive use of local knowledge that is already in place and can be used effectively and emphasized and helped to flourish. NGOs can be a large part of the process: "We believe a focus on processes and institutions that work, rather than policies that work, will lead to more effective interventions by governments, donors and development agencies."[48]

Priority must be given to the development of domestic and regional markets rather than exports. Countries should have sufficient flexibility for domestic policy measures—which may include supply management tools—that protect domestic producers from a surge in imports or a significant decline in import prices. Vorley puts forward four recommendations on how intervention should work: (1) negotiate agreement on the functions and objectives of smallholder and family-based farming; (2) create the right environment for peasant organizations and new social movements to be partners in decentralization; (3) agree on the roles of NGOs, community groups, and the public sector; and (4) create the right environment for fair trade between small farmers and agribusiness, for democratic control over markets.[49]

Vorley's observations highlight the alienation that many, especially in rural and remote villages, feel in relation to national structures and provincial governments. The way that he speaks of governance taps into what is already known about Papua New Guinea. Decentralized policy implementation in Papua New Guinea would happen at the provincial, ward, and village levels, and care in governance would be most important:

> *Governance that works* will achieve sustainability through *policies and processes that work*. In real life, this could allow a family to stay on land that may have been in the family for generations, a region to be secure in food, the use of farming practices that conserve productive resources and the environment, and a population that can negotiate with state and business from a position of strength, having the freedom to choose lasting improvements in their livelihoods.[50]

Land and Housing

Issues of landowning and housing in Papua New Guinea are complex, particularly in the cities and towns. The greatest issue is finding a way to accommodate indigenous landholders' rights and the needs of new urban communities as people move to urban centers and hinterland zones from elsewhere in the country. This urban shift was intensified in the postcolonial period as restrictions on movement such as vagrancy laws were lifted and *wantok*s and *pasindia*s relocated into bourgeoning informal (squatter) settlements.[51] In the period immediately after independence, short-distance migration was rightly seen as a good thing, creating a stronger relation between the country and the city (see, for example, the community profiles on Inuma and Alepa), but movement later became much more long-distance and widespread than anticipated. In a customary sense, anyone coming in to an urban center from the outside is crossing clan boundaries. In Port Moresby, Lae, and Madang, there is also prejudice against outsiders (Highlanders in particular) even when they are occupying "legitimate" low-covenant housing. As John Connell shows, these prejudices extend beyond clan rivalries to views inherited from colonial administrations,[52] and they have been reinforced as entrepreneurial Highlanders have become more successful in coastal cities through employment as taxi and PMV drivers and as security guards through both informal and semiformal arrangements.

In part because of a failure to address adequately the problems that have intensified with urban migration, Port Moresby has been regularly named on the *Economist*'s Liveability Index as one of the "worst cities in the world." In 2007 it was fourth "worst" in their list of 140 cities behind Harare, Dhaka, and Algiers. In 2002 it was the worst. As dramatic as they sound, those lists barely touch the issues at hand and in many ways are misleading. Nevertheless, they point to questions of place and community that have left the city as a difficult locale in which to live. More broadly, the tension between the need to find homes for a more mobile population and the claims of customary tenure are part of a long-term issue that crosses the Global South.[53] Papua New Guinea is far from unique in experiencing violent interventions and fights linked to squatting with occasional forced expulsions and regular calls for the Vagrancy Acts to be reinstated. The recent migration of outsiders onto Motu/Koita land in Port Moresby has only added further pressure on housing as relatives visit or move in over time. Initiatives such as the Morata self-help group and the provision of Housing Commission homes have emerged as local responses to try to deal with issues of violence and intra- and intercommunity tensions.

Michael Goddard argues that there was already a difference in status among Papua New Guineans on the basis of the distinction between those in low-covenant and no-covenant housing. He links the persistence of colonial perspectives and prejudices to current concerns about squatters: migrants tend to be stereotyped as unemployed, squatters as criminals, and house dwellers differentially according to the type of housing in which they live. The social reality is more complex, with people who work in the informal economy living in covenant housing, squatters working in the formal sector, and formal-sector high-covenant housing dwellers breaking the law. Internal/regional chauvinism, Goddard argues, is used by politicians, heightening tensions that are real enough, and this is exacerbated by a rolling discourse that lurches from disparagement to charity:

> Most residents of Port Moresby, including the *elites*, are migrants or, in the case of the younger generation, the children of migrants. And most, if they did not live in informal housing, have *wantoks* who do. Given the currency of the *elites/grassroots* imagery, the cross-cutting social ties, and the discontinuities between the realities of informal housing and the "homogenising" notion of "settlements," it is possible for people to vacillate between benign and censorious settlement imagery.[54]

Economic discussions of the informal sector, including informal or squatter settlements, have in general become more liberal in tone in the past fifteen years. However, the discourse vacillates between disparagement and tightly directed applause. In line with one direction of the neoliberal turn, some economists have moved toward praising informal sector initiatives as long as they come in the form of entrepreneurial opportunities. As we have been arguing, our concern about this arises when it is premised on a vision of progress that treats customary relations, including tribal land, as something to be overcome as the country "matures" toward having a one-dimensional modern economic realm. Unthinkingly moving in this direction would be disastrous, but there are points to be taken from these discussions. Satisfying a bank's requirements for legal title to land or any mentality based on the preeminence of private property seems a very poor reason to rush to formalize title when it can have long-lasting effects on clan-held land. However, while the drive to formalize titles gains strong impetus from banks and developers who want clear title before they will make loans or secure mortgages, there are other methods for negotiating loans in the informal sector, as we will discuss in relation to microcredit in the next chapter (Chapter 8). Codifying land title in urban and periurban zones may be a valuable exercise *if* (and the "if" here is a strong qualifier) handled through community consultation and with the recognition that it is an intensely modernizing process that will put stress on customary relations and different memories of land tenure. With the remarkable situation in Papua New Guinea in which 97 percent of land across the country is still unalienated as customary land, there is a need in cities to clarify boundaries and sovereignty, but the usual unqualified modern kind of cadastral mapping will miss the point completely.

Globalizing modernism and state-led development activities have led to both integration, on the one hand, and social exclusion and informalization, on the other. A significant proportion of Papua New Guinea's remote, rural people and urban underclass continue to find it difficult to function, live, and work within the modernizing systems characterized by market forces, discipline, contract, exchange, value, speed, and the bureaucracy of the state organization. Many appear to be attempting to exit from such economic, social, and political arrangements (which ironically also render many people unemployed or push them to seek refuge in informal production, trade, housing, and transportation). They are seeking alternative informal institutions and relations. The rapidly growing secondhand clothes street vendors, for example, circulating among the growing lower-income new Asian migrant community and the Papua New Guinea growing urban underclass and extending into the Highlands, are the latest products of this age. This livelihood is fiercely guarded—and visits to markets such as Boroka in Port Moresby reveals a tight network of vendors who control the open spaces where their wares are displayed and who circulate the market and its surrounds, expelling any unfamiliar traders who may be perceived to threaten their livelihoods. Vendors in these spaces protect an apparently passive network, which can rapidly turn (positively) to active communication and cooperation among themselves, and resistance to outside interference, disruption, or (negatively) engagement. In a parallel process, as Asef Bayat writes,

> Quiet and gradual grassroots activism tends to contest many fundamental aspects of state prerogatives, including the meaning of order, the control of public space, access to public and private goods, and the relevance of moder-

nity....A key attribute of quiet encroachment is that while advances are made quietly, individually, and gradually, defence of these gains is often (although not always) collective and audible.[55]

This form of grass-roots activism has an intuitive appeal, but unfortunately it says little about how individuals, local communities, and the state might work together to enhance the productivity of the informal economy. The reluctance of people to participate in "self-help" or "community" activities is one of the reasons that many projects that depend on an assumed communitarian sentiment fail in Papua New Guinea. The "community" as a singular, locality-framed, and village-based entity is a colonial artifact, and in many villages in Papua New Guinea different social divisions (such as clans, families, or other genealogical lineages) within a village provide the strongest basis for mutual support and group-based action. These groups of people tend to be seen as divisive, as they often perceive their interests to be separate from those of an imagined "village community." Women in particular seem to define their interests first with respect to their family and lineage and then in terms of church-based activities.[56]

Conclusion

At its simplest, the formal sector is generally taken to encompass economic activity taking place within legal, governmental regulation—which includes acquiring land and working for a taxed wage or running an incorporated business. So, in these terms, the informal sector is said to comprise low-level extralegal and illegal income generation operating outside formal regulation by government agencies. In this chapter, we have argued for a refinement of the concept in two ways: first, we have suggested that informality and low-level economic activity should not be equated. There are different kinds of informality across all economies ranging from reciprocal tribal to electronic financial exchange. Second, we analytically distinguish between different kinds of exchange/production and argue that in Papua New Guinea the informal sector should be taken to include both modern petty entrepreneurialism and customary exchange, with the latter substantially more important than the former. The approach to enhancing informal economies needs to be very different in Papua New Guinea from the approach used in a place where this ratio is reversed.

Arguments about what should be done in relation to supporting or regulating the informal sector vary greatly. Victor Tokman, for example, gives three policy recommendations to address a growing informal sector. He, like others, warns that, if the sector is left unregulated, it can lead to entrenched poverty and in particular the impoverishment of women and children. He argues that policy and procedures should be formulated that will assist producers (greater training), support workers (with targeted welfare), and legalize activities (with workable and appropriate regulation). He also argues for decentralization: "In order to take decisions, local governments need the authority and capability to answer and settle the claims that originate in the informal sector.... At the same time, the power to take a decision locally could enhance the efficiency of the state and national governments. In addition, conflicts will be decentralized, which may result in the attainment of more stable democracies."[57] This point about decentralization is made by many commentators, even if with different motivations. Anthony Power, for example, usefully calls for a buffer at the village level—one that involves specialization within the village and involves exchanges within the village and with the nearest town before entering into the wider national and international economy: "In PNG, we have a subsistence economy spinning out slightly into the national economy, but mostly into the international economy of traded commodities. Our village economy is a merry-go-round economy where cash from trading commodities comes into the village and then straight out again with little circulation in the village."[58]

All these suggestions are potentially useful, but they need to be framed by community negotiation in relation to two issues raised above: what is the mix of more extended and more localized production and exchange, and what is the balance of customary and petty entrepreneurial exchange? What, then, should be the appropriate role of the state? Two distinct policy approaches have emerged since the early 1990s.[59] The first approach recognizes the poverty and low productivity characteristic of the informal sector and argues that the state needs to provide supportive interventions through credit, technical support, and infrastructure. The second approach, one that has been developed by the World Bank, argues that state intervention, control, and restrictions have caused market distortions and instability—and what is required is not state intervention but deregulation and the freeing up of the economy to the flows and demands of the market. We suggest another path that neither assumes the involvement of the state nor presumes its substantial withdrawal. The nature of the state involvement needs to depend on whether the informal realm in question is "unregulated" capitalist exchange and services (including modern petty entrepreneurialism) or customary production-exchange relations (including tribal subsistence and extended-subsistence living) or occurs across the intersection between them, including roadside markets.

While the formal sector is inextricably dependent on state legislation however minimal, the customary informal sector is relatively independent of the state and can therefore work sustainably under many conditions, with or without its intervention. State involvement in the customary informal sector needs to be negotiated carefully, based on community consultation and independent disinterested research that is attuned to tensions across the ontologically layered world of communities. In other words, different informal economies have different needs; but, more than that, it is not just a matter of providing technical support and infrastructure and assuming that it will be useful—or even used. Here the community learning and development process (Chapter 12) provides one point of entry.

The informal sector undeniably plays an important role within Global South countries, including Papua New Guinea—it creates numerous jobs and absorbs a rising proportion of the unemployed, including the rising number of urban migrants. Looking at the informal sector from the standpoint of conventional economics and finance, we argue, is simply inadequate. Despite well-documented and widespread understanding that the informal sector is underpinned by its own social and cultural complexity, this sector continues to be analyzed through its monetary meaning, not its life meaning. What we are arguing for entails redefining the concept of "livelihood" in this broader context of the domain of the economic, but with awareness that livelihood crosses all domains of the circle of sustainability: economics, ecology, politics, and culture. The complex impact of many factors from global economic processes to local demographic changes means that there are no simple answers. Learning and training, infrastructure support such as providing minimally regulated spaces for market transactions, support with transport and supply-chain negotiation, and careful legal intervention into fair trade and employment guidelines would be possible examples of issues to be negotiated, with that negotiation including the terms on which support might be provided. It is the last point that is crucial—a Melanesian approach to deliberative democracy. This form of negotiation would recognize the very different places from which different stakeholders come.

Notes

1. Mike Davis, *Planet of Slums*, Verso, London, 2006, ch. 8.

2. Klarita Gerxhani, *The Informal Sector in Developed and Less-Developed Countries*, Amsterdam Institute for Advanced Labor Studies, Amsterdam, 2004.

3. Jim Thomas, *Informal Economic Activity*, Harvester Wheatsheaf, London, 1992.

4. P. W. Daniels, "Urban Challenges: The Formal and Informal Economies in Mega-Cities," *Cities*, vol. 21, no. 6, 2004, pp. 501–511.

5. On London see Mary George, *London Life in the Eighteenth Century*, Peregrine, London, (1925) 1966; Gareth Stedman Jones, *Outcast London*, Peregrine, Harmondsworth, revised edition, 1984.

6. Keith Hart, "Small Scale Entrepreneurs in Ghana and Development Planning," *Journal of Development Studies*, vol. 6, no. 4, 1970, pp. 104–120; Keith Hart, "Informal Income Opportunities and Urban Development in Ghana," *Journal of Modern African*

Studies, vol. 11, no. 1, 1973, pp. 61–89. In the first article the analysis centers on the category of what Hart calls "small-scale" or "indigenous" entrepreneurs, not on the informal economy as such.

7. M. Swaminathan, *Understanding the Informal Sector, a Survey*, WIDER WP 95, Finland, 1991.

8. Maghendra Reddy, "Modelling Poverty Dimensions of Urban Informal Sector Operators in a Developing Economy," *The European Journal of Development Research*, vol. 19, no. 3, 2007, pp. 459–479.

9. International Labour Organization, *Employment, Income and Equality: A Strategy for Increasing Productive Employment in Kenya*, ILO, Geneva, 1972; International Labour Organization, *ILO Compendium of Official Statistics on Employment in the Informal Sector*, ILO, Geneva, 2002.

10. Even under the neoliberal ideology and practice of the minimal and deregulating state, *regulation* for market "freedom" is fundamental to the practices of exchange and production.

11. Reddy, "Modelling Poverty Dimensions of Urban Informal Sector Operators."

12. Jütting, Parlevliet, and Xenogiani, *Informal Employment Re-Loaded*, p. 11.

13. Reddy, "Modelling Poverty Dimensions of Urban Informal Sector Operators," pp. 462–464; Michael P. Todaro, *Economic Development*, Longman, New York, fifth edition, 1994, pp. 250–258.

14. A. K. Ferej, "The Integration of Youth into the Informal Sector: The Kenyan Experience," 2000, http://www.cinterfor.org.uy/public/spanish/regional/ampro/cinterfor/temas/youth/eventos/korea/pon/ing/kenya, as cited in Reddy, "Modelling Poverty Dimensions of Urban Informal Sector Operators," p. 464.

15. Daniels, "Urban Challenges," p. 503.

16. Urjit R. Patel and Pradeep Srivastava, "Macroeconomic Policy and Output Co-movement: The Formal and Informal Sectors in India," *World Development*, vol. 24, no. 12, 1996, p. 1920.

17. Reddy, "Modelling Poverty Dimensions of Urban Informal Sector Operators."

18. Ibid.

19. R. G. Ward, "Urbanisation in the South Pacific," paper for UNESCO MOST Conference, USP, Suva, 1998.

20. Yoshiaki Azuma and Herschel I. Grossman, "A Theory of the Informal Sector," Working Paper, Brown University, Department of Economics, 2002, p. 1; also at http://www.econ.brown.edu/fac/Herschel_Grossman/papers/pdfs/informal.pdf, accessed 27 March 2009.

21. Reddy, "Modelling Poverty Dimensions of Urban Informal Sector Operators," pp. 459–479.

22. M. H. Malik, "Urban Poverty Alleviation through Development of the Informal Sector," *Asia-Pacific Development Journal*, vol. 3, no. 2, 1996, pp. 31–48.

23. Hernado de Soto, *The Other Path: The Invisible Revolution in the Third World*, Harper and Row, New York, 1989.

24. Anaya Roy and Nezar Alsayyad, eds., *Urban Informality: Transnational Perspectives from the Middle East, Latin America and South Asia*, Lexington Books, Lanham, 2003.

25. Roger Bromley and Chris Gerry, *Casual Work and Poverty in Third World Cities*, Wiley and Sons, Chichester, 1979.

26. Davis, *Planet of Slums*, p. 179.

27. Ibid., pp. 180–185. The following quotes also come from this source.

28. Here our point in characterizing Papua New Guinea as intensely patriarchal is that men tend to have public power even where that power is organized through matrilineal processes.

29. The Consultative Implementation and Monitoring Council was established in 1998 by the National Executive Council at its summit in February 1998. The consultative council is seen as an independent organization consisting of private sector, government partners, and civil society members who will develop policy and directly influence government decisions on PNG development strategies. The council secretariat is based in Port Moresby and administered through the Institute of National Affairs.

30. Concept paper on National Economy Policy, prepared by the Technical Working Group for the National Consultative Committee on Informal Economy, Department of Community Development, Port Moresby, 2006.

31. John Connell, *Papua New Guinea: The Struggle of Development*, Routledge, London, 1997.

32. Donald Denoon and C. Snowden, eds., *A Time to Plant and a Time to Uproot*, Institute of Papua New Guinea Studies, Port Moresby, no date.

33. E. K. Fisk, "The Economic Structure," in E. K. Fisk, ed., *New Guinea on the Threshold: Aspects of Social, Political and Economic Development*, Australian National University Press, Canberra, 1966, pp. 23–24.

34. Ibid., p. 24.

35. See, for example, Frederick K. Errington and Deborah B. Gewertz, *Articulating Change in the "Last Unknown,"* Westview Press, Boulder, 1995, ch. 2: "Duelling Currencies in East New Britain."

36. Karl Benediktsson, *Harvesting Development: The Construction of Fresh Food Markets in Papua New Guinea*, University of Michigan Press, Ann Arbor, 2002; Malcolm P. Levett, "Consumption and Demand for Fruits and Nuts in Port Moresby," *Yagl-Ambu*, vol. 17, 1993, pp. 55–77; Malcolm P. Levett,. "Urban Gardening in Port Moresby: A Survey of the Suburb of Gerehu Yagl Ambu, Papua New Guinea," *Journal of the Social Sciences and Humanities*, vol. 16, no. 3, 1992, pp. 47–68; Malcolm P. Levett and Marakan Uvano, "Urban Gardening in Port Moresby: A Survey of the Suburbs of Morata and Waigani," *Yagl-Ambu*, vol. 16, 1992, pp. 69–91.

37. Levett and Uvano, "Urban Gardening in Port Moresby."

38. O. H. K. Spate, "Changing Native Agriculture in New Guinea," *Geographical Review*, vol. 43, no. 2, 1953, pp. 151–172.

39. It should be said that our conclusion is countered by newspaper stories about successful dry-land rice growing and in particular a series of Taiwanese-supported initiatives in Eastern, Western, and Simbu Provinces. For example, see the spread in the World Food Supplement to the *National*, 18 October 2006.

40. http://www.fao.org/ES/ess/toptrade/trade.asp, accessed 2 April 2009.

41. Tim Spencer and Peter Heywood, "Staple Foods in Papua New Guinea: Their Relative Supply in Urban Areas, 1971 to 1981," *Food and Nutrition Bulletin*, vol. 5, no. 3, 1983, http://www.unu.edu/unupress/food/8F053E00.htm, accessed 19 October 2009, p. 6.

42. Deborah Gewertz and Frederick Errington, *Cheap Meat: Flap Food Nations in the Pacific Islands*, University of California Press, Berkeley, 2010.

43. R. D. Macadam, "From Pushing Production Inputs to Empowering Community: A Case Study in the Transformation of an Extension Agency," *Australian Journal of Experimental Agriculture*, vol. 40, no. 4, pp. 585–594.

44. Gina Koczberski and George N. Curry, "Making a Living: Land Pressures and Changing Livelihood Strategies among Oil Palm Settlers in Papua New Guinea," *Agricultural Systems*, vol. 85, no. 3, 2005, pp. 324–339.

45. Nancy Sullivan and Thomas Warr, "Timpis Maror: The Social Impact Study of RD Tuna," *Catalyst: Social Pastoral Journal of Melanesia*, vol. 35, no. 1, 2005, pp. 4–14.

46. Sullivan, Warr, Rainbubu, Kunoko, Akauna, Angasa, and Wenda, "A Social Impact Study of Proposed RD Tuna Cannery at Vidar Wharf, Madang," pp. 118–119.

47. William Vorley, *Sustaining Agriculture: Policy, Governance, and the Future of Family-Based Farming*, IIED, London, 2002, http://www.poptel.org.uk/iied/docs/sarl/sust_agintro.pdf, accessed 19 October 2009, p. 24.

48. Ibid., p. 48.

49. Ibid., pp. 7–8.

50. Ibid., p. 15; emphasis in original.

51. A *pasindia* is a passenger, a traveler, often used with a derogatory meaning. In the case of Lae the expansion came earlier, in the late 1960s, with the opening of the Kassam Pass and the Highlands Highway to unrestricted traffic. By 1970, according to James Sinclair, there were eight thousand squatters living in shanty towns around Lae (*Golden Gateway: Lae and the Province of Morobe*, Crawford House, Bathurst, 1998, p. 318).

52. Connell, "Regulation of Space in the Contemporary Postcolonial Pacific City: Port Moresby and Suva," pp. 243–257.

53. Mark Cleary and Peter Eaton, *Tradition and Reform: Land Tenure and Rural Development in South-East Asia*, Oxford University Press, Kuala Lumpur, 1996.

54. Michael Goddard, *The Unseen City: Anthropological Perspectives on Port Moresby, Papua New Guinea*, Pandanus Books, Canberra, 2005, p. 44.

55. Asef Bayat, "Globalisation and the Politics of the Informals in the Global South," in Ananya Roy and Nezar Alsayyad, *Urban Informality*, Lexington Books, Lanham, 2004, p. 91.

56. Martha Macintyre, "Petztorme Women: Responding to Change in Lihir, Papua New Guinea," *Oceania*, vol. 74, 2003, pp. 120–133.

57. Victor E. Tokman, "Policies for a Heterogeneous Informal Sector in Latin America," *World Development*, vol. 17, no. 7, 1989, p. 1075.

58. Anthony P. Power, "Global Village: A Village of the Future for Papua New Guinea," http://www.pngbuai.com/300socialsciences/economy-village/global-village-model-1.html, accessed 12 November 2008.

59. As distinguished by Malik, "Urban Poverty Alleviation through Development of the Informal Sector."

Chapter 8

Microfinance and Community Development

MICROFINANCE, MICROCREDIT, AND other initiatives that support microenterprise have been in the spotlight for well over a decade. Many of these initiatives, especially in Asia, have reported tremendous successes and are increasingly touted as the solution for poverty alleviation, especially for the Global South. Some of these initiatives have also reported spectacular results in terms of their outreach as well as their lending and saving portfolios. Such has been the level of enthusiasm for microfinance that the UN General Assembly was moved to declare 2005 the International Year of Microcredit. In 2006 an influential microfinance provider, the Grameen Bank, and its founder, Muhammad Yunus, were jointly awarded the Nobel Peace Prize "for their efforts to create economic and social development from below."

However, despite the enthusiastic claims of its proponents, microfinance—and especially microcredit—are not without substantial risks and dangers. The sustainable circulation of money as capital for the expansion of profit taking requires a constant movement and renewal, producing its own fragilities. These are compounded to the extent that customary forms of production and exchange are undermined. Circulating capital crosses social boundaries in ways that can be problematic, rarely taking account of cultural and political specificities, and having a tendency to displace rather than complement other forms of production and exchange. Without denying that there can be significant successes through microfinance schemes, it is our argument here that their success or failure turns not only on the process and procedures adopted, but also on the context in which they are deployed and the way in which they mesh with existing economies.

Microfinance can be quite destructive in circumstances where it is effectively used to create petty entrepreneurs living on the edge of two economies—

customary and capitalist—neither having the community-based security of the
first or the regulated patterns and disciplinary regimes of the second. All too often microcredit is projected as part of a neoliberal politics that assumes that the
replacement of customary economies by a capitalist system of production and
exchange relations will inevitably bring a higher quality of life. Sometimes microcredit brings more money, but an increased weekly income does not always
mean better living when the cost of living changes dramatically, and the local
capacity for producing the basics of life are diminished. In this chapter, as we
continue our exploration of different processes for underpinning community
sustainability in Papua New Guinea, microfinance is assessed for it usefulness
and viability.

Microcredit as Part of a Broader Schema of Microfinance

The terms "microfinance" and "microcredit" vary in meaning and application. Microfinance is broadly defined as the provision of a broad range of financial services to low-income enterprises and households. Many would classify
this as a supply of loans and savings services to the poor. Other products might
also include community-based health insurance (see Chapter 9), leasing, and
money transfers. More narrowly, microcredit emphasizes the provision of credit
services to low-income individuals, groups, and households with few assets that
could otherwise be used as collateral, usually in the form of small loans for
microenterprise and income-generating activities. These small loans typically
have to be repaid within short time frames at high interest. In recent decades,
the provision of credit services has increasingly been seen as a crucial tool for
poverty alleviation in the Global South.[1] However, some commentators argue
that microcredit should really be called "microdebt." Certainly the use of microcredit lending is often associated with an inadequate appreciation of the value
of savings services to the poor. In most cases, the provision of savings services
in microcredit schemes simply involves the collection of compulsory deposit
amounts that are designed only to collateralize those loans. Where clients have
restricted access to their enforced savings, these savings also become a source
of institutional capital.[2]

Examples of microfinance providers are strongly evident across the Pacific.[3]
Some development banks have attempted to create specific lending programs
aimed at reaching borrowers located in isolated regions and the outer islands.
Countries in the Pacific have also had varying semiformal setups such as credit
unions in both urban and rural areas. Beyond that, in trying to link both the informal and the semiformal sectors, NGOs have had some success in setting up
microfinance enterprises. These include the much-documented Liklik Dinau
Abitore Trust in Papua New Guinea, the Women's Social and Economic De-

velopment Programme (WOSED) in Fiji, and the Vanuatu Women's Development Scheme (VANWODS). In all of these, a solidarity group lending model was applied.

Over the past few decades, Papua New Guinea has, as we have stressed, undergone profound and revolutionary social change. Encounters with colonialism and the forces of globalization have put Papua New Guineans in touch with processes of neoliberal state formation, late-capitalist culture, and the emergence of a complex network of transnational identities. In addition to shaping the contours of the nation-state, these developments are also affecting the nature of embodied experience. The rise of charismatic Christianity, changing gender configurations, and the growing use of consumerism as a means of defining new social and political hierarchies and a revival of community—undoubtedly related to the slow crisis of community and reassertions of belonging to place—also requires that any community development schemes such as the microfinance enterprise take into account these dramatic shifts. Models developed instrumentally simply to service entrepreneurialism have the potential to damage the complex layering and interweaving of practices that crisscross tradition, power, and gender. For example, microcredit schemes that operate narrowly within a neoliberal understanding of maximizing "return on investment" can be completely counterproductive. As David Kavanamur observes,

> There is an intertwining relationship between market failure and state failure. Market failure results from excessive transaction costs in dealing with poor people and small businesses generally, while state failure in the provision of physical infrastructure and local amenities in developing countries exacerbates these transaction costs. Moreover, imperfect or asymmetric information leads to market failure in finance. So the target market of microfinance institutions, the poor, makes financial self-sufficiency a nonsensical aim. If this market had the resources to achieve financial sustainability, the people in it would not be poor and would not require this service of microfinance institutions.[4]

This chapter provides an outline of the origin and operation of microfinance and microcredit schemes and introduces some of the major schemes applied in Papua New Guinea. Microcredit finance schemes remain very much a part of the PNG government's development strategies. In September 2008 a national-level conference was held in Port Moresby. The Papua New Guinea Asian Development Bank (PNG-ADB) through the Bank of Papua New Guinea (the central bank) targeted service providers, donors, central banks, microfinance networks, and practitioners from Asia and Africa and the PNG microfinance fraternity as conference attendees. The primary objective of this conference was to discuss and implement Papua New Guinea's microfinance industry for the next decade. While recognizing the possibilities of microfinance when handled well, this chapter presents a detailed critique of unqualified hopes that are often expressed with regard to such schemes. In keeping with other chapters in this book, our overall argument is that microfinance works best when embedded in community-based solidarity groups with some sort of informal institutionalization (for example, through community learning centers) and developed with community consultation not only about the possibilities on offer, but also about the cultural, political, ecological, and economic consequences and costs of this path to development.

The Development of Microfinance

Credit initiatives began emerging in the 1950s, when NGOs and other, mainly community development, organizations experienced the limitations of formal banking institutions in responding to the needs of those living in poverty. These initiatives first emerged in what were called "the developing countries." Poor people, it was suggested, needed access to loans in order to rise above poverty. Their poverty, however, meant that they could not get access to loans through mainstream financial institutions and, moreover, could not afford to pay high interest rates. These initial credit projects were generally donor or government funded, offering subsidized interest rates, and tended to be geared toward agricultural or income-generating enterprises. In addition, state-owned rural development banks were often used to provide targeted, subsidized lending to a limited sector of the population. However, results were not promising, either in terms of project viability or of effective poverty alleviation.[5] Assessments of peoples' capacity to repay loans were often unrealistic, and schemes were subject to the fluctuating whims of both governments and donors.[6] When funds dried up, the projects stopped. The failure of these initial efforts led to an overall reconsideration of this development approach and a call for a "market-based solution" to the problem posed by the lack of financial services for people living in poverty.[7] Policy makers, economists, and community development workers began looking for ways to reduce the high costs and risks that normally accompanied the provision of financial services to poor people. Doing so, it was argued, would make it possible to offer such services to people who had previously been excluded from the mainstream financial market.

The shift to a market-based model was cemented with the establishment of the Grameen Bank in Bangladesh in 1983. Emphasizing the provision of microcredit for the establishment of microenterprises, the founder of the bank, Muhammad Yunus, transformed approaches to microfinance through the use of group-lending strategies. In place of physical collateral, the Grameen Bank developed the concept of "social collateral" as a means for ensuring repayments and reducing risks for the lender. Instead of loaning to individuals, microfinance providers following the Grameen model give loans to borrowers who are organized into small groups. Within these groups, members are jointly responsible for each other's loans and pressure one another to meet their repayments. Self-selecting groups essentially screen each other, as borrowers are unlikely to enter into joint responsibility with someone whom they do not trust to meet repayments. In addition, members have to attend compulsory meetings, usually weekly, that serve to maintain commitment and involvement, and act as a collection point for repayments and savings deposits. Essentially, social pressure is used in the place of physical collateral; joint responsibility for loans reduces the risk to lenders.

Following the establishment of the Grameen Bank, market-based approaches to microfinance quickly grew in popularity. The Grameen model began to be replicated in countries across the Global South, and government and funding agencies became more concerned with supporting and creating institutions that could provide microfinance services on a sustainable, long-term basis.[8] While the Grameen Bank has often been criticized for its rigid rules and regulations, compulsory savings, social agenda, and costly delivery system, a body of research evidence indicates that the bank has often produced positive effects for its clients.[9] As the model has been adopted and replicated over the years, it has been modified according to experience, experimentation, and local conditions.[10] There are other, more recently established institutions that follow the Grameen Bank model in part. In Bangladesh these include the Association for Social Advancement and the Bangladesh Rural Advancement Committee, both of which have performed well in terms of outreach and financial sustainability, following minimalist and maximalist approaches respectively.

Providers soon shifted from subsidized credit to microcredit (the provision of small-loan services only) and then to microfinance (the provision of a broader range of financial services) and even to microbanking (the provision of a full range of commercial banking services through a licensed institution).[11] Accordingly, a process of "formalization" began, requiring microfinance initiatives and providers to be brought under a rubric of financial regulations and legislative frameworks. Prototype microfinance institutions also made their appearance in Papua New Guinea and other Pacific Island countries in the 1950s and 1960s. One type that was popular was the revolving fund scheme, usually managed by a local government or a women's group. Most of these schemes failed owing to the high rate of nonrepayment of these loans.[12]

Over time, most of the schemes came to adhere to a neoliberal conception of development that stresses the need for increased income, growth, and efficiency.[13] This conception helps to explain the emphasis on microcredit and self-employment through entrepreneurship. Morgan Brigg, for example, argues that the provision of microcredit for microenterprise is very much line with the neoliberal developmental approach advanced by institutions such as the World Bank.[14] At the heart of this approach is the idea that any person can create a job and lift himself or herself out of poverty if only he or she works hard enough and embraces the principles of the market. The dominant approaches to microfinance provision that have emerged since the early 1980s are deeply embedded within broader discourses and strategies around development. However, what is new about the second wave of microfinance models is their high repayment rates, market interest rates, savings products, and risk-aversion products. The rate and extent of outreach services that was achieved among previously considered "unbankable people" grew phenomenally.[15] The ambitious plan that was mooted for Papua New Guinea was to deliver such a "scheme to the 70–80 percent of PNG's approximately four million and other Pacific Island countries' two-million low-income populations into the next millennium."[16]

Approaches to Microfinance

Microfinance provision can take a wide variety of forms, and there are a number of different ways of distinguishing between approaches. For instance, a distinction can be drawn between minimalist and maximalist approaches. In the case of the former, microfinance institutions provide only microfinancial services. Institutions following the maximalist approach, by contrast, provide a range of financial services combined with social development services such as business skills training. Another way to distinguish between different approaches to microfinance is to categorize service providers into three sectors: formal, semiformal, and informal. Organizations within the formal sector— which include, for example, banks (commercial, rural, savings, postal, or cooperative); development banks, which could be either state owned or private; and finance companies, building societies, credit unions, pension funds, and insurance companies—are monitored through a high level of regulation and supervision. Organizations that fall into the semiformal category are not so formally regulated but are usually licensed and supervised by some form of official government agency. Savings and credit cooperatives, credit unions, employee saving funds, village banks, registered self-help groups, and nongovernmental groups (NGOs) primarily fall within this category. The informal sector, consisting of nonregistered self-help groups, rotating savings and credit associations, commercial moneylenders, traders, shopkeepers, NGOs, friends, and family is characterized by the absence of formal regulations and supervision—usually relying on informal networks and processes for action and accountability.[17]

Informal approaches typically involve locally created systems that rely on trust among community members. Such systems are often better understood as informal money systems rather than microfinance initiatives per se. Examples include self-help groups and rotating savings and credit associations. Also included here are informal providers such as friends and family, trade stores, and local moneylenders. It is important that such informal financial systems are recognized because they often have a history that long predates the emergence of more structured and formalized microfinance approaches. Moreover, the existence of such systems disproves the assumption that poor people cannot save. To the contrary, it is well established that savings and credit arrangements—whether in cash or "in-kind"—have long been among the ways in which poor groups of people have managed their livelihoods. In many cases it is not an exchange of "cash" but of labor or produce. Many households, clans, or tribal communities are linked by family and extended family ties—and this also creates a network and culture of obligations and expectations.

As an example, in some villages in India there is a notion of *kuuttu*—a form of collective savings activity. Each month, members of this collective contribute a sum. Each month, too, a member of the collective receives the full collection, and this goes in rotation. This enables the member to pay for a wedding event, school fees, or something that he or she would not have been able to do as a single person. The group decides on the need of the person—and usually a small amount is set aside to invest in a new project that is also then collectively managed. The Junin community in Ecuador uses a system of rotational labor, called the *minga*, in which each community member is called up to provide community service when it is needed.

To keep one's word means also to fulfill the obligations of embodied reciprocal exchange. In conditions of relative poverty, the keeping of one's word is the foundation for a social-cultural system of face-to-face trust (rather than more abstract fiduciary trust) that is not just culturally but also economically sustaining. As Susan Johnson and Ben Rogaly argue, financial service providers that are considering the introduction of microfinance services to a particular area need to be aware of what other exchange systems already exist and the ways in which they operate. Such systems, they write, "are capable of supporting poor people's livelihoods as well as perpetuating structures which undermine them."[18] As local exchange networks change in the context of different and more extended ways of understanding value, such systems can be both enabling and exploiting.

Semiformal microfinance institutions include credit unions, multipurpose cooperatives, and nongovernmental organizations. Such institutions often, but not necessarily, need a license from the central bank of the country in which they work. Many operate as incorporated companies, for instance as nongovern-mental organizations. Since they do not fall under the "banking" category, they are limited in their service provision—that is, they cannot provide a full range of banking services and often are not allowed to collect deposits. However, the industry has developed a bit of a grey zone in this area. Many microfinance in-stitutions, including those following the Grameen Bank model, collect savings as part of the loan product or as part of a group fund. Usually these are called compulsory savings, and the client is not allowed to withdraw the funds un-less the loan is repaid. Banking authorities, supportive of microfinance develop-ment, have often tolerated these arrangements. They are, however, not without risk to the depositor. Credit unions or credit cooperatives are different. They are regulated by government departments or by central banks and so can of-fer saving services to their members. Formal institutions are those that hold a license to operate as a bank or a nonbank financial institution. They include commercial banks and public and private development banks. Typically, their license is issued by the central bank of the country within which they operate, and subsequently they are subject to the rules, regulations, and supervision of the central bank. Their license gives them authorization to mobilize savings from the public and offer a full range of financial services.

While some microcredit service providers lend to individuals, most employ some sort of group-lending methodology. Where providers using individual lending tend to follow commercial banking practices, those using group- or peer-lending practices differ markedly from mainstream banking and financial service providers. Among those providers who use a group-lending methodol-ogy, there are two primary forms of service provision: first, the use of solidarity-group lending and, second, the use of community-based delivery mechanisms. Both have their own distinct lending methods and target clientele.[19] Microfi-nance institutions using the solidarity-group principle provide loans to individu-als within a self-selected group of people (a solidarity group), and use peer pres-sure and moral obligation among borrowers of the group as a substitute for the lack of collateral.

Community-Based Services

Community-based microfinance organizations developed as a bottom-up approach for the delivery of microfinance services. These initiatives are mem-ber based, mostly situated in rural areas, and often use a group-lending meth-odology. The two main forms of community-based delivery mechanisms for microfinance services are village banks and savings and loan associations.[20] The village-bank model, designed for a larger group of people, first emerged in the mid-1980s and has the characteristics of a community-managed revolving fund.[21] After having received some initial technical assistance from the sponsoring funding agency and the start-up capital required for an initial loan fund, the village bank manages the fund independently and "on-lends" to its members. During the lifetime of the loan fund, the members can take loans, make repayments, and deposit savings. On a set due date, the village bank has to repay the loan to the funding agency. It is anticipated that, through the members' savings, the village bank can gradually become more independent of the agency and eventually manage its own fund. The village-bank model is appealing in the sense that it is a community-based program that, through transferring many administrative functions to the village bank, allows poor communities in remote areas to be serviced while simultaneously keeping transaction and operating costs to a minimum.[22]

Microfinance services following the village-bank model have been established by a number of organizations. The United States–based provider FINCA has set up village banks within Latin America, Eurasia, Africa, and the Middle East. In Guatemala, a nongovernmental organization, CARE, has established a Women's Village Banking Program. Likewise, village banks have been established by Save the Children in El Salvador, Freedom from Hunger in Mali, and Catholic Relief Services in Benin. Even though adopted in various forms, the village bank is broadly characterized by its minimalist approach, its targeting of the most disadvantaged women in remote areas with low population density, its capacity-building efforts at a community level, and its decentralized institutional structure.[23]

Savings and loan associations or societies, usually known as credit unions, have been established in developing countries since the 1950s.[24] They target small enterprises in urban or semiurban areas, offer savings and credit services on a minimalist approach, and operate according to a cooperative principle whereby membership is defined by a common bond, with members having joint ownership of the institution. They may also be known as "mutualist organizations." Usually, savings and loan societies follow a savings-first approach, whereby the loan fund is generated through the savings contributions of members. Thus, there is no direct dependency on a funding agency.[25] These institutions are regulated by respective government authorities, which often results in inflexible product design, making it difficult for providers to meet the needs of microenterprise clients. In other cases, such as the thrift-and-credit movement in Sri Lanka (SANASA), the primary cooperatives are autonomous and can adopt services according to the local context, which, according to Hulme and Mosley, is one of their key strengths.[26] In Papua New Guinea, savings and loan societies are governed by the Central Bank, which explicitly sets loan terms and interest rates for loan and savings products.

Evaluating the Success of Microfinance Institutions

As the microfinance industry developed and moved increasingly toward a capitalist market-based paradigm, donors and external funding agencies became increasingly interested in evaluating the performance of microfinance institutions and initiatives. The extent to which microfinance initiatives can be considered successful depends on the ultimate goals of such initiatives. Increasingly, the ultimate goal of microfinance is seen to be the alleviation of poverty on a cost-covering basis, that is, without any external financial assistance.[27] However, within the microfinance industry, providers have found it consistently difficult to achieve both financial sustainability and outreach. Different approaches have tended to emphasize either one or the other, thus establishing different sets of criteria against which the performance of microfinance initiatives should be measured. These two main approaches are known as the (financial) sustainability approach and the poverty approach.

Financial Sustainability versus Poverty Alleviation

The key distinction between the sustainability approach and the poverty camp is that the former emphasizes the need for a commercial focus, while the latter views microfinance as a social force and emphasizes a welfare-based perspective.[28] Microfinance initiatives that follow the poverty approach, on the one hand, tend to gear their service provision toward very poor clients who are most costly to serve. The shortfall between revenue and the cost of supply is covered by donations. Those providers following the sustainability approach, on the other hand, tend to have less poor clients who exist on the fringe of the formal financial system, and the provider's goal is the long-term expansion of the frontiers of the mainstream economy. Here, donations cover start-up costs and are used to fund the search for innovations to reduce the cost of supply, with the aim of revenue ultimately covering costs.[29]

With external sources of funding becoming increasingly difficult to secure, advocates of financial sustainability argue that only viable institutions will be able to provide financial services on a long-term basis and achieve economies of scale. The question arises whether the term "viable" is a self-supporting kind of assertion, thereby presuming its own standard of the capability of sustaining life. The financial sustainability argument has been primarily developed and advanced by a group of scholars of the Ohio State University, the member agencies of the Consultative Group to Assist the Poorest (CGAP), the World Bank, the US Agency for International Development (USAID), as well as other major donors. Their work has resulted in the design of microfinance best practices, which are vehemently promoted by the CGAP.[30] In response, supporters of the poverty camp have sought to reassert the social focus of microfinance. They have raised concerns that a commercial approach and a focus on financial viability will lead to "mission drift" from the social goal of overcoming poverty and neglect of the poorest of the poor.

According to Zeller and other scholars, neither approach has yet provided convincing arguments or results.[31] For instance, a survey conducted for the *MicroBanking Bulletin* in 2003 showed that of 124 surveyed microfinance institutions, only 66 were financially sustainable, which suggests that a larger number of clients may be reached at the cost of sustainability. However, since microfinance initially emphasized credit services, most available empirical impact studies focus on microcredit programs, proving only that the poorest people are often reluctant to get further into debt through loans and thus are unable to benefit from a credit-driven program.[32] A full range of services in a flexible money-management or savings facility would probably assist poor people better in smoothing their economic-cycle needs. But most semiformal and informal microfinance providers are not authorized to take deposits and therefore cannot provide these services.

Neither of these two approaches has gained dominance, and recent writings suggest that they should be seen as complementary rather than contradictory.[33] The industry thus seems to have settled for two key criteria in measuring the performance of microfinance institutions: institutional sustainability and outreach.[34] The first of these is concerned with the degree to which an institution is able to cover its cost without dependence on external subsidies. Jacob Yaron defines two levels of sustainability: operational and financial self-sufficiency. Operational self-sufficiency gives an indication as to whether an institution is able to cover its operational cost with the income earned. Financial self-sufficiency calculates the level of sustainability once adjustments for inflation and subsidies have been taken into consideration. The second criterion, outreach, is defined in terms of both breadth and depth.[35] While breadth of outreach is concerned with the number of clients reached, depth of outreach is focused on the clients' level of poverty and is often measured in terms of loan size. Commercially oriented microfinance providers primarily use level of self-sufficiency and breadth of outreach as the key indicators for success. Poverty-oriented microfinance providers, however, focus on the direct improvement of their clients' livelihood and prefer depth of outreach as the measurement tool for success of their interventions. Our position tends toward the poverty approach but with much more emphasis on partnership rather than welfare and more emphasis on generating an economy layered across different social forms than on promoting a modern market-based economy.

The Benefits of a Market-Based Strategy and Its Costs

The debate between supporters of a poverty-oriented and a sustainability-oriented emphasis continues, but there has been a general shift to a market-based paradigm. While there are still heated debates about perceived "mission drift" through commercialization, the industry as a whole is moving toward the approach exemplified in the dictum that institutions that follow commercial banking principles will ultimately alleviate the most poverty.[36] Even though the approach and immediate objective of microfinance differs from standard commercial banking, its fundamental concepts are similar. Like banking, microfinance is a business, principally based on a market-exchange mechanism where the institution acts as a financial intermediary, matching money supply and demand for an agreed price, that is, interest. Supply is generated through people who have access to money and would like to invest. Demand is driven by people who are in need of liquidity. So, in the end, microfinance is in essence a modern capitalist enterprise. Like mainstream banking, microfinance institutions rely on their clients' familiarity with market exchanges and a clear understanding of the value and use of money. Typically this familiarity can be found in established cash economies. The value of microfinance for communities in Papua New Guinea depends on whether extending a capitalist financial exchange system to the grass roots involves the loss of alternative and prior forms of exchange, such as reciprocal and barter-exchange systems.

With a capitalist exchange system—however low-level that exchange might be—transactions are depersonalized and abstracted from the embodied relations of those doing the exchanging; that is, they carry no necessary ongoing social attachment and can thus be accepted or rejected without social repercussion (see the section "Practices of Exchange" in Chapter 3). This is different from reciprocal exchanges, where modern economic forces such as supply and demand are suppressed and social motives are the driving force for exchanges. Even though the outsider might perceive these as economic transactions with an ultimate profit aim, empirical anthropological studies explain these transactions socially as involving commensurable units of *cultural* value. For instance, they can include ritualized gift giving and other reciprocal ceremonial forms of exchange that have no modern economic character.

Nonmarket activities play an important role in the livelihoods of people within rural areas, and village economies are mostly characterized by farming, hunting, and fishing activities. In the simplest form of the village economic model—the subsistence economy—there is little market development per se. People produce goods and foodstuffs for their own consumption, primarily at the household level, although a small surplus might be traded at local markets and with other household units. These peripheral markets mostly do not involve institutional trading partners or financial intermediation but rather operate through personalized, trust-based, and face-to-face relations. Village economies tend not to be fully monetized. Moreover, where money *is* used in transactions and exchanges, it may be used to fulfill noncommercial needs in the context of reciprocal exchanges within these societies.

Benefits for the Poorest of the Poor

In evaluating the performance of microfinance initiatives in the Global South, several scholars have raised the point that microfinance providers often fail to assist the poorest of the poor. David Hulme contends that microfinance institutions virtually never work with the poorest, and many get much of their work from clients who are nonpoor.[37] Similarly, Diana Mitlin argues that it is often the poorest members of a community who are least able to participate in the market. Better-off households tend to take up the opportunities offered by microfinance initiatives and so "monopolize space."[38] First, within self-selecting peer-monitoring groups, the poorest are likely to be excluded in favor of the less poor, with whom borrowers prefer to enter into a joint-responsibility relationship.[39] Second, the better-off the borrower is, the greater the increase in income will be as a result of a loan. That is, borrowers who already have skills and assets benefit more from the provision of credit than do the poorest borrowers. Indeed, there is evidence that the provision of credit to the poorest may cause more harm than good. Thus, third, already vulnerable, the poorest are both less able to take risks and more subject to major crisis in the case of business failure.[40] Fourth, the emphasis of the microfinance industry on the provision of microcredit for microenterprise is often inappropriate in dealing with the very poor. Poor people need access to more financial services than just credit. Indeed, the most important factor for people in breaking the poverty cycle is social and economic security. Indeed, it is argued that access to credit can only be of benefit once poor people have achieved a basic level of social and economic security.

Achieving such security may be better assisted through savings and insurance, or through loans for emergency expenses or basic assets.[41] These expenses, such as funeral or wedding costs, costs incurred through natural disasters or the death of a breadwinner, or those for education or housing, are not necessarily or immediately profit making. In such instances, the industry focus on the provision of working capital for microenterprise is not appropriate. There is indeed a real danger of borrowers becoming burdened through excessive debt. Because of circumstances beyond their control (flood, sickness, drought, theft, and so on), lack of skills or knowledge, or poor decisions, many poor borrowers encounter difficulty in repaying loans. In Bangladesh, a number of debtors have reported being threatened by the staff of microfinance institutions or other group members. Some face violence, and there are regularly reported cases of women committing suicide when faced with repayments they cannot make.[42]

Thus, contrary to the claims of many of its supporters, microfinance is not the cure-all for poverty in developing countries. Its micro-level focus means that it does not challenge the political and economic structures that generate and maintain poverty. As Khandakar Elahi and Constantine Danooulos put it, the poverty in Global South countries was not caused by a lack of microcredit.[43] Moreover, the trend toward the commercialization of microfinance means that services are increasingly being delivered on a for-profit basis by private providers and not necessarily in order to reduce poverty.[44]

Empowerment of Women

Supporters of microfinance often advance the argument that microfinance initiatives have the capacity to enact progressive social change, particularly through empowering women, who make up the overwhelming majority of microfinance clients.[45] However, as most commentaries recognize, microfinance initiatives overwhelmingly target women because they have proved to be better clients. The industry's focus on women may have much less to do with empowerment and much more to do with financial objectives. Rutherford argues that the real reason behind the targeting of women in Bangladesh is that they are seen to be more accessible because they are at home during working hours, more likely to repay on time, more pliable and patient than men, and cheaper to service because providers can hire lower-paid female staff.[46] The Grameen Bank notes that very poor women tend to make repayments more faithfully than men and tend to use money in ways that are more beneficial to their families and wider communities.[47] Available research suggests that outcomes have been mixed. On the one hand, women may sometimes be able to use their access to credit to negotiate improved status within the household.[48] Yet women often have little or no control over the use of the loan, and some women have reported increased domestic violence resulting from disputes over cash for loan repayments.[49]

It would be wrong to say that there are no positive effects from microfinance provision in the Global South. Many schemes involving the provision of credit have produced significant benefits for their clients. Survey data collected from governments, NGOs, and banks have demonstrated that, when comparisons are made between households that have had access to microcredit and those who have not, results indicate that credit provision can enable increases in household income.[50] But it is important to recognize its limits: microfinance does carry substantial risks and can produce harmful effects for some borrowers and communities. Moreover, increased income (more money) does not always equate with a higher quality of living. Particular microfinance services are not appropriate or useful in many conditions. This is particularly the case with the provision of microcredit for microenterprise, and many borrowers, particularly among the poorest, may better benefit from savings services that do not require their taking on debt. Microfinance is best viewed as one tool that, in some circumstances, is beneficial for some people.

Microfinance in Papua New Guinea

Often it seems that models are applied with little variation in situations where the operating context is much different from that in which they were first developed. Transferring the lessons of South Asia to the South Pacific and Melanesia is a case in point. There are major constraints on the implementation of microfinance institutions in Melanesia that distinguish it from Asia: the cost of accessibility, cultural limitations on the participation of women in financial activities, the nature of government involvement, the need for appropriate training in basic accounting questions, and pressure to expand too soon.[51] These constraints are accentuated in Papua New Guinea. The provinces and regions are distinctively different from each other in terms of geography, culture, and languages. In the remote areas communities tend to speak their own *tok ples* (language of the place). The population is widely dispersed, with Papua New

The cash economy is becoming more and more crucial in Papua New Guinea. Here kina changes hands as a coffee manufacturer in Lae buys a bag of semidried beans, or "parchment," from a small landholder.

Guinea having one of the lowest population densities in the world (11.9 people per square kilometer in 2006).[52] And, given the lack of infrastructure and the fact that semisubsistence farming and fishing provide about 80 percent of the staple food supply for households,[53] it is difficult for many villages to develop extended markets that are necessary to making conventional microfinance useful.

Since the 1950s and 1960s, there have been prototype microfinance institutions in Papua New Guinea and also in other Pacific Island countries including Fiji, Solomon Islands, Vanuatu, Western Samoa, Tonga, Kiribati, Cook Islands, and Tuvalu. One major example was revolving fund schemes, and these were usually managed by a local government or women's group. Most of the schemes were forced into dormancy through a very high level of nonrepayment. PNG Banking Corporation figures show that, between 1985 and 1995, the number of commercial bank networks and agencies in Papua New Guinea declined by 55 percent from 305 to 138.[54] Moreover, only 30 percent of the population held deposit accounts, and less than 1 percent had loans with commercial banks. There is a huge gap in participation of the mostly rural and remote population in the PNG financial system.

The literature on microfinance initiatives in Papua New Guinea reiterates the fact that these projects applied methods and systems successfully implemented in Asian countries directly to PNG scenarios instead of developing new methodologies that might have been more compatible with the local sociocultural and geographic conditions.[55] For example, while Goroka was selected as a model in 1994 because of its good road network, transport system, low crime rate, and relatively high population density, the scheme collapsed in 2002.

Earlier Attempts at Financial Services Provision

The development of microfinance in Papua New Guinea can be described as a process of experimental trial and error. Most projects mounted during the 1980s and 1990s are no longer in existence.[56] Early attempts at financial services provision for low-income groups can be broadly categorized into informal and formal approaches. Papua New Guinea has a long history of informal money systems. Extended family and other *wantoks* provide a major part of the informal source of credit, followed by the trade-store owners in the rural areas, and moneylenders in more urban settings. There are informal savings and credit groups that fall under the rubric of rotating savings and credit associations (ROSCAS), adjusted to the Papua New Guinea context. In Papua New Guinea, mostly called *sande* or *wok meri,* they have been operating all over the country but are most active in the Highland regions.[57] According to Kavanamur they are often based on ethnic or peer groupings where people pool funds and receive credit on a rotating basis.[58] Some of these initiatives have become more formalized and have received funding through the national or provincial government, through the national or provincial council of women, or are donor-supported, in particular as part of support for women's initiatives. A number of these initiatives run more or less autonomously within an overall framework set up by the Department of Home Affairs in 1995.[59]

Two of the bigger and most documented initiatives are the Western Highlands Women's Council Credit Scheme and the North Simbu Rural Development Project, Micro Credit Scheme. The former was at first a collaborative effort between the Government of Papua New Guinea, the South Pacific Forum's Women's Bureau, and the National Council of Women in 1988.[60] By the late 1990s, further donors had joined the scheme after its initial apparent success. Loans were disbursed by the Provincial Council of Women to women's associations throughout the province, which would in turn lend money to women within the association. One evaluation reported good repayment rates (inclusive of interest) with proper recording at Western Highlands.[61] However, eventually repayment rates by the associations deteriorated. A rival women's credit scheme (Gomis Women's Credit Association) was established during that time, claiming that the seed capital was given as handouts by the credit scheme to related associations. The Western Highlands Women's Council Credit Scheme has since then collapsed.

The North Simbu Rural Development Project was a rural development project supported by the provincial government and council of women and the Austrian Volunteer Scheme.[62] The project applied a solidarity group lending approach. That is, loans were disbursed to individual women within a group, with a compulsory savings component. It connected with women through the district and ward offices, which functioned as "branches" to carry out financial transactions. The scheme received a lot of support from women in the province, who voluntarily dedicated much of their time. Awareness raising, the go-isi approach (an informal approach that enables the setting of a contextual pace), continuous improvement of procedures, and constant follow-up on loan repayments contributed to the success of the scheme.[63] However, because of the project's "informal" character, the scheme does not run on a sustainable basis, and it became dependent on donor funding. More formal approaches in financial service provision for the small enterprise and agricultural sector as well as low-income groups in Papua New Guinea are characterized by government-supported guarantee schemes and/or directed lending initiatives.

Credit Guarantee Schemes

The Small Business Guarantee Facility was provided through the Small Business Development Corporation.[64] Its main purpose under the Small Business Development Corporation Act was to "develop credit and business advisory service schemes aimed at promoting small business."[65] It provided business courses and guarantee schemes to promote the small-enterprise sector. Loan applicants had to go through Small Business Development Corporation business training as a precondition for loan disbursement. With the inception of the Small Business Guarantee Facility in 1996, the corporation placed term deposits with partnering financial institutions that provided loans to small and medium-sized enterprises against the Small Business Guarantee Facility guarantee with no risk for the partnering institution. According to reports, the program has not been successful, with few disbursements and high default rates.[66] Among reasons mentioned for the failure were the directed credit approach (that is, an unsuitable credit product for the target group), lack of proper screening and follow-up procedures, overly high loan amounts exceeding the repayment capacities of the clients, as well as willful defaulters.

PNG Government Credit Guarantee Scheme

Since 1976 the PNG government, under the patronage of the Department of Treasury and Finance, has made similar attempts to provide guarantee schemes in order to promote the entrepreneurial sector. These guarantees were provided to commercial banks, which in turn would disburse a loan for any productive purpose.[67] By the end of 2001, none of the guarantee schemes were still operating as all of them had had high default rates. Various reasons contributed to their failure: lack of monitoring and management capacity at the respective governments department, insufficient recovery processing by the commercial banks, and willful defaulters that considered government-supported schemes as handouts.

Rural Development Bank

In 1967 the Australian Administration in Papua New Guinea established the Rural Development Bank in order to provide services to small-scale farmers, who make up the majority of the country's rural poor. Donors have used the bank as an executing arm for rural development with directed lending and guarantee programs, one of which was the Smallholder Agricultural Credit Scheme. This scheme was introduced as a revolving loan fund in 1995 with seed capital from the government. It provided subsidized loans to agricultural and livestock farmers, relying primarily on their repayment capacity (there was no collateral). The scheme was discontinued in early 1999, experiencing problems similar to those of other guarantee schemes. The Rural Development Bank has not been sustainable, mainly owing to small outreach, high default, excessive overhead, and heavy reliance on government budgetary allocation or donor funds.[68] Political interference in the management and operation of the bank was apparent, and it was often used by parliamentarians in the lead-up to elections to disburse "voting" money (covered up as a credit scheme, with no intention for collection of returns).[69] Despite several unsuccessful attempts to restructure the bank, it has recently, under new management, taken the approach of privatizing and obtaining a full commercial banking license. In addition, expatriates have been appointed to fill key positions, such as lending management and microfinance.

Savings and Loan Societies

Savings and loan societies (credit unions) were first introduced to Papua New Guinea in the early 1960s by the Australian Administration in order to provide agricultural and financial services to farmers. The sector suffered serious problems from the mid-1970s to 1990s, when mismanagement, lack of accounting and internal controls, inappropriate lending policies, abuse of authority, and misuse of funds became apparent and caused the sector to collapse. Out of the 165 savings and loan societies only 21 are active today.[70] In 2000, Bank of Papua New Guinea launched a revitalization program, which focused on the introduction of standard policies and procedures, internal controls, and tighter supervision and control mechanisms. Savings and loan societies have to report quarterly to the Bank of Papua New Guinea, and interest rates for savings and loans are capped. With the support of the Australian Association of Credit Unions and the Bank of Papua New Guinea, the remaining savings and loan societies have gained strength and resilience.[71] They now offer simple standardized financial services to their members, with a clear focus on savings. This is quite different from previous initiatives that were clearly credit driven. The credit procedures are also distinctively different from those in previous schemes. Loans are extended up to the maximum savings account balance of the member in a 1:1 ratio. This means that a borrower has to save K100 before he or she can borrow K100. This unique feature presents no risk to the lending institution. In case of nonrepayment of loans, the savings and loan society is authorized to debit the savings account with the loan equivalent. There is some flexibility in the system where Bank of Papua New Guinea allows selected savings and loan societies to extend loans using a different ratio, say a 1:2 ratio.

A number of savings and loan associations have been performing extremely well, among them the community-based, East New Britain Savings and Loan Society. This was one of the first examples to show that rural, low-income, or self-employed people are bankable. However, because of strict regulations, all societies have to offer the same type of products—that is, not adjusted to the particular context in which they are operating. They can therefore only cater to the relatively easily accessible rural poor familiar with money and knowledge of banking procedures. The society benefits substantially from a continuous inflow of savings deposits from salaried employees, which during periods of high Treasury bill interest rates generated good profits. With the recent drop in interest rates, societies have experienced a greater challenge to remain profitable.

Commercial Banks

Commercial banks do not have a history of servicing the typical microfinance target market. The only example was the Papua New Guinea Banking Corporation, which was established in 1974 with the transfer of the Commonwealth Banking Corporation to the government as part of preparations for independence. This was supposed to be Papua New Guinea's people's bank with a dense network throughout the country. It was quite successful in mobilizing savings from the low-income market but was subsequently privatized and absorbed by Bank of South Pacific, thus losing its "people" focus, resulting, among other things, in the closure of many branch offices. ANZ Bank has recently become more involved in the low-income market through a number of linkage arrangements with microfinance providers for deposit taking. There are endeavors to move into the market through a partnership with Post PNG, the national postal service. However, so far this has not materialized.

Savings-First Approach

Many microcredit projects with a mere credit focus were unsustainable and either closed down or continued to depend on outside funding with limited outreach.[72] Over the years, a savings-first approach evolved, integrating credit union and village banking principles into the methodology. Two of these initiatives that started with much promise were the Bougainville Microfinance Scheme (Bougainville Haus Moni) and the Putim na Kisim project, also known as the Nazarin Church Credit Scheme. As part of the economic reconstruction efforts after the Bougainville crisis, the Bougainville Microfinance Scheme was initiated as an AusAID funded project by the Credit Union Foundation of Australia and Australian Volunteers International in cooperation with the Bougainville Administration in 1996. The purpose of this project was to provide financial services to the grass roots of Bougainville by considering lessons learned from previous microfinance initiatives and pursuing an active collaboration with the Bougainvillean people.[73] It was set up as a three-tier system whereby tier one comprised grass-roots microfinance institutions; tier two, district agencies; and tier three, Bougainville Haus Moni (apex body). Grass-roots microfinance institutions are informal savings and credit associations that are voluntarily linked to district agencies for reporting purposes. The district agencies provide training services to the grass-roots microfinance institutions; the Bougainville Haus Moni, as the apex body and head office, liaises with government and donor agencies and has an overall management function. Grass-roots microfinance institutions are mostly based on family or clan formations, using existing social and cultural structures. Thus, there is a clear sense of ownership.[74] In terms of outreach the Bougainville Microfinance Scheme has achieved significant results, but loan repayment, even though backed by savings, is still unsatisfactory. However, no progress has been made toward institutionalization and self-sufficiency, and the project is dependent on external funding.

Putim na Kisim was established by the Lutheran Development Service in 1995 as a result of a symposium of community church leaders in Morobe Province.[75] The name reveals the approach to the provision of rural finance facilities. *Putim na kisim* is the Pidgin term for "put and receive." Thus, members have to put money first (savings) before receiving money (loans). The project aims to develop savings cells at the village level as the basis for the provision of financial services. Using a bottom-up approach, it should still be flexible enough to adjust to varying community contexts. It uses the existing structure of the Yangpela Didiman (Young Farmer) community development program. Under this program volunteer village-development workers provide agricultural extension services, community development, spiritual development, and financial literacy skills to villagers. The saving cells collect savings from their members and—applying a savings and loan society methodology—disburse loans, the amount of which is determined by the individual savings balance.[76] Following a village-banking structure, a central Putim na Kisim agency provides support to the saving cells in terms of capacity building (record keeping, policies, and so forth), auditing, and investment of access funds. The scheme is ongoing; however, it relies on volunteer workers as well as funding from the Lutheran Development Service for the central Putim na Kisim agency to be able to provide continuous support to the saving cells.

Replication of Models Based in Asia

Liklik Dinau Arbitore Trust is probably the most documented and researched microfinance intervention in Papua New Guinea. It started operation in Goroka in 1994 under the auspices of the United Nations Development Program in partnership with several government and nongovernment agencies.[77] The aim was to provide credit and savings facilities to rural poor women.[78] As a direct replication it followed the Grameen Bank's stringent rules and regulations, especially in terms of targeting and credit policies.[79] For example, only women were allowed in the program. The focus was on credit using a solidarity-group lending principle. Savings were linked to the credit product. Progress was slow, and by mid-2001 the performance was well behind the ambitious target (in terms of outreach and sustainability) for a variety of reasons, among others slow outreach, high default rates, dried up operational funds, and lack of management capacity. Since donor funding was no longer forthcoming, the scheme collapsed in 2002.

Another example is Village Finance Limited, established as a subsidiary of Papua New Guinea Banking Corporation in 1999 in order to cater to the low-income market (loan amounts below K5,000). It applied an adjusted version of the Grameen Bank approach (group-lending principle, targeting women),[80] and—because of the financial institution license of Papua New Guinea Banking Corporation—it was able to collect savings from the public. Like Liklik Dinau Arbitore Trust it was credit focused, loans were not collateralized, and peer pressure was not enforced. Services were provided through various branch offices; thus, it had a more institutional like character. Performance was promising in terms of outreach, but it had a high portfolio at risk and continued to be dependent on funding from Papua New Guinea Banking Corporation. It was subsequently liquidated by Bank of South Pacific in mid-2002 during the process of the takeover of Papua New Guinea Banking Corporation.

It is possible that, if the role of the field assistant (mostly operating out of the branch office) was decentralized and the overall approach was modified to suit the geopolitical cultural context of the place and associated way of life, such a scheme might have survived. As Felix Bablis suggests based on his 1999 research on the Liklik Dinau Arbitore Trust, there is a need to further decentralize the role of the field assistant to "center chief."[81] This would have the advantage of minimizing any perceived, or actual, paternalism. It is important that people feel they "own" the process, not that it is something imposed on them. In practice, this means that the responsibility of center chiefs must be increased. They could take on the routine tasks that field assistants normally perform, like collecting loan repayments and checking on the use of loans. There might be additional training costs and (minimal) compensation for their role, but it might be worth the gains in project sustainability and outreach. For isolated hamlets or coral islands, a center chief could be the difference that makes a project successful.

Bablis' study further observed that most microfinance institutions established with good intentions by government turn out to be unsuccessful. A United Nations study of microfinance institutions in Papua New Guinea in 1999 highlighted problems such as loans given to wives of public servants, a lack of loan supervision, application of nonmarket interest rates, and individual loans given for inadequately specified or unspecified purposes.[82] Institutions with a structure more representative of the community or a cooperative style organization with a quasi-NGO structure might have worked better.

Recent Developments

With the inauguration of the Papua New Guinea Asian Development Bank Microfinance and Employment Project in 2002, the microfinance industry has received greater attention. The project's aim is to provide support to the microfinance industry with capacity-building services, such as technical assistance and training, product development and linkages, as well as the establishment of a Greenfield laboratory microbank. Since commencement of the project, a few new promising players have entered the microfinance field. As a component of the project, Wau Microbank was established in Wau, Morobe Province, in 2004. It was the first microbank of its kind in Papua New Guinea with a financial institution's license issued by the Bank of Papua New Guinea. It has operational self-sufficiency. There is no more current data to show how the Bank of Papua New Guinea has performed since in supporting such enterprises. It applies a similar approach to savings and loan societies in terms of savings-backed lending, which seems to work well and is clearly savings focused. Loan portfolio growth compared to savings growth is small. The Bank of Papua New Guinea has in the meantime opened a branch in Lae and initiated various linkage programs with microfinance providers in other provinces, such as Bogia Cooperative Society, East Sepik Council of Women, and Kainantu Credit Scheme.

Ok Tedi Microfinance in Western Province was formerly a branch of Village Finance Ltd. It was taken over by PNG Microfinance Limited in 2005 with shareholders, such as the Papua New Guinea Sustainable Development Fund, Bank of South Pacific, International Finance Corporation, and others. PNG Microfinance Limited operates with a financial institution license issued by the Bank of Papua New Guinea with the intention to operate a nationwide microfinance institution. Because of its shareholders it has a clear sustainability/commercial focus. Maintaining modified Grameen Bank principles, it offers varied yet simple savings accounts and both group and individual lending products. PNG Microfinance Limited has had impressive outreach since inception with the newly established Koki Branch (Port Moresby), for example, registering more than twenty thousand clients in the first six months. While the savings products are in high demand, it seems to have problems with the growth of the loan portfolio. Owing to the work and advocacy of the Papua New Guinea Asian Development Bank Microfinance and Employment Project, the microfinance arena in Papua New Guinea has received some new momentum.

Conclusion

While the microfinance model has been successful in some parts of the world, it has had problems in others. The magnitude of the figures in successful instances has led to a rush to replicate successful programs in almost all countries where poverty is pervasive. However, such haste does not always allow for in-depth consideration, and care should be taken to ensure that the provision of microfinance is truly demand driven rather than simply a means to satisfy donors' agendas. The Grameen model has shown mixed results, in particular, in relation to financial sustainability. For example, in Papua New Guinea the Liklik Dinau Arbitore Trust in Goroka, a direct Grameen Bank replication, has failed miserably and was subsequently closed down.

In the unique context of Papua New Guinea, the demanding physical settings and the absence of a thriving small enterprise culture have provided a challenging environment for microfinance, resulting in a need to reconsider conventional microfinance approaches. Ultimately, being a business concept, microfinance was created out of the notion that credit is needed to be able to earn additional money through income-generating activities and that it needs an enabling environment as a precondition. This worked well in countries such as Bangladesh, where borrowers used the loan money to start small enterprises in order to support their families because agriculture did not provide a sufficient staple food supply. In addition, infrastructure was well established in terms of roads and communication, there was a high population density, and Bangladeshis had long been using money as a means of exchange and a store of value.

The situation is different in Papua New Guinea. First, conventional microfinance approaches, such as Grameen Bank, are credit focused and base their lending activities on productive, income-generating activities of their clients. However, with the absence of a flourishing microenterprise sector in Papua New Guinea, these loans are mainly used for consumption purposes such as food supplements, school fees, household items, medical expenses, and clothes.[83] Thus there is no generated "profit" through which interest and installments can be paid. Second, low-income people typically cannot provide any collateral. In Papua New Guinea, even though there are strong kinship and *wantok* systems, the Grameen approach to group lending and social pressure in order to secure repayment did not produce good results in lending and consequently cannot be relied upon. Some microfinance institutions, such as Bougainville Haus Moni, seem to have used the *wantok* or family system successfully in order to group clients. The grouping appears to work well for the collection of savings, but, nevertheless, grass-roots microfinance institution managers all seem to have problems with loan repayments. Ironically, the *wantok* system is often cited in the literature as the reason for high default rates and lack of credit culture.

Over the years different methodologies, such as the savings-first approach or the savings-backed lending approach, were successfully tested by various microfinance institutions in Papua New Guinea. This approach appears to be more suitable in the PNG context, and it also provides a lower risk to the institutions than other methodologies. However there is a further consideration. There is no legal framework explicitly necessary for microfinance to work. Bangladesh, for example, does not have microfinance regulations, and its programs work extremely well, but the situation becomes more complicated when savings are collected from the public. Licensing then becomes necessary to safeguard the depositors. In Papua New Guinea this is of particular importance because of the fast money schemes that have been circulating since 1998. These have promised huge returns to investors and have left many Papua New Guineans deprived of millions of kina, consequently resulting in a deep mistrust of any institution dealing with money. The latest emerging microfinance models in Papua New Guinea (microbanks) are, therefore, licensed institutions that provide saving and—according to lessons learned—savings-backed lending services. These institutions will still face difficulties to run successfully or self-sufficiently in the long run because of the dispersal of people in rural and remote areas as well as limited physical infrastructure. In addition, financial institutions do not have a low cost to set up owing to the requirements from the Bank of Papua New Guinea (computer, strong vault, and so on).

More consideration should be given to unique local contexts. Even though cash has slowly been introduced in rural areas through small-scale commercial agriculture or smallholder production with sometimes seasonal income, in some parts of Papua New Guinea money circulation is still relatively limited, and cash income per person through cash-crop production is considered low.[84] Given limited access to financial services and the lack of markets for buying and selling produce, it can reasonably be assumed that this situation will continue in rural areas. Since microfinance relies on monetized economies and understanding of market principles, conventional finance approaches have to be adjusted if they are to operate successfully in such a diverse cultural and physical environment. Financial services are only beneficial if customers know how to use and understand money (interest, loan, fixed repayment terms), understand business concepts (profit/loss), and have income-earning opportunities to deposit money. If people do not have skills to start and manage their entrepreneurial activities or have no access to markets to sell their produce, money is mostly going to be wasted.

So what does this leave us with in Papua New Guinea? Donald Denoon describes a visit by Ernest Fisk to Goroka in the Highlands in 1971.[85] His colleague, Sir John Crawford, then Australia's leading economic policy maker and just appointed as director of the Australian National University's new Research School of Pacific Studies, had encouraged the visit. There Fisk discovered a paradox: "These people seemed to have more leisure, more adequate food supplies, and generally to be considerably better off than quite a lot of villages in South and

East Asia—whose average incomes were being recorded as being very much higher."[86] Customary production and exchange, embedded in a lifeworld that was often referred to as "primitive affluence," thus defied conventional economics. The chord struck by Fisk had a very different tone from the conventional cadence of Australian-PNG colonial history. Most Australian policy makers had a strange confidence in the classical march to "development." This attitude continues in the work of neoliberals, even left-wing ones such as Jeffrey Sachs. He uses the conventional metaphor of the ladder of development—"their climb is evident in rising personal incomes and the acquisition of goods such as cell phones, television sets and scooters."[87] The evidence in Papua New Guinea defies this "wisdom." During the period from mid-2007 to 2010, the roll-out of the Digicel and Telikom mobile network brought cell phones to an increasing number of Papua New Guineans, and it was accompanied by all the virtues of SMS banking, but in all the communities in which we worked there was no evidence of an improving standard of living. To the contrary, as *The Song of the Tribal Economist* presents, gaining a foothold on the ladder of marketization may not be the answer:

> The primitive farmer says…cash
> Is unsatisfactory trash:
> It won't keep off the rain
> And it gives me pain
>
> …
>
> Cash cropping is all well
> If you've got something to sell:
> But tell me, sir, why
> If there is nothing to buy
> Should I bother? You can all go to hell. [88]

A holistic approach, such as a cooperative scheme that uses different development tools carefully moderated in relation to each other, might be more appropriate. Cooperatives are licensed under the Department of Trade and Industry, and according to the Cooperative Societies Act 1986 they are entitled to provide agricultural wholesale services and financial services to their members.[89] Since a multipurpose cooperative can provide agricultural wholesale, marketing, social, and financial services, and with those it could respond to geographic, social, and economic issues, it might be a potential platform for sustainable microfinance service delivery in Papua New Guinea. For example, the Bogia Co-operative Society in Madang Province collects and buys as well as markets agricultural produce, mostly cocoa and copra, from and for its members and offers deposit and loan services. This closes the financial circle. In addition it is a member-owned institution, a community-based form of intervention, which will increase local ownership and responsibility and can, therefore, be designed according to customary values and relations, taking into consideration local social networks, understandings, and uses of money and exchange. This aspect is particularly important since financial literacy in rural areas is still relatively low.

While many talk of Papua New Guineans taking development into their own hands this may be a platitude, bedeviling all those who persist in talking about independence—as if it follows that something spontaneously arises to replace imported ideas. In relation to community finance, while the discourse has been to adapt microcredit to the Melanesian Way, the manifold pathways to social development have tended only to be signposted in one direction. And, like contemporary capitalism itself, the signposts give no destination other than the acquisition of more money and goods. We are attracted because the road is paved with the basest of aspirations. Some positive lessons have been learned from attempts to replicate experiences from other places. But, given the continuing emphasis in Papua New Guinea on big development, there are still major pitfalls. In this context, the question that now needs to be asked is whether an extensive and comprehensive reassessment of community needs is possible beyond rhetorical referencing. Cooperative schemes with much more grounded commitment—including collectivist movements like Gildipasi and Pariet Amman (Chapters 5 and 6)—we argue, may provide the projected communities of practice that could take alternative methods of financing forward in conjunction with processes of learning and innovation. And this might counter the current tendency for the prescribed application of a unitary and linear set of global "best practices."

Notes

1. This is discussed in A. Counts, *Give Us Credit*, Research Press, New Delhi, 1996; Joe Remenyi and Benjamin Quinones Jr., eds., *Microfinance and Poverty Alleviation: Case Studies from Asia and the Pacific*, Pinter, London, 2000; Renée Chao Beroff, *The Constraints and Challenges Associated with Developing Sustainable Microfinance Systems in Disadvantaged Rural Areas in Africa*, United Nations Capital Development Fund, New York, 1999; and Manfred Zeller and Richard Meyer, *The Triangle of Microfinance: Financial Sustainability, Outreach, and Impact*, Johns Hopkins University Press, Baltimore, 2003.

2. Joan Ledgerwood, *Microfinance Handbook: An Institutional and Financial Perspective*, World Bank, Washington, 1999.

3. Robyn Cornford, *Microcredit, Microfinance or Simply Access to Financial Services: What do Pacific People Need?* The Foundation for Development Co-operation, Brisbane, 2000.

4. David Kavanamur, *Re-positioning Non-bank Credit Service Strategy in Papua New Guinea*, Asia Pacific Press, Canberra, 2003.

5. Dale Adams, Douglas H. Graham, and J. D. von Pischke, *Undermining Rural Development with Cheap Credit*, Westview Press, Boulder, CO, 1984.

6. Susan Johnson and Ben Rogaly, *Microfinance and Poverty Reduction*, Oxfam, Oxford, 1997.

7. Joan Ledgerwood, *Microfinance Handbook: An Institutional and Financial Perspective*, World Bank, Washington, DC, 1999, p. 2.

8. One of the first articles to discuss this was Elisabeth Rhyne, "The Yin and Yang of Microfinance: Reaching the Poor and Sustainability," *MicroBanking Bulletin*, no. 2, 1998, pp. 6–8.

9. Helen Todd, *Cloning Grameen Bank: Replicating a Poverty Reduction Model in India, Nepal and Vietnam*, IT Publications, London, 1996; Abu Wahid, ed., *The Grameen Bank, Poverty Relief in Bangladesh*, Westview Press, Boulder, 1993; David Bornstein, *The Price of a Dream*, Simon and Schuster, New York, 1996.

10. Pankaj Jain and Mick Moore, "What Makes Microcredit Programmes Effective? Fashionable Fallacies and Workable Realities," IDS Working Paper 177, January 2003; Pankaj Jain, "Managing Credit for the Rural Poor: Lessons from the Grameen Bank," *World Development*, vol. 24, no.1, 1996, pp. 79–89.

11. See also discussions in Zeller and Meyer, *The Triangle of Microfinance*; Caimbatore K. Prahalad, *The Fortune at the Bottom of the Pyramid: Eradicating Poverty through Profits*, Wharton School Publishing, Upper Saddle River, New Jersey, 2004; and Stuart Rutherford, *The Poor and Their Money: An Essay about Financial Services for Poor People*, Oxford University Press, New Delhi, 2000.

12. I. P. Getubig, Joe Remenyi, and Benjamin Quinones Jr., *Creating the Vision: Microfinancing the Poor in Asia-Pacific*, report for the Asian and Pacific Development Centre, Kuala Lumpur, 1997.

13. Thomas Fisher and M. S. Sriram, *Beyond Micro-Credit: Putting Development Back into Micro-Finance*, Vistaar Publications, New Delhi, 2002.

14. Morgan Brigg, "Disciplining the Developmental Subject: Neoliberal Power and Governance through Microcredit," in Jude L. Fernando, *Microfinance: Perils and Prospects*, Routledge, London, and New York, 2006.

15. Jacob Yaron, Benjamin McDonald, and Piprek Gerda, "Rural Finance: Issues, Design and Best Practices," World Bank, Washington, DC, 1997.

16. Getubig, Remenyi, and Quinones, *Creating the Vision*, p. 112.

17. Ledgerwood, *Microfinance Handbook*, p. 97.

18. Johnson and Rogaly, *Microfinance and Poverty Reduction*, pp. 16–17.

19. See Ledgerwood, *Microfinance Handbook;* Elisabeth Rhyne and Mario Otero, "Financial Services for Microenterprises: Principles and Institutions," in Mario Otero and Elisabeth Rhyne, eds., *The New World of Microenterprise Finance: Building Healthy Financial Institutions for the Poor,* Kumarian Press, West Hartford, 1994; and Marguerite S. Robinson, *The Microfinance Revolution: Sustainable Finance for the Poor,* vol. 1, The World Bank, Washington, DC, 2001.

20. Also known under the term "credit union" or "credit cooperative."

21. Sharon L. Holt, "The Village Bank Methodology: Performance and Prospects," in Otero and Rhyne, *The New World of Microenterprise Finance.*

22. Ibid.

23. Ledgerwood, *Microfinance Handbook;* Candace Nelson, Barbara McNelly, Kathleen Stack, and Lawrence Yanovitch, *Village Banking: The State of Practice,* SEEP Network, Pact, New York, 1995.

24. John H. Magill, "Credit Unions: A Formal-Sector Alternative for Financing Microenterprise Development," in Otero and Rhyne, *The New World of Microenterprise Finance.*

25. Robert Witzeling, *Credit Union Handbook,* World Council of Credit Unions (WOCCU), Madison, Wisconsin, 1994.

26. See David Hulme and Paul Mosley, *Financing against Poverty,* vol. 2, Routledge, London, 1996, p. 199.

27. Robert Cull, Asli Demirguc-Kunt, and Jonathan Morduch, "Financial Performance and Outreach: A Global Analysis of Leading Microbanks," World Bank Policy Research Working Paper Series 3827, 2006.

28. Gary Woller, Christopher Dunford, and Warner Woodworth, "Where to Microfinance?" *Microcredit and Development Policy,* vol. 1. no. 1, 1999; Rhyne, "The Yin and Yang of Microfinance."

29. Marcus Schreiner, "Aspects of Outreach: A Framework for Discussion of the Social Benefits of Microfinance," *Journal of International Development,* vol. 14, no. 5, 2002, pp. 591–603.

30. Consultative Group to Assist the Poorest, "Key Principles of Microfinance," http://www.cgap.org/portal/site/CGAP/menuitem.64c03ec40a6d29506780801059101oa0/, accessed 1 August 2007. See also discussions in Stephanie Charitonenko, Anita Campion, and Nimal Fernando, *Commercialization of Microfinance: Perspectives from South and Southeast Asia,* Asian Development Bank, Manila, 2004; and Zeller and Meyer, *The Triangle of Microfinance.*

31. Zeller and Meyer, *The Triangle of Microfinance;* Woller, Dunford, and Woodworth, "Where to Microfinance?"; Beatriz Armendariz de Aghion and Jonathan Morduch, *The Economics of Microfinance,* Massachusetts Institute of Technology Press, Cambridge, MA, 2005.

32. Charitonenko, Campion, and Fernando, *Commercialization of Microfinance;*

Birgit Helms, *Access for All: Building Inclusive Financial Systems,* World Bank, Washington, DC, 2006.

33. Rhyne, "The Ying and Yang of Microfinance," p. 2; Charitonenko, Campion, and Fernando, *Commercialization of Microfinance,* p. 37; Woller, Dunford, and Woodworth, "Where to Microfinance?"; Stephanie Charitonenko and S. M. Rahman, *Commercialization of Microfinance,* Asian Development Bank, Manila, 2002.

34. See also discussions in David Snodgrass, "Assessing the Effects of Program Characteristics and Program Context on the Impact of Microenterprise Services: A Guide for Practitioners," AIMS Brief no. 17, 1997, http://www.microlinks.org/ev_en .php?ID=7959_201&ID2=DO_TOPIC, accessed 12 July 2007; Woller, Dunford, and Woodworth, "Where to Microfinance"; Ledgerwood, *Microfinance Handbook;* Jacob Yaron, "Assessing Development Finance Institutions: A Public Interest Analysis," World Bank Discussion Paper 174, The World Bank, Washington, DC, 1992.

35. Today the industry has developed various other measures of outreach described by scholars in Schreiner, "Aspects of Outreach"; Claudio Gonzales-Vega, "Microfinance: Broader Achievements and New Challenges," Occasional Paper No. 2518, Rural Finance Program, Ohio State University, Columbus, OH, 1998; Charitonenko, Campion, and Fernando, *Commercialization of Microfinance.* For our discussion we will focus on the two main, universally accepted, ones.

36. Charitonenko and Rahman, *Commercialization of Microfinance,* p. 617

37. David Hulme, "Is Microdebt Good for Poor People? A Note on the Dark Side of Microfinance," *Small Enterprise Development,* vol. 11, no. 1, 2000, p. 27.

38. Diana Mitlin, "Sustaining Markets or Sustaining Poverty Reduction?" *Environment and Urbanization,* vol. 14, no. 1, 2002, p. 176.

39. Johnson and Rogaly, *Microfinance and Poverty Reduction.*

40. Hulme and Mosley, *Financing against Poverty.*

41. Fisher and Sriram, *Beyond Micro-Credit,* p. 49.

42. Hulme, "Is Microdebt Good for Poor People?" pp. 26–27.

43. Khandakar Q. Elahi and Constantine P. Dadopoulos, "Microfinance and Third World Development: A Critical Analysis," *Journal of Political and Military Sociology,* vol. 32, no.1, 2004, pp. 61–77.

44. Mitlin, "Sustaining Markets or Sustaining Poverty Reduction?" p. 176.

45. Jude L. Fernando, "Microcredit and Empowerment of Women: Blurring the Boundary between Development and Capitalism," in Fernando, *Microfinance.*

46. Stuart Rutherford, *ASA: The Biography of an NGO, Empowerment and Credit in Rural Bangladesh,* Dhaka, Association for Social Advancement, 1995.

47. Kathryn N. Gow, "Banking on Women: Achieving Healthy Economies through Microfinance," *WE International,* vol. 48/49, 2000.

48. See discussion in Johnson and Rogaly, *Microfinance and Poverty Reduction,* pp. 13–14.

49. Anne Marie Goetz and Rina Sen Gupta, "Who Takes the Credit? Gender, Pow-

er and Control Over Loan Use in Rural Credit Programmes in Bangladesh," *World Development*, vol. 24, no. 4, 1996, pp. 45–63.

50. Johnson and Rogaly, *Microfinance and Poverty Reduction*.

51. Felix G. Bablis, "The Lessons and Potential for Sustainability and Outreach of Microfinance Institutions in Papua New Guinea and Other Pacific Island Countries," *Development Bulletin*, vol. 50, no. 4, 1999.

52. Information from http://www.australian-web.org/papua-neuguinea/index .php, accessed 5 July 2007.

53. John Gibson, "The Economic and Nutritional Importance of Household Food Production in PNG," in R. M. Bourke, M. G. Allen, and J. G. Salisbury, eds., *Food Security for Papua New Guinea: Proceedings of the Papua New Guinea Food and Nutrition 2000 Conference*, Papua New Guinea University of Technology, Lae, ACIAR Proceedings, no. 99, Australian Centre for International Agricultural Research, Canberra, 2001.

54. Bablis, "The Lessons and Potential for Sustainability and Outreach."

55. Paul McGuire, "South Asian Economic Models for the Pacific? The Case of Microfinance—A Comment," *Pacific Economic Bulletin*, vol. 15, no. 10, 2000; Chris A. Gregory, "South Asian Economic Models for the Pacific? The Case of Microfinance," *Pacific Economic Bulletin*, vol. 14, no. 2, 1999.

56. David Kavanamur, "Strategic Alliance Issues in Microfinance Management," *Development Bulletin*, vol. 60, no. 12, 2002.

57. Lorraine D. Sexton, *Mothers of Money, Daughters of Coffee: The Wok Meri Movement*, UMI Research Press, Michigan, 1986. *Sande* is the Pidgin word for Sunday, because the gatherings often happened on a Sunday after church. *Wok meri* is the Pidgin term for working woman; these are women-associated ROSCAS.

58. See David Kavanamur and Robert Turare, "Sustainable Credit Schemes for Rural Development in Papua New Guinea," *Development Bulletin*, vol. 50, no. 3, 1999.

59. McGuire, "South Asian Economic Models for the Pacific?"

60. Kavanamur and Turare, "Sustainable Credit Schemes for Rural Development"; David Kavanamur, "Australian Agency for International Development: Report on Rural Credit Study, Background Study to the Medium Term Development Strategy 2003–2007," INA Discussion Paper, no. 87, 2002, David Kavanamur, "Re-positioning Non-bank Service Strategy in Papua New Guinea."

61. E. Kopel, *An Interim Evaluation Report on a Provincial Government Microcredit Scheme in Papua New Guinea*, report prepared for the Western Highlands Provincial Government, University of Papua New Guinea, Waigani, 2002.

62. Jan C. Ennenbach *PNG Microfinance and Employment Project*, report for Asian Development Bank, Manila, Microbanking Competence Centre Bankakademie International, Frankfurt, 2000.

63. Personal conversation with the manager of the North Simbu Rural Development Project, May 2002.

64. Ratified through the Small Business Development Corporation Act, 1990.

65. Kavanamur, "Australian Agency for International Development," p. 16; Kavanamur, "Re-positioning Non-bank Service Strategy in Papua New Guinea," p. 13.

66. Kavanamur, "Australian Agency for International Development"; Kavanamur, "Re-positioning Non-bank Service Strategy in Papua New Guinea."

67. Kavanamur and Turare, "Sustainable Credit Schemes for Rural Development."

68. Kavanamur, "Re-positioning Non-bank Service Strategy in Papua New Guinea"; Chinna Kannapiran. "Institutional Rural Finance in PNG: The Lessons from Failures and the Need for Reforms," NRI Discussion Paper, no. 86, 1995.

69. Kannapiran, "Institutional Rural Finance in PNG."

70. Bank of Papua New Guinea website: http://www.bankpng.gov.pg/index.php?option=com_content&task=blogcategory&id=2&Itemid=101, accessed 9 March 2009; Helen Kopunye, Aua Purumo, and John Newsom, "Microfinance and Financial Intermediation in Rural Papua New Guinea: An Integrated Scheme," *Development Bulletin,* vol. 50, no. 3, 1999.

71. Kavanamur, "Re-positioning Non-bank Service Strategy in Papua New Guinea."

72. Nimal Fernando, "Improving Rural Institutional Finance: Some Lessons," *Papua New Guinea Journal of Agriculture, Forestry and Fisheries,* vol. 37, no. 1, 1994; Kavanamur, "Australian Agency for International Development"; Robin Cornford, *Microcredit, Microfinance or Access to Financial Services: What Do Pacific People Need?* Foundation for Development Cooperation, Brisbane, 2001; Mike Getubig, Joe Remenyi, and David Gibbons, *Financing a Revolution: An Overview of the Microfinance Challenge in Asia–Pacific,* Pinter, London, 2000; Kavanamur and Turare, "Sustainable Credit Schemes for Rural Development"; Kopunye, Purumo, and Newsom, "Microfinance and Financial Intermediation in Rural Papua New Guinea"; Remenyi and Quinones, *Microfinance and Poverty Alleviation.*

73. Kopunye, Purumo, and Newsom, "Microfinance and Financial Intermediation in Rural Papua New Guinea.

74. Kavanamur, "Australian Agency for International Development"; John Newsom "Bougainville Microfinance: Rebuilding Rural Communities after the Crisis," *Development Bulletin,* vol. 57, no. 2, 2002.

75. Kopunye, Purumo, Kisim, and Newsom, "Microfinance and Financial Intermediation in Rural Papua New Guinea."

76. Ennenbach, *PNG Microfinance and Employment Project,* p. 8.

77. Rebecca Fleischer, "Replicating Grameen Bank in Papua New Guinea," *Pacific Economic Bulletin,* vol. 11, no. 2, 1996.

78. Ennenbach, *PNG Microfinance and Employment Project.*

79. Fleischer, "Replicating Grameen Bank in Papua New Guinea."

80. Individual lending was introduced later on. See Ennenbach, *PNG Microfinance and Employment Project.*

81. Bablis, "The Lessons and Potential for Sustainability and Outreach," p. 20.

82. LDAT (Liklik Dinau Abitore Trust), *Project Document—(PNG/93/001/C/01/11)—Microcredit and Savings 1993*, Government of Papua New Guinea, Port Moresby, 1993.

83. See also the discussion in Kieran Donaghue, "Microfinance in the Asia Pacific," *Asian-Pacific Economic Literature*, vol. 18, no. 1, 2004, pp. 41–61.

84. Lucas W. Hanson, B. J. Allen, R. M. Bourke, and T. J. McCarthy, *Papua New Guinea Rural Development Handbook*, Australian National University, Canberra, 2001.

85. Donald Denoon, *A Trial Separation: Australia and the Decolonisation of Papua New Guinea*, Australian National University, Pandanus Books, 2005.

86. Ernest Fisk, *Hardly Ever a Dull Moment*, History of Development Studies Monograph 5, National Centre for Development Studies, Australian National University, 1995, pp. 230–231, as cited in Denoon, *Trial Separation*, p. 12.

87. Jeffrey Sachs, *The End of Poverty: How We Can Make It Happen in Our Lifetime*, Penguin, London, 2005, p. 19.

88. Fisk, *Hardly Ever a Dull Moment*, p. 236. Refer also to his "Planning in a Primitive Economy: Special Problems of Papua New Guinea," *The Economic Record*, vol. 38, no. 40, December 1962.

89. Government of Papua New Guinea, *Cooperative Societies, Rules and Regulations* (Chapter 389), Government of Papua New Guinea, Port Moresby, 1986.

Chapter 9

Health and Community Equity

PAPUA NEW GUINEA's national development strategy currently prioritizes economic growth led by the private sector. It works on the presumption that improved economic outcomes will equate to greater spending on health and will automatically improve health outcomes. However, this has not happened. In fact, the opposite is the case. Overall, the health services and health status of Papua New Guinea have been in a general decline since independence, and the health and life expectancy of people in Papua New Guinea are rated as the poorest in the Pacific. This is mainly due to an unequal distribution of resources with the country's most disadvantaged groups relatively excluded from quality health care. Drawing on both comparative and national research, we argue that what is needed instead is a more deliberate national commitment to health, with a focus on developing strategies for improving equitable access. In particular health equity and community-based insurance are highlighted as promising initiatives in the context of learning and development centers based in and run by communities themselves. The effectiveness of any health initiative linked to learning and development centers would rely on effective engagement with local communities, particularly as the means for identifying key barriers to health care and tailoring specific programs that would work toward removing these barriers. At the same time, the engagement requires government and local non-government and international support as well as a mechanism for financing it. In other words, an emphasis on community engagement requires more than just a "Third Way" return to the village envisaged as a completely self-reliant community. It requires layers of relationships and processes, including some state support.

The improvement of health outcomes, while an important goal in itself, also carries secondary benefits. Health and economic development are inextricably linked not just in Papua New Guinea but in the Global South generally.[1] Improved health status increases well-being and welfare, strengthens educational capacities, and improves the productivity of work. Across the globe in recent decades, however, the provision of health services to all sections of the population as a human right has receded in favor of the much more extensive private purchase of health services. In most of the Global South today, the major proportion of health care costs is paid out of pocket by the users of health services. This development is a product of the years of structural adjustment and economic reform that have been common since the 1980s.

Either through unavoidable austerity or as a consequence of a political commitment to market-based development, the relative level of government funding for health services has declined markedly in poorer countries across the past couple of decades. At the same time, in nearly every case the user-pays system in health care delivery has worked to exclude the poor from access to health services. Against this trend, a commitment to find and implement different methods of what is known as social health protection for the poor has emerged through various subsidized and prepayment schemes, along with longer-term moves toward systems of universal national health insurance coverage.[2] In this chapter we will first look at the national context of health policy and development in Papua New Guinea and then consider examples from other countries in the region from which lessons can be drawn. Finally, we will discuss possible paths for health financing and development in the PNG context.

Papua New Guinea's Health Situation

In the years since 1975, postcolonial Papua New Guinea has made unsteady progress toward sustained conventional economic development. The country still faces the dual challenges of providing adequate public health services and developing the mechanisms that will underwrite service provision and provide adequate protection for the poor. Despite some progress, Papua New Guinea remains in a state of slow socioeconomic crisis, and the weaknesses in the economic and political context have had a major unfavorable impact on health and the delivery of health services. The poor provision of social services constitutes part of a complex range of factors causing widespread poverty. Other factors, such as deteriorating infrastructure including roads and health centers, also affect service provision and in many cases have resulted in the cessation of health care delivery, particularly in rural areas.[3]

Provision of Health Services

In Papua New Guinea, health services are delivered by government and church providers (both financed primarily from public sector funds), by enterprise-based services such as the mines, by a small, modern private sector, and by customary healers. Within the public sector, the Department of Health manages the provincial hospitals, while provincial and local governments are responsible for all other services such as rural hospitals, health centers, subcenters, and aid posts, known collectively as "rural health services." Of the overall health budget, about 30 percent goes to urban services and 33 percent to rural services.

The fifth National Health Plan outlines policy directions and priorities for the period 2001–2010. The plan aims to "improve the health of all Papua New Guineans through the development of a health system that is responsive, effective, affordable, and accessible to the majority of our people."[4] Because resources are limited, the plan focuses on priority areas including increasing services to the rural majority, expanding health promotion and preventive services, restructuring the health system, capacity building, and improved infrastructure investment. Within this context, the government and the donor community are moving toward a sectorwide approach to health reform in which donor funding (including aid from AusAID and the Asian Development Bank) will be pooled and used in support of the national plan.

While the government is the largest provider of health care, the Church Health Service operates approximately half of the rural health centers and subcenters, demonstrative of the considerable integration between church and state in terms of undertaking health care. Under the Church Partnership Program, churches also run six of the nine training schools for nurses and fourteen training schools for community health workers. Most of the financing for church-run facilities originates from the state, while the church-based organizations manage the health facilities.[5] The national health system is based on the primary health care approach with a network of urban and rural facilities. The system includes 2,400 aid posts, 500 health centers, 19 provincial hospitals, a national hospital, and 45 urban clinics.

While these figures might create the impression of an expansive health network, the quality of provision is often marred by dysfunction and a lack of resources. Hundreds of rural health facilities have remained closed or are not fully functioning—including the research sites discussed in this book as in Wisini village. Many district health centers are either shut down or delivering extremely limited services. District-level health facilities face extensive problems related to low capacities of health staff, limited training, lack of supervision and support, inadequate equipment and supplies, and insufficient financial resources.[6] Because most of the available health services have been situated in urban areas, rural communities have typically had poor access to basic health services.[7] While health aid posts have commonly offered the only sources of medicine and basic health care, the number of posts dramatically declined throughout the 1990s.[8]

Health facilities lacking resources have often been unable to deliver basic minimum standards of services such as immunizations or obstetric care.

Access to Services

The poor level of infrastructure both causes and perpetuates low levels of access.[9] The proportion of the population living within five kilometers of a health facility declined from 85 percent in 1995 to 80 percent by 2000. The number of doctors and community health workers declined at the same time, and an increase in the number of nurses failed to keep pace with population growth. The decline in service delivery most affected people in the poorest income quintiles, and there are wide disparities in the delivery of services between poorer and wealthier households. The poor have also been those most affected by closure of health facilities, although there have been some recent improvements. There are also wide variations in access across provinces, with the most difficult conditions in the Highlands and Momase regions, a reflection partly of the proportion of the population living in urban settings and partly of differences in socioeconomic status among rural populations.

Despite good intentions, the decentralization process has contributed to the deterioration of health services, particularly in rural areas. In 1975, at the time of independence, health services were centrally administered by the Department of Public Health in Port Moresby through regional and provincial health offices. District officers had day-to-day control over public servants but typically did not exercise line authority. Through the first decentralization in 1977, many health functions were transferred to the provinces and/or otherwise delegated to lower bodies with some functions remaining at the national level. Provinces mostly adopted a standard administrative structure for provincial health services. Changes introduced in 1995 through the Organic Law on Provincial Government and Local-Level Government transferred responsibility for rural health services to local governments, thus limiting the role of the national Department of Health essentially to policy development, standard setting, and monitoring. As a result, the Department of Health lost control over the delivery of health services at subnational levels, while capacities in districts were extremely limited. The regions lacked technical knowledge, staff (who may have been officially transferred from the provinces but actually remained in their positions for the lack of physical facilities at the district level), and financial resources because funds were not transferred from provinces to districts.[10]

With regard to issues of state and governance, a number of factors influence the Department of Health and the health sector more broadly in their ability to deliver health services. These include the broader economic domain, which affects both the financial allocations to the sector as well as people's capacity to

The health center in Boera village is run by local women through the church.

access the health system. An unstable political domain, hotly contested elections and communal tensions, law-and-order concerns, and, until recently, frequent changes in ministerial leadership have all constrained policy development. In particular this combination of factors has often deterred people from using the health system, has prevented health personnel from taking on assignments in difficult areas, and, with deteriorating infrastructure, has frequently resulted in the closure of health services, particularly in rural areas. Health service users in general therefore face a number of barriers to accessing health services. On the supply side, health services often have uneven clinical skills, a lack of medical staff (especially in rural and remote areas), poor quality of care, poorly maintained facilities, inadequate availability of drugs, as well as weak referral and regulatory mechanisms. The associated difficulties for those seeking care are made even worse by the collapse and closure of many rural health facilities.

Barriers on the demand side include sociocultural factors such as linguistic difference and communal rivalries, reluctance to travel far from the home, lack of understanding of the benefits of the public health system, and a common preference for customary healers. There are also physical barriers such as distance to nearest public health facility; rugged terrain and the inability to provide adequate communications; poor, deteriorating roads and lack of transport; as well as inconsistent and sometimes nonexistent services at facilities. Poor service delivery often causes a lack of public confidence in health services. People may not access services in the cases where they know those services to be poor, and, even when there have been substantial improvements or a reduction in costs, there is not always a way of knowing about such changes. Inadequate communication between service provider and the public can contribute to patients' uncertainty about the real and hidden costs of the health services they are seeking to access, as does the lack of a clear system of phased or deferred payments or exemptions to protect the poor.

As has been mentioned here, frequently the most affected are those in rural areas where people commonly need to travel great distances to access health services, while their ability to do so is constrained by the associated transport costs. Aid posts, which are the only source of medicine and basic health care for many remote communities, have declined by half over the last ten years, and, for those that remain open, the quality of service delivery has also been deteriorating.[11] Despite some improvements in the 1990s, the services offered to poorer households have been of lower quality than those available to more prosperous households in terms of qualifications of staff, equipment available at health facilities, availability of medical supplies, and the extent of clinical supervision. For example, the Misima Island Hospital in Milne Bay Province is only half used, falling into disrepair, and is without any doctors.[12] In addition, health workers often leave for extended periods to obtain supplies, receive training, or go on holiday leave.

The lack of access has had significant impact across a range of health areas. For instance, disease control has been far from adequate, particularly among the poor, leading to constant problems with the spread of preventable diseases. In terms of family planning, there are large disparities between income groups with use of contraception lowest among the poorest two quintiles. In terms of maternal health, poor women have more complications during pregnancy and are less likely to receive antenatal care or a supervised delivery. Distance from health care appears to have a strong influence on the rate of supervised delivery but is not the only barrier to the uptake of services since many poor women living within five kilometers of a facility do not use it to deliver. Some progress has been recorded in reaching poorer households with immunization services (as judged by BCG coverage and first-dose triple antigen), but fewer children in poorer households complete the immunization schedule, and rates for completion of triple antigen immunization fell by approximately 10 percent in the 1990s. Poorer people have a higher incidence of self-reported illness, particularly fever, but are less likely to seek treatment. Poorer people are more likely to use government health centers, followed by aid posts and then mission health centers for treating children.

There are large differences in childhood mortality rates between income quintiles, mainly owing to differences in postneonatal mortality.[13]

These points together paint an overall bleak picture for many in Papua New Guinea who suffer in terms of access to health care in part because of the broader structural constraints of governance and state formation in postindependence Papua New Guinea. The search for other effective pathways can be illuminated by examples from other lower-income countries in the Asia-Pacific region, such as Cambodia and the Lao PDR, though we must keep in mind that conditions may vary widely between such countries. When we make such comparisons, we do so in order to answer the question of how to develop health services in Papua New Guinea with full regard to basic issues of effectiveness, coverage, equity, and access.

The Global Health Context

Currently more than half of the world's population is excluded from social health protection, and at least 1.3 billion people worldwide lack access to the most basic health care. As a result, millions become sick or die every year from preventable or curable medical conditions. The toll from treatable infections and preventable complications of pregnancy and delivery is more than 10 million deaths every year. It is estimated that each year more than 150 million individuals in 44 million households globally face financial ruin as a direct result of paying for health care. About 25 million households or more than 100 million individuals are pushed into poverty by the need to pay for health services. Yet, in low-income countries, it would take only about US$35 per person per year to finance a social health protection scheme able to provide basic health services, of which only US$15 to US$25 would likely be required from international donors.[14]

In 2002 global expenditure on health care totaled US$3.2 trillion, equivalent to 10 percent of global GDP (or total production). Only US$350 billion of this expenditure was spent in Global South countries. Higher-income countries typically spend about one hundred times more on health per capita than low-income countries (or thirty times more if adjusted for cost of living). However, the major burden of disease is in the Global South, which accounts for 84 percent of the global population, 90 percent of the global burden of disease, and only 12 percent of global health expenditure. Well over half of all health spending in the South is paid out of pocket by private individuals and households.

The global distribution of health care spending closely follows the global distribution of income. This uneven distribution can be pictured as a champagne glass where a narrow stem at the base supports nearly all the consumption at the top. Health spending is greatest where the burden of disease is least and least where the need is greatest. The proportion of total health spending funded through the public health system is 29 percent in low-income countries, 42 percent in lower-middle-income countries, 56 percent in upper-middle-income countries, and 65 percent in high-income countries.[15] By these statistics and on the basis of need, the case for redistributing global health spending toward poorer countries is strong. In general, we can summarize as follows: health gains usually emerge before rather than after economic improvements; the elasticity of demand for health care and the marginal productivity of health expenditures is greater at low income levels; increased equity improves health outcomes; and, therefore, poverty reduction and increased public health spending are essential.

But increasing the effectiveness of health care delivery is dependent on understanding the strict resource constraints that face planners in the South. Long ago, the *World Development Report, 1993*, noted that international donor assistance for health represented only 2.5 percent of all health spending in Global South countries, and the share of health in total aid spending had declined to only 6 percent during the 1980s.[16] The situation has improved only marginally since then. In 2001 the World Health Organization Commission on Macroeconomics and Health offered a new strategy for investing in health for economic development, especially in the world's poorest countries.[17] Such an effort would require both a scaling up of the resources currently spent on the health sector in poor countries and the elimination of financial and other barriers to accessing health services.

A great deal of care is needed, however, in interpreting the relationship between incomes and health status.[18] It is instructive, for example, that improved health status in nineteenth-century Britain was only seen after state intervention despite the preceding period of rapid economic growth.[19] Indeed, there is some evidence to suggest it may be possible for poor countries to make considerable progress in the health sphere through deliberative prioritization of health even in the absence of any significant economic growth. If, in general, economic growth follows health status improvements, then additional attention to improving health care in low-income countries will have a greater positive effect at low income levels. The link between income disparities and health status is well established,[20] and reducing inequity is known to be a powerful impetus to improved health.[21] Generally speaking then, we can say that the return on each additional dollar spent on health care at the lower end of the scale is far greater in terms of improved health outcomes than it is at higher levels of national income. Following this logic, redistributing resources to low income levels (for example, by providing free health care) can be expected to have a larger than proportional impact in terms of improved health.

A crucial question with regard to health in Papua New Guinea is how some low-income countries have achieved good health outcomes despite their economic disadvantage.[22] From the 1960s and 1970s (and still today), significant health improvements were observed in countries such as Cuba, China, Costa Rica, Sri Lanka, and Kerala State in southern India in the absence of major increases in per capita income. While some of these gains were eroded by economic, social, and structural adjustments in the 1990s,[23] the main causes of the earlier improved health status in these countries can be found in a more even income distribution and greater social equity, land reform, adequate physical infrastructure, accessible primary health care services, and improved conditions and status for women.[24]

In *Development as Freedom,* Amartya Sen draws on the conclusions of Sudhir Anand and Martin Ravallion, who demonstrate that a positive correlation between life expectancy and national per capita income occurs mainly through improving the incomes of the poor and increasing public expenditure, particularly on health care.[25] Anand and Ravallion show that these two factors alone account for nearly all the correlation and that the measure of income per capita alone adds little to the explanation. While this is only a single study and it needs to be confirmed by further research, it implies that increasing per capita income helps to raise life expectancy *through* poverty reduction and *through* public health spending. In other words, increased per capita income is unlikely to result in greatly improved health outcomes unless it reflects income improvements for low-income groups.

From User Fees to Social Health Protection

Across the world in recent decades, user fees for government health services have been promoted as a way to supplement revenues and ration the provision of health services in a more efficient way. In practice, user fees, even at a very low level, have acted to exclude the poor from health services. It has often been argued that poor patients can be protected by offering exemptions to user fees. In fact, in cases where exemption systems are unfunded, constitute a drain on health facility revenues, and rely on ad hoc methods for identification of poor patients, such methods have commonly failed to provide access to health services for the poor.[26]

In the past, access to adequate health care was regarded as a human right rather than as a commodity to be traded. In 1946, for instance, the World Health Organization defined health as a state of complete physical, mental, and social well-being and not merely the absence of disease or infirmity. By this understanding good health is both a personal and a social resource that allows individuals and groups to realize aspirations and satisfy needs.[27] As another example, the 1978 international declaration on primary health care identified health as a fundamental human right and a crucial worldwide social goal; it recognized that health status reflects environmental, social, and economic determinants and could be improved only through universal coverage of basic health services at the community level.[28]

However, in recent decades a neoliberal argument has emerged that makes the case that to increase efficiency and equity in health service delivery in the Global South countries it is necessary to impose user fees for government services.[29] The World Bank's *World Development Report* in 1993 underscored this new approach, arguing in favor of the delivery of no more than a cost-effective minimum package of activities through government facilities, leaving most health service delivery to the private sector.[30] The subsequent experience with user fees created widespread difficulties and led to a dramatic fall in use of government services in many cases. One attempt to moderate the approach and to restore the role of government, at least as the main steward of health service delivery, was made through the World Health Organization's 2000 *World Health Report.*[31] Adoption of the United Nations Millennium Development Goals reinforced the idea that basic health services needed to reduce child mortality, improve maternal health, and combat HIV/AIDS, malaria, and other diseases, and that it should be provided as a right through public means.[32]

The 2007 World Bank Strategy for Health Nutrition and Population returns to an emphasis on strengthening health systems, albeit within the context of continued fiscal austerity. The strategy proposes to improve health conditions, particularly of the poor and the vulnerable, through an economic program of "poverty alleviation" supported by government leadership and donor programs. It calls for assembling the right components (financing mechanisms, regulatory framework for private-public collaboration, governance, insurance, logistics, provider payment and incentive mechanisms, information, well-trained personnel, basic infrastructure, and supplies) to ensure equitable access to services. The strategy aims to prevent further impoverishment resulting from illness through a program of economic growth, global competitiveness, and fiscal sustainability as well as good governance, accountability, and transparency in the health sector.[33]

This discussion has led recently to widespread concern for social health protection. Social health protection is a strategy comprising different financing mechanisms (such as tax-based funding, community-based and employer insurance schemes, and social health insurance) designed to reduce financial barriers to health care and pave the way for universal health insurance coverage. Social protection in health tends to prioritize a rights-based, inclusive approach that emphasizes equity, social justice, and social solidarity. The need for social health protection has arisen because of many of the problems outlined so far: the decline in government funding for health care, the universal implementation of user fees for government health services, the dramatic rise in out-of-pocket payments, and the failure in many cases of official and unfunded fee-exemption systems.

A Model for Sustainable Health Financing

The main components of social health protection that allow for a national universal coverage for health care include social health insurance (involving compulsory insurance for civil servants and private sector employees), community-based health insurance (a voluntary, nongovernment, nonprofit, and locally based microinsurance scheme), and health-equity funds (which constitute a social transfer mechanism for the poor funded by donors, governments, or community contributions). Faced with funding and financing difficulties and the exclusion of the poor from health services, Global South countries can take a step forward by introducing the right combination of these measures depending on local circumstances.

Where for reasons of structural adjustment or other constraints governments are unable to mobilize sufficient resources to support health care delivery through the fiscal system, a broader strategy based on the principles of social health protection is needed. In considering such a strategy, a number of areas provide a structure for policy making and for initiatives that meet the needs of both the poor and the broader population. These areas include

Population structure. Mapping the geographic distribution of the population is essential in order to provide data on the proportion and placement of urban, rural, and more remote populations; the mapping should include demographic and ethnic distributions as well as a simple measure of socioeconomic status (e.g., very poor, poor, not so poor, not poor).

Economic and social context. Understanding the national economic situation is crucial, using indicators such as GDP per capita and Gini coefficients to provide information on the character and distribution of poverty; indicators of the social context will reveal the challenges related to urban-rural relations, gender relations, and other issues that need to be addressed.

Nature of poverty. Knowing the proportion of the population living below the poverty line (defined roughly as those who cannot afford any payments for health care or for prepayment) is essential to target needed support schemes; poverty status needs to be disaggregated by social and ethnic characteristics, location, gender, and other relevant criteria to improve the efficiency of targeting measures.

Health status. Knowing the key causes of morbidity and mortality is essential to an understanding of the types of health services and health care programs that are needed and their relative cost to users (or to government).

Health system. A prerequisite for the successful implementation of financing schemes that provide social health protection is accounting for the number and distribution of public health facilities. Mapping the number and distribution of clinics, health centers, and district hospitals is essential to determine where the population must go to access services.

Health expenditures. Planning a social health protection system requires a comprehensive understanding of the composition of national health expenditures, including the proportion of total expenditures provided by the budget, by insurance and other prepayment systems, by private out-of-pocket spending, and by international donors and charitable institutions; shifting the burden away from payment by households at the time of service is the aim of the exercise.

Barriers to access. Knowing the weight and impact of each of the main barriers to access to health services is essential to making a judgment about the allocation of resources between competing ends, such as infrastructure development, drug supply, staff incentives, prepayment mechanisms, and support for the poor.

Mixed model or universal system. While it is the long-term aim within most health systems to achieve a system of national universal health insurance coverage, implementing such a system is a long-term and difficult process; in preparation for such a move, most developing countries begin by implementing a range of different schemes tailored to the needs of different sections of the population within a mixed system; the need here is to manage the various components under the umbrella of a single agreed strategy.

In poorer countries like Cambodia and the Lao PDR, these principles are now being implemented and tested, with a number of original and innovative approaches. Understanding that conditions vary widely between countries, these experiences nonetheless provide valuable information and a number of lessons relevant to similar countries within the region, including Papua New Guinea.

Health Financing in Cambodia

Cambodia is ranked 129 out of 177 countries on the UN Human Development Index. With an annual population growth rate of 2 percent, the total population passed 14 million in 2005, of which more than 80 percent live in rural areas and are engaged mainly in subsistence agriculture. More than 90 percent of the population are ethnically Khmer and Buddhist (the remainder being Islamic Cham people, upland communities in the remote Mondulkiri and Rattanakiri Provinces, and immigrant groups). While Cambodia remains a low-income country, the economy has been growing rapidly in recent years, averaging 8 percent per annum over the last decade and reaching 13 percent in 2005. Development assistance plays a large role in the economy, though it is falling as a share of Gross National Income (GNI)—down to 10 percent in 2005 from more than 16 percent in 1995. Nonetheless, aid still constitutes a greater proportion of GNI than tax revenues.

Despite the overall advances in economic growth, poverty is extensive, and income disparities are widening. In 2005 annual per capita GNI was US$430 (in current USD), and in 2004 35 percent of the population was living below the national poverty line of US$0.59 per person per day. The Gini coefficient—a measure of income inequality—has increased from about 0.35 in 1995 to 0.42 in 2004, making income distribution in Cambodia more unequal than in most countries in the region. The growing inequality largely reflects rural-urban differences, differentiations within rural society, and geographic disparities.[34]

In terms of the impact on health, the situation is still precarious even though on some levels the increase in economic well-being has had a positive impact. Preventable diseases still dominate the main causes of morbidity and mortality, though the incidence of heart disease and cancers is on the rise. Even so, average life expectancy rose to 64 years for women and 58 years for men in 2005 from 58 and 54 years in 1998. Significant reductions in childhood mortality rates in recent years reflect improvements in the economy and in health service delivery, as infant mortality rate fell by almost 40 percent between 1998 and 2003, and the child mortality rate has fallen more gradually since 1982. However, despite the acknowledged progress, one in every twelve Cambodian children dies before reaching the age of five, and four-fifths of these deaths occur in the first year of life. At 472 per 100,000 live births, maternal mortality remains extremely high. Obstetric complications, malnutrition, respiratory infections, diarrhea, and dengue hemorrhagic fever are the main causes of this mortality.[35]

Building on health reforms that began in 1995, a number of supply-side initiatives have improved health care delivery, though the quality of medical services is still very limited. As well, demand-side initiatives have tackled chronically low rates of use of government facilities by breaking through barriers to access. In 1996 the right of public health facilities to levy official user fees was granted under the Health Financing Charter, which aimed mainly to provide revenue for staff incentives and to regulate or remove unofficial payments in a situation where under-the-table charges by public health staff were rife and expensive.[36]

Health financing in Cambodia is characterized by an unusually high level of total health expenditure, relatively low government spending, and high household out-of-pocket spending. The best current estimates indicate that, at approximately 8 percent of GDP in 2005 (or US$27 to US$37 per capita per year), total health expenditure is almost twice the level in comparable Global South countries. With recurrent budget spending at less than 2 percent of GDP, government health spending is relatively low, though it is steadily rising (reaching US$7 per capita in the 2007 budget). At US$114 million in 2005 (or US$8 per capita per year), donor funding for health care is high and rising. However, household out-of-pocket spending accounts for approximately two-thirds of all health expenditure (or approximately US$25 per capita per year).

While the supply of health services in Cambodia increased from the 1990s, the demand for services did not rise in proportion. This was principally due to the impact of a range of barriers to access to health services (especially for the poor). Long distances, lack of transport, and restricted hours of service deterred many people, especially in more remote areas. For those with easier access, the direct and indirect costs of health services (including user fees, travel, and food costs), the unpredictability of service charges, and opportunity costs due to time lost have been the most significant barriers. Most important was the failure of official exemption systems to cover the poor adequately. Real and perceived poor quality of care, facilities, and medication was an added disincentive, including poor staff attitudes toward patients and conflict of interest between health suppliers' public and private activities. Most users have therefore shown a lack of confidence in public health services. There is also a general lack of information about the nature and costs of public health service delivery. One result has been a cultural preference for home-based care and for customary and traditional healers.

Health-Equity Funds

In these circumstances, various health-equity funds emerged independently through the activities of numerous local and international nongovernment organizations working with the Ministry of Health to address financial barriers and, indirectly, the quality of health service delivery. Health-equity funds are the most innovative and most widespread of the social protection schemes currently operating in Cambodia.[37] The funds are third-party-payer schemes for indigent patients managed at the district level by a local agent (usually a local NGO), supervised by an international NGO, and funded by donors (or in some cases by government or through community collections). Some health-equity funds are run by local communities and organizations, and in all instances the poor are identified at or before the point of service and receive free care at the health facility. They are also reimbursed for associated treatment costs such as transport and food and the facility then receives payment for the cost of user fees exempted for the poor.

At the center of a typical health-equity fund structure is the managing agency, a third-party payer, which in Cambodia is commonly an international NGO. Donor funds normally flow directly to the managing agency but could in some cases be directed through the Ministry of Health (either into Ministry of Health accounts or through donor projects managed by the Ministry of Health). Health-equity funds in Cambodia are organized at the level of the health district. The managing agency usually contracts a local NGO as an agent or may use an independent committee comprising local Ministry of Health or hospital staff. The local health-equity fund identifies and represents beneficiaries and arranges payments to the health facilities.

In this simple schema the principles of transparency and accountability are maintained. In the years that followed their origin in three locations in 2000, the number of health-equity funds mushroomed across Cambodia, and today they cover about half of all health districts in the country. In 2007 the government initiated its own subsidy scheme for the poor in an additional ten health districts and at national hospitals, and Ministry of Health strategies for the years 2008–2015 include scaling-up health-equity fund schemes to cover all districts. The number of funds grew rapidly precisely because the schemes proved to be effective in increasing the use of health services (particularly district hospitals) by the poor and reducing the financial barriers to access.[38] With health-equity funds, especially when combined with strategies that strengthen health facility management and incentives (for example, a positive form of contracting that has been implemented in Cambodia), the underutilization of hospital capacity is in most cases eliminated. Bed occupancy rates (a uniform measure of the utilization of hospital capacity) typically rose in these health districts in Cambodia from a common level of around 50 percent to full utilization in a short period of time.

The purpose of the health-equity fund is to reduce or eliminate the barriers to access posed by user fees and other constraints on the poor. Table 9.1 defines the schemes that complement health-equity funds within this process in Cambodia. Community-based health insurance is used in a small number of locations in Cambodia to provide a microinsurance or local prepayment system for families that are not so poor.

Coverage by an equity fund leads to increased health care facility use, produces reduced levels of household health-related debt, and allows greater discretion in the use of household monies for health care. There are a number of caveats associated with judging the impact of equity funds: achieving increased access and use is dependent also on the nature and quality of public services delivered at hospitals and health centers; the outcomes are difficult to judge if the routine data supporting increases in use and access is inconsistent and

Table 9.1 Selected Health Financing Schemes

User fees	Decentralized, affordable user fees at public health facilities were introduced in Cambodia through the 1996 Health Financing Charter. The charter certified the imposition of official fees according to an agreed schedule at affordable rates following consultation with the community. The initiative to implement fees remains with hospitals and health centers, which retain 99 percent of fee income. A nonsubsidized exemption system is implemented as part of the user fee scheme.
Contracting	A scheme in which all government health services at the health district level (primary-level care at health centers and secondary-level care at district hospitals) are managed and delivered by a nongovernment operator (usually an international NGO) working under contract to the Ministry of Health, using Ministry of Health staff with performance agreements. Normally donor funded; may include a form of "internal contracting" managed through the Ministry of Health.
Health-equity funding	A third-party-payer scheme for indigent patients in which a fund is managed at district level by a local agent (usually a local NGO), supervised by an international NGO, and funded by donors (or in some cases by government or through community collections). The poor are identified at or before the point of service and receive free care at the health facility. They are also reimbursed for associated treatment costs such as transport and food. The facility then receives reimbursement monthly.
Community-based health insurance	Voluntary, nonprofit local-level insurance schemes funded by user premiums and managed commonly by an international or local NGO. The insurer contracts public health facilities to provide approved health services. Patients prepay insurance premiums to the scheme and receive free health care at designated facilities. In most cases, facilities receive a monthly capitation payment or case payment. May eventually be included under the umbrella of contributory social health insurance.

incomplete (although the data here are sufficient to substantiate the general gains); and the impact of vertical programs should be isolated, although present research does not yet allow us to do so. Even so, the example of Cambodia provides a number of lessons and raises important challenges for the delivery of health in Papua New Guinea.[39]

Isolated Districts and Ethnic Minorities: Lao PDR

While Cambodia has a relatively homogenous population, the Lao PDR has a diverse composition with a large number of ethnic minorities who live mostly in remote, mountainous regions. The Lao-Tai people comprise up to two-thirds of the population and live mainly in the riparian lowlands along the Mekong River and its tributaries. Ethnic minorities, speaking a large variety of local languages and dialects, comprise at least 32 percent of the population and live mainly in the more remote and less accessible highland areas. Laos is a lower-income country, ranked 133 on the 2006 UN Human Development Index. With a population of 5.9 million, it had a per capita GDP of US$500 in 2006. Only 20 percent of the population is classified as urban. Economic progress following the end of the American War in 1975 was modest, and market-based economic reforms that began in 1986 were initially prudent and slow-paced. However, with the recovery from the 1997 Asian economic crisis, Laos' acceptance into membership of ASEAN, improvements in communications, and an accelerated pace of private investment, economic growth has increased in recent years and reached 7.6 percent in 2006.

Led by the Lao People's Revolutionary Party, which first came to power in 1975, the Lao government continues to play the key role in economic and social affairs. Despite the beginning of market reforms, Laos maintains a strongly administrative system in which the implementation and development of public programs involves extensive cooperation from public authorities. Consequently, no local nongovernment organizations (NGOs) have emerged in Laos—as they have, for example, in Cambodia—though a number of "mass organizations" such as the Lao Front, Lao Youth, or the Lao Women's Union, play an important role in delivering social programs. The Lao Red Cross has a special mixed status, and a small number of international NGOs play an important role in the health sector.[40]

Poor health status remains an issue in the Lao PDR: life expectancy is low at sixty-one years; maternal mortality of 405 per 100,000 live births is high; and child mortality rates have improved little over the past decade (the infant mortality rate is at 70 per 1,000 live births; under-five mortality rate is 98 per 1,000 live births). The 2006 Common Country Assessment indicates that communicable diseases are still widespread.[41] Poor nutrition contributes to half of all child mortality, and diarrheal diseases including cholera account for one-quarter. These national averages conceal marked disparities between lowland populations and upland populations, as mortality rates, for instance, are even higher in isolated and remote communities.

The quantity and quality of health service delivery remain constrained and uneven. On the one hand, the public health-care network has expanded significantly in the last fifteen years, with the construction or renovation of the majority of planned provincial and district hospitals, and a network of more than seven hundred rural health centers is now completed. However, while officially it is claimed that 94 percent of the population has physical access at least to a village drug kit (which is very limited in terms of addressing health care needs), many deficiencies still exist in health care in remote areas. Use of public health facilities remains very low, with an average attendance rate of only 0.2 curative contacts per year per inhabitant. Inequalities in access to services are still evident in poorer districts, and in highland areas low population densities and limited physical access make the provision of health services difficult and expensive.

In total, a little more than 3 percent of GDP is spent on health care, even less than the average for Least Developed Countries, which is more than 4.5 percent. According to World Health Organization estimates, households account for approximately 60 percent of total health expenditure, donors for 30 percent, and the government health budget for 10 percent.[42] Generally, it is expected that recurrent costs at public health facilities are met mainly through user fees paid through revolving drug funds and from other service charges.[43]

Access to health care is limited by a range of financial, geographic, cultural, and other barriers. While under regulations legalizing the introduction of user charges provision was made for fee exemptions to the poor, these exemption systems were unfunded and inadequately implemented. Consequently, user charges have been a barrier to access to health services for the poor. Even where families otherwise have sufficient means of basic consumption, the subsistence nature of many communities and the lack of available cash to pay for services constitutes a special barrier to accessing services. The barriers to access are greater for ethnic minority communities living in remote districts. In addition to the lack of cash resources, these communities face a range of barriers related to sparse population settlement, long distances to facilities, linguistic differences, and cultural preferences related to medicine. In general, these communities are not always well served by the public health system.

With these constraints in mind, the Ministry of Health with the support of the World Bank drafted national guidelines for health-equity funding in the Lao PDR in 2007. These guidelines were based significantly on the experiences gained in neighboring Cambodia. Health-equity funding is being introduced into Laos as one part of a broader program working gradually toward the implementation of universal health insurance coverage nationally. As in Cambodia, compulsory health insurance schemes have been devised for civil servants and private sector employees and a community-based health insurance scheme has begun in some locations. Within this broader system, the pilot health-equity funds will operate under the direction of the Ministry of Health and within the structure of the Lao health system. The pilot funds will work as a third-party-payer system with a contracted managing agency and implemented by district hospital and health administration staff.

Comparing Papua New Guinea

In beginning our comparison between Cambodia and Lao PDR, on the one hand, and Papua New Guinea, on the other, we must note the distinct differences between the three locations. For instance, while in Cambodia near total destruction of the country as a result of war and political conflict resulted in key challenges to health care, in Papua New Guinea it is the terrain, geography, and pattern of settlement that pose the major constraints.[44] Given the differences, it is important to ask if health-equity systems like those implemented in Cambodia and the Lao PDR are appropriate for Papua New Guinea. Could they be effective in overcoming the barriers to access to health services, particularly for the poor or for communities in remote areas?

While there are differences between Papua New Guinea and countries in Asia such as Cambodia and the Lao PDR, there are also informative similarities in the cases discussed in this chapter that provide ground to imagine how lessons learned could be reapplied. Papua New Guinea became independent only in 1975, and through the 1990s it experienced high levels of instability and political fracturing. Cambodia may have gained independence in the 1950s, but civil conflict began in 1970 and continued until the end of the 1990s, including the period of absolute social, economic, and human destruction under the Khmer Rouge from 1975 to 1979. Laos gained independence in the 1950s also but, like Cambodia, was engulfed in the American war in Vietnam, emerging only in 1975 with real peace and self-determination. While these forms of political conflict and violence were fundamentally different in form, each of these countries experienced the struggles of postcolonial nation-states seeking to sustain and consolidate the national form in the wake of uneven development across the period of Anglo-European control. Furthermore, each of these countries has urban-rural divides, and each has significant portions of the population based in rural and isolated communities that engage in agricultural production.

In Papua New Guinea there has been a period of relative stability since the 2002 election, which created conditions for some economic and social progress. For example, after a long period of negative growth from 1995 until 2002, annual economic growth reached 4 percent in 2007 and has been going up since. Along with foreign aid, government expenditure plays a major role in the economy, reaching 34 percent of GDP in 2006. Should this period of relative political stability continue and should economic growth be sustained, it is conceivable that there will be an opportunity to find additional resources for social programs in health and education.[45]

Thus, a health-equity fund scheme, as outlined above, could be applied in Papua New Guinea. Such a system seems commensurate with key aspects of PNG society, fitting the need for the state to decentralize health services by integrating them into local communities, a point that may also help the health systems translate better in terms of local modes of organizing. With regard to the state, the recognition of the need to direct greater public resources into areas such as health is taken up in the government's Medium Term Development Strategy 2005–2010.[46] The overriding aim of the strategy, however, is to increase economic growth through private sector development; social programs do not receive equal attention. Nevertheless, the strategy calls for greater PNG ownership of development programs including rehabilitation of the transport infrastructure, primary health care, and HIV/AIDS prevention. Stronger management of the fiscal structure, rural development, and strengthening human resource capacity are key priorities; and investing in education and health as well as promoting economic growth is seen as a means to reduce poverty. The strategy calls for improving access to health care, including interventions to overcome the diseases that cause the largest number of deaths, such as malaria, pneumonia, measles, tuberculosis, diarrhea, and anemia. The nature of poverty in Papua New Guinea and the existing patterns of health financing suggest that the implementation of health-equity funds can address both the specific needs of the urban poor and the needs of poorly serviced populations in remote districts.

Nature and Distribution of Poverty

The most complete information on the nature and distribution of poverty is provided by the World Bank's 2004 Poverty Assessment.[47] About half the population in Papua New Guinea lives below the national poverty line, with 39 percent living on less than US$1 a day. The national distribution of income is particularly uneven; the Gini coefficient was measured at 0.48 in 2005 with little change over the previous ten years. The least developed districts are in Western Province, Sandaun, Madang, Morobe, Bougainville, the Western Highlands, the Eastern Highlands, the Southern Highlands, Enga, East Sepik, Central, the Gulf, and Simbu. The fourteen poorest districts in the country have poverty levels in excess of 50 percent of the population. The percentage of the poor within the population ranges from 66 percent (Middle Fly, Western) in the poorest districts to 9 percent (Goroka, Eastern Highlands).[48] As most education and cash-earning opportunities are found in the larger urban areas, there is a substantial urban-rural divide. Data from 1996 indicates that poverty was 16 percent in urban and 41 percent in rural areas; urban household access to piped water was 71.7 percent compared to 8.5 percent in rural areas. In 2000, urban infant mortality was 69 per 1,000 live births compared to 29 in rural areas, and 574 health staff were reported per 100,000 people in urban areas compared to 166 in rural areas. Nearly every social indicator is significantly worse in rural areas, and the available information suggests that the gap is widening.[49]

A similar gap in social well-being exists across provinces. Assessed in terms of five indicators relating to infant mortality, life expectancy at birth, literacy rates, the ratio of female-to-male literacy, and the poverty head-count index, among the lowest levels are found in the provinces of Madang, East Sepik and West Sepik, Enga, Gulf, and Morobe. Gender inequalities are prevalent and increasing: literacy rates are 61 percent for males and 51 percent for females, and men have a clear advantage in accessing the few available opportunities.[50] After a general decline in the 1990s, the health status of the population was at best plateauing according to Papua New Guinea's 2003 Health Sector Medium-Term Expenditure Framework. This is largely due to failings in the health system, especially in rural areas and at the district level. Among the most serious health concerns is the generalized HIV/AIDS epidemic, which is described in detail in Chapter 10 of this volume. The epidemic adds to the general burden of disease in adults. Among the common measures of health status, infant and under-five mortality rates are high (64 and 87 per 1,000 live births respectively in 2000), and malnutrition levels are considerably higher for the poor relative to the rich. Perinatal, maternal, nutritional, and communicable diseases account for most of the disease burden in the country (59 percent), followed by noncommunicable diseases (30 percent), and accidents and injuries (11 percent). Malaria remains an important contributor to morbidity and mortality.[51]

The complexities of poverty and how they intersect with health in Papua New Guinea indicate that a more adaptable system scaled to work within both urban and rural communities in Papua New Guinea could go some of the way to reducing current barriers to health care. As described in the following section, such a system may also assist in reducing the funding pressure on the PNG state.

Financing for Health Care in Papua New Guinea

Although the government was able to increase allocations significantly in the 1990s, health expenditures in Papua New Guinea remained unchanged and inadequate. Papua New Guinea has typically maintained the lowest proportion of health expenditure to GDP and also the lowest level of health expenditure per capita among its Pacific country neighbors. Spending in the public sector fell from 3 percent of GDP in 1990 to 2.8 percent in 1997; it then rose to 3.9 percent in 2001.[52] Within this overall allocation there are also significant variations between provinces. While public sector expenditures on health increased by 42 percent in real terms between 1996 and 2001, the majority of additional resources came from donor funding.[53] By 2002, 82 percent of the health budget went to paying salaries, maintaining buildings and equipment, and purchasing basic supplies rather than direct interventions to prevent or treat illnesses. At that time it was estimated that by 2004 only 4 percent of the health budget would be available for directly treating health and by 2007 only 1 percent.[54]

During this period, per capita domestic resources for health rose marginally, mainly by increasing the proportion of the national budget spent on health from 4.8 percent in 1996 to 6.2 percent in 1999. Public resources are supplemented to a significant extent by NGOs (principally the churches, which run about half of all rural centers) and to a lesser extent by the private sector. While the financial constraint on the provision of public health services may have been relieved, deeper structural issues became apparent, including deficiencies in leadership, lack of staff motivation, the impact of decentralization, and weak governance.[55]

Overall, it appears that despite these increases in health funding, health outcomes have not improved in a consistent way and have been particularly limited for poor and remote communities. A special study conducted by the Asian Development Bank on trends in health services delivery to the poor found that poor households in Papua New Guinea have the worst access to health facilities, lowest uptake of services, and the worst health outcomes.[56] The study confirmed that there are large disparities in the delivery of services between the poorer and better-off households and that the poor had been affected by closure of health facilities although toward the end of the period some improvements in the quality of services run by government facilities benefited the poor.

Conclusion

Conditions vary greatly between Papua New Guinea and the poorer countries of the Asian region, including Cambodia and the Lao PDR. While the Asian economies have experienced increased political stability and strong economic growth in recent years, the gains in Papua New Guinea since 2002 have been more modest and more uneven. Papua New Guinea is still at the stage of creating a stable central administration that has the capacity, even with the support of donor partners, to tackle the key problems associated with the provision of health services. Nonetheless, as in Cambodia and Laos, the role of equity in the provision of health services—especially in the delivery of adequate and affordable health services to rural, remote, and demographically diverse populations—is critical and central to the further development of the health system.

In these three countries, the inability to provide affordable and accessible health services is one of the chief causes, and also a major consequence, of widespread poverty. Addressing the health concerns of all citizens by making access to health care more equitable is therefore a key mechanism for alleviating poverty. International evidence suggests that investment in health care is important. However, such benefits do not happen spontaneously but require a genuine and deliberate commitment to researching, designing, developing, and implementing health programs that appropriately address the issues faced by poorer countries. Because the dimensions of poverty and the specific barriers to access vary from context to context, even between different local communities, engaging with communities in the development of programs is important as a means of identifying local circumstances and tailoring programs accordingly. Previous studies in Papua New Guinea have highlighted the wide differences in delivery of health services between poorer and wealthier households. These differences indicate the need for explicit programs that reach the poor, especially poor women and their children in rural areas. Both government and donor programs need to focus on this critical concern.

Notes

1. International Monetary Fund, *Health and Development: Why Investing in Health Is Critical for Achieving Economic Development Goals*, International Monetary Fund, Washington, DC, 2004; M. Merson et al., *International Public Health: Diseases, Programs, Systems, and Policies*, Aspen Publishers, Maryland, 2001; David Phillips and Yola Verhasselt, eds., *Health and Development*, Routledge, London, 1994; Jeffrey Sachs, "Executive Summary," in Commission on Macroeconomics and Health, *Investing in Health for Economic Development: Report of the Commission on Macroeconomics and Health*, World Health Organization, Geneva, 2001; World Bank, *World Development Report 1993, Investing in Health*, Oxford University Press, New York, 1993.

2. Pablo Gottret and George Schieber, *Health Financing Revisited, A Practitioners Guide*, World Bank, Washington, DC, 2006; World Health Organization, *The World Health Report 2000, Health Systems, Improving Performance*, World Health Organization, Geneva, 2000.

3. Joe Bolger et al., *Papua New Guinea's Health Sector: A Review of Capacity, Change and Performance Issues*, European Centre for Development Policy Management, 2005; Clement Malau and Sue Crockett, "HIV and Development the Papua New Guinea Way," *Development Bulletin*, vol. 52, 2000, pp. 58–60.

4. Steve Fabricant, *Cambodia Essential Health Services Cost Study: Final Report*, WHO/USAID/POPTECH, Phnom Penh, 2005; National Department of Health, *National Health Plan 2001–2010, Health Vision 2010, Policy Directions and Priorities*, vol. 1, National Department of Health, Port Moresby, 2001.

5. Joe Bolger et al., *Papua New Guinea's Health Sector*; Paul Nichols, *Report on Peer Review of Three Australian NGOs Working in PNG*, Adventist Development and Relief Agency, Anglican Board of Mission, Caritas Australia, Sydney, 2003. J. Izard and M. Dugue, *Moving toward a Sector-Wide Approach: Papua New Guinea, the Health Sector Development Program Experience*, Asian Development Bank, Manila, 2003.

6. Asian Development Bank, *Initial Poverty and Social Assessment*, ADF Grant–PNG, HIV/AIDS Prevention and Control in Rural Development Enclaves, 2005.

7. J. Connell, "Health in Papua New Guinea, A Decline in Development," *Australian Geographical Studies*, vol. 35, 1997, pp. 271–293.

8. G. Koczberski, "The Sociocultural and Economic Context of HIV/AIDS in Papua New Guinea," *Development Bulletin,* vol. 52, 2000, pp. 61–63.

9. Indu Bhushan et al., *Scaling-up Health Sector Activities for Poverty Reduction: Lessons from Papua New Guinea, Cambodia, and Sri Lanka,* Asian Development Bank, Manila, 2004.

10. Bolger et al., *Papua New Guinea's Health Sector;* Doug Campos-Outcalt, "Decentralising the Health System in Papua New Guinea," *Social Science and Medicine,* vol. 4, 1989; Doug Campos-Outcalt et al., "Decentralisation of Health Services in Western Highlands Province, Papua New Guinea: An Attempt to Administer Health Service at the Subdistrict Level," *Social Science and Medicine,* vol. 40, no. 8, 1995, pp. 1091–1098; Johann-Friedrich Ramm, "Rethinking Decentralization in Papua New Guinea," United Nations Centre for Regional Development, Nagoya, 1993.

11. Asian Development Bank, *Country Economic Review of Papua New Guinea,* Asian Development Bank, 2000; Government of Papua New Guinea, *Functional and Expenditure Review of Rural Health Services of 2001,* PSRMU, Government of Papua New Guinea, Port Moresby, 2001; Department of Health, *Papua New Guinea Health Sector Medium Term Expenditure Framework 2004–2006,* National Department of Health, Port Moresby, 2003.

12. Zarnaz Fouladi, "AIDS Narratives and Sexual Cultures in Tubetube, Papua New Guinea," University of Melbourne, Master's thesis, 2006.

13. Bhushan et al., *Scaling-up Health Sector Activities for Poverty Reduction.*

14. See, for example, International Labour Organization, "Social Health Protection, ILO Strategy towards Universal Access to Health–A Consultation," Global Campaign on Social Security and Coverage for All, Social Security Department, International Labour Organization, GTZ-ILO-WHO-Consortium on Social Health Protection in Developing Countries, Geneva, 2007, http//www.shi-conference.de/social_protection_health.php, accessed 20 January 2008; International Labour Organization, "Social Health Protection," http//www.ilo.org/public/english/protection/secsoc/areas/policy/social.htm, accessed 20 January 2008; World Health Organization, "Helping Countries Provide Social Health Protection," http//www.who.int/healthsystems/mediacentre/news/berlin/en/index.html, accessed 20 January 2008.

15. Gottret and Schieber, *Health Financing Revisited.*

16. World Bank, *World Development Report, 1993: Investing in Health,* Oxford University Press, New York, 1993.

17. Commission on Macroeconomics and Health, *Investing in Health for Economic Development: Report of the Commission on Macroeconomics and Health,* World Health Organization, Geneva, 2001; Sachs, "Executive Summary."

18. Fran Baum, *The New Public Health: An Australian Perspective,* Oxford University Press, Melbourne, 1998.

19. David Sanders and Richard Carver, *The Struggle for Health: Medicine and the*

Politics of Underdevelopment, Macmillan, London, 1985; S. Szreter, cited in Fran Baum, *The New Public Health*, p. 278.

20. R. Wilkinson, "Income Distribution and Life Expectancy," *BMJ (British Medical Journal)*, vol. 304, 1992, pp. 165–168.

21. Baum, *The New Public Health*.

22. Leon Bijlmakers et al., "Health and Structural Adjustment in Rural and Urban Settings in Zimbabwe: Some Interim Findings," in Peter Gibbon, ed., *Structural Adjustment and the Working Poor in Zimbabwe*, Nordiska Afrikainstitutet, Uppsala, 1995.

23. William Hsiao, *A Framework for Assessing Health Financing Strategies and the Role of Health Insurance*, The World Bank, Washington, DC, 1995.

24. Baum, *The New Public Health*; John C. Caldwell, "Routes to Low Mortality in Poor Countries," *Population and Development Review*, vol. 8, no. 3, 1986, pp. 11–16; David Werner, "Challenges Facing 'Health for All,'" presented at "The New World Order, A Challenge to Health For All by the Year 2000," University of the Western Cape, Capetown, 29–31 January 1997.

25. Amartya Sen, *Development as Freedom*, Alfred A. Knopf, New York, 1999.

26. Ricardo Bitran and U. Gideon, "Waivers and Exemptions for Health Services in Developing Countries," Social Protection Discussion Paper Series, World Bank, 2003.

27. World Health Organization, *Constitution of the World Health Organization*, World Health Organization, Geneva, 1946, http://www.who.int/hlt/historical/documents/constitution.html, accessed 25 November 1999.

28. World Health Organization, *Primary Health Care: Report of the International Conference on Primary Health Care, Alma-Ata, USSR*, World Health Organization, Geneva, 1978.

29. John Akin et al., *Financing Health Services in Developing Countries: An Agenda for Reform*, The International Bank for Reconstruction and Development, Washington, DC, 1987.

30. World Bank, *World Development Report, 1993*.

31. World Health Organization, *The World Health Report 2000: Health Systems, Improving Performance*, World Health Organization, Geneva, 2000.

32. A. Haines and A. Cassels, "Can the Millennium Development Goals Be Attained?" *BMJ (British Medical Journal)*, vol. 329, 2004, pp. 394–397; United Nations, *Millennium Declaration*, United Nations General Assembly, Geneva, 2000.

33. World Bank, *Healthy Development: The World Bank Strategy for Health, Nutrition, and Population Results*, Washington, DC, 2007.

34. Cambodia, Ministry of Planning, *Cambodia Socio-Economic Survey 2004*, Ministry of Planning, Phnom Penh, 2006; World Bank, *Halving Poverty by 2015–Cambodia Poverty Assessment 2006*, Phnom Penh, 2006; World Bank, *World Development Indicators 2007*, Washington, DC, 2007.

35. Cambodia, National Institute of Public Health and National Institute of Statistics, *Cambodia Demographic and Health Survey 2005,* National Institute of Public Health and National Institute of Statistics, Phnom Penh, 2006.

36. Sarah Barber et al., "Formalizing Under-the-Table Payments to Control Out-of-Pocket Hospital Expenditures in Cambodia," *Health Policy and Planning,* vol. 19, no. 4, 2004, pp. 199–208; Cambodia, Ministry of Health, *Health Coverage Plan Cambodia,* Ministry of Health, Planning and Statistics Unit, Phnom Penh, 1996; Cambodia, Ministry of Health, *National Charter on Health Financing in the Kingdom of Cambodia,* Ministry of Health, Conference on Financing of Health Services, 5–9 February 1996, Phnom Penh, 1996; Cambodia, Ministry of Health, *Mid-Term Review Report 2003–June 2006,* Health Sector Support Project, Ministry of Health, Phnom Penh, 2006; Cambodia, Ministry of Health, *Joint Annual Performance Review,* Department of Planning and Health Information, Ministry of Health, Phnom Penh, 2007.

37. Peter Leslie Annear et al., *Study of Financial Access to Health Services for the Poor in Camboda–Phase 2: In-Depth Analysis of Selected Case Studies,* Ministry of Health, WHO, AusAID, RMIT University (Melbourne), Phnom Penh, 2007; Peter Leslie Annear et al., *Study of Financial Access to Health Services for the Poor in Cambodia–Phase 1: Scope, Design, and Data Analysis,* Ministry of Health, WHO, AusAID, RMIT University (Melbourne), Phnom Penh, 2006.

38. Annear et al., *Study of Financial Access to Health Services for the Poor in Cambodia–Phase 1.*

39. Peter Leslie Annear and Jim Tulloch, "A Challenge for Australia's Health Aid Strategy, Access to Health Services for the Poor," *Development Bulletin,* vol. 72, 2007.

40. See, for example, Carol Perks et al., "District Health Programs and Health-Sector Reform:, Case Study in the Lao People's Democratic Republic," *WHO Bulletin,* vol. 84, no. 2, 2006, pp. 132–138.

41. United Nations and Lao PDR, *Common Country Assessment,* Vientiane, 2006.

42. Fabricant, *Cambodia Essential Health Services Cost Study.*

43. National health account series data for the year 2005 based on Laos, Ministry of Finance, *Official Gazette 2006, Volume 1, 13th Year,* Ministry of Finance, Vientiane, 2007.

44. Shiladitya Chatterjee et al., "Case Study: Papua New Guinea and Sri Lanka–Scaling up Health Interventions," presented at the conference "Reducing Poverty, Sustaining Growth, What Works, What Doesn't and Why," Shanghai, 25–27 May 2004.

45. United Nations Development Program, *Papua New Guinea United Nations Development Program Development Assistance Framework, 2003–2007,* Port Moresby, 2002.

46. Government of Papua New Guinea, *Medium Term Development Strategy 2005–2010,* Government of Papua New Guinea, Port Moresby, 2005.

47. Davidson R. Gwatkin, *Are Free Government Health Services the Best Way to Reach the Poor?* World Bank, Washington, DC, 2004.

48. S. Chand, "Papua New Guinea Economic Survey: Transforming Good Luck into Policies for Long-Term Growth," *Pacific Economic Bulletin*, vol. 19, no. 1, 2004, pp. 1–19.

49. Gwatkin, *Are Free Government Health Services the Best Way to Reach the Poor?*

50. M. de Bruyn, "Women and AIDS in Developing Countries," *Social Science and Medicine*, vol. 34, 1993, pp. 249–262; J. Clark and J. Hughes, "A History of Sexuality and Gender in Tari," in A Biersack, ed., *Papuan Borderlands, Huli, Duna, and Ipili Perspectives in the Papua New Guinea Highlands*, University of Michigan Press, Ann Arbor, 1995; L. Heise et al., "Violence against Women: A Neglected Public Health Issue in Less Developed Countries," *Social Science and Medicine*, vol. 39, 1994, pp. 1165–1179.

51. Gwatkin, *Are Free Government Health Services the Best Way to Reach the Poor?*

52. Bhushan et al., *Scaling-up Health Sector Activities for Poverty Reduction.*

53. National Department of Health, *Papua New Guinea Health Sector Medium Term Expenditure Framework 2004–2006.*

54. Health Secretary Dr. Nicholas Mann, reported in the *National*, 6 August 2003, cited in Bolger et al., *Papua New Guinea's Health Sector.*

55. Bhushan, et al., *Scaling-up Health Sector Activities for Poverty Reduction.*

56. Asian Development Bank, *Trends in the Distribution of Health and Health Services in PNG 1991–2000*, conducted under ADB TA 3762, PNG Health Sector Review, 2002.

Chapter 10

HIV/AIDS and Community Context

HIV/AIDS WAS FIRST REPORTED IN Papua New Guinea in 1987. Over the next decade, the numbers of confirmed HIV and HIV/AIDS cases increased steadily, causing a general but unhurried state of concern.[1] Since then heightened attention has been raised about the need to recognize an impending crisis. After an exponential statistical rise in HIV/AIDS cases since 2000, Papua New Guinea has been classified as suffering from a generalized epidemic of HIV and AIDS.[2] This means that HIV is firmly established in the general population through substantial sexual networking, while subpopulations may continue to spread HIV disproportionately. Such a classification is determined when HIV prevalence in pregnant women is consistently over 1 percent, which was documented at the Port Moresby General Hospital's antenatal clinic in 2002.[3] By the end of 2007, there were an estimated 59,537 people living with HIV. The urban prevalence was estimated at 1.38 percent of the national population and the rural at 1.65 percent, with the epidemic classified as heterosexual.[4] That is the official story.

However, while the reports are becoming more circumspect, a number of contestable claims have been made about the nature of the spread.[5] For a long time, sex workers were considered the highest risk group, followed by youth, and young women in particular.[6] Married persons were generally considered at the lowest risk for infection because it was presumed that they tended to be "faithful." These factors have been associated with the projection of an African-style epidemic in Papua New Guinea, with some arguing that the similarly lax controls on premarital sexuality will inevitably lead to high levels of sickness and death.[7] At first the epidemic was characterized as urban, but very recently the characterization has shifted just as problematically to a rural emphasis. Both claims are based on patchy evidence and limited reflection on the constant interrelation between the urban and the rural in Papua New Guinea. All of this has created considerable alarm, but it has also raised questions about the nature of the evidence, the framing of discourses about sexuality, and the most appropriate pathways to sustainable social health. The shift of emphasis from "High-Risk Groups" to "High Risk Settings" in 2004, for example, has been criticized as little more than a shifting of acronyms.[8] The issues actually are much broader. First, as Dennis Altman has described the process, local practices are bound up with a global sex industry—not just in the broader sense of the globalization of modern sensibilities of desire and embodiment, but also in relation to the medicalization of practices that surround the response to HIV.[9] Second, the social differences in locales require acute cultural sensitivity to the way in which local and global processes intersect and remake each other.

Conventionally, modern formal medical institutions are assumed to be the obvious and most effective avenues for the delivery of HIV-prevention services and education, along with the distribution of informative posters and street banners. However, given the poor state of Papua New Guinea's formal health services coupled with the cultural complexity of cross-cutting ontologies of embodiment and knowledge informal health care arrangements and cross-cultural knowledge systems are likely to play a more influential role in shaping behaviors and beliefs than previously supposed. Although modern epidemiological practices should not be sidelined, there is an urgent need to develop a complementary community-based model of engagement that crosses the boundaries of modern, traditional, and tribal understandings of well-being. For example, the continuing use of customary remedies for HIV/AIDS needs to be taken seriously rather than ridiculed or pushed underground.[10] Instead of dismissing such remedies—even if they clearly do not work in conventional ways as either preventive or curative measures against HIV—community discussion should recognize the cultural roles played by customary health practices in giving subjective comfort.

When street vendors sell herbal remedies for AIDS, cancer, sexually transmitted infections, and what seems like a medieval range of other ailments, it is indicative of the crossover of forms that they use modern forms of legitimation such as written testimony. Vendors hang large signs listing the ailments that the herb is purported to cure; they display newspaper articles and other information as supporting evidence of a remedy's efficacy; they use terms such as "100 percent pure herbs," akin to the attempts by complementary medicines to legitimize themselves in the West. Drawing out the complexity of the issues involved here would require ongoing community discussion, but they carry only a fraction of the complexity of the politics of sexuality, gender relations, and embodiment that needs to be addressed if the epidemic is to be brought under some control.

A street vendor in Lae, selling Nguna Juice as a response to ailments ranging from HIV/AIDS to back pain and elephant leg

The lack of research into the strategies that local people are adopting to treat and otherwise deal with HIV outside their contact with the official health system is one reason why recent efforts at prevention have yielded limited success. However, the need for community engagement goes much further. Not all PNG citizens recognize the unchallengeable authority of formal, Western-style health institutions, the main avenues through which the recent HIV prevention policies have sought to influence popular behavior. Further, a lack of communication between formal and informal health care providers has meant that those living with the disease have sometimes received mixed and contradictory information from different sources about causes, transmission, and treatment of HIV. This undermines their ability to interpret or utilize available information about the prevention or management of HIV. Of still greater importance, many of the most devastating effects of the epidemic are experienced at the social level, where fragmentation and disintegration of communities and caring networks leads to the generation of despair and hopelessness. As a result, effective strategies to prevent the spread of HIV or to manage its effects require a system of care that respects local cultures and belief systems and actively seeks to mobilize the resources within communities.

This chapter provides an overview of the HIV/AIDS epidemic in Papua New Guinea with the purpose of evaluating some of the major questions and gaps in knowledge about the disease. In doing so, it draws on the literature on HIV in Papua New Guinea as well as in the broader Global South. It highlights the limitations of conventional biomedical approaches that underpin most of Papua New Guinea's HIV research and policy making. We argue that such approaches tend to rely too heavily on two problematic assumptions: that statistics provide an accurate representation of the HIV situation in Papua New Guinea and that Western discourses around and definitions of HIV can be applied directly in the cultural environment of Papua New Guinea. Drawing on research from fields such as anthropology, sociology, and feminism, we argue that prevailing epidemiological approaches to HIV fail to take into account the complex cultural factors that influence beliefs, behaviors, and patterns of transmission of the disease. This omission, we argue, goes a long way toward explaining the limitations of HIV prevention efforts in Papua New Guinea.

Responding to the Epidemic

In 1998 and 1999, mounting international concern over an impending epidemic prompted the PNG government to establish the National AIDS Council (NAC) and the National AIDS Council Secretariat (NACS) to act as the main government advisory bodies on all matters of policy in relation to HIV/AIDS,[11] with the NACS supervising and managing the operations of the NAC. The two bodies were established as independent government organizations, with little affiliation to the National Department of Health. In addition, they were to manage the provincial AIDS committees, which in turn managed the activities of the district AIDS committees within each province. Most important, the NACS was to maintain and monitor statistics on HIV and AIDS in all of Papua New Guinea.

Even though NACS is the main government body that manages HIV/AIDS policies in Papua New Guinea, 90 percent of its funding comes from international donors, and of this 95 percent comes directly from AusAID, administered through the AusAID-managed National HIV/AIDS Support Project.[12] As a result of the balance of funding, the latter has largely determined Papua New Guinea's HIV/AIDS policies. Because AusAID draws largely on biomedical models of HIV/AIDS,[13] a majority of the resulting policy initiatives and research in Papua New Guinea has been determined by these frameworks, although in the last year or so there have been a number of marginal shifts in emphasis, with some recognition that different methodologies for working in communities can provide alternative forms of engagement. In mid-2007, for example, the PNG Sustainable Development Program partnered with a number of other organizations, including Save the Children and the Department for Community Development, to run workshops in the Eastern Highlands and Western Province. There, methodologies presented included the "Appreciative Enquiry" approach, community awareness through drama, the "Values-Based" approach used by the Bahai faith, the "AIDS-Competence" approach of the Salvation Army, and the "Community Conversations" method developed in the United Nations Development Program Community Enhancement initiative, the latter being similar to the approach used in our own ethnography. There the community-engaged approach of Elizabeth Reid and Catherine Levy became exemplary of another way of approaching the HIV epidemic.[14]

Overall, Papua New Guinea has the greatest rates of HIV infections and numbers of cases of AIDS in the Western Pacific. Working with the PNG government, international health organizations such as the Australian Agency for International Development and the World Health Organization have dramatically increased their funding for HIV/AIDS prevention in recent years. These, however, have had little impact on HIV/AIDS infection rates or on the developing social, economic, and health crisis. Even more disturbing is that these mea-

An article from the *PNG Post Courier* on a notice board in Losuia

sures have not significantly alleviated the rampant fear, confusion, and stigmatization associated with the disease. As a result, many people feel that they lack agency to resist impending sickness and death. Furthermore, those afflicted with HIV/AIDS or believed to be spreading the disease are becoming increasingly vulnerable to rejection and vilification by their communities. In this chapter, we argue that the failure to improve the HIV situation in Papua New Guinea despite massive funding and other efforts suggests that the prevailing biomedical approaches are unable to address the key factors underlying the epidemic.

The Biomedical Model

The definitions and understandings of the human immunodeficiency virus and acquired immune deficiency syndrome have been the subject of debate since AIDS was first recognized by the Centers for Disease Control in the United States in 1981. Nonetheless, virtually all international public health responses to HIV and AIDS have been dominated by the biomedically based fields of microbiology, pharmacology, psychology, and epidemiology. These fields have commanded the largest share of international funding for HIV and AIDS research. Claiming privileged access to objective and empirically verifiable "truth," these disciplines depend on a model of disease that assumes a relatively mechanistic concept of causality with respect to both biological functioning and social behavior.

Much of the science underlying the biological actions of the human immunodeficiency virus is, of course, well founded. Viral particles are passed between persons through the exchange of bodily fluids, such as blood or semen, or between mothers and babies. Sexual contact and intravenous drug use are particularly important modes of transmission.[15] In relation to sexual transmission, women are considered at a much higher risk of contracting the virus as a result of biological differences between the sexes, with the risks increased further by physiological immaturity, rough sex leading to vaginal abrasion and tearing, and certain methods of cleaning or treating the vagina, causing irritation. For both men and women, the presence of another sexually transmitted infection also increases the risk of contracting HIV.[16]

The clinical manifestations of AIDS vary between individuals and regions and are affected by various factors, including malnutrition, parasitic infections, and poor sanitation. Where one lives in the world and the services and resources available in that place can crucially affect the clinical effects of HIV infection. Furthermore, because AIDS is a clinical diagnosis,[17] it is, by definition, linked to certain disease markers, which may vary in prevalence and severity from place to place: in Papua New Guinea these may include weight loss, chronic diarrhea, prolonged fever, oropharyngeal candidiasis, and tuberculosis.[18] All these phenomena are present in populations independently of HIV and may not, therefore, invariably reflect the effects of the virus. A recent study in Papua New Guinea of 124 adult patients "diagnosed" with HIV or AIDS showed that in actuality 11 percent were not HIV seropositive, emphasizing the importance for clinicians, researchers, and policy makers of avoiding stereotypical categories and assumptions.

The rush for AIDS-related funding and the lack of research on sexuality allowed instrumental and biomedical approaches to gain dominance.[19] The claim from these perspectives is that their empirical methods provide an unbiased account of sexuality, which is both universalizing in its claim and reductive in its reference point—reducing sexuality to the physiological components of the sexual act itself, with sexual behavior posited as deterministic and individualistic.[20] These discourses argue that biomedical classifications of homosexuality, heterosexuality, and bisexuality are universal and constant.[21] This has led to a focus on risk groups, whose particular behaviors are categorized as "deviant" or "abnormal." From this perspective, risk groups are seen as the main vectors of HIV infection and "barriers" to prevention.[22] As a result, terms such as "homosexuality" in the Global North and "heterosexuality" and "sex workers" in the Global South have almost become synonymous with risk of HIV/AIDS. In Papua New Guinea, the epidemic is consistently termed "heterosexual," suggesting that persons engaging in intercourse with the opposite sex outside of marriage are promiscuous, with males and females equally at risk of HIV infection. Underlying this assumption is the notion that heterosexual sex occurs only between male and female genitalia, ignoring a multiplicity of other possible forms of sexual exchange.[23] On the whole, these stigmatized group constructions highlight the individual sexual act, never acknowledging the complexity of factors that shape a person's decision to engage in sexual exchange, the nature of the sexual exchange, or cultural constructions of sexuality.

The emphasis on risk behaviors leads naturally to the application of theories of behavior from social psychology that assume that individuals make rational choices to maximize their advantages and minimize costs when educated about risks. In effect, it presupposes that information, attitudes, and action form a logically connected and unidirectional sequence within an individual person.[24] As a result, these theories relegate the varying cultural and psychological contexts of individuals' lives as irrelevant to behavior change and thus outside the domain of intervention.

In accordance with these frameworks, epidemiological research has relied heavily on quantitative techniques, in Papua New Guinea and elsewhere, especially the so-called Knowledge, Attitudes, Practices, and Beliefs (KAPB or KAB) surveys. The focus of this research is largely on knowledge of transmission of HIV, frequency of sex acts, the use of condoms, and the occurrence of behaviors defined as risky. Basic background information such as age, sex, and marital status is also recorded.[25] The categories are used to decide how and what questions are asked. The basic assumption here is that the research participants will exhibit a Western, or at least "modern," theoretical rationality. Taken together, the surveys and other information about the incidence of HIV and AIDS form what is referred to as "surveillance data," which are then used to inform policies and programs directed at prevention and intervention, regardless of the cultural context.[26]

The most common focus of these putative preventive measures is the ABC model—abstinence, being faithful, and condom use—the same model that is dominant in Papua New Guinea's preventive policies. Though these measures seldom work in any cultural context,[27] this failure is understood not as limitations of the biomedical frameworks of understanding of the HIV/AIDS epidemic, but as the fault of culture and sexuality.[28] This failure within the prevailing conceptual systems indicates a disconnection between the biomedical frameworks, the intervention policies informed by them, and the social contexts of the people they seek to target.

Weaknesses in the Data Collection and Surveillance Systems

Within the biomedical framework statistics are treated as providing factual representations of reality and often dictate directions for policies, funding, and research.[29] In reality, epidemiological information must be critically examined to expose unstated assumptions underlying the gathering, presentation, and interpretation of data.

A careful critical analysis of surveillance data raises doubts about the projections regarding HIV/AIDS in Papua New Guinea. As one of the most difficult issues to consider, the number of HIV and AIDS cases appears by some measures to comprise only a small percentage of the total population. A cumulative *reported* total of 9,851 HIV/AIDS cases from 1987 to 2004 is equal to 0.19 percent of the total estimated population of 5.2 million. This percentage, however, is far below the HIV prevalence of the two antenatal clinics that showed a greater than 1 percent seroprevalence in 2004. In addition, a majority of the total *reported* HIV and AIDS cases is occurring in the National Capital District. In 2004, 5,662 or 61 percent of HIV and AIDS cases were identified in the capital. In contrast, the next most significant province, Western Highlands Province, had 1,582 or approximately 16 percent of the cases identified. Following this was Morobe Province with 583 or approximately 6 percent. On these figures, the small percentage of the population with HIV/AIDS and the imbalance in reported cases per province suggest that it is misleading to conclude that the disease is rampant in Papua New Guinea's general population.

The imbalance in reported HIV and AIDS cases per province raises further questions about claims based on statistical data. The majority of testing facilities are located in urban areas within regions that have disproportionately been affected by modern development. In addition, many of the data from these areas are derived from women tested at antenatal clinics or from men at STI clinics.[30] In 2004 NACS monitored a total of only four antenatal clinics in the whole of Papua New Guinea. Consequently, the location of these facilities did not provide information about the "less developed" provinces or the predominantly rural population in PNG.[31] The 2006 collections drew more on rural collecting, leading to a reversal of earlier claims as a result of which the conclusion was drawn that "the trend of the epidemic in rural areas shows a late but strong increase. It appears that the HIV epidemic will become more rural as of 2007."[32] In reality, the facts remain inconclusive.

An alternative interpretation of the statistics is that the epidemic is concentrated in the capital and is not significant in other regions. If true, this could be attributable to increased migration from rural areas to the capital, particularly to the urban center of Port Moresby. Simultaneously, surveillance is more effective in the capital district than in other provinces, leading to an observer bias in this province. Testing facilities are naturally more available in the capital, and there is easier access to the National Reference Library,[33] the only laboratory allowed to make final confirmatory tests of HIV seropositive cases nationally.[34] Until 2006 all seropositive blood samples initially collected in the provinces and districts were sent to the National Reference Library for confirmatory testing.[35] Because samples and accompanying data are often poorly collected, samples often fail to reach the library, especially where transport is difficult, and results are often not delivered.[36] For these reasons, the systems used to monitor HIV and AIDS cases are inconsistent and unreliable, making conclusions about the disease unreliable.

The assumption that the epidemic is almost entirely heterosexual is also questionable. Caldwell, a leading experts on HIV/AIDS in Africa, argues for a "heterosexual" epidemic in Papua New Guinea because both the data collected from seropositive people and the near parity in HIV/AIDS cases between males and females suggest heterosexual transmission.[37] This, however, is a presumptuous statement given that HIV/AIDS Quarterly Reports consistently state that the mode of transmission in a majority of the cases is unknown. In 2002 and 2004, for example, these reports referred to 64 percent and 73 percent of the total cases of HIV/AIDS as having an unknown mode of transmission.[38] Therefore, the assumption of a heterosexual epidemic ignores the gaps in the available evidence as well as discounting other forms of sexual relations that fall outside dominant constructs of sexual classification. As was recognized in the

The grave site in Boera village of a young woman who died of HIV/AIDS

2008 *Country Progress Report*, there is no information about two-thirds of the recorded infections, throwing serious doubt on the data reproduced, despite the supposed precision quoted to two decimal places. [39]

A further possible discrepancy in the available data concerns the age distribution of the identified cases of HIV/AIDS. Data show that most of the persons diagnosed with either HIV or AIDS are young adults between the ages of twenty and twenty-nine. As a result, youth are considered to be at high risk of infection. This finding overlooks the fact that not only was information on age not available in almost 40 percent of cumulative cases from 1987 to 2004 but few people in Papua New Guinea actually know their chronological ages. A study by Lawrence Hammar of an STI clinic case registry at Daru General Hospital between the years 1981 and 1998 showed that a particular person's stated age could vary in successive visits by as much as fifteen years.[40] For example, one young woman visiting three times within seven months gave the sequential ages of nineteen, twenty-five, and twenty-four. Another man was aged thirty-five, fifty, and then forty in the years 1985, 1987, and 1989, respectively. Hammar argues that given the problematic nature of eliciting a person's age in Papua New Guinea, researchers and policy makers must "question the meaning and particular uses of conventional statuses and categories."[41] That is, classification of data according to epidemiological categories and classifications often omits an acknowledgment of the inherent uncertainties in gathering surveillance information in the PNG context. The records recognize some of these uncertainties: for example, in some presentations we see the category "unknown" as the largest category in the range. However, the age of a person as told at registration is still evidently taken at face value. [42]

Categories for assessing HIV designed for a Western setting are not necessarily appropriate for Papua New Guinea because the quality and meaning of statistics are profoundly influenced by underpinning cultural, political, social, and geographic contexts. Hence, an apparently straightforward statistical category (such as age distribution of a disease or mode of transmission) can refer to entirely different things in different cultural settings. However, it is important to emphasize that the failure of surveillance systems in Papua New Guinea is not due to their culturally ill-fitting structure alone: the PNG health system's limited resources and weak organizational and institutional arrangements, especially in relation to HIV management, are also major obstacles to effective surveillance.

Organizational, Institutional, and Infrastructural Barriers

It is worth remembering that, regardless of the ongoing HIV/AIDS epidemic, the health care systems of PNG are in a critically poor state, as described in Chapter 9. The general disintegration of the health system underlies the inability of the National Department of Health to provide adequate support to the National AIDS Council Secretariat for surveillance and prevention. The most obvious result is the limited number of testing facilities equipped to monitor HIV/AIDS statistics. In addition, although the National Department of Health has better access to the general population than the NACS does, it has often failed to educate its health staff about HIV and AIDS. Research on Tubetube Island in Milne Bay Province indicated that the health worker there had only attended two training workshops on HIV/AIDS, occurring ten and fifteen years previously, as a result of which the health worker was confused about issues surrounding HIV/AIDS. In addition, all the HIV/AIDS pamphlets and posters he had received from the National Department of Health were in Tok Pisin, a language that is not spoken in Milne Bay Province.[43] It is not uncommon for health workers to make moralizing claims about HIV and AIDS, often fueling local communities' fears: for example, some health workers are reluctant to provide condoms to single persons because they view condoms as a form of contraception only suitable for married people.[44] Overall, the lack of collaboration between the National Department of

Health and NACS has led to missed opportunities to integrate HIV/AIDS prevention within the already existing primary health care system.

Yet another problem is NACS' incapacity to manage national HIV/AIDS intervention and prevention activities effectively because of its inadequate relationship with the public health system. NACS was created independently from other government agencies, most notably the National Department of Health. As a result, HIV/AIDS has not been mainstreamed into other government sectors, with the exception of the Department for Community Development, and little political support has been given by government officials.[45] This has resulted in minimal inclusion of HIV/AIDS within primary health care. NACS often has difficulty accessing funds from the National HIV/AIDS Support Project, which controls a majority of NACS' funds.[46] This has led to considerable tension between the two organizations.[47] As a result of this inadequate funding, NACS does not have the necessary support and capacity for managing and coordinating nationwide HIV/AIDS preventive efforts. For example, the functions of the NAC and its corresponding committees at the provincial level are not well coordinated, leading to disorganization among provincial and district committee offices.[48] In addition, organizational shortcomings prevent effective collaboration with international agencies and discourage potential international NGOs with strong professional reputations in HIV/AIDS to work in Papua New Guinea.[49] Furthermore, this general lack of collaboration with outside sectors is also associated with NACS' minimal partnership with citizens, community organizations, and churches. These civil society organizations are integral to a successful HIV/AIDS campaign because they have direct access to and knowledge of local communities, which would include partnerships in learning programs conducted through community learning centers.[50] Overall, the fragmented and uncoordinated response to HIV/AIDS in Papua New Guinea has led to a lack of partnership with international agencies, government sectors, and civil society.

We have argued so far that the uncritical use of statistics relating to HIV in Papua New Guinea is problematic only in part because the country's surveillance systems are limited. These limits result from the lack of collaborative, organizational, and material capacities necessary for effective surveillance. However, just as important is the fact that surveillance systems are not properly tailored to local circumstances and therefore fail to capture a true representation of the proportions, distribution, and causes of the PNG epidemic. The apparent failure of intervention policies adopted so far suggests that the strategies employed by the international health agencies working with the PNG government have not addressed the factors that are shaping the HIV/AIDS epidemic. These policies often assume that HIV/AIDS is only a medical issue and consequently define the disease solely in terms of the pathology associated with it. It is assumed that risk is mitigated by universalistic interpretations of sexuality and that instruction about sexual practices will lead to behavior change. As we have argued, these assumptions are based on culturally specific biomedical definitions of HIV/AIDS and models of disease causation that support these constructions. In the PNG context, the result is that health policies generated on the basis of these assumptions are often ineffectual, inadequate, and inappropriate; fail to change behaviors; and exacerbate the stigmatization of already marginal groups.

In Papua New Guinea as well as internationally, there has been growing recognition of the limitations of purely biomedical accounts of HIV/AIDS. It is now acknowledged that HIV/AIDS cannot be understood as if it occurred in a biomedical vacuum; rather, the disease arises in conjunction with multiple conditions and processes of change within and across nations. A person's health is inextricably linked to the broader social, economic, and political forces acting in any one country. Efforts to prevent HIV/AIDS need to take these multiple factors into account.[51]

Dominant Research and Policy Making

Despite the deficiencies in the statistics and the interpretations generated by them, the increase in the numbers of HIV and AIDS cases in Papua New Guinea is deeply concerning and indicates the need both for improved surveillance systems and for research that addresses the pressing questions that will help generate effective policy responses. Unfortunately, most research done in Papua New Guinea uses inappropriate methods or cultural assumptions and lacks sensitivity to the local conditions and needs of the population. As indicated above, the relevance of approaches to prevention developed in other settings has been widely adopted as a starting point for work in Papua New Guinea. For example, in an interview in 2005 the director of Papua New Guinea's National AIDS Council Secretariat argued: "Getting the message across to people is not a problem, but it is changing attitudes and behavior that is the issue. People know AIDS has no cure but still continue to have sex without a condom.... We can say and do all we want, but if people at the individual level can't respond positively to prevent HIV, all we've done will count for nothing."[52] This statement takes for granted the abstinence, be faithful, condom use model of prevention, a model that has been shown to be ineffective across the globe. It continues to place blame on individuals, suggesting that irresponsible, promiscuous behavior is the root cause of the epidemic. Most important, it discounts the role of local cultural conditions in shaping sexuality and other aspects of social relationships.

As a result of the culturally limited approach to understanding HIV/AIDS in Papua New Guinea, research funding has overwhelmingly favored quantitative methodologies, risk-group classifications, and clinical research and has largely neglected interactive, community-based and participant-responsive methodologies. Until 2007 most studies were undertaken in major urban centers or in provinces with more dominant economies, ignoring most of the rural population in Papua New Guinea.

Much research has centered on risk groups defined as "sub-populations at high risk [who] may continue to contribute disproportionately to the spread of HIV,"[53] such as sex workers and transport workers.[54] In the mid-1990s this emphasis led to the Transex Project, which focused on reducing "high-risk behavior" among members of these populations, specifically transport workers and commercial sex workers and their clients in Port Moresby, Lae, the Highlands Highway, and along coastal shipping routes.[55] There is also much clinical-based biomedical research into HIV/AIDS,[56] and many studies have employed surveys, especially those using the standard KAPB (knowledge, attitudes, practices, and beliefs) model of HIV/AIDS.[57] Reports produced by international agencies have often focused on modeling disease incidence and on subsequent economic impact,[58] both of which are rather tenuous given the incompleteness of surveillance data and the lack of grounding of theoretical models in local conditions.[59] In general, these studies have contributed little to broadening the understanding of the nature or dynamics of the disease in Papua New Guinea.

Papua New Guinea's national prevention policies, principally defined by the National HIV/AIDS Support Project, focus on six main areas: (1) education, information, advocacy, and behavior change; (2) counseling, community care, and support; (3) clinical and laboratory services; (4) policy, legal, and ethical issues; (5) monitoring, surveillance, and evaluation; and (6) management support for the national response.[60] A recent evaluation of these policies showed that this approach has been largely ineffective,[61] although, surprisingly, there was little mention of the need for appropriately conducted, culturally responsive, qualitative and other evidence-based research to inform the national strategy.

Even if one were to accept the narrow biomedical perspective, the implementation of the current policies is deficient. For example, the focus on condom use is continually undermined by inadequate condom supplies and the inability to obtain condoms owing to social constraints. Condom distribution has largely been focused in selected urban areas, not only ignoring the rest of urban Papua New Guinea, but also never reaching the majority who live in rural areas.[62] Condom distribution lacked consistency in all the communities in which we worked, and in most rural and remote communities it had never happened.

A national program, funded by the Global Fund since 2005, has focused on providing antiretroviral treatment to a limited number of HIV seropositive persons in specified provinces. This program has been difficult to implement, in part because of a lack of medical staff,[63] but also because of difficulties reaching seropositive patients owing to fear of stigmatization and rejection by communities,[64] which highlight the failure of public discourses about HIV/AIDS to address key cultural and psychological issues. An additional recent policy initiative has focused on social mapping reports from provinces to identify factors contributing to HIV transmission.[65] Though these reports are presented in qualitative terms, in reality they are no more than summaries of questionnaires that were undertaken with little or no active communication with the participants about the social factors shaping HIV transmission.

A fully participatory research strategy that engages communities in respectful dialogues about the key issues raised by the HIV epidemic and what can be done in response to them remains to be put in place beyond the kind of interventions characterized by the work of Elizabeth Reid. The focus on biomedical models of disease, narrowly defined quantitative research strategies, and instrumental social policies together with the lack of acknowledgment of cultural complexity and the need to involve communities actively in both the understanding of the problems and the generation of solutions has severely limited the kinds of responses used to formulate national policy in Papua New Guinea.[66]

Cultural Complexities beyond the Biomedical Model

There are substantial resources on which an expansion of the conceptual framework for both research and policy development could call. In many cases these resources have been developed in difficult circumstances, often with limited financial assistance or institutional support.[67] Beyond the challenges of scarce funding, there is the sheer complexity of the ethnic composition of mostly rural Papua New Guinea, where there are over eight hundred languages and more cultural groups.[68] Sexual practices, for example, can vary from highly permissive, as in the Trobriand Islands during certain seasons, to extremely repressive, as among the Huli in the Highlands.[69] Furthermore, sexuality in Papua New Guinea is commonly shaped by strict sexual avoidance taboos, thus making it difficult to speak publicly or openly about sex. In addition to cultural diversity, shifts in political economy have also affected regions in various ways, changing the meanings and ways that sexuality is enacted. To accommodate this complexity, social research must acknowledge and seek to account for the overlapping and sometimes contending roles of social, cultural, political, and economic processes.

Culture and Sexuality

Much of the research into culture and sexuality in Papua New Guinea has centered on the need to move away from the static constructions that have dominated much of Western social science research in this field and to recognize the

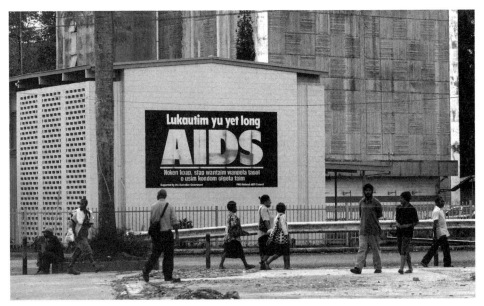

Awareness of HIV and AIDS is promoted predominantly through posters and signs both on the street and in public buildings. This poster is in the center of Lae, Morobe Province.

intertwining of shifting political economies and sexual cultures.[70] Bruce Knauft examines how tribal-traditional forms of ritualized homosexuality among the contemporary Gebusi were replaced by modern meanings of heterosexuality and masculinity, with shifting meanings attached to both local and modern Western discourses of sexuality.[71] He situates these shifting meanings within changes in the political economy, which include increased access to cash commodities and heightened desires for the trappings of the modern. He shows how, as a result, modern masculinity and "access" to women have become increasingly associated with Western-style clothing, popular music, and dance parties. These changing constructions of sexuality are typical across many communities in Papua New Guinea.[72]

Holly Wardlow examines local understandings of sexually transmitted infections among the Huli. She argues that culture must be understood as "mutable, strategic, often intimately tied to political economy," and that, as a result, people can often "deploy different logics about disease causality and that these logics can shape health-related behavior."[73] She examines the Huli people's shifting ways of understanding sexually transmitted infections not as biomedical constructs but as reflections of customary-tribal beliefs about heterosexual contact translated into a contemporary context characterized by rampant STIs. She writes how *gonolia*, the Huli term for sexually transmitted infections, is believed only to be contracted by men through contact with "passenger women"—women whose promiscuous behavior is considered undisciplined and amoral; that is, whose sexualities are outside sanctioned reproductive work and therefore polluting to others. It is believed that men cannot pass *gonolia* to women, as men's bodily fluids are not considered polluting. As a result, when Yerime, a faithful but barren wife, was biomedically diagnosed with having contracted an STI from her husband, Alembo, no one understood how this could be, because she had not committed any social transgressions and she could not get *gonolia* from her husband. In fact, the only way Yerime and her kin could make sense of it was to construct her contraction of *gonolia* from her husband in terms of a "malevolent and perverse desire on his part." Thus, sorcery and not the sexually transmitted infection or her husband's extramarital liaisons was seen as the cause of her infertility.

Wardlow's work raises a number of further issues that were confirmed in our fieldwork. Sexuality in tribal-traditional Papua New Guinea is commonly considered a social resource and in a sense a part of the clan, tribal, or community identity: that is, through the work of reproduction people establish and maintain bonds within their communities, ensuring the survival of that community. Accordingly, a woman's ability to reproduce is central to establishing her place in a community, and thus an infertile woman like Yerime is not held in high esteem in the community and can become marked as promiscuous. This is also confirmed by Jenny Hughes,[74] who consistently found that women were more concerned about their infertility than they were with knowing about or receiving treatment for their STIs, never making a cognitive connection between their STI and their consequent infertility. This failure to make a connection explains why it is not uncommon for both men and women to continue to have sexual relations despite knowing that they have a sexually transmitted disease.[75] Wardlow's study underscores how people in Papua New Guinea commonly understand health and illness in a manner that is independent of biomedical models of explanation.[76] It is often believed that HIV can be passed between bodies through touching, kissing, sharing things, or even sorcery.[77] Many married people consider themselves invulnerable to infection not only because of cultural beliefs, but also because the officially sponsored HIV/AIDS discourses promote marriage as a way to stay safe from HIV infection.[78] As Lawrence Hammar argues, the categories of husband, wife, boyfriend, and girlfriend are in fact insufficiently stable to rely upon in HIV prevention work.[79] His work on Daru, also confirmed by our discussions in various communities, revealed that a person could consider himself or herself married but not live with his or her partner, a husband living with his wife could in fact be paying his wife and other women for sex, and a brother or uncle could be selling his sister or niece to other men in exchange for money. Accordingly, a person's vulnerability to disease is determined by more than just the categories defined crudely within the official public health discourses.

Research in this area also raises a common conundrum within ABC models of prevention. Telling women to be faithful does not necessarily ensure their sexual health because it is not uncommon for husbands to have multiple partners outside of marriage. A national study found that 77 percent of women claimed that they knew or suspected that their husbands were having sex with other women.[80] What is more, multiple partnering by both men and women, married and unmarried, is generally a culturally accommodated yet hidden activity. Underlying this multipartnering is the common belief that conception cannot occur if one engages in brief sexual liaisons with numerous partners.[81] Increased outbound migration from villages by men in particular has created opportunities for sexual liaisons outside their communities.[82] This has created new opportunities for sexually transmitted infections to be exchanged and thereby brought back to the original communities.

Gender

Understanding gender relations in Papua New Guinea is integral to understanding why HIV could potentially reach epidemic levels. AIDS and STIs are evidence of sharp differences in power between men and women.[83] At the intersections of tribal relations (customary-based), traditional understandings (largely church-based), and modern practices (as, experienced for example, in the individualized citizenry of the postcolonial state), women tend to be ambiguously both respected and treated as subordinate. It is assumed that their sexual lives need to be overseen by male partners and relatives, for both customary (patriarchal) reasons and to satisfy contorted tribal-modern forms of ownership and trading. The subordination of women is compounded by their relatively poorer health and minimal access to a cash economy.[84] As a result, many of them have little power to control the timing, meaning, and implications of sexual intercourse. These gendered inequalities have made access to condoms by single and married women extremely difficult: in many cases, a woman who insists on condom use can be seen as promiscuous, leading to accusations, abandonment, and physical abuse.[85] In fact, people often view condoms as the cause of promiscuity. Even if a woman is able to negotiate condom use, most men and women do not understand how to use them properly, as a result of which they are unlikely to ensure safe sex. In addition, as illustrated in the notion of "passenger women," beliefs about female pollution often lead to blaming women as vectors of the epidemic, increasingly marginalizing their social status.[86] This is exacerbated by HIV/AIDS prevention discourses that focus on bodily fluids and that consistently place women at a higher risk for HIV infection.

Sexual Violence

The highly gender-differentiated relationships in Papua New Guinea often sanction sexual violence against women by men. Hospital visits by women have been strongly linked to treatment for sexual abuse.[87] Numerous studies have shown that rape and forced sex are common and normalized both within and outside of marriage.[88] The national study of sexuality showed that 55 percent of married women had been forced into sex by their husbands and that violence was used in one-third of these cases.[89] Often alcohol and marijuana use by men and women is associated with incidences of forced sex.[90] Rough sex can increase a woman's susceptibility of HIV infection in addition to other psychological, emotional, and physical health effects.[91] Worse, a raped woman becomes socially marked and fair game for future rapes.[92] Research has also brought attention to the violence involved in group sex, known as *lianup* or "single file," with numerous men having sex with one woman.[93] This not only heightens a woman's risk to HIV infection, but men are at risk of contracting HIV from the seminal fluids of other men either through the woman or by engaging in anal sex with another man during the incident. Overall, the research suggests that the issue of sexual violence has long historical underpinnings in Papua New Guinea and has been exacerbated by recent shifts in the nature of social and community life across Papua New Guinea. The chronic and continued normalization of sexual violence in Papua New Guinea presents one of the most difficult challenges of HIV/AIDS intervention efforts.[94]

Homosexuality, Heterosexuality, and Bisexuality

A multiplicity of forms of sexual contact are possible (vaginal-penile, anal-penile, oral-penile, oral-vaginal, and so forth) between bodies (male/male, female/female, or male/female), and increased access via modern means of communication to pornographic media, particularly by youth and men, has changed notions of how to engage in sexual intercourse.[95] As a result, anal and oral sex between men and women have become increasingly common throughout Papua New Guinea.[96] Furthermore, despite the decrease in ritualized customary homosexuality, other forms of male-male sexual relations have become more prevalent throughout Papua New Guinea. For example, because of economic constraints in urban areas, some young men offer sex to other men in exchange for money, though many of these men do not consider themselves homosexual. At the same time, there is also a growing use of the local term *geli-geli*—implicitly referring to the category of homoerotic heterosexuality.[97] Thus, the focus on heteroreproductive sex in dominant HIV/AIDS discourses does not address the differing ways of enacting sexuality, often leaving confusion and gaps in knowledge about modes of transmission.

Sexually Transmitted Infections

Sexually transmitted infections often act as cofactors in the increased transmission of HIV, as a result of which education and treatment of STIs is just as critical as any HIV/AIDS policy. STIs have remained at epidemic levels in Papua New Guinea since their introduction in the late nineteenth century with the arrival of colonialism.[98] In fact, the historical legacy of policies that often discriminated against people through systematic public humiliation and placing them in permanent quarantine continues through the current approaches to HIV/AIDS in Papua New Guinea.[99] This highlights the fact that the present epidemic must be understood in the historical context of previous experiences with sexually transmitted infections as well as of the broader medical system.

Compounding this historical legacy, practices associated with recent economic development in Papua New Guinea further exacerbate STI levels.[100] The increased development of mines, oil fields, logging camps, hydroelectric dams, and other major economic activities since 1975 have helped increase migration.[101] Consequently, new epidemics of STIs have been introduced into previously isolated areas.[102] For example, Hughes' ethnographic research of the Huli people shows how the development of the Highlands Highways near the Tari Basin increased mobility to and from the area and rapidly raised rates of STIs.[103] A clinical study of men and women in the Highlands showed a prevalence rate of 58 percent of one or more sexually transmitted infections.[104] Studies across Papua New Guinea have shown that sexually transmitted infections are an increasing problem among both rural and urban populations.[105] Most significant, few people are able to recognize the presence of an STI or understand their long-term effects, and most do not seek treatment even if they recognize that they have an infection. Moreover, many women do not have the social and economic means either to protect themselves against STIs or to seek treatment for themselves or their partners.

Sex Work

Sex work in Papua New Guinea is an ill-defined category. It does not correspond with assumptions of dominant discourses, which presume that sex workers are driven by economic necessity and operate within an organized industry.[106] Sometimes economic survival is a factor, as we found in our studies in Kananam (see Chapter 4). However, Holly Wardlow's work in rural Papua New Guinea shows how difficult it is to transfer this term to the local context of Huli passenger women.[107] She argues that these women do not engage in transactional sex because of economic need but as a way to protest against traditional social structures they feel have failed them: that is, through their social transgressions they enact a form of resistance to the increased focus on cash and the devaluation of women within the bride-wealth system. In this sense, they assert their agency to control their own sexuality and economic value without identifying as sex workers. In her studies Wardlow shows how these illicit sexual liaisons did not occur at brothels, through pimps, or in areas where women congregate to sell sex but were typically arranged through singing parties at now illegal customary courting parties that men previously attended to select their wives. In addition, she argues that men often engage in illicit liaisons with passenger women to resist changes brought about by shifts in the political economy, particularly the state's focus on controlling their sexuality. In contrast to Wardlow, Lawrence Hammar's work in the more urban areas of Daru Island in Western Province suggests that women's engagement in transactional sex may result from a lack of opportunities in a cash economy and, hence, from economic need.[108] Women who transact sex may do so under varying circumstances, such as being forced into sex work by a relative or networking on their own. Despite the differences between them, both authors agree that changes in the political economy have increased gender inequalities and commodified women's sexuality.[109] In effect, differences in history and geography—and the ways in which these developments have occurred—have generated different meanings and ways to negotiate sexual transactions.

Church

Sexual cultures in Papua New Guinea have also been shaped by the powerful presence of the church. In contemporary Papua New Guinea almost all individuals belong to a particular church denomination. Beyond religious services, churches provide an important means of communication between community members as well as more than half of the country's education and health services.[110] They therefore have a pivotal role to play in HIV/AIDS prevention. Yet many churches oppose the promotion of condoms and make "moral" claims against those who are afflicted with HIV/AIDS.[111] For example, Richard Eves writes how the Lelet community of New Ireland interprets, represents, and understands HIV/AIDS through Christian apocalyptic beliefs.[112] Underlying these cultural and religious discourses is a traditionalist view that transgression leads to illness and that HIV/AIDS is therefore a punishment for immoral behavior. As a result of such beliefs, in many areas of Papua New Guinea condoms are associated with shame and are increasingly difficult to obtain, particularly by youth.[113]

Charles Wilde examines how Gogodola men believe their allegiance to Christianity will save them from HIV/AIDS despite their acknowledged promiscuity.[114] This highlights the cognitive dissonance between HIV/AIDS messages and people's perceptions of their risk. Researching in the Finisterre Range of rural Papua New Guinea, Keck argues that understandings of HIV/AIDS must be contextualized within a dialogue that brings together *kastam* and the local church.[115] Similarly, Vicki Luker argues that churches must not be seen as obstacles to HIV/AIDS prevention but must be engaged with as a means to bridge the existing divide between communities and government services.[116]

Conclusion

This chapter has challenged the narrower versions of the biomedical model that underpins much of the prevailing HIV research and policy making in Papua New Guinea. We have questioned the limited conception of HIV/AIDS generated by these perspectives and has emphasized the need to take into account the diverse cultural, political, and economic factors that have shaped its development. We have also pointed out how these dominant conceptual frameworks have drawn on and taken for granted constructs of disease, sexuality, and behavior developed outside Papua New Guinea. These assumptions have led to rigid categories for mapping the effects and the spread of the infection, which often bear little relationship to the personal and social realities they are supposed to reflect.[117] Simplistic approaches at the local level are usually perpetuated at the level of national policy. Here too, cultural stereotypes and models derived in other settings have been doggedly applied, "no matter how ill the fit."[118] The most egregious example has been the reliance on the ABC approach to prevention despite its manifest lack of efficacy in any cultural setting, even in the West.

This chapter has also reflected critically on the kinds of data on which these flawed constructions of HIV/AIDS have relied. We have argued that the deficiency lies not merely in the conclusions, but also in the processes of gathering the information and composing the theories. Research into HIV in Papua New Guinea and elsewhere has focused on the collection of statistical and survey data on the basis of foreign, culturally specific categories and has often declined to engage communities in open participatory dialogues. The data generated on the basis of these categories have proven often to be misleading, and their uncertainties and biases are often ignored. In the limited cases where reliable ethnographic research data were available in relation to issues such as gender or sexual networking, these have gone largely unused by politicians, policy makers, physicians, politicians, and public health officials.[119] Like other research that has involved genuine engagement with individuals within their communities and cultural contexts, this ethnographic data has often drawn attention to the importance of understanding the complex social processes that shape personal relationships. If we are to understand and to respond effectively to Papua New Guinea's HIV epidemic, the basic concepts that are applied will need to reflect the changing boundaries of culture, gender relations, history, political economy, religion, and local beliefs about health and illness. We will need to understand how people actually talk about HIV/AIDS, imagine the disease, and experience it in different ways.[120]

Papua New Guinea presents a major challenge to researchers, practitioners, and policy makers to develop interventions that respond flexibly to changing contexts. Creative community-based approaches to developing an understanding of HIV/AIDS and fashioning responses that take into account the complexities of the lifeworlds of local communities offer an alternative perspective that ultimately may reflect more closely the needs and capacities of the people. Such endeavors not only would have to understand how social processes are shaping each community, but would also need to use an integrative and participatory approach to developing context-specific and realistic models for prevention. Projects designed along these lines would need to be able to evolve alongside changing political, cultural, and economic circumstances. They would involve ongoing efforts to ask questions and build on knowledge about how gender, sexual relations, political economy, and other issues create vulnerability to disease in a given context. These issues are still not well understood in the context of HIV/AIDS but could be better understood through more qualitative research, theoretical debate, evidence-based interventions, and community-based action.

Effective prevention strategies would require practical improvements, including greater access to and quality of basic social services, such as health care, schooling, HIV/AIDS education, sexual and reproductive health education, and economic opportunities. The strong relations with faith-based and community organizations developed in recent years and the growing emphasis on prevention through information, education, and communication supported by the NACS need to be extended, along with improved communication and collaboration between the National Department of Health, the NACS, and other institutions. Broader collaboration would involve the more challenging goal of integrating government AIDS policy with discussions in communities about how they want to approach the issue. It is such partnerships that will create spaces for individuals and groups within communities to begin openly communicating about their sexual practices. Most of all, there is a need to empower communities using their own languages and cultural logic and in ways that allow both men and women sufficient autonomy to negotiate the nature of sexual relationships. This will by no means be an easy task because no simple solutions are available.

Many of the issues outlined in this chapter lie at the heart of the model of community learning centers described in the next chapters of this book and are consistent with the outcomes of the UNESCO workshops on integrating HIV learning into community learning center activities.[121] In relation to HIV/AIDS, this proposed community-engaged model, drawing further on the experience of the 2007 PNG Sustainable Development workshops, is intended as a step in the direction of a more responsive approach to disease prevention that is embedded in the local cultural circumstances of different communities. Given the complex issues outlined in this chapter, it would be overly optimistic to anticipate any model serving as a singular solution to the HIV epidemic. Rather, the community learning center model is anticipated to produce practical outcomes that vary in the different local settings in which it is applied. In other words, the roles, activities, and focuses of different community learning centers established in different communities would need to adapt to locally identified areas of need. The common thread, however, will be a focus on bringing together different sections of the community with the aim of exchanging knowledge in ways that produce creative, evolving, and culturally appropriate responses.

Notes

1. Clement Malau, Michael O'Leary, Carol Jenkins, and Nicholas Faraclas, "HIV/AIDS Prevention and Control Programme in Papua New Guinea: The Experience of a Country with Low Prevalence but Potential for Transmission," *AIDS,* vol. 8, supplement 2, 1994, pp. S117–S124. AIDS is the acronym for acquired immunodeficiency syndrome. In 1987 the National Department of Health developed its first national policy document on HIV/AIDS control focusing on diagnosis, prevention, and care. These initial plans spanned 1987–1995 and saw the development of the Short-Term and Medium-Term Plans, both of which relied heavily on biomedical frameworks for prevention. These early policies were rather ineffective largely owing to a lack of political support for a serious national HIV/AIDS prevention campaign. See Clement Malau, "The Evolving AIDS Epidemic: Challenges and Responses in Papua New Guinea," *Development Bulletin,* vol. 50, 1999, pp. 70–71; and Carol Jenkins, "AIDS in Papua New Guinea," *Papua New Guinea Medical Journal,* vol. 39, 1996, pp. 164–165.

2. According to UNAIDS definitions. United Nations AIDS and World Health Organization, "Guidelines for Second Generation HIV Surveillance Working Group on Global HIV/AIDS and STI Surveillance," United Nations AIDS and World Health Organization, Geneva, 2000; Australian Agency for International Development (AusAID), "Potential Economic Impacts of an HIV/AIDS Epidemic in Papua New Guinea," Australian Agency for International Development, Canberra, 2002; John C. Caldwell and Geetha Isaac-Toua, "AIDS in Papua New Guinea: Situation in the Pacific," *Journal of Health, Population, and Nutrition,* vol. 20, no. 2, 2002, pp. 104–111; M. Howe, "Papua New Guinea Faces HIV Epidemic," *Lancet Infectious Diseases,* vol. 2, no. 7, 2002, p. 386.

3. AusAID, *Evaluation of the PNG National HIV/AIDS Support Project,* Evaluation and Review Series, no. 38, Australian Agency for International Development, Canberra, 2006.

4. National AIDS Council Secretariat and Partners, *UNGASS 2008, Country Progress Report*, NACS, Port Moresby, 2008, p. 11. However, in the 2010 UNGASS report this was not expressed so adamantly.

5. Detailed anthropological studies and community engagements have had little effect on policy. For a sense of the range of such studies, see, for example, Leslie Butt and Richard Eves, eds., *Making Sense of AIDS: Culture, Sexuality, and Power in Melanesia*, University of Hawai'i Press, Honolulu, 2008.

6. Carol Jenkins, *Youth in Danger: AIDS and STDs among Young People in Papua New Guinea*, PNG Institute of Medical Research and United Nations Population Fund, Port Moresby, 1997; Carol Jenkins and the National Sex and Reproduction Research Team, *Women and the Risk of AIDS in Papua New Guinea*, Women and AIDS Research Program, Papua New Guinea Institute of Medical Research, Goroka, Papua New Guinea, 1993.

7. John C. Caldwell, "AIDS in Melanesia," in AusAID, *It's Everyone's Problem: HIV/AIDS and Development in Asia and the Pacific*, Australian Agency for International Development, Canberra, 2000.

8. Lawrence J. Hammar, "Fear and Loathing in Papua New Guinea: Sexual Health in a Nation under Siege," in Butt and Eves, eds., *Making Sense of AIDS*.

9. Dennis Altman, *Global Sex*, Allen and Unwin, Sydney, 2001.

10. In an article with which we otherwise have much sympathy, Lawrence Hammar ("Epilogue: Homegrown in PNG: Rural Responses to HIV and AIDS," *Oceania*, no. 77, 2007, pp. 72–94) is scathing about tribal remedies for HIV.

11. David Stephens and Katherine Lepani, "Evaluation of the IMR Transex Project: Port Moresby, Lae and Goroka," unpublished report for AusAID, 1998.

12. AusAID, *Evaluation of the PNG National HIV/AIDS Support Project*.

13. For an example see Tim O'Connor, "HIV/AIDS and Australia's International Approach," AID/Watch, Erskineville, 2004. More recently, there have been some signs of reconsideration of this emphasis.

14. Papua New Guinea Sustainable Development Program and Save the Children, *Learning Workshops on Strengthening Community engagement with the HIV Epidemic and Its Driving Forces*, Papua New Guinea Sustainable Development Program and Save the Children, 2007. On a human rights approach see Elizabeth Reid, "Putting Values into Practice in PNG: The Poro Sapot Project and Aid Effectiveness," *eJournal of the Australian Association for the Advancement of Pacific Studies*, nos. 1.2 and 2.1, 2010.

15. In Papua New Guinea, HIV is only believed to be transmitted through sexual relations and from mother to baby. Infection by intravenous drug use is not generally considered an issue in Papua New Guinea at the present. This chapter will focus mostly on the sexual transmission of HIV in Papua New Guinea, as it is the most common way that HIV is believed to be infecting the general population.

16. The term used for a sexually acquired infection has shifted since biomedicine

first identified such diseases. Beginning with the earliest term, these include "venereal disease" (VD), "sexually transmitted disease" (STD), and the now-accepted term, "sexually transmitted infection" (STI). In addition, "reproductive tract infection" (RTI) is now used to identify infections not acquired through sexual intercourse.

17. Lawrence Hammar, "4,275 and Counting: Telling Stories about STDs on Daru," *Papua New Guinea Medical Journal*, vol. 47, nos. 1–2, 2004, pp. 88–113.

18. A. Seaton et al., "Clinical Manifestations of HIV Infection in Melanesian Adults," *Papua New Guinea Medical Journal*, vol. 39, 1996, pp. 181–182.

19. Carole Vance, "Anthropology Rediscovers Sexuality: A Theoretical Comment," in Richard Parker and Peter Aggleton, eds., *Culture, Society and Sexuality: A Reader*, UCL Press, Philadelphia, 1999.

20. Richard Parker and John Gagnon, *Conceiving Sexuality: Approaches to Sex Research in a Postmodern World*, Routledge, New York, 1995; Lincoln Chen, Jaime Sepulveda Amor, and Sheldon Segal, *AIDS and Women's Reproductive Health*, Plenum Press, New York, 1991; Gary Dowsett, "Some Considerations on Sexuality and Gender in the Context of AIDS," *Reproductive Health Matters*, vol. 11, no. 22, 2003, pp. 21–29.

21. Robert A. Padgug, "Sexual Matters: On Conceptualizing Sexuality in History," in Parker and Aggleton, *Culture, Society and Sexuality*.

22. Pat Caplan, *Risk Revisited*, Pluto Press, London, 2000.

23. Heterosexual intercourse is often conflated with reproductive sex—that is, between penis and vagina. This may have to do with the historical focus in the Global South on reproduction issues. See Chen, Amor, and Segal, *AIDS and Women's Reproductive Health*; Gary Dowsett, "Some Considerations on Sexuality and Gender in the Context of AIDS." For a discussion of this in Papua New Guinea, see also Vicki Luker, "Gender, Women and Mothers: HIV/AIDS in the Pacific," Australian National University, Canberra, 2001.

24. M. H. Becker, "The Health Belief Model and Personal Health Behavior," *Health Education Monographs*, vol. 2, 1974, pp. 324–508.

25. Caplan, *Risk Revisited*; Chen, Amor, and Segal, *AIDS and Women's Reproductive Health*; John Cleland and Benoit Ferry, *Sexual Behavior and AIDS in the Developing World*, Taylor and Francis, London, 1995.

26. United Nations AIDS and World Health Organization, "Initiating Second Generation Surveillance Systems: Practical Guidelines," Working Group on Global HIV/AIDS/STI Surveillance, United Nations AIDS, Geneva, 2002.

27. Fiona E. Greig and Cheryl Koopman, "Multilevel Analysis of Women's Empowerment and HIV Prevention: Quantitative Survey Results from a Preliminary Study in Botswana," *AIDS and Behavior*, vol. 7, no. 2, 2003, pp. 195–208; E. Lagarde et al., "Educational Level is Associated with Condom Use within Non-Spousal Partnerships in Four Cities in Sub-Saharan Africa," *AIDS*, vol. 15, no. 11, 2001, pp. 1399–1408.

28. C. Airhihenbuwa and R. Obregon, "A Critical Assessment of Theories/Models

Used in Health Communications for HIV/AIDS," *Journal of Health Communication*, vol. 5, supplement, 2000, pp. 5–10.

29. Stephen McNally, "Linking HIV/AIDS to Development," *Development Bulletin*, vol. 52, 2000, pp. 9–11.

30. Carol Jenkins, "Situation Analysis of HIV/AIDS in Papua New Guinea September, 2002," unpublished report, 2002; Malau, O'Leary, Jenkins, and Faraclas, "HIV/AIDS Prevention and Control Programme in Papua New Guinea."

31. Testing women at antenatal clinics also overlooks the fact that women with recurrent or untreated STIs are often infertile. In addition, these women are often reluctant to go to STI clinics for social, cultural, and economic reasons. Thus, both antenatal clinics and STI clinics are not necessarily testing a representative sample of women in rural and urban areas.

32. National AIDS Council Secretariat and Partners, *UNGASS 2008, Country Progress Report*, p. 19.

33. Malau, O'Leary, Jenkins, and Faraclas, "HIV/AIDS Prevention and Control Programme in Papua New Guinea."

34. Jenkins, "Situation Analysis of HIV/AIDS in Papua New Guinea."

35. Diro Babona, George Slama, and Elliot Puiahi, "Laboratory Diagnosis of HIV Infection in Papua New Guinea," *Papua New Guinea Medical Journal*, vol. 39, 1996, pp. 200–204.

36. For example, clinicians at the local hospital on Misima Island in Milne Bay Province indicated that there were eight initially confirmed HIV seropositive cases in 2004 that had never been confirmed by the National Reference Library, which meant that these people were never informed that they most likely were HIV seropositive. See Fouladi, "AIDS Narratives and Sexual Cultures in Tubetube, Papua New Guinea."

37. Caldwell and Isaac-Toua, "AIDS in Papua New Guinea."

38. National AIDS Council Secretariat and Department of Health, "HIV/AIDS Quarterly Report, March 2002," National AIDS Council Secretariat and Department of Health, Boroko, 2002.

39. National AIDS Council Secretariat and Partners, *UNGASS 2008, Country Progress Report*, p. 21.

40. Hammar, "4,275 and Counting."

41. Ibid., p. 56.

42. National AIDS Council Secretariat and Partners, *UNGASS 2008, Country Progress Report*, p. 22.

43. Fouladi, "AIDS Narratives and Sexual Cultures in Tubetube."

44. Verena Keck, "Knowledge, Morality and 'Kastom': SikAIDS among Young Yupno People, Finisterre Range, Papua New Guinea," *Oceania*, vol. 77, no. 1, 2007, pp. 43–57.

45. Asian Development Bank, *Proposed Asian Development Fund Grant Papua New*

Guinea: HIV/AIDS Prevention and Control in Rural Development Enclaves Project, ADB, 2006.

46. AusAID, *Evaluation of the PNG National HIV/AIDS Support Project.*

47. Personal communication with Kal Indistange, a former employee at NACS.

48. Asian Development Bank, *Proposed Asian Development Fund Grant Papua New Guinea.*

49. AusAID, *Evaluation of the PNG National HIV/AIDS Support Project;* United Nations AIDS, AusAID and National AIDS Council of Papua New Guinea, *HIV/AIDS Stakeholder Mapping in Papua New Guinea,* United Nations AIDS, Australian Agency for International Development, and National AIDS Council of Papua New Guinea, 2004.

50. Vicki Luker, "Civil Society, Social Capital and the Churches: HIV/AIDS in Papua New Guinea," paper delivered at the Governance in Pacific States Development Research Symposium, 30 September–2 October, 2003, University of the South Pacific, Suva, Fiji, http://classshares.student.usp.ac.fj/, accessed 28 December 2008.

51. Lawrence Hammar, "Sexual Health, Sexual Networking and AIDS in Papua New Guinea and West Papua," *Papua New Guinea Medical Journal,* vol. 47, nos. 1–2, 2004, p. 8.

52. Trevor Cullen, "HIV/AIDS in Papua New Guinea: A Reality Check," *Pacific Journalism Review,* vol. 12, no. 1, 2006, p. 156.

53. See United Nations AIDS and World Health Organization, "Guidelines for Second Generation HIV Surveillance Working Group on Global HIV/AIDS and STI Surveillance," p. 24.

54. R. Fiti-Sinclair, "Female Prostitutes in Port Moresby, Papua New Guinea: STDs and HIV/AIDS Knowledge, Attitudes, Beliefs and Practices," in Mary Spongberg, Jan Larbalestier, and Margaret Winn, eds., *Women Sexuality Culture: Cross Cultural Perspectives on Sexuality,* Women's Studies Centre, Sydney, 1996; Janet Gareet et al., "High Prevalence of Sexually Transmitted Infections among Female Sex Workers in the Eastern Highlands Province of Papua New Guinea: Correlates and Recommendations," *Sexually Transmitted Diseases,* vol. 32, no. 8, 2005, pp. 466–473; Carol Jenkins, *Behavioural Risk Assessment for HIV/AIDS among Workers in the Transport Industry, PNG,* final report to AIDSCAP/FHI, Bangkok, 1994; Charles Mgone et al., "Human Immunodeficiency Virus and Other Sexually Transmitted Infections among Female Sex Workers in Two Major Cities in Papua New Guinea," *Sexually Transmitted Diseases,* vol. 29, no. 5, 2002, pp. 265–270.

55. For an evaluation of the project, see Stephens and Lepani, "Evaluation of the IMR Transex Project." Also, for a comparative review of the project, see Carol Jenkins, *Female Sex Worker HIV Prevention Projects: Lessons Learnt from Papua New Guinea, India, and Bangladesh,* UNAIDS, Geneva, 2000.

56. See the many examples in the bibliography of this volume.

57. Fiti-Sinclair, "Female Prostitutes in Port Moresby, Papua New Guinea"; H. Friesen et al., "Assessment of HIV/AIDS Knowledge, Attitudes and Behaviour of High School Students in Papua New Guinea," *Papua New Guinea Medical Journal*, vol. 39, 1996, pp. 208–213; National Research Institute, *Evaluation of the Impact and Effectiveness of the PNG HIV/AIDS Awareness Program in Selected Secondary Schools and High Schools in the National Capital District*, National Research Institute, Port Moresby, 2004.

58. AusAID, *Impacts of HIV/AIDS 2005–2025 in Papua New Guinea, Indonesia and East Timor: Final Report of HIV Epidemiological Modeling and Impact Study*, AusAID, Canberra, 2006; AusAID, *Potential Economic Impacts of an HIV/AIDS Epidemic in Papua New Guinea*, AusAID, Canberra, 2002.

59. AusAID, *Potential Economic Impacts of an HIV/AIDS Epidemic in Papua New Guinea*.

60. National AIDS Council Secretariat, *Papua New Guinea National HIV/AIDS Medium Term Plan*, National AIDS Council Secretariat, Port Moresby, 2002.

61. AusAID, *Evaluation of the PNG National HIV/AIDS Support Project*.

62. Asian Development Bank, *Proposed Asian Development Fund Grant Papua New Guinea*.

63. National AIDS Council, *Situational Analysis for Strategic Planning at District Level: Milne Bay Province, Social Mapping Project*, National HIV/AIDS Support Project, National AIDS Council, Papua New Guinea, 2005.

64. Fouladi, "AIDS Narratives and Sexual Cultures in Tubetube."

65. National AIDS Council, *Situational Analysis for Strategic Planning at District Level*.

66. Malau and Crockett, "HIV and Development the Papua New Guinea Way."

67. See Hammar, "Sexual Health, Sexual Networking and AIDS in Papua New Guinea and West Papua," p. 1.

68. Malau and Crockett, "HIV and Development the Papua New Guinea Way."

69. Carol Jenkins, *HIV/AIDS, Culture, and Sexuality in Papua New Guinea*, Asian Development Bank, Manila, 2006.

70. The concept of sexual cultures refers to "a set of symbolic meanings and practices that regulate sexual conduct." See Gilbert Herdt, "Stigma and the Ethnographic Study of HIV: Problems and Prospects," *AIDS and Behavior*, vol. 5, no. 2, 2001, pp. 141–149. For discussion of political economy, culture, and sexuality, see the following: B. de Zalduondo and J. Bernard, "Meanings and Consequences of Sexual-Economic Exchange," in Parker and Gagnon, *Conceiving Sexuality*; Paul Farmer, *AIDS and Accusation: Haiti and the Geography of Blame*, University of California Press, Berkeley, 1992; Phillip Setel, *A Plague of Paradoxes: AIDS, Culture and Demography in Northern Tanzania*, University of Chicago Press, Chicago, 1999; Patricia Symonds, "Political Economy and Cultural Logics of HIV/AIDS among the Hmong in Northern Thailand," in Merrill Singer, ed., *The Political Economy of AIDS*, Baywood, Amityville, 1998.

71. Bruce M. Knauft, *Whatever Happened to Ritual Homosexuality? The Incitement of Modern Sexual Subjects in Melanesia and Elsewhere*, International Association for the Study of Sexuality, Culture and Society, Melbourne, 2001.

72. Fouladi, "AIDS Narratives and Sexual Cultures in Tubetube"; Carol Jenkins and Michael Alpers, "Urbanization, Youth and Sexuality: Insights for an AIDS Campaign for Youth in Papua New Guinea," *Papua New Guinea Medical Journal*, vol. 39, 1996, pp. 248–251.

73. Holly Wardlow, "Giving Birth to Gonolia: 'Culture' and Sexually Transmitted Disease among the Huli of Papua New Guinea," *Medical Anthropology Quarterly*, vol. 16, no. 2, 2002, p. 154.

74. Jenny Hughes, "Impurity and Danger: The Need for New Barriers and Bridges in the Prevention of Sexually-Transmitted Disease in the Tari Basin, Papua New Guinea," *Health Transition Review*, vol. 1, no. 2, 1991, pp. 131–140; Jenny Hughes, "Sexually Transmitted Infections: A Medical Anthropological Study from the Tari Research Unit 1990–1991," *Papua New Guinea Medical Journal*, vol. 45, nos. 1–2, 2002, pp. 128–133.

75. Hammar, "AIDS, STDs, and Sex Work in Papua New Guinea"; Carol Jenkins and the National Sex and Reproduction Research Team, *National Study of Sexual and Reproductive Knowledge and Behaviour in Papua New Guinea*, Papua New Guinea Institute of Medical Research Monograph no. 10, Papua New Guinea Institute of Medical Research, Goroka, 1994.

76. In another similar example, Lepani discusses how HIV/AIDS has been understood through the customary disease of *sovasova* on the Trobriands. Katherine Lepani, "Sovasova and the Problem of Sameness: Converging Interpretive Frameworks for Making Sense of HIV and AIDS in the Trobriands," *Oceania*, vol. 77, no. 1, 2007, pp. 12–28.

77. For discussion about beliefs regarding HIV transmission through touching or sharing, see Alison Dundon and Charles Wilde, "Introduction: HIV and AIDS in Rural Papua New Guinea," *Oceania*, vol. 77, no. 1, 2007, pp. 1–11; Fouladi, "AIDS Narratives and Sexual Cultures in Tubetube." On transmission through sorcery see, for example, Hammar, "AIDS, STDs, and Sex Work in Papua New Guinea," in Laura Zimmer-Tamakoshi, ed., *Modern Papua New Guinea*, Thomas Jefferson University Press, Kirksville, Missouri, 1998.

78. Fouladi, "AIDS Narratives and Sexual Cultures in Tubetube."

79. Lawrence Hammar, "Bad Canoes and Buffalo: The Political Economy of Sex on Daru Island, Western Province, Papua New Guinea," in T. Foster, C. Siegel, and E. Barry, eds., *Genders 23: Bodies of Writing, Bodies of Performance*, New York University Press, New York, 1996, p. 214.

80. Jenkins and the National Sex and Reproduction Research Team, *National Study of Sexual and Reproductive Knowledge and Behaviour in Papua New Guinea*.

81. Ibid.

82. Hammar, "Bad Canoes and Buffalo"; Jenny Hughes, "Sexually Transmitted"; Holly Wardlow, *Wayward Women: Sexuality and Agency in a New Guinea Society,* University of California Press, Berkeley, 2006.

83. Hammar, "AIDS, STDs, and Sex Work in Papua New Guinea."

84. Maria Kopkop, "The Status of Women in Papua New Guinea," in Tukutau Taufa and Caroline Bass, eds., *Population Family Health and Development,* University of Papua New Guinea Press, Port Moresby, 1993; Martha Macintyre, "The Persistance of Inequality," in Zimmer-Tamakoshi, *Modern Papua New Guinea.*

85. Fouladi, "AIDS Narratives and Sexual Cultures in Tubetube"; Hammar, "AIDS, STDs, and Sex Work in Papua New Guinea"; Lori Heise and Christopher Elias, "Transforming AIDS Prevention to Meet Women's Needs: A Focus on Developing Countries," *Social Science and Medicine,* vol. 40, no. 7, 1995, pp. 931–943.

86. Hammar, "AIDS, STDs, and Sex Work in Papua New Guinea."

87. Anou Borrey, "Sexual Violence in Perspective: The Case of Papua New Guinea," in S. Dinnen and A. Ley, eds., *Reflections on Violence in Melanesia,* Hawkins and Asia Pacific Press, Sydney, 2000.

88. Cyndi Banks, "Contextualizing Sexual Violence: Rape and Carnal Knowledge in Papua New Guinea," in S. Dinnen and A. Ley, eds., *Reflections on Violence in Melanesia;* Anou Borrey and B. Kombako, *The Reality of Sexual Violence in Papua New Guinea,* National Research Institute, Port Moresby, 1997.

89. Carol Jenkins and the National Sex and Reproduction Research Team, *National Study of Sexual and Reproductive Knowledge and Behaviour in Papua New Guinea.*

90. Banks, "Contextualizing Sexual Violence"; Leslie Butt, Jenny Munro, and Joanna Wong, "Border Testimonials: Patterns of AIDS Awareness across the Island of New Guinea," *Papua New Guinea Medical Journal,* vol. 47, nos. 1–2, 2004, pp. 65–76; Carol Jenkins, "The Homosexual Context of Heterosexual Practice in Papua New Guinea," in Peter Aggleton, ed., *Bisexualities and AIDS, International Perspectives,* Taylor and Francis, London, 1996.

91. J. C. Campbell, "Health Consequences of Intimate Partner Violence," *The Lancet,* vol. 359, 2002, pp. 1331–1336.

92. Carol Jenkins and the National Sex and Reproduction Research Team, *National Study of Sexual and Reproductive Knowledge and Behaviour in Papua New Guinea.*

93. Jenkins, "The Homosexual Context of Heterosexual Practice in Papua New Guinea."

94. The only national response to sexual violence occurred under the Transex Project, where police were targeted as the main perpetrators of sexual violence toward sex workers. The project resulted in minimal changes in men's behaviors. See Carol Jenkins, *Female Sex Worker HIV Prevention Projects: Lessons Learnt From Papua New Guinea, India, and Bangladesh,* UNAIDS, Geneva, 2000.

95. Fouladi, "AIDS Narratives and Sexual Cultures in Tubetube;" Jenkins and

Alpers, "Urbanization, Youth and Sexuality"; Holly Wardlow, *"Free Food, Free Food!": "Traditional" Rituals of "Modern" Manhood among the Huli of Papua New Guinea*, International Association for the Study of Sexuality, Culture and Society, Melbourne, 2001.

96. Carol Jenkins and the National Sex and Reproduction Research Team, *National Study of Sexual and Reproductive Knowledge and Behaviour in Papua New Guinea*.

97. Jenkins, "The Homosexual Context of Heterosexual Practice in Papua New Guinea."

98. Jenny Hughes, "A History of Sexually Transmitted Diseases in Papua New Guinea," in M. Lewis, S. Bamber, and M. Waugh, eds., *Sex, Disease and Society: A Comparative History of Sexually Transmitted Diseases and HIV/AIDS in Asia and the Pacific*, Greenwood Press, Westport, Connecticut, 1997.

99. Fouladi, "AIDS Narratives and Sexual Cultures in Tubetube"; Ian Riley, "Lessons from Sexually Transmitted Disease Epidemics," in AusAID, *It's Everyone's Problem: HIV/AIDS and Development in Asia and the Pacific*, AusAID, Canberra, 2000.

100. Similar to HIV/AIDS surveillance, monitoring STI rates in Papua New Guinea nationally is also a problematic endeavor. See Steven Tiwara et al., "High Prevalence of Trichomonal Vaginitis and Chlamydial Cervicitis among a Rural Population in the Highlands of Papua New Guinea," *Papua New Guinea Medical Journal*, vol. 39, 1996, pp. 234–238. For discussion of the most common STIs in Papua New Guinea today, see Hammar, "AIDS, STDs, and Sex Work in Papua New Guinea."

101. Migration patterns and increased mobility are considered to be critical factors in the spread of HIV infection across the developing world. There has been particular focus on sex workers, transport workers, and miners. For Papua New Guinea see Koczberski, "The Sociocultural and Economic Context of HIV/AIDS in Papua New Guinea." For international literature see the following: J. Decosas, F. Kane, J. Anarfi, K. Sodii, and H. Wagner, "Migration and AIDS," *The Lancet*, no. 346, 1995, pp. 826–828; Paul Farmer, *AIDS and Accusation;* K. Jochelson, M. Mothibeli, and J. Leger, "Human Immunodeficiency Virus and Migrant Labor in South Africa," in N. Krieger and M. Glenn, *AIDS: The Politics of Survival*, Baywood Publishing Co., Amityville, NY, 1994.

102. Jenkins, "Situation Analysis of HIV/AIDS in Papua New Guinea."

103. Jenny Hughes, "Impurity and Danger"; Jenny Hughes, "Sexually Transmitted Infections"; J. Clark and Jenny Hughes, "A History of Sexuality and Gender in Tari."

104. Tiwara et al., "High Prevalence of Trichomonal Vaginitis and Chlamydial Cervicitis."

105. Madeline Lemeki, Megan Passey, and Philip Setel, "Ethnographic Results of a Community STD Study in the Eastern Highlands Province," *Papua New Guinea Medical Journal*, vol. 39, 1996, pp. 239–242, Sebeya Lupiwa, Nathan Suve, Karen Horton, and Megan Passey, "Knowledge about Sexually Transmitted Diseases in Rural and Periurban Communities of the Asaro Valley of Eastern Highlands Province: The Health Education Component of an STD Study," *Papua New Guinea Medical Journal*,

vol. 39, 1996, pp. 243–247; Megan Passey et al., "Community Based Study of Sexually Transmitted Diseases in Rural Women in the Highlands of Papua New Guinea: Prevalence and Risk Factors," *Sexually Transmitted Infections*, vol. 74, 1998, pp. 120–127; B. Suligoi et al., "Infection with Human Immunodeficiency Virus, Herpes Simplex Virus Type 2, and Human Herpes Virus 8 in Remote Villages of Southwestern Papua New Guinea," *American Journal of Tropical Medical Hygiene*, vol. 72, no. 1, 2005, pp. 33–36.

106. The sex trade in Papua New Guinea varies both within and between urban and rural areas. For example, in urban areas women who work in the sex trade often depend on the sale of sex for income. These women may be single, married, or divorced. However, in rural areas women can expect to be paid for sex, accept cash to be nice, or accept gifts such as beer, food, and clothes. In addition, these exchanges can occur with boyfriends or within casual sexual encounters. See Jenkins, *HIV/AIDS, Culture, and Sexuality in Papua New Guinea.*

107. Holly Wardlow, *"Prostitution," "Sexwork," and "Passenger Women": When Sexualities Don't Correspond to Stereotypes,* International Association for the Study of Sexuality, Culture and Society, Melbourne, 2001; Holly Wardlow, "Passenger-Women: Changing Gender Relations in the Tari Basin," *PNG Medical Journal*, vol. 45, nos. 1–2, 2002, pp. 142–146; Holly Wardlow, "Anger, Economy, and Female Agency: Problematizing 'Prostitution' and 'Sex Work' among the Huli of Papua New Guinea," *Signs: Journal of Women in Culture and Society*, vol. 29, no. 4, 2004, pp. 1017–1040; Holly Wardlow, *Wayward Women: Sexuality and Agency in a New Guinea Society,* University of California Press, Berkeley, 2006.

108. Hammar, "Bad Canoes and Buffalo"; Lawrence Hammar, "Sex and Political Economy in the South Fly: Daru Island, Western Province, Papua New Guinea," Ph.D. dissertation, City University of New York, 1996.

109. For another similar example see J. Clark, "Gold, Sex, and Pollution: Male Illness and Myth at Mt. Kare, Papua New Guinea," *American Ethnologist*, vol. 20, no. 4, 1993, pp. 742–757.

110. Luker, "Civil Society, Social Capital and the Churches: HIV/AIDS in Papua New Guinea."

111. Dundon and Wilde, "Introduction: HIV and AIDS in Rural Papua New Guinea"; National AIDS Council, *Situational Analysis for Strategic Planning at the District Level: Southern Highlands Province, Social Mapping Project.*

112. Richard Eves, "AIDS and Apocalypticism: Interpretations of the Epidemic from Papua New Guinea," *Culture, Health, and Sexuality*, vol. 5, no. 3, 2003, pp. 249–264.

113. This has resulted in incidences of youth breaking into health clinics in order to obtain condoms. For example, see National AIDS Council, *Situational Analysis for Strategic Planning at the District Level: Southern Highlands Province, Social Mapping*

Project. In another incidence of condom theft, on Misima Island, the health worker responded by ceasing to stock condoms, never acknowledging that the youths stole the condoms because they wanted the right to have access to condoms (field notes, January 2006).

114. Charles Wilde, " 'Turning Sex into a Game': Gogodala Men's Response to the AIDS Epidemic and Condom Promotion in Rural Papua New Guinea," *Oceania,* vol. 77, no. 1, 2007, pp. 58–71.

115. Keck, "Knowledge, Morality and 'Kastom.' "

116. Vicki Luker, "Civil Society, Social Capital and the Churches: HIV/AIDS in Papua New Guinea," State, Society and Governance in Melanesia Project, working paper 2004/1, Canberra, 2004.

117. Lawrence Hammar, "Epilogue: Homegrown in PNG—Rural Responses to HIV and AIDS."

118. Ibid., p. 80.

119. Ibid.

120. S. R. Layton, "Living with Dignity Project," *Papua New Guinea Medical Journal,* vol. 47, nos. 1–2, 2004, pp. 13–21.

121. UNESCO, *Regional Planning Workshop: Integrating HIV/AIDS Projects into Community Learning Centres,* UNESCO, Bangkok, 2007.

IV   COMMUNITY LEARNING

Chapter 11

Learning beyond Formal Education

EDUCATION HAS LONG BEEN RECOGNIZED AS a powerful tool for social change and development. It can empower individuals and communities by stimulating reflective citizenship and active participation in cultural, political, and economic life, and by enabling people and communities to negotiate the increasing challenges and changes of their lifeworlds. Education can also be a force of disruption, inculcation of external values, and social abstraction—lifting people out of relatively stable contexts into new cultures of high expectation and ungrounded desire. In Boera, for example, as we discussed earlier, modern education has displaced older forms of learning. Now, only one woman left in the village knows how to make the sacred Hiri trade clay pots as a generation of young women who would otherwise have been eligible to learn were drawn away from the village to study at boarding schools in Port Moresby and elsewhere. This does not mean that the intersection of different kinds of education cannot enrich each other—quite the opposite. However, modern education has the power to remove knowledge from lifeworld contexts. It is both difficult to get right and also central to sustainable development.

One of the problems is that formal education is treated as an essential good. Well-considered learning practices, approached with reflexive care about the principles of engagement, provide a strong basis for good living. In recent years, a succession of international declarations and agreements have all asserted the importance of education, beginning with the United Nations Declaration of Human Rights and continuing with the 1990 UNESCO World Declaration on Education for All, and more recently the pledge to achieve universal primary education contained within the Millennium Development Goals. However, these worthy goals have to be seen in the context of a succession of postindependence reports in Papua New Guinea that bring up important questions. A report on Boera village includes the following concerns:

> From a village perspective, much of the school curriculum seems irrelevant at best, and disadvantageous at worst. From that perspective, what is the relevance of rain gauges, millimetres and millilitres, local government council, National Parliament, physical education skills, making a rainbow with a mirror and water, or pressing water here and causing it to rise there? What have these to do with activities such as fishing, hunting, gardening and collecting things for subsistence purposes? Also, is it not disadvantageous to systematically (though unintentionally) turn children against the cooperative values of the village life in favour of market driven individualism, which leaves them

Preschool children at Kira Kira Settlement near Vanagi, Port Moresby, attending informal-education classes supported by their local village

socially and economically dysfunctional in the village where the majority will live for most of their lives?[1]

Part of the problem with the assumption that education is good is that it tends to equate learning with formal education. Formal schooling systems in the Global North are by and large considered the primary vehicle for education. However, in many places around the world, including Papua New Guinea, formal school systems are inaccessible to many people or in some localities do not exist at all. This uneven access to formal schooling makes nonformal learning particularly important, although the latter should not be seen as simply a substitute for the former.

A parallel part of the problem is that in Papua New Guinea, as elsewhere, there is a tendency to fetishize formal education as a pathway to material wealth. In Colin Swatridge's words, modern education in reading and writing has become a means of "delivering the goods."[2] In other words, formal education (together with religiously framed knowledge) is often taken by Papua New Guineans to be better at delivering the bounty of material returns than informal education processes that include a customary knowledge dimension. While an important minority of people in Papua New Guinea can see how it is possible to walk in both worlds at the same time, there is a continuing and dominant view that sees modern formal education as the exclusive answer in the learning stakes.

In addition, we face the difficulty of integrating the two systems of modern and customary knowledge. It is modern training that generates local doctors, engineers, and school teachers, not informal learning—and we know all too well that Papua New Guinea is crying out for such specialists. A particular focus of this chapter is on strategies that may enable nonformal learning undertaken in Papua New Guinean communities to be recognized for the purposes of employment, entry to, and credit in formal education and training. We are concerned not to simply reproduce the dual societies of many other postcolonial nation-states—the modern-educated and relatively wealthy sector and the customary-educated and relatively poor sector. Setting up pathways between the two ways of learning is not a simple process of imposing a modern formalized set of protocols on a "both-ways" informal system. The discussion is framed by the recognition that the vast majority of Papua New Guineans continue to derive their livelihood from informal sector activities, whether in urban centers or rural villages, and articulated pathways from informal to formal learning may not be useful. Moreover, we recognize that the intersection of different modes of knowledge is not straightforward. Approaches to learning in Papua New Guinea thus need at once to recognize the diversity of social formations, livelihood activities, and formal and informal economies, while also responding to the complex interconnections between them. This is what Martin Nakata calls the "cultural interface."[3]

In this chapter we explore the contribution that nonformal and informal learning can make toward the realization of sustainable development and the strengthening of local communities and livelihoods in Papua New Guinea. The terms "nonformal" and "informal" learning encompass a broad range of activities and initiatives that take place outside the formal school system.[4] Nonformal learning tends to be defined as learning undertaken through unaccredited courses delivered in community learning centers and other community settings, and in workplaces. However, many of the initiatives discussed in this chapter also refer to what is normally defined as "informal learning": that is, activities associated with family, community, and leisure pursuits, where learning accompanies the primary purpose of the activity. Examples include planting and nurturing crops, preparing food, and producing artifacts, or, at the other end of the spectrum, practicing a new sporting technique.[5]

For the purposes of this discussion, informal learning will be drawn into a broader definition of nonformal learning. This is the term used by the PNG Department for Community Development to cover all learning for individuals and communities that takes place outside of the formal school system through community learning centers and informal learning networks. Instances of nonformal learning in Papua New Guinea include short courses and workshops run by church or government agencies, for example, on sewing or the use of new agricultural techniques; HIV/AIDS awareness workshops; adult literacy and numeracy training; community-based vernacular preschools; and vocational training. However, it is important to remember that nonformal learning also includes practices and forms of tribal education that have been part of Papua New Guinean community life for thousands of years: learning how to fish or make gardens; passing on customary skills such as canoe making, dancing, or building houses from bush materials; or teaching local stories, songs, and the histories of clans and families.

Political Relations of Formal and Nonformal Learning

Such is the value placed on formal educational structures and practices that it is commonplace for nonformal learning to be regarded as being of lesser worth: lacking in quality, rigor, or discipline. This is not necessarily the case. The quality, rigor, and discipline applied to any learning is a consequence of many factors—the quality of the teaching, the nature of the resources, the aptitude and motivation of learners, relevance, timeliness, and so on—apart from its institutional relations. What nonformal learning does lack is consistency and comparability from one learning site to another. Unlike formal education with its universalizing routines and structures—the "school day," curriculum, classroom architecture, textbooks, and examinations—nonformal learning derives its ways of being from multiple local community and workplace settings, unconstrained by school time and the structure and content of accredited qualifications.

Nonformal learning is characteristically experience based, integrated with other elements of daily life, and often tacit.[6] Nonformal learning usually takes place in the context of its application: meeting the needs of the individuals and organizations directly involved in the learning rather than the interests of educational authorities.[7] While the extension of formal schooling remains a goal in nations wrestling with issues of community sustainability and modernization, there is at the same time a growing understanding of the value of nonformal learning as a pathway to the acquisition of new skills in a time of rapid technological and cultural change.

Notions of the *learning organization*,[8] *communities of practice*,[9] *situated learning*,[10] and *lifelong and lifewide learning*[11] all signal a shift in the discourse of education away from the singularity of the school and toward a multiplicity of forms that acknowledge and can work with cultural and economic change and diversity. In Papua New Guinea, where the majority of the population lives in rural areas, with limited access to formal education and income-earning opportunities, attention has similarly turned to nonformal learning as a cost-effective and flexible strategy to address the need for literacy and skill development, as a pathway into formal education, and as a bridge between local and global economies.

The strength of nonformal learning—its capacity to address multiple local agendas in its multiple and varied sites—is also a weakness at the level of policy and regulation. How can relevant authorities be sure that necessary standards of teaching, assessment discipline, and health and safety are maintained when they do not have jurisdiction over learning sites and practitioners? And how can educational institutions and employers know that levels of knowledge and skill emerging from multiple learning sites are consistent? The strategies for measuring formal educational outcomes—via time served and national/state examinations—do not have currency beyond the confines of the academy. Moreover, by its very nature nonformal learning does not trade in currencies that readily apply as a systemic medium of exchange. As we will discuss, they are not readily assimilated as "social capital."

The need for common systematic practices that accord formal recognition of skills nonformally learned has become ever more pressing. It is a reality that needs to be faced, particularly in the context of globalizing economies where the movement of workers in pursuit of employment has brought with it the problem of reconciling different skill standards across regions and national borders.

Moreover, as cultural, linguistic, and educational diversity increases in the context of globalizing economies, governments are looking to their schooling systems to smooth over differences and secure social cohesion under new circumstances. Schooling systems that have in the past constituted effective sites for the production of regulated social stability now struggle to meet new economic and social demands under conditions of complexity and rapid change. As the school becomes a less likely site for the timely production of skills in demand, it also becomes less able to accommodate cultural diversity using regulatory forms that demand uniformity.

Development of the Formal Education System

Processes of learning and education in contemporary Papua New Guinea—both formal and nonformal—are strongly marked by the country's experience of colonization and missionization. During most of the period of Australian colonial administration, the formal state education system was largely inaccessible to Papua New Guineans beyond the early years. Mission training schools mixed customary and modern learning to prepare people for life as Christians and to train them for employment in mines and plantations, as clerical staff, or as service workers. Women were trained to be good Christian mothers and wives, and the bulk of nonformal learning available to Papua New Guinean women continues to be in skill areas loosely grouped under the heading of "home economics"—cooking, sewing, handicrafts, and nutrition. The state of education was such that by 1960 only a hundred Melanesians had completed secondary school, and there were no university graduates.[12] With national independence a fast-approaching inevitability, the colonial authorities sought to rectify the embarrassing situation by pushing for establishment of formal education for Papua New Guineans in the 1960s and 1970s.

The formal education system established by the colonial administration reflected the values, instructional methods, and format of the Australian school system. In this regard, Papua New Guinea was not dissimilar to other Pacific Island countries, and today education systems throughout Melanesia continue to display a strong Western bias. In the newly established system in Papua New Guinea, both government and religious agencies became providers of formal education. By the 1980s, several years after independence, there were approximately 2,600 community schools in operation, along with roughly 120 provincial high schools, 4 national high schools, a distance education system, a small number of private education services, and various vocational colleges and training centers. The University of Papua New Guinea was established in Port Moresby in 1965, with the PNG Institute of Higher Technical Education established in the same year; in 1973 the latter became the University of Technology,

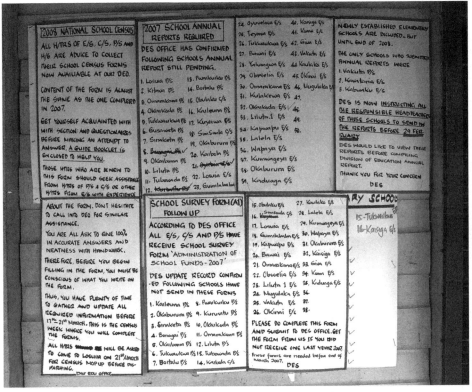

School notice board at Kiriwina High School for the National School Census

Lae. Not surprisingly perhaps, very few students reached the level of tertiary studies. Formal education at all levels was conducted in English, enrollment was not compulsory, and fees were charged most of the time. The system was marked by inordinately high attrition rates at the community school level and a pervasive problem of inaccessibility at the secondary level. Only one in six children was able to obtain a postprimary education, and less than 2 percent of students enrolled in grade one reached grade twelve. Marked gender imbalances were found in access to primary education and subsequent progression to secondary level.[13]

In 1986 an influential report was commissioned and later adopted by the national government. *The Ministerial Committee Report on a Philosophy of Education*—better known as the Matane Report after its principal author—prompted a substantial reform of the formal education system: "The philosophy is for every person to be dynamically involved in the process of freeing himself or herself from every form of domination and oppression so that each individual will have the opportunity to develop as an integrated person in relationship to others. This means that education must aim for integrating and maximizing: socialization, participation, liberation, and equality."[14] The report criticized the use of English as the only language of instruction and drew attention to the need for education to be provided in vernacular languages, particularly at the level of early childhood learning. Consequently, an Education Sector Review was established in 1991, prompting a major reform of the formal education system that is still ongoing. Under the new system elementary schools cater to students from preparatory level through grade two, followed by primary schools for grades three to eight. Two levels of secondary education—lower and upper secondary— teach grades nine to ten, and eleven to twelve respectively. Adult education and distance education streams feed into secondary levels, which in turn allow for entry into the tertiary sector, be it vocational colleges or one of the five universities now in operation in the country. At the elementary and primary levels, and in adult education, local languages are increasingly adopted in favor of English. The administration and governance of the formal system is decentralized to the provinces, and three district organizational units as well as churches and missions remain major education providers.

Formal Education in Papua New Guinea Today

Unfortunately, the formal education system in Papua New Guinea today remains inadequate to meet the learning needs of the population. First, a substantial section of the population either does not receive education through the schooling system or receives only a partial basic education. While the goal of universal primary education (one of the Millennium Goals) remains a key objective of the UNESCO Education For All framework to which the national government subscribes, the Department of Education has stated that it considers the realization of universal primary education to be unachievable until primary education is made compulsory, which in turn depends on its being available without charge. The department has declared free primary education unfeasible without significant improvements in infrastructure and law and order throughout the country.[15] School fees remain prohibitive for many families, and when parents are forced to choose which of their children are able to attend school, it is often girls who miss out. Remote communities are disadvantaged further—schools may be many hours away from villages, and paying fees becomes more difficult for communities where the dominant form of production is subsistence agriculture and the cash economy is peripheral. At the secondary school level and beyond, problems of geographic and financial inaccessibility are exacerbated as there are fewer educational institutions and attendance for many students requires leaving home and boarding.

The second substantial weakness in the formal education system is that it is overwhelmingly geared toward preparing students for waged employment within the formal sector. Notwithstanding the vernacular reforms begun in the early 1990s, the orientation of the Papua New Guinean school system continues to reflect strongly the Western modern approaches to education on which it is modeled. While such an instrumental approach to learning is riddled with problems in any context, it becomes particularly so in a country where well over 90 percent of the total labor force is engaged in the informal sector. As the Department of Education itself made clear in a 1985 report, "Education does not create jobs."[16] Around 80,000 school leavers graduate from education institutions in Papua New Guinea each year, a number that massively outstrips available employment opportunities. Indeed, only 5 percent of those graduates will be absorbed into jobs in the formal sector.[17] Many more remain in or return to informal livelihood activities within subsistence agriculture–based villages; others join the burgeoning ranks of the urban unemployed, scraping out a living from the urban informal economy and living in overcrowded settlements in Papua New Guinea's cities and towns.

A third, related, issue is that the Western-based model of formal education currently employed in Papua New Guinea sits in uneasy contrast to the forms of learning and education customarily found in Melanesian societies. Francyne Huckaby has written about her experiences working in village schools with the South Foré tribal people in the Eastern Highlands in the late 1990s. She draws on ethnographic observations to paint a picture of training in modern temporality and spatiality. While the South Foré village people would gather together in loosely organized groupings, children at school were always organized spatially into strict, straight lines. "I only see lines," she wrote in her field notes at the time, "at banks and post offices, in stores—and in schools."[18] Similarly, she notes the rigid approach to time and punctuality. The formal roll calls at the beginning of classes stood out in contrast to the understanding of time she observed in other parts of village life, where time spent waiting was time used for cementing relationships, making *bilums*, talking story, and other deceptively simple relational acts essential for maintaining community. "School was not about Papua New Guinean culture or tradition. A large portion of schooling in PNG was about order and learning rules. These rules began at each morning's assembly and continued in the classroom and lessons."[19] The reality of the formal education system, then, is a far cry from the eloquent vision outlined by Matane over two decades ago.

Toward the Development of Nonformal Education

Attempts at coordinating and developing nonformal education in Papua New Guinea have consistently been articulated in response to these recognized deficiencies in the formal education sector: namely, its inaccessibility for many, its orientation toward the formal economic sector, and its dominant Western bias. Nonformal education—with its learner-centered approach to education, its adaptability to local circumstance, and its capacity to incorporate diverse forms of knowledge and learning—has much to offer. Still, despite a plethora of reports, policy recommendations, and declarations, nonformal learning continues to be plagued by problems, which have been stated many times: it is under-resourced and underfunded; coordination between initiatives and providers is poor; there is a lack of clear and consistent policy at a governmental level; and nonformal learning is persistently perceived to have a second-rate status when compared to the formal education system. As Reymer notes, "The history of non-formal education is a history of stalled starts and failed attempts to establish policies and structures that would ensure a well-coordinated, stable, dynamic and well resourced system."[20] Nevertheless, at a rhetorical level at least, there is recognition among both government and nongovernment agencies of the potentialities of and need for nonformal education. It is instructional, then, to examine more closely some of these stalled starts and failed attempts, and to consider what might be done now to truly develop nonformal learning as a strategy for sustainable, strong communities and livelihoods in Papua New Guinea.

National Nonformal Education Initiatives

In 1985, ten years after independence, over 150 people involved in nonformal education initiatives in all the Papua New Guinean provinces gathered in Goroka with the specific purpose of examining nonformal education.[21] In the same year and following on from this significant event, a report commissioned by the Ministry of Education was released.[22] It noted the emergence of nonformal education initiatives across the country, including short courses, skills workshops, field training, project assistance, and print and radio materials. It recorded the broad range of national and provincial government departments involved in nonformal programs as well as initiatives run by churches and NGOs. There was no coordination of these activities at a national level and little opportunity for sharing ideas and resources.

In response, the commissioned report made an extensive series of recommendations, essentially outlining a proposal for a broad-ranging, national approach to the development and coordination of nonformal education. Three key areas of concern in approaching nonformal education were identified: (1) the coordination of existing programs; (2) basic education including information about government and nongovernment services, literacy and numeracy training, and short-term skills training aimed at the rural village population; and (3) vocational education. The recommendations of the report included a national officer to be employed to serve the needs of provisional nonformal education officers; provincial databases of all agencies involved in village learning programs; district nonformal education representation in Department of Education decision-making processes; training services for trainers, including in literacy/ numeracy, translation techniques, village instructor training, and customary learning styles; and information banks in all provinces for early access to information by village group representatives. Importantly, it recognized the need for systems of nonformal education to complement but also stand independently of the formal education system and so proposed the establishment of a National Association for Basic Education to complement the Department of Education but with a dedicated focus on nonformal education.

Invoking the concept of a "Melanesian way," it called for locally appropriate education suited to the needs and motivations of communities, with networks to allow communication between locales and the sharing of strategies and experiences, as well as an emphasis on self-reflection and evaluation by communities themselves. However, the recommendations of the Ministry of Education report were never implemented.

Instead, nonformal education continues to take place in an ad hoc manner without substantial coordination or communication. Both provincial governments and the national Department of Education focus overwhelmingly on adult literacy and on vocational training centers, which are the most closely aligned with the formal sector of all the strands of nonformal education. The lack of an institutional body with a dedicated focus on the provision of nonformal education—be it a National Association for Basic Education or some other equivalent—stands as an ongoing hindrance to the achievement of a comprehensive, well-coordinated, and well resourced system of nonformal education.

The Community-Based Nonformal Education Movement

The government-led reform of the education system and discussions of the role of nonformal education were themselves pursuant to the emergence of a significant community- and NGO-based grass-roots movement across Papua New Guinea in the 1980s. The community-based nonformal education movement emphasized, as Matane subsequently did in his 1985 report, the importance of local vernacular languages, particularly at the level of early childhood learning. A key outcome of the movement was the establishment of hundreds of village preschools teaching in vernacular languages, known as *tok ples priskuls*. The first of these was the *viles tok ples skul* (village vernacular school) established in North Solomons Province in 1979, and by 1991 there were 386 *tok ples priskuls* teaching in ninety-one languages and found in every province of the country.[23] The *priskuls* were, in each case, established by local communities, who built the classrooms and decided on curricula and teaching materials. Teachers were usually volunteers, selected by the community on the basis of their knowledge of the local language and culture. Church organizations and other NGOs played important roles in providing support and teacher training. Within a short while after their emergence, the *tok ples priskuls* were being lauded as enormously successful. Children given initial literacy training through the vernacular preschools were found to be academically outperforming other students when they went on to primary education in the formal system. In addition, feedback from teachers and parents indicated that community well-being at the local level was improving as relationships to local language and culture were celebrated and enhanced.

Formal evaluations of the *tok ples priskuls* began in the late 1980s and confirmed officially what was being reported anecdotally. They found conclusively that initial education in children's first tongue improved their success in later education, and they affirmed the social and cultural benefits of the *tok ples priskul* programs, including active and proud participation by students in their communities, the retention of local language, and increased knowledge of local culture. Significantly, it was noted that the *tok ples priskul* programs were enjoying strong levels of support by the communities themselves. Indeed, community participation and ownership of the *tok ples priskuls* was identified as a key factor in their success. In their review of the *viles tok ples skul* system in North Solomons Province, Delpit and Kemelfield wrote:

> What made mother tongue education realisable in Papua New Guinea was first, decentralisation of education policy-making and administrative powers, and second, the community enthusiasm for the scheme which inspired enough support that buildings, teachers, and other resources could be acquired at the local level. Certainly, were the backing of the people not behind the project, it could not have progressed as it has, an important lesson to those wishing to engage in education reform.[24]

The notable success of the community-based, nonformal education movement created the climate in which the official education reforms in Papua New Guinea took place. While the implementation of vernacular education is commendable, the reforms have focused on the formal system, largely ignoring the nonformal sector out of which the *tok ples priskuls* originally emerged. The 1991 Department of Education *Education Sector Review,* which triggered the education reform, noted the importance of supporting nonformal education and called for the creation of a National Non-Formal Education Council and Secretariat. However, this and other proposals relating to nonformal education were not implemented by the government, which chose to focus instead on restructuring the formal school system. In this sense, the long-standing disparity in the status afforded to nonformal learning has been maintained, suggesting that the important lessons of the *tok ples priskul* scheme have yet to be fully embraced.

Particular concern has arisen over the relationship between the *tok ples priskuls* and the new elementary schools. With the introduction of the elementary prep level as part of the education reforms—catering to the same age group that was already being taught through the nonformal vernacular preschools—some educators voiced their concern that the *tok ples priskuls* would be taken over by the national government and amalgamated into the formal system. In their 1995 report published by the National Research Institute, Ahai and Bopp noted emphatically that "community ownership and control is the heart of these programs."[25] The worry was that this vital element would be lost if the *tok ples priskuls* were replaced by elementary schools. Likewise, concern was expressed over the potential centralization of *tok ples priskul* schemes under national government control, arguing that the *tok ples priskul* "ceases to be a vehicle for a community to transfer its language and values to its young if control over what is taught and by whom is relinquished by the community to a National Organisation."[26] Another consideration is that the new elementary school system is heavily dependent on external funding—to pay for teachers, training, resources, and infrastructure—while one of the strengths of the *tok ples priskul* scheme is that it requires little financing, its success stemming from community input and cooperation. There is no denying that an injection of funding into the nonformal sector is both needed and desirable; our point is that, as with so many other development projects, money alone is no assurance of success. What is crucially important, however, is community support and ownership of the programs that affect them. The closing down of *tok ples priskuls* reflects as much the lack of sustained bottom-up capacity to carry the program through as the inadequacy of top-down support.

Regional Nonformal Education Initiatives

Most recently, attempts at creating better organized and coordinated approaches to nonformal education have occurred at the regional level, through workshops, conferences, and bodies such as the Pacific Islands Forum, an intergovernmental grouping of independent Pacific states. A 1995 workshop held in Port Vila, with government and nongovernment agencies from Papua New Guinea, the Solomon Islands, Vanuatu, and Fiji, was the first regional attempt to address questions concerning nonformal education. The meeting was hosted by the National Centre for Development Studies at the Australian National University and affirmed a commitment to developing a "Melanesian model" of nonformal education. More than a decade later, in November 2006, participants at another workshop—jointly organized by the University of the South Pacific and UNESCO in Lautoka—agreed to undertake a study of nonformal education with a view to developing a regional strategy under the auspices of the Pacific Islands Forum.[27] The efforts to produce a regional nonformal education scheme were situated within the context of the Pacific Plan, which aims to strengthen region- al cooperation and integration through sustainable development. The resulting blueprint, "Non-Formal Education in Pacific Islands Countries," was presented to the Pacific Islands Forum Secretariat's Education Ministers Meeting in Auck- land in November 2007.

The Pacific Islands Forum blueprint draws on and affirms the commit- ment of Pacific Island states to the goals set out in the World Declaration on Education for All signed in Jomtien, Thailand, in 1990. The Education for All Declaration in turn builds on the understanding articulated in the Universal Declaration of Human Rights that "everyone has a right to education."[28] Specifi- cally, the Jomtien Declaration calls for universal access to basic education for all children, youth, and adults. Basic education is understood as occurring through learning tools such as literacy, numeracy, problem solving, and oral expression; and in terms of the learning content—knowledge, skills, values, and attitudes— "required by human beings to be able to survive, to develop their full capacities, to live and work in dignity, to participate fully in development, to improve the quality of their lives, to make informed decisions, and to continue learning." Pri- mary schooling is considered to be the main vehicle for the delivery of such ba- sic education outside the family. In situating itself in relation to the goals of the Jomtien Declaration while simultaneously recognizing the current limits of the formal primary school system, the regional blueprint developed by the Pacific Islands Forum specifically highlights the importance of nonformal education in the provision of basic education.[29]

The report recommends the creation of mobile training teams and the de- velopment of management skills for nonformal education facilitators. It empha- sizes the need for innovative curriculum materials and confirms the importance of teaching learning methods in vernacular languages. The key recommenda- tion, however, is that the Pacific Islands Forum member states move toward the long-term goal of developing a regional accreditation system. There are cur- rently no comprehensive national accreditation systems throughout the Pacific, although the Cook Islands, Tonga, and Samoa are in the process of developing national qualification mechanisms for some vocational initiatives or else stan- dardizing with the New Zealand Qualifications Authority. Likewise, the PNG national government in 1994 began developing a program for vocational and technical education and training. In these instances, where qualifications are accredited by national qualifications authorities, they are added to a register maintained by the South Pacific Board for Educational Assessment. The Pacific Islands Forum proposes to move beyond this patchwork approach to develop a system of accreditation for the region as a whole. Such a system would allow for the recognition and transference of skills and training across national boundaries within the region, while also facilitating the integration of nonformal learning with the formal school system, potentially allowing training done through the nonformal sector to be counted toward the achievement of formal qualifications and entry to the formal workplace. It would also serve as a means to better facilitate the collating and sharing of best practices, curricula, and materials, while allowing for quality control across the diverse range of nonformal education initiatives and providers. Indeed, the Pacific Islands Forum blueprint identifies quality assurance of programs across the region as the key challenge in the development of nonformal education.

In calling for the creation of a regional accreditation system, the focus of the Pacific Islands Forum is in keeping with a broader global trend toward the development of systems and frameworks that allow qualifications to be easily transferred across industry and national boundaries. In part, this trend is a response to the increased demands of the globalizing economy for a mobile, flexible workforce suitable to mobile and multisited industry. Reymer is one commentator who has raised concerns about the push toward qualifications frameworks reflecting a broader advancement of neoliberal market-based policies. Pointing to the close relationship between development and education policies, she argues that the prevailing development orthodoxy—of economic liberalization, deregulated markets, and integration into a global economy—is reflected in the dominant discourse around education, which sees education as having narrowly defined instrumental outcomes, namely, the preparation of individuals for jobs in a formal market economy.[30] In this sense, there is a danger that the emphasis on creating accreditation systems and qualification frameworks—whether at the national or regional level—will mirror and perpetuate an existing weakness within the Papua New Guinean education system, its prevailing orientation toward waged employment in the formal economy. Although significant benefits could result from the development of such systems, they need to be developed as critical elements within a broader strategy for nonformal education that encompasses and supports the broad range of nonformal education activities, acknowledges the diversity of learning needs and forms of knowledge, and holds the modern in relation to the continuing importance of tribal and traditional ways of life.

Looking at the history of attempts to coordinate and develop nonformal education in Papua New Guinea and the Pacific region, it is clear that a strong and effective system of nonformal education will need to hold in balance the coexisting needs for coordination and systematization, on the one hand, and local adaptability, and community ownership and agency, on the other. The success of the community-based nonformal education movement and the *tok ples priskuls* shows clearly the importance of genuine local engagement in the processes of learning and education. Where there is such engagement, communities are much more likely to actively support nonformal education initiatives, providing vital resources, energy, and enthusiasm. Moreover, learning in such a context takes on a collective dimension, with whole communities engaged in the celebration and passing on of their language, culture, stories, skills, and history in ways that allow the benefits of education to extend well beyond individual students.

At the same time, however, it is clear that nonformal education cannot be organized solely at the level of the local. The need for coordination and the provision of resources at the provincial, national, and perhaps even regional levels is starkly evident. And while local knowledge and skills are vitally important, there are types of learning content existing beyond the level of the local—including modern skills and knowledge—that may have applicability for many Papua New Guinean communities and that would best be coordinated at the provincial or national levels. Examples of such learning content include literacy in English or Tok Pisin, vocational skills training, HIV/AIDS awareness training, education about government services, the teaching of new agricultural techniques, training in income management, education about development and globalization, or education about the impacts of climate change and rising water tables. The challenge, then, is to create models for the development of nonformal education that allow for systematization, coordination, and sharing of resources without suffocating local vitality and community agency.

The argument of the present book is that sustainable communities, sustainable livelihoods, and sustainable development must form the backbone of Papua New Guinea's approach to development. In realizing this, the key imperative is to create effective, reciprocal links between the local, national, regional, and global. Likewise, sustainable, equitable development cannot be dominated by the imposition of the modern, just as it cannot retreat to a parochial cultural conservatism. Rather, it must seek to hold in balance the complex intersection of social formations, ways of life, and forms of knowing and being in contemporary Papua New Guinea. Approaches to nonformal learning should be in keeping with this broader approach to development, recognizing the vital contribution that nonformal learning can make toward the achievement of sustainable communities and livelihoods. The vision for community learning and development centers laid out in Chapter 12 offers a space that can accommodate the diverse range of nonformal learning activities, drawing on a range of educational resources including elders, local knowledges and oral histories, customary skills, as well as modern teaching materials and curricula as required by the particular needs and circumstances of a community at a given time. Community coordination of the community learning centers will allow for genuine local ownership of the physical space and learning processes, while a network of district and provincial focal points, connected in turn to the national government, will provide the means through which local communities can obtain outside and expert forms of knowledge when such knowledge is appropriate and desired. At the national level, responsibility for the learning center structure will lie with the Department for Community Development, ensuring that the frequently voiced rhetorical support for nonformal education is matched by the existence of an institutional body with the committed focus, political will, and access to the necessary resources to make nonformal education a success. It is expected that other government departments and agencies will be actively involved in the learning center system, including the Departments for Women, Youth, Health, Primary Industries, and Education.

An important component of a coordinated approach to nonformal education will be a system for the provision of recognition for learning activities. Such a system serves a number of purposes: (1) it validates the work of educators, students, and engaged community members in the community learning centers; (2) when combined with processes through which learning centers voluntarily report back on their activities, it assists with the collection and sharing of information among local learning centers and with the provincial and national levels; (3) it allows learners to demonstrate their particular competencies for the purposes of gaining employment or access to further training, where this is appropriate; and (4) it provides possible pathways into the formal education system. In some instances—for example, in the case of vocational skills training or adult literacy—nonformal learning activities conducted through the learning centers would be well suited to recognition through regional or national accreditation systems and qualification frameworks. Such systems, however, are ill-suited to the recognition of other types of nonformal learning—for example, the teaching of locally specific histories, cultural dances and ceremonies, or customary skills such as clay-pot making in the Indigenous Motuan communities of the Papuan Gulf. In these cases, the dominant purpose of learning is clearly not to prepare individuals for waged employment or to fill gaps where the formal education system is absent. Accordingly, the formalized accreditation of learning should be seen as one aspect within an approach to nonformal education in which there are many *layers of recognition*, appropriately reflecting the diversity of nonformal education initiatives and the purposes they serve.

School-age youths sitting outside Donna's Trading Store, Wau, during school hours. The man standing against the wall works in one of the local houses.

In the remaining sections of this chapter, we examine in detail the development of accreditation systems and qualification frameworks in the global context, keeping in mind both the possibilities and the limitations inherent in them. Much of the literature in this area is drawn from Europe, Australia, and other places where the Western and the modern are dominant, and so a key consideration is to think through how it can be made relevant to Papua New Guinea and the Melanesian region. Toward the end of the chapter, the Yirrkala Landcare Project in an Indigenous community, Australia's Arnhem Land, is explored as a successful example of the development of nonformal learning in ways that can feed into formal industry competency standards while remaining locally appropriate and continuing to meet community cultural and social needs.

Emerging Forms of Educational Management

In attempting to address manifold education and training issues arising as a consequence of globalization, successive governments in the United Kingdom, Australia, and member nations of the European Union have moved to establish more flexible forms of educational management that can work around the structural inertia of the school and across jurisdictional boundaries. These are massive initiatives, involving legislation, complex governance and management structures, ongoing policy revision, and the design of new regulatory forms. Foremost among these new regulatory forms are tools that have agency beyond formal education, including taxonomies of general and vocational capability in the form of competency standards and taxonomies of learning outcomes in the form of qualification frameworks, evidence-based assessment strategies, and quality assurance authorities with jurisdiction over government institutions and nongovernment providers. These tools are in one way or another translation devices, able to relate educational outcomes achieved under different conditions and to authorize agreed common points of reference. Both the possibilities and the pitfalls of this direction in educational management will be illustrated with reference to the work undertaken in the United Kingdom, Europe, and Australia.

Occupational Standards and National Qualification Frameworks

The role of occupational standards is to specify the skills and knowledge required for competent work performance. As such, they can enable different courses of study related to the same occupational outcomes to be compared and aligned. The first such occupational standards appeared in the United Kingdom in the mid-1980s under the auspices of the National Council for Vocational Qualifications.[31] Today the main use for what are now known as National Occupational Standards and administered by the Qualifications and Curriculum

Authority is to design National Vocational Qualifications. In turn, the National Vocational Qualifications are used as standards against which a plethora of locally accredited qualifications from an array of awarding bodies can be certified according to a common scale.[32] While its aims were laudable, the National Vocational Qualifications process is seen by many employers as cumbersome and bureaucratic, with little relevance to "real" work.[33] As Page and Hillage note, the extent of paperwork associated with the qualifications may help to explain the reluctance of businesses, and particularly small and medium-sized enterprises, to deliver National Vocational Qualifications or to use them as a benchmark for the recognition of nonformal work-based training.[34]

The Australian National Training Board was similarly looking to use nationally developed qualifications to bridge differences between different regulatory regimes when they adopted the British competency standards model. In this case, the challenge was to enable the portability of vocational qualifications between the eight Australian states and territories that retained the constitutional authority to accredit education and training qualifications. Between 1990 and 1992, the National Training Board oversaw the development of standards for skilled occupations in most major industry sectors. These standards were taken on by the Australian Committee on Training Curriculum as the framework for developing standard national courses, which were then handed over to the states and territories, where they were duly reformatted according to local custom and accredited by the eight differently constituted training accreditation authorities. Such unwieldy processes neither pleased Australian industry nor afforded individuals an easier pathway to skill recognition.

Qualification Frameworks and the Lifelong Learning Agenda

Qualification frameworks are scaffolding devices that express the relative value of one or more classifications of qualifications. Typically a qualification framework will name and display different levels of qualification within a classification (e.g., Certificate Level 1, Certificate Level 2, Diploma), describe the primary and distinguishing characteristics of each qualification, and spell out the way in which individuals can progress from one to another. Qualification frameworks may also align qualifications in one classification to those of another—for instance, to those of related but different sectors of education.

Qualification frameworks are commonly used for two purposes: first, to achieve parity between vocational education and training outcomes and academic credentials; and, second, to integrate nonformal learning with formal education and training sectors so that individuals whose learning has been undertaken in nonformal settings can have their skills and knowledge counted toward national and in some cases international qualifications, and for entry to the workforce. The Australian Qualifications Framework contains the specifications for and aligns qualification levels in senior secondary schools, the vocational education and training sector, and universities. Because Australian states enable private education and training providers to be registered to deliver government-accredited courses, the Australian Qualifications Framework acts as a device both to regulate the work of public and private institutions and to relate the qualifications they issue to a common standard.

In 2001 interest in "lifelong learning" as a slogan under which to promote the benefits of adult education and training—at a time when traditional "unskilled" jobs had declined and new labor market skills were in demand—led the OECD to launch a project to investigate the role of national qualifications systems in promoting lifelong learning. The project involved investigations of the qualification systems in participating countries and the exploration of three key themes: the use of qualification frameworks as a vehicle for reforming qualification systems; the relationship between national qualifications systems and the quality of and access to lifelong learning and the recognition of nonformal and informal learning; and relations between different individual and institutional stakeholders in the development of qualification frameworks as well as occupational standards and vocational qualifications.[35]

Recently the European Parliament has initiated a resolution to adopt a European Qualifications Framework, the aim of which is to enable all member nation qualification systems to be aligned against a set of standard levels and descriptors. The core element of the framework is a set of eight reference levels describing what a learner knows, understands, and is able to do—their "learning outcomes"—regardless of the system through which a particular qualification was acquired. As an instrument for the promotion of lifelong learning, the framework encompasses general and adult education, vocational education and training, as well as higher education. The eight levels cover the entire span of qualifications from those achieved at the end of compulsory education to those awarded at the highest level of academic and professional or vocational education and training.[36] The significance of the European Qualifications Framework is found in its "reference levels," which shift the focus away from the traditional academic approach to accreditation and recognition that emphasizes learning inputs (length of a course, type of institution, course content) and learning outcomes (what can be achieved through the course).

Recognition through Multiple Learning Pathways

The unifying underlying theme of the reforms to the education and training systems in European and OECD member nations has been recognition of learning through multiple pathways—within and across education and training sectors, between state jurisdictions, and between nonformal and formal learning. Recognition of different pathways has typically been enabled through standardized assessment protocols known as Recognition of Prior Learning that were first developed in the United Kingdom in the mid-1980s and refined in Australia since 1992 in the context of the national training system. In that system Recognition of Prior Learning is defined as follows: "A process through which people can gain entry to, or credit in, recognized courses based on competencies gained. The competencies may have been gained through experience in the workplace, in voluntary work, in social or domestic activities or through informal or formal training."[37]

Recognition of Prior Learning involves evaluating evidence of knowledge and skill by an applicant with reference to the qualification/area of competency in which recognition is sought. Assessment regimes have tended to be cumbersome—in order to demonstrate validity, they are sometimes more rigorous than the standard assessments of course outcomes, demanding that applicants compile massive portfolios of evidence. Recognition of Prior Learning has been something of a sleeper in the reform of education and training: working the margins between sectors and systems and, as an essentially individualized mode of assessment, sitting somewhat awkwardly alongside standard qualifications. Nevertheless, it is a concept that has taken hold as a means of managing diversity and complexity and achieving parity across multiple jurisdictions. Since the publication in 1996 of the European Commission White Paper *Towards the Learning Society*, a majority of the European Union member states have moved to enable the identification, assessment, and accreditation of learning that takes place beyond formal education and training.[38]

The successful implementation of strategies for the recognition for nonformal learning requires four key tools and procedures to be in place: (1) clear statements of competency or capability that specify the standard to be assessed; (2) evidence-based assessment tools; (3) assessment protocols that allow for competency to be benchmarked directly to the required standard rather than to courses of study based on the standard(s); (4) a standards-based quality assurance regime: that is, quality assurance that encourages practitioners to engage in reflective practice, taking responsibility for quality at a grass-roots level.

The National Australian VET System and Nonformal Learning

The tools and systems that were invented to overcome the problem of interstate portability and timeliness of training proved to be equally useful as devices for bridging nonformal and formal learning. Thousands of Australian organizations took advantage of the opportunity to become registered as Registered Training Organizations (RTOs). In addition to private colleges, enterprises, and industry associations, the ranks of RTOs include secondary schools and a range of community organizations: learning centers, sporting associations, community networks, and charitable institutions. Thus an unanticipated but nevertheless now well-supported outcome of national training reform was the creation of a system to recognize people whose skills and knowledge were developed through nonformal learning and to award them with nationally endorsed qualifications. It is now possible for, say, a voluntary community development worker to achieve a formal qualification for competencies gained through voluntary work, without having to attend a course of study, by having his or her competency assessed against relevant units of competency in the Community Services Training Package. If the organization he or she worked with was an RTO, this organization could conduct the assessment and award the relevant qualification.

Recognition of Community Learning

The Yirrkala Landcare Project

Yirrkala is an Aboriginal community in northeast Arnhem Land, on the western tip of the Gulf of Carpentaria in Australia's north. One of the major community organizations is Gamarrwa Nuwul Landcare, constituted through the Yirrkala Dhanbul Council. Five Yolngu families—from the Rirratjingu and Gumatj clans—formed the association in response to the social fragmentation and environmental impacts occurring as a result of contact with the white community in Australia, and particularly as a result of the bauxite mine. The primary objective of the Gamarrwa Nuwul Association was, and remains, to advocate for and support Indigenous development toward self-governance for community-based resource management. Landcare has set the long-term goal of becoming an independent and economically sustainable body, enabling Yolngu people to establish and maintain autonomous control over land management issues.[39] Through the Community Development Employment Program Gamarrwa Nuwul Landcare has become Yirrkala Dhanbul Community Council's largest employer of Yolngu people. Landcare runs a diverse range of services for the community—from care of recreational facilities and public community grounds, to waste management and water quality monitoring, to major land rehabilitation and revegetation projects. Landcare also runs a nursery through which it carries out indigenous seed collection and propagation and conducts community education programs and comprehensive training for its own staff.[40]

The association between the Globalism Research Centre, RMIT University, and Gamarrwa Nuwul Landcare was formed during the Garma Festival in August 2002.[41] At that time the Landcare training program was nonformal and work based, with occasional support from external agencies including Charles

Darwin University and Batchelor College of Indigenous Education. While both institutions were most willing to enroll Landcare employees in formal training programs, they regarded this as the only legitimate pathway to recognized qualifications and could see no way to recognize the training offered by Landcare. As the Landcare coordinator, Banduk Marika, explained at the time, formal training was an unacceptable solution for both practical and philosophical reasons. First, enrollment at either of the major Northern Territory educational institutions meant traveling over a thousand kilometers to Darwin or Alice Springs and staying for either the duration of the course or for study blocks interspersed by periods of distance learning—a costly exercise in terms of both time and money.[42] Second, there were local income-earning opportunities for which there were no recognized formal training programs, such as the creation of work for cultural advisors who needed cultural knowledge and management skills. Landcare wanted to develop their own programs using national units of competency and locally designed units but could not get these recognized by the formal educational institutions. Third and most important, Banduk Marika and others at Landcare regarded the formal programs as essentially inappropriate—based as they were on the learning of theory for later application at work and assessment through written examinations. Training at Landcare was entirely integrated into daily routines. Supervising staff took on the roles of coaches and mentors, showing staff new skills and discussing the application of new knowledge. Any expedition to collect indigenous seeds was a learning exercise. Yirrkala elders who held specialist local horticultural knowledge participated in expeditions to pass on this knowledge and to advise on where to find rare plants and on propagation methods.[43] The essential characteristic of all Landcare training was that it fit with the flow of the organization's work and with the cultural life of the community. Knowledge about how to transact the business of Landcare was communicated in a way that respected the social and cultural basis of Yolngu knowledge. What the Landcare leaders wanted from formal education institutions was that they come to Yirrkala, observe the way that training was organized, and participate in joint planning. "We don't want to send our people away to be lonely and without support in Darwin: we want the educators to come here and work with us, and we will learn together."[44]

This is what Gamarrwa Nuwul Landcare sought from RMIT: a partnership to revise and extend the Landcare training program so that it met national industry competency standards, at the same time continuing to meet local workplace and cultural needs. The Landcare Council saw this as extending the principle of "both-ways learning" that was first instituted in the design of the curriculum for the Yirrkala primary and secondary school in the 1980s. This concept, which has come to indicate the acceptance of a mixing of Western and Indigenous knowledge and of teaching Indigenous culture and language alongside West-ern disciplines, was an initiative of a number of Yolngu people who trained as teachers and took on leading roles in the Yirrkala school.[45] Both-ways learn-ing materializes a powerful Yolngu metaphor that refers to a confluence of two streams of water—one from the land and one from the sea—into a mangrove lagoon on Caledon Bay in northeast Arnhem Land. This was articulated by two researchers who worked closely with the Yolngu people to develop both-ways learning as follows:

> The theory of this confluence, called *ganma,* holds (in part) that the forces of the stream combine and lead to deeper understanding and truth. It is an ancient metaphor, one which has served Yolngu people well in the past. In recent discussions amongst the Yolngu and non-Aboriginal Australians they have chosen to work with them, *ganma* theory has been applied to the meeting of two cultures—Aboriginal and Western. Thus we may use the term 'ganma' in English to refer to the situation where a river of water from the sea (Western knowledge) and a river of water from the land (Yolngu knowledge) engulf each other on flowing into a common lagoon and becoming one.[46]

The Gamarrwa Nuwul Landcare leaders and staff sought to enact this prin-ciple of *ganma* in the development of their training program through a partner-ship between themselves and policy makers and educators with expertise in the Australian national vocational education and training (VET) system. The na-tional VET regulatory tools turned out to be surprisingly amenable in working between two systems. In a negotiated and negotiable space, the tools through which governance in the Australian system is enacted—Training Packages, the Australian Qualifications Framework, and the Australian Quality Training Framework—also came to occupy a space between Western and Yolngu ways of approaching learning, operating at the point where the two systems merge and acting as a tool for both-ways translation.

Taking Nonformal Learning into Account

In the millennial moves to manage growing complexity in formal educa-tion and training and a multiplicity of nonformal learning modes, it is possible to imagine the emergence of a new form of learning. The significance of the reforms enacted in Europe, Australia, and more recently China,[47] Sikkim,[48] and Singapore is twofold. First, the hegemony of academic assessment meth-ods such as the essay and the end-of-course examination of internalized facts and theories has been challenged: there is now a widespread understanding among educators that assessment of knowledge and skill can take a number of different forms that does not necessarily always include documentary evidence. Second, through the use of standards that transcend institutional boundaries, nonformal learning sites can be both integrated with and allowed to remain separate from formal learning. That is, nonformal learning can be the pathway to formal qualifications without fundamentally altering its own practices and internal regulation.

Nonformal learning can continue to be located in an infinitely diverse range of community and in-work settings, using whatever learning strategies suit its learners and deploying different locally available resources. At the same time, it can be accounted for on the same scales as formal learning and therefore count toward further learning and employment in the formal economy. This is significantly different from the delivery of formal qualifications in a community or work setting, where a slice of the academy is relocated from its institutional home to the community, bringing with it the familiar paraphernalia of curriculum, lectures, textbooks, and tests; or where a fieldwork component is offered as part of a formal academic qualification, as is common in social work, teaching, nursing, and increasingly in other areas of vocational learning; or where an apprentice learns on the job alongside a day or more per week spent in the academy. Standards such as Training Packages act as boundary objects[49] that communicate between different institutions, translating from one (technical) language/meaning to another. In the case of learning, this means translating meaning in the nonformal learning arena into the formal arena and visa versa. Both remain what they are, and each can talk meaningfully to the other, achieving currency in each other's jurisdiction. In this imaginary the political relations of educational management and regulation generate recognition of nonformal learnings (multiple in practice and origin) as legitimate pathways into formal qualifications and work, and as having value in their own right and on their own terms, not only when supervised by the academy.[50]

Conclusion

The Department for Community Development's strategy for integrated community development identifies community learning as one of four "prongs of development," while recognizing community learning centers and networks as the vehicles for development. A lot is resting on the capacity of communities to design and implement locally effective strategies for learning. Moreover, success rests on the capacity of national and provincial officials to allow local strategies to flourish—even, perhaps, in the face of criticism from national educators who may not adequately value nonformal approaches. Unless specifically challenged, formal educational systems tend to bring with them curricula and pedagogies that are alien to learners. And this is not just a problem of "developing nations": ask Australian secondary teachers about the numbers of post-compulsory students for whom academic curricula and desk-bound text-based learning resembles a cruel and unnatural punishment.

We noted earlier in this chapter that customary informal learning in Papua New Guinea uses methods that are now regarded as innovative by educational researchers in developed nations. Such researchers also argue that literacy is much more than the capacity to read and write, and that multiple forms of literacy are critical to effective communication and meaning making. As Mary Kalantzis and Bill Cope put it, being *multi*literate means that one can understand and communicate across a range of different modalities of expression and meaning—linguistic, audio, visual, gestural, and spatial.[51] This idea can be pushed further to argue that structured oral communication may form a bridge to literacy and that practical hands-on learning supported by structured talk, multiple forms of recording oral communication, and skilled practice can form a bridge to recognition of learning by formal education systems. Talking about skills and their embedded knowledge and applications in the performance of both subsistence and income-generating activities not only yields data on skills in demand and enables the previously implicit to be recognized and documented, it also provides nonliterate practitioners of those skills with a vocabulary with which to name their technical knowledge explicitly and the confidence that comes with technical knowledge and rhetorical capabilities. Moreover, emphasis on oral communication can give written literacy meaning by having it clearly related to practice—for example, as an official and portable record of local skills.

Not everyone has to be literate at the outset for literacy to be manifested as a powerful tool of community development. A workable strategy is for selected members of the community to act as scribes with priority being given to the technical skills to operate video and voice-recording equipment that will provide records of proceedings accessible to all. What is important is that everyone has a voice and is able to participate fully in the talk from which an integrated approach to community development will emerge. In all of the communities in which we worked, community members actively engaged in the process of researching the patterns of local forms of learning, health, and livelihoods.

Finally, it is important that the talk is appropriately structured and kept on track, and here the Integrated Community Development policy can be used as a device for framing leading questions and setting agendas. By asking questions about what competencies are needed and having communities articulate these, a local iteration of national competency standards can be produced and then given general currency through a both-ways dialogue and the use of standards as translating devices. In this way standards and templates for translation can become engines for reform. Local networks can be empowered to decide on their own learning programs—what to learn and how to teach it—working in the framework of regional infrastructure and processes that guide, monitor, support, and resource, and in the context of national standards and frameworks that enable mobility and comparability.

Notes

1. Daro Avei, *Identifying the Motu Knowledge Base for Inclusion in School Curriculum: The Boera Experience*, National Research Institute, Division of Education Research, Report No. 69, Port Moresby, 1995.

2. Colin Swatridge, *Delivering the Goods: Education as Cargo in Papua New Guinea*, Manchester University Press, Manchester, 1985.

3. Martin Nakata, *Disciplining the Savages, Savaging the Disciplines*, Aboriginal Studies Press, Canberra, 2007, ch. 10.

4. The literature on adult and vocational education distinguishes between formal, nonformal, and informal learning on the basis of the location, structure, and intent. Formal learning, conducted in an education or training institution, leads to the award of an accredited qualification; nonformal learning, while having intended learning outcomes, is undertaken outside an educational institution, for example, through programs of study offered in workplaces, community centers, or professional associations. Informal learning happens as a consequence of other activities—usually unplanned but nevertheless producing valuable skills and knowledge. See Organisation for Economic and Cooperative Development, *Lifelong Learning for All*, OECD, Paris, 1996; Louise Watson, *Lifelong Learning in Australia*, University of Canberra/Department of Education, Science and Training, Canberra, 2003. International agencies and governments adopt variations of this distinction. For instance, the OECD classifies formal learning as a program of study that is recognized through a qualification and nonformal learning as a program that does not lead to a qualification. The Australian Department of Education and Science uses this definition, whereas, for example, the Swedish Agency for Education draws the distinction solely on the basis of location, defining formal learning as being undertaken in an institution designed primarily for that purpose. See Terry Clark, "Lifelong, Life-Wide or Life Sentence?" *Australian Journal of Adult Learning*, vol. 45, no. 1, 2005, pp. 47–62.

5. This distinction is being blurred in contemporary educational policy discussions, where Basil Yeaxlee's 1929 concept of "lifelong education" is brought into association with Eduard Lindeman's 1926 writings on the link between adult education and community development to promote a notion of lifelong and lifewide learning in a range of work, educational, and community settings. See Eduard C. Lindeman, *The Meaning of Adult Education*, Oklahoma Research Center for Continuing Professional and Higher Education, 1989.

6. Victoria Marsick and Karen Watkins, *Informal and Incidental Learning in the Workplace*, Routledge, London, 1990, pp. 15–24.

7. Bob Hoffman, *Informal Learning: Managing the Training Function*, Information Lifeline, 2005.

8. Peter M. Senge, *The Fifth Discipline: The Art and Practice of the Learning Organisation*, Doubleday, New York, 1990.

9. Etienne Wenger, *Communities of Practice: Learning, Meaning and Identity*, Cambridge University Press, Cambridge, 1998.

10. Jean Lave and Etienne Wenger, *Situated Learning: Legitimate Peripheral Participation*, Cambridge University Press, Cambridge, 1991.

11. European Commission, *A Memorandum on Lifelong Learning*, European Commission, Brussels, 2000.

12. Christina Reymer, "Breathing New Life into Education for Life: A Reconceptualisation of Non-formal Education with a Focus on the Melanesian Pacific," paper presented to the joint AARE/NZARE Conference, Melbourne 1999, http://www.aare.edu.au/99pap/rey99228.htm, accessed 28 May 2008.

13. John Josephs, *Education for All Assessment 2000: Papua New Guinea Country Report*, UNESCO, Port Moresby, 2000, http://www.unesco.org/education/wef/countryreports/papua_new_guinea/contents.html, accessed 16 June 2008.

14. Paulias Matane, *A Philosophy of Education for Papua New Guinea*, Ministerial Committee Report, Port Moresby, National Department of Education, 1986, p. 6.

15. Geoff Thompson, *The State of Education in Papua New Guinea*, Port Moresby, National Department of Education, 2003.

16. National Department of Education, *Growth of Education Since Independence 1975–1985*, Port Moresby, National Department of Education, 1985, p. 47.

17. Pacific Islands Forum Secretariat, *Non-Formal Education in Pacific Island Countries*, Suva, Pacific Islands Forum Secretariat, 2007.

18. Francyne M. Huckaby, "When Worlds Collide: A Critical Decolonizing View of Western-Based Schooling in Papua New Guinea Village Education," *Journal of Curriculum Theorizing*, vol. 20, no. 4, 2004, p. 80.

19. Ibid., p. 81.

20. Reymer, "Breathing New Life into Education for Life," p. 27.

21. The conference was convened as the Tenth Extraordinary Meeting of the Faculty of Education at the University of Papua New Guinea.

22. Michael Olsson, Ephraim Apelis, and Jacqueline Wasilewski, *The Coordination, Development and Implementation of Nonformal Education in Papua New Guinea*, Port Moresby, Ministry of Education, 1985.

23. Jeff Siegel, "Formal vs. Non-Formal Vernacular Education: The Education Reform in Papua New Guinea," *Journal of Multilingual and Multicultural Development*, vol. 18, no. 3, 1997.

24. Lisa D. Delpit and Graeme Kemelfield, *An Evaluation of the Viles Tok Ples Skul Scheme in the North Solomons Province,* Port Moresby, University of Papua New Guinea, 1985, p. 122.

25. Naihuwo Ahai and Michael Bopp, *Missing Links: Literacy, Awareness and Development in Papua New Guinea,* Educational Research Report, no. 67, Boroko, National Research Institute, 1995, p. 95.

26. L. Yeoman and M. Obi, *The Management of Government-Based Literacy Projects in Papua New Guinea,* Deloitte Touche Tohmatsu, Management Consultants, 1993, p. 17.

27. The Pacific Islands Forum is an intergovernmental grouping of independent states in the Pacific Ocean. Originally established in 1971 as the South Pacific Forum, it changed its name in 2000. The group has sixteen member states—Australia, the Cook Islands, the Federated States of Micronesia, Fiji, Kiribati, the Marshall Islands, Nauru, New Zealand, Niue, Palau, Papua New Guinea, Samoa, Solomon Islands, Tonga, Tuvalu, and Vanuatu. New Caledonia and French Polynesia attained associate member status in 2006.

28. UNESCO, "World Declaration on Education for All," http://www.unesco.org/education/efa/ed_for_all/background/jomtien_declaration.shtml, accessed 9 July 2008.

29. Pacific Islands Forum Secretariat, *Non-Formal Education in Pacific Island Countries,* p. 15.

30. Reymer, "Breathing New Life into Education for Life."

31. Institute of Scientific and Technical Communicators, "National Occupational Standards," http://www.istc.org.uk/Communication_Resources/National_Occ_Standards/nos_home.htm, accessed 26 July 2007.

32. R. Page and J. Hillage, *Vocational Education and Training in the UK: Strategies to Overcome Skill Gaps in the Workforce,* Social Science Research Centre, Berlin, 2006, p. 9.

33. Irena Grugulis, "The Contribution of National Vocational Qualifications to the Growth of Skills in the UK," *British Journal of Industrial Relations,* vol. 41, no. 3, 2003, pp. 457–475.

34. Page and Hillage, *Vocational Education and Training in the UK.*

35. Organisation for Economic and Cooperative Development, *The Role of National Qualifications Systems in Promoting Lifelong Learning: Report from Thematic Group 1: The Development and Use of "Qualification Frameworks" as a Means of Reforming and Managing Qualifications Systems,* OECD, Paris, 2004.

36. European Commission, "The European Qualifications Framework: A New Way to Understand Qualifications across Europe," http://ec.europa.eu/education/policies/educ/eqf/index_en.html, accessed 3 April 2007.

37. Office of Training and Tertiary Education, Statistical Data Guidelines, Melbourne, Office of Training and Tertiary Education, 2007.

38. A current initiative of the European Commission, the Valuing Prior Learning (VPL) Project, whose partners are the Netherlands, Norway, and France, includes as an outcome recommendations for the European Qualifications Framework on the recognition of prior learning. See European Centre for the Valuation of Prior Learning, "VPL 4 EU—Expected Outcomes," http://www.vpl4.eu/projectinformation/expectedoutcomes.php, accessed 24 March 2007.

39. Banduk Marika, Colin Lane, Helen Smith, and Leanne Reinke, "Working Towards an Indigenous Training Model: Learning from Gamarrwa Nuwul Landcare, Yirrkala," in Kaye Bowman, ed., *Equity in Vocational Education and Training: Research Readings*, National Centre for Vocational Education Research, Adelaide, 2004, p. 81.

40. Yirrkala Dhanbul Community Association Inc., "Landcare," http://www.yirrkaladhanbul.nt.gov.au/council/content/view/full/122, accessed 14 November 2007.

41. Garma is sponsored and managed through the Yothu Yindi Foundation, see "Garma Festival," Available at: http://www.garma.telstra.com/aboutgarma.htm, accessed 14 November 2007.

42. Although both institutions had campuses in the nearby township of Nhulunbuy, in 2002 neither offered programs there in skill areas that met Landcare's training needs.

43. Landcare also brought in external experts—for example, to advise on the commercial viability of local plants (Gamarrwa Nuwul Landcare, Monthly Report, February 2002)—and collaborated with other local organizations to offer technical training—for example, the YNOTS program that has been conducted since 2001 by ALCAN Gove with support from Landcare. See Landcare reports from 1999 to 2002.

44. Banduk Marika, Landcare coordinator, discussion at Yirrkala, August 2002.

45. A major force in this development was Mandawuy Yunupingu, a Yolngu leader who became principal of the Yirrkala school in 1986. Other local teachers who led this movement include Nalwarri Nurruwutthun and Raymattja Marika.

46. Helen Watson and Wade Chambers, *Singing the Land, Signing the Land*, Deakin University, Geelong, 1989, p. 5.

47. Through the British Council, several provincial and municipal government departments in China, including Chongqing, Hubei, and Guangdong, have adopted key elements of the UK and Australian competency-based systems. See British Council, "Vocational Education: Sino-UK Education Links," http://www.britishcouncil.org/china-education-sinouklinks-vocational.htm, accessed 6 August 2011.

48. In 2001 the national government of Sikkim received World Bank funding to develop approaches to vocational training that in part were modeled on the Australian national VET system.

49. Susan Leigh Star and James R. Griesemer, "Institutional Ecology, Translations and Boundary Objects: Amateurs and Professionals in Berkeley's Museum of Vertebrate Zoology, 1907–39," *Social Studies of Science*, vol. 19, 1989, pp. 387–420.

50. Maev O'Collins, *Social Development in Papua New Guinea 1972–1990: Searching for Solutions in a Changing World,* Political and Social Change Monograph No. 18, Department of Political and Social Change, Australian National University, Canberra, 2005.

51. Bill Cope and Mary Kalantzis, eds., *Multiliteracies: Literacy Learning and the Design of Social Futures,* Routledge, London, 2000.

Chapter 12

Learning Centers for Sustainable Living

THE GLOBAL LITERATURE ON community learning needs a complete reworking. Notwithstanding the limits of theory, practical application through learning centers has become one of the dominant means of addressing informal educational programs across the globe. International organizations including United Nations bodies have taken up various community learning approaches with positive dedication. UNESCO and the United Nations Development Program, for example, are using community learning centers to address a range of social equity issues in the Global South.[1] Most commonly they focus on the improvement of basic vernacular literacy levels or offer education initiatives aimed at creating sustainable livelihoods. Given that formal education still reaches proportionally fewer people in the Global South—and was even less likely to have done so in the youth of the current adults—there are a wide range of applications for informal education where lifelong learning approaches would seem to be appealing. On this basis and others, we argue strongly for such learning centers as an informal institutional basis for sustainable community development in the Global South. However, as will become clear, our responses to current literature and practice range from qualified support to deeply critical concern. In some cases, otherwise well-intentioned approaches are marred by deeply problematic assumptions in discrete areas; in other examples, the approaches would benefit from critical reflection on their general framing presuppositions.

Part of the purpose of this chapter is to analyze the current writing on community learning and community learning centers or networks, and to assess its relevance to Papua New Guinea. From the outset it is important to acknowledge that the work on learning centers and community learning is well-intentioned and directed to improving people's lives and livelihoods. However, as in all fields, the literature also needs careful and critical assessment. While there are exceptions, most of the writings on community learning centers carry implicit assumptions formulated within modernist and progressivist theoretical traditions of the Global North.[2] Here progress is still taken to be a movement toward modernist ideals—universal literacy and numeracy, time discipline, social capital appreciation, and money-management sensitivity. Projects tend to be based on the experiences of urban settings and on modern social subjectivities that self-consciously emphasize the accumulation of more and more information.

However, it is not clear that such approaches are directly applicable across different cultural settings in rural Papua New Guinea—or at least not without concerted efforts to rework some of their precepts. For example, simply taking away the "directive teacher" in the learning experience does not guarantee good practice; mishandled it can raise self-esteem and raise expectations while doing nothing to improve structural disadvantage. Simply providing modern information technologies and techniques for learning such as computers and computer-aided teaching can give the impression of progress and overcoming the "digital divide"; misdirected it can end up as an expensive and counterproductive process of short-term entertainment or expectation raising.[3] Constructing new community learning centers can efficiently use donor funds with impressive codifiable outcomes akin to building primary schools. However, unlike in formal education, where increased attendance figures can look impressive, it is difficult to evaluate community learning outcomes. And, in any case, it is not necessarily the buildings that make the most fundamental difference to community learning and sustainable development.

Community Learning Centers in Global Context

The idea of the community learning center as a place to promote "student-centered learning" and "lifelong learning" comes out of the dominant Western education theories of the past twenty-five years. What began as a theory for shifting from more didactic formal modes of education to more independent learning in primary and secondary school classrooms has been given wider application outside the formal education sector. This has primarily arisen out of concerns to improve the uptake of education among those who are less likely to obtain formal education, including in such cities as Los Angeles and Edinburgh. For example, Kelly Wilson's discussion of the Puente Learning Center would seem on the surface to have a connection to cross-cultural research, but it is about a highly funded community learning center in urban Los Angeles that is concerned more with the aesthetics of architecture and technology than the people for whom it is designed.[4] Or, to take another example, for over a decade now (since 1998) the United States Department of Education has poured money into its Twenty-first Century Community Learning Centers program, with US$1.081

billion allocated in 2008. This program is directed toward out-of-hours training for young students who come from high-poverty and low-performing schools with the aim of improving basic mathematics, English, school attendance, and classroom behavior.[5]

The predominant alternative to this approach that treats community-based learning as a supplement or fallback position emphasizes opening up and re-making the existing school system so that it engages with the community. How-ever, such approaches tend to assume a systematic and functional education system that can be built upon by mobilizing community resources.[6] In other words, whether community learning is treated as a supplement to bring stu-dents back into the formal system or communities are used as a resource to en-hance the formal system, the driving methodological and theoretical approach to learning centers comes out of North American and British *urban* examples di-rected at enhancing formal education. Despite early work, such as Paulo Friere's *Pedagogy of the Oppressed*, which drew its inspiration from the Global South, most of the examples of community learning centers come out of very specific historical, political, and sociological contexts that do not comfortably translate across to Melanesian, Pacific, and other customary villages.[7]

There are senses in which the literature in this area is helpful by infer-ence. Pat Millar and Sue Kilpatrick's work in disadvantaged communities in Hobart, Tasmania, argues that community learning centers can offer training programs for bringing early school leavers back into training in the technical and further education (TAFE) sector through informal learning.[8] This has some resonance for our study, though the level at which people leave school in Papua New Guinea is much earlier than the instances discussed here, and the kinds of training desired is completely different. Erping Zhu and Danilo M. Baylen's work takes as its object of study the communities of learning in universities. It is a solidly argued article but a bit upside down for our purposes, being mostly about tertiary-level learning for a community group in a thoroughly First World setting using e-mail, bulletin boards, and other electronic means of communi-cation. Nevertheless, it has a definition of community learning that does reflect one of our concerns:

> Community learning has not been clearly defined in the literature. For some people community learning aims at empowering people and enabling them to cope with and influence the factors affecting their lives, including work-ing towards getting a certificate/degree and functioning well in a certain com-munity. Community learning provides people with opportunities to improve employment prospects and the skills and information they need to participate in community life. For others, community learning implies programmes and

services coordinated by a community learning center.... Based on the literature, we define community learning as a pedagogical approach that employs
methods, programmes and services to develop individuals' knowledge, skills,
confidence and capacity for life-long learning and continuous services to the
community. As with learning communities, community learning is learner-
centered. Learners decide what and how they want to learn. However, the major difference is that community learning works with local communities and
their members rather than with educational establishments such as schools,
colleges or universities.[9]

It accords with the commonsense UNESCO definition, written into its terms of
reference, a definition that we are happy to use except for its implicit emphasis
on community learning as an internal "delivery mechanism" for externally provided literacy and knowledge training.[10]

A CLC is a local place of learning outside the formal education system. Located in both villages and other areas, it is usually set up and managed by
local people in order to provide various learning opportunities for community
development and improvement of the quality of life. A CLC doesn't necessarily require new infrastructure, but can operate from an existing health center,
temple, mosque, primary school or other suitable venue. CLCs have been recognized as effective delivery mechanisms of literacy and continuing education
programmes through community-based approaches.[11]

As an adjunct to formal education, community learning has also been used as
a means of drawing parents in as active participants in the process of both supporting their children and learning for themselves as part of lifelong education.[12]
It was in this context that the idea of "different knowledges" arose in response
to the particular needs of second-generation immigrant children whose parents
had traditional backgrounds, usually religiously framed. The adults were experiencing the social pressures of modernizing change and confronting children
with different values; the children were facing a generational shift. At their
best community learning centers became places for dialogue across difference.
While this concept of "different knowledges" has been used in a limited (plu-
ralist modern) way, it does also address another of our concerns—addressing
ontological difference.

A further dominant influence on the introduction of community learning
centers is in the area of environmental education. Environmental education in
the Global North is used from primary school onward to raise awareness of the
effects of pollution and to encourage recycling campaigns or develop awareness

of the ecosystems affecting both urban and rural plant and animal life.[13] The translation into community learning has its basis in concerns that come out of debates in the Global North, though the consequences for people in the Global South are often more immediate and more dire. Robert Hill's work, for example, on environmental activists organizing community awareness groups for both consciousness raising and political activism makes clear the tension between "ground-up" and external motivation in community learning. Reading between the lines of Hill's study, we find that, though North American grass-roots and bureaucratic educational initiatives are in political terms in opposition to each other, and even if the local knowledge (drawn from local expertise backed by empirical evidence) of effects of pollution was ignored by the scientific experts, both the grass-roots initiatives and the bureaucratic ones were actually working from the same educational premise of the progressive modernist accumulation of facts.[14] More relevant to Papua New Guinea, Adele Jones looks at initiatives in the Asia-Pacific region and activities in local settings focusing mainly on theater as a medium of education. Importantly, Jones notes that people are too often made to feel responsible for environmental change that is not their responsibility and/or beyond their power, and that transnational conglomerates escape culpability or responsibility by such strategies.[15]

Community learning centers have also been used in initiatives as diverse as adult education and mobilizing political activism. Community learning approaches have been used in community activism against large corporations in the developed world in places where industrial pollution is having an adverse impact on the health and well-being of local populations. It has been recognized that, while awareness of climate change and fostering care and responsibility for the environment is a social good—whether in relation to one's immediate surroundings or on a world scale—there is also a sense in which local campaigns can lead to an internalization of responsibility. For example, children are given a heightened sense of responsibility for urban water wastage that elides the structural causes and responsibilities for water shortages. In the context of Papua New Guinea, where large international logging, mining, fishing, and agricultural companies are the main agents destroying the viability of customary lands, one would neither want to make a community feel it was simply their fault that their land was polluted nor expect them to carry a greater burden of responsibility for the environmental health of the planet than people in the developed world, when other forms of livelihood (let alone sustainable livelihoods) are not within their reach. Environmental education that simply preaches "take matters into your own hands" are liable to confirm that sense of personal or local responsibility without the capacity to enact change. Sustained, consistent, and thoughtful support for dealing with environmental problems that are having a

direct impact on people's lives and livelihoods is required, along with appropriate approaches to identifying livelihoods that are not only environmentally sustainable but economically, socially, and culturally sustainable.

The most recent influence in the community learning area has come in the
last decade or so with the turn to information and communication technologies.
There is a common belief that, by overcoming the digital divide between the
Global North and the Global South, development will come to those currently
without enough information to follow the path already taken in the developed
countries. Various writings talk of the importance of community e-centers, tel-
ecenters, and information kiosks in "empowering" communities that have supposedly been "left behind in the shift to an information society."[16] Such writings
have appropriately begun to recognize that community ownership of an e-center
project is crucial, that training is integral to the process of information transfer, that projects need to be linked to government policy directions, and that
electronic communications development is slow and uncertain in its outcomes.
However, all this work takes for granted the idea, first, that the key dimension of
learning centers is the dissemination of information from those with the facts to
those without. Second, there is an overwhelming tendency to conflate information (instances of codified facts) and knowledge (different forms of understanding across different ontological formations) and to make little or no allowance
for the different communication needs of different knowledges (see Chapter 2).
In general, there is a tendency to foreground and fetishize digital communications technologies for their intrinsic learning and networking capacities rather
than to treat them as useful background tools that can be discriminately drawn
into the community learning context.

To draw together the discussion thus far, across most community learning
programs the intention has been to combat urban poverty and disadvantage,
socioeconomic hardship, and accompanying antisocial behavior through "empowerment," "capacity building," and responding to environmental degradation.
However, for all its good intentions, the mainstream approach has many un-
examined assumptions, particularly with respect to the nature of knowledge,
the meaning of information, and the means of their dissemination. Even Jerry
Schwab and Dale Sutherland's apparently sophisticated report for the Center for
Aboriginal Economic Policy Research on Indigenous Australia contains a basic
mismatch of social conditions and cultural forms, with most of the examples
drawn from the metropolitan West.[17] It may be possible to find commonalities
across the social distance between Washington Heights, New York, and Yirrkala,
Australia, or Vanagi Settlement, Papua New Guinea—and it is true that youth
in those places face similar issues of substance abuse, crime, truancy, and il-
literacy. However, the underlying social conditions are not the same, except

perhaps for the way in which there is a tendency by governments and international agencies to consider top-down dissemination of technologies, techniques, and technicalities, comfortably democratized by moments of consultation with the "communities in need." Without considerable subtlety of approach in the application of the theory of community learning centers, including an understanding of both-ways learning, there is a potential to contribute actively to the breakdown (rather than reflexive adaptation) of customary cultures. In some of the writings, a modern assimilationist potential is intended; in others it is the unintended consequences of assuming what is "best for them."

Assumptions Underlying the Community Learning Literature

The problems with the community learning literature are manifold. In this section we elaborate on just a few of the more prominent assumptions that block an understanding of the limitations we have outlined. Within most of this literature, the assumed background politics framing the development of learning centers in the Global South is, first, liberal capitalism—with participatory democracy sometimes added for good measure—and, second, modern learning-as-dissemination, with community empowerment added in as a descriptive flourish.[18] Third, the theory behind community learning centers is premised, on either a form of self-active and autonomous individualism that is prevalent in urban Western societies but not relevant to much of Papua New Guinea or a romantic notion of the integrated community that is hard to find anywhere.[19] When communities do become the center of discussion, the literature tends to deploy loose and imprecise terms such as "empowerment" and "capacity building." Too often such concepts are used with little sense of applied outcomes beyond increased basic literacy as a technical signifier of a particular liberal political persuasion—"education for all."[20] Being able to read and write does not necessarily equip students for the complexities of their different worlds. Feeling empowered does not necessarily make one powerful, nor does enhancing the capacity of people necessarily entail improved conditions for them. The structural conditions that frame the learning process are as important as individual subjectivities and motivations.

Questions of What and Who Are Being Addressed

All too often the mainstream approach to community learning centers begins with an inherently negative agenda. In other words, instead of describing the intricate play between strengths and weaknesses, the need for instituting a learning center is premised onesidedly on problems to be addressed. For example, the *Manual for the Implementation of Community Learning Centres* for UNESCO, the United Nations Development Program, and the Government of

Thailand does not ask: "What is good about this community?" "What is working?" "How can we make that better and stronger?" The program is premised on a "needs assessment" of what the community is doing wrong and what needs to be fixed.[21] In other words, the process begins with the negative. The Thai implementation pamphlets also assume a top-down form of managerialism: a leader, who "directs and monitors operations," members who "perform jobs as assigned," and supporters who secure materials and equipment. This makes some sense where lack of education and training are the material influences affecting disadvantage and where few people are likely to have the skills assumed to break out of the limits of poor education, but the rationale for such a negative assumption are left undiscussed. More important, this is not the only effective structure that could be proposed. There are different kinds of leadership and organizational expertise in such villages that could be drawn into contention.

Another problematic aspect of the UNESCO *Manual* is that people who do not fit the plan are not considered when discussing "members of the community." There is no room in the definition of community in this lengthy paper for people who dissent or differ in any way. Given that one of the main issues in Papua New Guinea is the pressures brought on by community dissenters (squatters, *raskols*, women unhappy with conventional gender inequalities, and other out-groups), this would seem an unhelpful approach. A more recent UNESCO report has recognized the importance of people living with HIV as an out-group for whom education might help diminish stigmatization, but here again the emphasis is on *dissemination* of information to respond to a negative problem rather than community dialogue.[22] As Lawrence Hammar and others have illustrated, and as we have discussed in Chapter 10, there is no paucity of information circulating around Papua New Guinea about HIV/AIDS;[23] the problem is that much of the information is misleading, misses the point, or is distorted in the necessary translation that occurs between different knowledge systems—tribal, traditional, and modern—and between different uses of knowledge: abstract technical knowledge (*teche*) and practical contextualized knowledge (*mētis*).[24] The assumption in much of the literature is that the practical local knowledge embedded in the day-to-day life of village people is lesser knowledge.

Another UNESCO initiative, implemented in neighboring Burma—*Myanmar: The Community Learning Centre Experience*—has some of the same problems of beginning with the negative as found in the Thai study, but it is more thoughtfully written. The author and editor acknowledge that in practice things do not go according to plan. They acknowledge, for example, that concerted efforts need to be made "to understand the dynamics of the community—such as who make the decisions, who are the followers, and what are the main obstacles

to inter-personal interactions. Understanding the dynamics may prevent the unfortunate situation which sometimes happens—that few community members
capitalize on the community learning center, while the majority of the villagers
remain marginalized."[25] This report recognizes the worth of local knowledge—
particularly the knowledge of the elders. It is also sensitive to gender differences. It makes clear in its statistics that the bodies or committees constituted
within the program that have the most power are dominated by men. The editor
acknowledges that women are less likely to take up formal education opportunities that might stem from such initiatives. The report also acknowledges that
there is a large and thorny issue in relation to the improvement of literacy levels
around an imposed national language, particularly when minority languages are
under threat. However, the report has some internal tensions. At certain points
it rejects other methods of knowledge transmission in favor of a "scientific"
Western results-based learning capacity that is then imposed over older forms
of learning. The problem is that this does not work even in its own terms. If in
the culture of the learners, for example, there is an entrenched traditional understanding of education as rote learning of truths, as there is in traditional East
Asian settings, or if there is a tribal understanding of learning through stories,
as is the case in much of Papua New Guinea, it is difficult to see how results-
based learning and Western scientific notions of information acquisition are not
in tension with each other. Furthermore, it is difficult to know how to measure
the results beyond the ability of participants to repeat back what they are supposed to have learned.

Questions of the Nature of Knowledge

In the literature, practitioners and implementers of community learning centers often open their discussions by justifying what they are doing in
terms of inclusiveness and respect for "different" knowledges. For the reasons
outlined earlier—see the section called "Defining Ontological Formations" in
Chapter 2—we would argue that those "different" *knowledges* are generally (different) sets of *information* constituted in one (singular) register of *knowledge*.
That is, they may be plural and various sets of understandings and facts, but
they fall within the recognizable range of technical and analytical knowledge in
societies framed by the dominance of modernism. In the current literature there
is little space for truly different knowledges (tribal, traditional). Analogical and
cosmological knowledge is usually confined to the religious sphere or reduced
to proto-knowledge that will be made comprehensible when it comes into contact with the kind of knowledge that comes down from international bodies or
the government bodies who want to meet progress-oriented goals.

This is most evident in publications such as the UNESCO/United Nations

Development Program *Manual for the Implementation of Community Learning Centres*. The *Manual* contains many statements along the lines of "When community analysis has been done, the community members then perceive what they need." That is, implicitly, it requires external intervention before people are able properly to "know." Despite all the rhetoric to the contrary, the process of perception tends not to be treated in a substantial way as the organic negotiated outcome of community consultation; it is more the product of a process managed and directed from the outside. As Graham Roberts' writing unintentionally exemplifies, apparently unaware of any tension between the two sides of his claim to community engagement a generalizable design model, engagement tends to work from the top down: "Kadavu provides a health promotion model that is generated and legitimated by local communities, rather than by government ministries or external agencies.... The Kadavu Rural Health Project (1994–97), an Australian Agency for International Development project of which the author was the Team Leader, was designed as a potential model for rural health projects in Fiji and the Pacific."[26]

A variation on the theme is *A Case Study on Community Learning Centre for Development,* submitted to the Asia Pacific Cultural Centre for UNESCO. This is a case study of the implementation of community learning centers in Nepal. Within the report is a disarmingly simple passage illustrative of the lack of respect for "different knowledges." Without being at all patronizing or offensive, in effect it says, "We are simply bringing new knowledge, and that new knowledge is better":

> Most people of the community learning center are farmers who are depending on a business of animal husbandry especially buffalo rearing. But they are still following a traditional way of cattle rearing. So, to train them in the scientific and modern way of cattle rearing, community learning center has formed a buffalo group in each sub-community learning center and is providing different training on animal husbandry to the group members about different diseases of buffaloes and their protection against those and also about fodder production and marketing techniques.[27]

The issue here is not that scientific and modern techniques are being communicated to people who have been using other forms of knowledge. A dialogue *between* and about different forms of knowledge can, if handled well, be very creative. It is rather that the report shows no recognition of the strengths and weaknesses—or indeed appropriateness and cultural implications—of other forms of knowledge. Modern, technical, and scientific epistemologies are taken for granted as part of good development. In this case, agricultural science finds a natural affinity with the *business* of animal husbandry—and indeed it does if "business" is defined in modern market terms. However, the report says nothing about the nature of the different forms of knowledge and how they might intersect, undercut each other, or exist alongside each other. In other words, it does not reflect on its own claims regarding community learning. This discussion of reflecting on learning can be taken further through elaborating on the question of reflexivity.

Questions of Reflexivity and Social Capital

Among the names evoked in the field of education is Pierre Bourdieu.[28] Unfortunately, however, there is a consistent misuse of Bourdieu's social theory in this literature. This misapprehension has trickled down to the community learning sector and has important implications for how community learning centers have been put into practice. The first misuse hinges on the difference between "reflection" and "reflexivity." In brief, reflection can be defined as the examination of things and meanings in the world, while reflexivity is a double process that requires both reflection as normally understood *and* reflection upon the process of reflection. That is, the notion of reflexivity turns on more than the repeated reflection upon things and meanings. In the way that we have been using it throughout this book, it entails analysis of the meaning of the practice of reflection and the consequences of lifting different patterns of knowledge into a more reflective mode.

Reflexivity involves reflection on the consequences of reflection and learning, including on how power and knowledge are bound up with each other.[29] For example, it is often said that "knowledge is power," but, without reflection on the ontological layers of knowledge in different social settings, an unreflexive modernist response is to conclude that therefore increased dissemination of knowledge (read: information) will give those receiving all that information more power. It is one of the liberal modern illusions, among others such as "more interconnectivity will bring about stronger social integration" or "more inclusion makes for stronger communities." Within the community learning center literature these two quite different concepts of "reflection" and "reflexivity" are thus often conflated.

The second misuse of Bourdieu's work concerns the notion of "cultural capital." Bourdieu puts education within a complex of comparably powerful fields in which people have more or less social "expertise"—art, food, sport, health, religion, and so on. Knowing how to work in these different fields, including how to relate to others, leads to the accumulation of what he terms "cultural capital," or the wealth of cultural knowledge and standing that we acquire throughout our lives. Bourdieu's ideas about cultural capital are reworked by writers such as Robert Putnam using the term "social capital."[30] However, in Putnam's hands or in the work of sociologist Anthony Giddens,[31] the term "social capital" becomes a cultural-political version of market-based capital—a transferable resource able to be drawn upon and used instrumentally by individuals.[32] In thinking about community learning centers, it would be more in keeping with Bourdieu's politics to return to his anthropological method in the *Outline of Practice*, which pays acute attention to local expertise within a cultural context. The shallow concept of "social capital" is as easily coopted by ultraconservatives as by liberal social reformers and has little in common with either the deeply nuanced concept of "cultural capital" in Bourdieu's terms or the lived experience of many village people of Papua New Guinea.

To give a pointed example, Mary Ann Brocklesby and Eleanor Fisher have summarized the sustainable livelihoods approach as emphasizing different forms of capital:

First, people are conceived of living within a *vulnerability context* in which they are exposed to risks, through sudden shocks, trends over time and seasonal change. Second, people have a number of *capital assets*, which they draw upon to make their livelihoods: these include *social capital* (social networks and relationships of trust), *natural capital* (natural resource stocks), *financial capital* (savings, income, credit), *physical capital* (transport, shelter, water, energy, communications) and *human capital* (skills, knowledge, labour). These five assets are put together to form an "*asset pentagon*," which is used to assess people's overall asset base. Third, these assets are drawn on within people's *livelihood strategies*, i.e. choices and activities through which people seek to generate a living or positive *livelihood outcomes*. Fourth, *policies, institutions and processes* are held to shape people's access to assets and livelihood activities, as well as the vulnerability context in which they live.[33]

The problem here is not that considerations regarding social life are analytically abstracted as various forms of capital—this is, at one level, what modern forms of epistemology, and in particular what is sometimes called *instrumental rationality*, have made possible, with extraordinary extensions of productivity.[34] The problem is (1) in theory such an analysis tends to be one-dimensional in its understanding—assets are simply accountable assets in the modern sense, able to be weighed, counted, codified, and therefore added to by simple accretion. (2) In practice, such considerations tend to take over and reconstitute all other ways of considering the meaning of relations and things. Forests become resources for exploiting—in tension with being lived places for grounding oneself. People become human capital to be instrumentally used—in tension with being considered family, associates, *wantok*, and enemies with whom relations have to be nurtured or negotiated. (3) Even in its own terms of aiming for productivity gains, the sustainable livelihoods approach tends to fail in practice because, while it takes into account *externalities* (the indirect costs of a particular process of production), it tends not to take into account what might be called *internalities* (the indirect consequences of "enhancing" or even just drawing on a particular form of "capital"). For example, relations of embodied personal trust can be used to enhance the flow of financial capital through intracommunity loans (see Chapter 8 on microfinance), but it may have the effect of changing the nature of trust in that community from embodied trust to more abstract trust based on fiduciary accountability such as the "known" ability of a category of person to pay back.

Even in one of the more compelling reports that we have discussed above—*Building Indigenous Learning Communities*, a study of community learning centers in a rural Indigenous community in Australia—its authors, Jerry Schwab and Dale Sutherland, are in thrall to the concept of "social capital" and associated concepts such as "capacity building" and "empowerment":

> Indigenous learning communities, as we conceive them, would take these ideas [of social capital] in to the context of Indigenous communities. They would be vehicles for the local development of social capital and tools for the construction of local capacity. Importantly, Indigenous learning communities would aim to unite families, schools and communities to identify and address local needs through drawing upon local resources.[35]

The report argues for Western education and the need for Indigenous youth to "succeed" because "the social role of education is increasingly aligned with the economy."[36] It then looks to predominantly US examples in urban settings, such as the Twenty-first Century Community Learning Centers program (touched upon earlier), which sets out to address what the US education system is not geared to deal with—and what supposedly the Australian education system should be. By contrast, as Brocklesby and Fisher suggest, sustainable livelihoods initiatives under the UN Millennium Development Goals and social capital approaches do not so comfortably mesh with notions of community development.[37] Schwab and Sutherland do, however, end with several important points that we need to take seriously in envisioning a better form of community learning center: third-party evaluation, cultural awareness and cultural sensitivity (everything is political), and outreach to uninvolved parents.

Propositions for an Alternative Approach

The approach that we have taken here, based on comparative research as well as extensive discussions with communities in Papua New Guinea and elsewhere in the Asia-Pacific region, turns on a number of propositions about the nature of community learning, the meaning of knowledge, and the kinds of pedagogical engagement.

> Proposition 1. The development of the community learning process should proceed mutually, both from within the community and from without, with careful negotiation over the level and nature of outside involvement.

Without substantial local community involvement and democratic engagement, the whole process is likely to become another top-down intervention that will require substantial ongoing financial support. However, without sensitive external support—even if only to develop a policy framework in dialogue with communities that gives learning centers legitimacy and suggests pathways for communities to seek support if they want it—local community groups can find the whole process difficult to keep going after the initial enthusiasm. Thus, the first proposition is that community learning should not be attempted using the top-down model implicit in the current literature. The kinds of community learning center programs in the Global South that organizations such as the United Nations have initiated or supported to date have been implemented in a concentrated way in small geographic areas, with limited numbers of participants and substantial external infrastructure, for a set period of time. These have then been "handed over" to communities, who are then left to find their own way with ongoing resource needs. In practice, this can be disempowering. If there is too much top-down infrastructure building, when the "top" leaves, the initiative tends slowly to dissipate, leading to disillusionment and resentment.

> Proposition 2. While provision should be made for developing or acquiring appropriate infrastructure to support community learning centers—a place to learn and tools and techniques to learn with—infrastructure is secondary to the issue of reflexively working through the conditions of community engagement and dialogue, both internally and across the internal-external divide.

In Papua New Guinea, many villages either have a place for talking or are capable of building a suitable facility to accommodate a community learning center out of bush materials. They have already grasped the concept with both hands and need people to come and give them some guidance around training. All that seems to be required is encouragement for that to continue and for basic accommodation to be supplied within the village for those who are invited in to conduct training or dialogue sessions. Tokain, for example, has a community learning center with a large room at the back for the basic but comfortable accommodation of visitors (see Chapter 5). Vagani Settlement, to take another example (see Chapter 4), has a village hall that doubles as a learning center, a preschool, and a church. One of the issues that is rarely thought through is that certain cultural boundaries mean that some themes and sensitivities cannot be talked about in public outdoor spaces. Moreover, the public/private, outdoor/indoor distinctions are often intensely gendered—in many cultures men are the public, outdoor orators; indoor spaces are the places for women's concerns. This is further complicated by another issue—"indoor" civil spaces and the church tend to be bound up with each other in Papua New Guinea. That is, there are very few indoor spaces large enough for community gatherings in villages and settlements that are not church buildings. Given that some congregational settings would silence or make certain learning discussions uncomfortable—for example in relation to HIV and sexuality—finding a suitable place for dialogue is not just about physical availability.[38]

Provision of infrastructure thus has to be handled very carefully. To take an example a different kind of infrastructure, while there is a strong contemporary emphasis on e-learning and computers for development, in many cases little attention is given to the needs of the communities themselves. For example, Nancy Hafkin and Helen Hambly Odame's report recommends the use of information communication technologies as a key mechanism for enhancing gender equity, but it is not clear how computer-mediated communication will make such a difference in places where computers are peripheral to daily life. It discusses implementation strategies for community learning centers, including through electronic-connected workshops for mutual interchange, but relies heavily on technologies that for the most part are used as abstracted dissemination networks for accessing unfiltered information.[39] It is also a bit more basic than that—go five kilometers outside any major center, and few people have the infrastructure and electricity—or a crank-computer—to support such strategies. They are lucky if they have a battery-powered radio.

> Proposition 3. Sustainable community learning is best conceived by bringing local knowledge (and local people, experts, and otherwise) into a productive relation with external expert knowledge (and outside purveyors of that knowledge).

This proposition does not sound very radical, but it is extraordinary how often learning centers are treated as places either to dump books and computers or to disseminate information. Such practices are often made on the basis of a decision made by an expert outsider who talks the language of community in the abstract but does not have time to develop any understanding of a particular community's needs. As Brocklesby and Fisher write of mainstream sustainable livelihoods approaches:

> Knowledge is located within a compartmentalized category of "human capital" in which it is seen as a "building block" for the utilization of other forms of capital. This raises the question of whether a sustainable livelihoods approach can contribute to an understanding of knowledge interfaces and the way different forms of knowledge come together, with a potential to generate conflict as well as consensus? Or whether the notion of human capital is too limited for understanding people's world views and experiences upon which any form of community development must be based?[40]

Developing a productive relation with communities involves considered respect on both sides of the insider/outsider divide. Ironically, it sometimes entails local people in customary settings developing a less *uncritical* acceptance of the magic of modern analytical knowledge. A refreshing report in this respect is *Diverse Ways of Learning, Life, Thoughts, Meanings, and Cognition.*[41] It is markedly different from many other approaches in that it does challenge Western assumptions and models of development. For example, the report includes a list from a prior workshop held in Udaipur, India, of *"10 lies my school taught me"*— a possible reference to the *David Letterman Show*—the first entry in which is "Western science and technology can solve all our problems." It takes a contrary view to much of the literature with regard to the implicit devaluation of customary and traditional knowledge and the overconfidence in scientific approaches, particularly in relation to agricultural practices.

Proposition 4. Sustainable community learning ideally involves working through multiliteracies—that is, it most adequately engages different means of learning communication, including through talking, writing, illustrating, and doing.[42]

Sustainable community learning engages different means of pedagogy that can range from practical workshops, storytelling, puppetry, theater, and drawing to written and electronic texts including videos, CDs, and web-based downloads.[43] Moreover, rather than assuming the use of global English or the national language, the practice of multiliteracy also takes seriously the matter of which language is chosen for learning and communication. Instead of the usual formal curriculum emphasis on teaching in official language(s), local first languages are often the most productive initial basis of learning, with national and global languages introduced alongside local languages as an integrated and complementary process.

> Proposition 5. Sustainable community learning concerns dialogue over the nature of knowledge rather than just the dissemination of information; it therefore needs to recognize that knowledge is a complicated entity, crossing not just different languages and different fields, but also fundamentally different ontologies of knowing and different modes of inquiry.

The starkest boundaries that need to be taken into account are the onto-logical differences between tribal, traditional, modern, and postmodern knowl-edges. They cannot be simply mapped onto each other as four ways of saying the same thing. Practices of community learning can only benefit from an ongoing reflexive approach that takes the strengths of different modes of inquiry—per-ceptual-analogical, cosmological, analytical, and aesthetic-relativist—and brings them into the same house of dialogue and translation.[44] In other words, there are different ways of producing and reproducing knowledge—and modern ana-lytical learning, including science, is only one of them. Customary tribal and tra-ditional ways of knowing and learning are also important. The most thoughtful practitioners of community learning have begun to openly recognize this need to bring different kinds of knowing and learning into contention.

This makes the conception of dialogue very important. Dialogue across dif-ferent formations of knowledge is not an easy process, even if these different ways of knowing are held as practical consciousness in the head of each of the participants in the process. Such dialogue requires going back to basics to con-tinually ask, "What is the epistemological status of what I am saying/they are saying?" It involves asking in colloquial terms, "Where are they coming from?" As Paulo Freire has emphasized:

> In order to understand the meaning of dialogical practice, we have to put aside the simplistic understanding of dialogue as a mere technique. Dialogue does not represent a somewhat false path that I attempt to elaborate upon and real-ize in the sense of involving the ingenuity of the other. On the contrary, dia-logue involves an epistemological relationship. Thus in this sense, dialogue is a way of knowing and should never be viewed as a mere tactic to involve students in a particular task.[45]

> Proposition 6. The organization form of a community learning center needs itself to be handled reflexively with continuous grappling over ba-sic issues of relations between those involved or potentially involved—

issues such as negotiation over relations of participation-authority, inclusion-exclusion, and difference-identity.

In relation to questions of participation, those who come forward to take part in community learning initiatives are in practice self-selecting. They are the people who are most likely to be socially active or form an interest group, which is not the whole community in its broadest sense. Interest groups will also have their own politics or agenda. This is a recognized facet of participatory community research, and it requires real dedication to ensure that those who are least likely to participate or speak up are heard. Gender is a basic issue for participation. This then extends to questions of authority—tribal, traditional, and modern. From the first stages of community consultation to later stages of external community support and community self-management, it is crucial to recognize that the most basic forms of politics will inform the dynamics of such initiatives. Without sensitivity to local, internal politics and without (paradoxically) some reflexively generated authority to engage otherwise, there is every possibility that the loudest voices, the most senior customary elders (usually men), or the most articulate translators of modern knowledge will carry the day. And there is no reason why those voices will reflect what the greater population or smaller groups within that population either want or need. It is a delicate balancing act in any social or cultural setting, but it becomes all the more important in a cross-cultural context to both respect customary social structures and ensure that voices that have little customary power are also heard. [46]

Imagining Other Learning Strategies

The legislation and policies for the recognition of nonformal learning discussed in this chapter and the last have evolved from institutional formations of the Global North, where community learning centers are modern institutions that take formal education into communities so that the communities are obliged to bend to accommodate the intervention. Even in nations of the Global North, such top-down interventions have encountered active or passive resistance from their primary target groups. For Papua New Guinea, the offer of strategies that are now adopted widely in the Global North carries the risk of a similar form of educational imperialism to that of the 1970s, when education was used as a vehicle for national development with little thought to how it might serve the diverse needs of rural populations and traditional economic bases. If knowledge and skill standards are to serve PNG community needs, they will need to be derived from indigenous ontologies and epistemologies in such a way that each of the imported tools are populated with local meaning.

However, as the case study of the Yirrkala Landcare Project discussed in Chapter 11 demonstrates, Global North legislation and policies can be used to support multiple and diverse community needs. In the concluding section of this chapter, we want to draw together the discussion in this chapter and the last to make some broad suggestions toward the formulation of a program of action in the context of the vision of the Department for Community Development. As space does not permit us to embark on a detailed exploration of customary and Western systems of education in Papua New Guinea, the following remarks should be regarded as a generalized gloss that serves as a way into further and more rigorously framed discussions of community learning options and possibilities.

Nonformal Learning in Papua New Guinea and New Directions in Community Development

Western researchers have noted that Papua New Guinean community life has traditionally been supported by well-developed systems of nonformal and formal learning that were embedded in the daily life of the community. Children and young people developed technical and social skills through observation, trial and error, and practice—guided by adult members of their family and community.[47] Learning was a lifelong endeavor, with technical and social skills being successively honed through practice and critique, and elements of sacred knowledge being taught by nominated community leaders under formal educational arrangements well into adulthood.[48] Indeed, customary formal education in the sacred knowledge that underpinned community life and leadership and gave meaning to technical and personal skills is described as being solely the province of adult learners.[49] Not only was this pattern of learning locally sustainable and relevant to community needs, it was also characterized by what are now recognized by Western educators as progressive and transformative pedagogical practices that include adult mentoring of children, peer coaching and guidance, and customized learning.

In contrast, the systems of formal and nonformal postprimary schooling in Papua New Guinea have frequently struggled to meet both national goals and local needs, suffering from inadequate resourcing and a lack of relevance to local social and economic conditions; access has remained a major issue for many communities as well. Establishing and maintaining the institutional apparatus of formal postprimary schooling in a diverse and decentralized jurisdiction is fraught and not always of value to people living on the margins of or outside the formal economy (see Chapter 7). As Richard Guy from the National Research Institute in Boroko remarks: "Vocational education has long been oriented toward the formal employment sector of the economy in Papua New Guinea. That sector is in decline but the informal sector is growing rapidly. There is little evidence of vocational education responding to this significant change in the work place despite extensive efforts to reform all sectors of education over the past five years."[50] Solutions to such problems faced by both the formal and nonformal national educational systems in Papua New Guinea have commonly fallen into two broad categories. In the first, the "developing" nation sets a determined path to national economic growth, even in the face of the failure of such strategies in the past. In what they describe as an "emergent and strident discourse of modernism," Peter Rushbrook and Edward Wanigasekera report on recent neoliberal analyses that deem the failure of Pacific economies to rest in customary and traditional forms of landownership and collectivism, and advocate the aggressive pursuit of modernity through the encouragement of a culture of competitive individualism and the privatization of customary land.[51] The second category is constructed around a discourse of sustainability that argues against a linear model of material and technoscientific progress and for the restoration of Pacific Island nation cultural values of "trust, reciprocity, creativity, restraint, compassion and their interdependence."[52] This view sees the reclaiming of indigenous knowledge systems as integral to Pacific Island nation sustainable development and its obverse—adherence to Western rationalism and corporate culture—as "anti-educational" and missing "the whole point of development altogether."[53]

Strategies for Implementing an Integrated Community Development Policy

In the messiness of everyday life, solutions are rarely found in a clear-cut choice between opposing discourses. Successful strategies tend to be multiple and contingent, adapting external models to work alongside embedded local systems and practices. This is reflected in the Department for Community Development's policy "Revitalising Local Communities and the Nation," which talks of "'bottom-up' planning and meaningful participation of people in the development process...designed to strengthen the process of decentralization and strengthen the very base of our society—the extended family system at the community level."[54] This policy approach, represented by a four-pronged garden fork, has clans and ethnic groups collaborating on the key strategies of community governance, community learning, local economic development, and sustainable environment. All four strategies are employed together in the establishment of community learning and development centers and learning networks. Importantly, this policy move is not about building new infrastructure but about using existing resources and building on the successful efforts of churches, NGOs, and communities that currently deliver literacy programs, skills training, agricultural programs, leadership training, family and conflict resolution programs, and income-generating activities.[55]

Implementation of community development in this PNG policy regime, operating locally in the framework of broad national and provincial policy directions and resourcing arrangements, will rest on the establishment of effective "both-ways" political relations and reflexive practice. Such arrangements would have government ministries and external agencies, on the one hand, and local communities, on the other, explicitly naming and taking responsibility for respective political positions and goals, meeting on middle ground to transact agreements and employing simple planning tools to design solutions and maintain links between the "center" and multiple local sites. This is the approach advocated in the Department for Community Development strategy paper, where a chain of advisory and implementation mechanisms at national, provincial, district, and local levels are ascribed roles and both-ways communicative relationships.[56] The policy envisages the community learning centers as the engine for development, operating as sites for the development of adult literacy and numeracy and skills for improved livelihoods, income generation, community governance and leadership, life skills and customary knowledges, and cultural and recreational activities including sports, storytelling, arts, and drama.[57]

A key implementation issue is to find ways of articulating this vision in practical terms so that members of each community can see how it can work for them, and can talk the vision into local realization. Three broad and concurrent strategies are suggested here as a way forward in the constituting of community learning centers and networks as local nodes in a system of nationally supported community development:

Use of community conversations about the purpose and operational arrangements for community learning centers and networks in each community to constitute the centers and ways of going forward.

Critical analysis of the principles and protocols underpinning tools and systems imported from the Global North to identify relevant models and work out what needs to be changed to reflect local needs and values.

Development of local ways of working and being with imported tools and systems, so that their practices are aligned to/modified for local needs.

The purpose of community conversation is threefold: (1) to enable local involvement and ownership; (2) to build confidence and team skills in those participating in the planning process; and (3) to act as a vehicle for the development of leadership skills—with potential leaders being supported by peer coaching and by expert mentors who may be external to the community. The question of leadership is critical. It is important that there be a shared understanding of the form that learning leadership will take in each community and that leadership models do not simply involve "taking away the directing teacher."[58] There needs to be an active process of deciding what will work, using relevant community learning and development center models as a point of departure and a source of ideas. Similarly, in determining what sort of management systems and tools will best achieve national needs for coordination and consistency, local needs for multiple approaches, and individual needs for particular programs of learning and for recognition of skills for the labor market and further study purposes, it is important that international management models are not adopted uncritically. Both customization to meet national needs and translation into multiple local knowledges will be necessary.

Conclusion

Most of the writings on community learning and community learning centers make statements of positive intent about changing the lifeworlds of the people at whom learning centers are directed. However, if one reads the writings regarding community learning centers, it is clear that it takes more than an initial reflection and statement of purpose to avoid stalling at the point of good intentions. All too often the different approaches (inadvertently or otherwise) impose a modernist model of information dissemination on communities that are supposedly choosing it for themselves. Considerations such as reflexivity in instituting the community learning centers, care about how outsiders engage, translation and dialogue across different forms of knowledge, and sensitivity to multiliteracies—as distinct from simply asking community members to reflect on their limitations and problems and then having them learn ways of enhancing social capital—are all central to rethinking the direction of community learning centers. Reflection on one's place within the process needs to be returned to at every step, and (the inevitable) failures need to be acknowledged as well as successes celebrated. Questions of the form of institutionalization and the nature of the learning need to be negotiated at the community level in an ongoing way. There are no easy answers, or even answers that can be given conclusively from a theoretical or geographic distance. In an important sense then, instituting a community learning center entails much more than just setting up a physical resource center with some learning materials and facilitators. For the community itself, it means in effect becoming a projected community of persons that together and across various divides—gender, generation, family and clan, place of origin—agree to act upon a shared and continually reinvigorated/contested vision of future challenges and possibilities. For the outsiders it means listening and talking with care about what the dialogue means.

Notes

1. UNESCO—United Nations Educational, Scientific and Cultural Organization—began its community learning center APPEAL program in 1998: Asia-Pacific Programme of Education for All, now operating in twenty-four countries.

2. See, for example, Rosa-Maria Torres, *Life-long Learning: A New Momentum and a New Opportunity for Adult Basic Learning and Education (ABLE) in the South,* a study commissioned by SIDA (Swedish International Development Cooperation Agency), Buenos Aires, 2002. This is a long, well-informed, and comprehensive report on the introduction of lifelong learning strategies in many places around the world. It is not directly applicable here, but it does give a good overview of the history of community learning centers as they have been implemented by international aid organizations, particularly United Nations agencies.

3. Leanne Reinke and Paul James, "Learning Reflexively: Technological Mediation and Indigenous Cultures," in Peter Kell, Sue Shore, and Michael Singh, eds., *Adult Education @ 21st Century,* Peter Lang, New York, 2004, pp. 221–235.

4. See, for example, Kelly R. Wilson, "The Puente Learning Center: A Building and a Program," *Journal of Urban Technology,* vol. 5, no. 2, 1998, 47–59.

5. http://www.ed.gov/programs/21stcclc/index.html, accessed 1 January 2009.

6. See, for example, Steve R. Parsons, *Journey into Community: Looking inside the Community Learning Center,* Eye on Education, West Larchmont, 2004.

7. Paulo Freire, *Pedagogy of the Oppressed,* Continuum International, New York, 2000 (1968).

8. Pat Millar and Sue Kilpatrick, "How Community Development Programmes Can Foster Re-engagement with Learning in Disadvantaged Communities: Leadership as Process," *Studies in the Education of Adults,* vol. 37, no.1, 2005, pp. 18–30.

9. Erping Zhu and Danilo M. Baylen, "From Learning Community to Community Learning: Pedagogy, Technology and Interactivity," *Educational Media International,* vol. 42, no. 3, September 2005, pp. 251–268, cited from p. 254.

10. As opposed to "both-ways learning" as discussed in Chapter 11.

11. UNESCO, *Strengthening Community Learning Networks through Linkages and Networks,* UNESCO, Bangkok, 2007, p. 1.

12. Jacquie Widin, Heidi Norman, Anne Ndaba, and Keiko Yasukawa, "An Indigenous Community Learning Centre to Promote a Culture of Learning," paper given at the Adult Learning Australia Forty-fourth Annual National Conference, "Bridging Cultures," University of Technology, Sydney, 2004. This is a report on a research project by academics from University of Technology, Sydney, at an urban Indigenous learning center, involved at least in part in teaching parents in community learning center settings how to motivate their children to remain within the formal education system.

13. For example, Alex Downie and Deidre Elrick, "Weaving the Threads: Community Development and Organizing around the Environment: A Scottish Perspective," *Community Development Journal,* vol. 35, no. 3, 2000, pp. 245–254.

14. Robert Hill, "Fugitive and Codified Knowledge: Implications for Communities Struggling to Control the Meaning of Local Environmental Hazards," *International Journal of Lifelong Education,* vol. 23, no. 3, 2004, pp. 221–242.

15. Adele M. Jones, "Mobile Training for Community Environmental Education: A Non-Formal Approach," in *Developing Alternatives: Community Development Strategies and Environmental Issues in the Pacific*, Victoria University, Melbourne, 1996, pp. 15–27.

16. United Nations Economic and Social Commission for Asia and the Pacific (UNESCAP) and the Asian Development Bank Institute, *Building e-Community Centres for Rural Development: Report of the Regional* Workshop, Bali, Indonesia, United Nations Publications, Thailand, 2005, p. 8.

17. R. G. Schwab and D. Sutherland, "Building Indigenous Learning Communities," Centre for Aboriginal Economic Policy Research Discussion Paper No. 225, 2001.

18. Against this tendency, one report records the overt arguments of its workshop participants against the overwhelmingly Global Northern approach to community development issues: Rania Saheli, *Diverse Ways of Learning, Life, Thoughts, Meanings, and Cognition*, report from the Diversity in Ways, Settings, Thought, and Discourse of Learning Workshop, Arab Education Forum and UNESCO, Ain Saadeh, Lebanon, 2004.

19. See, for example, Michael F. Reber, *An Alternative Framework for Community Learning Centers in the 21st Century: A Systemic Design Approach Toward the Creation of a Transformational Learning System*, Universal-Publishers, Boca Raton, 2003, which emphasizes self-actualization by autonomous individuals in a modern context.

20. See for example, UNESCO, *Community Empowerment through Community Learning Centres: Experiences from Thailand*, UNESCO and United Nations Development Program, Bangkok, 2002.

21. UNESCO, *Manual for the Implementation of Community Learning Centres*, UNESCO PROAP and Asia-Pacific Programme of Education for All (APPEAL), Bangkok, 1999.

22. UNESCO, *Regional Planning Workshop: Integrating HIV/AIDS Projects into Community Learning Centres*, UNESCO, Bangkok, 2007.

23. Hammar, "Epilogue: Homegrown In PNG: Rural Responses to HIV and AIDS."

24. On this distinction see James C. Scott, *Seeing like a State*, ch. 9. Modern knowledge is indeed associated with the dominance of *techne* over local contextualized knowledge, but it should be said that the modern/traditional/tribal distinction does not map directly onto the distinction between *techne* and *mētis*.

25. Baudouin Duvieusart, ed., *Myanmar: The Community Learning Centre Experience*, UNESCO Asia and Pacific Regional Bureau for Education, Bangkok, 2002, p. 11.

26. Graham Roberts, "The Kadavu Health Promotion Model, Fiji," *Health Promotion International*, vol. 12, no. 4, p. 283.

27. National Resource Centre for Non Formal Education, *A Case Study on Community Learning Centre for Development*, Asia Pacific Cultural Centre for UNESCO, Tokyo, 2001, p. 13.

28. Pierre Bourdieu, *In Other Words: Essays towards a Reflexive Sociology*, Polity Press, Oxford, 1990; and his *The Logic of Practice*.

29. This is therefore quite different from Ulrich Beck's discussion of "reflexive modernization" as the modernization of modernization, occurring autonomously, "undesired and unseen" as a "self-confrontation with effects of risk society that cannot be dealt with and assimilated in the system of industrial society" (Ulrich Beck in his book with Anthony Giddens and Scott Lash, *Reflexive Modernization*, p. 6).

30. Robert D. Putnam, *Bowling Alone: The Collapse and Revival of American Community*, Simon and Schuster, New York, 2000.

31. Anthony Giddens, *The Third Way: The Renewal of Social Democracy*, Polity, London, 1998.

32. See, for example, Douglas D. Perkins, Joseph Huey, and Paul W. Speer, "Community Psychology Perspectives on Social Capital Theory and Community Development Practice," *Journal of the Community Development Society*, vol. 33, no. 1, 2002, pp. 33–52.

33. Mary Ann Brocklesby and Eleanor Fisher, "Community Development in Sustainable Livelihoods Approaches: An Introduction," *Community Development Journal*, vol. 38, no. 3, 2003, p. 187; emphasis in original.

34. The critique of instrumental reason is most strongly associated with the Frankfurt School and its intellectual heirs, in particular Jürgen Habermas. See his *The Theory of Communicative Action*, vol. 2: *Lifeworld and System*, Polity Press, Cambridge, 1987.

35. Schwab and Sutherland, "Building Indigenous Learning Communities," p. 3.

36. Ibid., p. 8.

37. Brocklesby and Fisher, "Community Development in Sustainable Livelihoods Approaches."

38. Holly Wardlow, "You Have to Understand: Some of Us Are Glad AIDS Has Arrived," in Leslie Butt and Richard Eves, *Making Sense of AIDS*.

39. Nancy Hafkin and Helen Hambly Odame, *Gender, ICTs and Agriculture: A Situation Analysis for the 5th Consultative Expert Meeting of CTA's ICT Observatory Meeting on Gender and Agriculture in the Information Society*, CTA (Technical Centre for Agricultural and Rural Cooperation), Wageningen, Netherlands, 2002.

40. Brocklesby and Fisher, "Community Development in Sustainable Livelihoods Approaches," p. 195.

41. Saheli, *Diverse Ways of Learning*.

42. Bill Cope and Mary Kalantzis, eds., *Multiliteracies: Literacy Learning and the Design of Social Futures*, Routledge, London, 2000.

43. See, for example, the Burma experience described by Jørn Middelborg and Baudouin Duvieusart, *Myanmar: The Community Learning Centre Experience*, UNESCO Asia and the Pacific regional Bureau for Education, Bangkok, 2002.

44. James, *Globalism, Nationalism, Tribalism*, p. 120.

45. Freire, *Pedagogy of the Oppressed*, p. 17.

46. Cross-cultural can mean across clan groups or provinces or between national agencies and local wards, not just between Papua New Guineans and external/international providers.

47. D. McLaughlin and Tom O'Donoghue, *Community Teacher Education in Papua New Guinea*, PNG BUAI, Port Moresby, 1996.

48. P. McLaren, "Schools and Knowledge in Astrolabe Bay," in J. Brammell and R. May, eds., *Education in Melanesia*, Australian National University, Canberra, 1974; McLaughlin and O'Donoghue, *Community Teacher Education in Papua New Guinea*.

49. McLaughlin and O'Donoghue, *Community Teacher Education in Papua New Guinea*.

50. R. Guy, "Work-Related Skilling in Primary and Secondary Schools in Papua New Guinea," paper presented at the Australian Vocational Education and Training Research Association Annual Conference, 1999, p. 1.

51. Peter Rushbrook and Edward Wanigasekera, "Towards Papua New Guinea's First Vocational Education Degree: Reconciling Modernism and Cultural Sustainability," paper presented at the Australian Vocational Education and Training Research Association Annual Conference, Canberra, 2004, p. 3. Two such neoliberal analyses cited by the authors are Helen Hughes, "Aid Has Failed the Pacific," Issue Analysis, no. 33, Centre for Independent Studies, 2003; and Susan Windybank and Mike Manning, "Papua New Guinea on the Brink," Issue Analysis, no. 30, Centre for Independent Studies, 2003.

52. K. H. Thaman, "Shifting Sights: The Cultural Challenge of Sustainability," *Higher Education Policy*, no. 15, 2002, p. 135.

53. Ibid., p. 140.

54. Department for Community Development, *Revitalizing Local Communities and the Nation: A Four-Pronged Approach to Community Development in PNG*, Department for Community Development, Port Moresby, 2004, p. 2.

55. Ibid., p. 3.

56. Department for Community Development, *Integrated Community Development Policy: Promoting Peaceful Families and Communities by Creating Opportunities for Learning and Development for All in Papua New Guinea*, DFCD, Port Moresby, 2006, pp. 51–56.

57. Ibid., pp. 33–35.

58. Ibid., p. 37.

Chapter 13

Recommendations for Community Learning

PAPUA NEW GUINEA IS AT a critical point in its history. Overall we recommend that an engaged community learning process be used to strengthen the sovereignty and self-reliance of local communities, while at the same time drawing those communities into relationships beyond the local to the district and national levels, and through to the global. In other words, the community learning and development process should become part of a critical re-creation of the concept of the "global village," while leaving behind the usual romantic overtones associated with that suspect concept. Global and national processes are already having a profound impact on local communities in Papua New Guinea—via agents as diverse as Pentecostal churches, public-private mobile phone services, international aid agencies, global commodity traders, and mining, logging, and export-oriented agricultural companies. Instead of leaving this process to market vagaries or the fluctuations of philanthropic and donor emphases, the community learning process that we have outlined is intended to provide a systematic framework in which communities can obtain support and communicate with both governments and other communities. It is only one pathway among many, but it heads in the right direction.

Community learning and development centers (CLDCs) are best placed in local communities and organized from the ground up, but in order to work they will need a mediating point of liaison with government-supported focal points. These district-level focal points would provide a new face between communities and government, potentially responding to some of the problems of communication that the various layers of government—ward, local level, district, provincial, and national—have thus failed to overcome. The Organic Law and its focus on provincial political representation has not worked to mediate relations between local communities and the national polity. Community centers, supported by district focal points, would support this process of mediation. The remainder of this chapter comprises an outline of our recommendations for the establishment of community learning and development centers.

Principles Underlying Our Recommendations

1. The establishment of a network of community learning and development centers should be supported within local communities (and across Papua New Guinea by government and nongovernment organizations through such mechanisms as district-level focal points). This should be based upon the principles outlined within the Integrated Community Development Policy, with a particular emphasis on community self-reliance, sustainability, partnership, and recognition of the importance of the cultural foundations of Melanesian society.

2. Both local knowledge and external expert knowledge should be respected and related to each other in context, with care taken over the translation between different forms of knowledge, the appropriate storage of sensitive cultural knowledge, and the tendency for scientific knowledge to be misconstrued, taken out of context, or taken at face value.

3. Learning and development centers should be supported to identify and strengthen existing traditions and local ways of learning, including recognizing the importance of oral communication and dialogue. If technologies such as computers and audio recorders are to be used, they need to be incorporated into local learning needs. If pamphlets, books, and other written documents are used, they should be balanced by an emphasis on the spoken word—with the facilitation of visiting speakers, discussion forums, and provision of space for local elders to impart knowledge.

4. The learning centers should be linked to delivery of health and welfare services. In other words, community learning and development centers should take on a broad range of services for the reproduction of community life and its sustainable development.

5. The importance of existing structures and resources should be recognized, supported, and extended. Outside funding should be secured for supporting these existing foundations with new resources directed through community-led initiatives.

6. The centers should be based—as much as is possible and sustainable—on existing processes of local governance, leadership, and agency, including the work of existing community-based and faith-based organizations.

7. The centers should continue to draw on currently existing local resources rather than waiting for government or other funding. When funding

does come for community-led initiatives as coordinated grants channeled through the focal points, local community funding, or in-kind labor support, such a process should always be negotiated with communities.

8. The governance of the centers needs to be managed through self-reflexive negotiation over issues such as the complex relations of inclusion and exclusion in local community life. Here the emphasis should be on enhancing collaborative reciprocity and cooperation across and between families, clans, and tribes.

9. There must be a commitment to ensuring that there are not barriers to the participation of women. One of the complex issues in the positive inclusion of women, particularly regarding sensitive issues of sexuality and health, entails sometimes excluding men (and vice-versa).

10. Cross-community collaboration, dialogue, and exchange are encouraged between different community learning centers.

Recommendations—General

1. The institutionalized support of local community learning centers shall become a local community, district, and national priority in Papua New Guinea.

2. The implementation of district-level focal points as a key way of supporting local community learning centers shall becomes a district, provincial, and national priority.

3. The ongoing implementation process shall be based on the Integrated Community Development Policy (January 2007) recommendations.

4. The learning centers shall become places for interchange between communities and others outside those communities—including different levels of governance, NGOs, and international organizations. This means that, for example, aid-based projects in communities, HIV/AIDS awareness activities, or informal training exercises are to be conducted through or in consultation through the focal points to the community learning centers, rather than as stand-alone projects.

5. Policies regarding informal sector livelihood, skills training, and learning shall be developed in conjunction with the implementation of the Integrated Community Development Policy.

6. An ongoing process of assessment shall be implemented, including setting up an *informal* register of learning and development centers, and encouraging feedback from communities about positive and negative outcomes, including collecting and communicating inspiring and instructive narratives about learning practices and their consequences. Here "infor-

mal register" should not be taken to imply the usual compulsory registration process, including the extensive filling in of forms associated with the distribution of aid money.

7. An ongoing process of research and social mapping shall be encouraged, with that research coordinated through a national-level board or steering group (see under "Governance Structures" below).

8. The learning model shall be based on three dimensions:

   - *National agendas*—based on previous and continuing nationwide research on community sustainability and development, including that done by the Department for Community Development and its partners.
   - *Local agendas*—based on the complex layering of local community life, including customary tribal, traditional, and modern structures and understandings, and on perceived local community needs in relation to learning, livelihoods, and health.
   - *Futures agendas*—based on providing a space for young people to come together to engage actively across local, national, regional, and global domains for developing and sustaining local programs in a local setting.

9. An annual forum on community learning and development shall be instituted to be coordinated in relation to one of the festivals in the annual calendar of festivals across Papua New Guinea. This forum should have the following characteristics:

   - It would be held in a different community each year, with the host community being part of the process of organization. The host community would be chosen on the basis of expressions of interest by a national committee in a place where there is an active community learning center.
   - It would be organized around a single strategic theme and oriented toward thinking through how best to respond in local communities to the basic problems and opportunities that such a theme brought up. That theme would be chosen by a national committee based on advice and discussion in local, regional, and national forums.
   - It would include a customary leaders' forum to discuss responses to the chosen theme.
   - It would also include a youth forum as the "third face" of futures thinking to discuss responses to the chosen theme. Delegates to the forum would be chosen from persons nominated by local advisory committees in each of the learning centers.
   - It would include invited experts on that theme both from inside Papua

New Guinea and internationally to give talks at plenary sessions and in the longer term to be an ongoing part of the community learning process.

- A secretariat from the Department for Community Development shall record and register the recommendations of the forum for public dissemination and possible future policy implementation.
- The media shall be invited to take note of the recommendations, to witness the community governance process, and to disseminate its debates across the country.

Recommendations—Learning Materials and Themes

10. The existing written literature developed by different agencies, government departments, and international organizations shall be assessed for its suitability for provision to community learning centers.
11. Both local knowledge and expert knowledge shall be included in the development of content, with neither being privileged but with translation pathways being provided between them.
12. In developing content there shall be recognition that sometimes the domains of men and women's knowledge and engagement will be different.
13. Without being exclusive, the community learning centers shall frame their thinking around the following key themes (these are based on the major concerns reported by forty communities during our research):

Economics
- Livelihoods, including agriculture, aquaculture, and livestock
- Financial management and income generation
- Resource management (linked to ecological concerns)
- Skills training, in keeping with the needs of particular communities

Culture
- Multiliteracy for children and adults
- Local and national histories and identities
- Customary values and traditional ways of life
- Nutrition and health, including dealing with HIV/AIDS and sexual health

Politics
- Different forms of governance from the customary to the modern
- Community legal issues and local adjudication processes
- Processes of reconciliation
- Domestic and community violence

Ecology
- Environmental and human impact on place
- Development in the context of local, national, and global environmental issues
- Water and sanitation issues
- Climate change adaptation issues

Recommendations—Governance Structures

14. A national board or steering group shall be confirmed as an ongoing committee and given the status of an interdepartmental committee or a similar status. It needs to be supported by government but to draw more widely for its membership from government and national administration, civil society, the research community, and the business community.

15. The national board shall have the following terms of reference:

- To promote awareness and provide advice on the role of integrated community development approaches in addressing key development issues in Papua New Guinea
- To identify key strategies and targeted priority areas for action
- To make recommendations about the best available and most appropriate support technologies, including information and communication technologies, and to work with local, national, and international agencies, governments, and corporations to find ways of supplying those to local communities
- To provide a framework and an initial point of reference for civil society, donors, and other stakeholders engaged in community work, such as tertiary institutions and the private sector
- To make recommendations about the best available learning materials
- To advocate for the community learning model and critically respond to its strengths and weaknesses
- To offer advice on the implementation of the community learning process to the secretariat and implementation group
- To decide on the locality and the theme for the annual forum on community learning and development (see Point 9 above)

16. The national advisory board should be supported by a governmental secretariat with that secretariat having all or some of the following responsibilities:

- To provide information on the progress and development of the community learning process to the national advisory board and to the overseeing minister or ministers

- To support the operation and long-term development of the community learning process
- To contribute to providing a framework within which provincial governments, district administrations, and local-level governments can develop their specific community development policies and plans
- To develop an informal register of community learning and development centers in Papua New Guinea
- To develop a repository of positive and working examples of community learning practices for the purpose of guiding communities on what is possible
- To advise on the best available learning materials and to work with local, national, and international agencies to deliver those to local communities
- To explore avenues to mapping existing activities such as resource centers, community learning centers, and knowledge exchange networks, and to provide a central point for coordinating and sometimes integrating the various kindred activities currently being conducted by communities, NGOs, community development organizations, and churches
- To provide a venue for critical feedback from communities
- To evaluate the community learning program annually

17. The CLDC National Advisory Committee shall be constituted of a group of key people, including representatives from agencies such as the following:

   - The National Youth Council
   - The PNG Council of Churches
   - The National Women's Council
   - The national academic community
   - The Melanesian peak NGO association
   - The Department for Community Development (the secretary or a nominee)
   - The Department for Community Development Implementation Steering Group
   - The Department for Intergovernment Relations (the secretary or a nominee)
   - The Department of Health (the secretary or a nominee)
   - The Department of Agriculture and Livestock (the secretary or a nominee)

18. Each community shall have its own community learning advisory committee, and each community shall develop the terms and membership of its own committees under the principles of the community learning process.

19. The government, in coordination with national and international funding bodies, shall work toward providing a small operating fund for each community learning center.

20. In the rollout of service delivery and training programs, consideration shall be given to generating coordination and cooperation between learning centers. This will effectively reduce costs and the demands on human resources both from the overseeing department(s) and for the communities. For example, groups of villages within reasonable walking distance of each other can be encouraged to agree to share the responsibility for any training forthcoming from the department(s) within a given period. That is, if you have four villages with community learning centers and four training sessions available in a particular year and people agree that each village community learning center will host one module and the three others will join that village for that session, then each village takes one-quarter of the load. That way the tokens of appreciation left with the hosting village (for being hosted and for food and accommodation) are shared equitably, and at the same time the people giving the training can reach four villages with one presentation and do a number of those trainings in an area in a week. This would require that the training sessions for a given period (a year is a good measure) match the number of community learning centers in a cluster of villages, but it would be time- and cost-effective for everyone and should allow more training to be provided. One team of trainers could reach four times as many people in each session and potentially cover much greater areas in any two-week delivery schedule.

Project Partnerships and Coordination

Overall Coordination Group

Paul James, RMIT (Project Director)

Karen Haive, First Assistant Secretary, Department for Community Development (Coordinator, Papua New Guinea)

Victoria Stead, Research Project Officer, Community Sustainability Program, RMIT

Overall Project Advisors

Dame Carol Kidu, Minister for Community Development

Joseph Klapat, Secretary of the Department for Community Development

Jalal Paraha, Deputy Secretary, Community Development Division, Department for Community Development

Department for Community Development Research Location Leaders

Mollie Willie, First Assistant Secretary, Community Development

Sama Arua, Marriage Registration Officer

Jean Eparo, First Assistant Secretary, Community Governance

Beno Erepan, Assistant Secretary, Community Environment

Andrew Kedu, Executive Officer to the Secretary

Leonie Rakanangu, Assistant Secretary, Community Economics

Isabel Salatiel, Director, Child Welfare

Kema Vegala, Death Registration Officer

Betty Gali-Malpo, Policy Officer

Kila Aoneka, Information Officer

Community Leaders

Gerard Arua, Vanapa, Central Province

Monica Arua, Yule Island, Central Province

Viki Avei, Boera, Central Province

Sunema Bagita, Provisional Community Development Advisor, Milne Bay Province

Mago Doelegu, Alotau, Milne Bay Province

Clement Dogale, Vanagi, Central Province
Jerry Gomuma, Alepa, Central Province
Alfred Kaket, Simbukanam/Tokain, Madang Province
Yat Paol, Bismarck Ramu, Madang Province
Joseph Pulayasi, Omarakana, Milne Bay Province
Bing Sawanga, Yalu, Morobe Province
Alexia Tokau, Kananam, Madang Province
Naup Waup, Wisini village, Morobe Province

Globalism Research Centre Researchers and Administrators, 2004–2010

Todd Bennet, Research Administrator (project administration)
Kate Cregan, Researcher (community learning centers)
Kellie Donati, Research Assistant (informal sector and sustainable development)
Zarnaz Fouladi, Research Assistant (HIV/AIDS)
Julie Foster-Smith, Senior Research Associate (community facilitation)
Elizabeth Kath, Researcher (health)
Debbie Lozankoski, Financial Officer (project finance)
Stephanie Lusby, Research Assistant (foreign aid)
Martin Mulligan, Senior Researcher (research methods)
Yaso Nadarajah, Senior Researcher (locale engagement)
Peter Phipps, Researcher (research methods training)
Chris Scanlon, Researcher (research methods)
Helen Smith, Senior Researcher (vocational education)
Sabine Spohn, Research Assistant (microfinance)
Nicky Welch, Researcher (statistical methods)

Adams, Dale, Douglas H. Graham, and J. D. von Pischke, *Undermining Rural Development with Cheap Credit*, Westview Press, Boulder, 1984.

Ahai, Naihuwo, and Michael Bopp, *Missing Links: Literacy, Awareness and Development in Papua New Guinea*, Educational Research Report, no. 67, Boroko, National Research Institute, 1995.

Airhihenbuwa, C., and R. Obregon, "A Critical Assessment of Theories/Models Used in Health Communications for HIV/AIDS," *Journal of Health Communication*, vol. 5, supplement, 2000, pp. 5–10.

Akin, David, and Joel Robbins, eds., *Money and Modernity: State and Local Currencies in Melanesia*, University of Pittsburgh Press, Pittsburgh, 1999.

Akin, John, et al., *Financing Health Services in Developing Countries: An Agenda for Reform*, The International Bank for Reconstruction and Development, Washington, DC, 1987.

Allen, B., "Can We Predict the Impact of HIV/AIDS in Rural Melanesia and Southeast Asia?" in Godfrey Linge and Doug Porter, eds., *No Place for Borders: The HIV/AIDS Epidemic and Development in Asia and the Pacific*, Allen and Unwin, Sydney, 1997.

Allen, B. J., "Land Management: Papua New Guinea's Dilemma," *The Asia-Pacific Magazine*, no. 1, 1996, pp. 36–42.

Altman, Dennis, *Global Sex*, Allen and Unwin, Sydney, 2001.

Annear, Peter Leslie, et al., "Providing Access to Health Services for the Poor: Health Equity in Cambodia," in *ITM Antwerp Studies in Health Service Organisation and Policy–Health and Social Protection Experiences from Cambodia, China and Lao PDR*, no. 23, Health Policy and Financing Unit of the Department of Public Health of the Institute of Tropical Medicine, Antwerp, 2008.

———, *Study of Financial Access to Health Services for the Poor in Cambodia–Phase 1: Scope, Design, and Data Analysis*, Ministry of Health, WHO, AusAID, RMIT University (Melbourne), Phnom Penh, 2006.

———, *Study of Financial Access to Health Services for the Poor in Cambodia–Phase 2: In-Depth Analysis of Selected Case Studies*, Ministry of Health, WHO, AusAID, RMIT University (Melbourne), Phnom Penh, 2007.

Annear, Peter Leslie, and Jim Tulloch, "A Challenge for Australia's Health Aid Strategy, Access to Health Services for the Poor," *Development Bulletin*, vol. 72, 2007.

Appadurai, Arjun, *Modernity at Large: Cultural Dimensions of Globalization*, University of Minnesota Press, Minneapolis, 1996.

Armendariz de Aghion, Beatriz, and Jonathan Morduch, *The Economics of Microfinance*, Massachusetts Institute of Technology Press, Cambridge, Massachusetts 2005.

Asian Development Bank (ADB), *Asian Development Outlook 2006: Papua New Guinea*, ADB, Manila, 2006.

———, *Country Economic Review of Papua New Guinea*, ADB, 2000.

———, *Country Gender Assessment: Papua New Guinea*, ADB, Manila, 2006.

———, *Financial Sector Development in the Pacific Developing Member Countries*, vol. 2: *Country Reports*, ADB, Manila, 2001.

———, *Initial Poverty and Social Assessment*, ADF Grant–PNG, HIV/AIDS Prevention and Control in Rural Development Enclaves, 2005.

———, *Proposed Asian Development Fund Grant Papua New Guinea: HIV/AIDS Prevention and Control in Rural Development Enclaves Project*, ADB, 2006.

———, *Trends in the Distribution of Health and Health Services in PNG 1991–2000*, conducted under ADB TA 3762, PNG Health Sector Review, 2002.

Australian Agency for International Development (AusAID), *Evaluation of the PNG National HIV/AIDS Support Project*, Evaluation and Review Series, no. 38, AusAID, Canberra, 2006.

———, *Impacts of HIV/AIDS 2005–2025 in Papua New Guinea, Indonesia and East Timor: Final Report of HIV Epidemiological Modeling and Impact Study*, AusAID, Canberra, 2006.

———, "Papua New Guinea: Country Programs," http://www.ausaid.gov.au/ country/ papua.cfm, accessed 24 July 2010.

———, *Potential Economic Impacts of an HIV/AIDS Epidemic in Papua New Guinea*, AusAID, Canberra, 2002.

Australian Strategic Policy Institute (ASPI), *Strengthening Our Neighbour: Australia and the Future of Papua New Guinea*, ASPI, Canberra, 2004.

Australian Web, http://www.australian-web.org/papua-neuguinea/index.php, accessed 5 July 2007.

Avalos, Beatrice, "Ideology, Policy and Educational Change in Papua New Guinea," *Comparative Education*, vol. 29, no. 3, 1993, pp. 275–292.

Avei, Daro, *Identifying the Motu Knowledge Base for Inclusion in School Curriculum: The Boera Experience*, National Research Institute, Division of Education Research, Report No. 69, Port Moresby, 1995.

Axelson, Henrik, et al., "The Impact of the Health Care Fund for the Poor in Poor Households in Two Provinces in Vietnam," paper presented at Forum 9, Mumbai, India, 12–16 September 2005, Global Forum for Health Research, August 2005.

Azuma, Yoshiaki, and Herschel I. Grossman, "A Theory of the Informal Sector," Working Paper, Brown University, Department of Economics, 2002, http://www.econ.brown .edu/fac/Herschel_Grossman/papers/pdfs/informal.pdf, accessed 27 March 2009.

Bablis, Felix G., "The Lessons and Potential for Sustainability and Outreach of Microfinance Institutions in Papua New Guinea and Other Pacific Island Countries," *Development Bulletin*, vol. 50, no. 4, 1999, pp. 19–21.

Babona, Diro, George Slama, and Elliot Puiahi, "Laboratory Diagnosis of HIV Infection in Papua New Guinea," *Papua New Guinea Medical Journal*, vol. 39, 1996, pp. 200–204.

Baer, Hans, Merrill Singer, and Ida Susser, *Medical Anthropology and the World System*, Praeger Publishers, Westport, 2003.

Banduk, M. *Gamarrwa Nuwul Land-Care Department: Background Paper*, Yirrkala Dhanbul Community Association, Yirrkala, 2000.

Bank of Papua New Guinea, http://www.bankpng.gov.pg/index.php?option=com_content &task=blogcategory&id=2&Itemid=101, accessed 9 March 2009.

Banks, Cyndi, "Contextualizing Sexual Violence: Rape and Carnal Knowledge in Papua New Guinea," in S. Dinnen and A. Ley, eds., *Reflections on Violence in Melanesia*, Hawkins and Asia Pacific Press, Sydney, 2000.

Banks, Glenn, "Landowner Equity in Papua New Guinea's Minerals Sector: Review and Policy Issues," *Natural Resources Forum*, no. 27, 2003, pp. 223–234.

———, "Marginality and Environment in Papua New Guinea: The Strickland River Area," *Asia Pacific Viewpoint*, vol. 41, no. 3, 2000, pp. 217–230.

———, "Mining and the Environment in Melanesia: Contemporary Debates Revisited," *Contemporary Pacific*, vol. 14, no. 1, 2002, pp. 39–67.

Barber, Sarah, et al., "Formalizing Under-the-Table Payments to Control Out-of-Pocket Hospital Expenditures in Cambodia," *Health Policy and Planning*, vol. 19, no. 4, 2004, pp. 199–208.

Baum, Fran, *The New Public Health: An Australian Perspective*, Oxford University Press, Melbourne, 1998.

Bauman, Zygmunt, *Liquid Modernity*, Polity Press, Cambridge, 2000.

Bayat, Asef, "Globalisation and the Politics of the Informals in the Global South," in Ananya Roy and Nezar Alsayyad, *Urban Informality*, Lexington Books, Lanham, 2004.

Beck, Ulrich, Anthony Giddens, and Scott Lash, *Reflexive Modernization: Politics, Tradition, Aesthetics in the Modern Social Order*, Polity Press, Cambridge, 1994.

Becker, M. H., "The Health Belief Model and Personal Health Behavior," *Health Education Monographs*, vol. 2, 1974, pp. 324–508.

Benediktsson, Karl, *Harvesting Development: The Construction of Fresh Food Markets in Papua New Guinea*, University of Michigan Press, Ann Arbor, 2002.

Bhushan, Indu, et al., *Scaling-up Health Sector Activities for Poverty Reduction: Lessons from Papua New Guinea, Cambodia, and Sri Lanka,* Asian Development Bank, Manila, 2004.

Bijlmakers, Leon, et al., "Health and Structural Adjustment in Rural and Urban Settings in Zimbabwe: Some Interim Findings," in Peter Gibbon, ed., *Structural Adjustment and the Working Poor in Zimbabwe,* Nordiska Afrikainstitutet, Uppsala, 1995.

Bismarck Ramu, poster, "Industrial Logging is Giaman Development," first produced in 2003.

Bitran, Ricardo, and U. Gideon, "Waivers and Exemptions for Health Services in Developing Countries," Social Protection Discussion Paper Series, World Bank, 2003.

Bolger, Joe, et al., *Papua New Guinea's Health Sector: A Review of Capacity, Change and Performance Issues,* European Centre for Development Policy Management, 2005.

———, *Papua New Guinea's Health Sector: Paul Nichols, Report on Peer Review of Three Australian NGOs Working in PNG,* Adventist Development and Relief Agency, Anglican Board of Mission, Caritas Australia, Sydney, 2003.

Booth, Anne, "Development Challenges in a Poor Pacific Economy: The Case of Papua New Guinea," *Pacific Affairs,* vol. 68, no. 2, 1995, pp. 207–230.

Booth, Tim, and Wendy Booth, "In the Frame: Photovoice and Mothers with Learning Difficulties," *Disability and Society,* vol. 18, no. 4, 2003, pp. 431–442.

Bornstein, David, *The Price of a Dream,* Simon and Schuster, New York, 1996.

Borrey, Anou, "Sexual Violence in Perspective: The Case of Papua New Guinea," in S. Dinnen and A. Ley, eds., *Reflections on Violence in Melanesia,* Hawkins and Asia Pacific Press, Sydney, 2000.

Borrey, Anou, and B. Kombako, *The Reality of Sexual Violence in Papua New Guinea,* National Research Institute, Port Moresby, 1997.

Bourdieu, Pierre, *In Other Words: Essays towards a Reflexive Sociology,* Polity Press, Oxford, 1990.

———, *The Logic of Practice,* Polity Press, Cambridge, 1990.

Bouten, Mathew, "Sex Education to Grade Seven Students in Papua New Guinea, Yes or No?" *Papua New Guinea Medical Journal,* vol. 39, 1996, pp. 225–227.

———, "Sharing the Pain: Response of the Churches in Papua New Guinea to the AIDS Pandemic," *Papua New Guinea Medical Journal,* vol. 39, 1996, pp. 220–224.

Brigg, Morgan, "Disciplining the Developmental Subject: Neoliberal Power and Governance through Microcredit," in Jude L. Fernando, ed., *Microfinance: Perils and Prospects,* Routledge, London and New York, 2006.

British Council, "Vocational Education: Sino-UK Education Links," http://www.britishcouncil.org/china-education-sinouklinks-vocational.htm, accessed 24 July 2010.

Brocklesby, Mary Ann, and Eleanor Fisher, "Community Development in Sustainable Livelihoods Approaches: An Introduction," *Community Development Journal,* vol. 38, no. 3, 2003, pp. 185–198.

Bromley, Roger, and Chris Gerry, *Casual Work and Poverty in Third World Cities,* Wiley and Sons, Chichester, 1979.

Brown, Tim, Roy Chan, Doris Mugrditchian, Brian Mulhall, Rabin Sarda, and Werasit Sittitrai, *Sexually Transmitted Diseases in Asia and the Pacific,* Venereology Publishing, Armidale, Australia, 1998.

Brunton, Brian, "The Perspective on a Papua New Guinean NGO," in Glenn Banks and Chris Ballard, eds., *The Ok Tedi Settlement: Issues, Outcomes and Implications,* National Centre for Development Studies and Resource Management in Asia-Pacific, Australian National University, Canberra, 1997, pp. 167–182.

Bryld, Erik, "Potentials, Problems, and Policy Implications for Urban Agriculture in Developing Countries," *Agriculture and Human Values,* vol. 20, 2003, pp. 79–86.

Bukenya, Gilbert, "Sanitation and Health in Urban Settlements of Papua New Guinea," in Tukutau Taufa and Caroline Bass, eds., *Population Family Health and Development,* vol. 1, University of Papua New Guinea, Port Moresby, 1993.

Burawoy, Michael, et al., *Global Ethnography: Forces, Connections, and Imaginations in a Postmodern World,* University of California Press, Berkeley, 2000.

Butt, Leslie, and Richard Eves, eds., *Making Sense of AIDS: Culture, Sexuality, and Power in Melanesia,* University of Hawai'i Press, Honolulu, 2008.

Butt, Leslie, Jenny Munro, and Joanna Wong, "Border Testimonials: Patterns of AIDS Awareness across the Island of New Guinea," *Papua New Guinea Medical Journal,* vol. 47, nos. 1–2, 2004, pp. 65–76.

Butt, Leslie, Gerdha Numbery, and Jake Morin, *Preventing AIDS in Papua: Revised Research Report,* Family Health International, Jakarta, 2002.

Caldwell, John C., "AIDS in Melanesia," in Australian Agency for International Development (AusAID), *It's Everyone's Problem: HIV/AIDS and Development in Asia and the Pacific,* AusAID, Canberra, 2000.

———, "Rethinking the African AIDS Epidemic," *Population and Development Review,* vol. 26, no. 1, 2000, pp. 117–135.

———, "Routes to Low Mortality in Poor Countries," *Population and Development Review,* vol. 8, no. 3, 1986, pp. 11–16.

Caldwell, John C., and Geetha Isaac-Toua, "AIDS in Papua New Guinea: Situation in the Pacific," *Journal of Health, Population, and Nutrition,* vol. 20, no. 2, 2002, pp. 104–111.

Cambodia, Ministry of Health, *Health Coverage Plan Cambodia,* Ministry of Health, Planning and Statistics Unit, Phnom Penh, 1996.

———, *Joint Annual Performance Review,* Department of Planning and Health Information, Ministry of Health, Phnom Penh, 2007.

———, *Mid-Term Review Report 2003–June 2006,* Health Sector Support Project, Ministry of Health, Phnom Penh, 2006.

———, *National Charter on Health Financing in the Kingdom of Cambodia,* Ministry of

Health, Conference on Financing of Health Services, 5–9 February 1996, Phnom Penh, 1996.

Cambodia, Ministry of Planning, *Cambodia Socio-Economic Survey 2004*, Ministry of Planning, Phnom Penh, 2006.

Cambodia, National Institute of Public Health and National Institute of Statistics, *Cambodia Demographic and Health Survey 2005*, National Institute of Public Health and National Institute of Statistics, Phnom Penh, 2006.

Cammack, Diana, *Chronic Poverty in Papua New Guinea*, Chronic Poverty Research Centre, Manchester, 2008.

Campbell, J. C., "Health Consequences of Intimate Partner Violence," *The Lancet*, vol. 359, 2002, pp. 1331–1336.

Campos-Outcalt, Doug, "Decentralising the Health System in Papua New Guinea," *Health Policy and Planning*, vol. 4, no. 4, 1989, pp. 347–353.

Campos-Outcalt, Doug, et al., "Decentralisation of Health Services in Western Highlands Province, Papua New Guinea: An Attempt to Administer Health Service at the Subdistrict Level," *Social Science and Medicine*, vol. 40, no. 8, 1995, pp. 1091–1098.

Caplan, Pat, *Risk Revisited*, Pluto Press, London, 2000.

Catton, Michael, "Virological Aspects of Human Immunodeficiency Virus Infections," *Papua New Guinea Medical Journal*, 39, 1996, pp. 166–173.

Centre for International Economics, *Potential Economic Impacts of an HIV/AIDS Epidemic in Papua New Guinea*, AusAID, Canberra, 2002.

Certeau, Michel de, *The Practice of Everyday Life*, translated by Steven Rendall, University of California Press, Berkeley, 1988.

Chand, S., "Papua New Guinea Economic Survey: Transforming Good Luck into Policies for Long-Term Growth," *Pacific Economic Bulletin*, vol. 19, no. 1, 2004, pp. 1–19.

Chao Beroff, Renée, *The Constraints and Challenges Associated with Developing Sustainable Microfinance Systems in Disadvantaged Rural Areas in Africa*, United Nations Capital Development Fund, New York, 1999.

Charitonenko, Stephanie, Anita Campion, and Nimal Fernando, *Commercialization of Microfinance: Perspectives from South and Southeast Asia*, Asian Development Bank, Manila, 2004.

Charitonenko, Stephanie, and S. M. Rahman, *Commercialization of Microfinance*, Asian Development Bank, Manila, 2002.

Chatterjee, Shiladitya, et al., "Case Study: Papua New Guinea and Sri Lanka–Scaling up Health Interventions," presented at the conference "Reducing Poverty, Sustaining Growth, What Works, What Doesn't and Why," Shanghai, 25–27 May 2004.

Chen, Lincoln, Jaime Sepulveda Amor, and Sheldon Segal, *AIDS and Women's Reproductive Health*, Plenum Press, New York, 1991.

Chickering, A. Lawrence, and Mohamed Salahadine, "The Informal Sector's Search for

Self-Governance," in A. Lawrence Chickering and Mohamed Salahadine, eds., *The Silent Revolution: The Informal Sector in Five Asian and Near Eastern Countries*, ICS Press, San Francisco, 1991.

Clark, J., "Gold, Sex, and Pollution: Male Illness and Myth at Mt. Kare, Papua New Guinea," *American Ethnologist*, vol. 20, no. 4, 1993, pp. 742–757.

Clark, J., and Jenny Hughes, "A History of Sexuality and Gender in Tari," in A. Biersack, ed., *Papuan Borderlands: Huli, Duna, and Ipili Perspectives in the Papua New Guinea Highlands*, Ann Arbor, University of Michigan Press, 1995.

Clark, Terry, "Lifelong, Life-Wide or Life Sentence?" *Australian Journal of Adult Learning*, vol. 45, no. 1, 2005, pp. 47–62.

Cleary, Mark, and Peter Eaton, *Tradition and Reform: Land Tenure and Rural Development in South-East Asia*, Oxford University Press, Kuala Lumpur, 1996.

Cleland, John, and Benoit Ferry, *Sexual Behavior and AIDS in the Developing World*, Taylor and Francis, London, 1995.

Connell, John, "Health in Papua New Guinea: A Decline in Development," *Australian Geographical Studies*, vol. 35, no. 3, 1997, pp. 271–293.

———, *Papua New Guinea: The Struggle of Development*, Routledge, London, 1997.

———, "Regulation of Space in the Contemporary Postcolonial Pacific City: Port Moresby and Suva," *Asia Pacific Viewpoint*, vol. 44, no. 3, 2003, pp. 243–257.

Constitution of the Independent State of Papua New Guinea, Papua New Guinea Consolidated Legislation, Constitutional Laws Library, http://www.paclii.org/pg/legis/consol_act/cotisopng534/, accessed 21 May 2007.

Consultative Group to Assist the Poorest, "Key Principles of Microfinance," http://www.cgap.org/portal/site/CGAP/menuitem.64c03ec40a6d2950678080105910100a/, accessed 1 August 2007.

Coombes, M.. and S. Raybould, "Public Policy and Population Distribution: Developing Appropriate Indicators of Settlement Patterns," *Environment and Planning C: Government and Policy*, vol. 19, no. 2, 2001, pp. 223–248.

Cope, Bill, and Mary Kalantzis, eds., *Multiliteracies: Literacy Learning and the Design of Social Futures*, Routledge, London, 2000.

Cornford, Robin, *Microcredit, Microfinance or Access to Financial Services: What Do Pacific People Need?* Foundation for Development Cooperation, Brisbane, 2001.

Counts, Alex, *Give Us Credit*, Research Press, New Delhi, 1996.

Crockett, Sue, "The Future State and Predictions of HIV/AIDS in Papua New Guinea," *Pacific AIDS Alert*, vol. 20, 2000, pp. 12–15.

Cull, Robert, Asli Demirguc-Kunt, and Jonathan Morduch, "Financial Performance and Outreach: A Global Analysis of Leading Microbanks," World Bank Policy Research, Working Paper Series 3827, 2006.

Cullen, Trevor, "HIV/AIDS in Papua New Guinea: A Reality Check," *Pacific Journalism Review*, vol. 12, no. 1, 2006, pp. 153–165.

Curtin, Tim, "Scarcity Amidst Plenty: The Economics of Land Tenure in Papua New Guinea," in T. Curtin, H. Holzknecht, and P. Larmour, eds., *Land Registration in Papua New Guinea: Competing Perspectives,* Research School of Pacific and Asian Studies, State Society and Governance in Melanesia Project, Discussion Paper 2003/1, Canberra, 2003, pp. 6–17.

Dalton, George, ed., *Tribal and Peasant Economies,* Natural History Press, New York, 1967.

Daniels, P. W., "Urban Challenges: The Formal and Informal Economies in Mega-Cities," *Cities,* vol. 21, no. 6, 2004, pp. 501–511.

Davis, Mike, *Planet of Slums,* Verso, London, 2006.

de Bruyn, M., "Women and AIDS in Developing Countries," *Social Science and Medicine,* vol. 34, 1993, pp. 249–262.

Decosas, J., F. Kane, J. Anarfi, K. Sodii, and H. Wagner, "Migration and AIDS," *The Lancet,* no. 346, 1995, pp. 826–828.

Delanty, Gerhard, *Community,* Routledge, London, 2003.

Delpit, Lisa D., and Graeme Kemelfield, *An Evaluation of the Viles Tok Ples Skul Scheme in the North Solomons Province,* Port Moresby, University of Papua New Guinea, 1985.

Demerath, Peter, "The Cultural Production of Educational Utility in Pere Village, Papua New Guinea," *Comparative Education Review,* vol. 43, no. 2, 1999, pp. 162–192.

Denoon, Donald, "Papua New Guinea's Crisis: Acute or Chronic?" *World Affairs,* vol. 164, no. 3, 2002, pp. 115–122.

———, *Public Health in Papua New Guinea: Medical Possibility and Social Constraint 1884–1984,* Cambridge University Press, Cambridge, 1989.

———, *A Trial Separation: Australia and the Decolonisation of Papua New Guinea,* Australian National University, Pandanus Books, 2005.

Denoon, Donald, and C. Snowden, eds., *A Time to Plant and a Time to Uproot,* Institute of Papua New Guinea Studies, Port Moresby, no date.

Department for Community Development (DFCD), *Corporate Plan, 2005–2007,* DFCD, Port Moresby, 2005.

———, *Integrated Community Development Policy: Promoting Peaceful Families and Communities by Creating Opportunities for Learning and Development for All in Papua New Guinea,* DFCD, Port Moresby, 2006.

———, *New Policy Direction: Revitalizing Local Communities and the Nation,* DFCD, Port Moresby, 2004.

———, *Revitalizing Local Communities and the Nation: A Four-Pronged Approach to Community Development in PNG,* DFCD, Port Moresby, 2004.

Department of Health, *Papua New Guinea Health Sector Medium Term Expenditure Framework 2004–2006,* National Department of Health, Port Moresby, 2003.

de Soto, Hernando, *The Other Path: The Invisible Revolution in the Third World,* Harper and Row, New York, 1989.

de Zalduondo, B., and J. Bernard, "Meanings and Consequences of Sexual-Economic Exchange," in Richard Parker and John Gagnon, eds., *Conceiving Sexuality: Approaches to Sex Research in a Postmodern World,* Routledge, New York, 1995.

Diamond, Jared, *Guns, Germs, and Steel,* Vintage, London, 1998.

Dickson-Waiko, Anne, "The Missing Rib: Mobilizing Church Women for Change," *Oceania,* no. 74, 2003, pp. 98–119.

Donaghue, Kieran, "Microfinance in the Asia Pacific," *Asian-Pacific Economic Literature,* vol. 18, no. 1, 2004, pp. 41–61.

Downie, Alex, and Deidre Elrick, "Weaving the Threads: Community Development and Organizing around the Environment," *Community Development Journal,* vol. 35, no. 3, 2000, pp. 245–254.

Dowsett, Gary, "Some Considerations on Sexuality and Gender in the Context of AIDS," *Reproductive Health Matters,* vol. 11, no. 22, 2003, pp. 21–29.

Duesberg, Peter, *Infectious AIDS: Have We Been Misled?* North Atlantic Books, Berkeley, California, 1995.

Duesberg, Peter, Claus Koehnlein, and David Rasnick, "The Chemical Bases of the Various AIDS Epidemics: Recreational Drugs, Anti-Viral Chemotherapy and Malnutrition," *Journal of Bioscience,* vol. 28, 2003, pp. 383–412.

Duncan, Ron, and Ila Temu, "Papua New Guinea: Longer Term Developments and Recent Economic Problems," *Asian-Pacific Economic Literature,* vol. 9, no. 2, 1995, pp. 36–54.

Dundon, Alison, "Mines and Monsters: A Dialogue on Development in Western Province, Papua New Guinea," *Australian Journal of Anthropology,* vol. 13, no. 2, 2002, pp. 139–154.

———, "Warrior Women, the Holy Spirit and HIV/AIDS in Rural Papua New Guinea," *Oceania,* vol. 77, 2007, pp. 29–42.

Dundon, Alison, and Charles Wilde, "Introduction: HIV and AIDS in Rural Papua New Guinea," *Oceania,* vol. 77, no. 1, 2007, pp. 1–11.

Duvieusart, Baudouin, ed., *Myanmar: The Community Learning Centre Experience,* UNESCO Asia and Pacific Regional Bureau for Education, Bangkok, 2002.

Dwyer, J., and S. Lovell-Jones, "Editorial: The Gathering Storm That Is the HIV Epidemic in Papua New Guinea," *Australia and New Zealand Journal of Medicine,* vol. 27, no. 1, 1997, pp. 3–5.

Edwards, Keith, "Rural Health Service Crisis in Papua New Guinea: Causes, Implications and Possible Solutions," *PNG Medical Journal,* vol. 37, no. 3, 1994, pp. 145–151.

Elahi, Khandakar Q., and Constantine P. Dadopoulos, "Microfinance and Third World Development: A Critical Analysis," *Journal of Political and Military Sociology,* vol. 32, no.1, 2004.

Ellis, Frank, and James Sumberg, "Food Production, Urban Areas and Policy Responses," *World Development,* vol. 26, no. 2, 1998, pp. 213–225.

Ennenbach, Jan C., *PNG Microfinance and Employment Project*, report for Asian Development Bank, Manila, Microbanking Competence Centre Bankakademie International, Frankfurt, 2000.

Errington, Frederick K., and Deborah B. Gewertz, *Articulating Change in the "Last Unknown*," Westview Press, Boulder, Colorado, 1995.

———, *Yali's Question: Sugar, Culture, & History,* University of Chicago Press, Chicago, 2004.

Etzioni, Amitai, "Introduction: A Matter of Balance, Right and Responsibilities," in *The Essential Communitarian Reader,* Rowman and Littlefield, Lanham, Maryland, 1998.

European Centre for the Valuation of Prior Learning, "VPL 4 EU—Expected Outcomes," http://www.vpl4.eu/projectinformation/expectedoutcomes.php, accessed 24 March 2007.

European Commission, "The European Qualifications Framework: A New Way to Understand Qualifications across Europe," http://ec.europa.eu/education/policies/educ/eqf/index_en.html, accessed 3 April 2007.

———, *A Memorandum on Lifelong Learning,* European Commission, Brussels, 2000.

European Conference of Ministers Responsible for Spatial/Regional Planning (CEMAT), *Glossary of Key Expressions Used in Spatial Development Policies in Europe,* CEMAT, Lisborne, 2006, http://www.mzopu.hr/doc/14CEMAT_6_EN.pdf, accessed 15 August 2007.

Eves, Richard, "AIDS and Apocalypticism: Interpretations of the Epidemic from Papua New Guinea," *Culture, Health, and Sexuality,* vol. 5, no. 3, 2003, pp. 249–264.

———, "Money, Mayhem and the Beast: Narratives of the World's End from New Ireland (Papua New Guinea)," *Journal of the Royal Anthropological Institute,* no. 9, 2003, pp. 527–547.

———, "Waiting for the Day: Globalisation and Apocalypticism in Central New Ireland, Papua New Guinea," *Oceania,* vol. 71, no. 2, 2000, pp. 73–91.

Fabricant, Steve, *Cambodia Essential Health Services Cost Study: Final Report,* WHO/USAID/POPTECH, Phnom Penh, 2005.

Fakade, Wabulem, "Deficits of Formal Urban Land Management and Informal Responses under Rapid Urban Growth: An International Perspective," *Habitat International,* vol. 24, 2000, pp. 127–150.

Farmer, Elaine, "AIDS and the Community," *Papua New Guinea Medical Journal,* vol. 39, 1996, pp. 214–217.

Farmer, Paul, *AIDS and Accusation: Haiti and the Geography of Blame,* University of California Press, Berkeley, 1992.

Feeny, Simon, "The Impact of Foreign Aid on Economic Growth in Papua New Guinea," *Journal of Development Studies,* vol. 41, no. 6, 2005, pp. 1092–1117.

Ferej, A. K. "The Integration of Youth into the Informal Sector: The Kenyan Experience," 2000, http://www.cinterfor.org.uy/public/spanish/regional/ampro/cinterfor/temas/youth/eventos/korea/pon/ing/kenya.

Fernando, Jude L., "Microcredit and Empowerment of Women: Blurring the Boundary between Development and Capitalism," in Jude L. Fernando, ed., *Microfinance: Perils and Prospects*, Routledge, London and New York, 2006.

Fernando, Nimal, "Improving Rural Institutional Finance: Some Lessons," *Papua New Guinea Journal of Agriculture, Forestry and Fisheries*, vol. 37, no. 1, 1994, pp. 92–103.

Fife, Wayne, "The Look of Rationality and the Bureaucratization of Consciousness in Papua New Guinea," *Ethnology*, vol. 34, no. 2, 1995, pp. 129–142.

Firth, Raymond, *Elements of Social Organization*, Massachusetts Institute of Technology Press, Boston, third edition, 1963.

Fisher, Thomas, and M. S. Sriram, *Beyond Micro-Credit: Putting Development Back into Micro-Finance*, Vistaar Publications, New Delhi, 2002.

Fishery Status Reviews: Torres Strait Lobster Fishery, http://www.affashop.gov.au/PdfFiles/03_FSR07_tslf.pdf, accessed 9 January 2009.

Fisk, Ernest Kelvin, "The Economic Structure," in E. K. Fisk, ed., *New Guinea on the Threshold: Aspects of Social, Political and Economic Development*, Australian National University Press, Canberra, 1966.

——, *Hardly Ever a Dull Moment*, History of Development Studies Monograph 5, National Centre for Development Studies, Australian National University, 1995.

——, "Planning in a Primitive Economy: Special Problems of Papua New Guinea," *The Economic Record*, vol. 38, no. 4, December 1962, pp. 462–478.

Fiti-Sinclair, R., "Female Prostitutes in Port Moresby, Papua New Guinea: STDs and HIV/AIDS Knowledge, Attitudes, Beliefs and Practices," in Mary Spongberg, Jan Larbalestier, and Margaret Winn, eds., *Women, Sexuality, Culture: Cross Cultural Perspectives on Sexuality*, Women's Studies Centre, Sydney, 1996.

Fleischer, Rebecca, "Replicating Grameen Bank in Papua New Guinea," *Pacific Economic Bulletin*, vol. 11, no. 2, 1996, pp. 23–37.

Food and Agricultural Organization of the United Nations, http://www.fao.org/ES/ess/toptrade/trade.asp, accessed 2 April 2009.

Forde, Daryll, and Mary Douglas, *Primitive Economies*, in G. Dalton, ed., *Tribal and Peasant Economies*, Natural History Press, New York, 1967, pp. 13–28.

Foster, Robert J., *Materializing the Nation: Commodities, Consumption, and Media in Papua New Guinea*, Indiana University Press, Bloomington, 2002.

——, ed., *Nation Making: Emergent Identities in Postcolonial Melanesia*, University of Michigan Press, Michigan, 1995.

——, "Print Advertisements and Nation Making in Metropolitan Papua New Guinea," in Robert J. Foster, ed., *Nation Making: Emergent Identities in Postcolonial Melanesia*, University of Michigan Press, Ann Arbor, 1995.

Fouladi, Zarnaz, "AIDS Narratives and Sexual Cultures in Tubetube, Papua New Guinea," University of Melbourne, Master's thesis, 2006.

Fox, Daniel, and Elizabeth Fee, *AIDS: The Burdens of History*, University of California Press, Berkeley, 1988.

Frankel, S., *The Huli Response to Illness*, Cambridge University Press, Cambridge, 1984.

Freire, Paulo, *Pedagogy of the Oppressed*, Continuum International, New York, 2000 (1968).

Friesen, H., R. Danaya, P. Doonar, A. Kemiki, W. Lagani, G. Mataio, T. Rongap, and J. Vince, "Assessment of HIV/AIDS Knowledge, Attitudes and Behaviour of High School Students in Papua New Guinea," *Papua New Guinea Medical Journal*, vol. 39, 1996, pp. 208–213.

Gamarrwa Nuwul Landcare, Monthly Report, February 2002.

Gare, Janet, Tony Lupiwa, Dagwin Suarkia, Michael Paniu, Asibo Wahasoka, Hanna Nivia, Jacinta Kono, William Yeka, John Reeder, and Charles Mgone, "High Prevalence of Sexually Transmitted Infections among Female Sex Workers in the Eastern Highlands Province of Papua New Guinea: Correlates and Recommendations," *Sexually Transmitted Diseases*, vol. 32, no. 8, 2005, pp. 466–473.

Garma Festival, http://www.garma.telstra.com/aboutgarma.htm, accessed 14 November 2007.

Gavamani Sivarai (monthly government newspaper), vol. 5, no. 1, 2008.

Gegeo, David Welchman, and Karen Ann Watson-Gegeo, "Whose Knowledge? Epistemological Collisions in Soloman Islands Community Development," *The Contemporary Pacific*, vol. 14, no. 2, 2002, pp. 377–409.

George, Mary, *London Life in the Eighteenth Century*, Peregrine, London, (1925) 1966.

Gershuny, J. I., "The Informal Economy: Its Role in Post-Industrial Society," *Futures*, February 1979, pp. 3–15.

Gerxhani, Klarita, *The Informal Sector in Developed and Less-Developed Countries*, Amsterdam Institute for Advanced Labor Studies, Amsterdam, 2004.

Getubig, I. P., Joe Remenyi, and Benjamin Quinones Jr., *Creating the Vision: Microfinancing the Poor in Asia-Pacific*, report for the Asian and Pacific Development Centre, Kuala Lumpur, 1997.

Getubig, Mike, Joe Remenyi, and David Gibbons, *Financing a Revolution: An Overview of the Microfinance Challenge in Asia–Pacific*, Pinter, London, 2000.

Gewertz, Deborah B., *Sepik River Societies: A Historical Ethnography of the Chambri and Their Neighbors*, Yale University Press, New Haven, 1983.

Gewertz, Deborah B., and Frederick K. Errington, *Cheap Meat: Flap Food Nations in the Pacific Islands*, University of California Press, Berkeley, 2010.

———, *Emerging Class in Papua New Guinea: The Telling of Difference*, Cambridge University Press, Cambridge, 1999.

———, *Twisted Histories, Altered Contexts: Representing the Chambri in a World System*, Cambridge University Press, Cambridge, 1991.

Gibson, John, "The Economic and Nutritional Importance of Household Food Production in PNG," in R. M. Bourke, M. G. Allen, and J. G. Salisbury, eds., *Food Security for Papua New Guinea: Proceedings of the Papua New Guinea Food and Nutrition 2000 Conference,* Papua New Guinea University of Technology, Lae, ACIAR Proceedings, no. 99, Australian Centre for International Agricultural Research, Canberra, 2001, pp. 37–44.

Giddens, Anthony, *The Third Way: The Renewal of Social Democracy,* Polity, London, 1998.

Gildipasi Community, "Gildipasi Community Organisation Working Document," Gildipasi, unpublished paper, October 2007.

Gladman, Darren, David Mobray, and John Duguman, eds., From *Rio to Rai: Environment and Development in Papua New Guinea,* vols. 1–6, University of Papua New Guinea Press, Port Moresby, 1996.

Goddard, Michael, "From Rolling Thunder to Reggae: Imagining Squatter Settlements in Papua New Guinea,'" *The Contemporary Pacific,* vol. 13, no. 1, 2001, pp. 1–32.

———, *The Unseen City: Anthropological Perspectives on Port Moresby, Papua New Guinea,* Pandanus Books, Research School of Pacific and Asian Studies, Australian National University, Canberra, 2005.

———, ed., *Villagers and the City: Melanesian Experiences of Port Moresby, Papua New Guinea,* Sean Kingston Publishing, Wantage, UK, 2010.

Godelier, Maurice, *The Enigma of the Gift,* Polity Press, Cambridge, 1999.

Goetz, Anne Marie, and Rina Sen Gupta, "Who Takes the Credit? Gender, Power and Control Over Loan Use in Rural Credit Programmes in Bangladesh," *World Development,* vol. 24, no. 4, 1996, pp. 45–63.

Goldman, L. R., J. Duffield, and C. Ballard, "Fire and Water: Fluid Ontologies in Melanesian Myth," in L. R. Goldman and C. Ballard, eds., *Fluid Ontologies: Myth, Ritual and Philosophy in the Highlands of Papua New Guinea,* Bergin and Garvey, Westport, 1998.

Gonzales-Vega, Claudio, "Microfinance: Broader Achievements and New Challenges," Occasional Paper No. 2518, Rural Finance Program, Ohio State University, Columbus, 1998.

Gottret, Pablo, and George Schieber, *Health Financing Revisited: A Practitioners Guide,* World Bank, Washington, DC, 2006.

Government of Papua New Guinea, *Cooperative Societies, Rules and Regulations* (Chapter 389), Government of Papua New Guinea, Port Moresby, 1986.

———, *Functional and Expenditure Review of Rural Health Services of 2001,* PSRMU, Government of Papua New Guinea, Port Moresby, 2001.

———, *Medium Term Development Strategy 2005–2010,* Government of Papua New Guinea, Port Moresby, 2005.

Gow, Kathryn N., "Banking on Women: Achieving Healthy Economies through Microfinance," *WE International,* vol. 48/49, 2000, pp. 11–13.

Gregory, C. A., *Gifts and Commodities,* Academic Press, London, 1982.

———, *Savage Money: The Anthropology and Politics of Commodity Exchange*, Harwood
    Academic Publishers, Amsterdam, 1997.

———, "South Asian Economic Models for the Pacific? The Case of Microfinance,"
    Pacific Economic Bulletin, vol. 14, no. 2, 1999, pp. 82–92.

Greig, Fiona E., and Cheryl Koopman, "Multilevel Analysis of Women's Empower-
    ment and HIV Prevention: Quantitative Survey Result from a Preliminary Study
    in Botswana," *AIDS and Behavior*, vol. 7, no. 2, 2003, pp. 195–208.

Grossman, Larry, "The Cultural Ecology of Economic Development," *Annals of the As-
    sociation of American Geographers*, vol. 71, no. 2, 1981, pp. 220–236.

Grugulis, Irena, "The Contribution of National Vocational Qualifications to the Growth
    of Skills in the UK," *British Journal of Industrial Relations*, vol. 41, no. 3, 2003, pp.
    457–475.

Guy, R., "Work-Related Skilling in Primary and Secondary Schools in Papua New
    Guinea," paper presented at the Australian Vocational Education and Training
    Research Association Annual Conference, 1999.

Gwatkin, Davidson R., *Are Free Government Health Services the Best Way to Reach the
    Poor?* World Bank, Washington, 2004.

Habermas, Jürgen, *The Theory of Communicative Action*, vol. 2: *Lifeworld and System*,
    Polity Press, Cambridge, 1987.

Hafkin, Nancy, and Helen Hambly Odame, *Gender, ICTs and Agriculture: A Situation
    Analysis for the 5th Consultative Expert Meeting of CTA's ICT Observatory Meeting
    on Gender and Agriculture in the Information Society*, Wageningen, Netherlands,
    2002.

Haines, A., and A. Cassels, "Can the Millennium Development Goals Be Attained?"
    BMJ (British Medical Journal), vol. 329, 2004, pp. 394–397.

Hammar, Lawrence, "AIDS, STDs, and Sex Work in Papua New Guinea," in Laura
    Zimmer-Tamakoshi, ed., *Modern Papua New Guinea*, Thomas Jefferson Univer-
    sity Press, Kirksville, Missouri, 1998.

———, "Bad Canoes and Buffalo: The Political Economy of Sex on Daru Island, West-
    ern Province, Papua New Guinea," in T. Foster, C. Siegel, and E. Barry, eds., *Gen-
    ders 23: Bodies of Writing, Bodies of Performance*, New York University Press, New
    York, 1996.

———, "Caught between Structure and Agency: Gendered Violence and Prostitu-
    tion in Papua New Guinea," *Transforming Anthropology*, vol. 8, nos. 1–2, 1998, pp.
    77–96.

———, "Epilogue: Homegrown in PNG—Rural Responses to HIV and AIDS," *Ocea-
    nia*, vol. 70, no. 1, 2007, pp. 72–94.

———, "Fear and Loathing in Papua New Guinea: Sexual Health in a Nation under
    Siege," in Leslie Butt and Richard Eves, eds., *Making Sense of AIDS: Culture, Sexu-
    ality, and Power in Melanesia*, University of Hawai'i Press, Honolulu, 2008.

————, "4,275 and Counting: Telling Stories about STDs on Daru," *Papua New Guinea Medical Journal,* vol. 47, nos. 1–2, 2004, pp. 88–113.

————, "Sex and Political Economy in the South Fly: Daru Island, Western Province, Papua New Guinea," Ph.D. dissertation, City University of New York, 1996.

————, "Sex Industries and Sexual Networking in Papua New Guinea: Public Health Risks and Implications," *Pacific Health Dialogue,* vol. 5, no. 1, 1998, pp. 47–53.

————, "Sexual Health, Sexual Networking and AIDS in Papua New Guinea and West Papua," *Papua New Guinea Medical Journal,* vol. 47, nos. 1–2, 2004, pp. 1–12.

————, "Sexual Transactions on Daru," *Research in Melanesia,* vol. 16, 1992, pp. 21–54.

Hannerz, Ulf, "Many Sites in One," in Thomas Hylland Eriksen, ed., *Globalisation: Studies in Anthropology,* Pluto, London, 2003.

Hanson, Lucas W., B. J. Allen, R. M. Bourke, and T. J. McCarthy, *Papua New Guinea Rural Development Handbook,* Australian National University, Canberra, 2001.

Harper, D., "Meaning and Work: A Study in Photo Elicitation," *International Journal of Visual Sociology,* vol. 2, no. 1, 1984, pp. 20–43.

Hart, Keith, "Informal Income Opportunities and Urban Development in Ghana," *Journal of Modern African Studies,* vol. 11, no. 1, 1973, pp. 61–89.

————, "Small Scale Entrepreneurs in Ghana and Development Planning," *Journal of Development Studies,* vol. 6, no. 4, 1970, pp. 104–120.

Hart, Maureen, *Guide to Sustainable Community Indicators, Sustainable Measures,* Hart Environmental Data, North Andover, 2nd edition, 1999.

Hayden, Bill, "The Ethics of Development: Aid—a Two Way Process?" in Susan Stratigos and Philip J. Hughes, eds., *The Ethics of Development: The Pacific in the 21st Century,* University of Papua New Guinea Press, Port Moresby, 1987, pp. 54–59.

Heise, Lori L., Alanagh Raikes, Charlotte H. Watts, and Anthony B. Zwi, "Violence against Women: A Neglected Public Health Issue in Less Developed Countries," *Social Science and Medicine,* vol. 39, 1994, pp. 1165–1179.

Heise, Lori L., and Christopher Elias, "Transforming AIDS Prevention to Meet Women's Needs: A Focus on Developing Countries," *Social Science and Medicine,* vol. 40, no. 7, 1995, pp. 931–943.

Helms, Birgit, *Access for All: Building Inclusive Financial Systems,* The World Bank, Washington, DC, 2006.

Herdt, Gilbert, *Ritualized Homosexuality in Melanesia,* University of California Press, Berkeley, 1984.

————, "Stigma and the Ethnographic Study of HIV: Problems and Prospects," *AIDS and Behavior,* vol. 5, no. 2, 2001, pp. 141–149.

Hill, Robert, "Fugitive and Codified Knowledge: Implications for Communities Struggling to Control the Meaning of Local Environmental Hazards," *International Journal of Lifelong Education,* vol. 23, no. 3, 2004, pp. 221–242.

Hoffman, Bob, *Informal Learning: Managing the Training Function*, Information Lifeline, 2005.

Holt, Sharon L., "The Village Bank Methodology: Performance and Prospects," in Maria Otero and Elisabeth Rhyne, eds., *The New World of Microenterprise Finance:
Building Healthy Institutions for the Poor*, Kumarian Press, West Hartford, Connecticut, 1994, pp. 156–185.

Holzknecht, Hartmut, "Customary Land Tenure Systems: Resilient, Appropriate and
Productive," in T. Curtin, H. Holzknecht, and P. Larmour, eds., *Land Registration
in Papua New Guinea: Competing Perspectives*, Research School of Pacific and
Asian Studies, State Society and Governance in Melanesia Project, Discussion Paper 2003/1, Canberra, 2003, pp. 18–23.

Holzknecht, Horst, "Past, Present and Future: Building on Papua New Guinea's Customary Strengths in Resource Management," *Development Bulletin*, vol. 50, 1999,
pp. 29–31.

Hopkins, Sarah, Graham Ogle, Lisette Kaleveld, John Maurise, Betty Keria, William
Louden, and Mary Rohl, "'Education for Equality' and 'Education for Life'": Ex-
amining Reading Literacy and Reading Interest in Papua New Guinea Primary
Schools," *Asia-Pacific Journal of Teacher Education*, vol. 33, no. 1, 2005, pp. 77–96.

Howe, M., "Papua New Guinea Faces HIV Epidemic," *Lancet Infectious Diseases*, vol. 2,
no. 7, 2002, p. 386.

Hsiao, William, *A Framework for Assessing Health Financing Strategies and the Role of
Health Insurance*, The World Bank, Washington, DC, 1995.

Huckaby, Francyne M., "When Worlds Collide: A Critical Decolonizing View of Western-Based Schooling in Papua New Guinean Village Education," *Journal of Curriculum Theorizing*, vol. 20, no. 4, 2004, pp. 75–90.

Hudson, Bernard, Willem van der Meijden, and Tony Lupiwa, "A Survey of Sexually
Transmitted Diseases in Five STD Clinics in Papua New Guinea," *Papua New
Guinea Medical Journal*, vol. 37, no. 3, 1994, pp. 152–160.

Huffer, Elise, "Governance, Corruption, and Ethics in the Pacific," *The Contemporary
Pacific*, vol. 17, no. 1, 2005, pp. 118–140.

Hughes, Helen, "Aid Has Failed the Pacific," *Issue Analysis*, Centre for Independent
Studies, no. 33, 2003.

———, "Can Papua New Guinea Come Back from the Brink?" *Issue Analysis*, Centre
for Independent Studies, no. 49, 2004.

Hughes, Jenny, "A History of Sexually Transmitted Diseases in Papua New Guinea,"
in M. Lewis, S. Bamber, and M. Waugh, eds., *Sex, Disease and Society: A Comparative History of Sexually Transmitted Diseases and HIV/AIDS in Asia and the Pacific*,
Greenwood Press, Westport, 1997.

———, "Impurity and Danger: The Need for New Barriers and Bridges in the Prevention of Sexually-Transmitted Disease in the Tari Basin, Papua New Guinea," *Health Transition Review*, vol. 1, no. 2, 1991, pp. 131–140.

———, "Sexually Transmitted Infections: A Medical Anthropological Study from the Tari Research Unit 1990–1991," *Papua New Guinea Medical Journal*, vol. 45, nos. 1–2, 2002, pp. 128–133.

Hughes, Jenny, and T. Dyke, "Barriers and Bridges to the Spread of Sexually Transmitted Diseases among the Huli of Southern Highlands Province," in T. Taufa and C. Bass, eds., *Population, Family Health and Development*, vol. 2, University of Papua New Guinea Press, Port Moresby, 1993.

Hugo, Graeme, Anthony Champion, and Alfredo Lattes, "Toward a New Conceptualization of Settlements for Demography," *Population and Development Review*, vol. 29, no. 2, 2003, pp. 277–297.

Hulme, David, "Is Microdebt Good for Poor People? A Note on the Dark Side of Microfinance," *Small Enterprise Development*, vol. 11, no. 1, 2000, p. 26.

Hulme, David, and Paul Mosley, *Financing against Poverty*, vol. 2, Routledge, London, 1996.

Hyndman, David, "Academic Responsibilities and Representation of the Ok Tedi Crisis in Postcolonial Papua New Guinea," *The Contemporary Pacific*, vol. 13, no. 1, 2001, pp. 33–54.

Imbun, Benjamin Y., "Mining workers or 'Opportunistic' Tribesmen? A Tribal Workforce in a Papua New Guinean Mine," *Oceania*, vol. 71, no. 2, 2000, pp. 129–149.

Indistange, Kal, personal communication (a former employee at the National AIDS Council Secretariat).

Institute of Scientific and Technical Communicators, "National Occupational Standards," http://www.istc.org.uk/Communication_Resources/National_Occ_Standards/nos_home.htm, accessed 26 July 2007.

International Labour Organization (ILO), *Employment, Income and Equality: A Strategy for Increasing Productive Employment in Kenya*, ILO, Geneva, 1972.

———, *ILO Compendium of Official Statistics on Employment in the Informal Sector*, ILO, Geneva, 2002.

———, "ILO Strategy towards Universal Access to Health—A Consultation," Global Campaign on Social Security and Coverage for All, Social Security Department, International Labour Organization, GTZ-ILO-WHO-Consortium on Social Health Protection in Developing Countries, Geneva, 2007, http://www.shi-conference.de/social_protection_health.php, accessed 20 January 2008.

———, "Social Health Protection," http://www.ilo.org/public/english/protection/secsoc/areas/policy/social.htm, accessed 20 January 2008.

International Monetary Fund (IMF), *Health and Development: Why Investing in Health Is Critical for Achieving Economic Development Goals*, IMF, Washington, DC, 2004.

Itoh, Makato, and Costas Lapavitsas, *Political Economy of Money and Finance,* Macmillan Press, London, 1999.

Izard, J., and M. Dugue, *Moving toward a Sector-Wide Approach: Papua New Guinea, the Health Sector Development Program Experience,* Asian Development Bank, Manila, 2003.

Jain, Pankaj, "Managing Credit for the Rural Poor: Lessons from the Grameen Bank," *World Development,* vol. 24, no.1, 1996, pp. 79–89.

Jain, Pankaj, and Mick Moore, "What Makes Microcredit Programmes Effective? Fashionable Fallacies and Workable Realities," IDS Working Paper 177, Institute of Development Studies, Brighton, 2003.

James, Paul, *Globalism, Nationalism, Tribalism: Bringing Theory Back In,* Sage Publications, London, 2006.

James, Paul, and Andy Scerri, "Globalizing Life-Worlds: Consuming Capitalism," in Phillip Darby, ed., *Postcolonializing the International,* University of Hawai'i Press, Honolulu, 2006.

Jenkins, Carol, "AIDS in Papua New Guinea," *Papua New Guinea Medical Journal,* vol. 39, 1996, pp. 164–165.

———, *Behavioural Risk Assessment for HIV/AIDS among Workers in the Transport Industry, PNG,* final report to AIDSCAP/FHI, Bangkok, 1994.

———, *Female Sex Worker HIV Prevention Projects: Lessons Learnt From Papua New Guinea, India, and Bangladesh,* UNAIDS, Geneva, 2000.

———, *HIV/AIDS, Culture, and Sexuality in Papua New Guinea,* Asian Development Bank, Manila, 2006.

———, "The Homosexual Context of Heterosexual Practice in Papua New Guinea," in Peter Aggleton, ed., *Bisexualities and AIDS, International Perspectives,* Taylor and Francis, London, 1996.

———, "Situation Analysis of HIV/AIDS in Papua New Guinea September, 2002," unpublished report, 2002.

———, *Youth in Danger: AIDS and STDs among Young People in Papua New Guinea,* PNG Institute of Medical Research and United Nations Population Fund, Port Moresby, 1997.

Jenkins, Carol, and Michael Alpers, "Urbanization, Youth and Sexuality: Insights for an AIDS Campaign for Youth in Papua New Guinea," *Papua New Guinea Medical Journal,* vol. 39, 1996, pp. 248–251.

Jenkins, Carol, and the National Sex and Reproduction Research Team, *National Study of Sexual and Reproductive Knowledge and Behaviour in Papua New Guinea,* Papua New Guinea Institute of Medical Research Monograph No. 10, Papua New Guinea Institute of Medical Research, Goroka, 1994.

———, *Women and the Risk of AIDS in Papua New Guinea,* Women and AIDS Research Program, Papua New Guinea Institute of Medical Research, Goroka, Papua New Guinea, 1993.

Jochelson, K., M. Mothibeli, and J. Leger, "Human Immunodeficiency Virus and Migrant Labor in South Africa," in N. Krieger and M. Glenn, *AIDS: The Politics of Survival*, Baywood Publishing Co., Amityville, 1994.

Johnson, Susan, and Ben Rogaly, *Microfinance and Poverty Reduction*, Oxfam, Oxford, 1997.

Jones, Adele M., "Mobile Training for Community Environmental Education: A Non-Formal Approach," in *Developing Alternatives: Community Development Strategies and Environmental Issues in the Pacific*, Victoria University, Melbourne, 1996, pp. 15–27.

Jones, Gareth Stedman, *Outcast London*, Peregrine, Harmondsworth, revised edition, 1984.

Jorgensen, Dan, "Third Wave Evangelism and the Politics of the Global in Papua New Guinea: Spiritual Warfare and the Recreation of Place in Telefolmin," *Oceania*, vol. 75, 2005, pp. 44–61.

Josephs, John, *Education for All Assessment 2000: Papua New Guinea Country Report*, UNESCO, Port Moresby, 2000, http://www.unesco.org/education/wef/countryreports/papua_new_guinea/contents.html, accessed 16 June 2008.

Jütting, Johannes, Jante Parlevliet, and Theodora Xenogiani, *Informal Employment Reloaded*, OECD Development Centre, Paris, 2008.

Kaima, Sam, "The Politics of 'Payback': Villager Perceptions of Elections in the Markam Open," a paper presented at the "Political Culture, Representation and Electoral Systems in the Pacific" conference, University of the South Pacific, Vanuatu, July 2004.

Kannapiran, Chinna, "Institutional Rural Finance in PNG: The Lessons from Failures and the Need for Reforms," NRI Discussion Paper, no. 86, Natural Resources Institute, Kent, 1995.

Kavanamur, David, "Australian Agency for International Development: Report on Rural Credit Study, Background Study to the Medium Term Development Strategy 2003–2007," INA Discussion Paper, no. 87, Institute of National Affairs, Port Moresby, 2002.

———, "Re-positioning Non-bank Service Strategy in Papua New Guinea," *Labour and Management in Development Journal*, vol. 3, no. 6, 2003, pp. 1–24.

———, "Strategic Alliance Issues in Microfinance Management," *Development Bulletin*, vol. 60, no. 12, 2002, pp. 87–90.

Kavanamur, David, and Robert Turare, "Sustainable Credit Schemes for Rural Development in Papua New Guinea," *Development Bulletin*, vol. 50, no. 3, 1999, pp. 11–14.

Kavanamur, David, Charles Yala, and Quinton Clements, *Building a Nation in Papua New Guinea: Views of the Post-Independence Generation,* Pandanus Books, Canberra, 2003.

Kean, Peter, "Economic Development in the Siki Settlement Scheme, West New Britain," *Critique of Anthropology,* vol. 2, no. 2, 2000, pp. 153–172.

Keck, Verena, "Knowledge, Morality and 'Kastom': SikAIDS among Young Yupno People, Finisterre Range, Papua New Guinea," *Oceania,* vol. 77, no. 1, 2007, pp. 43–57.

Kila, Rai, "Dilemmas in AIDS Care," *Papua New Guinea Medical Journal,* vol. 39, 1996, pp. 218–219.

Kirsch, Stuart, "Anthropologists and Global Alliances: Comment," *Anthropology Today,* vol. 12, no. 4, 1996, pp. 14–16.

———, "Return to Ok Tedi," *Meanjin,* vol. 55, no. 4, 1996, pp. 657–666.

Knauft, Bruce, *Exchanging the Past: A Rainforest World of Before and After,* University of Chicago Press, Chicago, 2002.

———, *From Primitive to Postcolonial in Melanesia and Anthropology,* University of Michigan Press, Ann Arbor, 1999.

———, *What Ever Happened to Ritual Homosexuality? The Incitement of Modern Sexual Subjects in Melanesia and Elsewhere,* International Association for the Study of Sexuality, Culture and Society, Melbourne, 2001.

Koczberski, Gina, "Pots, Plates and *Tinpis*: New Income Flows and the Strengthening of Women's Gendered Identities in Papua New Guinea," *Development: Local/ Global Encounters,* vol. 45, no. 1, 2002, pp. 88–92.

———, "The Sociocultural and Economic Context of HIV/AIDS in Papua New Guinea," *Development Bulletin,* vol. 52, 2000, pp. 61–63.

Koczberski, Gina, and George N. Curry, "Divided Communities and Contested Landscapes: Mobility, Development and Shifting Identities in Migrant Destination Sites in Papua New Guinea," *Asia Pacific Viewpoint,* vol. 45, no. 3, 2004, pp. 357–371.

———, "Making a Living: Land Pressures and Changing Livelihood Strategies among Oil Palm Settlers in Papua New Guinea," *Agricultural Systems,* vol. 85, no. 3, 2005, pp. 324–339.

Koczberski, Gina, George N. Curry, and John Connell, "Full Circle or Spiralling Out of Control? State Violence and the Control of Urbanisation in Papua New Guinea," *Urban Studies,* vol. 38, no. 11, pp. 2017–2036.

Kopel, Elizabeth, *An Interim Evaluation Report on a Provincial Government Microcredit Scheme in Papua New Guinea,* report prepared for Western Highlands Provincial Government, University of Papua New Guinea, Port Moresby, 2002.

———, "Street Vending in Port Moresby: A Positive Step Towards Self-Help or an Eyesore for the City?" in D. Gladman, D. Mowbray, and J. Duguman, eds., *From Rio to Rai: Environment and Development in Papua New Guinea up to 2000 and Beyond,*

Papers from the Twentieth Waigani Seminar, Port Moresby, vol. 6, pp. 153–165, University of Papua New Guinea Press, Port Moresby, 1996.

Kopkop, Maria, "The Status of Women in Papua New Guinea," in Tukutau Taufa and Caroline Bass, eds., *Population Family Health and Development*, University of Papua New Guinea Press, Port Moresby, 1993.

Kopunye, Helen, Aua Purumo, and John Newsom, "Microfinance and Financial Intermediation in Rural Papua New Guinea: An Integrated Scheme," *Development Bulletin*, vol. 50, no. 3, 1999, pp. 15–18.

Kramer, P. B., "Knowledge about AIDS and Follow Up Compliance in Patients Attending a Sexually Transmitted Disease Clinic in the Highlands of Papua New Guinea," *Papua New Guinea Medical Journal*, vol. 38, no. 3, 1995, pp. 178–190.

Lagarde, E., et al., "Educational Level Is Associated with Condom Use within Non-Spousal Partnerships in Four Cities in Sub-Saharan Africa," *AIDS*, vol. 15, no. 11, 2001, pp. 1399–1408.

Lagisa, Leonard, and Regina Scheyvens, "Mining in Papua New Guinea," in John Overton and Regina Scheyvens, eds., *Strategies for Sustainable Development: Experiences from the Pacific*, UNSW Press, Sydney, 1999, pp. 125–141.

Laos, Ministry of Finance, *Official Gazette 2006, Volume 1, 13th Year*, Vientiane, Ministry of Finance, 2007.

Larmour, Peter, *Customary Land Tenure: Registration and Decentralisation in Papua New Guinea*, Monograph 29, National Research Institute, Boroko, 1991.

Latouche, Serge, "The Ethical Implications of Development: A Philosophic Reflection on an Economic Process," in Susan Stratigos and Philip J. Hughes, eds., *The Ethics of Development: The Pacific in the 21st Century*, Papers from the Seventeenth Waigani Seminar, Port Moresby, University of Papua New Guinea Press, Port Moresby, 1987, pp. 130–147.

———, *In the Wake of the Affluent Society: An Exploration of Post-Development*, translated by Martin O'Connor and Rosemary Arnoux, Zed Books, London and New Jersey, 1993.

Lave, Jean, and Etienne Wenger, *Situated Learning: Legitimate Peripheral Participation*, Cambridge University Press, Cambridge, 1991.

Lavu, E. K., N. Kutson, C. Connie, G. Tau, and P. Sims, "Total Lymphocyte Counts in Adult HIV/AIDS Patients in Port Moresby General Hospital," *Papua New Guinea Medical Journal*, vol. 47, nos. 1–2, 2004, pp. 31–38.

Layton, S. R., "Living with Dignity Project," *Papua New Guinea Medical Journal*, vol. 47, nos. 1–2, 2004, pp. 13–21.

LDAT (Liklik Dinau Abitore Trust), *Project Document—(PNG/93/001/C/01/11)—Microcredit and Savings 1993*, Government of Papua New Guinea, Port Moresby, 1993.

Ledgerwood, Joan, *Microfinance Handbook: An Institutional and Financial Perspective*, World Bank, Sustainable Banking with the Poor Program, Washington, DC, 1999.

Lemeki, Madeline, Megan Passey, and Philip Setel, "Ethnographic Results of a Community STD Study in the Eastern Highlands Province," *Papua New Guinea Medical Journal*, vol. 39, 1996, pp. 239–242.

Lepani, Katherine, "Sovasova and the Problem of Sameness: Converging Interpretive Frameworks for Making Sense of HIV and AIDS in the Trobriands," *Oceania*, vol. 77, no. 1, 2007, pp. 12–28.

Levett, Malcolm P., "Consumption and Demand for Fruits and Nuts in Port Moresby," *Yagl-Ambu*, vol. 17, 1993, pp. 55–77.

———, "Urban Gardening in Port Moresby: A Survey of the Suburb of Gerehu Yagl Ambu, Papua New Guinea," *Journal of the Social Sciences and Humanities*, vol. 16, no. 3, 1992, pp. 47–68.

Levett, Malcolm P., and Marakan Uvano, "Urban Gardening in Port Moresby: A Survey of the Suburbs of Morata and Waigani," *Yagl-Ambu*, vol. 16, 1992, pp. 69–91.

Levine, Hal B., and Marlene Levine, *Urbanization in Papua New Guinea*, Cambridge University Press, Cambridge, 1979.

Lewis, Nancy Davis, and Moshe Rapaport, "In a Sea of Change: Health Transitions in the Pacific," *Health and Place*, vol. 1, no. 4, 1995, pp. 211–226.

Lindeman, Eduard C., *The Meaning of Adult Education*, Oklahoma Research Center for Continuing Professional and Higher Education, Oklahoma, 1989.

Linge, Godfrey, and Doug Porter, *No Place for Borders: The HIV/AIDS Epidemic and Development in Asia and the Pacific*, Allen and Unwin, Sydney, 1997.

LiPuma, Edward, *Encompassing Others: The Magic of Modernity in Melanesia*, University of Michigan Press, Ann Arbor, 2001.

Lombange, Candy, "Trends in Sexually Transmitted Disease Incidence in Papua New Guinea," *Papua New Guinea Medical Journal*, vol. 27, nos. 3–4, 1984, pp. 145–157.

Lucatelli, S., S. Savastano, and M. Coccia, "Health and Social Services in Rural Umbria," *Materiali UVAL*, issue 12, 2006, http://www.dps.mef.gov.it/documentazione/uval/materiali_uval/Muval12_Sviluppo_rurale_inglese.pdf, accessed 13 August 2007.

Luker, Vicki,, "Civil Society, Social Capital and the Churches: HIV/AIDS in Papua New Guinea," paper delivered at the Governance in Pacific States Development Research Symposium, 30 September–2 October 2003, University of the South Pacific, Suva, Fiji, http://classshares.student.usp.ac.fj/, accessed 28 December 2008.

———, "Civil Society, Social Capital and the Churches: HIV/AIDS in Papua New Guinea," State, Society and Governance in Melanesia Project, working paper 2004/1, Canberra, 2004.

———, *Gender, Women and Mothers: HIV/AIDS in the Pacific*, Australian National University, Canberra, 2001.

Lupiwa, Sebeya, Nathan Suve, Karen Horton, and Megan Passey, "Knowledge about Sexually Transmitted Diseases in Rural and Periurban Communities of the Asaro

Valley of Eastern Highlands Province: The Health Education Component of an STD Study," *Papua New Guinea Medical Journal*, vol. 39, 1996, pp. 243–247.

Luteru, P. H., and G. R. Teasdale, "Aid and Education in the South Pacific," *Comparative Education*, vol. 29, no. 3, 1993, pp. 293–306.

Macadam, R. D., "From Pushing Production Inputs to Empowering in the Community: A Case Study in the Transformation of an Extension Agency," *Australian Journal of Experimental Agriculture*, vol. 40, 2000, pp. 585–594.

Macintyre, Martha, "The Persistence of Inequality," in Laura Zimmer-Tamakashi, ed., *Modern Papua New Guinea*, Thomas Jefferson University Press, Kirksville, Missouri, 1998.

———, "Petztorme Women: Responding to Change in Lihir, Papua New Guinea," *Oceania*, vol. 74, 2003, pp. 120–133.

Macintyre, Martha, and Simon Foale, "Politicized Ecology: Local Responses to Mining in Papua New Guinea," *Oceania*, vol. 74, no. 3, 2004, pp. 231–251.

Magill, John H., "Credit Unions: A Formal-Sector Alternative for Financing Microenterprise Development," in Maria Otero and Elisabeth Rhyne, eds., *The New World of Microenterprise Finance: Building Healthy Institutions for the Poor*, Kumarian Press, West Hartford, 1994.

Malau, Clement, "The Evolving AIDS Epidemic: Challenges and Responses in Papua New Guinea," *Development Bulletin*, vol. 50, 1999, pp. 70–71.

Malau, Clement, and Sue Crockett, "HIV and Development the Papua New Guinea Way," *Development Bulletin*, vol. 52, 2000, pp. 58–60.

Malau, Clement, Micheal O'Leary, Carol Jenkins, and Nicholas Faraclas, "HIV/AIDS Prevention and Control Programme in Papua New Guinea: The Experience of a Country with Low Prevalence but Potential for Transmission," *AIDS*, vol. 8, supplement 2, 1994, pp. S117–S124.

Malik, M. H., "Urban Poverty Alleviation through Development of the Informal Sector," *Asia-Pacific Development Journal*, vol. 3, no. 2, 1996, pp. 31–48.

Malinowski, Bronislaw, *Argonauts of the Western Pacific: An Account of Native Enterprise and Adventure in the Archipelagoes of Melanesian New Guinea*, London, Routledge and Kegan Paul, (1922) 1972.

Mallet, Shelley, *Conceiving Cultures: Reproducing People and Places on Nuakata, Papua New Guinea*, University of Michigan, Ann Arbor, 2003.

Maloney, William F., "Informality Revisited," *World Development*, vol. 32, no. 7, 2004, pp. 1159–1178.

Manning, H. J., and Ciaran O'Faircheallaigh, "Chapter 24: Papua New Guinea," *American Journal of Economics and Sociology*, vol. 59, no. 5, 2000, pp. 385–395.

Marcus, George, "Ethnography in/of the World System: The Emergence of Multi-sited Ethnography," *Annual Review of Anthropology*, vol. 24, 1995, 95–117.

Marika, Banduk, Colin Lane, Helen Smith, and Leanne Reinke, "Working towards an

Indigenous Training Model: Learning from Gamarrwa Nuwul Landcare, Yirrka-la," in Kaye Bowman, ed., *Equity in Vocational Education and Training: Research Readings*, National Centre for Vocational Education Research, Adelaide, 2004, pp. 72–89.

Marsick, Victoria, and Karen Watkins, *Informal and Incidental Learning in the Workplace*, Routledge, London, 1990.

Martin, Imran, David Hulme, and Stuart Rutherford, "Finance for the Poor: From Microcredit to Microfinancial Services," *Journal of International Development*, vol. 14, no. 2, 2002, pp. 273–294.

Mase, Margaret, "Development, Life-Modes and Language in Papua New Guinea," *Development Bulletin*, vol. 50, 1999, pp. 67–69.

Matane, Paulias, *A Philosophy of Education for Papua New Guinea*, Ministerial Committee Report, Port Moresby, National Department of Education, 1986.

May, Patricia, and Margaret Tuckson, *The Traditional Pottery of Papua New Guinea*, University of Hawai'i Press, Honolulu, 2000.

May, Ron, ed., *Micronationalist Movements in Papua New Guinea*, Research School of Pacific Studies, Canberra, 1982.

McBride, W. J. and D. Bradford, "Antiretroviral Therapy for HIV-Infected People in Papua New Guinea: Challenges and Opportunities," *Papua New Guinea Medical Journal*, vol. 47, 2004, pp. 22–30.

McGuire, Paul, *Microfinance in the Pacific Island Countries*, Foundation for Development Cooperation, Brisbane, 1997.

———, "South Asian Economic Models for the Pacific? The Case of Microfinance: A Comment," *Pacific Economic Bulletin*, vol. 15, no. 10, 2000, pp. 168–172.

McLaren, P., "Schools and Knowledge in Astrolabe Bay," in J. Brammell and R. May, eds., *Education in Melanesia*, Australian National University, Canberra, 1974.

McLaughlin, D., and Tom O'Donoghue, *Community Teacher Education in Papua New Guinea*, PNG BUAI, Port Moresby, 1996.

McNally, Stephen, "Linking HIV/AIDS to Development," *Development Bulletin*, vol. 52, 2000, pp. 9–11.

Merson, M., et al., *International Public Health: Diseases, Programs, Systems, and Policies*, Aspen Publishers, Maryland, 2001.

Mgone, Charles, Sebeya Lupiwa, and William Yeka, "High Prevalence of Neisseria Gonorrhoeae and Multiple Sexually Transmitted Diseases among Rural Women in the Eastern Highlands Province of Papua New Guinea, Detected by Polymerase Chain Reaction," *Sexually Transmitted Diseases*, December, 2002, pp. 775–779.

Mgone, Charles, Megan Passey, Joseph Anang, Wilfred Peter, Tony Lupiwa, Dorothy Russell, Diro Babona, and Michael Alpers, "Human Immunodeficiency Virus and Other Sexually Transmitted Infections among Female Sex Workers in Two

Major Cities in Papua New Guinea," *Sexually Transmitted Diseases*, vol. 29, no. 5, 2002, pp. 265–270.

Middelborg, Jørn, and Baudouin Duvieusart, *Myanmar: The Community Learning Centre Experience*, UNESCO Asia and Pacific Regional Bureau for Education, Bangkok, 2002.

Millar, Pat, and Sue Kilpatrick, "How Community Development Programmes Can Foster Re-engagement with Learning in Disadvantaged Communities: Leadership as Process," *Studies in the Education of Adults*, vol. 37, no. 1, 2005, pp. 18–30.

Mitlin, Diana, "Sustaining Markets or Sustaining Poverty Reduction?" *Environment and Urbanization*, vol. 14, no. 1, 2002, pp. 173–177.

Mola, Glen, "HIV Infections in Obstetrics and Gynaecology," *Papua New Guinea Medical Journal*, vol. 39, 1996, pp. 190–195.

Moore, Mike, "Poverty Is Not Inevitable," *The National*, 29 February 2008.

Morduch, Jonathan, "The Microfinance Schism," *World Development*, vol. 28, no. 4, 2000, pp. 617–629.

Mulgan, G., *Connexity: How to Live in a Connected World*, Chatto and Windus, London, 1997.

Mulligan, Martin, Paul James, Kim Humphery, Chris Scanlon, Pia Smith, and Nicky Welch, *Creating Community: Celebrations, Arts and Wellbeing within and across Local Communities*, VicHealth and the Globalism Research Centre, Melbourne, 2007.

Mulligan, Martin, and Yaso Nadarajah, "Local-Global Relations and Community-Engaged Research," *Globalism Institute Annual Report*, 2007, pp. 11–22.

Nadarajah, Yaso, "A Community in Transition: Propagating a Yield of Conflict and Violence," in Alejandro Cervantes-Caron and Ilse Lazaroms, eds., *Meaning and Violence: Readings across Disciplines*, Inter-Disciplinary Press, Oxford, 2007.

Nakata, Martin, *Disciplining the Savages, Savaging the Disciplines*, Aboriginal Studies Press, Canberra, 2007.

NASFUND Newsletter, 1999–2011.

Nash, Manning, "The Organisation of Economic Life," in George Dalton, ed., *Tribal and Peasant Economies*, Natural History Press, New York, 1967.

National AIDS Council (NAC), *Monitoring the Declaration of Commitment on HIV/ AIDS*, NAC, Port Moresby, 2005.

——, *Review of Policy and Legislative Reform Relating to HIV/AIDS in Papua New Guinea*, NAC, Port Moresby, 2001.

——, *Situational Analysis for Strategic Planning at District Level: Milne Bay Province, Social Mapping Project*, National HIV/AIDS Support Project, NAC, Port Moresby, 2005.

——, *Situational Analysis for Strategic Planning at the District Level: Southern High-*

lands Province, Social Mapping Project, National HIV/AIDS Support Project, NAC, Port Moresby, 2005.

National AIDS Council Secretariat (NACS), *Papua New Guinea National HIV/AIDS Medium Term Plan*, NACS, Port Moresby, 2002.

National AIDS Council Secretariat and Department of Health, *HIV/AIDS Quarterly Report, March 2002*, NACS and Department of Health, Boroko, 2002.

National AIDS Council Secretariat and Partners, *UNGASS 2008, Country Progress Report*, NACS, Port Moresby, 2008.

National Consultative Committee on Informal Sector, *Concept paper on National Economy Policy*, prepared by the Technical Working Group for the Department of Community Development, Port Moresby, 2006.

National Department of Education, *Growth of Education Since Independence 1975–1985*, Port Moresby, National Department of Education, 1985.

National Department of Health, *National Health Plan 2001–2010, Health Vision 2010, Policy Directions and Priorities*, vol. 1, National Department of Health, Port Moresby, 2001.

———, *Papua New Guinea Health Sector Medium Term Expenditure Framework 2004–2006* NDH, Port Moresby, 2003.

National Resource Centre for Non Formal Education, *A Case Study on Community Learning Centre for Development*, Asia Pacific Cultural Centre for UNESCO, Tokyo, 2001.

National Research Institute, *Evaluation of the Impact and Effectiveness of the PNG HIV/AIDS Awareness Program in Selected Secondary Schools and High Schools in the National Capital District*, National Research Institute, Port Moresby, 2004.

Nelson, Candace, Barbara McNelly, Kathleen Stack, and Lawrence Yanovitch, *Village Banking: The State of Practice*, SEEP Network, New York, 1995.

Nesse, Randolph M., and George C. Williams, *Evolution and Healing: The New Science of Darwinian Medicine*, Weidenfeld and Nicolson, London, 1995.

Newsom, John, "Bougainville Microfinance: Rebuilding Rural Communities after the Crisis," *Development Bulletin*, vol. 57, no. 2, 2002, pp. 85–88.

Nihill, M., "New Women and Wild Men: 'Development,' Changing Sexual Practice and Gender in Highland Papua New Guinea," *Canberra Anthropology*, vol. 17, no. 2, 1994.

O'Collins, Maev, *Social Development in Papua New Guinea 1972–1990: Searching for Solutions in a Changing World*, Political and Social Change Monograph No. 18, Department of Political and Social Change, Australian National University, Canberra, 2005.

O'Connor, Tim, "HIV/AIDS and Australia's International Approach," AID/Watch, Erskineville, 2004.

Office of Training and Tertiary Education, *Statistical Data Guidelines*, Office of Training and Tertiary Education, Melbourne, 2007.

Okole, Henry, "Political Participation in a Fragmented Democracy: Ethnic and Religious Appeal in Papua New Guinea," *Development Bulletin*, University of Papua New Guinea, Port Moresby, 2002.

Olsson, Michael, Ephraim Apelis, and Jacqueline Wasilewski, *The Coordination, Development and Implementation of Nonformal Education in Papua New Guinea*, Port Moresby, Ministry of Education, 1985.

Organisation for Economic and Cooperative Development (OECD), *Lifelong Learning for All*, OECD, Paris, 1996.

————, *The Role of National Qualifications Systems in Promoting Lifelong Learning: Report from Thematic Group 1: The Development and Use of "Qualification Frameworks" as a Means of Reforming and Managing Qualifications Systems*, OECD, Paris, 2004.

Overton, John, and Regina Scheyvens, eds., *Strategies for Sustainable Development: Experiences from the Pacific*, UNSW Press, Sydney, 1999.

Pacific Islands Forum Secretariat, *Non-Formal Education in Pacific Island Countries*, Pacific Islands Forum Secretariat, Suva, 2007.

Padgug, Robert A., "Sexual Matters: On Conceptualizing Sexuality in History," in Richard Guy Parker and Peter Aggleton, *Culture, Society and Sexuality*, Routledge, Abingdon, UK, 2007.

Page, R., and J. Hillage, *Vocational Education and Training in the UK: Strategies to Overcome Skill Gaps in the Workforce*, Social Science Research Center, Berlin, 2006.

Papua New Guinea Informal Sector Study: Review of Constraints to Informal Sector Development, A Report to the Informal Sector Committee of the Consultative Implementation and Monitoring Council (CIMC), Institute of National Affairs, Port Moresby, 2001.

Papua New Guinean Informal Sector Training Manual: A Training Guide for Informal Business, Consultative Implementation and Monitoring Council (CIMC) Informal Sector Committee, Uramina and Nelson, Port Moresby, 2006.

Papua New Guinea Sustainable Development Program and Save the Children, *Learning Workshops on Strengthening Community Engagement with the HIV Epidemic and Its Driving Forces*, Papua New Guinea Sustainable Development Program and Save the Children, 2007.

Parker, Richard, "Sexuality, Culture, and Power in HIV/AIDS Research," *Annual Review of Anthropology*, vol. 30, 2001, pp. 163–179.

Parker, Richard, and John Gagnon, *Conceiving Sexuality: Approaches to Sex Research in a Postmodern World*. Routledge, New York, 1995.

Parsons, Steve R., *Journey into Community: Looking inside the Community Learning Center*, Eye on Education, West Larchmont, 2004.

Passey, Megan, "Issues in the Management of Sexually Transmitted Diseases in Papua New Guinea," *Papua New Guinea Medical Journal*, vol. 39, 1996, pp. 252–260.

Passey, Megan, Charles Mgone, Sebeya Lupiwa, Nathan Suve, S. Tiwara, T. Lupiwa,

A. Clegg, and Michael Alpers, "Community Based Study of Sexually Transmitted Diseases in Rural Women in the Highlands of Papua New Guinea: Prevalence and Risk Factors," *Sexually Transmitted Infections*, vol. 74, 1998, pp. 120–127.

Patel, Urjit R., and Pradeep Srivastava, "Macroeconomic Policy and Output Comovement: The Formal and Informal Sectors in India," *World Development*, vol. 24, no.12, 1996, pp. 1915–1923.

Perkins, Douglas D., Joseph Hughey, and Paul W. Speer, "Community Psychology Perspectives on Social Capital Theory and Community Development Practice," *Journal of the Community Development Society*, vol. 33, no. 1, 2002, pp. 33–52.

Perks, Carol, et al., "District Health Programs and Health-Sector Reform, Case Study in the Lao People's Democratic Republic," *WHO Bulletin*, vol. 84, no. 2, 2006, pp. 132–138.

Phillips, David, and Yola Verhasselt, eds., *Health and Development*, Routledge, London, 1994.

Phipps, Peter, "Community Sustainability Research: The Challenge of Reciprocity," *Local-Global Journal*, vol. 1, 2005, pp. 79–89.

Pitts, Maxine, *Crime, Corruption and Capacity in Papua New Guinea*, Asia Pacific Press, Canberra, 2002.

Polanyi, Karl, Conrad Arensberg, and Harry Pearson, eds., *Trade and Markets in Early Empires: Economies in History and Theory*, Glencoe Free Press, Illinois, 1957.

Polier, Nicole, "Culture, Community and the Crisis of Modernity in Papua New Guinea," *Political and Legal Anthropology Review*, vol. 22, no. 1, 1999, pp. 55–65.

———, "Of Mines and Min: Modernity and its Malcontents in Papua New Guinea," *Ethnology*, vol. 35, no. 1, 1996, pp. 1–16.

Power, Anthony P., "Global Village: A Village of the Future for Papua New Guinea," http://www.pngbuai.com/300socialsciences/economy-village/global-village-model-1.html, accessed 12 November 2008.

Prahalad, Caimbatore K., *The Fortune at the Bottom of the Pyramid: Eradicating Poverty through Profits*, Wharton School Publishing, Upper Saddle River, New Jersey, 2004.

Pryor, Frederic L., *The Origins of the Economy*, Academic Press, New York, 1977.

Purdie, Nick, "Pacific Islands Livelihoods," in John Overton and Regina Scheyvens, eds., *Strategies for Sustainable Development: Experiences from the Pacific*, UNSW Press, Sydney, 1999, pp. 64–79.

Putnam, Robert D., *Bowling Alone: The Collapse and Revival of American Community*, Simon and Schuster, New York, 2000.

Rabinow, Paul, *Reflections on Fieldwork in Morocco*, University of California Press, Berkeley, 1977.

Ramm, Johann-Friedrich, "Rethinking Decentralization in Papua New Guinea," United Nations Centre for Regional Development, Nagoya, 1993.

Ramoi, Gabriel, "Ethics and Leadership," in Susan Stratigos and Philip J. Hughes, eds., *The Ethics of Development: The Pacific in the 21st Century*, University of Papua New Guinea Press, Port Moresby, 1987, pp. 88–96.

Randell, Ruth, *Gender Equality and Democratic Governance in the City of Port Moresby*, UNIFEM Pacific, 2008.

Reber, Michael F., *An Alternative Framework for Community Learning Centers in the 21st Century: A Systemic Design Approach toward the Creation of a Transformational Learning System*, Universal-Publishers, Boca Raton, Florida, 2003.

Reddy, Maghendra, "Modelling Poverty Dimensions of Urban Informal Sector Operators in a Developing Economy," *The European Journal of Development Research*, vol. 19, no. 3, 2007, pp. 459–479.

Reid, Elizabeth, "Putting Values into Practice in PNG: The Poro Sapot Project and Aid Effectiveness," *eJournal of the Australian Association for the Advancement of Pacific Studies*, nos. 1.2 and 2.1, 2010.

Reinke, Leanne, and Paul James, "Learning Reflexively: Technological Mediation and Indigenous Cultures," in Peter Kell, Sue Shore, and Michael Singh, eds., *Adult Education @ 21st Century*, Peter Lang, New York, 2004.

Remenyi, Joe, and Benjamin Quinones Jr., eds., *Microfinance and Poverty Alleviation: Case Studies from Asia and the Pacific*, Pinter, London, 2000.

Reymer, Christina, "Breathing New Life into Education for Life: A Reconceptualisation of Non-formal Education with a Focus on the Melanesian Pacific," paper presented to the joint AARE/NZARE conference, Melbourne 1999, http://www.aare.edu.au/99pap/rey99228.htm, accessed 28 May 2008.

Rhyne, Elisabeth, "The Yin and Yang of Microfinance: Reaching the Poor and Sustainability," *MicroBanking Bulletin*, no. 2, 1998, pp. 6–8.

Rhyne, Elisabeth, and Mario Otero, "Financial Services for Microenterprises: Principles and Institutions," in Mario Otero and Elisabeth Rhyne, eds., *The New World of Microenterprise Finance: Building Healthy Financial Institutions for the Poor*, Kumarian Press, West Hartford, Connecticut, 1994, pp. 11–26.

Riley, Ian, "Lessons from Sexually Transmitted Disease Epidemics," in Australian Agency for International Development (AusAID), *It's Everyone's Problem: HIV/AIDS and Development in Asia and the Pacific*, AusAID, Canberra, 2000.

Robbins, Joel, *Becoming Sinners: Christianity and Moral Torment in a Papua New Guinea Society*, University of California Press, Berkeley, 2004.

———, "The Globalization of Pentecostal and Charismatic Christianity," *Annual Review of Anthropology*, vol. 33, pp. 117–143.

———, "The Humiliations of Sin: Christianity and the Modern Subject," in Joel Robbins and Holly Wardlow, eds., *The Making of Global and Local Modernities in Melanesia: Humiliation, Transformation and the Nature of Cultural Change*, Ashgate, Aldershot, 2005.

Robbins, Joel, and Holly Wardlow, eds., *The Making of Global and Local Modernities in Melanesia: Humiliation, Transformation and the Nature of Cultural Change*, Ashgate, Aldershot, 2005.

Roberts, Graham, "The Kadavu Health Promotion Model, Fiji," *Health Promotion International*, vol. 12, no. 4, pp. 283–290.

Robinson, Marguerite S., *The Microfinance Revolution: Sustainable Finance for the Poor*, vol. 1, World Bank, Washington, DC, 2001.

Robinson, William, *James Chalmers, Missionary and Explorer of Rarotonga and New Guinea*, F. H. Revell, New York, 1888.

Root-Bernstein, Robert, *Rethinking AIDS: The Tragic Cost of Premature Consensus*, Free Press, New York, 1993.

Rose, Nikolas, *Powers of Freedom: Reframing Political Thought*, Cambridge University Press, Cambridge, 1999.

Rostow, W. W., *How It All Began: Origins of the Modern Economy*, McGraw-Hill, New York, 1975.

Rothman, Kenneth, *Epidemiology: An Introduction*, Oxford University Press, New York, 2002.

Rowley, C. D., *The New Guinea Villager: A Retrospect from 1964*, Cheshire, Melbourne, 1965.

Roy, Anaya, and Nezar Alsayyad, eds., *Urban Informality: Transnational Perspectives from the Middle East, Latin America and South Asia*, Lexington Books, Lanham, 2003.

Rushbrook, Peter, and Edward Wanigasekera, "Towards Papua New Guinea's First Vocational Education Degree: Reconciling Modernism and Cultural Sustainability," paper presented at the Australian Vocational Education and Training Research Association Annual Conference, Canberra, 2004.

Rutherford, Stuart, *ASA: The Biography of an NGO, Empowerment and Credit in Rural Bangladesh*, Dhaka, Association for Social Advancement, 1995.

———, *The Poor and Their Money: An Essay about Financial Services for Poor People*, Oxford University Press, New Delhi, 2000.

Sachs, Jeffrey, *The End of Poverty: How We Can Make It Happen in Our Lifetime*, Penguin, London, 2005.

———, "Executive Summary," in Commission on Macroeconomics and Health, *Investing in Health for Economic Development: Report of the Commission on Macroeconomics and Health*, World Health Organization, Geneva, 2001.

Saheli, Rania, *Diverse Ways in Learning, Life, Thoughts, Meanings, and Cognition*, report from the Diversity in Ways, Settings, Thought, and Discourse of Learning Workshop, Arab Education Forum and UNESCO, Ain Saadeh, Lebanon, 2004.

Sahlins, Marshall, "The Economics of Develop-man in the Pacific," in Joel Robbins and Holly Wardlaw, eds,, *The Making of Global and Local Modernities in Melanesia:*

Humiliation, Transformation and the Nature of Cultural Change, Ashgate, Aldershot, 2005.

————, *Stone Age Economics*, Tavistock, London, 1974.

Samana, Utula, *Papua New Guinea: Which Way?* Arena Publications, Melbourne, 1988.

Sanders, David, and Richard Carver, *The Struggle for Health: Medicine and the Politics of
Underdevelopment*, Macmillan, London, 1985.

Scerri, Andy, and Paul James, "Accounting for Sustainability: Combining Qualitative
and Quantitative Research in Developing 'Indicators' of Sustainability," *International Journal of Social Research Methodology*, vol. 13, no. 1, 2010, pp. 41–53.

————, "Communities of Citizens and 'Indicators' of Sustainability," *Community Development Journal*, vol. 45, no. 2, 2010, pp. 219–236.

Schreiner, Marcus, "Aspects of Outreach: A Framework for Discussion of the Social
Benefits of Microfinance," *Journal of International Development*, vol. 14, no. 5,
2002, pp. 591–603.

Schwab, R. G., and D. Sutherland, "Building Indigenous Learning Communities,"
Centre for Aboriginal Economic Policy Research Discussion Paper No. 225, Australian National University, Canberra, 2001.

Scott, Ben, *Re-Imagining PNG: Culture, Democracy and Australia's Role*, Lowy Institute,
Double Bay, 2005.

Scott, James C., *Seeing like a State: How Certain Schemes to Improve the Human Condition Have Failed*, Yale University Press, New Haven, 1998.

Seaton, A., J. Ombiga, J. Wembri, P. Armstrong, S. Naraqi, D. Linge, I. Kevau, B. Mavo,
A. Saweri, A. Sengupta, A. K. Sinha, E. Puiahi, G. Glama, J. Igo, and D. Babona,
"Clinical Manifestations of HIV Infection in Melanesian Adults," *Papua New
Guinea Medical Journal*, vol. 39, 1996, pp. 181–182.

Seeley, Janet, and Kate Butcher, "'Mainstreaming' HIV in Papua New Guinea: Putting
Gender Equity First," *Gender and Development*, vol. 14, no. 1, 2006, pp. 105–114.

Seibel, Hans D., and Dolores Torres, "Are Grameen Replications Sustainable, and Do
They Reach the Poor? The Case of CARD Rural Bank in the Philippines," *Journal
of Microfinance*, vol. 1, no. 1, 1999, pp. 117–130.

Sen, Amartya, *Development as Freedom*, Alfred A. Knopf, New York, 1999.

Senge, Peter M., *The Fifth Discipline: The Art and Practice of the Learning Organisation*,
Doubleday, New York, 1990.

Setel, Phillip, *A Plague of Paradoxes: AIDS, Culture and Demography in Northern Tanzania*, University of Chicago Press, Chicago, 1999.

Sexton, Lorraine D., *Mothers of Money, Daughters of Coffee: The Wok Meri Movement*,
UMI Research Press, Ann Arbor, Michigan, 1986.

Sharp, Nonie, *Stars of Tagai: The Torres Strait Islanders*, Aboriginal Studies Press, Canberra, 1993.

Siegel, Jeff, "Formal vs. Non-Formal Vernacular Education: The Education Reform in

Papua New Guinea," *Journal of Multilingual and Multicultural Development*, vol. 18, no. 3, 1997, pp. 206–222.

Sinclair, James, *Golden Gateway: Lae and the Province of Morobe*, Crawford House, Bathurst, 1998.

Smith, Linda Tuhiwai, *Decolonizing Methodologies: Research and Indigenous Peoples*, Zed Books, London, 1999.

Smith, M. F., *Village on the Edge: Changing Times in Papua New Guinea*, University of Hawai'i Press, Honolulu, 2002.

Snodgrass, Donald, "Assessing the Effects of Program Characteristics and Program Context on the Impact of Microenterprise Services: A Guide for Practitioners," AIMS Brief No. 17, 1997, http://www.microlinks.org/ev_en.php ?ID=7959_201&ID2=DO_TOPIC, accessed 12 July 2007.

Spate, O. H. K., "Changing Native Agriculture in New Guinea," *Geographical Review*, vol. 43, no. 2, 1953, pp. 151–172.

———, "Problems of Development in New Guinea," *Geographical Journal*, vol. 122, no. 4, 1956, pp. 430–436.

Spencer, Tim, and Peter Heywood, "Staple Foods in Papua New Guinea: Their Relative Supply in Urban Areas, 1971 to 1981," *Food and Nutrition Bulletin*, vol. 5, no. 3, 1983, http://www.unu.edu/unupress/food/8F053e/8F053E00.htm, accessed 19 October 2009.

Star, Susan Leigh, and James R. Griesemer, "Institutional Ecology, Translations and Boundary Objects: Amateurs and Professionals in Berkeley's Museum of Vertebrate Zoology, 1907–39," *Social Studies of Science*, no. 19, 1989, pp. 387–420.

Stephens, David, and Katherine Lepani, "Evaluation of the IMR Transex Project: Port Moresby, Lae and Goroka," unpublished report for AusAID, 1998.

Strathern, Andrew J., and Gabriel Stürzenhofecker, eds., *Migration and Transformations: Regional Perspectives on Papua New Guinea*, University of Pittsburgh Press, Pittsburgh, 1994.

Suligoi, B., R. T. Danaya, L. Sarmati, I. L. Owen, S. Boros, E. Pozio, M. Andreoni, and G. Rezza, "Infection with Human Immunodeficiency Virus, Herpes Simplex Virus Type 2, and Human Herpes Virus 8 in Remote Villages of Southwestern Papua New Guinea," *American Journal of Tropical Medical Hygiene*, vol. 72, no. 1, 2005, pp. 33–36.

Sullivan, Nancy, ed., *Culture and Progress: The Melanesian Philosophy of Land and Development in Papua New Guinea*, DWU Press, Madang, 2002.

Sullivan, Nancy, Joseph Rainbubu, Kritoe Keleba, Yunus Wenda, and Chris Dominic, *European Union's Rural Coastal Fisheries Development Project BaseLine Study: Follow-up RRA for Madang*, Nancy Sullivan Ltd., Madang, 2004.

Sullivan, Nancy, and Thomas Warr, "Tinpis Maror: The Social Impact Study of RD Tuna," *Catalyst: Social Pastoral Journal of Melanesia*, vol. 35, no. 1, 2005, pp. 4–14.

Sullivan, Nancy, Thomas Warr, Joseph Rainbubu, J. Kunoko, F. Akauna, M. Angasa, and Yunus Wenda, "A Social Impact Study of Proposed RD Tuna Cannery at Vidar Wharf, Madang," unpublished report for Bismarck Ramu Group and Gadens Ridgeway Attorneys at Law, 2003.

Swaminathan, M., *Understanding the Informal Sector: A Survey*, WIDER WP 95, Finland, 1991.

Swatridge, Colin, *Delivering the Goods: Education as Cargo in Papua New Guinea*, Manchester University Press, Manchester, 1985.

Symonds, Patricia, "Political Economy and Cultural Logics of HIV/AIDS among the Hmong in Northern Thailand," in Merrill Singer, ed., *The Political Economy of AIDS*, Baywood, Amityville, 1998.

Tawaii, Kumalu, *Signs in the Sky: Poems by Kumalu Tawaii*, Papua Pocket Poems, Port Moresby, 1970.

Taylor, J. E. and Adelman, I., *Village Economies*, Cambridge University Press, Cambridge, 1996.

Thaman, K. H., "Shifting Sights: The Cultural Challenge of Sustainability," *Higher Education Policy*, no. 15, 2002, p. 135.

Thaman, R. R., "Urban Food Gardening in the Pacific Islands: A Basis for Food Security in Rapidly Urbanising Small-Island States," *Habitat International*, vol. 19, no. 2, 1995, pp. 209–224.

Thomas, Jim, *Informal Economic Activity*, Harvester Wheatsheaf, London, 1992.

Thompson, Geoff, *The State of Education in Papua New Guinea*, Port Moresby, National Department of Education, 2003.

Tiwara, Steven, Megan Passey, Alison Clegg, Charles Mgone, Sebeya Lupiwa, Nathan Suve, and Tony Lupiwa, "High Prevalence of Trichomonal Vaginitis and Chlamydial Cervicitis among a Rural Population in the Highlands of Papua New Guinea," *Papua New Guinea Medical Journal*, vol. 39, 1996, pp. 234–238.

Todaro, Michael P., *Economic Development*, Longman, New York, fifth edition, 1994.

Todd, Helen, *Cloning Grameen Bank: Replicating a Poverty Reduction Model in India, Nepal and Vietnam*, IT Publications, London, 1996.

Todd, Ian, *Papua New Guinea: Moment of Truth*, Angus and Robertson, Sydney, 1974.

Tokman, Victor E., "Policies for a Heterogenous Informal Sector in Latin America," *World Development*, vol. 17, no. 7, 1989, pp. 1067–1076.

Tönnies, Ferdinand, *Community and Society*, Harper and Row, New York, (1887) 1963.

Torres, Rosa-Maria, *Life-Long Learning: A New Momentum and a New Opportunity for Adult Basic Learning and Education (ABLE) in the South*, Swedish International Development Cooperation Agency, Buenos Aires, 2002.

Tsing, Anna L., *Friction: An Ethnography of Global Connection*, Princeton University Press, Princeton, 2005.

Tully, James, *Strange Multiplicity: Constitutionalism in the Age of Diversity*, Cambridge University Press, Cambridge, 1995.

United Nations (UN), *Papua New Guinea Common Country Assessment*, UN, Port Moresby, 2001.

————, *Millennium Declaration*, United Nations General Assembly, Geneva, 2000.

United Nations AIDS (UNAIDS), Australian Agency for International Development (AusAID), and National AIDS Council of Papua New Guinea (NACPNG), *HIV/AIDS Stakeholder Mapping in Papua New Guinea*, UNAIDS, AusAID, and NACPNG, Canberra, 2004.

United Nations AIDS and World Health Organization, "Guidelines for Second Generation HIV Surveillance Working Group on Global HIV/AIDS and STI Surveillance," United Nations AIDS and World Health Organization, Geneva, 2000.

————, "Initiating Second Generation Surveillance Systems: Practical Guidelines," Working Group on Global HIV/AIDS/STI Surveillance, United Nations AIDS, Geneva, 2002.

United Nations and Lao PDR, *Common Country Assessment*, Vientiane, 2006.

United Nations Development Program (UNDP), *Millennium Development Goals: Progress Report for Papua New Guinea 2004*, UNDP, 2004, http://www.undp.org.pg/documents/mdgs/National_MDG_Progress_Report_2004.pdf, accessed 6 May 2008.

————, *Papua New Guinea United Nations Development Program Development Assistance Framework, 2003–2007*, Port Moresby, 2002.

————, *UNDP Human Development Report: Millennium Development Goals—A Compact among Nations to end Human Poverty*, UNDP, New York, 2003.

United Nations Economic and Social Commission for Asia and the Pacific (UNESCAP) and the Asian Development Bank Institute, *Building e-Community Centres for Rural Development: Report of the Regional* Workshop, Bali, Indonesia, United Nations Publications, Thailand, 2005.

United Nations Educational, Scientific and Cultural Organization (UNESCO), *Community Empowerment through Community Learning Centres: Experiences from Thailand*, UNESCO and United Nations Development Program, Bangkok, 2002.

————, *Manual for the Implementation of Community Learning Centres*, UNESCO PROAP and Asia-Pacific Programme of Education for All (APPEAL), Bangkok, 1999.

————, *Regional Planning Workshop: Integrating HIV/AIDS Projects into Community Learning Centres*, UNESCO, Bangkok, 2007.

————, "World Declaration on Education for All," http://www.unesco.org/education/efa/ed_for_all/background/jomtien_declaration.shtml, accessed 9 July 2008.

United Nations Global Compact, Cities Programme (UNGCCP), *Circles of Sustainability: An Integrated Approach to Developing Sustainability Indicators*, UNGCCP, Melbourne and New York, 2008, http://www.citiesprogramme.org, accessed 14 January 2011.

United Nations Statistics Division (UNSD), *Principles and Recommendations for Population and Housing Censuses*, series M, no. 67, rev. 1, UNSD, New York, 1998.

United States Agency for International Development (USAID), *Health Profile: Papua New Guinea*, USAID, Washington, DC, 2005.

An Urban Social Charter for Papua New Guinea, no date (but circa 2005).

Vance, Carole, "Anthropology Rediscovers Sexuality: A Theoretical Comment," in Richard Parker and Peter Aggleton, eds., *Culture, Society and Sexuality: A Reader*, UCL Press, Philadelphia, 1999.

Van Helden, Flip, *Between Cash and Conviction: The Social Context of the Bismarck-Ramu Integrated Conservation and Development Project*, National Research Institute, Boroko, 1998.

Vietnam, Ministry of Health, *Health Care Support to the Poor of the Northern Uplands and Central Highlands, Overall Work Plan 2006–2010*, Ministry of Health, Project No. 2004/ 16 810, Budget Line, BGUE—B 2004—19 10 01, Hanoi, 2006.

Vorley, William, *Sustaining Agriculture: Policy, Governance, and the Future of Family-Based Farming*, IIED, London, 2002, http://www.poptel.org.uk/iied/docs/sarl/sust_agintro.pdf, accessed 19 October 2009.

Voth, Donald E., and Zola K. Moon, "Defining Sustainable Communities," paper presented at the "Rural Infrastructure as a Cause and Consequence of Rural Economic Development and Quality of Life" conference, 1997, Birmingham, Alabama, http://www.uark.edu/depts/hesweb/hdfsrs/sustcom.pdf, accessed 31 July 2003.

Vuylsteke, Bea, Rose Sunkutu, and Marie Laga, "Epidemiology of HIV and Sexually Transmitted Diseases in Women," in Jonathan M. Mann and Daniel J. M. Tarantola, eds., *AIDS in the World, II: Global Dimensions, Social Roots and Responses*, Oxford University Press, New York, 1996.

Wahid, Abu, ed., *The Grameen Bank, Poverty Relief in Bangladesh*, Westview Press, Boulder, Colorado, 1993.

Waiko, John D., "Introduction: A Plea for an Ethical Stocktake," in Susan Stratigos and Philip J. Hughes, eds., *The Ethics of Development: The Pacific in the 21st Century*, University of Papua New Guinea Press, Port Moresby, 1987, pp. 1–8.

Walmsley, Jim, "The Nature of Community: Putting Community in Place," *Dialogue*, vol. 25, no.1, 2006, pp. 5–12.

Wanek, Alexander, *The State and Its Enemies in Papua New Guinea*, Curzon Press, Richmond, 1996.

Wang, C., and M. A. Burris, "Photovoice; Concept, Methodology and Use for Participatory Needs Assessment," *Health and Behaviour*, vol. 24, no. 3, 1997, pp. 369–387.

Wang, C., and C. A. Pies, "Family, Maternal, and Child Health through Photovoice," *Maternal and Child Health Journal*, vol. 8, no. 2, 2004, pp. 95–102.

Wang, C., and Y. A. Redwood-Jones, "Photovoice Ethics: Perspectives from Flint Photovoice," *Health Education and Behavior*, vol. 28, no. 5, 2001, pp. 560–572.

Ward, R. G., "Urbanisation in the South Pacific," paper for UNESCO MOST Conference, USP, Suva, 1998.

Wardlow, Holly, "Anger, Economy, and Female Agency: Problematizing 'Prostitution' and 'Sex Work' among the Huli of Papua New Guinea," *Signs: Journal of Women in Culture and Society*, vol. 29, no. 4, 2004, pp. 1017–1040.

———, *"Free Food, Free Food!": "Traditional" Rituals of "Modern" Manhood among the Huli of Papua New Guinea*, International Association for the Study of Sexuality, Culture and Society, Melbourne, 2001.

———, "Giving Birth to Gonolia: 'Culture' and Sexually Transmitted Disease among the Huli of Papua New Guinea," *Medical Anthropology Quarterly*, vol. 16, no. 2, 2002, pp. 151–175.

———, *Love, Marriage and HIV: A Multisite Ethnographic Study of Gender and HIV Risk*, 2005, http://www.mailman.hs.columbia.edu/sms/cgsh/lmhiv1.html, accessed 29 January 2007.

———, "Passenger-Women: Changing Gender Relations in the Tari Basin," *PNG Medical Journal*, vol. 45, nos. 1–2, 2002, pp. 142–146.

———, *"Prostitution," "Sexwork," and "Passenger Women": When Sexualities Don't Correspond to Stereotypes*, International Association for the Study of Sexuality, Culture and Society, Melbourne, 2001.

———, "Public Health, Personal Beliefs: Battling HIV in Papua New Guinea," *Cultural Survival Quarterly*, vol. 26, no. 3, 2002, http://www.culturalsurvival.org/publications/csq/csq-article.cfm?id=1563, accessed 29 January 2007.

———, *Wayward Women: Sexuality and Agency in a New Guinea Society*, University of California Press, Berkeley, 2006.

———, "You Have to Understand: Some of Us Are Glad AIDS Has Arrived," in Leslie Butt and Richard Eves, eds., *Making Sense of AIDS: Culture, Sexuality, and Power in Melanesia*, University of Hawai'i Press, Honolulu, 2008.

Watson, Helen, and Wade Chambers, *Singing the Land, Signing the Land*, Deakin University, Geelong, 1989.

Watson, Louise, *Lifelong Learning in Australia*, University of Canberra and the Department of Education Science and Training, Canberra, 2003.

Webber, M. M., "Order in Diversity: Community without Propinquity," in L. Wirigo, ed., *Cities and Space*, Johns Hopkins University Press, Baltimore, 1963.

Weeks, Sheldon G., "Education in Papua New Guinea 1973–1993: The Late-Development Effect?" *Comparative Education*, vol. 29, no. 3, 1993, pp. 261–273.

Weiner, Annette B., *Inalienable Possessions: The Paradox of Keeping-While-Giving*, University of California Press, Berkeley, 1992.

Weiner, James F., "Introduction: Depositings," in Alan Rumsey and James F. Weiner, eds., *Mining and Indigenous Lifeworlds in Australia and Papua New Guinea*, Sean Kingston, Oxon, 2004.

————, *The Lost Drum: The Myth of Sexuality in Papua New Guinea and Beyond*, University of Wisconsin Press, Madison, 1995.

Wenger, Etienne, *Communities of Practice: Learning, Meaning and Identity*, Cambridge University Press, Cambridge, 1998.

Werner, David, "Challenges Facing 'Health for All,'" paper presented at "The New World Order, A Challenge to Health for All by the Year 2000," University of the Western Cape, Capetown, 29–31 January 1997.

Wesley-Smith, Terence, "Self-Determination in Oceania," *Race and Class*, vol. 48, no. 3, 2007, pp. 29–46.

West, F. J., "Colonial Development in Central New Guinea," *Pacific Affairs*, vol. 29, no. 2, 1956, pp. 161–173.

West, Paige, *Conservation Is Our Government Now: The Politics of Ecology in Papua New Guinea*, Duke University Press, Durham, 2006.

Widin, Jacquie, Heidi Norman, Anne Ndaba, and Keiko Yasukawa, "An Indigenous Community Learning Centre to Promote a Culture of Learning," paper given at the Adult Learning Australia Forty-fourth Annual National Conference, "Bridging Cultures," University of Technology, Sydney, 2004.

Wilde, Charles, "'Turning Sex into a Game': Gogodala Men's Response to the AIDS Epidemic and Condom Promotion in Rural Papua New Guinea," *Oceania*, vol. 77, no. 1, 2007, pp. 58–71.

Wilkinson, R., "Income Distribution and Life Expectancy," *BMJ* (*British Medical Journal*), vol. 304, 1992, pp. 165–168.

Wilson, Kelly R., "The Puente Learning Centre: A Building and a Program," *Journal of Urban Technology*, vol. 5, no. 2, 1998, pp. 47–59.

Windybank, Susan, and Mike Manning, "Papua New Guinea on the Brink," *Issue Analysis*, Centre for Independent Studies, no. 30, 2003, pp. 1–16.

Wingti, Paias, "The Power of the People," in Susan Stratigos and Philip J. Hughes, eds., *The Ethics of Development: The Pacific in the 21st Century*, University of Papua New Guinea Press, Port Moresby, 1987, pp. 84–87.

Witzeling, Robert, *Credit Union Handbook*, World Council of Credit Unions (WOCCU), Madison, 1994.

Woller, Gary, Christopher Dunford, and Warner Woodworth, "Where to Microfinance?", *International Journal of Economic Development*, vol. 1, no. 1, 1999, pp. 29–64.

World Bank, *Addressing HIV/AIDS in East Asia and the Pacific*, Health, Nutrition, and Population Series, World Bank, Washington, DC, 2004.

————, *Halving Poverty by 2015—Cambodia Poverty Assessment 2006*, Phnom Penh, 2006.

————, *Healthy Development: The World Bank Strategy for Health, Nutrition, and Population Results*, World Bank, Washington, DC, 2007.

——, *Papua New Guinea: Improving Governance and Performance*, Report No. 19288—PNG, Poverty Reduction and Economic Management Sector Unit, East Asia and Pacific Region, World Bank, Washington, DC, 1999.

——, *Papua New Guinea Poverty Assessment*, World Bank, Washington, DC, 2004.

——, *World Development Indicators 2007*, World Bank, Washington, DC, 2007.

——, *World Development Report 1993: Investing in Health*, Oxford University Press, New York, 1993.

World Commission on Environment and Development, *Our Common Future*, Oxford University Press, Oxford, 1997.

World Food Supplement to *The National*, 18 October 2006.

World Health Organization, Commission on Macroeconomics and Health, *Investing in Health for Economic Development: Report of the Commission on Macroeconomics and Health*, World Health Organization, Geneva, 2001.

World Health Organization, *Constitution of the World Health Organization*, World Health Organization, Geneva, 1946, http://www.who.int/hlt/historical/documents/constitution.html, accessed 25 November 1999.

——, "Helping Countries Provide Social Health Protection," http://www.who.int/healthsystems/mediacentre/news/berlin/en/index.html, accessed 20 January 2008.

——, *HIV/AIDS in Asia and the Pacific Region 2003*, World Health Organization, Geneva, 2004.

——, *Primary Health Care: Report of the International Conference on Primary Health Care, Alma-Ata, USSR*, World Health Organization, Geneva, 1978.

——, *The World Health Report 2000: Health Systems, Improving Performance*, World Health Organization, Geneva, 2000.

Yala, Charles, *Rethinking Customary Land Tenure Issues in Papua New Guinea*, National Research Institute, Port Moresby, paper presented at Oceania Development Network Conference, Port Moresby, 1–14 October 2005.

Yaron, Jacob, "Assessing Development Finance Institutions: A Public Interest Analysis," World Bank Discussion Paper 174, World Bank, Washington, DC, 1992.

Yaron, Jacob, Benjamin McDonald, and Piprek Gerda, "Rural Finance: Issues, Design and Best Practices," World Bank, Washington, DC, 1997.

Ye, Yimin, Jim Prescott, and Dennis Darren, "Sharing the Catch of Migratory Rock Lobster (*Panulirus ornatus*) between Sequential Fisheries of Australia and Papua New Guinea," http://www.fish.wa.gov.au/docs/events/ShareFish/papers/pdf/papers/YiminYe.pdf, accessed 9 January 2009.

Yeaxlee, Basil, *Lifelong Education*, Cassell, London, 1929.

Yeoman, L., and M. Obi, *The Management of Government-Based Literacy Projects in Papua New Guinea*, Deloitte Touche Tohmatsu, Management Consultants, 1993.

Yirrkala Dhanbul Community Association Inc., "Landcare," http://www.yirrkaladhanbul .nt.gov.au/council/content/view/full/122, accessed 14 November 2007.

Young, Iris M., *Inclusion and Democracy*, Oxford University Press, Oxford, 2000.

———, *Justice and the Politics of Difference*, Princeton University Press, Princeton, New Jersey, 1990.

Zeller, Manfred, and Meyer, Richard, *The Triangle of Microfinance: Financial Sustainability, Outreach, and Impact*, Johns Hopkins University Press, Baltimore, 2003.

Zhu, Erping, and Danilo M. Baylen, "From Learning Community to Community Learning: Pedagogy, Technology and Interactivity," *Educational Media International*, vol. 42, no. 3, 2005, pp. 251–268.

Zimmer-Tamakoshi, Laura, "Nationalism and Sexuality in Papua New Guinea," *Pacific Studies*, vol. 16, no. 4, 1993, pp. 61–97.

INDEX

Page numbers in **boldface** refer to photographs